Nov 29   29 + 1

28   A·4

PRINCIPLES OF ACCOUNTING
INTRODUCTORY

PRENTICE-HALL ACCOUNTING SERIES

H. A. Finney, Editor

PRINCIPLES
OF ACCOUNTING

————INTRODUCTORY————

by

H. A. FINNEY, Ph.B., C.P.A.

and

HERBERT E. MILLER, Ph.D., C.P.A.

Professor of Accounting, University of Michigan

FOURTH EDITION

Englewood Cliffs, N. J.

PRENTICE-HALL, INC.

Copyright, 1932, 1936, 1938, 1940, 1948, 1953, by
PRENTICE-HALL, INC.
Englewood Cliffs, N. J.

FOURTH EDITION

L. C. Cat. Card No. 53-6779

First printing .... *April, 1953*
Second printing ...... *September, 1953*
Third printing .... *October, 1953*
Fourth printing .... *May, 1954*
Fifth printing .... *May, 1955*
Sixth printing .... *January, 1956*

PRINTED IN THE UNITED STATES OF AMERICA
70395

Preface

In the preparation of this revision, we have been largely guided by the helpful suggestions of teachers. Some of the differences and similarities between this edition and the preceding one are mentioned below.

Introduction to the accounting cycle. It is important to acquaint the student, at the very earliest possible point in the course, with the entire cycle of bookkeeping procedures: journalizing, posting, taking a trial balance, preparing working papers and statements, and adjusting and closing the books. In the preceding edition, this cycle, with the exception of adjusting entries, was covered in the first four chapters. In this edition, the first four chapters are again devoted to the cycle, but they include some basic considerations of adjusting entries. This change has been made for two reasons: Making adjusting entries is part of the accounting cycle; working papers become more purposeful when adjustments are included in them.

In the preceding edition, the journal was not introduced until the second chapter, and entries were made directly in ledger accounts. In this edition, the journal is introduced in the first chapter, after a basic discussion of the nature of accounts. Thus, in conformity with one of the main objectives of the revision, the student's work, in his first assignments, is in closer accord with reality.

The discussion of changes in the proprietorship equity has been postponed to the second chapter. By limiting Chapter 1 to the consideration of the recording of the original investment and changes in assets and liabilities, and by devoting the second chapter to changes in the proprietorship equity, the student is introduced more gradually to the whole framework of accounts. Also, by devoting an entire chapter to changes in proprietorship, it is possible, in the first discussion of the subject, to give a realistic and sequential presentation of the use and closing of income, expense, and dividend accounts.

Corporate approach. The prefaces of preceding editions contained the following statement: "Students should obtain, at the very beginning of the course, a clear concept of net worth, or capital. When the course begins with the individual proprietorship, a needless source of confusion is introduced, as students find it difficult to distinguish between the capital of the business and the aggregate net worth of the proprietor." Reaction to the corporate approach seems to have been very generally favorable, and that approach has been retained. However, material on individual proprietorships and partnerships appears much earlier in this edition than in preceding editions.

Beginning with a nontrading business. In this edition, as in all preceding editions, the illustrations and problems in the introductory chapters are based on the accounts of companies which derive their income from fees for services rather than from merchandise sales. It is thus possible to show more clearly how income and expense affect the proprietorship equity, and to avoid the inventory complications in the first explanations of working papers, statements, and closing entries.

Perpetual inventories in first merchandise chapter. To postpone further the troublesome feature of dealing with an end-of-period inventory not shown by the accounts, the first chapter dealing with merchandising businesses (Chapter 5) utilizes a simple perpetual inventory procedure. After the student has been introduced to merchandise accounting, he is shown, in Chapter 6, how to deal with periodic inventories.

Reduced emphasis on notes and bills of exchange. The chapter coverage on promissory notes has not been materially reduced, but two-party drafts have been somewhat de-emphasized, and the discussion of three-party commercial bills has been deleted, as their use in business has been largely discontinued. Fewer note and acceptance transactions appear in the terminal practice set than heretofore.

Theory. To give an opportunity for review and synthesis, the chapter on theory toward the end of the book has been retained, with considerable revision. In addition, an effort has been made to give greater consideration throughout the text to matters of theory.

Assignment material. There are more problems and practice sets than in any preceding edition, and there is a wide assortment of problems—short and long, easy and difficult. As in the past, they have been designed to be specifically applicable to the related text material. There are five kinds of assignment material:

Questions.

Group A problems. Envelopes of forms have been provided for this assignment material; the forms are tailor-made to suit the requirements of the problems, and numerous devices have been employed to reduce the student's expenditure of time.

Group B problems. Some teachers like to have their students prepare solutions to some problems on ordinary columnar paper, without using the time- and labor-saving material provided for the A problems. Therefore the supplies provided for the Group B problems consist of a pad of ruled forms—mostly journal, ledger, and analysis paper.

Practice sets. An additional practice set has been provided for assignment after Chapter 11 (Specialized Books of Original Entry); the content of the other practice set, designed for assignment during the latter part of the second semester, has been materially reduced. Books of original entry, ledgers, and other materials required for the solution of the practice sets are included in the envelopes of forms for the A problems.

A workbook. The material in the workbook has been designed as a quick, but comprehensive, test of the material in the related chapters.

We wish to acknowledge our obligation to the following people, for their generous co-operation: Marcus H. Bean, Rutgers University; Thomas A. Budd, University of Pennsylvania; Albert H. Cohen, University of Michigan; Thomas M. Dickerson, Western Reserve University; Oscar S. Gellein, University of Denver; Harold B. Goodall, Henry Ford Community College; Douglas R. Haines, Rutgers University; H. M. Heckman, University of Georgia; S. R. Hepworth, University of California; Charles E. Johnson, University of Oregon; Robert E. Linde, University of Michigan; Louis W. Matusiak, University of Detroit; Stuart B. Mead, Michigan State College; Carl L. Nelson, University of Minnesota; Wayne E. Shroyer, University of Denver; Warren L. Slagle, University of Tennessee; Robert T. Sprouse, University of Minnesota; D. L. Sweeney, State University of Iowa; D. A. Thomas, University of Michigan; William C. Tuthill, University of Michigan; Harry H. Wade, State University of Iowa; S. M. Wedeberg, University of Maryland; John T. Wheeler, University of Minnesota; Mrs. Nina L. Youngs, University of Minnesota.

Accounting research bulletins of the American Institute of Accountants are copyrighted by the Institute. Quotation in this text is by their permission.

H. A. Finney
Herbert E. Miller

Foreword

The nature of accounting and its significance in the business world can be described by noting the variety of work performed by persons trained in the field of accounting.

(1) *Installation of accounting systems:* As a general rule, the first accounting work performed for any business involves the development of an accounting system. The accountant studies the nature of the business, determines the types of transactions that probably will occur, and plans or selects the necessary forms and records in which the transactions of the business may be recorded. As a business grows, it is customary to review the accounting system from time to time, and to initiate any desirable amplifications or modifications.

(2) *Record keeping:* After the accounting system has been designed and installed, the results of business transactions are recorded in the accounting forms and records.

(3) *Preparation of financial statements:* At regular intervals the accountant, using the financial data accumulated in the accounting records, prepares statements showing the financial position of the business and the results of its operations. Such statements furnish important information to management, owners, investors, bankers, and governmental agencies.

(4) *Auditing:* Auditing is a procedure by which the accounting records and statements are examined to safeguard against fraud and error and to give assurance that these records and statements are in accord with accepted accounting principles. Auditing is of two general classes:

  (a) Continuous internal audit. Large businesses usually have on their own payroll a staff of accountants whose duty it is to make continuous checks of the work performed by the accounting department.

  (b) Periodic audit by public accountants. To give added assurance to the management and to outsiders, a business may engage the services of an outside, independent accountant to determine whether the statements present fairly the financial position of the business and the results of operations in accordance with generally accepted accounting principles, and to express, in his audit report, an opinion on these matters.

It should be mentioned that auditing is not the only service performed by public accountants. They may, among other things, install accounting systems, prepare or review tax returns, and make special studies for their clients.

(5) *Tax accounting:* Most accountants have some contact with tax matters, and many accountants specialize in this field.

(6) *Budgeting:* Although the preparation of budgets (plans and forecasts for the future) may not be the exclusive responsibility of the accountant, his understanding of the accounting records and procedures and of the information previously recorded makes him an important participant in budget preparation.

(7) *Cost accounting:* Many accountants specialize in the field of cost accounting. If a business manufactures the goods which it sells, it is essential that it keep adequate detailed records showing the cost of material, labor, and other items used in the production of the various kinds of goods. Cost records may also be maintained for the selling or distribution phases of the business. The cost accountant participates in determining how cost data shall be accumulated in the records, and generally is charged with the responsibility of interpreting cost information for management.

(8) *Controllership:* The controller is the chief accounting officer of a business and the financial advisor to its management. Controllership is a specialized field of accounting calling for broad and thorough training in accounting and business management.

(9) *Special investigations:* Frequently, special investigations requiring a thorough knowledge of accounting principles and procedures must be made for such purposes as establishing a price for the sale of an entire business or a department thereof, deciding whether a given activity is or might be profitable, or determining the feasibility of retirement or bonus plans.

From the above discussion of the work of the accountant, it is obvious that record keeping is only one part of this broad field of activity. However, once the accounting system has been designed and installed, the work of record keeping is extremely important, because the satisfactory accomplishment of most of the other accounting activities depends, to a great extent, upon the accuracy and completeness of the accounting records. Therefore, a major objective of the first course in accounting is to expose the student to the procedures of record keeping. To master this phase of the subject, problem and practice work is essential.

But a knowledge of procedures is not the only objective. To understand *why* things are recorded as they are requires a knowledge of accounting principles. And finally, the end product of the accounting process, the financial statements, should be understood.

Some knowledge of accounting is valuable even to those who do not expect to earn a living as accountants. Too often business executives, investors, and others who need the information contained in accounting statements but who have had no training in accounting are unable to grasp wholly the significance of the reports prepared for their guidance. A knowledge of the fundamentals of accounting would enable them more adequately to analyze the reports of companies with whose management they are charged, or in which they have placed their funds or contemplate placing them.

Accounting is now recognized as one of the very important professions. Employment opportunities are varied and numerous, and the compensation to be expected compares very favorably with that in other professions. There is always an opportunity for qualified accountants to obtain satisfactory employment with government agencies, private business, and public accounting firms.

As in any other honorable calling, the accountant should be a person of integrity; he must also be possessed of a high degree of analytical ability; he must not be averse to dealing with vast amounts of detail; he should be tactful; and he should maintain a personal appearance consistent with his professional status.

Contents

CONTENTS

11. SPECIALIZED BOOKS OF ORIGINAL ENTRY (*Continued*).

Receipts Book: Interest Income; Sales; Prepaid Interest Expense; Collection and Exchange. Other Special-Purpose Columns in the Cash Disbursements Book: Interest Expense; Purchases, Freight In, and Freight Out; Special columns to be used. Transactions Recorded on Two Lines of a Cash Book or in a Cash Book and the General Journal: Two entries in the General Ledger column; Entry in a cash book and the general journal; Locating errors.

12. DEPARTMENTAL OPERATIONS 165

Departmental profits; Determining gross profits by departments; Columnar sales and purchase records; Cash sales and cash purchases; Cash discounts; Departmental inventories in the balance sheet; Gross profit less selling expenses by departments; Dangers of approximations; Net income by departments; Significance of the statement; Contribution to overhead; Adjusting and closing entries.

13. MANUFACTURING ACCOUNTS 185

Manufacturing costs; Operating statements; Statement of cost of goods sold; Surplus statement; Balance sheet; Working papers; Adjusting and closing entries; Apportioned items in the working papers.

14. THE VOUCHER SYSTEM 194

Vouchers; Preparing the voucher; Recording the voucher; Filing the voucher until payment; Paying the voucher; Recording the payment; Filing the paid voucher; Vouchers for immediate disbursements; Extended illustration; Posting from the voucher register; Posting from the check register; Elimination of accounts payable ledger; Balance sheet title for liability; Partial payments; Exchange charges; Returned purchases and allowances; Notes payable.

15. ALTERNATIVE ADJUSTMENT PROCEDURES. 215

Accrued Income: Procedures previously described; Alternative procedure; Why reversing entries are desirable. Accrued Expense: Procedures previously described; Alternative procedure; Desirability of reversing entries. Apportionments of Recorded Costs: Procedure previously described; Alternative procedure; The two procedures illustrated; Reason for the reversing entry; A second alternative procedure; Custom and convenience affect choice of method. Apportionments of Recorded Income: Procedure previously described; Alternative procedure; The two procedures illustrated; Second alternative procedure. Determining When Adjustments Are Required and the Amounts Thereof.

16. PARTNERSHIPS (CONCLUDED). 226

Miscellaneous Methods of Dividing Profits and Losses: Determinants of an equitable division; Methods of dividing profits and losses; Basis of illustrations; Salaries and/or interest in excess of net income. Changes in Personnel: Procedures generally applicable to changes in personnel; Admission of a partner by purchase; Admission of a partner by investment; Retirement of a partner; Death of a partner. Liquidation of the Partnership: Disposal of assets; Division of the profit or loss; Distribution of cash; Partner with a debit balance.

17. CORPORATIONS 242

Nature of the corporation; Organization of a corporation; Organization costs; Corporate management; Elements of net worth; Capital stock. Re-

CONTENTS

What is cash? Internal check; Cash receipts; Cash disbursements; Bank columns in the cash books; Petty, or imprest, cash; Cash over and short. Dealings with the Bank: Opening a bank account; Deposits; Maintaining a record of the bank balance; Miscellaneous transactions; The bank statement; Reconciling the bank account; Certified checks; Adjustments after reconciliation; Payroll bank account; Dividend bank account; Bank overdraft.

Accounts Receivable: Accounts receivable in the balance sheet; Accounts receivable and payable with same party; Ledger headings; Account and statement at one impression; C.O.D. sales; Red balances in subsidiary ledgers; Aging the receivables; Bad debt recoveries; Reserves for returns and allowances, cash discounts, and freight; Discounts on returned sales; Freight paid and discount taken by customer; Sales discount on customers' partial payments; Uncollectible notes receivable. Discounting Notes and Acceptances Receivable: Purposes of discounting notes and acceptances receivable; Same methods apply to notes and acceptances; Endorsements; Proceeds; Discounting notes receivable at the bank; Discounting notes receivable with a creditor; Discounted note paid by maker at maturity; Discounted note dishonored by maker; Disposition of Notes Receivable Discounted account; Protest; Purpose of Notes Receivable Discounted account; Notes receivable and notes receivable discounted in the balance sheet; Discounted notes taken from debtor on account.

Definitions; Charging fixed asset costs to operations; Classification of fixed assets; Valuation of fixed assets; Depreciation; Computing and recording depreciation; Depreciation vs. provision for replacement; Expenditures during ownership; Disposal of fixed assets; Trade-ins; Depreciation program revisions; Subsidiary records. Natural Resources: Valuation; Depletion. Intangible Fixed Assets Normally Subject to Amortization: Reason for amortization; Patents; Copyrights; Franchises; Leaseholds and leasehold improvements. Intangible Fixed Assets Not Normally Subject to Amortization: Trademarks; Goodwill; Methods of computing goodwill; Proper book value of goodwill. Fixed Assets in the Balance Sheet.

Classes of inventories; Inventory all goods owned; Importance of accuracy in taking and pricing the inventory; Procedure of inventory taking; Inventory pricing; Cost; Cost selection for inventory pricing; Specific identification; Weighted-average method; First-in, first-out method; Last-in, first-out method; Cost or market, whichever is lower; Application of cost or market; Effect of cost-or-market rule on gross profits; Obsolete and damaged merchandise; Valuation basis should be disclosed; Gross profit method of estimating inventories.

Purpose of chapter; Accounting principles; Shift in emphasis; Periodic statements. Income: The nature of income; When is income earned? Income from production and sales activities; Income from services; Unrealized appreciation; Income and savings. Costs: Terminology; The cost principle; Departures from the cost basis; Classification of cost out-

CHAPTER 1

Assets, Liabilities, and Owners' Equity

The balance sheet. One of the major purposes of accounting is to provide the information required for the preparation of a statement showing the financial position of a business on a stated date. This statement, called a *balance sheet*, shows the assets of the business, its liabilities, and the owners' equity. Following is a simple illustrative balance sheet.

COMMUNITY TELEVISIONS

Balance Sheet

August 31, 19—

Assets		Liabilities and Owners' Equity		
Cash	$2,895.00	Liabilities:		
Accounts receivable	1,250.00	Accounts payable		$1,300.00
Installation and repair parts	3,800.00			
Land	1,500.00	Owners' equity:		
		Capital stock	$8,000.00	
		Earned surplus	145.00	8,145.00
	$9,445.00			$9,445.00

Observe that the heading of the balance sheet shows (1) the name of the business, (2) the name of the statement, and (3) the date.

It will help us to understand the balance sheet if we consider the nature of its elements: assets, liabilities, and owners' equity.

Assets. Assets are things of value owned. Cash, accounts receivable, notes receivable, merchandise, land, buildings, machinery and other equipment, and patents are some of the assets that may be owned by a business.

Things may have value for several reasons. Cash has value because other things can be acquired with it. Accounts and notes receivable have value because they can be collected in cash. Merchandise has value because it can be sold for cash or can be sold on account and the account can be collected in cash.

But things may have value although there is no intention to convert them into cash. Land, buildings, machinery, and equipment are assets of this nature; although it may be possible to sell them, their value to a business lies primarily, not in their salability, but in their usefulness in operations. Other assets, such as patents, copyrights, and franchises, have value because of the special rights that they give to their owners and because they help to make operations profitable.

Liabilities.   Liabilities are debts; they are amounts owed to creditors.   Accounts payable, notes payable, mortgages payable, wages payable, and taxes payable are some of the liabilities that may be owed by a business.

Owners' equity.   The excess of the assets over the liabilities of a business is the owners' equity.

For instance,

If a business has assets in the amount of	$9,445.00
And has liabilities of	1,300.00
The owners' equity is	$8,145.00

Sources of owners' equity.   The owners' equity in a corporation may come from the following sources:

From stockholders' investments—Shown in the illustrative balance sheet as Capital Stock.

From earnings—Shown in the illustrative balance sheet as Earned Surplus.

In this chapter, we shall deal only with the portion of the owners' equity produced by stockholders' investments.

The balance sheet equation.   The assets of a business are always equalled by the sum of the liabilities and the owners' equity. This fact can be expressed in the form of an equation, thus:

$$\text{ASSETS} = \text{LIABILITIES} + \text{OWNERS' EQUITY}$$
$$\$9,445 = \quad \$1,300 \quad + \quad \$8,145$$

The illustrative balance sheet on page 1 is an expression of this equation.

Continuing balance sheet equality.   The totals of the two sides of a balance sheet are always equal because, no matter what transactions occur, the assets of a business are always equalled by the interests of the creditors and the owners.   To demonstrate this fact, let us consider a number of transactions of a business, prepare a balance sheet after each transaction, and observe the equality of the two sides of each balance sheet.

Issuance of capital stock.   J. C. White, Henry Dobson, and J. B. Hudson organized a corporation called Community Televisions. The charter obtained from the state authorized the corporation to issue eighty shares of capital stock of $100 par value per share; this gave the corporation an authorized capital stock of $8,000. We shall assume that White invested $4,000, and that each of the other men invested $2,000.

Investments in a corporation are evidenced by stock certificates.   An illustration of a stock certificate appears on page 3.

Certificate No. ___1___   ___20___ Shares

CAPITAL STOCK $8,000.00
80 Shares of $100.00 Par Value

THIS CERTIFIES THAT _____Henry Dobson_____ is the

owner of _____Twenty_____ Shares of the Capital Stock of

COMMUNITY TELEVISIONS

transferable only on the books of the Corporation by the holder hereof in person or by attorney upon the surrender of this Certificate properly endorsed.

    IN WITNESS WHEREOF, the said Corporation has caused this Certificate to be signed by its duly authorized officers, and to be sealed with the seal of the Corporation at ___Chicago, Illinois___ this __20th__ day of ___July___ , 19 __——__

J. B. Hudson
Secretary

J. C. White
President

Stock Certificate

    As evidence of his investment, Dobson received this certificate for 20 shares of stock, with a total par value of $2,000. Certificates were issued to the other incorporators for their investments.

    After the issuance of $8,000 par value of capital stock for cash on July 20, the company's balance sheet appeared as follows:

COMMUNITY TELEVISIONS
Balance Sheet
July 20, 19—

Assets		Owners' Equity	
Cash	$8,000.00	Capital stock	$8,000.00

    Purchase of land. The company planned to erect its own shop building, and purchased two adjoining pieces of land on July 22 for $1,500 each, paying cash. As a result of this transaction, the company acquired a new asset (land) and decreased its cash. After this transaction, the company's balance sheet appeared as follows:

COMMUNITY TELEVISIONS
Balance Sheet
July 22, 19—

Assets		Owners' Equity	
Cash	$5,000.00	Capital stock	$8,000.00
Land	3,000.00		
	$8,000.00		$8,000.00

Sale of land. The management decided that more land had been purchased than was needed, and one of the lots was sold to G. E. Dutton on July 27 for $1,500, the amount it had cost the company. No cash was received from Dutton on this date. This transaction produced an account receivable asset of $1,500, and correspondingly decreased the land asset. After this transaction, the balance sheet appeared as follows:

COMMUNITY TELEVISIONS
Balance Sheet
July 27, 19—

Assets		Owners' Equity	
Cash	$5,000.00	Capital stock	$8,000.00
Account receivable—G. E.			
Dutton	1,500.00		
Land	1,500.00		
	$8,000.00		$8,000.00

Purchase of installation and repair parts. To conduct its operations, the company will need a considerable quantity of antennas and other installation and repair parts. Mr. White found a dealer, O. E. Maltby, who was going out of business, and purchased the dealer's entire stock of such parts for the company on July 28. Mr. Maltby said that he thought he could easily obtain at least $4,000 for the parts by selling them at auction, but was willing to accept $3,800 for them at a quick sale. It is a generally recognized accounting principle that the accounting basis for assets, at the date of their acquisition, is the cost thereof, regardless of value; therefore, the parts are shown in the following balance sheet at their $3,800 cost. Delivery was postponed until the company acquired or rented a building. No cash payment was made to Maltby on this date.

By this transaction, the company acquired a new asset (installation and repair parts) and incurred an account payable liability. After this transaction, the balance sheet appeared as follows:

COMMUNITY TELEVISIONS
Balance Sheet
July 28, 19—

Assets		Liabilities and Owners' Equity	
Cash	$ 5,000 00	Liabilities:	
Account receivable—G. E.		Account payable—O. E.	
Dutton	1,500.00	Maltby	$ 3,800.00
Installation and repair parts	3,800.00		
Land	1,500.00	Owners' equity:	
		Capital stock	8,000.00
	$11,800.00		$11,800.00

Collection on an account receivable. On July 29, $1,000 in cash was received from G. E. Dutton, in partial settlement of his account. This transaction increased the cash asset and decreased the account receivable asset. The balance sheet after this transaction appeared as follows:

COMMUNITY TELEVISIONS
Balance Sheet
July 29, 19—

Assets		Liabilities and Owners' Equity	
Cash....................	$ 6,000.00	Liabilities:	
Account receivable—G. E.		Account payable—O. E.	
Dutton................	500.00	Maltby...............	$ 3,800.00
Installation and repair parts.	3,800.00		
Land....................	1,500.00	Owners' equity:	
		Capital stock...........	8,000.00
	$11,800.00		$11,800.00

Payment on an account payable. On July 31, the company paid $2,500 to O. E. Maltby to apply on account. This transaction decreased the account payable liability and also decreased the cash. After this transaction, the balance sheet appeared as follows:

COMMUNITY TELEVISIONS
Balance Sheet
July 31, 19—

Assets		Liabilities and Owners' Equity	
Cash....................	$3,500.00	Liabilities:	
Account receivable—G. E.		Account payable—O. E.	
Dutton................	500.00	Maltby...............	$1,300.00
Installation and repair parts..	3,800.00		
Land....................	1,500.00	Owners' equity:	
		Capital stock...........	8,000.00
	$9,300.00		$9,300.00

Accounts. It would be impracticable to prepare a balance sheet for a business after each transaction. Instead, the transactions are recorded in the accounting records, and the information accumulated in these records is used for the preparation of balance sheets at periodic intervals.

Transactions cause increases and decreases in the assets, the liabilities, and the owners' equity. These increases and decreases are recorded in *accounts*. The following illustration shows an account form:

DATE	EXPLANATION	REF.	AMOUNT	DATE	EXPLANATION	REF.	AMOUNT

You will observe that the account form has two sides, with identical columns. The column headings (*Date, Explanation, Ref.,* and *Amount*) shown in the preceding illustration do not usually appear in accounts, but are included in the illustration to indicate the purpose of each column.

The *Date* column shows the date of the transaction.

The *Explanation* column may contain some short comment indicating the reason for the entry. This column is used only on rare occasions when it may be desirable to describe some unusual transaction.

Ref. is an abbreviation of *Reference.* The use of this column is explained later in the chapter.

The *Amount* column shows the dollar amount of the entry.

Accounts usually are kept in a loose-leaf binder or in a file. The binder or file, together with the accounts therein, is called a *ledger.*

A separate account is kept for each asset, each liability, and each element of the owners' equity. The July 31 balance sheet of Community Televisions on page 5 shows that, in order to record the July transactions, the company needed the accounts listed below. The accounts should be arranged in the ledger in the order in which they will appear in the balance sheet, and they should be numbered. The following list shows that some numbers have not been assigned to any accounts; these numbers have been reserved for other accounts which can be added in balance sheet sequence later if required.

	Account Number
Assets:	
Cash	1
G. E. Dutton	2
Installation and repair parts	10
Land	15
Liabilities:	
O. E. Maltby	20
Owners' equity:	
Capital stock	50

Debit and credit. The left side of an account is called the *debit* side; the right side is called the *credit* side. An entry on the left side of an account is called a *debit entry*, or merely a *debit;* an entry on the right side is called a *credit entry*, or a *credit.* The words *debit* and *credit* are also used as verbs. When you make an entry on the left side of an account, you are *debiting* the account. When you make an entry on the right side, you are *crediting* the account.

The difference between the total debits and the total credits in an account is called the *balance*. If the debits exceed the credits, the account has a debit balance; if the credits exceed the debits, the account has a credit balance.

Debit and credit entries in accounts. As previously stated, transactions cause increases and decreases in assets, in liabilities, and in owners' equity. Accounts have two sides so that increases can be recorded on one side and decreases can be recorded on the other side. The nature of the account determines the side to be used for increases and the side to be used for decreases.

Asset accounts. Assets are shown on the left side of the balance sheet. Consistency suggests that asset accounts should therefore have balances on the left, or debit, side. For an asset account to have a debit balance, it is necessary that increases and decreases in the asset be recorded thus:

Any Asset Account	
Increases	Decreases

Liability and owners' equity accounts. Since the liabilities and the owners' equity are shown on the right side of the balance sheet, consistency also suggests that increases and decreases in liabilities and increases and decreases in owners' equity be recorded thus:

Any Liability Account or Any Owners' Equity Account	
Decreases	Increases

Summary statement of debit and credit procedure. The procedures stated above may be summarized as follows:

In ASSET accounts:
  Increases are recorded by debits.
  Decreases are recorded by credits.
In LIABILITY and OWNERS' EQUITY accounts:
  Increases are recorded by credits.
  Decreases are recorded by debits.

Recording transactions. To illustrate the debiting and crediting of accounts, let us review the transactions of Community Televisions, analyze each transaction to see what increases or decreases occurred, and observe the debit and credit entries which record these increases and decreases. To simplify the illustration, skeleton accounts (often called "T-accounts") are used and only the amounts of the debits and credits are shown. To help you identify the entries, the debit and credit for each successive transaction are shown in italics. Asset accounts are shown below at the left; liability and owners' equity accounts are shown at the right.

Capital stock was issued for cash, $8,000.

The cash asset was increased   —Debit Cash.

The owners' equity was increased—Credit Capital Stock.

Cash		Capital Stock	
8,000			8,000

Land was purchased for cash, $3,000.

The land asset was increased—Debit Land.

The cash asset was decreased—Credit Cash.

Land	
3,000	

Cash	
8,000	3,000

Land was sold to G. E. Dutton on account, $1,500.

An account receivable asset was acquired—Debit G. E. Dutton.

The land asset was decreased—Credit Land.

G. E. Dutton	
1,500	

Land	
3,000	1,500

Installation and repair parts were purchased from O. E. Maltby on account, $3,800.

A new asset (installation and repair parts) was acquired—Debit Installation and Repair Parts.

An account payable liability was incurred—Credit O. E. Maltby.

Installation and Repair Parts		O. E. Maltby	
3,800			3,800

Cash was collected from G. E. Dutton to apply on account, $1,000.

The cash asset was increased—Debit Cash.

The account receivable asset was decreased—Credit G. E. Dutton.

Cash

| 8,000 | 3,000 |
| 1,000 | |

G. E. Dutton

| 1,500 | 1,000 |

Cash was paid to O. E. Maltby to apply on account, $2,500.

The account payable liability was decreased—Debit O. E. Maltby.

The cash asset was decreased—Credit Cash.

Cash		O. E. Maltby	
8,000	3,000	*2,500*	3,800
1,000	*2,500*		

How the words *debit* and *credit* came into use. The first accounts kept were accounts with debtors. The account with each debtor showed the amounts of sales made to him on account and the amounts of subsequent collections. An entry for a sale was the first entry in a debtor's account and was recorded on the left side of the debtor's account, thus:

Name of Debtor

| June 20   Sale | 25.00 | |

When a collection was received from the debtor, it was recorded on the right side of the account, thus:

Name of Debtor

| June 20   Sale | 25.00 | July 12   Cash | 10.00 |

As long as the customer owed anything, his account had a balance on the left side; this balance was called a *debit* (a Latin word meaning "he owes") balance.

The next accounts kept were those with creditors, and the procedure already developed for debtors' accounts was applied to creditors' accounts. This procedure may be stated thus:

Name of Debtor or Creditor

| Things given to him on account | Things received from him on account |

As long as anything was owed to a creditor, his account had a balance the right side; this balance was called a *credit* (Latin for "he trusts") balance.

Now that accounts are kept with such things as cash and land, which cannot owe or trust, the words *debit* and *credit* are no longer used in their original meanings. *Debit* merely indicates the left side of an account, and *credit* indicates the right side.

Journal and ledger. Although transactions *could be* recorded directly in the ledger accounts, it is customary (for reasons stated later) to use at least two bookkeeping records:

(1) *A Journal.*

The first record of a transaction is made in a journal.

The procedure of recording transactions in the journal is called *journalizing*. A journal is called a *book of original entry*.

The entry for each transaction shows what accounts will later be debited and credited in the ledger.

(2) *A Ledger.*

The debits and credits to the various accounts, as shown by the journal entries, are entered in the accounts by a process called *posting*.

Journalizing. On page 11 are journal entries recording, in chronological order, the transactions of Community Televisions previously mentioned. Following is the procedure for journalizing:

Analyze each transaction by asking yourself the question:

In what ways were the assets, the liabilities, or the owners' equity of the business increased or decreased by this transaction? The answer to this question will indicate the accounts to be debited and credited.

After each transaction is analyzed, it is recorded in the journal in the following manner:

Write the date of the transaction in the Date column; the year, month, and day of the month should be written in the first journal entry on each page; entries on the same page for subsequent transactions in the same year and month need show only the day of the month.

Write the name of the account to be debited, and enter the amount of the debit in the left money column.

On the next line, write the name of the account to be credited, and enter the amount of the credit in the right money column. The name of the account credited should be indented.

Write an explanation of the transaction.

Leave a blank line after each journal entry.

The account names written in journal entries should be the *exact* names of the accounts as they appear in the ledger.

The journal of Community Televisions appears below. The transactions have been journalized, but the journal entries have not been posted.

Journal   (Page 1)

DATE	ACCOUNT DEBITED ACCOUNT CREDITED	L.F.	DEBIT AMOUNT	CREDIT AMOUNT
July 20	Cash		8 0 0 0 00	
	Capital stock			8 0 0 0 00
	Issuance of 80 shares of stock at $100 par value.			
22	Land		3 0 0 0 00	
	Cash			3 0 0 0 00
	Purchase of two building lots for $1,500 each; paid in cash.			
27	G. E. Dutton		1 5 0 0 00	
	Land			1 5 0 0 00
	Sale to G. E. Dutton of 1 lot at the price it cost the company. Sale made on account.			
28	Installation and repair parts		3 8 0 0 00	
	O. E. Maltby			3 8 0 0 00
	Purchase of installation and repair parts on account.			
29	Cash		1 0 0 0 00	
	G. E. Dutton			1 0 0 0 00
	Collection on account.			
31	O. E. Maltby		2 5 0 0 00	
	Cash			2 5 0 0 00
	Payment on account.			

Advantages of the journal. The journal serves three useful purposes. In the first place, it reduces the possibility of error. If transactions were recorded directly in the ledger, there would be considerable danger of omitting the debit or the credit entry, or of making two debit entries or two credit entries. This danger is reduced to a minimum by using the journal. In the journal, the debits and credits for each transaction are recorded together, where an error of this kind would be readily observed. Of course, similar errors may be made in posting to the ledger, but such errors can be readily detected by tracing the account entries back to the journal.

In the second place, the journal shows offsetting debit and credit entries for each transaction, and thus provides a complete record of the transaction in one place.   Also, the journal provides ample space for an explanation of the transaction.

In the third place, the journal shows all of the pertinent facts about the transactions in their *chronological order*.

Posting.   *Posting* is the process of recording in the ledger accounts the debits and credits indicated by the journal entries.

The procedure of posting consists of the steps stated below:

> First post the debit member of the entry:
> Turn to the account to be debited.
> Enter on the debit side of the account:
> In the Date column—the date.
> In the Reference column—the number of the journal page *from* which the entry was posted.
> In the money column—the amount of the debit.
> Turn to the journal and, in the "L. F." (which means *ledger folio* or page or account number) column at the left of the money column, enter the number of the account *to* which the entry was posted.
> Post the credit member of the journal entry in a similar manner.

Entering the journal page number in the ledger and the account number in the journal serves two purposes:

> *While* the bookkeeper is posting, it shows how much of the posting has been done.   Thus, if the bookkeeper is called away before the posting is completed, he knows that the work should be taken up again with the first journal entry showing no account number in the L. F. column.
> *After* the posting has been completed, the numbers serve as cross references between the journal and the ledger.   This is particularly helpful if the bookkeeper, when looking at some account, wishes to find the journal entries from which the postings were made.

The first journal entry of Community Televisions is repeated below to show how the account numbers are entered in the ledger folio column.

Journal   (Page 1)

19—					
July 20	Cash	1	8,000 00		
	Capital stock	50		8,000 00
	Issuance of 80 shares of stock at $100 par value.			

After this journal entry is posted, the accounts affected appear as follows:

Cash   (*Account No. 1*)

July 20		1	8,000 00			

Capital Stock   (*Account No. 50*)

				July 20	1	8,000 00

After the completion of the posting of all of the journal entries, the accounts appear as follows:

Cash   (Account No. 1)

19— July	20 29	1 1	8,000 00 1,000 00	19— July	22 31	1 1	3,000 00 2,500 00

G. E. Dutton   (Account No. 2)

19— July	27	1	1,500 00	19— July	29	1	1,000 00

Installation and Repair Parts   (Account No. 10)

19— July	28	1	3,800 00				

Land   (Account No. 15)

19— July	22	1	3,000 00	19— July	27	1	1,500 00

O. E. Maltby   (Account No. 20)

19— July	31	1	2,500 00	19— July	28	1	3,800 00

Capital Stock   (Account No. 50)

				19— July	20	1	8,000 00

Computing balances of accounts. Account balances may be computed, and shown in the accounts, in the manner described below:

Add the debit column of the account, and enter the total in small pencil figures at the bottom of the column.

Add the credit column of the account, and enter the total in small pencil figures at the bottom of the column.

Enter the balance in small pencil figures in the Explanation column: on the line of the last debit entry if the account has a debit balance; on the line of the last credit entry if the account has a credit balance.

The following illustration shows the procedure.

Cash

19—						19—				
July	20			1	8,000 00	July	22		1	3,000 00
	29	3,500.00		1	1,000 00		31		1	2,500 00
					9,000 00					5,500 00

If only one entry appears on either side of an account, a pencil total of that side is, of course, unnecessary. If an account contains only one entry, the amount of that entry is the balance of the account, and it is unnecessary to write the balance again in the Explanation column.

If an account contains only debit entries or credit entries, the pencil total of the column shows the balance of the account, and therefore it is unnecessary to enter the balance in the Explanation column.

The trial balance. Double-entry bookkeeping derives its name from the fact that the recording of each transaction requires debit and credit entries of equal amount. Since the debit and credit entries for each transaction are equal, it is obvious that the total debit entries in all of the accounts should be equal to the total credit entries. It is equally true that the total of the debit balances in the accounts should be equal to the total of the credit balances.

It is customary to check the equality of the debit and credit balances in a ledger by listing and totaling them. Such a list is called a *trial balance*. Following is the July 31 trial balance of Community Televisions:

COMMUNITY TELEVISIONS
Trial Balance
July 31, 19—

Cash..	3,500.00	
G. E. Dutton................................	500.00	
Installation and repair parts..............	3,800.00	
Land.......................................	1,500.00	
O. E. Maltby...............................		1,300.00
Capital stock..............................		8,000.00
	9,300.00	9,300.00

Uses of the trial balance. A trial balance is useful in checking the *mathematical* correctness of the ledger. But it should be understood that a trial balance proves nothing more than the equality of the debit and credit entries. The trial balance will still "balance" even though a transaction was not journalized, or though a wrong account was debited or credited in the journal, or though a debit or credit was posted to a wrong account in the ledger, or though there was a failure to post both the debit and credit of a journal entry.

A trial balance is also useful to an accountant whenever periodic statements are to be prepared. Although it is possible for the accountant to prepare such statements by working directly from the ledger, it is much easier to use the account balances shown by a trial balance. You will observe that the account balances shown in the above trial balance are the same as those shown in the balance sheet on page 5.

Accounts receivable and payable in the balance sheet. If there are several accounts receivable and accounts payable, they may be detailed and totaled in the balance sheet in the manner illustrated below:

Accounts receivable:			Accounts payable:		
John Doty	$300.00		A. B. Sutton	$1,000.00	
Fred Hoyt	175.00		Davis & Co	650.00	$1,650.00
Frank Lane	80.00	$555.00			

However, in most businesses there are so many accounts receivable and accounts payable that listing them would make the balance sheet cumbersome. Moreover, balance sheets are often given to outsiders, such as bankers and other creditors, and are frequently included in published reports; it might be inexpedient for a business to disclose the names of its debtors and creditors. For these reasons it is the usual custom to show, in the balance sheet, only the totals of the accounts receivable and accounts payable, thus:

Accounts receivable...... $555.00   Accounts payable...... $1,650.00

Notes receivable and payable. Although a separate account is maintained for each account receivable and each account payable, a separate account is not maintained for each note receivable and note payable. All notes received may be debited to a single Notes Receivable account, and all notes given may be credited to a single Notes Payable account. The balances of these accounts appear in the balance sheet without detailing of the individual notes receivable or payable.

Compound journal entries. Sometimes the recording of a transaction requires more than one debit and one credit. For instance, assume that land which cost $10,000 was sold at cost, and that U. S. Government bonds worth $6,000 and cash in the amount of $4,000 were received in settlement; the entry to record the transaction is:

U. S. Government bonds	6,000.00	
Cash	4,000.00	
Land		10,000.00
Sale of land.		

Such entries, having more than one debit and/or more than one credit, are called *compound journal entries.*

CHAPTER 2

Changes in Owners' Equity. Closing the Books

Causes of changes in owners' equity. The principal causes of increases and decreases in the owners' equity in a corporation are stated below:

Discussed in Chapter 1:
Investments by stockholders.
Discussed in this chapter:
Income.
Expenses.
If the income of a business exceeds the expenses, a net income is earned. If the expenses exceed the income, a net loss is incurred.
Dividends to stockholders.

As an introduction to the accounting for income, expenses, and dividends, we shall continue the Community Televisions illustration through the month of August.

Income. Business operations are conducted with the object of earning income. Community Televisions has a contract with George Sloan, a television dealer, under which it expects to earn income in the following ways:

Selling television sets on a commission basis.
Installing television sets and antennas.
Making inspections of television sets within thirty days from the date of sale.
Repairing television sets.

Because of the time required for setting up its shop, the only income earned by Community Televisions during August consisted of commissions on the sale of television sets.

Expenses. Community Televisions incurred two kinds of expense during August:

Salaries expense—the three stockholders worked for the company; their salaries, totaling $900 per month, were expenses.
Office expense—Pending the time when the company could move into its own quarters, Mr. White arranged with an acquaintance for telephone, stenographic, and other office services at a monthly cost of $125.

Dividends.   Dividends are distributions of assets to stockholders.   Such distributions usually are made in cash.   Dividends reduce the owners' equity, but they are *not* an expense.   The company paid an $80 dividend at the end of August.

Debit and credit procedure.   The first chapter stated a general rule for recording increases and decreases in the owners' equity. This rule was:

In OWNERS' EQUITY accounts:
    Increases are recorded by credits.
    Decreases are recorded by debits.

In accordance with this general rule,

    Income, which increases the owners' equity, is credited to income accounts.
    Expenses, which decrease the owners' equity, are debited to expense accounts.
    Dividends, which decrease the owners' equity, are debited to a Dividends account.

To provide detailed information about the operating activities of a business, accountants customarily use a separate income account for each class of income, and a separate expense account for each class of expense.

Illustrative entries.   The transactions of Community Televisions during August are stated and journalized below.

Income.   On August 16, Community Televisions collected $500 cash from George Sloan for commissions on television sales made during the first half of the month.   The journal entry to record this transaction was:

```
Aug. 16   Cash...................................... 500.00
                 Commissions earned....................      500.00
           Commissions for first half of August.
```

On August 31, the company billed Sloan $750 for commissions earned during the last half of August; no cash was received on this date.   The journal entry for the transaction was:

```
Aug. 31   George Sloan............................. 750.00
                 Commissions earned....................      750.00
           Commissions for second half of August.
```

Expenses.   The salaries and office expense previously mentioned were paid on August 31.   The journal entries were:

```
Aug. 31   Salaries expense.......................... 900.00
                 Cash..................................      900.00
           Salaries for August.
```

Aug. 31	Office expense................................ 125.00	
	Cash....................................	125.00
	Use of office facilities during August.	

Dividend. The dividend payment was made on August 31, and was recorded as follows:

Aug. 31	Dividends................................ 80.00	
	Cash....................................	80.00
	Payment of dividend to stockholders.	

Complete journal. Following is Community Televisions' journal containing entries for all of its August transactions:

Journal   (Page 2)

19—				
Aug.	16	Cash...................................	500 00	
		Commissions earned.......................		500 00
		Commissions for first half of August.		
	31	George Sloan............................	750 00	
		Commissions earned.......................		750 00
		Commissions for second half of August.		
	31	Salaries expense..........................	900 00	
		Cash.................................		900 00
		Salaries for August.		
	31	Office expense...........................	125 00	
		Cash.................................		125 00
		Use of office facilities during August.		
	31	Dividends...............................	80 00	
		Cash.................................		80 00
		Payment of dividend to stockholders.		

Ledger. Following is the ledger of Community Televisions after the posting of the August entries. The August entries are shown in italics. Balances have been computed in all accounts containing more than one entry.

Cash   (1)

19—					19—				
July	20		1	8,000 00	July	22		1	3,000 00
	29		1	1,000 00		31		1	2,500 00
Aug.	16	2,895.00	2	500 00	Aug.	31		2	900 00
				9,500 00		31		2	125 00
						31		2	80 00
									6,605 00

G. E. Dutton   (2)

19—					19—				
July	27	500.00	1	1,500 00	July	29		1	1,000 00

George Sloan   (3)

19—				
Aug.	31		2	750 00

Installation and Repair Parts (10)

19—									
July	28		1	3,800	00				

Land (15)

19—						19—					
July	22	1,500.00	1	3,000	00	July	27		1	1,500	00

O. E. Maltby (20)

19—						19—					
July	31		1	2,500	00	July	28	1,300.00	1	3,800	00

Capital Stock (50)

						19—					
						July	20		1	8,000	00

Dividends (52)

19—									
Aug.	31		2	80	00				

Commissions Earned (61)

						19—					
						Aug.	16		2	500	00
							31		2	750	00
										1 250	00

Salaries Expense (71)

19—									
Aug.	31		2	900	00				

Office Expense (72)

19—									
Aug.	31		2	125	00				

Trial balance. The following trial balance was taken from the foregoing ledger.

COMMUNITY TELEVISIONS

Trial Balance

August 31, 19—

Cash..	2,895.00	
G. E. Dutton...............................	500.00	
George Sloan..............................	750.00	
Installation and repair parts...................	3,800.00	
Land......................................	1,500.00	
O. E. Maltby..............................		1,300.00
Capital stock..............................		8,000.00
Dividends.................................	80.00	
Commissions earned........................		1,250.00
Salaries expense...........................	900.00	
Office expense.............................	125.00	
	10,550.00	10,550.00

Statement of income and expense. Most businesses are engaged in a continuing "stream" of operations which are conducted with the object of earning a net income. The success of a business is largely judged by the amount of its net income.

Not until a business has ceased to function as a going concern and has disposed of its assets and paid its liabilities is it possible to compute, *with absolute accuracy*, the amount of its entire net income or net loss. But it obviously would be unsatisfactory to make no attempt to measure the results of the operations of a business until its life span had been completed. To get an idea of the success of a business, it is customary to prepare periodic statements of income and expense. Such statements usually are prepared at least once a year; they may be prepared more frequently.

Illustrative statement. Following is the income and expense statement of Community Televisions for August. It was prepared by using the balances of the income and expense accounts shown in the trial balance.

COMMUNITY TELEVISIONS

Statement of Income and Expense

For the Month of August, 19—

Income:
Commissions earned.................................... $1,250.00
Expenses:
Salaries expense.............................. $900.00
Office expense................................ 125.00   1,025.00
Net income... $ 225.00

Observe that the heading of the statement shows: (1) the name of the business, (2) the name of the statement, and (3) the period covered. The heading of a balance sheet and the heading of a statement of income and expense differ in this important particular: the heading of a balance sheet shows the *date* on which the stated financial condition existed; the heading of the statement of income and expense shows the *period* covered by the statement.

Earned surplus. The *earned surplus* of a corporation is the portion of the owners' equity derived from earnings. It is the excess of the company's aggregate net income since organization over all dividends distributed to stockholders.

Recently it has been suggested that the words "retained earnings" be used instead of "earned surplus." Such substitute terminology is gaining popularity. It is favored by many accountants who believe that the words *retained earnings* are more descriptive and less subject to misunderstanding.

It is important to make a distinction between capital stock and earned surplus, and to maintain this distinction in the statements and accounts, because the amount of the earned surplus usually has a bearing on the amount of dividends which a corporation can legally distribute. Furthermore, many statement users consider it helpful to know how much of the owners' equity resulted from investments by stockholders and how much is attributable to the retention of earnings.

Illustrative statement. The amount of the retained earnings of Community Televisions on August 31 is shown by the following statement:

COMMUNITY TELEVISIONS
Statement of Earned Surplus
For the Month of August, 19—

Net income for the month—per statement of income and expense	$225.00
Deduct dividend...	80.00
Earned surplus, August 31, 19—..........................	$145.00

If a company has any earned surplus at the beginning of the period for which the statement is being prepared, this beginning-of-period balance should be shown in the statement. See the illustration on page 52.

Balance sheet. Using information presented in the trial balance and the statement of earned surplus, the following balance sheet may be prepared.

COMMUNITY TELEVISIONS
Balance Sheet
August 31, 19—

Assets		Liabilities and Owners' Equity		
Cash......................	$2,895.00	Liabilities:		
Accounts receivable........	1,250.00	Accounts payable.........		$1,300.00
Installation and repair parts..	3,800.00			
Land......................	1,500.00	Owners' equity:		
		Capital stock..	$8,000.00	
		Earned surplus.	145.00	8,145.00
	$9,445.00			$9,445.00

Periodic nature of income, expense, and dividend accounts. The statement of income and expense and the statement of earned surplus cover a period of time. Therefore, the income, expense, and dividend accounts used in the preparation of these statements should show the increases and decreases in the earned surplus *during that period.*

It is a business custom to prepare statements annually: for the twelve months ended on December 31 if the company is on a calendar-year basis of accounting, or ending on some other date if the company is on a fiscal-year basis. At the end of the *accounting year,* whenever it may be, the income, expense, and dividend accounts should show the changes in the earned surplus during the year.

Statements may also be prepared at monthly intervals. For instance, assume that a company on a calendar-year basis prepares statements at the end of January; the accounts will show data for January, and the statement will cover that month. If the company prepares statements at the end of February, the accounts will show data for January and February, and the statements will cover the two-month period. And so on, throughout the year.

Closing the books. At the end of the *accounting year* (whether it be a calendar year or a fiscal year), the books should be "closed." The process of *closing the books* accomplishes two purposes:

> A balance is produced in the Earned Surplus account which is the amount of the earned surplus at the end of the year.
>
> The income, expense, and dividend accounts are left with no balances, so that, when entries are made in them during the succeeding year, the account balances will show the results of transactions during the succeeding year only, and will therefore furnish the data required for the preparation of statements for such succeeding year.

Although it is customary to close the books only at the end of the accounting year, we shall close the books of Community Televisions at the end of August, to illustrate the procedure.

Closing income accounts. Income accounts are closed by making and posting journal entries which transfer their credit balances to the credit side of a new account called Profit and Loss. Community Televisions has only one income account; it is closed by the following journal entry:

		Journal					(Page 3)
19—							
Aug.	31	Commissions earned........................	61	1,250	00		
		Profit and loss...........................	55			1,250	00
		To close the income account.					

The account numbers in the folio column of the journal show that the postings have been made. Following are the two accounts affected by this journal entry. In the following ledger accounts, the debit and credit of each successive journal entry are shown in italics, as an aid in identifying them.

			Commissions Earned					(61)
19—					19—			
Aug.	31		3	*1,250* *00*	Aug.	16	2	500 00
						31	2	750 00
				1,250 00				1,250 00

					Profit and Loss					(55)
					19—					
					Aug.	31		3	1,250	00

The Commissions Earned account has now been closed; that is, it has no balance. This fact is indicated by the totals and rulings. The closing entry transferred the credit balance of the Commissions Earned account to the credit of Profit and Loss.

Closing expense accounts. Expense accounts are closed by transferring their debit balances to the debit of the Profit and Loss account. Community Televisions has two expense accounts; they are closed by making and posting the following journal entries:

		Journal				(Page 3 Continued)	
31	Profit and loss.................................	55	900	00			
	Salaries expense..........................	71				900	00
	To close the Salaries Expense account.						
31	Profit and loss.............................	55	125	00			
	Office expense............................	72				125	00
	To close the Office Expense account.						

The accounts affected by these closing entries are shown below.

				Salaries Expense				(71)
19—				19—				
Aug.	31	2	900	00	Aug.	31	3	900	00

				Office Expense				(72)
19—				19—				
Aug.	31	2	125	00	Aug.	31	3	125	00

				Profit and Loss				(55)
19—					19—				
Aug.	31	3	900	00	Aug.	31	3	1,250	00
	31	3	125	00				

The two expense accounts are closed. The Profit and Loss account has a credit balance of $225, which is the amount of the net income; the balance of this Profit and Loss account should, and does, agree with the net income shown by the statement of income and expense on page 21.

Ruling closed accounts. You should observe the method of ruling closed accounts. In the Commissions Earned account, note the single rulings on the same line in the debit and credit money columns, the totals, and the double rulings in three places on the line below the totals. Since the expense accounts contain only one entry on each side, totals are unnecessary, and the accounts are ruled with double lines only.

Single rulings extend across the money columns only, whereas the double rulings extend across the date, reference, and money columns.

Graphic summary. The effect of these closing entries is shown graphically below. The amounts of the closing entries are shown in italics. The numbers in parentheses indicate the sequence in which the closing entries are made.

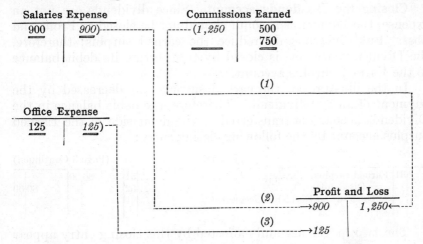

Closing the Profit and Loss account. The earned surplus was increased by the $225 of net income earned during August. Therefore, the Profit and Loss account is closed by transferring its $225 credit balance to the Earned Surplus account.

Journal				(Page 3 Continued)	
31	Profit and loss............................	55	225 00		
	Earned surplus...........................	51		225 00	
	To close the Profit and Loss account and credit Earned Surplus with the net income for August.				

The two accounts affected by this closing entry are shown below:

Profit and Loss							(55)	
19—				19—				
Aug.	31	3	900 00	Aug.	31	3	1,250 00	
	31	3	125 00					
	31	3	225 00					
			1,250 00				1,250 00	

Earned Surplus						(51)	
			19—				
			Aug.	31	3	225 00	

The nature and purpose of the Profit and Loss account should now be clearly apparent. It is used only when the books are closed. It has no balance before the closing procedure is begun, and it has no balance after the closing procedure is completed. It is used to assemble, in the ledger, the data required for the computation of the net income, and it is closed when the net income is transferred from Profit and Loss to Earned Surplus.

Closing the Dividends account. Since dividends are not an expense, the Dividends account should not be closed to Profit and Loss. But dividends do reduce the earned surplus; therefore, the Dividends account is closed by transferring its debit balance to the Earned Surplus account.

In the illustration, the earned surplus was decreased by the payment of an $80 dividend. Therefore, the debit balance in the Dividends account is transferred to the debit side of the Earned Surplus account by the following closing entry:

Journal (Page 3 Continued)

31	Earned surplus...............................	51	80	00	
	Dividends..................................	52			80	00
	To close the Dividends account.				

The two ledger accounts affected by this closing entry appear below:

Dividends (52)

19—				19—				
Aug.	31	2	80	00	Aug.	31	3	80	00

Earned Surplus (51)

19—				19—				
Aug.	31	3	80	00	Aug.	31	3	225	00

The Earned Surplus account now has a credit balance of $145, the amount of the earned surplus on August 31, 19—, as shown by the statement on page 22.

Summary of closing entries. The procedure of closing the books (that is, closing the income, expense, and dividend accounts) is summarized as follows:

Close the income and expense accounts to the Profit and Loss account. The balance of the Profit and Loss account then shows the net income *for the period.*

Close the Profit and Loss account and the Dividends account to Earned Surplus. The balance of the Earned Surplus account then shows the accumulated, undistributed earnings *at the end of the period.*

The complete closing procedure is shown graphically below.

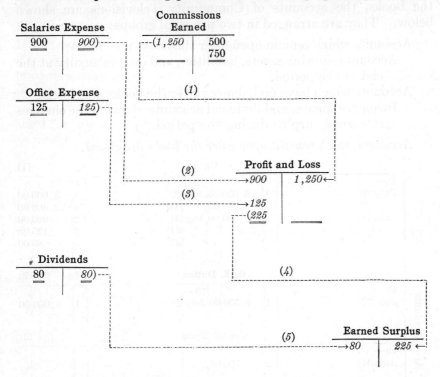

Journal with closing entries. The journal page containing all of the closing entries, with posting references included, is shown below:

		Journal		(Page 3)	
19— Aug.	31	Commissions earned............................	61	1,250 00	
		Profit and loss.............................	55		1,250 00
		To close the income account.			
	31	Profit and loss................................	55	900 00	
		Salaries expense............................	71		900 00
		To close the Salaries Expense account.			
	31	Profit and loss................................	55	125 00	
		Office expense.............................	72		125 00
		To close the Office Expense account.			
	31	Profit and loss................................	55	225 00	
		Earned surplus.............................	51		225 00
		To close the Profit and Loss account and credit Earned Surplus with the net income for August.			
	31	Earned surplus................................	51	80 00	
		Dividends.................................	52		80 00
		To close the Dividends account.			

Ledger. To indicate as clearly as possible the effect of closing the books, the accounts of Community Televisions are shown below. They are arranged in two principal groups:

Accounts which remain open after the books are closed:
  Accounts showing assets, liabilities, and owners' equity at the end of the period.
Accounts which have no balances after the books are closed:
  Income, expense, and dividend accounts, showing the changes in earned surplus during the period.

Accounts which remain open after the books are closed.

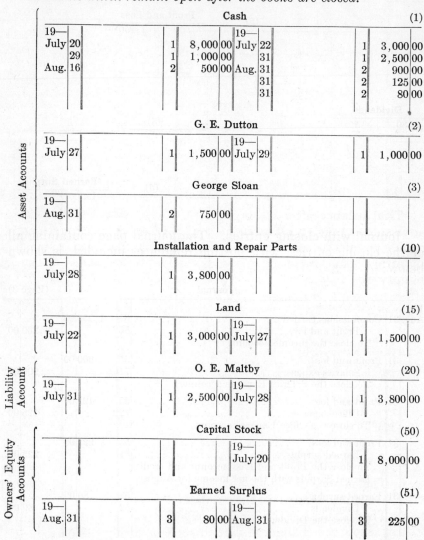

Asset Accounts

Cash (1)

19—					19—			
July	20	1	8,000	00	July	22	1	3,000	00
	29	1	1,000	00		31	1	2,500	00
Aug.	16	2	500	00	Aug.	31	2	900	00
						31	2	125	00
						31	2	80	00

G. E. Dutton (2)

19—					19—			
July	27	1	1,500	00	July	29	1	1,000	00

George Sloan (3)

19—				
Aug.	31	2	750	00

Installation and Repair Parts (10)

19—				
July	28	1	3,800	00

Land (15)

19—					19—			
July	22	1	3,000	00	July	27	1	1,500	00

Liability Account

O. E. Maltby (20)

19—					19—			
July	31	1	2,500	00	July	28	1	3,800	00

Owners' Equity Accounts

Capital Stock (50)

					19—			
					July	20	1	8,000	00

Earned Surplus (51)

19—					19—			
Aug.	31	3	80	00	Aug.	31	3	225	00

Accounts which have no balances after the books are closed.

Dividends (52)

19—						19—				
Aug.	31		2	80	00	Aug.	31	3	80	00

Profit and Loss (55)

19—						19—				
Aug.	31		3	900	00	Aug.	31	3	1,250	00
	31		3	125	00					
	31		3	225	00					
				1,250	00				1,250	00

Commissions Earned (61)

19—						19—				
Aug.	31		3	1,250	00	Aug.	16	2	500	00
							31	2	750	00
				1,250	00				1,250	00

Salaries Expense (71)

19—						19—				
Aug.	31		2	900	00	Aug.	31	3	900	00

Office Expense (72)

19—						19—				
Aug.	31		2	125	00	Aug.	31	3	125	00

Trial balance after closing. After the books are closed, it is advisable to take an *after-closing* trial balance, to be sure that the equality of debits and credits in the ledger has not been destroyed by errors made in closing the books. The trial balance of Community Televisions after closing on August 31 is shown below:

COMMUNITY TELEVISIONS
After-Closing Trial Balance
August 31, 19—

Cash..	2,895.00	
G. E. Dutton.................................	500.00	
George Sloan.................................	750.00	
Installation and repair parts.................	3,800.00	
Land...	1,500.00	
O. E. Maltby.................................		1,300.00
Capital stock................................		8,000.00
Earned surplus...............................		145.00
	9,445.00	9,445.00

Before the books are closed:

The balance in the Earned Surplus account shows the earned surplus, if any, at the beginning of the period.

The balances in the income, expense, and dividend accounts show the changes in earned surplus during the period.

After the books are closed:

> The balance in the Earned Surplus account shows the earned surplus at the end of the period.
>
> The income, expense, and dividend accounts have no balances. They are therefore ready for recording the changes in earned surplus during a subsequent period.

Sequence of accounting procedures. The various accounting procedures thus far explained are performed in the following sequence:

> Journalize.
> Post.
> Take a trial balance.
> Prepare a statement of income and expense for the period.
> Prepare a statement of earned surplus for the period.
> Prepare a balance sheet showing the financial condition at the end of the period.
> Make and post the journal entries necessary to close the books.
> Take an after-closing trial balance.

Punctuating numbers. When numbers are written on columnar-ruled paper, it is unnecessary to indicate decimal locations by using commas and periods; the rulings accomplish this purpose. Numbers written on paper which does not have money-column rulings should be punctuated, thus: 2,356,457.87.

Use of zeros and dashes. In books of original entry, ledger accounts, and trial balances, the use of two zeros or a dash in the cents column is a matter of choice. Thus, an amount may be written 1 257 00 or 1 257 —. Many bookkeepers feel that a dash is more easily written than two zeros, and that the use of dashes facilitates the addition of the cents column.

In balance sheets and other statements it is preferable, for the sake of appearance, to use zeros.

Dollar signs. Dollar signs need not be written in books of original entry, ledger accounts, and trial balances. They should be used in balance sheets and other formal statements. In such statements, a dollar sign should be written:

> Beside the first amount in each column. Look at the income statement on page 21 and observe the dollar signs in $1,250.00 and $900.00.
>
> Beside each amount appearing below an underline. Look at the same statement and observe the dollar sign in $225.00.

CHAPTER 3

Adjustments at the End of the Period

Transactions and adjustments. The statements prepared at the end of the period should reflect, as correctly as possible, the income earned and the expenses incurred during the period, and the assets, liabilities, and owners' equity at the end of the period.

In some instances, the statements will conform to this requirement when they are prepared from accounts which contain no entries other than those for transactions. But usually this is not the case. Usually it is necessary to make adjusting entries at the end of the period for some or all of the following:

Accruals of unrecorded:
  Expense.
  Income.
Apportionments of recorded:
  Costs.
  Income.

Adjustments of all of these classes are illustrated in this chapter.

Basis of illustration. For purposes of explanation, we shall continue the Community Televisions illustration through September. The company's operations for that month, and the related entries, are described below under the following captions:

Income and expense correctly reflected by transaction entries only.
Adjustments required for accruals.
Adjustments required for apportionments.

Income and Expense Correctly Reflected by Transaction Entries Only

Income. The company had three kinds of income during September which were correctly reflected by entries for transactions, without any adjusting entries at the end of the month.

Commissions earned. On September 3 the company collected from George Sloan the $750 which he was billed on August 31 for commissions on sales of television sets during the last half of August. The entry to record this transaction does not contain a credit to an income account; the income was earned in August and

31

an entry was made on August 31 debiting George Sloan and crediting Commissions Earned $750. The following entry records the collection of the receivable.

Sept. 3   Cash.. 750.00
         George Sloan................................   750.00
         Collection of commission billings for last half
         of August.

On September 16 the company collected $625 from Sloan for commissions on sales during the first half of September.

Sept. 16   Cash.. 625.00
         Commissions earned......................   625.00
         Collection of commissions for first half of
         September.

On September 30 the company billed Sloan $700 for commissions on sales during the last half of the month.

Sept. 30   George Sloan.............................. 700.00
         Commissions earned......................   700.00
         Commission billing for last half of September.

After these entries are posted, the Commissions Earned account will have a credit balance of $1,325, the amount of the commission income for the month.

Repair service income. All repair work done by Community Televisions on sets and antennas is done on orders from Sloan. On September 27 the company received $160 from Sloan for repair work done for his customers during the first 26 days of September.

Sept. 27   Cash.. 160.00
         Repair service income....................   160.00
         For repair work done Sept. 1 through Sept. 26.

On September 30 the company billed Sloan $35 for repair work done from September 27 to September 30, inclusive.

Sept. 30   George Sloan.............................. 35.00
         Repair service income....................   35.00
         Amount billed Sloan for repair work done from
         Sept. 27 to Sept. 30, inclusive.

After these entries are posted, the Repair Service Income account will have a credit balance of $195, the amount of the repair income for the month.

Installation income. When a television set is sold, Community Televisions is given the job of installing the set and of installing an outside antenna if one is required. The company is paid by Sloan at the end of the month for all such work done during the month. The amount collected on September 30 was $825. The entry for the collection is on page 33.

```
Sept. 30  Cash...................................  825.00
              Installation income.....................          825.00
          For television set and antenna installations
          during September.
```

The $825 credited to the income account in this transaction entry is the amount of the installation income for the month.

Expense. The company had two classes of expense which were correctly reflected by transaction entries for the month.

Building rent. The company management decided to rent quarters instead of erecting a building. The building rent for September, $250, was paid on September 1.

```
Sept. 1  Building rent...............................  250.00
             Cash...................................          250.00
         Payment of rent for September.
```

The $250 debited to the expense account correctly reflects the rent expense for the month.

Salaries. Salaries for the month, in the amount of $1,150, were paid on September 30.

```
Sept. 30  Salaries expense........................  1,150.00
              Cash............................          1,150.00
          Paid salaries for the month.
```

The $1,150 is the salaries expense for the month.

Adjustments Required for Accruals

The words *accrual* and *accrued* are applied to income which has been earned or expenses which have been incurred for which no transaction entry has been recorded.

Accrued income. The company had one item of accrued income at the end of September.

Interest income. When the company decided, on September 1, to rent a building instead of erecting one, it sold the land, receiving $500 in cash and taking a $1,000 mortgage. The transaction was recorded as follows:

```
Sept. 1  Cash...................................    500.00
         Mortgage receivable....................  1,000.00
             Land...............................          1,500.00
         To record the sale of land.
```

The mortgage bore 6% interest, payable semiannually. Although no interest was *collected* during September, one month's interest, or $5 ($1,000 × .06 × $\frac{1}{12}$), was *earned* during that month. Therefore, the following adjusting entry was required:

```
Sept. 30  Accrued interest receivable.....................  5.00
              Interest income...........................          5.00
          One month's interest on mortgage.
```

The debit balance in the Accrued Interest Receivable account will be shown in the balance sheet as an asset. The credit balance in the Interest Income account will be shown in the statement of income and expense.

The following general rule may be stated for making adjusting entries for accrued income: *If a company has earned income for which no transaction entry has been made, debit an asset account and credit an income account.*

Accrued expense. The company had one item of accrued expense at the end of the month.

Truck rent. The company rented a truck at a rate of ten cents a mile. The rent for each month was payable on the first day of the following month. Since there was no rent payment in September, there was no transaction entry for that month. But the company drove the truck 2,400 miles during September, and thus incurred a rent expense of $240 during the month. The following adjusting entry for the accrual was therefore required at the end of September:

```
Sept. 30   Truck rent...............................  240.00
              Truck rent payable.....................          240.00
              Expense and liability for use of truck during
              September.
```

The following general rule may be stated for making adjusting entries for accrued expenses: *If a company has incurred an expense for which no transaction entry has been made, debit an expense account and credit a liability account.*

Adjustments Required for Apportionments

Income apportionments. Collections may be received in payment for services to be rendered in the future. The accounting procedures to be used in such cases are stated below:

If the service will be completely performed, and the total income thereby earned, during the accounting period in which the collection is received, an income account should be credited at the time of the collection.

If the service will not be completely performed during the accounting period in which the collection is received:

The entire amount of the collection should be credited to an unearned income account;

At the end of the period, the portion of the income earned during the period by the performance of service should be transferred, by an adjusting entry, from the unearned income account to an income account.

Community Televisions had one source of income which required an unearned income account and an adjusting entry.

Inspection service.   When a television set is sold, Sloan agrees to have it inspected within thirty days from the date of sale. Community Televisions does this work, and Sloan pays the company $5 for service on each set sold.   Regardless of when the inspection is made, Sloan makes a payment at the middle of each month for inspection service on all sets sold during the first half of the month, and another payment on the last day of the month for service on all sets sold during the last half of the month.   Collections from Sloan during September were:

```
September 15................................................. $100
          30.................................................  150
```

Because Community Televisions has thirty days from the date of each sale to make the inspection, it is obvious that the total amount collected during the month will not be earned by the performance of service during the month.   Therefore, the amounts of the collections are credited to an unearned income account.

```
Sept. 15   Cash....................................  100.00
               Unearned inspection income............       100.00
           For inspection service to be done on 20 sets
           sold during the first half of September.

Sept. 30   Cash....................................  150.00
               Unearned inspection income............       150.00
           For inspection service to be done on 30 sets
           sold during the last half of September.
```

By the end of September, Community Televisions had inspected 12 sets, and therefore had earned $60.   This $60 is transferred from the unearned income account to an income account by the following adjusting entry:

```
Sept. 30   Unearned inspection income..................  60.00
               Inspection service income................       60.00
           Income earned by inspection of 12 sets.
```

The posting of the transaction entries and the adjusting entry will produce the following accounts:

Unearned Inspection Income

19—							19—				
Sept.	30			6	60	00	Sept.	15		5	100	00
								30		5	150	00

Inspection Service Income

							19—				
							Sept.	30		6	60	00

The $60 credit balance in the Inspection Service Income account will be shown in the statement of income and expense. The $190 credit balance in the Unearned Inspection Income account (sometimes called a deferred income account) will be shown on the liability side of the balance sheet; it represents an obligation to render inspection service in the future.

Cost apportionments. An expenditure is a payment, or the incurring of an obligation to make a future payment, for a benefit received or to be received. The amount of the expenditure is the cost of the benefit.

If the expenditure benefits only the period in which it is made, the cost should be debited to an expense account. This was the case with the expenditures for building rent and salaries.

Business concerns often make expenditures for things which are assets at the date of the expenditure but which are used up during several periods as the result of operations or the passage of time. If an expenditure will benefit more than one period, it is properly chargeable to an asset account, but at the end of each period it is necessary to determine how much of the cost should be charged as an expense of the period and what portion of the cost should still be shown in the balance sheet as an asset. The accounting procedure to be used in such cases is stated below:

At the date of the expenditure, debit the entire cost to an asset account.

At the end of each period benefited by the expenditure, an appropriate portion of the cost should be transferred from the asset account to an expense account.

Illustrations applicable to Community Televisions are presented below.

Insurance. On September 1, the company bought a one-year fire insurance policy at a cost of $120. This $120 is the cost of an asset—a very valuable right to collect from the insurance company in the event of a fire. Therefore, an asset account, Unexpired Insurance, was debited.

```
Sept. 1   Unexpired insurance........................ 120.00
              Cash...................................          120.00
          Cost of one-year fire insurance policy.
```

One-twelfth of this asset expires each month. The cost expiration is an expense, and the following adjusting entry is required:

```
Sept. 30  Insurance expense.......................... 10.00
              Unexpired insurance.....................          10.00
          Insurance expense for the month.
```

The posting of this entry will affect the two accounts as follows:

Unexpired Insurance

19—						19—					
Sept.	1			5	120 00	Sept.	30			6	10 00

Insurance Expense

19—					
Sept.	30			6	10 00

The $10 debit balance in the Insurance Expense account will appear in the statement of income and expense. The $110 debit balance in the Unexpired Insurance account will be shown on the asset side of the balance sheet.

Installation and repair parts used. In July the company purchased antennas and other parts at a cost of $3,800, which was debited to an asset account called Installation and Repair Parts. In its installation and repair work during September, the company used antennas and parts which cost $270. To give recognition to the expense and the reduction in the asset, the following adjusting entry is required at the end of September:

```
Sept. 30   Installation and repair parts expense........  270.00
                 Installation and repair parts.............       270.00
           Expense for the month.
```

Installation and Repair Parts

19—						19—					
July	28			1	3,800 00	Sept.	30			6	270 00

Installation and Repair Parts Expense

19—					
Sept.	30			6	270 00

The $3,530 debit balance in the Installation and Repair Parts (asset) account will appear on the asset side of the balance sheet. The $270 debit balance of the Installation and Repair Parts Expense account will appear in the statement of income and expense.

Depreciation of equipment. To conduct its operations, Community Televisions purchased equipment on September 1, at a cost of $2,400. Payment was made in cash and the purchase was recorded by the following entry:

```
Sept. 1   Equipment.............................  2,400.00
                Cash............................       2,400.00
          Purchase of equipment.
```

The equipment is an asset, with an expected useful life of ten years. Since its cost will become an expense during the ten-year period, a portion of the cost should be recognized as an expense during each accounting period. In other words, there is a monthly cost expiration of $\frac{1}{120}$ of $2,400, or $20. This cost expiration, which is called *depreciation*, is recorded by an adjusting entry.

The monthly adjusting entry for depreciation includes a debit to Depreciation of Equipment—an expense account. The credit *might* be made to the Equipment (asset) account. However, it usually is desirable to have the balance of such an asset account show the original cost of the asset. Therefore, it is customary to credit a separate account. Reserve for Depreciation has long been, and is here, used as the title of this account. Some accountants prefer the account title, Allowance for Depreciation.

Following is the September 30 adjusting entry:

```
Sept. 30   Depreciation of equipment..................... 20.00
                 Reserve for depreciation—Equipment......        20.00
           Depreciation for September.
```

Equipment

19—										
Sept.	1			5	2,400	00				

Reserve for Depreciation—Equipment

				19—						
				Sept.	30			6	20	00

Depreciation of Equipment

19—										
Sept.	30			6	20	00				

The asset and reserve account balances will appear in the balance sheet, thus:

```
Equipment.................................... $2,400.00
    Less reserve for depreciation...............   20.00 $2,380.00
```

The balance in the Depreciation of Equipment account will appear as an expense in the statement of income and expense.

It should be noted that the balance of the Depreciation of Equipment (expense) account is transferred to Profit and Loss when the books are closed, but the reserve account remains open and its balance is increased by the periodic adjusting entries for depreciation.

Journal—Transaction entries. On page 39 is the journal of Community Televisions containing all of the entries for September transactions previously mentioned and an entry to record the payment of a dividend.

Journal

(Page 5)

19—				
Sept.	1	Cash...................................	500 00	
		Mortgage receivable.......................	1,000 00	
		Land..................................		1,500 00
		To record the sale of land.		
	1	Building rent..............................	250 00	
		Cash..................................		250 00
		Payment of rent for September.		
	1	Equipment................................	2,400 00	
		Cash..................................		2,400 00
		Purchase of equipment.		
	1	Unexpired insurance.......................	120 00	
		Cash..................................		120 00
		Cost of insurance policy.		
	3	Cash.....................................	750 00	
		George Sloan.........................		750 00
		Collection of commission billing for last half of August.		
	15	Cash.....................................	100 00	
		Unearned inspection income...............		100 00
		For inspection service to be done on 20 sets sold during the first half of September.		
	16	Cash.....................................	625 00	
		Commissions earned.......................		625 00
		Collection of commissions for first half of September.		
	27	Cash.....................................	160 00	
		Repair service income.....................		160 00
		For repair work done Sept. 1 through Sept. 26.		
	30	George Sloan.............................	700 00	
		Commissions earned.......................		700 00
		Commission billing for last half of September.		
	30	Cash.....................................	825 00	
		Installation income.......................		825 00
		For television set and antenna installations during September.		
	30	Cash.....................................	150 00	
		Unearned inspection income...............		150 00
		For inspection service to be done on 30 sets sold during the last half of September.		
	30	George Sloan.............................	35 00	
		Repair job income........................		35 00
		Amount billed Sloan for repair work done from Sept. 27 to Sept. 30, inclusive.		
	30	Salaries expense..........................	1,150 00	
		Cash..................................		1,150 00
		Paid salaries for the month.		
	30	Dividends................................	80 00	
		Cash..................................		80 00
		Payment of dividend.		

Trial balance after posting transaction entries. The following trial balance shows the balances of the accounts after the completion of the posting of the entries for the September transactions.

COMMUNITY TELEVISIONS

Trial Balance

September 30, 19—

Cash	2,005.00	
G. E. Dutton	500.00	
George Sloan	735.00	
Installation and repair parts	3,800.00	
Unexpired insurance	120.00	
Mortgage receivable	1,000.00	
Equipment	2,400.00	
O. E. Maltby		1,300.00
Unearned inspection income		250.00
Capital stock		8,000.00
Earned surplus		145.00
Dividends	80.00	
Commissions earned		1,325.00
Repair service income		195.00
Installation income		825.00
Salaries expense	1,150.00	
Building rent	250.00	
	12,040.00	12,040.00

Journal—Adjusting entries. Following is the journal of Community Televisions containing all of the September 30 adjusting entries. The first entry is for an accrued income; the second entry is for an accrued expense; the third entry is for an income apportionment; the last three entries are for cost apportionments.

Journal   (Page 6)

19—				
Sept.	30	Accrued interest receivable	5 00	
		Interest income		5 00
		One month's interest on mortgage.		
	30	Truck rent	240 00	
		Truck rent payable		240 00
		Expense and liability for use of truck during September.		
	30	Unearned inspection income	60 00	
		Inspection service income		60 00
		Income earned by inspection of 12 sets.		
	30	Insurance expense	10 00	
		Unexpired insurance		10 00
		Insurance expense for the month.		
	30	Installation and repair parts expense	270 00	
		Installation and repair parts		270 00
		Expense for the month.		
	30	Depreciation of equipment	20 00	
		Reserve for depreciation—Equipment		20 00
		Depreciation for September.		

Trial balances before and after adjustments. Below are shown the trial balances of the company before and after the posting of the adjusting entries.

COMMUNITY TELEVISIONS
Trial Balances
September 30, 19—

	Before Adjustments		After Adjustments	
Cash.	2,005		2,005	
G. E. Dutton.	500		500	
George Sloan.	735		735	
Accrued interest receivable.			5	
Installation and repair parts.	3,800		3,530	
Unexpired insurance.	120		110	
Mortgage receivable.	1,000		1,000	
Equipment.	2,400		2,400	
Reserve for depreciation—Equipment.				20
O. E. Maltby.		1,300		1,300
Truck rent payable.				240
Unearned inspection income.		250		190
Capital stock.		8,000		8,000
Earned surplus.		145		145
Dividends.	80		80	
Commissions earned.		1,325		1,325
Repair service income.		195		195
Installation income.		825		825
Inspection service income.				60
Interest income.				5
Salaries expense.	1,150		1,150	
Building rent.	250		250	
Truck rent.			240	
Insurance expense.			10	
Installation and repair parts expense.			270	
Depreciation of equipment.			20	
	12,040	12,040	12,305	12,305

Locating errors. If a trial balance does not balance, the amount of the difference should be determined; the following steps may be taken to locate the error:

(1) Refoot the trial balance.
(2) See that the balances have been carried correctly from the ledger to the trial balance. Watch for:
    (a) Differences between the balances in the accounts and the balances shown in the trial balance.
    (b) Debit balances in the accounts entered on the credit side of the trial balance, and vice versa.
    (c) Ledger balances omitted from the trial balance.
(3) Recompute the ledger balances; this will involve the following steps:
    (a) Refooting the debit side and the credit side of each account.
    (b) Recomputing the difference between the two sides of each account.

(4) Check the postings from the journal to the ledger. Beginning with the first journal entry, see whether each debit and credit has been correctly posted. Watch for:

(a) Errors in amounts.

(b) Postings to wrong accounts.

(c) Posting a journal debit to the credit side of the ledger, or a journal credit to the debit side of the ledger.

As each entry in the journal is traced to the ledger, place a check mark ($\sqrt{}$) beside the amount in the journal and also beside the amount in the ledger. A check mark usually is placed at the right of an amount. After the checking of the postings has been completed, look for:

(a) Unchecked entries in the journal—see whether these items have been posted.

(b) Unchecked entries in the ledger—see whether these items belong in the ledger; it is possible that a journal entry has been posted twice, that one ledger entry has been checked, and that the unchecked ledger entry is a duplicate posting.

(5) See that the debit and credit amounts in each journal entry are equal.

In looking for errors, be constantly on the watch for:

Transpositions—such as $79.85 posted as $78.95.
Slides   —such as $.75 posted as $75.00.

Erasures should not be made in accounting records. When an error is discovered, the incorrect amount or other item in the entry should be struck out by drawing a line through it, and the correct entry should be inserted above the incorrect one.

CHAPTER 4

Working Papers and Their Uses

Working papers. *Working papers* are a columnar device employed by accountants as a convenient and orderly way of organizing the accounting data to be used in the preparation of adjusting entries, periodic statements, and closing entries.

If the ledger contains only a few accounts, working papers are not necessary, and the accounting procedures are performed in the following order:

Make and post the entries for transactions.
Take a trial balance.
Make and post the adjusting entries.
Take an adjusted trial balance.
Prepare the statement of income and expense, the statement of earned surplus, and the balance sheet.
Make and post entries to close the books.
Take an after-closing trial balance.

If the ledger contains a considerable number of accounts, working papers are very useful. Since one of their purposes is to indicate the adjusting entries which should be made, the above-stated sequence of procedures is changed as follows:

Make and post the entries for transactions.
Take a trial balance.
Prepare working papers.
Prepare the statement of income and expense, the statement of earned surplus, and the balance sheet.
Make and post adjusting and closing entries.
Take an after-closing trial balance.

These procedures, in total, constitute an *accounting cycle*. In actual business, this cycle, including closing the books, usually is completed only once a year, because the books ordinarily are not closed more frequently. In the illustrations and problems in this text it is often assumed, for convenience and simplicity, that the cycle is completed monthly.

Illustrative working papers. The account balances of Community Televisions at the end of September and the related adjustment data, presented in the preceding chapter, will be used

43

for purposes of illustration.   There are so few accounts that an experienced accountant probably would not consider it worth while to prepare working papers; but in a textbook it is advisable to begin with a relatively simple illustration.

The steps in the preparation of the working papers are stated and illustrated below.

First step.   Headings were written; the ledger account balances before adjustments were entered in the Trial Balance columns; and these columns were totaled to determine their equality.

The working papers after the completion of this step are shown on page 45.

Second step.   The required adjustments were entered in the Adjustments columns.   These adjustments are the same as those mentioned in Chapter 3.   Observe that the nature of each adjustment is stated at the bottom of the working papers, with a key letter referring to the debit and credit entries in the Adjustments columns.   These letters not only key the debit and credit entries to the explanatory data but also make it easier to match an entry in the Adjustments debit column with its related credit.   The Adjustments columns were totaled as a check against errors.

The working papers after the completion of this step are shown on page 46.   Read the explanation of each adjustment at the bottom of the working papers, and observe the related debit and credit entries in the Adjustments columns.   Also observe that, if the adjustment requires the use of an account which does not appear in the trial balance, the name of the account is written below the trial balance.

Third step.   The account balances (after the application of adjustments, if any) were entered in the Adjusted Trial Balance columns.   Observe how the adjustments were applied.   For instance, on the Installation and Repair Parts line, the $3,800 in the Trial Balance debit column minus the $270 in the Adjustments credit column is $3,530, the amount entered in the Adjusted Trial Balance debit column.

The Adjusted Trial Balance columns were totaled as a test of accuracy.   The working papers after the completion of this step are shown on page 47.

Fourth step.   Each account balance appearing in the Adjusted Trial Balance columns was entered in a column at the right corresponding to the statement in which it should appear.

Debit balances were entered in debit columns; credit balances were entered in credit columns.

The working papers after the completion of this step are on page 48.   (Continued on page 51.)

Step 1

COMMUNITY TELEVISIONS
Working Papers
For the Month of September, 19—

	Trial Balance		Adjustments	Adjusted Trial Balance	Income and Expense Statement	Earned Surplus Statement	Balance Sheet
Cash	2,005						
G. E. Dutton	500						
George Sloan	735						
Installation and repair parts	3,800						
Unexpired insurance	120						
Mortgage receivable	1,000						
Equipment	2,400						
O. E. Maltby		1,300					
Unearned inspection income		250					
Capital stock		8,000					
Earned surplus		145					
Dividends	80						
Commissions earned		1,325					
Repair service income		195					
Installation income		825					
Salaries expense	1,150						
Building rent	250						
	12,040	12,040					

Step 2

COMMUNITY TELEVISIONS
Working Papers
For the Month of September, 19—

Account	Trial Balance (Dr)	Trial Balance (Cr)	Adjustments (Dr)	Adjustments (Cr)	Adjusted Trial Balance	Income and Expense Statement	Earned Surplus Statement	Balance Sheet
Cash	2,005							
G. E. Dutton	500							
George Sloan	735							
Installation and repair parts	3,800			270e				
Unexpired insurance	120			10d				
Mortgage receivable	1,000							
Equipment	2,400							
O. E. Maltby		1,300						
Unearned inspection income		250	60c					
Capital stock		8,000						
Earned surplus		145						
Dividends	80							
Commissions earned		1,325						
Repair service income		195						
Installation income		825						
Salaries expense	1,150							
Building rent	250							
	12,040	12,040						
Accrued interest receivable			5a					
Interest income				5a				
Truck rent			240b					
Truck rent payable				240b				
Inspection service income				60c				
Insurance expense			10d					
Installation and repair parts expense			270e					
Depreciation of equipment			20f					
Reserve for depreciation—Equipment				20f				
			605	605				

Adjustments

a—Accrued interest income on mortgage.
b—Accrued truck rent expense.
c—Portion of inspection service income earned during September.
d—Portion of insurance cost expired during September.
e—Cost of parts used during September.
f—Depreciation of equipment during September.

Step 3

COMMUNITY TELEVISIONS
Working Papers
For the Month of September, 19—

Account	Trial Balance Dr	Trial Balance Cr	Adjustments Dr	Adjustments Cr	Adjusted Trial Balance Dr	Adjusted Trial Balance Cr	Income and Expense Statement	Earned Surplus Statement	Balance Sheet
Cash	2,005				2,005				
G. E. Dutton	500				500				
George Sloan	735				735				
Installation and repair parts	3,800			270e	3,530				
Unexpired insurance	120			10d	110				
Mortgage receivable	1,000				1,000				
Equipment	2,400				2,400				
O. E. Maltby		1,300				1,300			
Unearned inspection income		250	60c			190			
Capital stock		8,000				8,000			
Earned surplus		145				145			
Dividends	80				80				
Commissions earned		1,325				1,325			
Repair service income		195				195			
Installation income		825				825			
Salaries expense	1,150				1,150				
Building rent	250				250				
	12,040	12,040							
Accrued interest receivable			5a		5				
Interest income				5a		5			
Truck rent			240b		240				
Truck rent payable				240b		240			
Inspection service income				60c		60			
Insurance expense			10d		10				
Installation and repair parts expense			270e		270				
Depreciation of equipment			20f		20				
Reserve for depreciation—Equipment				20f		20			
			605	605	12,305	12,305			

Adjustments

a—Accrued interest income on mortgage.
b—Accrued truck rent expense.
c—Portion of inspection service income earned during September.
d—Portion of insurance cost expired during September.
e—Cost of parts used during September.
f—Depreciation of equipment during September.

Step 4

COMMUNITY TELEVISIONS
Working Papers
For the Month of September, 19—

Account	Trial Balance Dr	Trial Balance Cr	Adjustments Dr	Adjustments Cr	Adjusted Trial Balance Dr	Adjusted Trial Balance Cr	Income and Expense Statement Dr	Income and Expense Statement Cr	Earned Surplus Statement Dr	Earned Surplus Statement Cr	Balance Sheet Dr	Balance Sheet Cr
Cash	2,005				2,005						2,005	
G. E. Dutton	500				500						500	
George Sloan	735				735						735	
Installation and repair parts	3,800			270e	3,530						3,530	
Unexpired insurance	120			10d	110						110	
Mortgage receivable	1,000				1,000						1,000	
Equipment	2,400				2,400						2,400	
O. E. Maltby		1,300				1,300						1,300
Unearned inspection income		250	60c			190						190
Capital stock		8,000				8,000						8,000
Earned surplus		145				145				145		
Dividends	80				80				80			
Commissions earned		1,325				1,325		1,325				
Repair service income		195				195		195				
Installation income		825				825		825				
Salaries expense	1,150				1,150		1,150					
Building rent	250				250		250					
	12,040	12,040										
Accrued interest receivable			5a		5						5	
Interest income				5a		5		5				
Truck rent			240b		240		240					
Truck rent payable				240b		240						240
Inspection service income				60c		60		60				
Insurance expense			10d		10		10					
Installation and repair parts expense			270e		270		270					
Depreciation of equipment			20f		20		20					
Reserve for depreciation—Equipment				20f		20						20
			605	605	12,305	12,305						

Adjustments

a—Accrued interest income on mortgage.
b—Accrued truck expense.
c—Portion of inspection service income earned during September.
d—Portion of insurance cost expired during September.
e—Cost of parts used during September.
f—Depreciation of equipment during September.

Step 5

COMMUNITY TELEVISIONS
Working Papers
For the Month of September, 19—

Account	TB Dr	TB Cr	Adj Dr	Adj Cr	Adj. TB Dr	Adj. TB Cr	Inc. & Exp. Dr	Inc. & Exp. Cr	Earned Surplus Dr	Earned Surplus Cr	Bal. Sheet Dr	Bal. Sheet Cr
Cash	2,005				2,005						2,005	
G. E. Dutton	500				500						500	
George Sloan	735				735						735	
Installation and repair parts	3,800			270e	3,530						3,530	
Unexpired insurance	120			10d	110						110	
Mortgage receivable	1,000				1,000						1,000	
Equipment	2,400				2,400						2,400	
O. E. Maltby		1,300				1,300						1,300
Unearned inspection income		250	60c			190						190
Capital stock		8,000				8,000						8,000
Earned surplus		145				145				145		
Dividends	80				80				80			
Commissions earned		1,325				1,325		1,325				
Repair service income		195				195		195				
Installation income		825				825		825				
Salaries expense	1,150				1,150		1,150					
Building rent	250				250		250					
	12,040	12,040										
Accrued interest receivable			5a		5						5	
Interest income				5a		5		5				
Truck rent			240b		240		240					
Truck rent payable				240b		240						240
Inspection service income				60c		60		60				
Insurance expense			10d		10		10					
Installation and repair parts expense			270e		270		270					
Depreciation of equipment			20f		20		20					
Reserve for depreciation—Equipment				20f		20						20
			605	605	12,305	12,305						
Net income							470			470		
							2,410	2,410				

Adjustments

a—Accrued interest income on mortgage.
b—Accrued truck expense.
c—Portion of inspection service income earned during September.
d—Portion of insurance cost expired during September.
e—Cost of parts used during September.
f—Depreciation of equipment during September.

Final Step

COMMUNITY TELEVISIONS
Working Papers
For the Month of September, 19—

	Trial Balance		Adjustments		Adjusted Trial Balance		Income and Expense Statement		Earned Surplus Statement		Balance Sheet	
Cash	2,005				2,005						2,005	
G. E. Dutton	500				500						500	
George Sloan	735				735						735	
Installation and repair parts	3,800			270e	3,530						3,530	
Unexpired insurance	120			10d	110						110	
Mortgage receivable	1,000				1,000						1,000	
Equipment	2,400				2,400						2,400	
O. E. Maltby		1,300				1,300						1,300
Unearned inspection income		250	60c			190						190
Capital stock		8,000				8,000						8,000
Earned surplus		145				145				145		
Dividends	80				80				80			
Commissions earned		1,325				1,325		1,325				
Repair service income		195				195		195				
Installation income		825				825		825				
Salaries expense	1,150				1,150		1,150					
Building rent	250				250		250					
	12,040	12,040										
Accrued interest receivable			5a		5						5	
Interest income				5a		5		5				
Truck rent			240b		240		240					
Truck rent payable				240b		240						240
Inspection service income				60c		60		60				
Insurance expense			10d		10		10					
Installation and repair parts expense			270e		270		270					
Depreciation of equipment			20f		20		20					
Reserve for depreciation—Equipment				20f		20						20
			605	605	12,305	12,305						
Net income							470			470		
							2,410	2,410				
Earned surplus, September 30, 19—									535			535
									615	615	10,285	10,285

Adjustments

a—Accrued interest income on mortgage.
b—Accrued truck expense.
c—Portion of inspection service income earned during September.
d—Portion of insurance cost expired during September.
e—Cost of parts used during September.
f—Depreciation of equipment during September.

Fifth step. The net income for the month, amounting to $470, was determined by computing the balance of the Income and Expense columns. The $470 was entered in the Income and Expense debit column as a balancing figure; and, since the net income increases the earned surplus, it was also entered in the Earned Surplus credit column. The Income and Expense columns were then totaled. The working papers after the completion of this step are on page 49.

Final step. The earned surplus balance at the end of the month, in the amount of $535, was determined by computing the balance of the two Earned Surplus columns. The $535 was entered as a balancing figure in the Earned Surplus debit column; and, since the earned surplus also appears in the balance sheet, the $535 was also entered in the Balance Sheet credit column.

The Earned Surplus columns were totaled.

The two Balance Sheet columns were totaled and found to be in agreement. If the Balance Sheet columns did not have the same totals, an error some place in the working papers would be indicated.

The completed working papers are on page 50.

Statements prepared from working papers. The working papers furnish in a convenient form the information required for the periodic statements.

Statement of income and expense. The following statement shows the amounts which appear in the Income and Expense columns of the working papers.

COMMUNITY TELEVISIONS

Statement of Income and Expense

For the Month of September, 19—

Income:

Commissions earned		$1,325.00
Repair service income		195.00
Installation income		825.00
Inspection service income		60.00
Interest income		5.00
Total		$2,410.00
Deduct expenses:		
Salaries expense	$1,150.00	
Building rent	250.00	
Truck rent	240.00	
Insurance expense	10.00	
Installation and repair parts expense	270.00	
Depreciation of equipment	20.00	
Total		1,940.00
Net income		$ 470.00

Statement of earned surplus. The following statement shows the amounts which appear in the Earned Surplus columns of the working papers.

COMMUNITY TELEVISIONS
Statement of Earned Surplus
For the Month of September, 19—

Earned surplus, August 31, 19—...............................	$145.00
Add net income for the month—Per statement of income and expense..	470.00
Total...	$615.00
Deduct dividends..	80.00
Earned surplus, September 30, 19—.........................	$535.00

Balance sheet. The following statement shows the amounts which appear in the Balance Sheet columns of the working papers.

COMMUNITY TELEVISIONS
Balance Sheet
September 30, 19—
Assets

Cash..		$ 2,005.00
Accounts receivable...................................		1,235.00
Accrued interest receivable...........................		5.00
Installation and repair parts..........................		3,530.00
Unexpired insurance...................................		110.00
Mortgage receivable..................................		1,000.00
Equipment...............................	$2,400.00	
Less reserve for depreciation................	20.00	2,380.00
		$10,265.00

Liabilities and Owners' Equity

Liabilities:		
Accounts payable.........................	$1,300.00	
Truck rent payable........................	240.00	
Unearned inspection income................	190.00	
Total...		$ 1,730.00
Owners' equity:		
Capital stock.............................	$8,000.00	
Earned surplus—Per statement of earned surplus	535.00	
Total...		8,535.00
		$10,265.00

A balance sheet in which the assets appear at the left and the liabilities and owners' equity at the right is sometimes called an *account form* balance sheet. The term *report form* is sometimes applied to a balance sheet in which the liabilities and owners' equity appear below the assets.

Adjusting entries. The amounts in the Adjustments columns of the working papers, together with the information in the key to adjustments at the bottom of the working papers, furnish the information for the following adjusting entries to be recorded in the journal and posted to the ledger.

Journal (Page 6)

19—				
Sept.	30	Accrued interest receivable.....................	5 00	
		Interest income............................		5 00
		One month's interest on mortgage.		
	30	Truck rent...................................	240 00	
		Truck rent payable......................		240 00
		Expense and liability for use of truck during September.		
	30	Unearned inspection income....................	60 00	
		Inspection service income.................		60 00
		Portion of income earned.		
	30	Insurance expense............................	10 00	
		Unexpired insurance......................		10 00
		Insurance expense for the month.		
	30	Installation and repair parts expense...........	270 00	
		Installation and repair parts..............		270 00
		Expense for the month.		
	30	Depreciation of equipment....................	20 00	
		Reserve for depreciation—Equipment.......		20 00
		Depreciation for September.		

Closing entries. The closing entries can be prepared from the data in the Income and Expense columns and the Earned Surplus columns of the working papers.

Journal (Page 7)

19—				
Sept.	30	Commissions earned..........................	1,325 00	
		Repair service income........................	195 00	
		Installation income...........................	825 00	
		Interest income..............................	5 00	
		Inspection service income.....................	60 00	
		Profit and loss...........................		2,410 00
		To close the income accounts.		
	30	Profit and loss...............................	1,940 00	
		Salaries expense..........................		1,150 00
		Building rent.............................		250 00
		Truck rent...............................		240 00
		Insurance expense........................		10 00
		Installation and repair parts expense.......		270 00
		Depreciation of equipment.................		20 00
		To close the expense accounts.		
	30	Profit and loss...............................	470 00	
		Earned surplus...........................		470 00
		To transfer the net income to Earned Surplus.		
	30	Earned surplus...............................	80 00	
		Dividends................................		80 00
		To close the Dividends account.		

In the illustrative closing entries in Chapter 2, a separate journal entry was made for the closing of each income and expense account. This was done for purposes of clear explanation. The closing procedure can be greatly simplified by making compound journal entries. The foregoing closing entries, prepared from data in the working papers, are illustrative of compound entries.

The Profit and Loss and Earned Surplus accounts after the posting of the closing entries will appear as follows:

Profit and Loss (55)

19—					19—				
Sept.	30		7	1,940 00	Sept.	30		7	2,410 00
	30		7	470 00					
				2,410 00					2,410 00

Earned Surplus (51)

19—					19—				
Aug.	31		3	80 00	Aug.	31		3	225 00
Sept.	30		7	80 00	Sept.	30		7	470 00

Accrual adjustments and entries in subsequent periods. If an expense accrual is made in the books at the end of a period, it must be remembered when payment is made in a subsequent period. For instance, in Chapter 3 the following adjusting entry was made for an expense accrual:

Sept. 30　Truck rent.............................. 240.00
　　　　　　　Truck rent payable.................... 240.00
　　　　　　　Expense and liability for use of truck during
　　　　　　　September.

Assume, first, that payment is made on October 10; the entry should be:

Oct. 10　Truck rent payable........................ 240.00
　　　　　　Cash................................. 240.00
　　　　　　Payment of truck rental for September.

Assume, second, that payment is made on October 15, at which date another $150 of truck rent has accrued, and that the entire $390 is paid; the entry should be:

Oct. 15　Truck rent payable........................ 240.00
　　　　　　Truck rent............................. 150.00
　　　　　　Cash................................. 390.00
　　　　　　Payment of September truck rent, and $150
　　　　　　of October rent accrued to date.

Assume, third, that no payment is made in October, that the rent accrual for use of the truck during October is $270, and that the $510 total for September and October rent is paid on November 5.

An adjusting entry should be made at the end of October for the rent accrued during that month, as follows:

Oct. 31   Truck rent............................. 270.00
            Truck rent payable....................   270.00
            Expense and liability for use of truck during
            October.

The entry for the payment of the rent would be:

Nov. 5   Truck rent payable....................... 510.00
            Cash.................................   510.00
            Payment of truck rent for September and
            October.

If an income accrual is made in the books at the end of a period, it should similarly be borne in mind when the collection is received in a subsequent period.

CHAPTER 5

Merchandise Operations—Perpetual Inventory Method

Illustrative statement of income and expense. In the illustrations in the preceding chapters, the business operations consisted of rendering services. Many businesses, however, derive all or a large portion of their earnings from selling merchandise. A statement of income and expense for a company whose entire income is derived from selling merchandise is presented below.

THE MORTON COMPANY
Statement of Income and Expense
For the Month of April, 19—

Sales...		$3,600.00
Cost of goods sold.....................................		2,700.00
Gross profit on sales..................................		$ 900.00
Deduct expenses:		
Advertising expense...........................	$ 25.00	
Depreciation expense—Equipment..............	10.00	
Rent expense.................................	75.00	
Salaries expense.............................	500.00	
Total expenses.......................		610.00
Net income for the month..............................		$ 290.00

Notice the new feature introduced by the merchandising operations: namely, the appearance in the statement of income and expense of the "gross profit on sales." The gross profit is the excess of the selling price over the cost of the goods sold.

Some accountants, perhaps because of the appearance of the "gross profit," prefer to give the above statement the heading "Statement of Profit and Loss" or "Profit and Loss Statement." All of these statement headings are acceptable, and all are used in this text in order to familiarize the student with such variations.

Perpetual and periodical inventory methods. There are two basic accounting methods for the determination of the cost of goods sold and the cost of goods remaining on hand: The perpetual inventory method is described in this chapter; the periodical inventory method is described in the next chapter.

Basis of illustration. For purposes of illustration, it is assumed that The Morton Company deals in room air-conditioners, which it buys at wholesale for $300 and sells at retail for $400. The company has been in business for some time; its account balances after the books had been closed on March 31 are shown on page 57.

56

Account Balances—March 31, 19—

Cash...	3,700.00	
Inventory (4 units costing $300 each)..............	1,200.00	
Equipment.......................................	1,200.00	
Reserve for depreciation—Equipment..............		300.00
Capital stock...................................		5,000.00
Earned surplus..................................		800.00
	6,100.00	6,100.00

Included in the above list of accounts is an Inventory account. When used as an account title, the term "inventory" refers to the merchandise which a business purchases for resale to its customers. Such merchandise is recorded at cost.

The illustration covers the month of April.

Inventories, purchases, sales, and cost of goods sold. The procedures, by the perpetual inventory method of accounting for inventories, purchases, sales, and the cost of goods sold, are described below.

Inventory at beginning of period. The inventory at the beginning of April was shown in the Inventory (asset) account as follows:

Inventory (3)

19—				
March 31	Balance		1,200 00	

Purchases. Purchases increase the merchandise asset and are therefore debited to the Inventory account. One purchase transaction occurred during April:

April 3—Ten air-conditioning units costing $300 each were purchased from George White on account.

The journal entry to record this transaction was:

Journal (Page 11)

19—					
April	3	Inventory...............................		3,000 00	
		George White........................			3,000 00
		Purchased ten air-conditioning units on account.			

After this entry was posted, the Inventory account appeared as follows:

Inventory (3)

19—				
March 31	Balance		1,200 00	
April 3		11	3,000 00	

Sales. A sale of merchandise is recorded in the same way as a "sale" of service—that is, by a credit to an income account. The Sales account is used for this purpose. One sale occurred during April:

> April 18—Nine air-conditioning units were sold to Bailey Apartments on account, for $400 each.

The journal entry to record the sale was:

Journal			(Page 11)
19— April 18	Bailey Apartments........................ Sales................................ Sale of nine units on account.	3,600 00	3,600 00

After this entry was posted, the Sales account appeared as follows:

		Sales		(13)
		19— April 18	11	3,600 00

Cost of goods sold. When the perpetual inventory method is used, entries for sales are followed by companion entries for the cost of the goods sold. These entries transfer the cost of the goods sold from the Inventory account to a Cost of Goods Sold account. The transfer entry for the sale mentioned above was:

Journal			(Page 11)
19— April 18	Cost of goods sold........................ Inventory............................ Cost of nine units sold transferred from Inventory to Cost of Goods Sold. $300 × 9.	2,700 00	2,700 00

After this entry was posted, the accounts affected appeared as follows:

		Cost of Goods Sold		(14)
19— April 18	11	2,700 00		

			Inventory		(3)
19— March 31 Balance April 3		11	1,200 00 3,000 00	19— April 18	11	2,700 00

Inventory at end of period. The inventory on April 30, to appear in the balance sheet, is the balance of the Inventory account, $1,500. Since, under the perpetual inventory method, all purchases of merchandise are debited to the Inventory account and the cost of all goods sold is credited to the Inventory account, the Inventory account balance should show the cost of goods in the inventory at the end of the period, provided that no merchandise has been lost or stolen.

Detailed inventory records. In most instances where the perpetual inventory method is in use, a running record in terms of quantities is maintained for each of the various types of goods held for sale. Cost data may also be included. In the case of The Morton Company, which sells only one type of merchandise, such a supplementary record, in terms of quantities, can be illustrated as follows:

INVENTORY CARD			
Description Room air-conditioners			
Date	Quantity		
	Purchased	Sold	Balance
19—			
April 1			4
3	10		14
18		9	5

As a check on the accuracy of these detailed records, it is advisable and customary to make occasional counts of merchandise on hand.

April journal. In addition to the transactions already mentioned, the following transactions occurred in April:

April 1—The store rent for the month, $75, was paid in cash.
    15—Salaries for the first half of April, $250, were paid in cash.
    26—A cash payment of $1,500 was made to George White, to apply on account.
    27—A cash collection of $1,750 was received from Bailey Apartments, to apply on account.
    30—A cash dividend of $50 was declared and paid.

The complete journal is on page 60. Observe that the sales entry is immediately followed by the related entry for the cost of goods sold.

Journal   (Page 11)

19—				
April	1	Rent expense.................................	75 00	
		Cash.....................................		75 00
		Payment of store rent for April.		
	3	Inventory....................................	3,000 00	
		George White...........................		3,000 00
		Purchase of merchandise on account. Ten units at $300 each.		
	15	Salaries expense............................	250 00	
		Cash.....................................		250 00
		Salaries for the first half of April paid in cash.		
	18	Bailey Apartments..........................	3,600 00	
		Sales.....................................		3,600 00
		Sale of merchandise on account. Nine units at $400 each.		
	18	Cost of goods sold...........................	2,700 00	
		Inventory.................................		2,700 00
		Cost of nine units sold transferred from Inventory to Cost of Goods Sold. $300 × 9.		
	26	George White...............................	1,500 00	
		Cash.....................................		1,500 00
		Payment to White to apply on account.		
	27	Cash.......................................	1,750 00	
		Bailey Apartments........................		1,750 00
		Collection from Bailey Apartments to apply on account.		
	30	Dividends...................................	50 00	
		Cash.....................................		50 00
		Payment of dividend to stockholders.		

Trial balance. The trial balance in the working papers on page 61 shows the balances that would appear in the ledger as of April 30 after the preceding journal entries were posted.

Completed working papers. Completed working papers for The Morton Company are presented on page 62. Adjustments were made for the following matters:

(a) Salaries for the last half of April have not been paid; there are accrued salaries in the amount of $250.

(b) Accrued advertising; there was an unrecorded liability for April newspaper advertising in the amount of $25.

(c) Depreciation for April; the depreciation rate for the equipment is 10 per cent per annum. The depreciation for one month is therefore $10.

Equipment..	$1,200
Depreciation rate per year...........................	10%
Depreciation per year...............................	$ 120
Depreciation per month..............................	$ 10

THE MORTON COMPANY
Working Papers
For the Month of April, 19—

	Trial Balance		Adjustments		Adjusted Trial Balance		Statement of Income and Expense		Statement of Earned Surplus		Balance Sheet	
Cash	3,575											
Bailey Apartments	1,850											
Inventory	1,500											
Equipment	1,200											
Reserve for depreciation—Equipment		300										
George White		1,500										
Capital stock		5,000										
Earned surplus		800										
Dividends	50											
Sales		3,600										
Cost of goods sold	2,700											
Rent expense	75											
Salaries expense	250											
	11,200	11,200										

THE MORTON COMPANY
Working Papers
For the Month of April, 19—

	Trial Balance		Adjustments		Adjusted Trial Balance		Statement of Income and Expense		Statement of Earned Surplus		Balance Sheet	
Cash	3,575				3,575						3,575	
Bailey Apartments	1,850				1,850						1,850	
Inventory	1,500				1,500						1,500	
Equipment	1,200				1,200						1,200	
Reserve for depreciation—Equipment		300		10c		310						310
George White		1,500				1,500						1,500
Capital stock		5,000				5,000						5,000
Earned surplus		800				800				800		
Dividends	50				50				50			
Sales		3,600				3,600		3,600				
Cost of goods sold	2,700				2,700		2,700					
Rent expense	75				75		75					
Salaries expense	250		250a		500		500					
	11,200	11,200										
Accrued salaries payable				250a		250						250
Advertising expense			25b		25		25					
Accrued advertising payable				25b		25						25
Depreciation expense—Equipment			10c		10		10					
			285	285	11,485	11,485						
Net income							290			290		
							3,600	3,600				
Earned surplus, April 30, 19—									1,040			1,040
									1,090	1,090	8,125	8,125

Adjustments

a—Accrued salaries for the last half of April.
b—Accrued advertising.
c—Depreciation of equipment for April.

Statements prepared from working papers.   After the working papers are completed, the accountant has the information he needs for purposes of statement preparation.   The financial statements of The Morton Company, prepared from the preceding working papers, appear below:

THE MORTON COMPANY
Statement of Income and Expense
For the Month of April, 19—

Sales...		$3,600.00
Cost of goods sold......................................		2,700.00
Gross profit on sales..................................		$ 900.00
Deduct expenses:		
Advertising expense...........................	$ 25.00	
Depreciation expense—Equipment..............	10.00	
Rent expense.................................	75.00	
Salaries expense.............................	500.00	
Total expenses...................................		610.00
Net income...		$ 290.00

THE MORTON COMPANY
Statement of Earned Surplus
For the Month of April, 19—

Earned surplus, March 31, 19—..........................	$ 800.00
Net income for the month..............................	290.00
Total...	$1,090.00
Deduct dividends......................................	50.00
Earned surplus, April 30, 19—.........................	$1,040.00

THE MORTON COMPANY
Balance Sheet
April 30, 19—

Assets			Liablilties and Owners' Equity		
Cash.....................		$3,575.00	Liabilities:		
Accounts receivable........		1,850.00	Accounts payable.........	$1,500.00	
Inventory..................		1,500.00	Accrued salaries payable......	250.00	
Equipment.......	$1,200.00		Accrued advertising payable	25.00	$1,775.00
Less reserve for depreciation..	310.00	890.00	Owners' equity:		
			Capital stock...	$5,000.00	
			Earned surplus.	1,040.00	6,040.00
		$7,815.00			$7,815.00

Recording the adjusting and closing entries.   Adjusting and closing entries for a merchandising company using the perpetual inventory method are made in the same manner as those for a service enterprise, which were illustrated in the preceding chapters. In the case of The Morton Company, the adjusting journal entries on the following page are required.

Journal   (Page 12)

19—					
April	30	Salaries expense...............................	250	00	
		Accured salaries payable..................			250	00
		Accrued salaries for the last half of April.				
	30	Advertising expense...........................	25	00	
		Accrued advertising payable..............			25	00
		To record liability for April newspaper adver-tising not recorded before the trial balance was prepared.				
	30	Depreciation expense—Equipment..............	10	00	
		Reserve for depreciation—Equipment.......			10	00
		To record depreciation for one month. $1,200 × 10% ÷ 12 = $10.				

The following entries close the accounts of The Morton Company. The closing entries are based on the information in the working papers.

Journal   (Page 12)

19—					
April	30	Sales..	3,600	00	
		Profit and loss............................			3,600	00
		To close the income account.				
	30	Profit and loss...............................	3,310	00	
		Cost of goods sold.........................			2,700	00
		Rent expense..............................			75	00
		Salaries expense...........................			500	00
		Advertising expense........................			25	00
		Depreciation expense—Equipment...........			10	00
		To close the expense accounts.				
	30	Profit and loss...............................	290	00	
		Earned surplus............................			290	00
		To close the Profit and Loss account.				
	30	Earned surplus...............................	50	00	
		Dividends.................................			50	00
		To close the Dividends account.				

Ledger accounts after adjusting and closing. The following ledger accounts are those of The Morton Company after the entries for the transactions for April and the adjusting and closing entries have been posted.

Cash   (1)

19—						19—				
March	31	Balance		3,700	00	April	1		11	75	00
April	27		11	1,750	00		15		11	250	00
							26		11	1,500	00
							30		11	50	00

Bailey Apartments (2)

19—						19—					
April	18		11	3,600	00	April	27		11	1,750	00

Inventory (3)

19—						19—					
March	31	Balance		1,200	00	April	18		11	2,700	00
April	3		11	3,000	00						

Equipment (4)

19—					
March	31	Balance		1,200	00

Reserve for Depreciation—Equipment (5)

					19—					
					March	31	Balance		300	00
					April	30		12	10	00

George White (6)

19—						19—					
April	26		11	1,500	00	April	3		11	3,000	00

Accrued Salaries Payable (7)

					19—					
					April	30		12	250	00

Accrued Advertising Payable (8)

					19—					
					April	30		12	25	00

Capital Stock (9)

				19—					
				March	31	Balance		5,000	00

Earned Surplus (10)

19—						19—					
April	30		12	50	00	March	31	Balance		800	00
						April	30		12	290	00

Dividends (11)

19—						19—					
April	30		11	50	00	April	30		12	50	00

Profit and Loss (12)

| 19—
April | 30
30 | | | | 12
12 | 3,310|00
290|00 | 19—
April | 30 | | 12 | 3,600|00 |
| | | | | | | 3,600|00 | | | | | 3,600|00 |

Sales (13)

| 19—
April | 30 | | | | 12 | 3,600|00 | 19—
April | 18 | | 11 | 3,600|00 |

Cost of Goods Sold (14)

| 19—
April | 18 | | | | 11 | 2,700|00 | 19—
April | 30 | | 12 | 2,700|00 |

Depreciation Expense—Equipment (15)

| 19—
April | 30 | | | | 12 | 10|00 | 19—
April | 30 | | 12 | 10|00 |

Advertising Expense (16)

| 19—
April | 30 | | | | 12 | 25|00 | 19—
April | 30 | | 12 | 25|00 |

Rent Expense (17)

| 19—
April | 1 | | | | 11 | 75|00 | 19—
April | 30 | | 12 | 75|00 |

Salaries Expense (18)

| 19—
April | 15
30 | | | | 11
12 | 250|00
250|00 | 19—
April | 30 | | 12 | 500|00 |
| | | | | | | 500|00 | | | | | 500|00 |

Net loss for period. If the expenses exceed the gross profit for the period, the statement of profit and loss will appear as illustrated below:

THE *A B* COMPANY
Statement of Profit and Loss
For the Month of February, 19—

Sales..	$5,000.00
Deduct cost of goods sold...............................	4,500.00
Gross profit on sales...................................	$ 500.00
Deduct expenses.......................................	600.00
Net loss..	$ 100.00

Since the operations resulted in a loss, the Profit and Loss account will have a debit balance, and will be closed by an entry debiting Earned Surplus and crediting Profit and Loss.

In the working papers, the Income and Expense columns will be balanced by entering the net loss in the credit column. The net loss will also be entered in the debit Earned Surplus column.

Loss on sales. If the cost of goods sold exceeds the sales, the operations will result in a loss on sales instead of in a gross profit, and the statement will be prepared as follows:

THE *X Y* COMPANY

Statement of Profit and Loss

For the Month of July, 19—

Sales	$10,000.00
Deduct cost of goods sold	10,200.00
Loss on sales	$ 200.00
Add expenses	500.00
Net loss	$ 700.00

Deficit. The occurrence of net losses may cause the Earned Surplus account to have a debit balance. Should the Earned Surplus account have a debit balance, it is described in the balance sheet as a Deficit and is deducted from the capital stock as follows:

Owners' equity:		
Capital stock	$40,000.00	
Deduct deficit	10,000.00	$30,000.00

Two principal sources of income. If a company has two principal sources of income, one from merchandising operations and the other from rendering services, its statement of income and expense may be presented as follows:

THE *M N* COMPANY

Statement of Income and Expense

For the Month of August, 19—

Sales	$8,000.00
Deduct cost of goods sold	5,000.00
Gross profit on sales	$3,000.00
Income from services	2,000.00
Total	$5,000.00
Deduct expenses	4,000.00
Net income	$1,000.00

CHAPTER 6

Merchandise Operations—Periodical Inventory Method

Determining cost of goods sold and ending inventory. The sum of the inventory at the beginning of the period and the purchases during the period is the cost of goods available for sale. To prepare a statement of income and expense and a balance sheet for a merchandising company, it is necessary to divide this total into two portions:

The cost of goods sold during the period—to be shown in the statement of income and expense.

The cost of goods remaining in the inventory at the end of the period—to be shown in the balance sheet.

There are two methods for making this division.

Perpetual inventory method. This method, which was described in the preceding chapter, can be used when it is practicable to determine and record the merchandise cost applicable to each sale. Using the data in Chapter 5, we may express the procedures as follows:

Bookkeeping procedure:

	Inventory	Cost of Goods Sold
Inventory at beginning of period..............	1,200	
Purchases during period......................	3,000	
Cost of goods sold...........................	2,700	2,700

Statement procedure:

The $1,500 balance in the Inventory account is shown in the balance sheet as an asset.

The $2,700 balance in the Cost of Goods Sold account is shown in the statement of income and expense, as illustrated below:

Statement of Income and Expense

Sales..	$3,600.00
Deduct cost of goods sold..............................	2,700.00
Gross profit on sales....................................	$ 900.00

Periodical inventory method. When it is impracticable, because of the large number of small sales or for any other reason, to determine and record the merchandise cost applicable to each sale, the procedures stated on page 69 are used.

Bookkeeping procedure:

	Inventory
Inventory at beginning of period...................... 1,200	

	Purchases
Purchases during period............................ 3,000	

Statement procedure:

The end-of-period inventory is determined by counting and listing all merchandise on hand held for sale, and pricing such merchandise in terms of cost. This is called "taking a physical inventory."

The inventory thus determined is shown in the balance sheet as an asset.

The end-of-period inventory is also shown in the income and expense statement as a deduction from the cost of goods available for sale, to determine the cost of goods sold, as illustrated below:

Statement of Income and Expense

Sales..		$3,600.00
Deduct cost of goods sold:		
Inventory at beginning of period..............	$1,200.00	
Add purchases.............................	3,000.00	
Total goods available for sale.................	$4,200.00	
Deduct inventory at end of period.............	1,500.00	
Cost of goods sold...................................		2,700.00
Gross profit on sales....................................		$ 900.00

Comparative summary of bookkeeping procedures. As indicated in the preceding paragraphs of this chapter, the bookkeeping procedures for recording transactions by the perpetual inventory method and the periodical inventory method are identical, with the following exceptions:

By the perpetual inventory method:
Purchases are debited to the Inventory account.
The cost of goods sold is recorded by a debit to Cost of Goods Sold and a credit to Inventory.
By the periodical inventory method:
Purchases are debited to the Purchases account.
No entry is made for the cost of goods sold.

Comparative trial balances. The trial balances on the following page show the account balances under each inventory method. Asterisks appear where differences in methods affect the account balances.

THE MORTON COMPANY
Trial Balances (Before Adjustments)
April 30, 19—

	Perpetual Inventory Method		Periodical Inventory Method	
Cash	3,575.00		3,575.00	
Bailey Apartments	1,850.00		1,850.00	
*Inventory	1,500.00		1,200.00	
Equipment	1,200.00		1,200.00	
Reserve for depreciation—Equipment		300.00		300.00
George White		1,500.00		1,500.00
Capital stock		5,000.00		5,000.00
Earned surplus		800.00		800.00
Sales		3,600.00		3,600.00
*Purchases			3,000.00	
*Cost of goods sold	2,700.00			
Rent expense	75.00		75.00	
Salaries expense	250.00		250.00	
Dividends	50.00		50.00	
	11,200.00	11,200.00	11,200.00	11,200.00

Working papers—Periodical inventory method. Working papers in various stages of completion appear on pages 72, 73, and 74. They are based on the data of The Morton Company shown on the preceding pages of this chapter.

Observe the following features in the working papers:

(1) The term *Profit and Loss* has been used in place of *Income and Expense* as a column heading. As noted earlier, either terminology is considered acceptable.

(2) Columns for the Adjusted Trial Balance have been omitted. Many accountants prefer to extend the trial balance amounts, as modified by the data in the Adjustments columns, directly to the statement columns.

(3) All of the accounts in the ledger, except the Profit and Loss account, have been listed in the trial balance, including accounts having no balances when the trial balance was prepared. In the ledger of an established business, there may be several accounts that normally have no balances when the trial balance is prepared but acquire balances from the adjusting entries. Depreciation expense accounts and accrued accounts are examples. The accountant may find it desirable to list such "no balance" accounts in their statement order in the trial balance in the working papers; this procedure, by avoiding the addition of account titles below the trial balance, results in having the working-paper information more nearly in statement order.

Stage 1. The working papers identified as Stage 1 (see page 72) show the condition of the papers after the following steps have been taken:

(1) All working-paper headings entered.
(2) The trial balance entered.
(3) The adjustments entered.

Stage 2. Page 73 shows how the working papers appear after the completion of the following additional steps:

(1) The balances in the (beginning) Inventory and Purchases accounts appearing in the trial balance have been extended to the Profit and Loss debit column. The sum of these two debits, $4,200, is the cost of goods which were available for sale during the period.

(2) The ending inventory, $1,500, which does not appear in the trial balance, has been entered in the working papers in two places:

(*a*) In the Profit and Loss column, because it will appear in the profit and loss statement as an element of the computation of the cost of goods sold. It is entered in the credit column because it is a deduction from the opening inventory and purchases, which are debits. The Profit and Loss columns now have a debit balance of $2,700, the cost of goods sold.

(*b*) In the Balance Sheet debit column, because the ending inventory will be shown in the balance sheet as an asset.

Stage 3. Page 74 shows the completed working papers.

Stage 1

THE MORTON COMPANY
Working Papers
For the Month of April, 19—

	Trial Balance		Adjustments		Profit and Loss		Earned Surplus		Balance Sheet	
Cash...............................	3,575									
Bailey Apartments.................	1,850									
Inventory, March 31, 19—..........	1,200									
Equipment.........................	1,200									
Reserve for depreciation—Equipment.		300		10c						
George White......................		1,500								
Accrued salaries payable..........				250a						
Accrued advertising payable.......				25b						
Capital stock.....................		5,000								
Earned surplus....................		800								
Dividends.........................	50									
Sales.............................		3,600								
Purchases.........................	3,000									
Advertising expense...............			25b							
Depreciation expense—Equipment....			10c							
Rent expense......................	75									
Salaries expense..................	250		250a							
	11,200	11,200	285	285						

Adjustments

a—Accrued salaries for the last half of April.

b—Accrued advertising.

c—Depreciation of equipment for April.

Stage 2

THE MORTON COMPANY
Working Papers
For the Month of April, 19—

	Trial Balance		Adjustments		Profit and Loss		Earned Surplus		Balance Sheet	
	Dr	Cr	Dr	Cr	Dr	Cr	Dr	Cr	Dr	Cr
Cash....................	3,575									
Bailey Apartments.........	1,850									
Inventory, March 31, 19—..	1,200				1,200					
Equipment...............	1,200									
Reserve for depreciation—Equipment..		300		10c						
George White.............		1,500								
Accrued salaries payable....				250a						
Accrued advertising payable..				25b						
Capital stock.............		5,000								
Earned surplus............		800								
Dividends................	50									
Sales....................		3,600								
Purchases................	3,000				3,000					
Advertising expense........			25b							
Depreciation expense—Equipment.			10c							
Rent expense.............	75									
Salaries expense..........	250		250a							
	11,200	11,200	285	285						
					1,500				1,500	
Inventory, April 30, 19—..........										

Adjustments

a—Accrued salaries for the last half of
   April.
b—Accrued advertising.
c—Depreciation of equipment for April.

Stage 3

THE MORTON COMPANY
Working Papers
For the Month of April, 19—

	Trial Balance Dr.	Trial Balance Cr.	Adjustments Dr.	Adjustments Cr.	Profit and Loss Dr.	Profit and Loss Cr.	Earned Surplus Dr.	Earned Surplus Cr.	Balance Sheet Dr.	Balance Sheet Cr.
Cash	3,575								3,575	
Bailey Apartments	1,850								1,850	
Inventory, March 31, 19—	1,200				1,200					
Equipment	1,200								1,200	
Reserve for depreciation—Equipment		300		10c						310
George White		1,500								1,500
Accrued salaries payable				250a						250
Accrued advertising payable				25b						25
Capital stock		5,000								5,000
Earned surplus		800						800		
Dividends	50						50			
Sales		3,600				3,600				
Purchases	3,000				3,000					
Advertising expense			25b		25					
Depreciation expense—Equipment			10c		10					
Rent expense	75				75					
Salaries expense	250		250a		500					
	11,200	11,200	285	285						
Inventory, April 30, 19—						1,500			1,500	
Net income					290			290		
					5,100	5,100		1,090		
Earned surplus, April 30, 19—							1,040			1,040
							1,090	1,090	8,125	8,125

Adjustments

a—Accrued salaries for the last half of April.
b—Accrued advertising.
c—Depreciation of equipment for April.

Financial statements—Periodical inventory method. The following profit and loss statement was prepared from the preceding working papers. It is presented in order to show the computation of the cost of goods sold.

THE MORTON COMPANY

Statement of Profit and Loss

For the Month of April, 19—

Sales...		$3,600.00
Deduct cost of goods sold:		
Inventory, March 31, 19—...................	$1,200.00	
Purchases....................................	3,000.00	
Cost of goods available for sale.............	$4,200.00	
Deduct inventory, April 30, 19—.............	1,500.00	
Cost of goods sold.................................		2,700.00
Gross profit on sales....................................		$ 900.00
Deduct expenses:		
Advertising expense.........................	$ 25.00	
Depreciation expense—Equipment............	10.00	
Rent expense................................	75.00	
Salaries expense.............................	500.00	
Total..		610.00
Net income...		$ 290.00

The statement of earned surplus and the balance sheet would be identical with those on page 63 of Chapter 5.

Adjusting journal entries—Periodical inventory method. The adjusting entries are not affected by the inventory method. They are the same as those in the preceding chapter.

Closing entries—Periodical inventory method. The closing entries under the periodical inventory method are presented below. Observe that, in these entries, the beginning inventory is removed from the Inventory account by a credit, and the ending inventory is debited to the Inventory account.

Journal   (Page 12)

19—			
April 30	Sales...	3,600 00	
	Inventory....................................	1,500 00	
	Profit and loss............................		5,100 00
	To close the Sales account and set up the ending inventory.		
30	Profit and loss...............................	4,810 00	
	Inventory.................................		1,200 00
	Purchases................................		3,000 00
	Advertising expense......................		25 00
	Depreciation expense—Equipment.........		10 00
	Rent expense.............................		75 00
	Salaries expense.........................		500 00
	To close the expense accounts and to remove the beginning inventory from the Inventory account.		

Journal   (Page 12 Concluded)

19—				
April	30	Profit and loss.................................	290 00	
		Earned surplus............................		290 00
		To close the Profit and Loss account.		
	30	Earned surplus...............................	50 00	
		Dividends.................................		50 00
		To close the Dividends account.		

After the above entries are posted, the Inventory account will appear as follows:

Inventory

19—					19—				
March	31		10	1,200 00	April	30		12	1,200 00
April	30		12	1,500 00					

Special note regarding a newly organized business. A newly organized business may start operations without a beginning inventory. The cost of goods sold during its *first* accounting period will be computed by simply deducting the ending inventory from the purchases.

Office Routines; Documents

Duties of the accounting department. The work of the accounting department includes:

(1) Writing up various documents, such as sales invoices, checks, and notes. Most of these documents are delivered to the parties with whom the company does business; duplicates of some of them (duplicate sales invoices, for instance) may be retained in the company's files for future reference and as evidence of the propriety of the entries for the transactions.

(2) Checking similar documents received from the parties with whom the company does business, to determine whether or not they have been prepared in accordance with the facts of the transactions. After having been checked, the documents are filed as evidence of the transactions.

(3) Recording the transaction facts indicated by the documents written up in the office or received from other parties.

Internal control. The office and accounting procedure should be so organized that errors will be prevented so far as possible, and that, if errors are made (by the company's employees or in documents received from people with whom the company does business), they probably will be discovered. Moreover, the work of the various members of the organization should be so interrelated and checked that fraud cannot be committed and concealed without the collusion of two or more persons. The method of effecting these safeguards is called the *system of internal check* or *internal control.*

It should be understood that the discussion in this chapter relative to office routines is intended to indicate methods which *may be* used to provide for internal control. It is not intended to describe procedures used in every business.

The number of copies of each document prepared in any given business may be more or less than the number stated in the following comments. Also, the office routines depend on the size of the business and on the ideas of the company's accountant regarding the relative advantages of different procedures.

Purchase Routine

Purchase requisitions. All purchases may be made by the purchasing agent, who obtains information concerning requirements from purchase requisitions sent to him by other members of the organization. Requisition forms are of various kinds; the following is illustrative.

R. E. JOHNSON & COMPANY

Requisition No. __M135__   Date __July 2, 19--__

Please purchase for delivery __before July 6__

Quantity	Description
10 cases	XXXX Strawberry preserves
15 cases	Acorn Peanut butter
10 cases	Acorn peas

Requisitioned by _C. E. Walters_   Approved by _J. E. White_

Purchasing Agent's Memorandum of Order

Purchase Order No. __17C5__   Issued to __The Osborne Co.__

Date of Order __July 2__   __Chicago__

Purchase Requisition

Purchase requisitions may be filled out by various persons, depending on the nature and size of the business.

In the case of staple merchandise, the merchandise manager may fix a minimum quantity below which the stock must not be allowed to fall without reordering. When the stock is reduced to the minimum quantity determined by the merchandise manager, the stock clerk enters the description of the article on a requisition; he may also enter the quantity to be ordered (if a standard quantity to be purchased has been established), or the quantity may be entered on the requisition by the merchandise manager.

In the case of non-staple merchandise, the requisition may be prepared in the office of the merchandise manager after consultation with the sales manager regarding quantities which probably will be required.

Purchase order. The purchasing agent places the order by filling out a purchase order. Purchase orders vary in form; the following is illustrative.

Purchase Order   No. 1705

R. E. JOHNSON & COMPANY
2913 North Western Avenue
Chicago

To_The Osborne Company_   Date____July 2, 19--____

_____   Deliver____Before July 6____

215 West Canal Street   Ship via____Your truck____

_____   F. O. B. _____

Chicago_____   Terms____1/10; n/30____

Quantity	Description	Price
10 cases	XXXX Strawberry Preserves	27.80
15 cases	Acorn Peanut Butter	9.20
10 cases	Acorn Peas	12.40

R. E. Johnson & Company

Req. No.__M135__   By__L. K. Bacon__
                                         Purchasing Agent

Purchase Order

Three copies of the purchase order may be made, and disposed of as follows:

Original—sent to the supplier from whom the goods are being purchased.

First carbon—retained in the purchasing department files.

Second carbon—sent to the receiving department.

The uses subsequently made of the first and second carbon copies of the purchase order are described in a subsequent section of this chapter.

Invoice. The purchaser receives an invoice from the seller. The invoice describes the merchandise shipped, shows the amount charged therefor, and gives other important information. An illustrative invoice appears below.

THE OSBORNE COMPANY
215 West Canal Street
Chicago, Illinois

Invoice No. **2397**

Customer's Order No. 1705

Date of Order 7/2/19--   Invoice Date July 3, 19--

Sold to R. E. Johnson & Company   Terms 1/10; n/30

2913 North Western Ave.

Chicago, Ill.   F. O. B.

Shipped to Same   Date Shipped July 3

How Shipped Truck

Car. No. & Initials

Quantity	Description	Unit Price	Amount
10 cases	XXXX Strawberry Preserves	27.80	278.00
15 cases	Acorn Peanut Butter	9.20	138.00
10 cases	Acorn Peas	12.40	124.00
			540.00

Invoice

Purchaser's verification of invoice. When the invoice is received, it is sent to the purchasing department, where a check sheet in the following general form is pasted to it, or a rubber stamp imprint of the same form is made on it.

```
Goods checked to invoice                          _____
Invoice checked to purchase order for:
    Merchandise                                   _____
    Prices                                        _____
    Discount terms                                _____
    Freight terms                                 _____
Invoice footings and extensions checked           _____
Approved for payment                              _____
Paid by Check No._____Date_____
```

Check Sheet

Before the purchase is recorded, the purchasing company should know that:

(1) The goods invoiced have been received.

The second carbon of the purchase order was sent to the receiving department. When the goods are received, the receiving clerk:

Inspects the merchandise to see that it is in good condition.

Counts, weighs, or otherwise determines the quantities received, and enters these quantities on his copy of the purchase order. This copy was made with a narrow carbon, so that the quantities ordered were not typed on it; such a practice assures a careful count by the receiving clerk instead of a perfunctory checking of typed quantities.

Initials the copy of the purchase order and sends it to the purchasing department, where it is filed in a binder called a *receiving record*.

A clerk in the purchasing department compares the quantities received (shown by the receiving record) with the quantities billed (shown by the invoice). If they agree, he initials the check sheet on the "Goods checked to invoice" line.

(2) The invoice agrees with the purchase order.

The first carbon of the purchase order was retained in the purchasing department files. A clerk checks the invoice against this carbon of the purchase order to see that the merchandise invoiced is the same as the merchandise ordered, and that the prices, the discount terms, and the freight terms are correct. He indicates the accuracy of these matters by initialing the check sheet on the four lines provided therefor.

(3) The extensions and footings of the invoice are correct.

The computations are checked by a clerk in the accounting department, and their accuracy is indicated by his initials on the "Invoice footings and extensions checked" line of the check sheet.

After the invoice has been checked, an entry is made to record the purchase.

Payment of the invoice. The terms of the invoice received from The Osborne Company were 1/10; n/30. This is read as follows: *1% in 10 days; net 30**. It means that 1% cash discount will be allowed if the invoice is paid within ten days from its date, July 3, and that the invoice is due in thirty days without discount.

To be sure that all invoices are paid within the discount period, they may be filed in a *tickler*, which is a card file with index cards bearing dates. The Osborne invoice will be filed in front of the card for July 12, the date on which the check should be mailed to reach the creditor before the expiration of the discount period.

When the payment date arrives, the invoice is taken from the tickler and sent to the treasurer. If funds are available for the payment of the invoice, the treasurer signs or initials the check sheet on the "Approved for payment" line and sends the invoice to the cashier, who:

(1) Draws a check;

(2) Enters the check number and date of payment on the check sheet attached to the invoice;

(3) Sends the check to the treasurer for his signature. The check is clipped to the invoice so that the treasurer can be sure that the check he is signing is in payment of an approved invoice.

The treasurer signs the check and sees that it is mailed to the creditor. The invoice is sent to the bookkeeper, who records its payment. The invoice is then filed for future reference as evidence of the propriety of the entries for the purchase and the payment.

---

* The expression *net* is a misnomer, because the gross amount of the invoice (not the net amount) is payable after 10 days.

Checks, advices, and receipts. When a remittance is sent to a creditor, it is important that the creditor be given information which will indicate the particular invoice which is being paid. A debtor may owe several bills; he has a legal right to specify that his remittance shall apply to a certain bill or certain bills, and the debtor's and the creditor's records should show which bills are being paid. It is also desirable to obtain a receipt from the creditor. Several methods may be used to accomplish these purposes; two methods in common use are described below:

(1) The check form may be a simple one, similar to the following illustration:

FIRST NATIONAL BANK 2-1	No. 1668
	Chicago, July 12, 19--
Pay to the order of ____ The Osborne Company ____	$ 534.60
EXACTLY $534 AND 60 CTS.	Dollars
	R. E. Johnson & Company
	Peter Oldham Treasurer

Check

When the purchaser sends the seller the check, he may send with it a letter, stating that the check is sent in payment of the creditor's invoice 2397 of July 3, in the amount of $540, less 1% cash discount.

This method has two disadvantages:

(*a*) It necessitates writing a letter.
(*b*) Although the creditor's endorsement of the check is a receipt for $534.60, it is not an acknowledgment of the payment of a particular invoice.

(2) Data with respect to the invoice that is being paid may be shown in a space provided for that purpose at the left of the check, as illustrated on page 83.

The back of the left end of the check contains the following or similar words: "Endorsement of this check by the payee shall constitute a receipt for the items described on the face thereof." A receipt for specific items is thus obtained from the creditor.

Date	Invoice	Amount	FIRST NATIONAL BANK 2-1	No. 1668

Date	Invoice	Amount
7/3/19--	2397	540.00

Chicago, _____July 12,_____ 19<u>--</u>

Pay to the order of _____The Osborne Company_____ $ 534.60

EXACTLY $534 60 CTS. _____ Dollars

Total		540.00
Discount		5.40
Net		534.60

R. E. Johnson & Company

Peter Oldham

Treasurer

Check with Space for Data at Left

Sales Routine

Sales. The office and accounting procedures with respect to sales differ in retail and wholesale businesses; they also depend on the nature and size of the business. The procedures described in the following paragraphs are typical and illustrative; but you should understand that, although they are indicative of methods of establishing internal control, other procedures may be used with equal effectiveness.

In retail stores, where the orders in most cases are oral, the clerk may merely ring up the sale on the cash register. If it is a charge sale, the salesman may make out a sales ticket in duplicate, showing the name and the address of the customer and the items purchased; one copy will be given to the customer, and the other copy will be sent to the bookkeeping department for entry in the records. If the order is to be filled from stock in the storeroom, a third copy may be made for use in filling the order.

In wholesale businesses, most orders are received in written form from the company's salesmen or customers, the sales are made on account, and the goods are shipped or otherwise delivered to the customers. The procedure may be somewhat as follows:

(1) The order goes to the credit department for approval of the customer's credit rating. If the approval is given,

(2) The order goes to a billing clerk who types an invoice in triplicate. The three copies are used as follows:

The second carbon is sent to the stock room for order filling, and thence (with the merchandise) to the shipping room for packing and shipment. After the goods have been shipped, this copy of the invoice is initialed by the shipping clerk and sent to the accounting department, where it is filed, in invoice-number sequence, in a binder which serves as a shipping record. Maintaining a record relative to the shipment of goods is important. In the first place, it serves as evidence of the propriety of the entry debiting the customer and crediting the Sales account; in the second place, if the goods are delayed or lost in transit, it furnishes information which may be of assistance in tracing the shipment or in substantiating a claim for loss.

The first carbon remains in the accounting department, where it is checked to determine that it is in agreement with the order, and that the prices, terms, and computations are correct. After the second carbon is returned to the accounting department (thus showing that the goods have been shipped), the first carbon is filed in a sales binder and used by the bookkeeper in making his entries.

The original is mailed to the customer after the goods are shipped.

Statements. In many lines of business, merchants send their customers monthly statements. Such statements show:

(1) The balance owed by the customer at the beginning of the month.
(2) Charges to the customer during the month, for sales.
(3) Credits to the customer during the month, for cash remittances, returns and allowances, and so forth.
(4) The balance owed by the customer at the end of the month.

Statement

R. E. JOHNSON & COMPANY
2913 North Western Avenue
Chicago

J. K. Larson,
Whitney, Oklahoma   July 31, 19--

Date	Charges	Credits	Balance
June 30			39.85
July 7	47.88		87.73
9		39.85	47.88
18	40.50		88.38

CHAPTER 7

Additional Income and Expense Accounts— Classified Statements

Introductory note. Starting with this chapter, it will be assumed in all instances that the *periodical* inventory method is the one in use. Any differences in accounts and procedures necessitated by the use of the perpetual inventory method in place of the periodical inventory method are presented in Chapter 28.

Expense classification. The expense accounts kept by each business depend upon the kinds of expenses which the business incurs and the amount of detailed information desired by the management. Frequently it is possible to distinguish between those expenses incurred in connection with selling activities and those incurred in the general administration of the business. Whenever such a classification can be made, it may increase the informative value of the profit and loss statement to so classify the expenses. Such a classification is illustrated below.

Partial Profit and Loss Statement

Gross profit on sales		$29,000.00
Deduct expenses:		
Selling:		
Store rent	$5,000.00	
Advertising	2,000.00	
Delivery expense	500.00	
Salesmen's salaries	9,000.00	
Miscellaneous selling expenses	750.00	
Total selling expenses		$17,250.00
General:		
Insurance	$ 450.00	
Taxes	125.00	
Office salaries	2,500.00	
Office expenses	3,260.00	
Miscellaneous general expenses	400.00	
Total general expenses		6,735.00
Total expenses		23,985.00

Transportation charges. Freight, express, and other transportation costs applicable to goods purchased are part of the cost of obtaining the goods; therefore, they are added to the purchases in the statement of profit and loss, as shown in the illustration on the following page.

Partial Profit and Loss Statement

Sales..		$60,500.00
Deduct cost of goods sold:		
Inventory, June 30, 19—..................	$115,700.00	
Purchases................... $50,100.00		
Freight in................... 525.00	50,625.00	
Cost of goods available for sale..........	$166,325.00	
Deduct inventory, July 31, 19—..........	117,320.00	
Cost of goods sold.................................		49,005.00
Gross profit on sales..................................		$11,495.00

Freight, express, and other expenses incurred in delivering goods to customers should be shown in the profit and loss statement under the Selling Expenses caption.

Freight terms.   Freight terms are expressed thus:

F. o. b. destination.   This means free on board cars at destination.   In other words, the seller bears the freight charges.

F. o. b. shipping point.   This means that the seller bears the cost of putting the merchandise on board the cars, but the purchaser pays the freight charges.

Returned sales and allowances.   Customers, after receiving merchandise sold to them, may:

(1) Return the goods because they are not of the kind or quality ordered.   When the returned goods are received, the selling company should make entries as follows:

If the customer has paid for the goods, and cash is returned to him:

Returned sales and allowances...........	500.00	
Cash...............................		500.00

If the customer is given credit for the returned goods:

Returned sales and allowances...........	500.00	
Customer's account..................		500.00

(2) Request and receive an allowance on the price.   If an allowance is granted, the seller should make entries as follows:

If cash is sent to the customer for the amount of the allowance:

Returned sales and allowances.............	40.00	
Cash...............................		40.00

If the customer is given credit for the allowance:

Returned sales and allowances.............	40.00	
Customer's account...................		40.00

The notice sent to the customer that his account has been credited for a return or an allowance may be in the form of a letter, or a credit memorandum may be issued to him. A form for a credit memorandum is illustrated below:

R. E. JOHNSON & COMPANY
2913 North Western Avenue
Chicago

_____   Credit Memo No. _____

_____   Date _____

_____

We credit your account as follows:

Reason for Credit	Amount

R. E. Johnson & Company

Per_____

Credit Memorandum

Credit memorandums should be made in duplicate. The original is usually signed by an officer or an employee of the company and is sent to the customer. The carbon copy, which should be initialed by the person who signed the original (as evidence that the credit was properly authorized), should be filed in a credit memo binder to give the bookkeeper the information he will need in recording the allowance. The initialed copies of the credit memorandums also serve as evidence of the propriety of the entries crediting the customers' accounts and debiting Returned Sales and Allowances.

The debit balance in the Returned Sales and Allowances account should be shown in the profit and loss statement as a deduction from the gross sales, as illustrated in the following partial profit and loss statement:

Partial Statement of Profit and Loss

Gross sales	$5,000.00
Deduct returned sales and allowances	350.00
Net sales	$4,650.00

Returned purchases and allowances. Goods purchased may be found unsatisfactory and may be returned. Or the goods may be kept if the concern from which they were purchased grants an allowance from the purchase price. Entries for purchase returns or allowances are illustrated below:

```
Davis and Company................................. 375.00
     Returned purchases and allowances................        375.00
     To charge Davis and Company for goods returned.
or,

Cash.............................................. 50.00
     Returned purchases and allowances..................        50.00
     To record return of goods to Osborne Corporation and
     cash received therefor.
```

The credit balance of the Returned Purchases and Allowances account should be deducted in the profit and loss statement from the debit balance of the Purchases account, as illustrated below:

```
Cost of goods sold:
   Inventory, August 31, 19—........................... $ 6,900.00
   Add net cost of purchases:
      Purchases............................. $3,215.00
      Deduct returned purchases and allowances..   122.00
      Net purchases......................... $3,093.00
      Add freight in........................    275.00   3,368.00
   Cost of goods available for sale...................... $10,268.00
```

Trade discounts. Trade discounts are deductions from the list price allowed for various reasons, such as:

(a) To avoid frequent publication of catalogues; the prices can be changed merely by changing the discount rates.

(b) To allow dealers a deduction from an advertised retail price; this practice is followed, for instance, by publishers whose advertisements state the retail prices of their books, dealers being allowed a discount from the published, or list, price.

Trade discounts may be stated as a single rate or as a series of rates. For instance, assume that the list price of merchandise is $1,200 and that a trade discount of 35% is allowed; the net price is computed as follows:

```
List price............................................... $1,200
Less trade discount—35% of $1,200........................    420
Net price...............................................  $  780
```

Or, assume that the list price is $2,000, and that trade discounts of 30% and 10% are allowed; the net price is computed on the following page.

List price...	$2,000
First discount—30% of $2,000............................. ...	600
Remainder after first discount...............................	$1,400
Second discount—10% of $1,400............................	140
Net price..	$1,260

No entries are made in the accounts for trade discounts; entries for sales and purchases are made at the net price. For instance, assume that Wharton and Company sold goods to James Benton at a list price of $2,000, subject to trade discounts of 30% and 10%. Wharton and Company would make the following entry:

James Benton...................................	1,260.00	
Sales......................................		1,260.00

and Benton's entry would be:

Purchases..	1,260.00	
Wharton and Company.....................		1,260.00

Cash discounts.   Cash discounts are deductions allowed to customers to induce them to pay their bills within a definite time. Cash discount terms are stated on the invoice in the following manner: 2/10; n/30.

Discount on sales.   If we refer to the preceding illustration and assume that Benton paid the bill within the ten-day discount period and deducted the two per cent cash discount, Wharton and Company's entry would be:

Cash..	1,234.80	
Discount on sales.............................	25.20	
James Benton.............................		1,260.00
To record collection of invoice of June 19, less 2% cash discount.		

Since discounts on sales reduce the amount received for sales, they are shown in the profit and loss statement as a deduction from sales, thus:

Partial Profit and Loss Statement

Gross sales...		$23,560.00
Deduct:		
Returned sales and allowances.................	$365.00	
Discount on sales............................	197.00	562.00
Net sales..		$22,998.00

Discount on purchases.   Benton's entry would be:

Wharton and Company..........................	1,260.00	
Discount on purchases.......................		25.20
Cash..		1,234.80
To record payment of invoice of June 19, less 2% cash discount.		

Because purchase discounts reduce the amount paid for merchandise, they are shown in the profit and loss statement as a deduction, thus:

Partial Profit and Loss Statement

Net sales..			$22,998.00
Deduct cost of goods sold:			
Inventory, May 31, 1953.............................		$ 5,450.00	
Add net cost of purchases:			
Gross purchases........................	$17,500.00		
Deduct:			
Returned purchases and allowances.....................	$235.00		
Discount on purchases........	315.00	550.00	
Net purchases........................	$16,950.00		
Add freight in........................	415.00	17,365.00	
Cost of goods available for sale........................		$22,815.00	
Deduct inventory, May 31, 1954......................		7,815.00	
Cost of goods sold...			15,000.00
Gross profit on sales...			$ 7,998.00

Accounting for bad debts. At the end of 1953 (the first year of operations), a company prepared the following statements:

THE X Y COMPANY
Statement of Profit and Loss
For the Year Ended December 31, 1953

Sales...	$100,000.00
Deduct cost of goods sold.............................	80,000.00
Gross profit on sales.................................	$ 20,000.00
Deduct expenses.....................................	12,000.00
Net income...	$ 8,000.00

THE X Y COMPANY
Balance Sheet
December 31, 1953

Assets		Liabilities and Owners' Equity		
Cash.....................	$ 6,000.00	Accounts payable.........		$ 5,000.00
Accounts receivable........	13,000.00	Owners' equity:		
Inventory.................	19,000.00	Capital stock	$25,000.00	
		Earned surplus.......	8,000.00	33,000.00
	$38,000.00			$38,000.00

Both the statement of profit and loss and the balance sheet are incorrect because no consideration has been given to the probable loss from bad debts.

The balance sheet shows that there are $13,000 of accounts receivable on the books. But it is a rare thing for merchants to collect all their accounts receivable; some losses are almost certain to occur. Therefore, if the balance sheet is to present fairly the financial position of the company, it should show the *net* amount which probably will be collected from the accounts receivable; this will be less than $13,000.

Moreover, the statement of profit and loss for each period should include all losses and expenses applicable to the period. Bad debt losses should therefore be deducted in the statement of profit and loss for the period in which the losses are incurred. In what period are they incurred? Bad debt losses result from selling merchandise to customers who do not pay their accounts; such losses are therefore incurred in the period in which the sales are made. If goods were sold in 1953 to customers whose accounts were found in 1954 to be worthless, the loss was *incurred* in 1953. The loss was not *incurred* in 1954; it was merely *discovered* in that year.

Thus it is evident that both the balance sheet and the statement of profit and loss will be incorrect unless recognition is given to probable losses on accounts receivable.

If it is estimated that only $12,000 will be collected from the receivables totaling $13,000, the bad debt losses are estimated at $1,000, and the following journal entry should be made at the end of 1953:

```
Bad debts.......................................  1,000.00
     Reserve for bad debts........................           1,000.00
     To provide for the estimated losses on uncollectible
     accounts.
```

The Bad Debts account, which was debited in the foregoing journal entry, is an expense account; in a statement in which the expenses are classified, bad debts may be shown in the general expense section, because passing on credits is usually an administrative function rather than a function of the sales force. The Bad Debts account, like other expense accounts, should be closed to Profit and Loss.

Nature of bad debt reserve. The estimated loss from bad debts cannot be credited to accounts receivable because, at the time the estimate is made, the particular customers' accounts which will finally prove worthless are unknown. Since we cannot credit any particular customers' accounts, we credit the reserve, which thus stands as a sort of blanket deduction from all of the accounts receivable. In other words, the total of the debit balances in the customers' accounts minus the credit balance in the Reserve for Bad Debts represents the estimated realizable value of the accounts receivable asset. Therefore, in the balance sheet, the credit balance in the Reserve for Bad Debts should be deducted from the total of the debit balances in the customers' accounts, as illustrated on page 92.

THE *X Y* COMPANY
Balance Sheet
December 31, 1953
Assets

Cash..		$ 6,000.00
Accounts receivable..........................	$13,000.00	
Deduct reserve for bad debts..............	1,000.00	12,000.00
Inventory...		19,000.00
		$37,000.00

Liabilities and Owners' Equity

Liabilities:		
Accounts payable...................................		$ 5,000.00
Owners' equity:		
Capital stock............................	$25,000.00	
Earned surplus...........................	7,000.00	32,000.00
		$37,000.00

The Reserve for Bad Debts is called a *valuation* account, or valuation reserve. Valuation reserves are sometimes called *contra* accounts or *offset* accounts. The nature of the reserve might be more clearly understood if some title such as Estimated Deduction for Bad Debts were used. The word *Reserve*, as used in accounting terminology, carries the same meaning.

Writing off bad accounts. After the adjusting journal entry shown on page 91 is made, the ledger contains the following balances:

Accounts receivable (total)...................	$13,000.00	
Reserve for bad debts.........................		$1,000.00

Let us now assume that an account with P. K. Lane, with a balance of $75, is determined to be uncollectible; it should be written off by the following journal entry:

Reserve for bad debts................................	75.00	
P. K. Lane.......................................		75.00
To write off the uncollectible account.		

It should be noted that the loss is charged to the reserve and not to the Bad Debts (expense) account. If we debited the Bad Debts account with *estimated* losses when the reserve is set up and later with *ascertained* losses, a double charge to expense would result.

After Lane's account is written off, the ledger contains the following balances:

Accounts receivable (total)......................	$12,925.00	
Reserve for bad debts...........................		$925.00

Methods of estimating bad debt provisions. The amount to be debited to Bad Debts and credited to the Reserve for Bad Debts at the end of a period is frequently computed as a percentage of the net sales for the period.   For example, assume that the ledger contains the following balances on December 31:

```
Accounts receivable (total).................. $20,000.00
Reserve for bad debts.......................           $    315.00
Sales.......................................            215,000.00
Returned sales and allowances..............  1,500.00
```

Assume, further, that experience shows that the reserve should be credited with a provision for bad debts equal to ½ of 1% of the sales for the year less returns and allowances.   The provision is computed as follows:

```
Sales................................................. $215,000
Deduct returned sales and allowances......................   1,500
Sales less returns and allowances..........................  $213,500
    Reserve provision = ½ of 1% of $213,500 = $1,067.50
```

This amount is debited to Bad Debts and credited to the reserve.

The total reserve is now $315.00 + $1,067.50, or $1,382.50, and the accounts receivable will be shown in the balance sheet as follows:

```
Accounts receivable......................... $20,000.00
    Less reserve for bad debts...............  1,382.50  $18,617.50
```

The amount to be added to the reserve is sometimes computed by giving consideration to the probable collectibility of each customer's account, and thereby estimating the total probable reserve requirement.   The Bad Debts account is then debited and the reserve is credited with an amount sufficient to increase the reserve to the required balance.   For example, suppose that the management reviewed the accounts receivable totaling $20,000 (see the preceding illustration) and decided that a $1,500 reserve might be required.   The provision to be made at the end of the year would be computed as follows:

```
Total reserve required...................................... $1,500
Present balance in the reserve..............................    315
Amount to be debited to Bad Debts and credited to the reserve. $1,185
```

The accounts receivable would appear in the balance sheet as follows:

```
Accounts receivable......................... $20,000.00
    Less reserve for bad debts...............  1,500.00  $18,500.00
```

Payroll and Sales Taxes

Payroll taxes and employees' income taxes withheld.   The subject of payroll taxes is presented in considerable detail in

Appendix 1. The subject is introduced here in an abbreviated form; the objective is to present the basic debit-credit procedures for recording such taxes.

Old Age Benefits Taxes:

If covered by social security, employees are taxed* at $1\frac{1}{2}\%$ of the first \$3,600 of their annual wages or salaries. The taxes levied on employees are withheld by the employers. The employers' tax is equal to the amount of tax withheld from the employees' pay.

The taxes assessed against the employer and the amount the employer has withheld must be remitted monthly or quarterly, depending on the amount.

Unemployment Insurance Taxes:

Taxes are levied against employers (but not against employees) under the Federal Unemployment Tax Act to obtain funds required to meet the provisions of the Social Security Act relative to unemployment insurance, sometimes called *unemployment compensation.*

The federal unemployment insurance tax rate is 3%; wages in excess of \$3,000 paid to any one individual during any one calendar year are not subject to the tax.   Although the tax rate is 3%, the employer is entitled to a credit for taxes paid to the states and territories under their unemployment compensation laws.   This credit cannot be more than 90% of the tax assessed by the federal government at the 3% rate.   Because of this provision in the federal law, the states have generally established a 2.7% unemployment compensation tax rate.   Since taxable wages are generally (although subject to some minor exceptions) computed in the same manner for both federal and state taxes, the tax rates are usually considered to be as follows:

Federal tax—Payable after close of year....................... .3%
State tax—Payable after close of quarter...................... 2.7
Total... 3.0%

Income taxes withheld:

As a general rule, employers are required to withhold federal income taxes from the wages and salaries of employees. The amount withheld from each employee depends on the amount earned, the applicable income tax rates, and the number of the exemptions of the employee.

The amounts withheld must be remitted either monthly or quarterly, depending on the amount.

---

* At the date of this writing.

The entries in connection with income and payroll taxes are presented below.

Entries at payroll date:

Wages expense..	400.00	
Salaries expense......................................	600.00	
Federal O. A. B. taxes withheld...................		15.00
Federal income taxes withheld...................		120.00
Wages and salaries payable......................		865.00
To record wages and salaries and withholding taxes thereon.		
Wages and salaries payable...........................	865.00	
Cash...		865.00
To record payment of wages and salaries.		
Payroll taxes..	45.00	
Federal O. A. B. taxes payable....................		15.00
Federal unemployment taxes payable.............		3.00
State unemployment taxes payable...............		27.00
To record liability for payroll taxes.		

Entries when taxes are paid:

Federal income taxes withheld........................	120.00	
Cash...		120.00
To record payment of income taxes withheld from employees' pay.		
Federal O. A. B. taxes withheld.......................	15.00	
Federal O. A. B. taxes payable.......................	15.00	
Cash...		30.00
To record payment of O. A. B. taxes withheld from employees' pay and our O. A. B. liability.		
Federal unemployment taxes payable..................	3.00	
Cash...		3.00
To record payment of federal unemployment tax.		
State unemployment taxes payable....................	27.00	
Cash...		27.00
To record payment of state unemployment tax.		

Statement presentation.   The following accounts are liability accounts and their balances are shown in the balance sheet: Federal Income Taxes Withheld, Federal O. A. B. Taxes Withheld, Federal O. A. B. Taxes Payable, Federal Unemployment Taxes Payable, State Unemployment Taxes Payable.

The tax expense is presented in the profit and loss statement, either classified as a general expense or apportioned among the expense classifications according to the payroll apportionment. In other words, the payroll tax on a salesman's salary may be classified as a selling expense and the payroll tax on a bookkeeper's salary may be classified as a general expense.

Sales taxes.   A number of taxes that are levied on the consumer are collected by the business man. The business man, in turn, remits such collections to the unit of government levying the tax. Such taxes include sales taxes, luxury taxes, transportation taxes, and gasoline taxes. The accounting for such taxes can be illustrated by an example based on a 2% retail sales tax.

Entries for sales include credits to Liability for Sales Taxes for the amount of the tax collected or charged to the customer.

When the tax is remitted to the government, the liability account is debited and Cash is credited. If the tax law specifies that the amount to be remitted is to be computed by multiplying the sales for the period by 2%, the amount due may differ from the amount collected from customers and credited to Liability for Sales Taxes. Any excess due is a tax expense; if the amount due is less than the amount collected, a miscellaneous income is realized.

Miscellaneous Matters

Income tax expense. Income taxes should be charged to an expense account in the period in which the taxable income was earned. As a general rule, the balance of the Income Tax Expense account is shown as the last expense item in the profit and loss statement in the manner illustrated on page 97.

Other income. Merchandising companies sometimes earn incidental income from transactions other than sales of merchandise. Such earnings may be shown in the profit and loss statement under the caption Other Income, after the net income from merchandising operations. Examples include interest income, rent income, and dividend income on shares of stock owned by the business.

Other expense. Expenses may be incurred which cannot properly be classified either as selling expense or as general expense. Interest expense is an example. Such expenses are presented in the profit and loss statement under the caption Other Expense, as illustrated on page 97.

Illustrative statements. The accounts introduced in this chapter are included in the financial statements presented on pages 97 to 99.

Exhibit letters. It will be noted that the balance sheet is called *Exhibit A*, the earned surplus statement is called *Exhibit B*, and the profit and loss statement is called *Exhibit C*.

The balance sheet shows the earned surplus at the end of the year, and refers to Exhibit B, where further details regarding the earned surplus can be found.

The earned surplus statement shows the earned surplus at the beginning of the year, the net income and the dividends for the year, and the earned surplus at the end of the year. The net income shown in this statement carries a reference to Exhibit C, where details of income and expense can be found.

THE POTTER COMPANY   Exhibit C

Statement of Profit and Loss

For the Year Ended December 31, 1953

Gross sales			$103,500.00
Deduct:			
Returned sales and allowances		$ 900.00	
Discount on sales		1,800.00	
Total deductions from sales			2,700.00
Net sales			$100,800.00
Deduct cost of goods sold:			
Inventory, December 31, 1952		$25,000.00	
Add net cost of purchases:			
Purchases	$65,000.00		
Deduct:			
Returned purchases and allowances	$1,000.00		
Discount on purchases	1,200.00		
Total deductions from purchases	2,200.00		
Net purchases	$62,800.00		
Add freight in	2,000.00		
Total		64,800.00	
Cost of goods available for sale		$89,800.00	
Deduct inventory, December 31, 1953		26,000.00	
Cost of goods sold			63,800.00
Gross profit on sales			$ 37,000.00
Deduct selling and general expenses:			
Selling:			
Store rent	$ 6,000.00		
Advertising	2,500.00		
Depreciation expense—Delivery equipment	500.00		
Other delivery expense	2,200.00		
Freight out	1,800.00		
Salesmen's salaries	8,000.00		
Miscellaneous selling expenses	600.00		
Total selling expenses		$21,600.00	
General:			
Bad debts	$ 504.00		
Insurance	300.00		
Taxes, other than income and payroll	596.00		
Payroll taxes	495.00		
Office salaries	3,000.00		
Office expenses	2,130.00		
Total general expenses		7,025.00	
Total selling and general expenses			28,625.00
Net operating income			$ 8,375.00
Add other income:			
Rent income from land	$ 1,200.00		
Interest income	930.00		
Total other income		$ 2,130.00	
Deduct other expense:			
Interest expense		30.00	
Other income less other expense			2,100.00
Net income before income taxes			$ 10,475.00
Income taxes			3,200.00
Net income			$ 7,275.00

Some accountants prefer to omit the words *Add* and *Deduct* and such lines as "Cost of goods sold" and "Total selling expenses." A statement illustrating such omissions is shown below.

THE POTTER COMPANY   Exhibit C

Statement of Profit and Loss

For the Year Ended December 31, 1953

Gross sales...			$103,500.00
Returned sales and allowances........................		$ 900.00	
Discount on sales..................................		1,800.00	2,700.00
Net sales...			$100,800.00
Cost of goods sold:			
Inventory, December 31, 1952.......................		$25,000.00	
Purchases.............................	$65,000.00		
Returned purchases and			
allowances...............	$1,000.00		
Discount on purchases.......	1,200.00	2,200.00	
Net purchases.....................		$62,800.00	
Freight in.........................		2,000.00	64,800.00
Cost of goods available for sale....................		$89,800.00	
Inventory, December 31, 1953......................		26,000.00	63,800.00
Gross profit on sales...			$ 37,000.00
Selling expenses:			
Store rent.............................	$ 6,000.00		
Advertising.............................	2,500.00		
Depreciation expense—Delivery equipment	500.00		
Other delivery expense...................	2,200.00		
Freight out...........................	1,800.00		
Salesmen's salaries.....................	8,000.00		
Miscellaneous selling expenses...........	600.00	$21,600.00	
General expenses:			
Bad debts.............................	$ 504.00		
Insurance.............................	300.00		
Taxes, other than income and payroll......	596.00		
Payroll taxes...........................	495.00		
Office salaries........................	3,000.00		
Office expenses........................	2,130.00	7,025.00	28,625.00
Net operating income...			$ 8,375.00
Other income:			
Rent income from land..................	$ 1,200.00		
Interest income.......................	930.00	$ 2,130.00	
Other expense:			
Interest expense.............................		30.00	2,100.00
Net income before income taxes.................................			$ 10,475.00
Income taxes..			3,200.00
Net income...			$ 7,275.00

THE POTTER COMPANY   Exhibit B

Statement of Earned Surplus

For the Year Ended December 31, 1953

Earned surplus, December 31, 1952.................................	$ 25,950.00
Add net income, per Exhibit C.............................	7,275.00
Total..	$ 33,225.00
Deduct dividends..	5,000.00
Earned surplus, December 31, 1953.....	$ 28,225.00

In the following balance sheet, "net worth" has been used instead of "owners' equity." The term "net worth" was in general use for many years. Although it has been supplanted to a very considerable extent by "owners' equity" and other similar expressions, the term "net worth" is still frequently used, and therefore it is desirable that accounting students be familiar with it.

THE POTTER COMPANY   Exhibit A

Balance Sheet

December 31, 1953

Assets

Current assets:

Cash	$18,325.00	
Securities	8,000.00	
Notes receivable	3,000.00	
Accounts receivable	$16,120.00	
Less reserve for bad debts	620.00	15,500.00
Accrued interest receivable		100.00
Inventory		26,000.00
Prepaid rent		500.00
Unexpired insurance		50.00 $71,475.00

Other assets:

Land (Held for future use)	$15,000.00	
Securities	12,000.00	27,000.00

Fixed assets:

Delivery equipment	$ 3,000.00	
Less reserve for depreciation	1,500.00	1,500.00
		$99,975.00

Liabilities and Net Worth

Current liabilities:

Accounts payable	$ 6,190.00	
Notes payable	1,000.00	
Accrued salaries	400.00	
Accrued income taxes	3,200.00	
Liability for sales taxes	600.00	
Federal income taxes withheld	180.00	
Federal O.A.B. taxes withheld	45.00	
Federal O.A.B. taxes payable	45.00	
Federal unemployment taxes payable	9.00	
State unemployment taxes payable	81.00	$11,750.00

Long-term liability:

Liability for pensions	15,000.00

Net worth:

Capital stock	$45,000.00	
Earned surplus, per Exhibit B	28,225.00	73,225.00
		$99,975.00

Balance sheet classifications. The balance sheet illustrated above is called a *classified* balance sheet. The classifications used in a balance sheet depend upon the nature of the business and the types of balance sheet accounts appearing in the ledger. The principal balance sheet categories are stated on the next page.

Assets:

Current assets: Cash and other assets, such as temporary investments in securities, accounts receivable, inventory, and prepaid expense, that presumably will be converted into cash or used during a normal operating cycle. Such items are held to be indicative of short-run debt-paying ability.

An operating cycle can be described as follows: business operations consist of a round of conversions—cash to inventories and prepaid expenses, to receivables, to cash; the average time required to complete this round is an *operating cycle.* The time period of an operating cycle varies, depending on the nature of the business.

The current assets are customarily listed in the following order: cash, securities, receivables, accrued receivables, inventories, and prepaid expenses. Prepaid expenses are regarded as current assets because, from the standpoint of ability to pay current debts, a company with, say, $950 of cash and $50 of unexpired insurance is in essentially the same position as a company with $1,000 of cash but faced with the necessity of immediately spending $50 for insurance.

Other assets: Any assets, such as land held for future use or permanent investments in securities, which do not fall into the other classifications.

Fixed assets: Property of a relatively permanent nature, such as land, buildings, furniture and fixtures, office equipment, and delivery equipment, used in the operations of the business and not intended for sale. Accounts listed under the fixed assets caption are customarily listed according to their use-life, assets with the longest use-life being listed first, assets with the shortest use-life being listed last.

Liabilities and net worth:

Current liabilities: The debts or obligations that will, according to reasonable expectations, be settled by the use of assets properly classifiable as current assets. Items of income collected in advance, which are to be earned by the future performance of services or delivery of merchandise, are properly classifiable as current liabilities, because the earning of such income normally requires the utilization of current assets.

The relative amounts of current assets and current liabilities are indicative of the ability of a business to pay its currently maturing obligations.

Long-term liabilities: Bonds, mortgages, and other debts not due in the near future.

Net worth: The capital stock and earned surplus.

Depreciation for fractional periods.   If fixed assets are acquired during an accounting period, depreciation must be computed and recorded for a fractional period.   Since depreciation is an estimate, it seems unnecessary to compute fractional-period depreciation in terms of days.   Depreciation is not that precise.   As a general rule, fractional-period depreciation is computed in terms of months or fractions of months.   This is illustrated below, where it is assumed that the company's accounting period ends on December 31.

Asset	Date Acquired	Cost	Depreciation Rate	Annual Charge for Depreciation	Months Asset in Use First Year	Fraction of Year	Depreciation Charge for First Year
Delivery equipment..	March 31	$4,000	20 %	$800	9	9/12	$600
Office machine.......	September 17 (treated as Sept. 15 for fractional-period purposes)	1,200	10 %	120	3-1/2 (7 half-months)	7/24	35

CHAPTER 8

Individual Proprietorships.   Partnerships

This chapter deals with accounts and procedures peculiar to a business owned by an individual proprietor and with some elementary matters applicable to partnership accounting.   More advanced material relative to partnerships appears in Chapter 16.

The asset, liability, income, and expense accounts of an individual proprietorship or a partnership may be the same as those of a corporation in the same line of business.   The books of an individual proprietorship or a partnership necessarily differ from those of a corporation only in the net worth accounts.

Individual Proprietorships

Capital and drawing accounts.   In place of the Capital Stock, Earned Surplus, and Dividends accounts kept by a corporation, the books of an individual proprietor contain the following accounts:

Capital account:
> This account is credited with the proprietor's original investment and with any additional investments; by transfer from Profit and Loss, it is credited with the net income or debited with the net loss for the period.

Drawing account:
> Although all changes in a proprietor's net worth could be, and sometimes are, recorded in his capital account, it is a rather general custom to also have another account, variously called the *drawing* account, the *personal* account, or the *current* account.
>
> When such an account is kept, it is debited with:
> (*a*) Withdrawals of cash or other business assets.
>> When a proprietor takes merchandise for his own use, it is customary to charge him for it at cost. Debiting the proprietor at sales price and crediting the Sales account would be illogical; a withdrawal of merchandise is not a sale.   The debit to the proprietor's drawing account is offset by a credit to Inventory (if the perpetual inventory method of accounting is used) or to Purchases (if the periodical inventory method is used).

(b) Disbursements of business cash for the benefit of the proprietor—as, for instance, a purchase made for him.

Other entries in the drawing account are described under the caption "Closing the books."

The following accounts are illustrative:

James White, Capital

					19—					
					Jan.	1	Investment	1	7,500	00
					Feb.	15	Additional invest-ment	2	1,500	00

James White, Drawings

19—				3	900	00				
Mar.	25			3	900	00				
July	8			7	400	00				
Sept.	5			9	750	00				
Dec.	17			12	600	00				

Closing the books.   The procedure of closing the income and expense accounts to Profit and Loss is exactly the same in an individual proprietorship as in a corporation.   Assume that the net income for the year is $4,500; the Profit and Loss account is closed to the proprietor's capital account by the following entry:

```
Profit and loss...................................  4,500.00
     James White, capital.......................              4,500.00
     To close the Profit and Loss account and transfer
     the net income for the year to the proprietor's
     capital account.
```

The closing procedure is completed by transferring the balance of the drawing account to the capital account by the following entry:

```
James White, capital. ........................  2,650.00
     James White, drawings ... ................              2,650.00
     To close.
```

Proprietor's accounts after closing the books.   After the books are closed, the capital account and the drawing account appear as follows:

James White, Capital

19—				13	2,650	00	19—					
Dec.	31	Drawings		13	2,650	00	Jan.	1	Investment	1	7,500	00
							Feb.	15	Additional invest-ment	2	1,500	00
							Dec.	31	Net income	12	4,500	00

James White, Drawings

19—						19—				
Mar.	25		3	900	00	Dec.	31	To capital	13	2,650	00
July	8		7	400	00					
Sept.	5		9	750	00					
Dec.	17		12	600	00					
				2,650	00					2,650	00

Working papers. Instead of a pair of Earned Surplus columns, the working papers of an individual proprietorship contain a pair of Capital columns.

The working papers on page 105 do not contain Adjustment columns; it is assumed that no adjustments are required.

Statements. The profit and loss statement of an individual proprietorship does not necessarily differ from that of a corporation in the same line of business.

JAMES WHITE — Exhibit C

Statement of Profit and Loss

For the Year Ended December 31, 19—

Sales..		$48,000.00
Less returned sales and allowances........................		1,000.00
Net sales...		$47,000.00
Less cost of goods sold:		
Purchases...............................	$35,000.00	
Less returned purchases and allowances......	500.00	
Net purchases...........................	$34,500.00	
Less inventory, December 31, 19—..........	4,000.00	
Cost of goods sold.................................		30,500.00
Gross profit on sales....................................		$16,500.00
Less expenses..		12,000.00
Net income...		$ 4,500.00

No income tax is shown because the proprietor's total tax is usually affected by other matters not related to the business.

Instead of the earned surplus statement prepared for a corporation, a statement of the proprietor's capital is prepared.

JAMES WHITE — Exhibit B

Statement of Proprietor's Capital

For the Year Ended December 31, 19—

Investment, January 1, 19—............................		$ 7,500.00
Add:		
Additional investment......................	$1,500.00	
Net income for the year—Exhibit C..........	4,500.00	6,000.00
Total..		$13,500.00
Deduct withdrawals.....................................		2,650.00
Balance, December 31, 19—............................		$10,850.00

The investment at the beginning of the year and the additional investment during the year were determined from the capital account.

JAMES WHITE
Working Papers
Year Ended December 31, 19—

	Trial Balance		Profit and Loss Statement		Statement of Capital		Balance Sheet	
Cash.	3,850.00						3,850.00	
Accounts receivable.	9,000.00						9,000.00	
Notes receivable.	2,000.00						2,000.00	
Accounts payable.		6,000.00						6,000.00
Notes payable.		2,000.00						2,000.00
Sales.		48,000.00		48,000.00				
Returned sales and allowances.	1,000.00		1,000.00					
Purchases.	35,000.00		35,000.00					
Returned purchases and allowances.		500.00		500.00				
Expense.	12,000.00		12,000.00					
James White, capital.		9,000.00				9,000.00		
James White, drawings.	2,650.00				2,650.00			
	65,500.00	65,500.00						
Inventory, December 31, 19—				4,000.00			4,000.00	
Net income—to Capital.			4,500.00			4,500.00		
			52,500.00	52,500.00				
Capital, December 31, 19—					10,850.00			10,850.00
					13,500.00	13,500.00	18,850.00	18,850.00

The balance sheets of an individual proprietorship and a corporation do not necessarily differ except in the net worth section. The balance sheet of an individual proprietorship shows the proprietor's capital in one amount, whereas the balance sheet of a corporation shows the capital stock and surplus.

JAMES WHITE   Exhibit A

Balance Sheet

December 31, 19—

Assets		Libalities and Net Worth	
Current assets:		Current liabilities:	
Cash	$ 3,850.00	Accounts payable	$ 6,000.00
Accounts receivable	9,000.00	Notes payable	2,000.00
Notes receivable	2,000.00	Total current liabilities.	$ 8,000.00
Merchandise inventory	4,000.00		
		Net worth:	
		James White, capital—Exhibit B	10,850.00
	$18,850.00		$18,850.00

Partnerships

Nature of a partnership. "A partnership," as defined by the Uniform Partnership Act, "is an association of two or more persons to carry on, as co-owners, a business for profit."

The partnership and the corporation are the two most common forms of organization by which two or more persons can join in a business enterprise. The partnership form is usually employed in comparatively small businesses requiring no more capital than can be contributed by a few partners; or in professional practices, such as law, medicine, and accounting, in which the relations of the firm to its clientele should involve a personal responsibility.

Some of the significant characteristics of the partnership form of business organization are briefly discussed below. For a comprehensive treatment of these matters, a text on the law of partnerships should be consulted.

No separate legal entity. Generally, a partnership has no legal status as an entity. The assets are owned, and the liabilities are owed, by the partners collectively. However, this common-law concept of the partnership has been somewhat modified by the Uniform Partnership Act, which, for instance, enables a partnership to hold real and personal property in its own name. The Uniform Partnership Act has not been adopted by all of the states.

Mutual agency. Each partner is an agent for all of the other partners in matters coming within the scope of partnership activities. Therefore, outsiders have a right to assume that the partnership is bound by the acts of any partner relative to the affairs of the partnership.

Unlimited liability. Each partner is individually liable for all of the debts of a partnership incurred during his membership in the firm; he may assume a liability for debts incurred before his admission to the partnership; and, unless proper notice of withdrawal is given to the public, he may be liable for partnership debts incurred after his retirement. If a partner pays partnership debts from his personal assets, he is entitled to reimbursement.

Limited partnerships are permissible in some states. A limited partner has no personal liability to creditors, but he must maintain his investment at the amount contributed at the time of organization. There must be at least one general partner who is liable to creditors for debts which cannot be paid from firm assets.

Limited right to dispose of interest. A partner has a legal right to assign his partnership interest to another person, although he may be subject to a suit for damages for any loss incurred by his partners as a consequence of such an assignment. But he cannot compel the other partners to accept the assignee as a partner.

Division of profits. Partnership profits may be divided among the partners in any manner to which they agree. Consequently, the division of profits is more flexible in a partnership than in a corporation.

Withdrawal of assets. Because the stockholders of a corporation generally have no personal liability for corporate debts, the law places limitations on the amounts of dividend payments or other asset distributions which may be made to corporate stockholders. There are no similar legal restrictions on partners' withdrawals of cash or other assets; the individual liability of the partners for the payment of partnership debts makes such creditor protection unnecessary. However, the partners may make agreements among themselves placing limitations on the amounts which they may withdraw.

Effect of partner's death. The death of a partner automatically dissolves the partnership of which he was a member. His heirs have a right to be paid the amount of his partnership interest, but they have no right (except by consent of the other partner or partners) to succeed him as a member of the firm.

The partnership contract. The partnership relation is created by a contract. The contract may be oral, but it is much better to have it in writing, because partners have been known to forget the features of oral agreements which prove ultimately to be to their disadvantage. A partnership contract is sometimes called *the partnership agreement*, and sometimes *the articles of partnership*. Among the more important things to be covered by the contract are those mentioned on the following page.

(1) The names of the partners and the name of the partnership.
(2) The date when the contract becomes effective.
(3) The nature of the business.
(4) The place where operations are to be conducted.
(5) The amount of capital to be contributed by each partner,
the assets to be invested and the valuations to be placed
on them.
(6) The rights and duties of the partners.
(7) The dates when the books are to be closed and the profits
ascertained and divided.
(8) The portion of the profits to be allowed to each partner.
(9) The drawings to be allowed each partner and the penalties,
if any, to be imposed because of excess withdrawals.
(10) The length of time the partnership is to continue.
(11) Conditions under which a partner may withdraw or may
be compelled to withdraw; the bases for the determination of his equity in the event of withdrawal; and agreements regarding the payment of his equity in full or in
installments.
(12) Procedures in the event of the death of a partner.
(13) Provision for arbitration in the event of disputes.
(14) The rights and duties of the partners in the event of
dissolution.

Capital and drawing accounts. The capital and drawing
accounts of a partnership are similar to those of an individual proprietorship. They are discussed below.

Capital account:
A capital account is kept with each partner and is credited
with the amount of his original investment and the
amounts of any additional investments. Other entries
which may be made in the capital accounts are described
under the caption "Closing the books."
Drawing account:
All changes in a partner's share of the net worth may be
recorded in his capital account, but it is customary to
use also a drawing (sometimes called a *personal* or
current) account.
When such an account is kept, it may be debited with:
(a) Withdrawals of cash or other partnership assets.
As a general rule, all such withdrawals are charged
to the drawing account. However, partners
sometimes agree that each partner may draw a

stipulated amount each month as his share of the estimated earnings, and that any withdrawals in excess of this amount shall be regarded as withdrawals of investments and shall be debited to his capital account.

What was said about withdrawals of merchandise by a single proprietor applies equally here.

(b) Disbursements of business cash for the benefit of a partner.

Other entries which may be made in the drawing accounts are described under the caption "Closing the books."

The following accounts are illustrative:

D. E. Snyder, Capital

						19—				
						Jan.	1	Investment	1	9,000 00
						June	1	Additional investment	10	1,000 00

D. E. Snyder, Drawings

19—									
Apr.	15			5	200 00				
Oct.	20			14	800 00				

J. O. Long, Capital

						19—				
						Jan.	1	Investment	1	15,000 00
						July	1	Additional investment	11	4,000 00

J. O. Long, Drawings

19—									
Mar.	10			4	500 00				
Nov.	5			15	700 00				

Loan accounts. A partnership may be in need of funds, which a partner is able to supply but which he is willing to furnish only temporarily. In such instances, the credit to the partner may be made in a loan account. Such loans should not be shown in the balance sheet as part of the net worth; they should be shown among the liabilities, but clearly distinguished from liabilities to outsiders.

On the other hand, a partner may wish to make a temporary withdrawal of funds in the form of a loan. A loan receivable account will then appear on the partnership books. In the balance sheet, such a loan should be shown separately from receivables from outsiders.

Opening the books. If all capital contributions are in the form of cash, no problems arise; the Cash account is debited and each partner's capital account is credited.

If non-cash assets are invested, it is extremely important that they be recorded at their fair values at the date of the investment. Assume, for instance, that a partner invests land and a building which he is carrying on his books at $20,000, which was the cost to him less depreciation. At the date when he invests this property in the partnership, it is worth $25,000. If the property were recorded on the partnership books at $20,000 and later sold for $25,000, all of the partners would share in the gain; this would not be fair to the partner who invested the property and who should have received a $25,000 credit for it.

If any liabilities of a partner are assumed by the partnership, they should, of course, be credited to liability accounts, and the partner's capital account should be credited with the net investment.

Goodwill. If a partner's investment consists of a going business, it may be equitable to give the partner a capital credit for the goodwill of the business. A business may have goodwill if it has exceptionally good earnings. The valuation of the goodwill is a matter of agreement among the partners, and should be based on the probable future amount of profits attributable to the business brought in by the partner. The amount, if any, agreed upon should be debited to a Goodwill account, with an offsetting credit to the partner's capital account.

The profit and loss ratio. The ratio in which partners divide their profits or losses is called the *profit and loss ratio*. In the illustration in this chapter, it is assumed that the partners have agreed to divide profits and losses equally. Other methods of dividing partnership profits and losses are discussed in Chapter 16.

If partners make no agreement regarding the division of profits and losses, the law assumes an agreement to divide them equally. If partners make an agreement regarding the division of profits, without any mention of losses, the agreed method for the division of profits applies also to the division of losses.

Closing the books. Income and expense accounts are closed to the Profit and Loss account in the same manner as those of an individual proprietorship or a corporation. The remaining closing entries depend upon whether the partners' capitals are to be maintained at fixed amounts.

Capitals maintained at fixed amounts. Partners sometimes agree that their capitals shall be maintained at fixed amounts, to be shown by the balances of their capital accounts. If there is

such an agreement, the Profit and Loss account should be closed
by transfer of the net income or loss to the partners' drawing
accounts.   The total or net amount of the balances in the capital
and drawing accounts of each partner is the amount to be included
in the net worth section of the balance sheet.

No agreement for fixed capitals.   If there is no agreement with
respect to fixed capitals, the Profit and Loss account is closed to
the partners' capital accounts, and each partner's drawing account
is closed to his capital account.   This is the more customary
procedure and it is illustrated below.   It is assumed that the net
income for the year was $8,000.

```
Profit and loss...................................  8,000.00
    D. E. Snyder, capital........................              4,000.00
    J. O. Long, capital..........................              4,000.00
    To divide the net income for the year equally.

D. E. Snyder, capital............................  1,000.00
    D. E. Snyder, drawings.......................              1,000.00
    To close the drawing account.

J. O. Long, capital..............................  1,200.00
    J. O. Long, drawings.........................              1,200.00
    To close the drawing account.
```

Working papers.   The working papers of a partnership contain a pair of columns for each partner, as shown in the illustration on page 112.

Profit and loss statement.   The profit and loss statement of a
partnership will be similar to that of an individual proprietorship
or a corporation in the same line of business.

SNYDER AND LONG   Exhibit C

Statement of Profit and Loss

For the Year Ended December 31, 19—

```
Sales...............................................................  $90,000.00
Less discount on sales..............................................      200.00
Net sales...........................................................  $89,800.00
Less cost of goods sold:
    Purchases...............................  $60,000.00
    Less discount on purchases..............      700.00
    Net purchases...........................  $59,300.00
    Less inventory at the end of the year...    5,000.00
    Cost of goods sold......................               54,300.00
Gross profit on sales...............................................  $35,500.00
Less expenses:
    Selling expenses........................  $13,000.00
    General expenses........................   14,500.00   27,500.00
Net income..........................................................  $ 8,000.00
```

This statement does not show any deduction for income taxes.
A partnership, as such, does not pay any federal income taxes, but
it is required to file an information return showing the results of its

SNYDER AND LONG
Working Papers
Year Ended December 31, 19—

	Trial Balance		Profit and Loss Statement		D. E. Snyder, Capital		J. O. Long, Capital		Balance Sheet	
Cash	14,800.00								14,800.00	
Accounts receivable	18,000.00								18,000.00	
Accounts payable		3,000.00								3,000.00
D. E. Snyder, capital		10,000.00				10,000.00				
D. E. Snyder, drawings	1,000.00				1,000.00					
J. O. Long, capital		19,000.00						19,000.00		
J. O. Long, drawings	1,200.00						1,200.00			
Sales		90,000.00		90,000.00						
Discount on sales	200.00		200.00							
Purchases	60,000.00		60,000.00							
Discount on purchases		700.00		700.00						
Selling expenses	13,000.00		13,000.00							
General expenses	14,500.00		14,500.00							
	122,700.00	122,700.00								
Inventory, December 31, 19—				5,000.00					5,000.00	
Net income—Divided equally			8,000.00			4,000.00		4,000.00		
			95,700.00	95,700.00						
Capitals at the end of the year:										
Snyder					13,000.00					13,000.00
Long							21,800.00			21,800.00
					14,000.00	14,000.00	23,000.00	23,000.00	37,800.00	37,800.00

operations and each partner's share of the net income or net loss. Each partner is subject to income tax on his share of the partnership net income, regardless of the portion thereof which he has withdrawn.

Statement of partners' capitals.   In order to prepare the following statement, it was necessary to refer to the capital accounts to determine the investments at the beginning of the year and the additional investments during the year.

	D. E. Snyder	J. O. Long	Total
SNYDER AND LONG Exhibit B			
Statement of Partners' Capitals			
For the Year Ended December 31, 19—			
Investments, January 1, 19—..............	$ 9,000.00	$15,000.00	$24,000.00
Add:			
Additional investments..................	1,000.00	4,000.00	5,000.00
Net income for the year—Exhibit C......	4,000.00	4,000.00	8,000.00
Totals..................................	$14,000.00	$23,000.00	$37,000.00
Deduct withdrawals......................	1,000.00	1,200.00	2,200.00
Balances, December 31, 19—..............	$13,000.00	$21,800.00	$34,800.00

Balance sheet.   The balance sheet of a partnership usually shows the capital of each partner, with a reference to the statement of partners' capitals, where details can be found.

SNYDER AND LONG   Exhibit A

Balance Sheet

December 31, 19—

Assets

Current assets:

Cash... $14,800.00

Accounts receivable.............................. ....   18,000.00

Merchandise inventory................................   5,000.00

$37,800.00

Liabilities and Net Worth

Current liabilities:

Accounts payable.................................... $ 3,000.00

Net worth—Exhibit B:

D. E. Snyder, capital.................:........ $13,000.00

J. O. Long, capital......................   21,800.00   34,800.00

$37,800.00

CHAPTER 9
Promissory Notes—Bills of Exchange

Notes

Definition. The following definition is quoted from the Uniform Negotiable Instruments Act:

> A negotiable promissory note within the meaning of this act is an unconditional promise in writing made by one person to another, signed by the maker, engaging to pay on demand or at a fixed or determinable future time a sum certain in money to order or bearer.

<u>$100.00</u>   <u>Chicago, Illinois, July 25, 19--</u>
<u>One month</u>   after date <u>I</u> promise to pay to
the order of <u>F. K. Hamilton</u>
<u>--One Hundred-no/100----------------------------</u> Dollars
Payable at <u>First National Bank of Chicago</u> .
Value received, with interest at <u>6%</u>
No. <u>17</u>   Due <u>August 25, 19--</u>   *C. H. Mather*

The original parties to a note are:

The payee—In the above illustration,
F. K. Hamilton.
The maker—In the above illustration,
C. H. Mather.

Every promissory note is a note receivable from the standpoint of the payee (since he expects to receive money) and a note payable from the standpoint of the maker (since he expects to pay money).

Maturity. Notes may be drawn to mature:

(1) On a date named in the note, thus: "On June 30, 19—, I promise to pay."
(2) On demand, thus: "On demand, I promise to pay."
(3) Upon the expiration of a stated period of time; the time may be stated in several ways, as indicated on the following page.

(a) Years, thus: "One year after date, I promise to pay."
Such notes will mature in a subsequent year on the
same day of the same month as the date of issue,
except that notes issued on February 29, payable
in a year having only 28 days in February, will
mature on February 28.

(b) Months, thus: "Three months after date, I promise
to pay." Such notes will mature in a subsequent
month on the same day of the month as the date of
issue, except that: (1) notes dated on the 31st of a
month and maturing in a month having only 30
days will mature on the 30th of the month; and
(2) notes dated on the 29th, 30th, or 31st of a
month and maturing in February will mature on
the last day of February.

(c) Days, thus: "One hundred and twenty days after
date, I promise to pay." The method of determining the maturity of such notes is illustrated by
the following computation of the maturity of a
120-day note dated December 15, 1954:

Remaining days in December	16
Days in January	31
	47
Days in February	28
	75
Days in March	31
	106
Days in April	14 Maturity
	120

Interest

Computing interest—General formula. The general formula
for computing interest may be expressed thus:

$$\text{Principal} \times \text{Interest Rate} \times \text{Time} = \text{Interest}$$

Interest rates, unless specifically qualified to the contrary, are per
annum rates. If a note is described as a 6% note, the interest is
at the rate of 6% per year.

If time is expressed in terms of months, interest is computed in
terms of months. For example, the interest on a $1,000, 6% note
for three months is computed as follows:

$$\$1,000 \times .06 \times \tfrac{3}{12} = \$15$$

If time is expressed in terms of days, the exact number of days
is used in the interest computation. However, for interest computation purposes, it is commonly assumed that there are 360 days

in a year.   For example, the interest on a 45-day 6% note for $1,000 is computed as follows:

$$\$1,000 \times .06 \times \tfrac{45}{360} = \$7.50$$

In the determination of the number of days between two dates, for purposes of computing interest, exclude the first day and include the last.   For instance, the time of a note dated June 17 and due August 4 would be computed as follows:

Remaining days in June	13
July	31
August	4
	48

Computing interest—Short methods.   There are several methods of computing simple interest.   Some of the shortest are explained below.   At 6% per annum,

The interest on $1.00 for 1 year is	$.06
The interest on 1.00 for 2 months (60 days) is	.01 (⅙ of $.06)
The interest on 1.00 for 6 days is	.001 (¹⁄₁₀ of $.01)

It is evident that interest on $1.00 for sixty days can be computed by moving the decimal point in the principal two places to the left, and that interest on $1.00 for six days can be computed by moving the decimal point in the principal three places to the left.   If this is true of $1.00, it is true of any principal, and a general rule may be developed in the manner shown below:

Given any principal, to find the interest at 6%:
For   6 days, point off three places to the left
"   60   "   ,   "   " two   "   "   "   "
"   600   "   ,   "   " one   place "   "   "
"   6,000   "   , the interest is the same as the principal.

Thus,   6 days' interest on $1,230.00 is $ 1.23
             60   "   "   "   1,230.00 "   12.30
            600   "   "   "   1,230.00 "   123.00
          6,000   "   "   "   1,230.00 "   1,230.00

Multiples and fractions.   The time, stated in days, may be separated into parts that are multiples or fractions of 6, 60, 600, or 6,000, and the interest for partial time periods may be added.   What is the interest on $137.65 for fifteen days?

Interest for 60 days = $1.3765
    "   " 15 "   = ¼ of $1.3765, or $.3441

What is the interest on $137.65 for eighty-eight days?

Interest for 60 days = $1.3765
    "   " 20 "   =   .4588 (⅓ of $1.3765)
    "   "   6 "   =   .13765
    "   "   2 "   =   .04588 (⅓ of $.13765)
    "   " 88 "   = $2.01883 or $2.02.

Interest for any number of days.   When the time cannot easily be divided into fractions or multiples of 6, 60, 600, or 6,000,

Point off three places.   (Amount is interest for six days.)
Multiply by the numbers of days.   (Product is interest for six times the
stated number of days.)
Divide by 6.   (Quotient is interest for the stated number of days.)

What is the interest on $137.65 at 6% for seventy-seven days?

Point off three places. . . . . $ .13765
Multiply by   77
Interest for 6 × 77 days $10.59905
Divide by 6: $10.59905 ÷ 6 = $1.7665 = $1.77, interest for 77 days.

Interchanging principal and time.   The principal and time may be interchanged if this procedure will simplify the computation. What is the interest on $1,000 for thirty-eight days?

Interchanging, what is the interest on $38.00 for 1,000 days?
Interest for 6,000 days   = $38.00
Divide by 6: $38.00 ÷ 6 =   6.33

Interest at other rates.   When the rate is other than 6%, it is convenient to compute the interest at 6%, and make the adjustments for the difference between 6% and the actual rate.
What is the interest on $360 for thirty days at 7%?

Compute the interest at 6%:
  Interest for 60 days = $3.60
  Interest for 30 days = $1.80
Add one sixth of $1.80   .30
Interest at 7% $2.10

What is the interest on $3,500 for forty-five days at $5\frac{1}{2}$%?

Compute the interest at 6%:
  Interest for 60 days = $35.00
  Interest for 45 days = $\frac{3}{4}$ of $35.00 $26.25
Deduct (for $\frac{1}{2}$ of 1%) $\frac{1}{12}$ of $26.25   2.19
Interest at $5\frac{1}{2}$% $24.06

Notes Receivable

Notes Receivable account.   Although it is customary to keep a separate account with each debtor who owes the business on open account, notes receivable from all debtors may be recorded in one account, thus:

Notes Receivable

19—					19—					
July	3	J. B. Gates 60 da.	1	a 1,000 00	Aug.	1	J. F. Cole	1	d 1,000 00
	7	C. L. Peters 30 da.	1	b 1,500 00					
	18	H. N. Burt 30 da.	1	c 1,000 00					
	22	J. F. Cole 10 da.	1	d 1,000 00					

Each debit entry shows the name of the maker and the time the note is to run. The credits are identified with the debits by names and cross-reference letters; thus, the credit records the collection of the Cole note, as evidenced by the reference *d*.

The number of days shown in each entry is the number of days the note runs. Since the note may bear a date earlier than that of the entry, the maturity of the note is not necessarily the stated number of days after the date of the entry.

Entries for note receivable transactions. Let us assume that we receive from Peter Dunlap a note for $1,000 due in 60 days. Illustrative entries for the receipt of the note and for its collection or dishonor at maturity are shown below:

(*A*) *Entries for the receipt of the note:*

> In studying the following illustrative entries, you will observe that the entry to be made when a note receivable is received always includes a debit to the Notes Receivable account; the credit depends upon other facts about the transaction.
>
> You will observe also that the following illustrative debit and credit entries for the receipt of a note are not affected by the fact that the note bears interest or does not bear interest. The only difference is in the explanation, which states whether the note is interest-bearing or non-interest-bearing.
>
> (1) Assume that the note is received for a cash loan to Dunlap (and that it bears 6% interest):

Notes receivable.............................. 1,000.00
    Cash.......................................   1,000.00
    Received a 60-day, 6% note from Peter Dunlap for
a loan.

> (2) Assume that Dunlap is indebted to us on an account receivable, and that we obtain the note from him to apply on account (and that it does not bear interest):

Notes receivable.............................. 1,000.00
    Peter Dunlap...............................   1,000.00
    Received a 60-day note, without interest, to apply
on account.

> (3) Assume that we sell merchandise to Dunlap and receive a note immediately for the amount of the invoice (and that the note bears 6% interest).
>
> The transaction *might be* recorded in the manner shown on the following page.

```
Notes receivable.............................  1,000.00
   Sales.....................................             1,000.00
   Received a 60-day, 6% note from Peter Dunlap for
   amount of sale today.
```

> However, it is considered better practice to make two
> entries, as illustrated below, so that all the facts will
> be shown in our account with Dunlap:

```
Peter Dunlap.................................  1,000.00
   Sales.....................................             1,000.00
   Sale of merchandise.

Notes receivable.............................  1,000.00
   Peter Dunlap..............................             1,000.00
   Received a 60-day, 6% note for amount of sale
   today.
```

(B) Entries for the collection of the note:

> The entries for the collection of a note *are* affected by the
> fact that it bears interest or does not bear interest.

> (1) Assume that the note mentioned in the preceding illus-
> trations does not bear interest; we will collect the
> face of the note, $1,000.

```
Cash.........................................  1,000.00
   Notes receivable..........................             1,000.00
   Collection of 60-day note from Peter Dunlap.
```

> (2) Assume that the note bears 6% interest; we will collect
> the face of the note and $10 interest.
> Interest is a fee charged for loaning money or extend-
> ing credit; it is income to the payee of the note,
> and should be credited by him to the Interest Income
> account.

```
Cash.........................................  1,010.00
   Notes receivable..........................             1,000.00
   Interest income...........................                10.00
   Collection of 60-day note and interest at 6%, from
   Peter Dunlap.
```

> If an adjusting entry was made for accrued interest
> during the life of the note, the amount of the accrual
> should be credited to Accrued Interest Receivable
> when the interest is collected, and the remainder
> should be credited to Interest Income.

(C) Entries if note is dishonored:

> If the maker of a note does not settle for it at maturity, the
> note is said to be dishonored. Some bookkeepers make

no entry whatever to show that a note receivable has been dishonored, and continue to carry it in the Notes Receivable account, with the hope that eventually it will be collected.

This is not the best practice. If we hold a note receivable and do not collect it at maturity, we should transfer the amount from the Notes Receivable account to an account receivable with the debtor, so that our account with the debtor will show, for credit information purposes, the fact that he has dishonored his note.

Illustrative entries to record the dishonoring of notes are shown below:

(1) Assume that Dunlap's note does not bear interest, and that he dishonors it:

```
Peter Dunlap....................................  1,000.00
    Notes receivable...........................              1,000.00
    Non-interest-bearing note dishonored.
```

(2) Assume that Dunlap's note bears 6% interest, and that he dishonors it:

```
Peter Dunlap....................................  1,010.00
    Notes receivable...........................              1,000.00
    Interest income............................                 10.00
    Dishonor of 6% note.
```

Observe that the Interest Income account is credited, even though the interest is not collected. The interest has been earned, and Dunlap owes us the interest as well as the face of the note.

(D) *Entries if note is partially collected:*

If at the maturity of a note we make only a partial collection, we should charge the maker's account with only the uncollected portion of the amount due, because the note is only partially dishonored.

(E) *Entries for a renewal note:*

At the maturity of a note, the maker may dishonor it and give us a new note for the full amount; or we may receive a partial collection in cash and a new note for the balance.

(1) Assume that Dunlap's note does not bear interest, and that, at maturity, he dishonors it and gives us a new note for the amount of the dishonored note. Our entries are as shown on the following page.

```
Peter Dunlap..................................  1,000.00
    Notes receivable.............................          1,000.00
    Dishonor of 60-day note due today.

Notes receivable..............................  1,000.00
    Peter Dunlap................................          1,000.00
    New 60-day note received.
```

(2) Assume that Dunlap's note bears interest, and that, at maturity, we collect the interest and $700 on the principal, and that we receive from Dunlap a new 60-day, 6% note for the balance. Our entries are:

```
Cash.........................................  710.00
    Notes receivable............................          700.00
    Interest income.............................           10.00
    Collection of portion of $1,000 note, and the interest.

Peter Dunlap.................................  300.00
    Notes receivable............................          300.00
    Dishonor of portion of 60-day note due today.

Notes receivable..............................  300.00
    Peter Dunlap................................          300.00
    New 60-day, 6% note for balance of note due today.
```

Notes Payable

Notes Payable account. Notes payable are also recorded in one account. Each credit entry shows the name of the payee and the time the note is to run. The debits recording payments are identified with the credits by writing the names of the payees and by using cross-reference letters, in the manner illustrated in the Notes Receivable account on page 117.

Entries for note payable transactions. Let us assume that we give George Weaver a note for $2,500, due in 60 days. Illustrative entries for the issuance and for the payment or dishonor of this note are shown below:

(A) *Entries for the issuance of the note:*

The entry to record the issuance of an interest-bearing note or a non-interest-bearing note always includes a credit to the Notes Payable account for the face amount of the note; the debit depends on other facts about the transaction, as illustrated below:

(1) Assume that the note is issued to Weaver for a cash loan (and that it bears 6% interest):

```
Cash.........................................  2,500.00
    Notes payable...............................          2,500.00
    Issued 60-day, 6% note to George Weaver for a
    loan.
```

(2) Assume that we are indebted to Weaver on an account payable, that we give him the note to apply on his account payable, and that the note does not bear interest:

George Weaver...............................	2,500.00	
Notes payable...............................		2,500.00
Issued a 60-day note, without interest, on account.		

(3) Assume that we purchase merchandise from Weaver and issue a note immediately for the amount of the invoice, and that the note bears 6% interest.

The transaction *might* be recorded by a single journal entry as follows:

Purchases......................................	2,500.00	
Notes payable...............................		2,500.00
Issued a 60-day, 6% note to George Weaver for amount of purchase today.		

However, it is considered better practice to make two entries, as illustrated below, so that all the facts will be shown in our account with Weaver:

Purchases......................................	2,500.00	
George Weaver...............................		2,500.00
Purchase of merchandise.		
George Weaver...............................	2,500.00	
Notes payable...............................		2,500.00
Issued a 60-day, 6% note for purchase today.		

(*B*) *Entries for the payment of the note:*

(1) Assume that the note does not bear interest; we will pay the face of the note, $2,500.

Notes payable................................	2,500.00	
Cash.......................................		2,500.00
Payment of 60-day note to George Weaver.		

(2) Assume that the note bears 6% interest; we will pay the face of the note and $25 interest.

Notes payable................................	2,500.00	
Interest expense................................	25.00	
Cash.......................................		2,525.00
Payment of 60-day note and 6% interest to George Weaver.		

If an adjusting entry was made for accrued interest during the life of the note, the amount of the accrual should be debited to Accrued Interest Payable when the interest is paid, and the remainder should be debited to Interest Expense.

(C) Dishonor of a note payable:

If we hold a note receivable and it is dishonored at maturity, we should charge it back to the maker's account, so that his account will show, for credit information purposes, that he has dishonored his note.

If we dishonor our note payable, we have no similar reason for transferring the amount of the note from the Notes Payable account to an account payable with the payee. Therefore, we will make no entry to show that we have dishonored the note.

If the note bears interest and we do not pay it, we should make an entry to record the interest expense and the liability for the interest. Thus, if our note to Weaver bears interest and we make no payment at maturity, we should make the following entry to record the accrued interest:

```
Interest expense.....................................  25.00
    Accrued interest payable.........................          25.00
    Interest accrued at 6% for 60 days on note payable to
    George Weaver, due today.
```

(D) Entries if note is partially paid:

If, at the maturity of our note payable, we pay a portion thereof, our only entry will be for the amount of the payment.

(1) Assume that the note to Weaver does not bear interest, and that we make a partial payment of $1,200 at maturity:

```
Notes payable................................. 1,200.00
    Cash .....................................          1,200.00
    Partial payment to George Weaver on note due
    today.
```

(2) Assume that the note to Weaver bears 6% interest, and that we make a partial payment of $1,200 at maturity. Since Weaver will presumably regard $25 as payment of interest, and will regard the remainder as a payment on the principal, our entry will be:

```
Interest expense...............................    25.00
Notes payable.................................. 1,175.00
    Cash......................................          1,200.00
    Payment of portion of principal of note to George
    Weaver, due today, and interest.
```

(*E*) *Entries for a renewal note:*

> At the maturity of our note payable, we may give a new note for the full amount, or we may make a partial payment and give a new note for the balance.
>
> (1) Assume that the Weaver note does not bear interest, and that, at maturity, we give him a new note due in 60 days for the amount of the old note. Our entry will be:

```
Notes payable.................................. 2,500.00
    Notes payable..............................          2,500.00
    Issuance of a new 60-day note to George Weaver
    for face of 60-day note due today.
```

> (2) Assume that the Weaver note bears 6% interest, and that, at maturity, we pay him the interest on the note and $1,000 on the principal, and give him a new 60-day, 6% note for the balance.

```
Notes payable.................................. 1,000.00
Interest expense...............................    25.00
    Cash.......................................          1,025.00
    Payment of portion of note due today, and total
    interest.

Notes payable.................................. 1,500.00
    Notes payable..............................          1,500.00
    Issuance of a new 60-day, 6% note to George
    Weaver for unpaid portion of note due today.
```

Discounting a note payable. When a note payable is issued to a bank for a loan, the note usually does not bear interest, but the interest is deducted in advance. For instance, assume that we give a bank a 60-day note for $1,000, and that the bank charges discount at 6%. The discount is $10, and we will receive the proceeds of $990.

Entry if note matures before the end of the accounting period:

```
Cash.......................................... 990.00
Interest expense..............................  10.00
    Notes payable.............................         1,000.00
    Note due in 60 days, discounted at bank.
```

Entry if note matures after the end of the accounting period:

```
Cash.......................................... 990.00
Prepaid interest expense......................  10.00
    Notes payable.............................         1,000.00
    Note due in 60 days, discounted at bank.
```

If the Prepaid Interest Expense account is used, an adjusting entry is required at the end of the accounting period to transfer the expense portion to Interest Expense.

Bills of Exchange

Definition.   The following definition is quoted from the Uniform Negotiable Instruments Act:

> A bill of exchange is an unconditional order in writing addressed by one person to another, signed by the person giving it, requiring the person to whom it is addressed to pay on demand or at a fixed or determinable future time a sum certain in money to order or to bearer.

The parties to a bill of exchange are:

The drawer—the person who signs the order.
The drawee—the person to whom the bill is addressed and who is ordered to make the payment.
The payee—the person to whom the required payment is to be made.

Classification.   Bills of exchange, often called *drafts*, may be classified as follows:

(*A*) As to the nature of the parties:
  (1) Bills drawn on banks; a bank check is an illustration of such a bill of exchange.
  (2) Bills drawn on parties other than banks; these are known as *commercial bills*. They are the only bills of exchange with which we are concerned in this chapter.
(*B*) As to the number of parties:
  (1) Three-party drafts—in which *A* orders *B* to pay *C*. Three-party commercial bills are now so rarely used in business that they are not discussed in this chapter.
  (2) Two-party drafts—in which *A* orders *B* to pay *A*. In such a draft, *A* is both the drawer and the payee.
  Since there are always three parties to a draft (drawer, drawee, and payee), it would be more precise to use the expression *two-person draft* when one person is both drawer and payee. However, *two-party draft* is the customary terminology.
(*C*) As to the time when payment is to be made:
  (1) Sight drafts—payable immediately upon presentation to the drawee.
  (2) Time drafts—payable after a lapse of time. Since we are concerned in this chapter with time paper, we shall deal only with time drafts.

Two-party time draft. A two-party time draft is illustrated below:

$100.00   Chicago, Illinois, __July 20,__ 19__
__Thirty days after date__ Pay to the order of OURSELVES
One Hundred-no/100--------------------------------Dollars
To __George Hill,__
__Freeport, Illinois__   *Peter Rowe*

Two-Party Time Draft

Acceptance. A time draft should be presented to the drawee to obtain his agreement to pay it at maturity. This agreement is called *acceptance* of the draft and is expressed by writing across the face of the draft:

Accepted
(Drawee's signature)

After a time draft has been accepted by the drawee, it is called an *acceptance*. Thus the word *acceptance* has two meanings: the act of accepting, and an accepted draft.

Time drafts may be payable:

(1) A certain period after the date of the paper; in such cases, the time is expressed thus:

"Thirty days after date, pay to the order of (etc.)."

A draft drawn on June 15, payable thirty days after date, will be due on July 15, regardless of the date on which it is accepted. Since the date of acceptance has no bearing on the maturity of the draft, the date of acceptance need not be shown.

(2) A certain period after the date when the draft is accepted by the drawee; the time may be expressed thus:

"Thirty days after sight, pay to the order of (etc.)," *or*
"At thirty days' sight, pay to the order of (etc.)."

A draft drawn on June 15, payable thirty days after sight, and accepted on June 20, will be due on July 20. Since the date of acceptance of such a draft determines the date of its maturity, the date of acceptance should be shown, thus:

Accepted
June 20, 19—
(Drawee's signature)

Accounts with notes and acceptances. An accepted time draft, like a promissory note, is a debtor's written agreement to pay a certain sum of money at a fixed or determinable future date.   Therefore, most accountants record acceptances receivable in the Notes Receivable account, and acceptances payable in the Notes Payable account.

Although a few accountants prefer to keep separate accounts with Notes Receivable and Acceptances Receivable, and separate accounts with Notes Payable and Acceptances Payable, this distinction is usually considered unnecessary.

Two-party time draft for collection purposes. Two-party time drafts are occasionally used to reduce a past-due account to a written promise to pay. If a debtor will not pay his account, he may consent to give a promissory note or accept a time draft.   If a time draft is used, it is drawn by the creditor and sent to the debtor for acceptance.

If the debtor accepts the draft, the following entries are made by the two parties:

Drawee's journal entry:

```
Creditor's name..................................... 100.00
    Notes payable.................................          100.00
    To record acceptance of draft.
```

Drawer's journal entry:

```
Notes receivable.................................... 100.00
    Debtor's name.................................          100.00
    To record receipt of acceptance.
```

Two-party time draft per terms of sale. Sometimes the terms of sale require the purchaser of merchandise to accept a time draft for the amount of the invoice. If the purchaser has established a credit standing with the seller, the merchandise is shipped on a straight bill of lading and the draft is sent to the purchaser for acceptance. To assure obtaining acceptance of the draft before delivery of the goods, a draft with an order bill of lading attached may be sent to a bank in the purchaser's city. The purchaser must accept the draft before the bank will release the bill of lading.

Sequence of Entries

Seller's entry at time of sale:

```
Customer's name.....................................  300.00
    Sales...........................................          300.00
    Sale of merchandise; terms, 30-day acceptance.
```

Purchaser's entry at time of receipt of goods and acceptance of draft:

```
Purchases..........................................  300.00
    Creditor's name.......  ........................          300.00
    Purchase of merchandise; terms, draft due 30 days after
    sight.

Creditor's name....................................  300.00
    Notes payable...................................          300.00
    Acceptance of 30-day draft for amount of purchase
    today.
```

Seller's entry when acceptance is received:

```
Notes receivable...................................  300.00
    Customer's name.................................          300.00
    Acceptance received.
```

A time draft drawn by the seller on the purchaser of goods sold, accepted by such purchaser, and bearing on its face the evidence that the draft arose from a sale of merchandise, is called a *trade acceptance.*

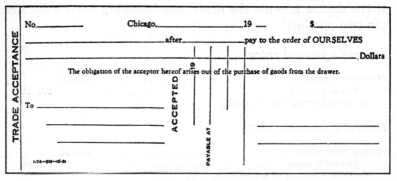

Trade Acceptance

Trade acceptances are used in connection with transactions of the nature just described.

Registers

Notes receivable register. If many notes and acceptances are received, it is desirable to keep a supplementary record called a Notes Receivable Register, where spaces are provided for more detailed information about the notes and acceptances than can be entered in the Explanation columns of the Notes Receivable account. This register is a supplementary book; the entries in it do not take the place of those in the journal and the ledger, but details can be omitted from the Explanation columns of the account.

An illustration is presented below. It shows (1) the illustrative transactions, (2) the entries (in journal form) to record them, (3) the Notes Receivable account, and (4) the notes receivable register.

Peterson note:

> On May 12, a 30-day, non-interest note for $1,000, dated May 12, payable at our office, was received from O. B. Peterson, to apply on account.

Notes receivable................................ 1,000.00
    O. B. Peterson.............................   1,000.00

> On June 11, the note was collected.

Cash... 1,000.00
    Notes receivable...........................   1,000.00

Smith note:

> On May 21, a 60-day, 6% note for $1,500, dated May 20, payable at the State Bank, was received from H. D. Smith to apply on account.

Notes receivable................................ 1,500.00
    H. D. Smith................................   1,500.00

> On July 19, when the note matured, the maker dishonored it, and it was charged back to his account.

H. D. Smith.................................... 1,515.00
    Notes receivable...........................   1,500.00
    Interest income............................   15.00

> On July 21, Smith paid us $315 in cash, and gave us a new 6% note, payable in three months at our office, for $1,200.

Cash...   315.00
    H. D. Smith................................   315.00
Notes receivable................................ 1,200.00
    H. D. Smith................................   1,200.00

Norton acceptance:

> On July 24, we drew a $900 draft on Henry Norton, payable 60 days after date. Norton accepted the draft, and returned it to us. We received it on July 25.

Notes receivable................................   900.00
    Henry Norton..............................   900.00

The acceptance has not yet matured.

Notes Receivable

19—					19—					
May	12			1,000	00	June	11		1,000	00
	21			1,500	00	July	19		1,500	00
July	21			1,200	00					
	25			900	00					

The notes receivable register appears on page 131. The letters in the first column indicate whether the paper is a note or an acceptance. The letters *J*, *F*, *M*, and so forth, at the head of the narrow columns indicate months of maturity, and the numbers in these columns indicate the dates of maturity.

The Notes Receivable account has a debit balance of $2,100. This balance is the total of the last two items in the register.

Notes payable register. An illustration of notes and acceptances payable transactions is presented below.

Bank loan:

> On March 1, we discounted at the First National Bank our 60-day note for $5,000; discount rate, 6%.

Cash... 4,950.00
Interest expense.............................. 50.00
    Notes payable............................   5,000.00

Slocum acceptance:

> On March 10, we accepted a 30-day sight draft for $1,150, drawn by Frank Slocum on March 9, payable at his office.

Frank Slocum................................ 1,150.00
    Notes payable............................   1,150.00

> On April 9, the acceptance was paid.

Notes payable............................... 1,150.00
    Cash....................................   1,150.00

Bailey note:

> On March 17, we gave George Bailey a 6%, two-month note for $750.

George Bailey............................... 750.00
    Notes payable............................   750.00

Notes Payable

19—					19—					
Apr.	9			1,150	00	Mar.	1		5,000	00
							10		1,150	00
							17		750	00

The notes payable register appears on page 131.

Notes Receivable Register

N/A	Date Received	Date of Paper	Maker or Drawee	Drawer or Endorser	Where Payable	Time Mo.	Time Da.	Int. Rate	Year	J	F	M	A	M	J	J	A	S	O	N	D	Amount	Date Paid	Remarks
N	19— May 12	19— May 12	O. B. Peterson		Our office		30	—	19—													1,000 00	19— June 11	Dishonored. See new note below.
N	21	May 20	H. D. Smith		State Bank		60	6%	19—							11						1,500 00		
N	21	July 21	H. D. Smith		Our office	3		6%	19—													1,200 00		
A	25	24	Henry Norton	Ourselves			60		19—									21	22			900 00		

Notes Payable Register

N/A	Date Given	Date of Paper	Payee	Endorser or Drawer	Where Payable	Time Mo.	Time Da.	Int. Rate	Year	J	F	M	A	M	J	J	A	S	O	N	D	Amount	Date Paid	Remarks
N	19— Mar. 1	19— Mar. 1	First National Bk.		Bank		60	Disc.	19—					30								5,000 00		
A	10	9	Frank Slocum		His office	2		—	19—					9								1,150 00	19— Apr. 9	
N	17	17	George Bailey				30	6%	19—					17								750 00		

CHAPTER 10

Columnar Journals. Controlling Accounts

Columnar Journals

Special columns to reduce postings. Accountants have given a great deal of thought to the development of accounting records which reduce labor. One of the simplest labor-saving devices is a journal in which special columns are provided for accounts frequently debited and credited. Such a journal is illustrated on page 133.

Observe that posting labor is saved because the individual entries in the special columns are not posted; only the column totals are posted. For instance:

> The three debits to Cash, entered in the first debit column, are not posted; instead, the $10,800 column total is posted.
> The two debits to Purchases, in the second column, are not posted; instead, the $4,000 column total is posted.

The account number at the foot of a column shows that a posting has been made. The only items individually posted are those for which special columns are not provided; these are in the Sundry columns. Since the individual entries in these columns are posted, the column totals are not posted.

Cross-footing columnar books of original entry. Before posting column totals of a book of original entry containing several debit and credit columns, you should always make sure that the sum of the debit-column totals agrees with the sum of the credit-column totals by a computation (which may be made on scratch paper) similar to the following proof of the equality of the debits and credits in the journal on page 133.

Debits	Credits
10,800.00	4,050.00
4,000.00	800.00
3,550.00	13,500.00
18,350.00	18,350.00

Determining the equality of the debit and credit totals of columnar books of original entry should never be omitted; if they are not in balance, the trial balance will not balance, and a great amount of work may have to be done before the error is located.

Journal

Debits Cash	Debits Purchases	Debits Sundry	Date	L.F.	Account	Credits Cash	Credits Sales	Credits Sundry
			19—					
10,000.00			June 1	30	Cash			
					Capital stock			10,000.00
					Issuance of 100 shares of $100 par value.			
	3,000.00		5	21	Purchases			
					Wilson & Co.			3,000.00
					Purchase on account.			
	1,000.00		9		Purchases			
					Cash	1,000.00		
					Cash purchase.			
		500.00	13	11	John Pierce			
					Sales		500.00	
					Sale on account.			
300.00			18		Cash			
					Sales		300.00	
					Cash sale.			
		3,000.00	22	21	Wilson & Co.			
					Cash	3,000.00		
					Payment on account.			
500.00			26		Cash			
					John Pierce			500.00
					Collection on account.			
		50.00	30	61	Expense			
					Cash	50.00		
					Payment of expense.			
10,800.00	4,000.00	3,550.00				4,050.00	800.00	13,500.00
(1)	(50)					(1)	(40)	

Controlling Accounts

Division of the ledger. If a business has numerous accounts receivable and accounts payable, it is advisable to divide the ledger into three sections, as follows:

> Accounts receivable ledger—containing all accounts with customers.
> Accounts payable ledger—containing all accounts with trade creditors.
> General ledger—containing all other accounts.

When this is done, the accounts receivable ledger and the accounts payable ledger are called *subsidiary ledgers*.

Controlling accounts. When the two subsidiary ledgers mentioned above are used, it is customary to keep the two following accounts in the general ledger:

> Accounts Receivable—the balance of this account shows the total amount receivable from all customers.
> Accounts Payable—the balance of this account shows the total amount payable to all trade creditors.

Posting to the subsidiary ledgers and also to the controlling accounts does not involve any great amount of extra work. The journal is provided with debit and credit columns for Accounts Receivable and Accounts Payable. The individual entries in these columns are posted to the accounts in the subsidiary ledgers, and the column totals are posted to the controlling accounts in the general ledger.

Controlling accounts help in locating errors. Without controlling accounts, it would be necessary to take a combined trial balance of the general ledger and the subsidiary ledgers. If they did not balance, it might be necessary to check all of the postings in search for errors. With controlling accounts, the three ledgers can be proved separately, as follows:

> General ledger—by taking a trial balance.
> Subsidiary ledgers—by seeing that the totals of their balances are in agreement with the balances of their related controlling accounts.
> > The sum of the balances in the accounts receivable ledger should be equal to the balance of the Accounts Receivable controlling account; and
> > The sum of the balances in the accounts payable ledger should be equal to the balance of the Accounts Payable controlling account.

Subsidiary ledger rulings. The ledger form most frequently used for personal accounts in the two subsidiary ledgers is provided with a column to show the balance after each transaction. Two illustrations are given below. Hudson's account is in the accounts receivable ledger; Murphy's account is in the accounts payable ledger. The purpose of each column may be indicated in a box heading, as in the first illustration; or the box headings may be omitted, as in the second illustration.

C. E. Hudson

Date		Explanation	Folio	Debit		Credit		Balance	
19—									
June	2		1	600	00			600	00
	11		1			600	00	—	
	19		2	760	00			760	00
	23		2			35	00	725	00
	28		3			725	00	—	
July	6		4	495	00			495	00

T. O. Murphy

19—									
Oct.	4		17			975	00	975	00
	13		17	975	00			—	
	22		18			856	00	856	00
	25		18			20	00	836	00
Nov.	1		19	836	00			—	
	9		20			425	00	425	00

If a balance appears in an account in the accounts receivable ledger, it is assumed to be a debit balance; if an account has a credit balance, this fact may be indicated by writing "Cr." after the amount of the balance. An account in the accounts payable subsidiary ledger is assumed to have a credit balance; a debit balance may be indicated by writing "Dr." after the balance.

If the balance in an account is composed of unsettled balances from more than one invoice, the bookkeeper may use letters to aid him in determining the elements of the account balance. The procedure is illustrated below:

B. R. Riley

19—									
Nov.	13		20	a	295	00		295	00
	16		21			a	15	00	280	00
	19		21	b	300	00		580	00
	24		22	c	179	00		759	00
	26		22			c	13	00	746	00
	28		23			b	300	00	446	00

The $446 balance in the account with B. R. Riley on the preceding page consists of the following elements:

Invoice, November 13	$295.00	
Less credit on November 16	15.00	$280.00
Invoice, November 24	$179.00	
Less credit on November 26	13.00	166.00
Total		$446.00

Illustration. The use of controlling account columns in the journal and the procedure of posting to the three ledgers and determining that they are in balance are illustrated on the following pages. You should trace all the postings from the journal on pages 137 and 138 to the three ledgers, which appear on the pages indicated below:

General ledger	139
Accounts receivable ledger	140
Accounts payable ledger	140

During the month, the entries in the Sundry columns were posted to the general ledger and the entries in the Accounts Receivable and Accounts Payable columns were posted to the subsidiary ledgers. The accounts in the subsidiary ledgers usually are arranged in alphabetical order and are not numbered. Since there are no subsidiary ledger account numbers, the bookkeeper indicates that postings have been made by entering check marks ($\sqrt{}$) in the L. F. column of the journal.

At the end of the month the column totals, including the totals of the controlling account columns, but excluding the totals of the Sundry columns, were posted to the general ledger.

Journal   (Page 1)

			DEBITS					CREDITS				
Date	L.F.		Cash	Purchases	Accounts Receivable	Accounts Payable	Sundry	Cash	Sales	Accounts Receivable	Accounts Payable	Sundry
19— July 1	30	Cash Capital stock Issuance of 250 shares.	25,000 00									25,000 00
2	√	Purchases Cash Cash purchase.		7,500 00				7,500 00				
3	√	Purchases Bacon & Company Purchase on account.		3,000 00							3,000 00	
5	60	Store rent Cash Payment of rent for July.					250 00	250 00				
8	√	Cash Sales Cash sale.	900 00						900 00			
10	√	John Phelps Sales Sale on account.			300 00				300 00			
11	51	Bacon & Company Returned purchases and allowances... Credit memo for defective goods.				150 00						150 00
12	41	Returned sales and allowances John Phelps... Merchandise returned.					20 00			20 00		
	√	Totals forward	25,900 00	10,500 00	300 00	150 00	270 00	7,750 00	1,200 00	20 00	3,000 00	25,150 00

Journal   (Page 2)

DEBITS

Cash	Purchases	Accounts Receivable	Accounts Payable	Sundry	Date	L.F.	Description
25,900 00	10,500 00	300 00	150 00	270 00	19— July 15	✓	Totals brought forward
		700 00				✓	Peter Mason / Sales............ / Sale on account.
	1,800 00				19	✓	Purchases / White and Davis...... / Purchase on account.
100 00					22	✓	Cash / John Phelps......... / Collection on account.
686 00				14 00	23	42	Cash / Discount on sales / Peter Mason...... / For sale on July 15, less 2%.
			2,000 00		25	✓	Bacon & Company / Cash............ / Payment on account.
		350 00			31	✓	John Nolan / Sales............ / Sale on account.
26,686 00	12,300 00	1,350 00	2,150 00	284 00			
(1)	(50)	(10)	(20)				

CREDITS

Cash	Sales	Accounts Receivable	Accounts Payable	Sundry
7,750 00	1,200 00	20 00	3,000 00	25,150 00
	700 00			
			1,800 00	
		100 00		
		700 00		
2,000 00				
	350 00			
9,750 00	2,250 00	820 00	4,800 00	25,150 00
(1)	(40)	(10)	(20)	

General ledger. The general ledger accounts appear below:

Cash (1)

Date			Amount	Date			Amount
19— July	31	2	26,686 00	19— July	31	2	9,750 00

Accounts Receivable (10)

Date			Amount	Date			Amount
19— July	31	2	1,350 00	19— July	31	2	820 00

Accounts Payable (20)

Date			Amount	Date			Amount
19— July	31	2	2,150 00	19— July	31	2	4,800 00

Capital Stock (30)

Date			Amount	Date			Amount
				19— July	1	1	25,000 00

Sales (40)

Date			Amount	Date			Amount
				19— July	31	2	2,250 00

Returned Sales and Allowances (41)

Date			Amount	Date			Amount
19— July	12	1	20 00				

Discount on Sales (42)

Date			Amount	Date			Amount
19— July	23	2	14 00				

Purchases (50)

Date			Amount	Date			Amount
19— July	31	2	12,300 00				

Returned Purchases and Allowances (51)

Date			Amount	Date			Amount
				19— July	11	1	150 00

Store Rent (60)

Date			Amount	Date			Amount
19— July	5	1	250 00				

Accounts receivable ledger. The accounts receivable subsidiary ledger appears below:

Peter Mason

19—							
July	15		2	700 00			700 00
	23		2		700 00		—

John Nolan

19—						
July	31		2	350 00		350 00

John Phelps

19—						
July	10		1	300 00		300 00
	12		1		20 00	280 00
	22		2		100 00	180 00

Accounts payable ledger. Following is the accounts payable subsidiary ledger:

Bacon & Company

19—						
July	3		1		3,000 00	3,000 00
	11		1	150 00		2,850 00
	25		2	2,000 00		850 00

White and Davis

19—						
July	19		2		1,800 00	1,800 00

Proving the ledgers. Following is the trial balance of the general ledger:

General Ledger Trial Balance
July 31, 19—

Cash	16,936.00	
Accounts receivable	530.00	
Accounts payable		2,650.00
Capital stock		25,000.00
Sales		2,250.00
Returned sales and allowances	20.00	
Discount on sales	14.00	
Purchases	12,300.00	
Returned purchases and allowances		150.00
Store rent	250.00	
	30,050.00	30,050.00

The subsidiary ledgers are proved by preparing the following schedules of their balances and finding that the totals thereof are in agreement with the balances of the respective controlling accounts in the general ledger.

Schedule of Accounts Receivable
July 31, 19—

John Nolan	350.00
John Phelps	180.00
Total (per balance of controlling account)	530.00

Schedule of Accounts Payable
July 31, 19—

Bacon & Company	850.00
White and Davis	1,800.00
Total (per balance of controlling account)	2,650.00

CHAPTER 11

Specialized Books of Original Entry

Division of labor. The columnar journal illustrated in the preceding chapter saves posting labor, but it does not provide for a division of labor. In a large business it is utterly impracticable to use a single book of original entry. To enable several bookkeepers to work at the same time, it is necessary to have several books of original entry. And, as we shall see in this chapter, by using specially designed books of original entry for different classes of transactions, the labor of journalizing can be greatly reduced.

Books to be illustrated. The special books to be used in any business will depend upon the nature of its operations, and upon whether transactions of a particular kind occur often enough to warrant having a special book of original entry in which to record them. The special books to be illustrated in this chapter are:

Sales book.	Cash receipts book.
Purchase book.	Cash disbursements book.

These books are sometimes called the *sales journal*, the *purchase journal*, and so forth. Since some transactions cannot be recorded in the special books of original entry, it is necessary also to have a journal in which to record these transactions; this book may be called the *general journal* or merely the *journal*.

If a transaction is recorded in one of the specialized books of original entry, it is not recorded in the general journal also; only those transactions which cannot be recorded in a specialized book of original entry are recorded in the general journal.

Sales book. A sales book is illustrated below.

Sales Book   (Page 1)

Date	√	Name	Invoice No.	Amount	
19—					
May 2	√	R. E. West.....................................	1	800	00
7	√	G. O. Davis...................................	2	450	00
12	√	S. E. Bates...................................	3	600	00
18	√	R. E. West....................................	4	850	00
23	√	G. O. Davis...................................	5	280	00
30	√	R. E. West....................................	6	300	00
				3,280	00
				(10)	(40)

The sales book is used for recording sales on account. It has the following advantages:

Saving of labor:
In recording transactions:
Each entry records a debit to a customer and a credit to Sales; but the credit to Sales need not be written; it is *implied* because the entry is in the sales book.

The sales book need not contain an explanation of each entry. A numbered invoice is given to the customer, and a carbon copy thereof is retained and filed. The sales book shows the number of the invoice. Information about the kinds of merchandise sold can be obtained by referring to the filed duplicate of the invoice indicated by the number.

In posting:
A separate book of original entry for sales, like the special Sales column in the journal in Chapter 10, saves posting labor because, instead of posting the amount of each sale separately to the Sales account, the bookkeeper posts the total of all entries to the Sales account. The column total is also posted to the Accounts Receivable controlling account.

Division of labor:
In recording transactions:
One bookkeeper can be engaged in recording sales while other bookkeepers are recording other kinds of transactions.

In posting:
An assistant bookkeeper can post to the accounts receivable subsidiary ledger, and the head bookkeeper can post to the general ledger.

The other special books of original entry described in this chapter have similar advantages.

Postings have been made from the illustrative sales book on page 142. The postings of the individual debits to customers were made during the month. The postings of the debit to Accounts Receivable controlling account (account 10) and the credit to Sales (account 40) were made at the end of the month.

Purchase book. Savings in journalizing and posting can be effected by using a special book of original entry for recording purchases on account. The entries in the purchase book on page 144 are equivalent to five entries debiting Purchases and crediting the parties from whom the merchandise was purchased.

Purchase Book (Page 1)

Date	√	Name	Invoice Date	Amount
19—			19—	
May 1	√	Price and Holmes.............................	May 1	2,000 00
9	√	Henderson's, Inc.............................	8	3,500 00
13	√	Osborne Company............................	10	2,600 00
18	√	Price and Holmes.............................	16	650 00
24	√	Henderson's, Inc.............................	23	1,300 00
				10,050 00
				(50) (20)

Postings were made as follows:

During the month, the individual entries were posted to the credit of the creditors' accounts in the subsidiary ledger.

At the end of the month, the column total was posted to general ledger accounts as follows:

To the debit of Purchases.

To the credit of Accounts Payable.

Cash receipts book. The cash receipts book on page 145 contains entries for the following transactions:

May 1—Issued capital stock for cash, $25,000.
3—Sold merchandise for cash, $150.
5—Collected from R. E. West amount of invoice of May 2, $260.
12—Sold merchandise for cash, $500.
15—Collected from G. O. Davis amount of invoice of May 7, $450, less 1% cash discount.
20—Collected a non-interest-bearing note from R. E. West, $500.
24—Collected from R. E. West amount of invoice of May 18, $850, less 1% cash discount.
31—Sold merchandise for cash, $400.

The illustrative cash receipts book contains two credit columns:

General Ledger—In this column are entered the amounts of the credits to all accounts other than accounts receivable.

Accounts Receivable—This column serves two purposes:

The accounts receivable subsidiary ledger bookkeeper can easily find the items that are to be posted to the accounts receivable subsidiary ledger.

The general ledger bookkeeper can post the total of the column to the Accounts Receivable controlling account.

The cash receipts book also contains two debit columns, to facilitate the recording of collections from customers who take a deduction for cash discounts. The amount of the discount is

Cash Receipts Book

(Page 1)

Date	Account Credited	Explanation	L.F.	General Ledger Amount	Accounts Receivable √	Accounts Receivable Amount	Discount on Sales	Cash
19— May 1	Capital stock	Investment	30	25,000 00				25,000 00
3	Sales	Cash sale	40	150 00				150 00
5	R. E. West	Invoice, May 2			√	260 00		260 00
12	Sales	Cash sale	40	500 00				500 00
15	G. O. Davis	Invoice, May 7, less 1%			√	450 00	4 50	445 50
20	Notes receivable	R. E. West note	15	500 00				500 00
24	R. E. West	Invoice, May 18, less 1%			√	850 00	8 50	841 50
31	Sales	Cash sale	40	400 00				400 00
				26,550 00		1,560 00	13 00	28,097 00
						(10)	(42)	(1)

entered in the Discount on Sales debit column; the amount of cash received is entered in the Cash debit column; and the total is entered in the Accounts Receivable credit column.

Each of the entries in the cash receipts book records a receipt of cash. The debits to Cash are not written (as they would have to be in the journal), but are indicated by the fact that the amounts are in the Cash debit column. The debits to Discount on Sales are indicated by the fact that the amounts are in the Discount on Sales debit column.

Postings were made as follows:

During the month:
    The head bookkeeper posted the entries in the General Ledger column to the credit of the accounts named under "Account Credited."
    The assistant bookkeeper posted the entries in the Accounts Receivable column to the credit of the accounts named under "Account Credited."

At the end of the month:
    The head bookkeeper posted column totals to accounts in the general ledger, as follows:
        Accounts Receivable column—to the credit of the Accounts Receivable controlling account, No. 10.
        Discount on Sales column—to the debit of the Discount on Sales account, No. 42.
        Cash column—to the debit of the Cash account, No. 1.

It will be observed that the two debit columns in the cash receipts book on page 145 are at the right of the two credit columns. In columnar books of original entry, any column sequence may be adopted so long as the headings clearly identify the debits and credits. The column arrangement shown above was adopted so that the columns in the cash receipts and cash disbursements books would be in the same sequence: general ledger, subsidiary ledger, discount, and cash.

Cash disbursements book. The cash disbursements book on page 147 contains two debit columns:

General Ledger—In this column are entered the amounts of the debits to all accounts other than Accounts Payable.
Accounts Payable—This column serves two purposes:
    The accounts payable subsidiary ledger bookkeeper can easily find the items that are to be posted to the accounts payable subsidiary ledger.
    The general ledger bookkeeper can post the total of the column to the Accounts Payable controlling account.

Cash Disbursements Book (Page 1)

Date	Account Debited	Explanation	L.F.	DEBITS General Ledger Amount	DEBITS Accounts Payable Amount	CREDITS Discount on Purchases	CREDITS Cash
19—May 1	Purchases	Cash purchase	50	5,000 00			5,000 00
1	Store rent	For May	61	300 00			300 00
7	Price and Holmes	Invoice, May 1, less 2%	✓		850 00	17 00	833 00
10	Purchases	Cash purchase	50	500 00			500 00
16	Henderson's, Inc.	Invoice, May 9, less 1%	✓		3,500 00	35 00	3,465 00
16	Salesmen's salaries		62	200 00			200 00
19	Osborne company	On account	✓		500 00		500 00
25	Notes payable	Price and Holmes	21	1,000 00			1,000 00
26	Purchases		50	350 00			350 00
31	Salesmen's salaries		62	200 00			200 00
				7,550 00	4,850 00	52 00	12,348 00
					(20)	(52)	(1)

The cash disbursements book also contains two credit columns, to facilitate the recording of payments to creditors with a deduction for cash discounts.

Postings were made as follows:

During the month:

The head bookkeeper posted the entries in the General Ledger column to the debit of the accounts named under "Account Debited."

The assistant bookkeeper posted the entries in the Accounts Payable column to the debit of the accounts named under "Account Debited."

At the end of the month:

The head bookkeeper posted column totals to accounts in the general ledger, as follows:

Accounts Payable column—to the debit of the Accounts Payable controlling account, No. 20.

Discount on Purchases—to the credit of the Discount on Purchases account, No. 52.

Cash—to the credit of the Cash account, No. 1.

Journal.   To facilitate the postings to the controlling accounts, it is desirable to use a six-column journal with special debit and credit columns for each controlling account.   See page 149.

Postings from the journal were made as follows:

During the month:

Entries in the Accounts Receivable columns were posted to accounts in the subsidiary accounts receivable ledger.

Entries in the Accounts Payable columns were posted to accounts in the subsidiary accounts payable ledger.

Entries in the General Ledger columns were posted to accounts in the general ledger.

At the end of the month, totals of the Accounts Receivable and Accounts Payable columns were posted to the controlling accounts—Accounts Receivable, No. 10, and Accounts Payable, No. 20.

References to books of original entry.   When several books of original entry are used, the ledger accounts must indicate the books from which the entries were posted.   Thus,

CR1 means cash receipts book, page 1.

CD1   "   cash disbursements book, page 1.

S1   "   sales book, page 1.

P1   "   purchase book, page 1.

J1   "   journal, page 1.

Journal

(Page 1)

Debits						Credits		
Accounts Receivable	Accounts Payable	General Ledger	Date	L.F.		General Ledger	Accounts Payable	Accounts Receivable
		40 00	19— May 3	41	Returned sales and allowances			
				√	R. E. West............................			40 00
					Credit memo No. 1.			
		500 00	5	15	Notes receivable			
				√	R. E. West............................			500 00
					Received 15-day, non-interest note to apply on account.			
	150 00		5	√	Price and Holmes			
				51	Returned purchases and allowances	150 00		
					Return of portion of goods purchased May 1.			
	1,000 00		7	√	Price and Holmes			
				21	Notes payable........................	1,000 00		
					Gave 18-day, non-interest note to apply on account.			
	1,150 00	540 00				1,150 00		540 00
	(20)					(10)		

You should trace all the postings from the foregoing books of original entry to the following ledger accounts, beginning with the first entry in the sales book and continuing to the last entry in the journal.

General ledger.   The general ledger accounts appear below:

Cash (1)

19—				CR1	28,097 00	19—		CD1	12,348 00
May	31					May	31		

Accounts Receivable (10)

19—				S1	3,280 00	19—		CR1	1,560 00
May	31					May	31	J1	540 00
							31		

Notes Receivable (15)

19—		R. E. West	J1		500 00	19—		R. E. West	CR1	500 00
May	5					May	20		

Accounts Payable (20)

19—				CD1	4,850 00	19—		P1	10,050 00
May	31			J1	1,150 00	May	31		
	31								

Notes Payable (21)

19—		Price and Holmes	CD1	1,000 00	19—		Price and Holmes	J1	1,000 00
May	25				May	7		

Capital Stock (30)

					19—		CR1	25,000 00
					May	1		

Sales (40)

					19—			
					May	3	CR1	150 00
						12	CR1	500 00
						31	CR1	400 00
						31	S1	3,280 00

Returned Sales and Allowances (41)

19—			J1	40 00		
May	3					

Discount on Sales (42)

19—			CR1	13 00		
May	31					

Purchases (50)

19—								
May	1	CD1	5,000	00				
	10	CD1	500	00				
	26	CD1	350	00				
	31	P1	10,050	00				

Returned Purchases and Allowances (51)

			19—				
			May	5		J1	150|00

Discount on Purchases (52)

			19—				
			May	31		CD1	52|00

Store Rent (61)

19—						
May	1	CD1	300|00			

Salesmen's Salaries (62)

19—						
May	16	CD1	200|00			
	31	CD1	200|00			

Accounts receivable ledger. After postings from the books of original entry are completed, the subsidiary accounts receivable ledger appears as follows:

S. E. Bates

19—							
May	12		S1	600|00		600|00

G. O. Davis

19—							
May	7		S1	450|00		450|00
	15		CR1		450	00	—
	23		S1	280|00		280|00

R. E. West

19—							
May	2		S1	800|00		800|00
	3		J1		40|00	760|00
	5		CR1		260|00	500|00
	5		J1		500	00	—
	18		S1	850|00		850|00
	24		CR1		850	00	—
	30		S1	300|00		300|00

Accounts payable ledger. The subsidiary accounts payable ledger appears as follows:

Henderson's, Inc.

19—						
May	9		P1		3,500 00	3,500 00
	16		CD1	3,500 00		—
	24		P1		1,300 00	1,300 00

Osborne Company

19—						
May	13		P1		2,600 00	2,600 00
	19		CD1	500 00		2,100 00

Price and Holmes

19—						
May	1		P1		2,000 00	2,000 00
	5		J1	150 00		1,850 00
	7		CD1	850 00		1,000 00
	7		J1	1,000 00		—
	18		P1		650 00	650 00

Proving the ledgers. Following are the trial balance of the general ledger and the schedules of the subsidiary ledgers.

General Ledger Trial Balance
May 31, 19—

Cash..	15,749.00	
Accounts receivable..........................	1,180.00	
Accounts payable.............................		4,050.00
Capital stock................................		25,000.00
Sales..		4,330.00
Returned sales and allowances................	40.00	
Discount on sales............................	13.00	
Purchases....................................	15,900.00	
Returned purchases and allowances............		150.00
Discount on purchases........................		52.00
Store rent...................................	300.00	
Salesmen's salaries..........................	400.00	
	33,582.00	33,582.00

Schedule of Accounts Receivable
May 31, 19—

S. E. Bates..	600.00
G. O. Davis..	280.00
R. E. West..	300.00
Total (per balance of controlling account)...............	1,180.00

Schedule of Accounts Payable
May 31, 19—

Henderson's, Inc...	1,300.00
Osborne Company..	2,100.00
Price and Holmes...	650.00
Total (per balance of controlling account)...............	4,050.00

Providing controlling account columns in books of original entry. It is desirable to provide special controlling account columns in the various books of original entry so that the postings to the controlling accounts, so far as practicable, will consist only of column totals.

Suppose, for example, that customers are frequently credited with returned merchandise after having paid their accounts in full. Their accounts will then have credit balances which may have to be paid in cash. If there are many such cash disbursements requiring debits to customers' accounts, it will be desirable to have an Accounts Receivable debit column in the cash disbursements book, as illustrated in the cash disbursements book on page 154.

The accounts receivable bookkeeper posted the two items in the Accounts Receivable column, and the general ledger bookkeeper posted the column total.

Posting to subsidiary ledgers from General Ledger column. Transactions of the nature mentioned in the preceding section may be too infrequent to justify providing a special column for them in the cash disbursements book; if it is not desired to have a special column, the amounts of the entries may be put in the General Ledger column and each entry will be posted twice: once by the accounts receivable bookkeeper to the subsidiary ledger, and once by the general ledger bookkeeper to the controlling account in the general ledger. See illustrative cash disbursements book on page 155.

The method illustrated in the cash disbursements book with no Accounts Receivable column (page 155) may be applied whenever entries affecting subsidiary ledgers and controlling accounts must be made in a book of original entry which does not have a special column for the controlling account affected. Great care should be exercised to see that items of this nature are posted to *both* the general ledger and the subsidiary ledger; if only one posting were made, the subsidiary ledger would be thrown out of agreement with its control.

Providing controlling account columns in books of original entry. It is ... the special controlling account columns in ... books of original entry, so that the postings to the controlling account were previously only of column ...

Suppose, for example, that customers are frequently credited with returned merchandise after having paid their accounts in full. Their accounts are then overdrawn; the balances which may have to be paid in ... If these sums represent cash disbursements requiring debits to customers' accounts, it were desirable to have an Accounts Receivable debit column in the cash disbursements book, as illustrated in the cash disbursements book on page 154.

The account payable bookkeeper posts the two items in the Accounts Payable column, and the general ledger bookkeeper posts the column total.

Posting to subsidiary ledgers. In the General Ledger column. Transactions of ... explained in the preceding section may be too infrequent to justify providing a separate column for them in the cash disbursements book; if it is not desired to have a special column, the amounts of the entries are entered in the General Ledger column and are individually posted twice: once by the accounts receivable bookkeeper to the subsidiary ledger, and once by the general ledger bookkeeper to the controlling account in the general ledger. See illustrative cash disbursements book on page 155.

The method illustrated in the cash disbursements book, with no Accounts Receivable column (page 155), may be applied whenever entries affecting subsidiary ledgers and controlling accounts must be made in a book of original entry which does not have a special column for the controlling account affected. Great care should be exercised to see that items of this nature are posted to both the general ledger and the subsidiary ledger; if only the posting were made, the subsidiary ledger would be thrown out of agreement with its control.

Cash Disbursement Book

Date	Account Debited	Explanation	L.F.	General Ledger Amount	Accounts Receivable (Debits) Amount	Accounts Payable (Credits) Amount	Discount on Purchases	Cash
19— Aug. 5	Purchases		50	500 00				500 00
11	Price and Holmes	On account				300 00	3 00	297 00
15	Salesmen's salaries		62	200 00				200 00
19	Price and Holmes	Invoice, August 12				250 00	2 50	247 50
20	G. O. Davis	Overpayment			25 00			25 00
23	Purchases		50	450 00				450 00
25	S. E. Bates	Overpayment			15 00			15 00
31	Salesmen's salaries		62	200 00				200 00
				1,350 00	40 00	550 00	5 50	1,934 50
					(10)	(20)	(52)	(1)

(Note the special Accounts Receivable controlling account debit column, which may be used if cash payments are frequently made to customers.)

Cash Disbursements Book

Date	Account Debited	Explanation	DEBITS General Ledger L.F.	DEBITS General Ledger Amount	DEBITS Accounts Payable L.F.	DEBITS Accounts Payable Amount	CREDITS Discount on Purchases	CREDITS Cash
19— Aug. 5	Purchases............		50	500 00				500 00
11	Price and Holmes......	On account			✓	300 00	3 00	297 00
15	Salesmen's salaries....		62	200 00				200 00
19	Price and Holmes......	Invoice, August 12			✓	250 00	2 50	247 50
20	G. O. Davis/Accounts receivable....	Overpayment	√/10	25 00				25 00
23	Purchases............		50	450 00				450 00
25	S. E. Bates/Accounts receivable....	Overpayment	√/10	15 00				15 00
31	Salesmen's salaries....		62	200 00				200 00
				1,390 00		550 00	5 50	1,934 50
				(✓)		(20)	(52)	(1)

The check marks and the account numbers (√/10) appearing in the L.F. column show that the accounts receivable bookkeeper and the general ledger bookkeeper have posted these entries.

Other Special-Purpose Columns in the Cash Receipts Book

A cash receipts book with several additional special columns appears on page 157. The additional columns and their uses are described below.

Interest Income. The cash receipts book shows that, on June 23, a $600 note and $1 of interest were collected from Oscar White. The entry for the transaction includes credits to Notes Receivable and Interest Income, and a debit to Cash. The special Interest Income credit column makes it possible to record the transaction on one line of the cash receipts book.

Sales. This column was provided because the Sales account is frequently credited. The special column reduces posting work.

Prepaid Interest Expense. On June 25, a $2,000 note payable was discounted at the bank. The entry for the transaction includes a credit to Notes Payable and debits to Prepaid Interest Expense and Cash. The special Prepaid Interest Expense debit column makes it possible to record the transaction on one line of the cash receipts book.

Collection and Exchange. On June 26, a $600 check was received from J. B. Turner to apply on account. When the check was deposited, the bank charged an exchange fee of $.25. The entry for the transaction includes a credit to J. B. Turner and debits to Collection and Exchange and Cash. The special Collection and Exchange debit column makes it possible to record the transaction on one line. This special column was also used to record the fee charged by the bank for the collection of the Peterson note.

Cash Receipts Book

						CREDITS				DEBITS		
			General Ledger		Accounts Receivable		Interest Income	Sales	Discount on Sales	Prepaid Interest Expense	Collection and Exchange	Cash
Date	Account Credited	Explanation	L.F.	Amount	✓	Amount						
19—												
June 11	R. T. Snowden	Invoice, June 5			✓	300 00			6 00			294 00
22	Notes receivable	Peter Dunlap	5	1,200 00								1,200 00
23	Notes receivable	Oscar White	5	600 00			1 00					601 00
25	Notes payable	Bank—60 days	13	2,000 00						20 00		1,980 00
26	J. B. Turner	On account			✓	600 00					25	599 75
27	Notes receivable	Leo Peterson	5	400 00							50	399 50
28	Sales	Cash sale						200 00				200 00
30	Sales	Cash sale						175 00				175 00
				4,200 00		900 00	1 00	375 00	6 00	20 00	75	5,449 25
						(2)	(23)	(21)	(22)	(30)	(28)	(1)

The cash receipts book has been footed and posted.

Other Special-Purpose Columns in the Cash Disbursements Book

A cash disbursements book with several additional special columns appears on page 159.

Interest Expense. The Interest Expense debit column makes it possible to record the payment of a note payable and interest on one line.

Purchases, Freight In, and Freight Out. These special columns were provided because the accounts are frequently debited in the cash disbursements book.

Special columns to be used. You should understand that the special columns shown in this chapter are purely illustrative. The special columns to be used in the cash books of a business will depend on the nature of the business and the frequency of certain types of cash transactions.

Cash Disbursements Book

Date	Account Debited	Explanation	L.F.	General Ledger Amount	Accounts Payable √	Accounts Payable Amount	Interest Expense	Purchases	Freight In	Freight Out	Discount on Purchases	Cash
19—												
June 10	W. E. Burton......	Invoice, June 3			√	1,000 00					10 00	990 00
25	Notes payable.....	John Henderson	13	750 00								750 00
26	Notes payable.....	Fred Hobson	13	900 00			1 50					901 50
27	Purchases.........	Cash purchase						85 00				85 00
27	Freight in........								60 00			60 00
28	Purchases.........	Cash purchase						200 00				200 00
28	Freight out.......									30 00		30 00
29	Freight...........								45 00	20 00		65 00
				1,650 00		1,000 00	1 50	285 00	105 00	50 00	10 00	3,081 50
						(12)	(30)	(25)	(26)	(29)	(27)	(1)

The cash disbursements book has been footed and posted.

Transactions Recorded on Two Lines of a Cash Book or in a Cash Book and the General Journal

It is theoretically desirable to have enough columns in the cash books so that each cash transaction can be recorded on a single line, but it is impracticable to provide columns for accounts which are infrequently used. Two procedures for dealing with situations in which special columns would be helpful but are not provided are discussed below and illustrated in the cash receipts book and journal on pages 161 and 162. Similar procedures can be used for recording cash disbursements.

Two entries in the General Ledger column. For purposes of illustration, assume that, on June 5, land which had been acquired as a building site at a cost of $12,000 was sold for $15,000 cash. The entry for the transaction requires a $15,000 debit to Cash, a $12,000 credit to Land, and a $3,000 credit to Gain on Sale of Land. The transaction is recorded on two lines of the cash receipts book on page 161; the two credits are entered in the General Ledger column.

Entry in a cash book and the general journal. Assume the same transaction except that $5,000 cash and a $10,000 mortgage were received. It is inconvenient to record the $10,000 debit to Mortgage Receivable in the cash receipts book because there is no General Ledger debit column. The accounting procedure follows.

The entire transaction is recorded in the general journal, in the manner illustrated on page 162. Observe that an "X" is placed beside the Cash debit to indicate that it is not posted.

The cash receipt is recorded in the cash receipts book. Observe that the cash amount appears in the General Ledger credit column as well as in the Cash debit column; this is necessary in order to make the debits and credits in the cash book equal. But no account name appears in the Account Credited section, and an "X" appears in the L.F. column at the left of the General Ledger credit column, to indicate that no credit is posted from the cash receipts book.

Observe that postings were made as follows:

	Debit	Credit
From the general journal:		
Mortgage receivable	10,000	
Land		12,000
Gain on sale of land		3,000
From the cash receipts book:		
Cash (included in column total)	5,000	

Transaction recorded on two lines of a cash book.

Cash Receipts Book

Date	Account Credited	Explanation	CREDITS						DEBITS			
			General Ledger		Accounts Receivable		Interest Income	Sales	Discount on Sales	Prepaid Interest Expense	Collection and Exchange	Cash
			L.F.	Amount	√	Amount						
19— June 5	Land............ Gain on sale of land	Sale of land	18 70	12,000 00 3,000 00								15,000 00

Transaction recorded in general journal and a cash book.

General Journal

	DEBITS			Date	L.F.		CREDITS		
	Accounts Receivable	Accounts Payable	General Ledger				General Ledger	Accounts Payable	Accounts Receivable
				19— June 5	X	Cash			
			5,000 00		13	Mortgage receivable			
			10,000 00		18	Land............	12,000 00		
					70	Gain on sale of land......	3,000 00		
						Sale of land.			

Cash Receipts Book

				CREDITS				DEBITS			
Date	Account Credited	Explanation	L.F.	General Ledger Amount	Accounts Receivable √ Amount	Interest Income	Sales	Discount on Sales	Prepaid Interest Expense	Collection and Exchange	Cash
19— June 5	Sale of land	Sale of land—See journal	X	5,000 00							5,000 00

Locating errors. When subsidiary ledgers and controlling accounts are used, it usually is possible to determine which ledger contains an error and which bookkeeper should be charged with the responsibility of locating it. For example:

If the general ledger is in balance, and the accounts receivable schedule agrees with its control, but the accounts payable schedule does not agree with its control, an error is indicated in the accounts payable ledger.

If the general ledger is in balance, and the accounts payable schedule agrees with its control, but the accounts receivable schedule does not agree with its control, an error is indicated in the accounts receivable ledger.

If the general ledger is not in balance, but the subsidiary ledgers are in agreement with their controls, an error is indicated in the general ledger, and this error is presumably not in the controlling accounts.

If the general ledger is not in balance, and the subsidiary ledgers are not in agreement with their controls, it usually is advisable to look for errors in the general ledger first. When these errors are located and the general ledger is in balance, it may be found that corrected balances in the controlling accounts will be in agreement with the subsidiary ledgers; if not, a search must be made for errors affecting the subsidiary ledgers.

Following is an outline of the procedures to be applied for the purpose of locating errors.

(A) When the general ledger trial balance does not balance, perform the following operations, in the order indicated:

(1) Refoot the general ledger trial balance.

(2) Compare the balances shown by the trial balance with those shown by the accounts in the general ledger.

(3) Check the computation of the balances of the general ledger accounts.

(4) Check the postings to the general ledger.

(5) Refoot the books of original entry which have only one column.

(6) See whether the sum of the totals of the debit columns is equal to the sum of the totals of the credit columns of the columnar books of original entry; if they are not in balance, refoot each column. If this does not disclose the error, see

whether the debits and credits in each entry are equal.

See whether any amounts are entered in wrong columns of columnar books of original entry.

(B) When the general ledger is in balance but a subsidiary ledger is out of agreement with its control:

(1) Refoot the schedule of the subsidiary ledger.

(2) See that the balances were carried correctly from the subsidiary ledger to the schedule.

(3) Recompute the balance of each subsidiary ledger account.

(4) Check the postings to the subsidiary ledger.

CHAPTER 12

Departmental Operations

Departmental profits. If a merchandising concern operates two or more departments, it is advisable for it to keep the accounts in such a way that a statement of profit and loss can be prepared showing the results of operations by departments.

Determining gross profits by departments. To determine the gross profits by departments, as shown in the illustrative profit and loss statement on page 168, the following departmental merchandise accounts were kept:

Inventory—Department *A*
Inventory—Department *B*

Sales—Department *A*
Sales—Department *B*

Returned Sales and Allowances—Department *A*
Returned Sales and Allowances—Department *B*

Discount on Sales—Department *A*
Discount on Sales—Department *B*

Purchases—Department *A*
Purchases—Department *B*

Returned Purchases and Allowances—Department *A*
Returned Purchases and Allowances—Department *B*

Discount on Purchases—Department *A*
Discount on Purchases—Department *B*

The trial balance in the working papers on pages 166 and 167 shows that only one Freight In account was kept. If, in a business with departments, it is practicable to analyze the freight bills to determine the freight costs applicable to each department, departmental Freight In accounts may be kept. In the illustration in this chapter it is assumed that the management prefers to make an approximate apportionment of the cost of freight in, rather than to incur the expense of analyzing the freight bills. The apportionment was made on the basis of purchases.

Department	Purchases	Per Cent	Freight In
A	$ 60,000	40%	$ 720
B	90,000	60	1,080
Total	$150,000	100%	$1,800

THE RANDALIA COMPANY
Working Papers
(Showing Gross Profit on Sales by Departments)
For the Year Ended December 31, 1954

Account	Trial Balance Dr	Trial Balance Cr	Adjustments Dr	Adjustments Cr	P&L Dept. A Dr	P&L Dept. A Cr	P&L Dept. B Dr	P&L Dept. B Cr	Unallocated	Earned Surplus Dr	Earned Surplus Cr	Balance Sheet Dr	Balance Sheet Cr
Cash	8,030											8,030	
Accounts receivable	14,800											14,800	
Reserve for bad debts		320		420d									740
Notes receivable	3,000											3,000	
Accrued interest receivable			30c									30	
Inventories—Dec. 31, 1953:													
Dept. A	17,000				17,000								
Dept. B	29,000						29,000						
Unexpired insurance	850			600a								250	
Delivery equipment	4,000											4,000	
Reserve for depreciation—D. E.		1,000		1,000e									2,000
Accounts payable		12,000											12,000
Notes payable		5,000											5,000
Federal income tax payable				1,000f									1,000
Accrued salaries payable				90b									90
Capital stock		50,000											50,000
Earned surplus—Dec. 31, 1953		5,995									5,995		
Dividends	5,000									5,000			
Sales:													
Dept. A		75,000				75,000							
Dept. B		125,000						125,000					
Returned sales and allowances:													
Dept. A	400				400								
Dept. B	900						900						
Discount on sales:													
Dept. A	600				600								
Dept. B	1,000						1,000						
Purchases:													
Dept. A	60,000				60,000								
Dept. B	90,000						90,000						
Returned purchases and allowances:													
Dept. A		600				600							
Dept. B		850						850					
Totals forward	234,580	275,765	30	3,110	78,000	75,600	120,900	125,850		5,000	5,995	30,110	70,830

Working Papers for the Year Ended December 31, 1954
(Concluded)

	Trial Balance		Adjustments		Profit and Loss						Earned Surplus		Balance Sheet	
					Department A		Department B		Unallocated					
Totals brought forward	234,580	275,765	30	3,110	78,000	75,600	120,900	125,850			5,000	5,995	30,110	70,830
Discount on purchases:														
Dept. A		390				390								
Dept. B		810						810						
Freight in	1,800				720		1,080							
Store rent	6,000								6,000					
Advertising	4,000								4,000					
Salesmen's salaries:														
Dept. A	6,000								6,000					
Dept. B	7,000								7,000					
Delivery expense	4,000								4,000					
Depreciation—Delivery equipment			1,000e						1,000					
Officers' salaries	10,000								10,000					
Office salaries	2,310		90b						2,400					
Insurance			600a						600					
Bad debts			420d						420					
Miscellaneous general expenses	1,200								1,200					
Interest income		50		30c						80				
Interest expense	125								125					
Federal income tax			1,000f						1,000					
	277,015	277,015	3,140	3,140										
Inventories—Dec. 31, 1954:														
Dept. A						13,000							13,000	
Dept. B								31,000					31,000	
Gross profit on sales					10,270		35,680			45,950				
					88,990	88,990	157,660	157,660	46,030	46,030				
Net income—to Earned Surplus									2,285			2,285		
Earned surplus—Dec. 31, 1954											3,280			3,280
											8,280	8,280	74,110	74,110

Adjustments

a—Insurance expired during year.
b—Accrued office salaries payable.
c—Accrued interest income.
d—Provision for bad debts.
e—Depreciation of delivery equipment.
f—Federal income tax for 1954.

Note. Payroll taxes have been omitted to simplify the illustration.

THE RANDALIA COMPANY
Statement of Profit and Loss
(Showing Gross Profit on Sales by Departments)
For the Year Ended December 31, 1954

	Department A			Department B			Total		
Gross sales			$75,000			$125,000			$200,000
Deduct:									
Returned sales and allowances	$ 400			$ 900			$ 1,300		
Discount on sales	600	1,000		1,000	1,900		1,600	2,900	
Net sales			$74,000			$123,100			$197,100
Deduct cost of goods sold:									
Purchases		$60,000			$90,000			$150,000	
Deduct:									
Returned purchases and allowances	$600			$850			$ 1,450		
Discount on purchases	390	990		810	1,660		1,200	2,650	
Net cost of purchases		$59,010			$88,340			$147,350	
Add freight in		720			1,080			1,800	
Total		$59,730			$89,420			$149,150	
Add inventory—December 31, 1953		17,000			29,000			46,000	
Total cost of goods available for sale		$76,730			$118,420			$195,150	
Deduct inventory—December 31, 1954		13,000			31,000			44,000	
Cost of goods sold			63,730			87,420			151,150
Gross profit on sales			$10,270			$ 35,680			$ 45,950
Deduct expenses:									
Selling expenses:									
Store rent							$ 6,000		
Advertising							4,000		
Salesmen's salaries:									
Department A							6,000		
Department B							7,000		
Delivery expense							4,000		
Depreciation of delivery equipment							1,000		
Total selling expenses								$ 28,000	
General expenses:									
Officers' salaries							$10,000		
Office salaries							2,400		
Insurance							600		
Bad debts							420		
Miscellaneous general expenses							1,200		
Total general expenses								14,620	
Total operating expenses									42,620
Net operating income									$ 3,330
Deduct net interest expense:									
Interest expense							$ 125		
Interest income							80	45	
Net income before federal income tax									$ 3,285
Deduct federal income tax								1,000	
Net income									$ 2,285

Columnar sales and purchase records. When departmental sales and purchases accounts are kept, it is advisable to use columnar books of original entry for sales and purchases. The sales book, for example, may have columns such as those illustrated below.

Sales Book

Date	Name	Invoice No.	L.F.	DEBIT	CREDITS	
				Accounts Receivable	Sales Dept. *A*	Sales Dept. *B*
19—						
Jan. 7	C. H. Holmes...............	1001	√	1,500 00	1,000 00	500 00
11	D. E. Whitely...............	1002	√	2,550 00	2,000 00	550 00
19	D. R. Long.................	1003	√	1,250 00	750 00	500 00
29	G. K. Jones................	1004	√	2,525 00	525 00	2,000 00
				7,825 00	4,275 00	3,550 00
				(1120)	(4001)	(4002)

The general ledger postings from this book were made as follows:

Debit: Accounts Receivable controlling account, for the total of the Accounts Receivable column.
Credits: Sales—Department *A*.
   Sales—Department *B*.
      For the totals of the Department *A* and Department *B* Sales columns.

The purchase book should have three columns:

Credit: Accounts Payable.
Debits: Purchases—Dept. *A*.
   Purchases—Dept. *B*.

Cash sales and cash purchases. Chapter 11 showed how special columns for cash sales and cash purchases may be included in the cash receipts book and the cash disbursements book. If a business has only two or three departments, the cash receipts book may contain a Sales column for each department, and the cash disbursements book may contain a Purchases column for each department. The totals of these columns can then be posted to the departmental sales and purchases accounts.

But if the business is divided into a great many departments, Sales and Purchases columns cannot be provided in the cash books without making these books so wide as to be inconvenient. Under such conditions it is advisable, in place of a Sales column for each department in the cash receipts book, to add a Cash debit column to the sales book and to have only one Sales column in the cash receipts book. Cash sales will then be recorded in the two books thus:

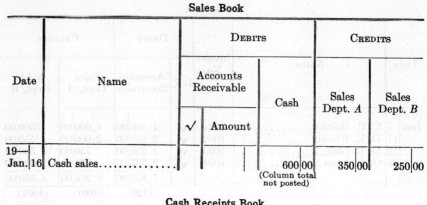

Sales Book

Date	Name	DEBITS			CREDITS	
		Accounts Receivable		Cash	Sales Dept. A	Sales Dept. B
		✓	Amount			
19—Jan. 16	Cash sales..............	✓		600 00 (Column total not posted)	350 00	250 00

Cash Receipts Book

Date	Account Credited	CREDITS				DEBITS	
		Sundry Accounts		Sales	Accounts Recievable	Discount on Sales	Cash
		L.F.	Amount		✓	Amount	
19—Jan. 16	Sales.....			600 00 (Column total not posted)			600 00

The debit to Cash (in the sales book) and the credit to Sales (in the cash receipts book) are not posted. The posted entries are, therefore:

From the cash receipts book: The debit to Cash.
From the sales book: The credits to the two
                    Sales accounts.

The illustrations on pages 172 and 173 show a sales book and a cash receipts book after the completion of footing and posting at the end of the month. The bookkeeper put an X at the foot of each of the two columns (Cash in the sales book, and Sales in the cash book) which were not to be posted. It will be noted that the totals of these two columns are equal, and the bookkeeper should always be sure that this is the case.

Cash purchases may be recorded in a similar manner.   That is:

The purchase book will contain a Cash credit column, the total of which will not be posted.

The cash disbursements book will contain a Purchases debit column, the total of which will not be posted.

Entries for cash purchases will be made in both books, the debits to the departmental Purchases accounts being posted from the purchase book, and the credits to Cash being posted from the cash disbursements book.

Cash discounts.   If a business has only a few departments, a Discount on Sales column for each department can be provided in the cash receipts book, and a Discount on Purchases column for each department can be provided in the cash disbursements book. If there are so many departments that it is impracticable to provide a column for each in both of the cash books, the cash receipts book may have a single Discount on Sales column (as in the illustration on page 173) and the cash disbursements book may have a single Discount on Purchases column.   Supplementary records may then be provided with discount columns for each department, postings being made from these supplementary records instead of from the cash books.   Or no supplementary records may be maintained, postings being made from the cash books to a Discount on Sales account and a Discount on Purchases account, and approximate apportionments of the balances of these accounts may be made for statement purposes.

Departmental inventories in the balance sheet.   In the balance sheet of a business with departments, the inventories may be set out separately, thus:

```
Inventories:
   Department A........ $13,000.00
   Department B........   31,000.00
      Total...................... $44,000.00
```

If there are very many departments, it is impracticable to detail the inventories in the balance sheet; hence, they may be shown in total.

Sales Book

Date	Name	Invoice No.	DEBITS			CREDITS	
			Accounts Receivable Amount	Cash		Sales Dept. A	Sales Dept. B
19— Jan. 7	C. H. Holmes.....	1001	1,500 00			1,000 00	500 00
11	D. E. Whitely.....	1002	2,550 00			2,000 00	550 00
16	Cash sale.....			600 00		350 00	250 00
19	D. R. Long.....	1003	1,250 00			750 00	500 00
25	Cash sale.....			725 00		400 00	325 00
29	G. K. Jones.....	1004	2,525 00			525 00	2,000 00
			7,825 00	1,325 00		5,025 00	4,125 00
			(1120)	X		(4001)	(4002)

Invoices are often made out for cash sales as well as for sales on account, in which case the invoice numbers for cash sales should be shown in the sales book.

Cash Receipts Book

Date	Account Credited	Explanation	Sundry Accounts L.F.	Sundry Accounts Amount	Sales	Notes Receivable	Interest Income	Accounts Receivable Amount	Discount on Sales	Collection and Exchange	Freight Out	Cash
						CREDITS				DEBITS		
19— Jan. 1	Rtd. P. & A.—Dept. B	Inv. Dec. 28	5179	125 00								125 00
7	C. D. Magee							1,000 00 √	10 00	15	5 00	984 85
16	Sales				600 00							600 00
19	Notes receivable	O. E. Davis				1,000 00	10 00					1,010 00
25	Sales				725 00							725 00
				125 00	1,325 00	1,000 00	10 00	1,000 00 √	10 00	15	5 00	3,444 85
				(X)	(X)	(1130)	(8135)	(1120)	(8201)	(7081)	(6061)	(1111)

Gross profit less selling expenses by departments. If it is desired to have the profit and loss statement show gross profit less selling expenses by departments (as in the illustration on page 177), departmental selling expense accounts should be kept to the extent practicable. The trial balance in the working papers shows that, in this illustration, only the following departmental expense accounts were kept:

Salesmen's Salaries—Department *A*
Salesmen's Salaries—Department *B*

In many cases it is not practicable to identify selling expenses by departments at the time they are incurred; in such cases, one account is kept for each type of expense and some basis of apportionment for statement purposes is adopted. The balances of such accounts are frequently apportioned to departments in the ratio of sales by departments; but this is only a "rough and ready" method and is not likely to be very accurate because the departmental expenses are rarely, if ever, proportionate to the departmental sales.

If possible, some accurate basis of apportionment should be used for each expense. In the illustration, it is assumed that the store rent was apportioned by departments on the basis of floor space occupied, and that the advertising was apportioned on the basis of advertising space occupied. In some businesses it may be possible to apportion delivery expenses on the basis of the number of deliveries made for each department, with proper consideration of differences in weight and bulk of the merchandise of the various departments. In this illustration it is assumed that such a procedure is impracticable, and the apportionments were made on the basis of sales, as follows:

Department	Sales	Per Cent	Delivery Expense	Depreciation—Delivery Equipment
A	$ 75,000	37.5%	$1,500	$ 375
B	125,000	62.5	2,500	625
Total	$200,000	100.0%	$4,000	$1,000

Dangers of approximations. To the extent that items of expense or income are allocated to departments by some method of approximation, the departmental profit and loss statement is affected by estimates and guesswork; judgments based on such a statement may be erroneous and misleading; and, unless management maintains a constant awareness of this element of guesswork and possible error, unwise policies may be adopted.

THE RANDALIA COMPANY
Working Papers
(Showing Gross Profit Less Selling Expenses by Departments)
For the Year Ended December 31, 1954

	Trial Balance Dr.	Trial Balance Cr.	Adjustments Dr.	Adjustments Cr.	P&L Dept. A Dr.	P&L Dept. A Cr.	P&L Dept. B Dr.	P&L Dept. B Cr.	Unallocated Dr.	Unallocated Cr.	Earned Surplus Dr.	Earned Surplus Cr.	Balance Sheet Dr.	Balance Sheet Cr.
Cash	8,030												8,030	
Accounts receivable	14,800												14,800	
Reserve for bad debts		320		420d										740
Notes receivable	3,000												3,000	
Accrued interest receivable			30e										30	
Inventories—Dec. 31, 1953:														
Dept. A	17,000				17,000									
Dept. B	29,000						29,000							
Unexpired insurance	850			600a									250	
Delivery equipment	4,000												4,000	
Reserve for depreciation—D. E.		1,000		1,000e										2,000
Accounts payable		12,000												12,000
Notes payable		5,000												5,000
Federal income tax payable				1,000f										1,000
Accrued salaries payable				90b										90
Capital stock		50,000												50,000
Earned surplus—Dec. 31, 1953		5,995										5,995		
Dividends	5,000										5,000			
Sales:														
Dept. A		75,000				75,000								
Dept. B		125,000						125,000						
Returned sales and allowances:														
Dept. A	400				400									
Dept. B	900						900							
Discount on sales:														
Dept. A	600				600									
Dept. B	1,000						1,000							
Purchases:														
Dept. A	60,000				60,000									
Dept. B	90,000						90,000							
Returned purchases and allowances:														
Dept. A	600					600								
Dept. B	850							850						
Totals forward	234,550	275,765	30	3,110	78,000	75,600	120,900	125,850			5,000	5,995	30,110	70,830

Working Papers for the Year Ended December 31, 1954
(Concluded)

	Trial Balance Dr.	Trial Balance Cr.	Adjustments Dr.	Adjustments Cr.	P&L Dept. A Dr.	P&L Dept. A Cr.	P&L Dept. B Dr.	P&L Dept. B Cr.	Unallocated Dr.	Unallocated Cr.	Earned Surplus Dr.	Earned Surplus Cr.	Balance Sheet Dr.	Balance Sheet Cr.
Totals brought forward	234,580	275,765	30	3,110	78,000	75,600	120,900	125,850			5,000	5,995	30,110	70,830
Discount on purchases:														
Dept. A		390				390								
Dept. B		810						810						
Freight in	1,800				720		1,080							
Store rent	6,000				2,400		3,600							
Advertising	4,000				1,600		2,400							
Salesmen's salaries:														
Dept. A	6,000				6,000									
Dept. B	7,000						7,000							
Delivery expense	4,000				1,500		2,500							
Depreciation—Delivery equipment			1,000e		375		625							
Officers' salaries	10,000								10,000					
Office salaries	2,310		90b						2,400					
Insurance			600a						600					
Bad debts			420d						420					
Miscellaneous general expenses	1,200								1,200					
Interest income		50		30c						80				
Interest expense	125								125					
Federal income tax			1,000f						1,000					
	277,015	277,015	3,140	3,140										
Inventories—Dec. 31, 1954:														
Dept. A						13,000							13,000	
Dept. B								31,000					31,000	
Departmental profit (loss*)						1,605*	19,555			17,950				
					90,595	90,595	157,660	157,660	18,030	18,030				
Net income—to Earned Surplus									2,285			2,285		
									18,030	18,030				
Earned surplus—Dec. 31, 1954											3,280			3,280
											8,280	8,280	74,110	74,110

Adjustments

a—Insurance expired during year.
b—Accrued office salaries payable.
c—Accrued interest income.
d—Provision for bad debts.
e—Depreciation of delivery equipment.
f—Federal income tax for 1954.

THE RANDALIA COMPANY
Statement of Profit and Loss
(Showing Gross Profit Less Selling Expenses by Departments)
For the Year Ended December 31, 1954

	Department A		Department B		Total	
Gross sales		$75,000		$125,000		$200,000
Deduct:						
Returned sales and allowances	$ 400		$ 900		$ 1,300	
Discount on sales	600	1,000	1,000	1,900	1,600	2,900
Net sales		$74,000		$123,100		$197,100
Deduct cost of goods sold:						
Purchases		$60,000		$ 90,000		$150,000
Deduct:						
Returned purchases and allowances	$600		$850		$1,450	
Discount on purchases	390	990	810	1,660	1,200	2,650
Net cost of purchases		$59,010		$ 88,340		$147,350
Add freight in		720		1,080		1,800
Total		$59,730		$ 89,420		$149,150
Add inventory—December 31, 1953		17,000		29,000		46,000
Total cost of goods available for sale		$76,730		$118,420		$195,150
Deduct inventory—December 31, 1954		13,000		31,000		44,000
Cost of goods sold		63,730		87,420		151,150
Gross profit on sales		$10,270		$ 35,680		$ 45,950
Deduct selling expenses:						
Store rent		$ 2,400		$ 3,600		$ 6,000
Advertising		1,600		2,400		4,000
Salesmen's salaries		6,000		7,000		13,000
Delivery expense		1,500		2,500		4,000
Depreciation of delivery equipment		375		625		1,000
		11,875		16,125		28,000
Departmental profit (loss*)		$ 1,605*		$ 19,555		$ 17,950
Deduct general expenses:						
Officers salaries						10,000
Office salaries						2,400
Insurance						600
Bad debts						420
Miscellaneous general expenses						1,200
						14,620
Net operating income						$ 3,330
Deduct net interest expense:						
Interest expense						125
Interest income						80
						45
Net income before federal income tax						$ 3,285
Deduct federal income tax						1,000
Net income						$ 2,285

Net income by departments. A profit and loss statement carried to the final point of net income or net loss is illustrated on page 179. It is assumed that:

(a) The bad debt losses by departments were determined by analyzing the accounts receivable.

(b) The office salaries, officers' salaries, and miscellaneous general expenses were apportioned to departments on the basis of sales, for want of a better basis.

Interest income was apportioned on the basis of sales, on the assumption that the interest was earned on notes received from customers.

Interest expense was apportioned on the basis of purchases on the assumption that funds were borrowed to finance purchases.

It is obvious that most of the foregoing assumptions are of doubtful validity and that the apportionments are subject to question. The computations are shown below:

Apportionments on Basis of Sales

	Total	Dept. A	Dept. B
Sales	$200,000	$75,000	$125,000
Per cent	100.0%	37.5%	62.5%
Office salaries	$ 2,400	$ 900	$ 1,500
Officers' salaries	10,000	3,750	6,250
Miscellaneous general expense	1,200	450	750
Interest income	80	30	50

Apportionment on Basis of Purchases

	Total	Dept. A	Dept. B
Purchases	$150,000	$60,000	$ 90,000
Per cent	100%	40%	60%
Interest expense	$ 125	$ 50	$ 75

(c) The insurance was apportioned to departments in the ratio of the average inventories on the assumption that the premiums were paid for insurance on the merchandise. (Automobile insurance was charged to Delivery Expense.) The computation is shown below:

	Total	Dept. A	Dept. B
Inventories, December 31, 1953	$ 46,000	$17,000	$ 29,000
Inventories, December 31, 1954	44,000	13,000	31,000
Total	$ 90,000	$30,000	$ 60,000
Average inventories	$ 45,000	$15,000	$ 30,000
Fractions		⅓	⅔
Insurance	$ 600	$ 200	$ 400

Special attention is directed to the treatment of income tax in the profit and loss statement. On the assumption of the correctness of the expense and income apportionments to departments, Department *A* suffered a loss, which reduced the income tax.

THE RANDALIA COMPANY
Profit and Loss Statement
(Showing Net Income by Departments)
For the Year Ended December 31, 1954

	Department A	Department B	Total
Gross sales	$75,000	$125,000	$200,000
Deduct:			
Returned sales and allowances	$ 400	$ 900	$ 1,300
Discount on sales	600	1,000	1,600
Net sales	$74,000	$123,000	$197,100
Deduct cost of goods sold:			
Purchases	$60,000	$90,000	$150,000
Deduct:			
Returned purchases and allowances	$ 600	850	$ 1,450
Discount on purchases	390	810	1,200
Net cost of purchases	$59,010	$ 88,340	$147,350
Add freight in	720	1,080	1,800
Total	$59,730	$ 89,420	$149,150
Add inventory—December 31, 1953	17,000	29,000	46,000
Total cost of goods available for sale	$76,730	$118,420	$195,150
Deduct inventory—December 31, 1954	13,000	31,000	44,000
Cost of goods sold	63,730	87,420	151,150
Gross profit on sales	$10,270	$ 35,680	$ 45,950
Deduct operating expenses:			
Selling expenses:			
Store rent	$2,400	$3,600	$ 6,000
Advertising	1,600	2,400	4,000
Salesmen's salaries	6,000	7,000	13,000
Delivery expense	1,500	2,500	4,000
Depreciation of delivery equipment	375	625	1,000
	$11,875	$ 16,125	$ 28,000
General expenses:			
Officers' salaries	$3,750	$6,250	$10,000
Office salaries	900	1,500	2,400
Insurance	200	400	600
Bad debts	150	270	420
Miscellaneous general expenses	450	750	1,200
	5,450	9,170	14,620
	17,325	25,295	42,620
Net operating income (loss*)	$ 7,055*	$ 10,385	$ 3,330
Deduct net interest expense:			
Interest expense	$ 50	75	125
Interest income	30	50	80
	20	25	45
Net income (loss*) before federal income tax	$ 7,075*	$ 10,360	$ 3,285
Federal income tax (credit #)	2,000#	3,000	1,000
Net income (loss*)	$ 5,075*	$ 7,360	$ 2,285

Although this assumption is of doubtful validity, consistency requires that Department *B* be charged with income tax in the amount which would have been payable on its net income, and that Department *A* be given credit for the tax reduction resulting from its net loss.

Significance of the statement. Because the apportionments of expenses are to such a large degree based on assumptions which may not be valid, complete reliance should not be placed on the amounts shown as net loss for Department *A* and net income for Department *B*.

Moreover, even if no assumptions had been made in the allocation of expenses to departments, the fact that Department *A* shows a loss should not be accepted as a conclusive reason for discontinuing the department. The discontinuance of Department *A* would result in eliminating all the gross profit resulting from its operations, but it would not result in eliminating all the expenses which were charged to it. Before reaching any decision with respect to the advisability of discontinuing Department *A*, the management should make a study of the expenses and the miscellaneous income for the purpose of determining the probable reductions which would result from such a discontinuance. The following statement is assumed to be the result of such a study.

Probable Reduction in Expenses and Miscellaneous Income Which Would Result from Discontinuance of Department *A*

	Charged to Department *A*	EFFECT OF DISCONTINUANCE OF DEPARTMENT *A*	
		Eliminated	Not Eliminated
Selling expenses:			
Store rent...................	$ 2,400.00		$2,400.00
Advertising................	1,600.00	$1,600.00	
Salesmen's salaries..........	6,000.00	6,000.00	
Delivery expense.............	1,500.00		1,500.00
Depreciation—Delivery equipment.....	375.00		375.00
Total selling expenses............	$11,875.00	$7,600.00	$4,275.00
General expenses:			
Office salaries...............	$ 900.00		$ 900.00
Officers' salaries............	3,750.00		3,750.00
Insurance...................	200.00	$ 200.00	
Miscellaneous general expense........	450.00	150.00	300.00
Bad debts..................	150.00	150.00	
Total general expenses............	$ 5,450.00	$ 500.00	$4,950.00
Interest income..............	$ 30.00	$ 30.00	
Interest expense..............	$ 50.00	$ 50.00	

The first column shows the items of expense and income which appear in the Department *A* columns of the profit and loss statement on page 179. The second column shows the items which, in the opinion of the management, would be eliminated if Department *A* were discontinued. The third column shows the items which the management believes would not be eliminated. The management's conclusions were reached as follows:

The store rent would not be reduced, because the entire space would have to be retained under the lease. The advertising and salesmen's salary charges could be eliminated. The delivery equipment and the driver would have to be retained to make deliveries for Department *B*. There is only one office employee, and no portion of her salary could be eliminated. The officers' salaries would not be reduced. Since the merchandise inventory of Department *A* would be eliminated, the insurance cost applicable to it would be eliminated. It is estimated that one-third of the miscellaneous general expense apportioned to Department *A* could be eliminated. With the discontinuance of sales by Department *A*, there would be no bad debt losses in that department. Without Department *A*, the interest income on receivables arising from Department *A* sales, and the interest expense incurred to make purchases for that department, would disappear.

The consequences of discontinuing Department *A* can now be estimated as follows:

Estimated Effect on Net Income Which Would Result from Discontinuance of Department *A*

Net income of Departments *A* and *B* before income tax..........		$3,285.00
Net income which would be lost by discontinuing Department *A*:		
Income lost:		
Gross profit on sales........................	$10,270.00	
Interest income...........................	30.00	
Total income lost........................	$10,300.00	
Expense reductions:		
Selling expenses..................	$7,600.00	
General expenses.................	500.00	
Interest expense..................	50.00	
Total expense reduction...................	8,150.00	
Net income lost..................................		2,150.00
Resulting net income before income tax.......................		$1,135.00

Surprising as it may at first seem, the foregoing statement indicates that, although the departmental profit and loss statement on page 179 shows that Department *A*'s operations resulted in a net loss of $7,075 before income tax adjustment, the elimination of that department would not increase the net income of the business as a whole but would reduce it from $3,285 to $1,135 before income taxes.

Contribution to overhead. Some accountants now prepare statements in which no attempt is made to show the net income, or even the gross profit less selling expenses, by departments. Instead, each department is credited with the income and charged with the expenses which, in the opinion of the management, would disappear if the department were discontinued. The excess of such income over the "direct" departmental expenses represents the contribution of the department to what may be called the overhead of the business as a whole, or non-departmental overhead. Such a statement is illustrated on page 183.

Adjusting and closing entries. The adjusting entries indicated by the working papers are:

<pre>
(a) Insurance.................................   600.00
        Unexpired insurance....................   600.00
        Insurance expired during the year.

(b) Office salaries............................   90.00
        Accrued salaries payable...............   90.00
        Unpaid salaries at the end of the year.

(c) Accrued interest receivable................   30.00
        Interest income........................   30.00
        Accrued interest on notes receivable.

(d) Bad debts..................................   420.00
        Reserve for bad debts..................   420.00
        To increase the reserve to 5% of the accounts
        receivable.

(e) Depreciation—Delivery equipment............ 1,000.00
        Res. for depr.—Delivery equipment......   1,000.00
        To provide for depreciation at the rate of 25%
        per annum.

(f) Federal income tax......................... 1,000.00
        Federal income tax payable.............   1,000.00
        Tax for 1954.
</pre>

The closing procedure need not be affected by the fact that the business is departmentalized. Below and on page 184 are the closing entries:

<pre>
1954
Dec. 31 Inventory—Dept. A.........................   13,000.00
         Inventory—Dept. B.........................   31,000.00
         Sales—Dept. A.............................   75,000.00
         Sales—Dept. B............................. 125,000.00
         Returned purchases and allowances—Dept. A....   600.00
         Returned purchases and allowances—Dept. B....   850.00
         Discount on purchases—Dept. A 390.00
         Discount on purchases—Dept. B..............   810.00
         Interest income...........................   80.00
              Profit and loss......................   246,730.00
         To record the December 31, 1954 inventories and
         close accounts with credit balances.
</pre>

THE RANDALIA COMPANY
Statement of Profit and Loss
For the Year Ended December 31, 1954

	Department A			Department B			Total		
Gross sales			$75,000			$125,000			$200,000
Deduct:									
Returned sales and allowances		$400			$900			$1,300	
Discount on sales		600			1,000			1,600	
Net sales			1,000			1,900			2,900
			$74,000			$123,100			$197,100
Deduct cost of goods sold:									
Purchases			$60,000			$90,000			$150,000
Deduct:									
Returned purchases and allowances	$600			$850			$1,450		
Discount on purchases	390			810			1,200		
Net cost of purchases		990			1,660			2,650	
		$59,010			$88,340			$147,350	
Add freight in		720			1,080			1,800	
Total		$59,730			$89,420			$149,150	
Add inventory—December 31, 1953		17,000			29,000			46,000	
Total cost of goods available for sale		$76,730			$118,420			$195,150	
Deduct inventory—December 31, 1954		13,000			31,000			44,000	
Cost of goods sold			63,730			87,420			151,150
Gross profit on sales		$10,270			$35,680			$45,950	
Add interest and other income		30			50			80	
Total gross profit and other income			$10,300			$35,730			$46,030
Deduct direct departmental expenses:									
Advertising		$1,600			$2,400			$4,000	
Salesmen's salaries		6,000			7,000			13,000	
Insurance		200			400			600	
Miscellaneous general expense		150			250			400	
Bad debts		150			270			420	
Interest expense		50			75			125	
Total direct departmental expenses			8,150			10,395			18,545
Contribution to nondepartmental overhead			$2,150			$25,335			$27,485
Deduct nondepartmental overhead:									
Store rent								$6,000	
Delivery expense								4,000	
Depreciation—Delivery equipment								1,000	
Officers' salaries								10,000	
Office salaries								2,400	
Miscellaneous general expense								800	
Total nondepartmental overhead									24,200
Net income before federal income tax									$3,285
Deduct federal income tax									1,000
Net income									$2,285

Dec. 31	Profit and loss.................................	244,445.00	
	Inventory—Dept. *A*......................		17,000.00
	Inventory—Dept. *B*......................		29,000.00
	Returned sales and allowances—Dept. *A*....		400.00
	Returned sales and allowances—Dept. *B*....		900.00
	Discount on sales—Dept. *A*................		600.00
	Discount on sales—Dept. *B*................		1,000.00
	Purchases—Dept. *A*......................		60,000.00
	Purchases—Dept. *B*......................		90,000.00
	Freight in................................		1,800.00
	Store rent................................		6,000.00
	Advertising...............................		4,000.00
	Salesmen's salaries—Dept. *A*..............		6,000.00
	Salesmen's salaries—Dept. *B*..............		7,000.00
	Delivery expense..........................		4,000.00
	Depreciation—Delivery equipment.........		1,000.00
	Officers' salaries..........................		10,000.00
	Office salaries............................		2,400.00
	Insurance................................		600.00
	Bad debts................................		420.00
	Miscellaneous general expenses.............		1,200.00
	Interest expense..........................		125.00
	Federal income tax.......................		1,000.00
	To close the accounts with debit balances.		
31	Profit and loss.............................	2,285.00	
	Earned surplus...........................		2,285.00
	To close the Profit and Loss account.		
31	Earned surplus.............................	5,000.00	
	Dividends................................		5,000.00
	To close the Dividends account.		

CHAPTER 13

Manufacturing Accounts

Manufacturing costs. A merchandising concern buys its goods ready for resale; its books, therefore, contain a Purchases account which shows the cost of merchandise purchased. A manufacturing concern buys raw materials, but the process of manufacture also involves expenditures for labor and for a great variety of manufacturing expenses; its books must, therefore, contain accounts in which to record all these manufacturing costs.

The following statement indicates the elements which enter into the computation of the cost of goods manufactured. Payroll taxes have been omitted to simplify the illustration.

THE *A B C* COMPANY   Exhibit D

Statement of Cost of Goods Manufactured
Year Ended December 31, 1954

Materials:			
Inventory, December 31, 1953			$ 12,000
Purchases		$94,000	
Deduct:			
Returned purchases and allowances	$1,500		
Discount on purchases	1,200	2,700	
Net purchases		$91,300	
Freight in		800	
Total			92,100
Total inventory and purchases			$104,100
Deduct inventory, December 31, 1954			9,000
Cost of materials used			$ 95,100
Direct labor			80,750
Manufacturing expenses:			
Indirect labor		$ 9,125	
Heat, light, and power		3,500	
Building and machinery repairs		300	
Depreciation:			
Buildings		3,500	
Machinery and equipment		6,000	
Insurance		950	
Taxes		1,400	
Factory supplies		3,500	
Miscellaneous factory expense		2,500	
Total manufacturing expenses			30,775
Total cost of manufacturing			$206,625
Add goods in process, December 31, 1953			15,000
Total			$221,625
Deduct goods in process, December 31, 1954			11,000
Cost of goods manufactured			$210,625

185

"Materials" include only those things which enter into and become a part of the finished product; supplies used in the operation of the factory are not classified as materials because they do not become part of the finished product.

The nature of direct labor can best be shown by distinguishing it from indirect labor. Employees who work on the product with tools, or who operate machines in the process of production, are direct laborers; but superintendents and foremen, who supervise the work of production, and engineers and janitors, whose services are incidental to the process of production, are indirect laborers.

Manufacturing expense, or manufacturing overhead, includes all costs incurred in production which cannot be classed as material or direct labor. Manufacturing expense includes, among other things, indirect labor, depreciation of the factory building and equipment, power, supplies, taxes and insurance on the assets used in manufacture, and repairs and upkeep of the factory.

The cost of finished goods manufactured during a given period cannot be determined, however, merely by adding the costs incurred during the period for materials, direct labor, and manufacturing expense. There may be unfinished goods, called *goods in process*, on hand at the end of the period, and the cost of these unfinished goods must be deducted to determine the cost of goods finished. Similarly, there may have been goods in process at the beginning of the period, and these must also be taken into consideration.

Operating statements. The operating statements of manufacturing companies do not necessarily differ from those of trading companies except in one particular: the statements of manufacturing companies show the cost of goods *manufactured* (as determined in the statement of cost of goods manufactured), whereas the statements of trading companies show the cost of goods *purchased*. The profit and loss statement follows.

<table>
<tr><td colspan="2">THE A B C COMPANY</td><td>Exhibit C</td></tr>
<tr><td colspan="3">Statement of Profit and Loss
Year Ended December 31, 1954</td></tr>
<tr><td>Gross sales...</td><td></td><td>$300,000</td></tr>
<tr><td>Deduct:</td><td></td><td></td></tr>
<tr><td>Returned sales and allowances..................</td><td>$ 2,000</td><td></td></tr>
<tr><td>Discount on sales...........................</td><td>2,500</td><td>4,500</td></tr>
<tr><td>Net sales...</td><td></td><td>$295,500</td></tr>
<tr><td>Deduct cost of goods sold:</td><td></td><td></td></tr>
<tr><td>Finished goods inventory, December 31, 1953....</td><td>$ 20,000</td><td></td></tr>
<tr><td>Cost of goods manufactured—per Exhibit D......</td><td>210,625</td><td></td></tr>
<tr><td>Total.......................................</td><td>$230,625</td><td></td></tr>
<tr><td>Deduct finished goods inventory, December 31, 1954</td><td>17,000</td><td></td></tr>
<tr><td>Cost of goods sold...................................</td><td></td><td>213,625</td></tr>
<tr><td>Gross profit on sales (forward)..........................</td><td></td><td>$ 81,875</td></tr>
</table>

Gross profit on sales (brought forward)........................ $ 81,875
Deduct expenses:
  Selling expenses:
    Advertising.......................... $ 9,000
    Salesmen's salaries.................. 20,360
    Salesmen's traveling expense......... 8,000
    Miscellaneous selling expense........ 2,500 $ 39,860
  General expenses:
    Officers' salaries.................... $18,000
    Office salaries....................... 3,040
    Stationery and printing.............. 400
    Office supplies...................... 300
    Depreciation of furniture and fixtures.. 750
    Bad debts............................ 800
    Miscellaneous general expense........ 700   23,990
  Total expenses... 63,850
Net income before federal income tax....................... $ 18,025
Federal income tax... 5,500
Net income.. $ 12,525

Statement of cost of goods sold. Some accountants prepare
a statement of cost of goods sold instead of a statement of cost of
goods manufactured. Such a statement would be similar to the
statement of cost of goods manufactured, on page 185, except that
the title would be changed from "Cost of Goods Manufactured"
to "Cost of Goods Sold," and would appear as follows:

THE *A B C* COMPANY   Exhibit D

Statement of Cost of Goods Sold
Year Ended December 31, 1954

and the finished goods inventories would appear in the statement,
as shown below:

Cost of goods manufactured............................... $210,625
Add finished goods inventory, December 31, 1953............ 20,000
Total.. $230,625
Deduct finished goods inventory, December 31, 1954........ 17,000
Cost of goods sold....................................... $213,625

The matter thus included in the statement of cost of goods
sold would be excluded from the profit and loss statement, which
would then show the computation of the gross profit as follows:

THE *A B C* COMPANY   Exhibit C

Statement of Profit and Loss
Year Ended December 31, 1954

Gross sales... $300,000
Deduct:
  Returned sales and allowances..................... $2,000
  Discount on sales................................. 2,500   4,500
Net sales.. $295,500
Deduct cost of goods sold—per Exhibit D.................. 213,625
Gross profit on sales.................................... $ 81,875

Surplus statement. There are no unusual features in the earned surplus statement of a manufacturing company. The statement of The *A B C* Company appears below.

THE *A B C* COMPANY   Exhibit B

Statement of Earned Surplus
Year Ended December 31, 1954

Balance, December 31, 1953	$71,450
Net income for the year, per Exhibit C	12,525
Total	$83,975
Less dividends	6,000
Balance, December 31, 1954	$77,975

Balance sheet. The balance sheet of a manufacturing company will usually contain three inventory accounts (finished goods, goods in process, and raw materials) and certain factory fixed asset account balances. The balance sheet of The *A B C* Company is shown on page 189.

Working papers. The illustrative statements were prepared from the working papers on pages 190 and 191. These working papers have a new pair of columns headed *Manufacturing*, which contain all of the amounts used in determining the cost of goods manufactured.

Adjusting and closing entries. Following are the adjusting entries; the closing entries are on pages 192 and 193.

Dec. 31	Bad debts	800.00	
	Reserve for bad debts		800.00
	To increase the reserve to $1,000.		
31	Depreciation of buildings	3,500.00	
	Reserve for depreciation—Buildings		3,500.00
	To provide for depreciation at 5% per annum.		
31	Depreciation of machinery and equipment	6,000.00	
	Reserve for depreciation—M. & E.		6,000.00
	To provide for depreciation at 10% per annum.		
31	Depreciation of furniture and fixtures	750.00	
	Reserve for depreciation—F. & F.		750.00
	To provide for depreciation at 15% per annum.		
31	Direct labor	750.00	
	Indirect labor	125.00	
	Salesmen's salaries	360.00	
	Office salaries	40.00	
	Accrued salaries and wages payable		1,275.00
	Salaries and wages accrued and unpaid at end of year.		
31	Insurance	950.00	
	Unexpired insurance		950.00
	Insurance expired during year.		
31	Federal income tax	5,500.00	
	Federal income tax payable		5,500.00
	Tax for 1954.		

Exhibit A

THE *A B C* COMPANY
Balance Sheet
December 31, 1954

Assets

Current assets:			
Cash			$25,000
Accounts receivable		$40,000	
Less reserve for bad debts		1,000	39,000
Inventories:			
Finished goods		$17,000	
Goods in process		11,000	
Raw materials		9,000	37,000
Unexpired insurance			300	$101,300
Fixed assets:			
Land			$10,000
Factory buildings		$70,000	
Less reserve for depreciation		15,500	54,500
Machinery and equipment		$60,000	
Less reserve for depreciation		21,000	39,000
Furniture and fixtures		$5,000	
Less reserve for depreciation		2,250	2,750
Total fixed assets—Cost less depreciation			106,250
			$207,550

Liabilities and Net Worth

Current liabilities:		
Accounts payable	$22,800	
Accrued salaries and wages	1,275	
Federal income tax payable	5,500	
Total current liabilities		$ 29,575
Net worth:		
Capital stock	$100,000	
Earned surplus, per Exhibit B	77,975	
Total net worth		177,975
		$207,550

THE A B C COMPANY
Working Papers
Year Ended December 31, 1954

Account	Trial Balance Dr	Trial Balance Cr	Adjustments Dr	Adjustments Cr	Manufacturing Dr	Manufacturing Cr	Profit and Loss Dr	Profit and Loss Cr	Earned Surplus Dr	Earned Surplus Cr	Balance Sheet Dr	Balance Sheet Cr
Cash	25,000										25,000	
Accounts receivable	40,000										40,000	
Reserve for bad debts		200		800 (A)								1,000
Raw materials inventory—Dec. 31, 1953	12,000				12,000							
Goods in process inventory—Dec. 31, 1953	15,000				15,000							
Finished goods inventory—Dec. 31, 1953	20,000						20,000					
Unexpired insurance	1,250			950(F)							300	
Land	10,000										10,000	
Buildings	70,000										70,000	
Reserve for depreciation—Buildings		12,000		3,500 (B)								15,500
Machinery and equipment	60,000										60,000	
Reserve for depreciation—M. & E.		15,000		6,000(C)								21,000
Furniture and fixtures	5,000										5,000	
Reserve for depreciation—F. & F.		1,500		750(D)								2,250
Accounts payable		22,800										22,800
Accrued salaries and wages payable				1,275 (E)								1,275
Federal income tax payable				5,500(G)								5,500
Capital stock		100,000										100,000
Earned surplus		71,450								71,450		
Dividends	6,000								6,000			
Sales		300,000						300,000				
Returned sales and allowances	2,000						2,000					
Discount on sales	2,500						2,500					
Purchases—Raw materials	94,000				94,000							
Returned purchases and allowances		1,500				1,500						
Discount on purchases		1,200				1,200						
Freight in	800				800							
Direct labor	80,000		750 (E)		80,750							
Indirect labor	9,000		125 (E)		9,125							
Heat, light, and power	3,500				3,500							
Building and machinery repairs	300				300							
Depreciation—Buildings			3,500 (B)		3,500							
Depreciation—Machinery and equipment			6,000(C)		6,000							
Insurance			950(F)		950							
Taxes	1,400				1,400							
Factory supplies	3,500				3,500							
Miscellaneous factory expense	2,500				2,500							
Totals forward	463,750	525,650	11,325	18,775	233,325	2,700	24,500	300,000	6,000	71,450	210,300	169,325

THE A B C COMPANY
Working Papers (Concluded)
Year Ended December 31, 1954

	Trial Balance		Adjustments		Manufacturing		Profit and Loss		Earned Surplus		Balance Sheet	
Totals brought forward	463,750	525,650	11,325	18,775	233,325	2,700	24,500	300,000	6,000	71,450	210,300	169,325
Advertising	9,000						9,000					
Salesmen's salaries	20,000		360 (E)				20,360					
Salesmen's traveling expense	8,000						8,000					
Miscellaneous selling expense	2,500						2,500					
Office salaries	18,000						18,000					
Officers salaries	3,000		40 (E)				3,040					
Stationery and printing	400						400					
Office supplies	300						300					
Depreciation—Furniture and fixtures			750 (D)				750					
Bad debts			800 (A)				800					
Miscellaneous general expense	700						700					
Federal income tax			5,500 (G)				5,500					
	525,650	525,650	18,775	18,775								
Inventories—Dec. 31, 1954:												
Raw materials						9,000					9,000	
Goods in process						11,000					11,000	
Finished goods								17,000			17,000	
Cost of goods manufactured					210,625	210,625	210,625					
					233,325	233,325						
Net income—to Earned Surplus							12,525			12,525		
							317,000	317,000				
Earned surplus—Dec. 31, 1954									77,975			77,975
									83,975	83,975	247,300	247,300

Adjustments

(A) Provision for bad debts, to bring total reserve to $1,000, estimated amount required.
(B) Provision for depreciation of factory buildings at 5% per annum.
(C) Provision for depreciation of machinery and equipment at 10% per annum.
(D) Provision for depreciation of furniture and fixtures at 15% per annum.
(E) Accrued salaries and wages, charged to expense accounts and credited to a liability account.
(F) Expired insurance transferred from Unexpired Insurance account to an expense account.
(G) Federal income tax for 1954.

The procedure for closing the books of a manufacturing concern involves setting up a Manufacturing account and debiting and crediting it with the totals of all of the items appearing in the Manufacturing columns of the working papers.

Dec. 31	Manufacturing.................................	233,325.00	
	Raw materials inventory (12/31/53).........		12,000.00
	Goods in process inventory (12/31/53).......		15,000.00
	Purchases—Raw materials..................		94,000.00
	Freight in................................		800.00
	Direct labor.............................		80,750.00
	Indirect labor............................		9,125.00
	Heat, light, and power....................		3,500.00
	Building and machinery repairs............		300.00
	Depreciation—Buildings...................		3,500.00
	Depreciation—Machinery and equipment.....		6,000.00
	Insurance................................		950.00
	Taxes....................................		1,400.00
	Factory supplies..........................		3,500.00
	Miscellaneous factory expense.............		2,500.00
	To close manufacturing accounts with debit balances.		
31	Returned purchases and allowances.............	1,500.00	
	Discount on purchases........................	1,200.00	
	Raw materials inventory (12/31/54)............	9,000.00	
	Goods in process inventory (12/31/54)...........	11,000.00	
	Manufacturing...........................		22,700.00
	To close manufacturing accounts with credit balances and record end-of-year inventories.		

The closing procedure is completed by debiting and crediting Profit and Loss with all of the items appearing in the Profit and Loss columns of the working papers and transferring the net income and the balance of the Dividends account to Earned Surplus.

Dec. 31	Profit and loss..............................	210,625.00	
	Manufacturing...........................		210,625.00
	To close the Manufacturing account.		
31	Profit and loss..............................	93,850.00	
	Finished goods inventory (12/31/53)........		20,000.00
	Returned sales and allowances.............		2,000.00
	Discount on sales..		2,500.00
	Advertising..............................		9,000.00
	Salesmen's salaries.......................		20,360.00
	Salesmen's traveling expense..............		8,000.00
	Miscellaneous selling expense..............		2,500.00
	Officers' salaries.........................		18,000.00
	Office salaries...........................		3,040.00
	Stationery and printing...................		400.00
	Office supplies...........................		300.00
	Depreciation—Furniture and fixtures.......		750.00
	Bad debts................................		800.00
	Miscellaneous general expense.............		700.00
	Federal income tax.......................		5,500.00
	To close accounts with debit balances.		

Dec. 31 Sales..................................... 300,000.00
         Finished goods inventory (12/31/54)............ 17,000.00
              Profit and loss...........................   317,000.00
              To close the Sales account and record end-of-
         year inventory of finished goods.

    31   Profit and loss.............................. 12,525.00
              Earned surplus...........................   12,525.00
              To transfer net income to Earned Surplus.

    31   Earned surplus...............................   6,000.00
              Dividends................................   6,000.00
              To close the Dividends account.

Apportioned items in the working papers. If an expense
charged to one expense account is to be apportioned (as between
manufacturing and selling expenses, or among manufacturing,
selling, and general expenses), the apportionment may be indicated in the working papers in the manner illustrated below.
Observe that, when a portion of an expense is classified as Selling
Expense and another portion of the same expense is classified as
General Expense, the two portions are identified by the letters
S and *G*. These letters may also be used if an expense is not
apportioned between Selling and General but the title of the
account does not clearly indicate whether the items should be
classified as Selling or General.

	Trial Balance	Manufacturing	Profit and Loss
Taxes............	3,000	2,000	{ 600 S { 400 G
Rent of building...	6,000	5,000	1,000 G

If an account balance is apportioned in part to manufacturing
and in part to selling and/or general expense, the journal entries
closing the books should give recognition to the apportionment.
A portion of the account balance should be transferred to the
Manufacturing account and the remainder should be transferred
to Profit and Loss.

CHAPTER 14

The Voucher System

Vouchers. In a small business the proprietor may check every invoice before it is recorded and sign every check. He is thus in a position to satisfy himself of the propriety of each entry recording a liability, and the propriety of drawing a check in payment of the liability. In large businesses this work must be delegated to others, and the system of office procedure and internal control should be such as to give assurance that responsible employees satisfy themselves as to the propriety of recording a liability and issuing a check in payment thereof. Also, there should be documents indicating which members of the organization satisfied themselves of the propriety of recording the liability and the propriety of issuing a check.

When the voucher system is used, the propriety of recording liabilities and issuing checks in payment thereof is evidenced by a voucher and supporting papers attached to it.

Preparing the voucher. The office procedures for the preparation of vouchers vary in different businesses. The procedures described below are indicative of the desired objectives and of one acceptable method of achieving them.

Chapter 6 contains a description of the method of checking invoices received from creditors. The illustration in that chapter was based on an invoice which is repeated on page 195.

It will be remembered that a check sheet in the following form was attached to the invoice, and was initialled by employees in the purchasing and accounting departments to show that they had made the indicated verifications.

Goods checked to invoice	_D.J._
Invoice checked to purchase order for:	
Merchandise	_WO_
Prices	_WO._
Discount terms	_WO_
Freight terms	_WO_
Invoice footings and extensions checked	_M.J._
Approved for payment	
Paid by Check No._____Date_____	

THE OSBORNE COMPANY
2 1 5 West Canal Street
Chicago, Illinois

Invoice No.____**2397**____

Customer's Order No.___1705___

Date of Order___7/2/19-- ___   Invoice Date _July 3, 19--_

Sold to_R. E. Johnson & Company_   Terms____1/10; n/30____

___2913 North Western Ave.___

___Chicago, Ill.___   F. O. B._____

Shipped to____Same____   Date Shipped___July 3___

How Shipped___Truck___

Car. No. & Initials_____

Quantity	Description	Unit Price	Amount
10 cases	XXXX Strawberry Preserves	27.80	278.00
15 cases	Acorn Peanut Butter	9.20	138.00
10 cases	Acorn Peas	12.40	124.00
			540.00

Invoice

If a voucher system is in use, the checking of the invoice is followed by the preparation of a voucher. The face and back of a voucher are illustrated on page 196.

The steps in the preparation of this voucher were as follows:

(a) Using the information shown by the invoice (with check sheet attached), a voucher clerk typed the information shown on the face of the voucher and in the Summary section on the back of the voucher.

(b) The voucher clerk attached to the face of the voucher the invoice and any other documents related to the transaction. He then sent the voucher to the controller.

R. E. JOHNSON & COMPANY
2913 North Western Avenue
Chicago, Illinois

Voucher No. 1693

Date July 6, 19--

Terms 1/10; n/30

Payee The Osborne Company,

Due July 12

215 West Canal Street,

Chicago, Illinois.

Check No. _____

Invoice Date	Invoice No.	Amount
July 3, 19--	2397	540.00
Cash Discount		5.40
Net		534.60

Approved *G. A. Oliver*   Passed for Payment _____
                     Controller   Treasurer

Face of Voucher

Distribution	Summary
Purchases............ _____	Voucher No. _____ 1693
Freight In............ _____	Date ____ July 6, 19--
Freight Out.......... _____	Date Due July 12, 19--
Advertising.......... _____	
Salesmen's Salaries..... _____	Date Paid_____
Delivery Expense...... _____	Check No._____
Misc. Selling Expense.. _____	Amount of check_____
Office Salaries......... _____	To The Osborne Company,
Officers' Salaries....... _____	215 W. Canal Street,
Office Supplies......... _____	Chicago, Illinois.
Stationery & Printing.. _____	
.... _____	Amount.......... 540.00
.... _____	
.... _____	Discount......... 5.40
.... _____	Net............. 534.60
.... _____	
Total_____	

(Voucher is folded here)

Back of Voucher

(c) The controller examined the voucher and the documents attached to it, and assured himself that the checking of the invoice, as described in Chapter 6, had been performed, and that R. E. Johnson & Company actually owed the amount of the voucher. The controller's signature on the voucher indicates that he made this examination.

Recording the voucher. In a large business, much of the bookkeeping work may be done by assistant bookkeepers who must be told what accounts to debit and credit. Therefore, the back of the voucher may be printed with the names of accounts most frequently debited, and blank lines may be left on which to write the names of other accounts which may be debited. Before the voucher was given to the assistant bookkeeper to be recorded, the head bookkeeper (or some other employee competent to do so) filled in the Distribution section on the back of the voucher to indicate the debit to be made by the assistant bookkeeper. The name of the account to be credited is not stated on the back of the voucher, *because all credits are made to a liability account called Vouchers Payable.* After the Distribution section was completed, the back of the voucher appeared as follows:

Distribution		Summary
Purchases............ *540.00*		Voucher No.____ 1693 ____
Freight In............ _____		Date____ July 6, 19-- ____
Freight Out.......... _____		Date Due July 12, 19--
Advertising.......... _____		
Salesmen's Salaries..... _____		Date Paid_____
Delivery Expense...... _____		Check No._____
Misc. Selling Expense.. _____		Amount of check_____
Office Salaries........ _____	(Voucher is folded here)	To The Osborne Company,
Officers' Salaries....... _____		215 W. Canal Street,
Office Supplies......... _____		Chicago, Illinois.
Stationery & Printing.. _____		
.... _____		Amount.......... 540.00
.... _____		Discount......... 5.40
.... _____		Net............. 534.60
.... _____		
.... _____		
Total____ *540.00*		

Back of Voucher

When a voucher system is in use, all vouchers are recorded in a special book of original entry called a *voucher register*, which contains numerous columns for accounts to be debited, thus providing many of the advantages of the columnar books of original entry discussed in preceding chapters.

Note the following facts with respect to the voucher register on page 199:

> Numerous explanatory columns are provided at the left for miscellaneous information about the transactions.

> The Vouchers Payable column is a credit column; *the amount of each voucher is recorded in this column,* and the column total is posted at the end of the month to the credit of Vouchers Payable.

> All the other columns are debit columns.   Special columns are provided for all accounts frequently debited.   (Later illustrations contain many more special columns.)   Debits to accounts for which special columns are not provided are recorded by entries in the *Sundry Accounts* debit section at the right of the register, where space is provided to write the names of the accounts debited as well as the amounts.

The entry in the voucher register to record voucher No. 1693 debits Purchases and credits Vouchers Payable.

Filing the voucher until payment.   After the voucher was recorded in the voucher register, it was folded (at the line indicated in the illustration, on page 196, of the back of the voucher) with the documents inside and was filed in a tickler.   A *tickler* is a file divided into sections by months, with a subdivision for each day.

The illustrative voucher shows that a 1% discount can be taken if payment is made within 10 days from the date of the invoice.   It also shows (on the Due line) the date when payment should be made so that the remittance will reach the creditor in time to justify taking the discount.   This date is July 12.   Therefore, the voucher is filed in the July 12 space of the tickler so that it will receive attention on that date.

You can now see the purpose of the Summary section on the back of the voucher.   This section shows most of the important facts relative to the voucher.   The voucher is filed with this section facing to the front; anyone looking through the voucher file for a particular voucher can locate it without being obliged to open the vouchers to read from the face.

Voucher Register

Voucher No.	Date	Payee	Explanation	Terms	Date Paid	Check No.	Credit Vouchers Payable	Purchases	Freight In	Sundry Accounts		
										Name of Account	L.F.	Amount
1693	19— July 6	The Osborne Company...	Invoice, July 3	1/10; n/30			540 00	540 00				

Paying the voucher. On July 12 the voucher was taken from the tickler and sent to the treasurer for approval of payment. The treasurer examined the documents and authorized the payment by signing the voucher on the line "Passed for Payment."

R. E. JOHNSON & COMPANY 2913 North Western Avenue Chicago, Illinois Payee The Osborne Company, 215 West Canal Street, Chicago, Illinois.	Voucher No. __1693__ Date __July 6, 19--__ Terms __1/10; n/30__ Due __July 12__ Check No. _____

Invoice Date	Invoice No.	Amount
July 3, 19--	2397	540.00
Cash Discount		5.40
Net		534.60

Approved _G.A.Oliver_ Passed for Payment _D.R.Holmes_
Controller   Treasurer

Face of Voucher

The cashier then performed the following operations:

(a) Drew a check.
(b) Entered in the Summary section, on the back of the voucher, the date of payment, the number of the check, and the amount of the check. The Summary section then appeared as shown on page 201.
(c) Sent the check to the creditor.
(d) Sent the voucher to the bookkeeper, to record payment.

Recording the payment. The notations made by the cashier in the Summary section on the back of the voucher (on the lines for Date Paid, Check No., and Amount of check) furnished the bookkeeper with all of the information that he required to record the payment. The recording of the payment included:

(a) Making an entry in a check register.

    A *check register* is a cash disbursements book under another name. Because every voucher is recorded in the voucher register with a credit to Vouchers Payable,

Distribution		Summary
Purchases............ *540.00*		Voucher No._____ 1693
Freight In........... ———		Date____ July 6, 19--
Freight Out.......... ———		Date Due_ July 12, 19--
Advertising.......... -———		
Salesmen's Salaries..... ———		Date Paid _July 12, 19--_
Delivery Expense..... . ———	(Voucher is folded here)	Check No._____ _1668_
Misc. Selling Expense . . ———		Amount of check _$534.60_
Office Salaries......... ———		To_The Osborne Company,
Officers' Salaries....... ———		
Office Supplies......... ——— .		215 W. Canal Street,
Stationery & Printing . . ———		Chicago, Illinois.
.... ———		
.... ———		Amount.......... 540.00
.... ———		Discount......... 5.40
.... ———		Net............. 534.60
.... ———		
Total_____ *540.00*		

Back of Voucher

every entry in the check register to record the payment
of a voucher includes a debit to Vouchers Payable.
The entries in the voucher register and the check register
for the recording of a voucher and its payment are:
> *Entry in voucher register:*
>> Debit the account (or accounts) chargeable with
>> the expenditure.   Credit Vouchers Payable.
> *Entry in the check register:*
>> Debit Vouchers Payable.   Credit Cash (and Dis-
>> count on Purchases, if a discount is taken).
The check register on page 202 shows how the payment of
voucher No. 1693 was recorded.   The entry shows the
number of the check issued and the number of the
voucher paid.   Vouchers Payable account is debited and
Discount on Purchases and Cash are credited.

(b) Writing notations in the Date Paid and Check No. columns of the voucher register.   Observe the notations
in these columns in the voucher register on page 202.

Filing the paid voucher.   After the entry was made in the
check register and the notations were made in the voucher register,
the voucher was filed in a paid voucher file.   Paid vouchers usually are filed in numerical order, so that they can be found easily.

Check Register

Check No.	Date	Payee	Voucher No.	Debit Vouchers Payable	Credits Discount on Purchases	Credits Cash
1668	19— July 12	The Osborne Company.............	1693	540 00	5 40	534 60

Voucher Register

Voucher No.	Date	Payee	Explanation	Terms	Date Paid	Check No.	Credit Vouchers Payable	Purchases	Freight In	Sundry Accounts Name of Account	L.F.	Amount
1693	19— July 6	The Osborne Company....	Invoice, July 3	1/10; n/30	July 12	1668	540 00	540 00				

Since each voucher is signed by persons having authority to approve the expenditure and has attached to it the creditor's invoice and any other supporting documents, it furnishes evidence of the propriety of the entries in the voucher and check registers.

Vouchers for immediate disbursements. The preceding discussion shows the procedure to be followed if some time elapses between the drawing of the voucher and its payment. The procedure is the same for transactions involving the immediate payment of a voucher except that the filing of the voucher in a tickler to await the payment date is omitted. The other steps are:

Preparing the voucher.
Recording the voucher in the voucher register.
Paying the voucher.
Recording the payment.
Filing the paid voucher.

Observe that *an entry is made in the voucher register crediting Vouchers Payable even though the voucher is immediately paid.* There are two reasons why this is done:

(1) When a voucher system is in operation, no check can be drawn without a voucher, and each voucher should be recorded in the voucher register so that all vouchers (which are prenumbered) will be accounted for.

(2) It is advantageous to use the special debit columns which are provided in the voucher register.

Extended illustration. A voucher register and a check register containing the record of a month's transactions appear on pages 206, 207, and 208. To provide a large number of distributive debit columns, the voucher register extends across two facing pages. (In the illustration, the left page is printed above the right page.) Observe how the following transactions are recorded in the voucher register and in the check register.

Summary of August Transactions and Entries

Aug. 1—Received merchandise from Barnard & Co.:

VOUCHER REGISTER	CHECK REGISTER
Purchases	
Vouchers payable	(Later)

3—Paid freight on merchandise purchased:

VOUCHER REGISTER	CHECK REGISTER
Freight in	Vouchers payable
Vouchers payable	Cash

The date paid and check number are entered in the voucher register. (This should be done each time a voucher is paid.)

Aug. 4—Paid Daily News for advertising:

VOUCHER REGISTER   CHECK REGISTER
  Advertising   Vouchers payable
    Vouchers payable   Cash

4—Paid freight:

VOUCHER REGISTER   CHECK REGISTER
  Freight in   Vouchers payable
  Freight out   Cash
    Vouchers payable

5—Paid Davis Supply Co. for office supplies and stationery:

VOUCHER REGISTER   CHECK REGISTER
  Office supplies   Vouchers payable
  Stationery and printing Cash
    Vouchers payable

7—Paid G. E. Wilson for note and interest:

VOUCHER REGISTER   CHECK REGISTER
  Notes payable   Vouchers payable
  Interest expense   Cash
    Vouchers payable

The debit to Notes Payable was entered in the Sundry Accounts section.

8—Paid Barnard & Co. voucher 1:

VOUCHER REGISTER   CHECK REGISTER
(Notations in Date Paid and Vouchers payable
  Check Number columns)   Discount on purchases
                 Cash

10—Received merchandise from L. N. Whitely:

VOUCHER REGISTER   CHECK REGISTER
  Purchases
    Vouchers payable   (Later)

15—Paid store rent for the month:

VOUCHER REGISTER   CHECK REGISTER
  Store rent   Vouchers payable
    Vouchers payable   Cash

The debit was entered in the Sundry Accounts section.

17—Received merchandise from F. R. Mason & Co.:

VOUCHER REGISTER   CHECK REGISTER
  Purchases
    Vouchers payable   (Later)

Aug. 19—Paid L. N. Whitely voucher 7:

VOUCHER REGISTER   CHECK REGISTER
(Notations in Date Paid and   Vouchers payable
Check Number columns.)   Discount on purchases
                                Cash

23—Paid Acme Garage for August rent:

VOUCHER REGISTER   CHECK REGISTER
Delivery expense   Vouchers payable
Vouchers payable   Cash

26—Received merchandise from George Martin:

VOUCHER REGISTER   CHECK REGISTER
Purchases
Vouchers payable   (Not paid in August)

26—Paid F. R. Mason & Co. voucher 9:

VOUCHER REGISTER   CHECK REGISTER
(Notations in Date Paid and   Vouchers payable
Check Number columns.)   Discount on purchases
                                Cash

28—Purchased postage stamps:

VOUCHER REGISTER   CHECK REGISTER
Postage   Vouchers payable
Vouchers payable   Cash

30—Received merchandise from Dalton & Doane:

VOUCHER REGISTER   CHECK REGISTER
Purchases
Vouchers payable   (Not paid in August)

31—Paid salaries for the month:

JOURNAL

Salesmen's salaries	500.00	
Delivery expense	350.00	
Office salaries	250.00	
Officers' salaries	600.00	
Federal income taxes withheld		316.00
Federal O. A. B. taxes withheld		25.50
Accrued payroll		1,358.50
To record salaries expense, tax withholdings, and net payroll liability.		
Payroll taxes	76.50	
Federal O. A. B. taxes payable		25.50
State unemployment taxes payable		45.90
Federal unemployment taxes payable		5.10
To record employers' taxes.		

VOUCHER REGISTER   CHECK REGISTER
Accrued payroll... 1,358.50   Vouchers payable 1,358.50
Vouchers pay-   Cash......... 1,358.50
able........ 1,358.50

You should understand that the illustration on these two pages represents two wide facing sheets of a voucher register. The left side of the register appears at the top of pages 206 and 207. The right side of the register appears at the bottom of the two pages.

Left page

Line No.	Voucher No.	Date			Payee	Explanation	Terms	Date Paid	
		19—						19—	
1	1	Aug.	1		Barnard & Co........	Invoice, Aug. 1	2/10; n/30	Aug.	8
2	2		3		C. N. W. Ry.........				3
3	3		4		Daily News..........	Bill dated Aug. 3	Cash		4
4	4		4		C. N. W. Ry.........				4
5	5		5		Davis Supply Co.....	Invoice 317	Cash		5
6	6		7		G. E. Wilson.........	Note dated July 8			7
7	7		10		L. N. Whitely........	Invoice, Aug. 9	1/10; n/30		19
8	8		15		B. N. Haines.........	Rent for August			15
9	9		17		F. R. Mason & Co....	Invoice 2425	2/10; n/30		26
10	10		23		Acme Garage.........	Rent for August			23
11	11		26		George Martin........	Invoice 1372	1/10; n/30		
12	12		28		Postmaster..........				28
13	13		30		Dalton & Doane......	Invoice 3639	2/10; n/30		
14	14		31		Payroll.............				31
15									
16									

Register

DEBITS

Line No.	Miscellaneous Selling Expense	Accrued Payroll			Office Supplies	Stationery and Printing	Postage	Interest Expense	
1									
2									
3									
4									
5					30	00	75	00			
6								5	00
7									
8									
9									
10									
11									
12							25	00		
13									
14		1,358	50						
15		1,358	50			30	00	75	00	25	00	5	00
16		(15)			(53)	(54)	(55)	(61)	

Voucher

Check No.	Credit Vouchers Payable	Purchases	Freight In	Freight Out	Advertising	Delivery Expense	Line No.
6	1,500 00	1,500 00					1
1	18 00		18 00				2
2	150 00				150 00		3
3	35 00		20 00	15 00			4
4	105 00						5
5	1,005 00						6
8	3,500 00	3,500 00					7
7	200 00						8
10	2,600 00	2,600 00					9
9	25 00					25 00	10
	1,750 00	1,750 00					11
11	25 00						12
	1,875 00	1,875 00					13
12	1,358 50						14
	14,146 50	11,225 00	38 00	15 00	150 00	25 00	15
	(11)	(31)	(35)	(41)	(42)	(45)	16

Right page

Sundry Accounts			Remarks	Line No.
Name of Account	L.F.	Amount		
				1
				2
				3
				4
				5
Notes payable..............	12	1,000 00		6
				7
Store rent..................	43	200 00		8
				9
				10
				11
				12
				13
				14
		1,200 00		15
				16

Check Register

Check No.	Date			Payee	Voucher No.	Debit Vouchers Payable	CREDIT	
							Discount on Purchases	Cash
	19—							
1	Aug.	3		C. N. W. Ry.............	2	18 00		18 00
2			4	Daily News.............	3	150 00		150 00
3			4	C. N. W. Ry.............	4	35 00		35 00
4			5	Davis Supply Co.........	5	105 00		105 00
5			7	G. E. Wilson.............	6	1,005 00		1,005 00
6			8	Barnard & Co............	1	1,500 00	30 00	1,470 00
7		15		B. N. Haines.............	8	200 00		200 00
8		19		L. N. Whitely...........	7	3,500 00	35 00	3,465 00
9		23		Acme Garage...........	10	25 00		25 00
10		26		F. R. Mason & Co.......	9	2,600 00	52 00	2,548 00
11		28		Postmaster.............	12	25 00		25 00
12		31		Payroll.................	14	1,358 50		1,358 50
						10,521 50	117 00	10,404 50
						(11)	(71)	(1)

Posting from the voucher register. The entries in the Sundry Accounts debit section should be posted during the month. At the end of the month, the columns of the voucher register are footed. The total of the footings of the debit columns should be compared with the footing of the Vouchers Payable credit column to see that the debits and the credits in the voucher register are equal. Postings are then made as follows:

Credit: Vouchers Payable—column total.
Debits: Totals of all special debit columns.

Posting from the check register. At the end of the month, the columns of the check register are footed, and the total of the Vouchers Payable debit column is compared with the sum of the totals of the two credit columns (Discount on Purchases and Cash). Postings are then made as follows:

Debit: Vouchers Payable—column total.
Credits: Discount on Purchases—column total.
Cash—column total.

Use the letters *Ch R* in the ledger accounts to indicate postings from the check register.

Elimination of accounts payable ledger. When a voucher system is in use, a subsidiary ledger with accounts payable is not required; it is possible to determine the individual liabilities at any date by merely noting the unpaid items in the voucher register. To illustrate, posting the totals of the Vouchers Payable column in the voucher register and the Vouchers Payable column in the check register in the preceding illustration will produce the following controlling account:

Vouchers Payable

19—					19—				
Aug. 31	....	ChR1	10,521	50	Aug. 31	....	VR1	14,146	50

This account has a credit balance of $3,625. The individual liabilities making up this total are the items in the voucher register with no notations in the Date Paid and Check Number columns. A schedule of the unpaid vouchers can be prepared as follows:

Schedule of Vouchers Payable
August 31, 19—

Voucher No.	Payee	Amount
11	George Martin..................................	1,750.00
13	Dalton & Doane...............................	1,875.00
	Total..	3,625.00

The elimination of the accounts payable subsidiary ledger is a major advantage of the voucher system, as a great deal of posting labor is thereby avoided.

Some companies like to be able to determine the purchases made from each creditor by keeping a file, with a card for each creditor, on which are listed the date and the number of each voucher payable to him. Such a card might appear as follows:

J. B. Henderson,					
1357 North Calumet Avenue,					
Chicago, Illinois					
Date	Vo. No.	Date	Vo. No.	Date	Vo. No.
Sep. 15	135				
Sep. 27	191				

This card can be referred to when it is desired to determine the numbers of the vouchers payable to each creditor, and the vouchers can be obtained from the file.

Or, carbon copies of all vouchers may be made, and carbon copies of the vouchers payable to each payee may be filed together.

Balance sheet title for liability. When a voucher system is in use, the total liability on open vouchers is sometimes called "Vouchers payable" in the balance sheet. The better-known title "Accounts payable" is probably preferable.

Partial payments. If, when an invoice is received, it is known that it will be paid in installments, a separate voucher should be made and recorded for each installment. If installment payments are decided upon after one voucher for the entire invoice has been made and recorded, a new voucher for each installment must be prepared and recorded.

To illustrate, assume that voucher number 200 was prepared on July 7 in the amount of $2,000, and recorded as shown in the voucher register on page 211. On July 20 it was decided to make an installment payment of $500; two new vouchers, numbers 255 and 256, were prepared and recorded in the register with a notation "See Voucher 200" in the Explanation column; the credits were recorded in the Vouchers Payable column; the debit was also to the Vouchers Payable account, and it was entered in the Sundry Accounts debit section. A notation "See 255 and 256" was made in the Date Paid and Check Number columns of the voucher register on the line for voucher 200, thus indicating how the liability on voucher 200 was cancelled. A check (number 945) was drawn in payment of voucher 255; it was recorded in the check register, and the date of payment and the check number were recorded in the voucher register on the line for voucher 255.

The voucher and check registers are shown on page 211.

Exchange charges. If, at the time a voucher is drawn and recorded, it is known that the payment will be made by a bank draft or in some other manner which will involve an exchange charge, the voucher may be made for the full amount of the prospective disbursement, including the exchange, and Collection and Exchange can be debited either in a special column of the voucher register or in the Sundry Accounts section.

If the exchange charge is not known until the disbursement is made, at some date after the recording of the voucher, an entry can be made in the journal, debiting Collection and Exchange and crediting Vouchers Payable. For instance:

On June 10, merchandise was purchased for $500; voucher 27 was prepared, and an entry was made in the voucher register debiting Purchases and crediting Vouchers Payable.

On June 25, a bank draft for $500 was purchased and mailed to the creditor; the bank draft was paid for by a check to the bank in the amount of $500.25, the $.25 being an exchange charge. (*Continued on page 212.*)

Voucher Register

Voucher No.	Date	Payee	Explanation	Date Paid	Check No.	Credit Vouchers Payable	Purchases	Name of Account	L.F.	Amount
	19—									
200	July 7	A. B. White	Invoice, July 6	See Vo.	255 & 256	2,000 00	2,000 00			
255	July 20	A. B. White	See Voucher 200	July 20	945	500 00		} Vouchers Payable	11	2,000 00
256	20	A. B. White	See Voucher 200	20		1,500 00				

(DEBITS: Purchases, Sundry Accounts)

Check Register

Check No.	Date	Payee	Voucher No.	Debit Vouchers Payable	Discount on Purchases	Cash
	19—					
945	July 20	A. B. White	255	500 00		500 00

(CREDITS: Discount on Purchases, Cash)

An entry should be made in the journal as follows:

```
Collection and exchange....................................... .25
    Vouchers payable (No. 27).............................        .25
    Exchange charged by bank on bank draft for $500 purchased
    for payment of voucher 27.
```

And an entry should be made in the check register debiting Vouchers Payable and crediting Cash, $500.25.

If exchange charges are frequently incurred, the journal entry procedure just described can be avoided by providing a Collection and Exchange debit column in the check register.

Returned purchases and allowances.   Assume that a purchase of merchandise, on invoice A1316, costing $500, with terms of 2/10; n/30, is made from Keith & Co. on November 5, and that voucher No. 2324 is prepared and recorded in the voucher register, as shown in the first voucher register on page 213.

Assume, further, that some of the merchandise is returned to Keith & Co. and that a credit memorandum for $45 is received on November 9.   An entry in the journal is made as follows:

```
Nov. 9   Vouchers payable (No. 2324)................... 45.00
            Returned purchases and allowances.........        45.00
         Credit memo No. 239.
```

A notation is made on the face of the voucher, so that, when it is taken out of the tickler for payment, the cashier will draw a check for only the net amount.   The credit memo is attached to the voucher.

The list of open vouchers prepared at the end of the month should show the *net* liability on each voucher.   To make it easy for the bookkeeper to prepare the list, the voucher register may be provided with Deductions columns in which a memorandum notation (*not to be posted, because postings are made from the general journal*) may be entered in the manner illustrated in the second voucher register on page 213.

If there are enough returns and allowances to warrant it, a returned purchases and allowances book may be used.   The entry in such a book would be made as follows:

Returned Purchases and Allowances Book

Date		Name	Explanation	Voucher No.	Amount	
19— Nov.	9	Keith & Co..............	Cr. Memo 239	2324	45	00

Voucher Register

Voucher No.	Date	Payee	Explanation	Terms	Deductions			Date Paid	Check No.	Credit Vouchers Payable	Debits	
					Date	Ref.	Amount				Purchases	Freight In
2324	19— Nov. 5	Keith & Co......	Inv. No. A1316	2/10; n/30						500 00	500 00	

Voucher Register

Voucher No.	Date	Payee	Explanation	Terms	Deductions			Date Paid	Check No.	Credit Vouchers Payable	Debits	
					Date	Ref.	Amount				Purchases	Freight In
2324	19— Nov. 5	Keith & Co......	Inv. No. A1316	2/10; n/30	19— Nov. 9	J5	45 00			500 00	500 00	

At the end of the month, the column total would be posted to the debit of Vouchers Payable and to the credit of Returned Purchases and Allowances.   Memorandum notations, of the nature previously described, would be made on the face of the voucher and in the Deductions columns of the voucher register.

Notes payable.   Several methods are available for dealing with notes payable issued for merchandise or other purchases.   The following method will usually be found satisfactory:

(1) Record the purchase in the usual way in the voucher register, debiting Purchases (or another appropriate account) and crediting Vouchers Payable.

(2) Make a journal entry for the issuance of the note, debiting Vouchers Payable and crediting Notes Payable.   In the voucher register, indicate the issuance of the note by a memorandum, "Canceled by note," in the Deductions section, and by entering the date of the issuance of the note in the Date Paid column.

(3) At the maturity of the note, make a new voucher and record it in the voucher register, debiting Notes Payable (and Interest Expense, if the note bears interest) and crediting Vouchers Payable.

(4) Record the payment of the note by an entry in the check register, debiting Vouchers Payable and crediting Cash.

Journal entries charging Vouchers Payable should show the number of the voucher, thus:

Vouchers payable (No. 3)
Notes payable

CHAPTER 15

Alternative Adjustment Procedures

Chapter 3 contains a discussion of adjustments for accruals of unrecorded income and expense, and for apportionments of recorded income and costs. On page 54 of Chapter 4 there is a statement of the procedures to be followed when income that had accrued and had been recorded by an adjusting entry at the end of one period is collected in a subsequent period, and when an expense, accrued and recorded by an adjusting entry at the end of one period, is paid in a subsequent period. For the sake of simplicity, no intimation was given in those chapters that alternative procedures are sometimes used. We shall now consider alternative procedures.

Accrued Income

Procedures previously described. The procedures described in Chapters 3 and 4 for recording adjustments for accrued income and the subsequent collection thereof were as follows:

Adjusting entry:
> If a business has earned income for which no transaction entry has been made, debit an asset account and credit an income account.

Entry for collection:
> When the income is subsequently collected, credit the asset account (set up by the adjusting entry) with the amount of the recorded accrual, and credit an income account with any amount collected in excess of the recorded accrual.

For instance, assume that a company receives a 60-day, 6% note for $1,000 on December 21, 1953, and collects the note and interest on February 19, 1954.

Adjusting entry—December 31, 1953:

Accrued interest receivable....................	**1.67**	
Interest income..........................		**1.67**
Accrued interest for 10 days on $1,000 note.		

Entry for collection—February 19, 1954:

Cash..	1,010.00	
Accrued interest receivable.................		1.67
Interest income............................		8.33
Notes receivable...........................		1,000.00
Collection of note and interest.		

Alternative procedure. An alternative procedure is described and illustrated below:

Adjusting entry—December 31, 1953 (Same as by the method previously described):

```
Accrued interest receivable....................    1.67
    Interest income...........................            1.67
    Accrued interest for 10 days on $1,000 note.
```

Reversing entry—January 1, 1954 (Reverses the adjusting entry):

```
Interest income...............................    1.67
    Accrued interest receivable.................            1.67
    To reverse adjusting entry.
```

Entry for collection—February 19, 1954 (No apportionment of income necessary):

```
Cash.........................................  1,010.00
    Interest income...........................            10.00
    Notes receivable..........................         1,000.00
    Collection of note and interest.
```

When this procedure is used, the Accrued Interest Receivable account and the Interest Income account appear as follows:

Accrued Interest Receivable

1953					1954					
Dec.	31	Adjustment		1	67	Jan.	1	Reversal	1	67

Interest Income

1953					1953					
Dec.	31	To Profit and Loss		1	67	Dec.	31	Adjustment	1	67
1954					1954					
Jan.	1	Reversal		1	67	Feb.	19	Collection	10	00

Observe that the Interest Income account now has a credit balance of $8.33, the amount of the interest income applicable to 1954.

Why reversing entries are desirable. The above illustration shows that the two procedures produce identical results. Many accountants believe that it is desirable to reverse the accruals, because subsequent transactions can then be recorded without any need to refer to prior accruals. In the preceding illustration, for instance, if the accrual is not reversed, it is necessary, on February 19, when the note and interest are collected, to look up the amount of interest accrued on December 31 in order to make the credit to Accrued Interest Receivable. If there are many notes receivable, this will be quite an inconvenience.

Accrued Expense

Procedures previously described. The procedures described
in Chapters 3 and 4 for recording adjustments for accrued expenses
and the entries for the subsequent payment thereof may be summarized as follows:

> *Adjusting entry:*
> If a business has incurred an expense for which no trans-
> action entry has been made, debit an expense account and
> credit a liability account.

> *Entry for payment:*
> When the expense is subsequently paid, debit the liability
> account (set up by the adjusting entry) with the amount
> of the recorded accrual, and debit an expense account with
> any amount paid in excess of the accrual recorded by the
> adjusting entry.

For instance, assume that a company issues a 60-day, 6%
note for $1,000 on December 21, 1953, and pays the note and
interest on February 19, 1954.

Adjusting entry—December 31, 1953:

Interest expense.................................	1.67	
Accrued interest payable.....................		1.67
Accrued interest for 10 days on note payable.		

Entry for payment—February 19, 1954:

Accrued interest payable........................	1.67	
Interest expense................................	8.33	
Notes payable................................	1,000.00	
Cash..		1,010.00
Payment of note and interest.		

Alternative procedure.   The alternative procedure is described
and illustrated below:

Adjusting entry—December 31, 1953 (Same as by method previously described):

Interest expense.................................	1.67	
Accrued interest payable.....................		1.67
Accrued interest for 10 days on note payable.		

Reversing entry—January 1, 1954 (Reverses the adjusting
entry):

Accrued interest payable........................	1.67	
Interest expense............................		1.67
To reverse adjusting entry.		

Entry for payment—February 19, 1954 (No apportionment of expense necessary):

Interest expense..................................	10.00	
Notes payable....................................	1,000.00	
Cash..		1,010.00
Payment of note and interest.		

When this procedure is used, the Accrued Interest Payable account and the Interest Expense account appear as follows:

Accrued Interest Payable

1954					1953				
Jan.	1	Reversal		1	67	Dec.	31	Adjustment	1	67

Interest Expense

1953					1953				
Dec.	31	Adjustment		1	67	Dec.	31	To Profit and Loss	1	67
1954					1954				
Feb.	19	Payment		10	00	Jan.	1	Reversal	1	67

Observe that the Interest Expense account now has a debit balance of $8.33, the amount of the interest expense applicable to 1954.

The words *Adjustment, Payment, Reversal,* and *To Profit and Loss* are included above for explanatory purposes only, and need not appear in the accounts.

Desirability of reversing entries. The remarks made in the comparable paragraph in the discussion of accrued income are equally applicable here.

Apportionments of Recorded Costs

Procedure previously described. The following procedure was described in Chapter 3:

If an expenditure benefits only the period in which it is made, the cost should be debited to an expense account.

If an expenditure will benefit more than one period, it is properly chargeable to an asset account; at the end of each period benefited by the expenditure, the portion of the cost *expired during the period* should be transferred, by an adjusting entry, from the asset account to an expense account.

Alternative procedure. An alternative procedure is stated below:

Charge all expense expenditures to expense accounts, regardless of the number of periods that will be benefited.

At the end of each period, the portion of the cost *unexpired at the end of the period* should be transferred, by an adjusting entry, from the expense account to an asset account.

At the beginning of the next period, reverse the adjusting entry.

The two procedures illustrated. Assume that a three-year fire insurance policy is purchased on January 2, 1954 at a premium cost of $300. Entries by the two procedures are shown below:

Original Debit to Asset Account

Original Debit to Expense Account

January 2, 1954 entry for expenditure:

Unexpired insurance	300		Insurance expense	300	
Cash		300	Cash		300
Three-year fire policy.			Three-year fire policy.		

December 31, 1954 entry for apportionment:

Insurance expense	100		Unexpired insurance	200	
Unexpired insurance		100	Insurance expense		200
To transfer one-third of premium to expense.			To set up as an asset the unexpired (two-thirds) portion of the three-year premium.		

January 1, 1955 reversing entry:

None.

Insurance expense	200	
Unexpired insurance		200
To reverse the adjusting entry.		

The acceptability of the above alternative procedures is evident when it is noted that the periodical statement results for 1954 by both procedures are identical. In both cases $100 is shown in the profit and loss statement as an expense, and $200 is shown in the balance sheet as an asset.

Reason for the reversing entry. To understand why the reversing entry is desirable, let us assume that no reversing entry was made and that another insurance policy was purchased in 1955 and charged to Insurance Expense. At the end of 1955, when it came time to make the annual adjusting entry, part of the apportionable costs would be in the Unexpired Insurance account and part would be in the Insurance Expense account. This would be a confusing situation, which the reversing entry avoids.

A second alternative procedure. A second alternative procedure for dealing with costs which are apportionable is described on page 220:

Charge all of the expenditures to a prepaid expense (asset) account, regardless of the number of periods benefited.

At the end of each period benefited by the expenditure, the portion of the cost *expired during the period* should be transferred, by an adjusting entry, from the prepaid expense account to an expense account.

This procedure has the advantage of the first alternative method, described on page 219, because it results in charging all expenditures of the same nature to a single account, instead of charging part to a prepaid expense account and part to an expense account on the basis of the number of periods benefited. And it has the advantage of the method described in Chapter 3, because it avoids the necessity of making a reversing entry.

The procedure is illustrated on page 221, and is contrasted with the first alternative procedure. Observe that the expenditures consist of a premium for a three-year policy and premiums for one-year policies. Observe also that the procedure of charging all of these expenditures to the Unexpired Insurance account makes reversing entries unnecessary.

Custom and convenience affect choice of method. When should an expenditure be charged to an asset account, and when should it be charged to an expense account? For certain transactions, the answer is apparent.

Use an asset account if there is no expectation that any portion of the expenditure will ever be chargeable to expense; an expenditure for the purchase of land is an example.

Use an expense account if no portion of the expenditure will benefit a future period; income tax expense is an example.

For other expenditures, when some or all of the cost will sooner or later be assigned to expense, custom and convenience are the factors which determine the selection of the account for the debit.

It is customary, for example, to debit an asset account at acquisition for all items properly classifiable as fixed assets. Amounts invested in fixed assets, if ultimately assignable to expense, reach expense accounts by way of depreciation entries. It would not be sensible to charge the cost of a fixed asset to a depreciation expense account at acquisition and later by adjusting entries remove the portion applicable to future periods.

It is sometimes impracticable for the person recording transactions to determine, with a reasonable degree of accuracy at the time of making the expenditure, whether the expenditure will benefit more than one period. For instance, how long will store

First Alternative Procedure
Premiums Charged to Insurance Expense

	Unexpired Insurance	Insurance Expense	Profit and Loss
Year 1:			
Jan. 1 One-year policy		100	
Jan. 1 Three-year policy		600	
Dec. 31 Adjusting entry	400 (b)	400	
Dec. 31 Closing entry		300	300
		700	300
		700	
Year 2:			
Jan. 1 Reversing entry	400	400	
Jan. 1 Renewal of one-year policy		100	
Dec. 31 Adjusting entry	200 (c)	200	
Dec. 31 Closing entry		300	300
		500	
		500	
Year 3:			
Jan. 1 Reversing entry	200	200	
Jan. 1 Renewal of one-year policy		100	
Dec. 31 No adjusting entry required.			
Dec. 31 Closing entry		300	300
		300	
		300	

Second Alternative Procedure
Premiums Charged to Unexpired Insurance

	Unexpired Insurance	Insurance Expense	Profit and Loss
Year 1:			
Jan. 1 One-year policy	100		
Jan. 1 Three-year policy	600		
Dec. 31 Adjusting entry	300	→300 (a)	
Dec. 31 Closing entry		300	300
Year 2:			
Jan. 1 Reversing entry			
Jan. 1 Renewal of one-year policy	100		
Dec. 31 Adjusting entry	300	→300 (a)	
Dec. 31 Closing entry		300	300
Year 3:			
Jan. 1 Reversing entry			
Jan. 1 Renewal of one-year policy	100		
Dec. 31 Adjusting entry	300	→300 (a)	
Dec. 31 Closing entry		300	300

a—One-year premium plus one-third of three-year premium.
b—Two-thirds of three-year premium.
c—One-third of three-year premium.

supplies last? In such cases the choice of procedure is largely a matter of accounting policy; some accountants would charge the expenditure to an asset account and make end-of-period transfers to expense; others would charge the expenditure to an expense account and make end-of-period transfers to an asset account, with reversing entries at the beginning of the succeeding period.

Even when the apportionment of an expenditure to periods to be benefited can be accurately made at the date of the expenditure, a strict application of the rule stated in Chapter 3 may be undesirable. For example, during any given year some expenditures for insurance might benefit only the current year whereas others might benefit a longer period of time. If the tentative rules stated in Chapter 3 were followed, some premiums (those on policies expiring before the end of the accounting period) would be charged to Insurance Expense and other premiums (those on policies not expiring before the end of the accounting period) would be charged to Unexpired Insurance. Such a procedure would result in the use of two insurance accounts for current transactions, which might cause some confusion. To avoid such confusion, it might be preferable to charge all premiums to *either* the asset or the expense account, and to make the adjusting and reversing entries consistent with the method adopted.

It is of some significance to recognize that, even if, at the time of making an expenditure, a determination were made of the period or periods affected by the transaction, adjusting entries would not necessarily be avoided nor would their number always be minimized. Referring to the immediately preceding paragraph, the use of both an Insurance account and an Unexpired Insurance account for the payment of premiums would not avoid the necessity of making an adjusting entry for the expired portion of the premiums charged to Unexpired Insurance.

Failure to adhere strictly to either the procedure stated in Chapter 3 or the alternative procedure stated in this chapter for recording expenditures cannot be considered to be *wrong* so long as the transaction entry and the adjusting and reversing entries together effect a correct apportionment of costs to the periods benefited. For instance, it would not be a *mistake* to charge insurance premiums to Unexpired Insurance, an asset account, even though the policies expired during the current accounting period. It would be *wrong* to leave the premium in the asset account at the end of the period and show it in the balance sheet as an asset when in fact the policy and the premium had expired.

The considerations noted above have created a situation in accounting practice where it is considered acceptable to charge an expense expenditure to either a prepaid expense (asset) account or an expense account, regardless of the number of time periods affected, provided that adjusting and reversing entries are made in such a way as to effect a proper apportionment of cost, for periodical statement purposes, between expired cost (expense) and unexpired cost (asset).

Apportionments of Recorded Income

Procedure previously described. Collections may be received for services to be rendered in the future. The following procedure for dealing with such collections was described in Chapter 3:

> If the service will be completely performed, and the total thereby earned, during the accounting period in which the collection is received, an income account should be credited at the time of the collection.
>
> If the service will not be completely performed during the period in which the collection is received, the entire amount should be credited to an unearned income account; at the end of each period during which service is performed, the portion of the income *earned during the period* should be transferred by an adjusting entry, from the unearned income account to an income account.

Alternative procedure. An alternative procedure is stated below:

> Credit all income collections to income accounts, regardless of the number of periods over which the income will be earned.
>
> At the end of each period, the portion of the income *unearned at the end of the period* should be transferred, by an adjusting entry, from the income account to an unearned income account.
>
> At the beginning of the next period, reverse the adjusting entry.

The two procedures illustrated. Assume that, on December 1, 1953, cash in the amount of $300 is collected as rent of a portion of our building for three months. Entries by the two procedures are shown below:

Original Credit to Unearned Income   **Original Credit to Income**
December 1, 1953 entry for collection:

Cash......................	300		Cash......................	300	
Unearned rent income.....		300	Rent income.............		300
Collection of rent for three months.			Collection of rent for three months.		

December 31, 1953 entry for apportionment:

Unearned rent income.......... 100
  Rent income.............. 100
  To transfer December rent
  from unearned income account to income account.

Rent income.................. 200
  Unearned rent income..... 200
  To transfer January and
  February rent to an un-
  earned income account.

January 1, 1954 reversing entry:

None.

Unearned rent income......... 200
  Rent income............. 200
  To reverse the adjusting
  entry.

The acceptability of the above alternative procedures is evident when it is noted that the periodical statement results for 1953 are identical. In both cases, $100 is shown in the profit and loss statement as income, and $200 is shown in the balance sheet as unearned income (under the current liabilities caption).

What was said in the discussion of apportionments of recorded costs, under the captions "Reason for reversing entry" and "Custom and convenience affect choice of method," is equally relevant in relation to apportionments of recorded income.

Second alternative procedure. An alternative procedure for dealing with income which is apportionable, comparable to the second alternative procedure described for dealing with apportionable costs, is described below:

Credit all income collections to unearned income accounts, regardless of the number of periods over which the income will be earned.

At the end of each period during which service is rendered and income thereby earned, the portion of the income *earned during the period* should be transferred, by an adjusting entry, from the unearned income account to an income account.

This procedure has advantages comparable to those discussed in connection with the second alternative method of dealing with the apportionment of recorded costs: (1) it avoids the confusion of credits to income accounts and unearned income accounts for income collections of the same nature; and (2) it avoids the necessity of making reversing entries.

Determining When Adjustments Are Required and the Amounts Thereof

An inspection of the trial balance of the general ledger will usually indicate the nature of the required adjustments. The existence of balances in certain classes of asset accounts may suggest the necessity for adjustments. For instance, an Accounts Receivable account suggests an adjustment for bad debts; fixed asset accounts suggest provisions for depreciation; a Notes Receivable account suggests the possibility of a required adjustment for accrued interest receivable.

The appearance of certain classes of liability accounts may call the accountant's attention to the necessity for an adjustment. For instance, a Notes Payable account suggests the possibility of a required adjustment for accrued interest payable.

If any prepaid expense accounts or unearned income accounts appear in the trial balance, they should immediately draw the accountant's attention to the fact that adjustments for cost or income apportionments may be required.

The accountant will do wisely to consider each income and each expense account and ask himself whether there is any possibility that an adjustment may be in order, either for an accrual or for an apportionment.

Although an inspection of the trial balance may suggest the *nature* of the required adjustments, it usually is necessary to have recourse to other sources of information to determine the *amounts* of the adjustments. For instance, the amount of the provision for bad debts may be based on loss experience or a review of the receivables; provisions for depreciation are governed by the established rates and the accounting policy with respect to depreciation for fractional periods; insurance premium apportionments may be determined by an inspection of policies or of an insurance register; and interest adjustments may be determined by an inspection of notes or of note registers.

CHAPTER 16

Partnerships (Concluded)

Chapter 8 dealt with some of the fundamentals of partnership accounting. This chapter deals with the following more advanced material: miscellaneous methods of dividing profits and losses; changes in personnel; and liquidation of the partnership.

Miscellaneous Methods of Dividing Profits and Losses

Determinants of an equitable division. Some of the things which should be given consideration in the determination of an equitable division of partnership profits are:

The relative amounts of capital furnished by the partners.

The relative values of the services rendered by the partners. These may differ because of differences in business ability and/or time devoted to partnership affairs.

Various matters, such as seniority, business contacts, profit potential of a going business contributed by a partner, and the degree of risk-taking. The degree of risk-taking depends on the dangers of loss and the relative amounts of the partners' capitals, as well as their outside assets to which the firm creditors may have recourse for the payment of partnership debts.

Methods of dividing profits and losses. Various methods of dividing partnership profits and losses are discussed below, under the following captions:

(1) In a fractional ratio.
(2) In a capital ratio.
(3) Interest on capitals, and the remainder in a fractional ratio.
(4) Salaries to partners, and the remainder in a fractional ratio.
(5) Salaries, interest, and the remainder in a fractional ratio.

Any agreement with respect to the division of profits applies also to the division of losses. In the absence of an agreement with respect to the division of profits, the law assumes an agreement to divide them equally.

Basis of illustrations. For purposes of illustration we shall assume that the capital accounts of two partners appear as follows:

J. L. Lane, Capital

1954					1954				
June	1	CD 6	500	00	Jan.	1	CR 1	10,000	00
Nov.	1	CD11	1,500	00	Aug.	1	CR 8	2,000	00

D. K. Burton, Capital

1954					1954				
Apr.	1	CD 4	1,000	00	Jan.	1	CR 1	20,000	00
Dec.	1	CD12	2,000	00	July	1	CR 7	2,000	00

The debit balances in the drawing accounts at the end of the year were: J. L. Lane, $3,000.00; D. K. Burton, $4,000.00.

The balances in the drawing accounts represent the totals of the agreed monthly drawings; the debits in the capital accounts record withdrawals in excess of the agreed monthly amounts.

The income and expense accounts have been closed, and the Profit and Loss account has a credit balance of $12,000, the amount of the net income for the year.

The illustrative closing entries are based on an assumption that there is no agreement to maintain fixed amounts of capitals; therefore, the Profit and Loss and drawing accounts are closed to the capital accounts.

(1) *Divisions in a fractional ratio.* The equal division of profits in Chapter 8 is an illustration of a division in a fractional ratio.

To illustrate another fractional-ratio division, let us assume that the partners, Lane and Burton, after consideration of the determinants of an equitable division of profits, agree that adequate recognition can be given to all of the determinants by dividing the profits in the ratio of one-fourth to Lane and three-fourths to Burton. The entries to close the books are:

Profit and loss..............................	12,000.00	
J. L. Lane, capital.........................		3,000.00
D. K. Burton, capital......................		9,000.00
To divide the net income in the ratio of 25% and 75%.		
J. L. Lane, capital...........................	3,000.00	
J. L. Lane, drawings.......................		3,000.00
To close Lane's drawing account.		
D. K. Burton, capital........................	4,000.00	
D. K. Burton, drawings....................		4,000.00
To close Burton's drawing account.		

The entries closing the drawing accounts are omitted from the remaining illustrations. They would be the same as those above.

(2) *Divisions in a capital ratio.* If the capital investments are the major source of income and the other determinants of an equitable division of profits are not pertinent, the total profits may be divided in a capital ratio. Two illustrations are given below:

Division in ratio of capitals at beginning of period. The capital accounts on page 227 show the following balances on January 1:

J. L. Lane	$10,000.00
D. K. Burton	20,000.00

The net income division on this basis is shown below:

Partner	Capitals at Beginning	Fraction	Amount
Lane	$10,000.00	⅓	$ 4,000.00
Burton	20,000.00	⅔	8,000.00
Total	$30,000.00		$12,000.00

Division in ratio of capitals at end of period. As an inducement for partners to refrain from making withdrawals of material amounts during the period for which income is being divided, and to encourage them to invest additional capital as needed, it may be preferable to divide the net income in the ratio of the capitals at the end of the period, thus:

Partner	Capitals at End	Fraction	Amount
Lane	$10,000.00	$10\frac{}{29}$	$ 4,137.93
Burton	19,000.00	$19\frac{}{29}$	7,862.07
Total	$29,000.00		$12,000.00

(3) *Interest on capitals; remainder in fractional ratio.* Suppose that the partners agree that *some* consideration should be given to capital investments, but that consideration should also be given to other determinants of an equitable division of the net income. Therefore, they agree to divide a portion of the net income in the capital ratio by allowing 6% interest on the capitals, and to divide the remainder in some other fractional ratio—say, equally. The interest may be computed on the capitals at the beginning or at the end of the year, as agreed; in the following entries, the interest is computed on opening capitals.

Profit and loss	1,800.00	
J. L. Lane, capital		600.00
D. K. Burton, capital		1,200.00

To allow interest on opening capitals.
Lane: 6% on $10,000 = $ 600
Burton: 6% on $20,000 = $1,200

Profit and loss	10,200.00	
J. L. Lane, capital		5,100.00
D. K. Burton, capital		5,100.00

To divide remaining net income equally.

(4) *Salaries to partners, and remainder in a fractional ratio.* Partners may agree to make a partial division of the net income in the form of salaries in order to give recognition to the difference in the value of their services. The remaining net income may be divided equally or in any other ratio to which the partners agree. One illustration will be sufficient: salaries and an equal division of the remainder.

For purposes of illustration, assume that Lane is allowed a salary of $3,600 a year and Burton is allowed a salary of $4,800. They are permitted to draw such amounts during the year as they desire, and at the end of the year their salaries are to be credited to them. The following entries will be made:

Profit and loss.................................. 8,400.00		
J. L. Lane, capital...........................	3,600.00	
D. K. Burton, capital.......................	4,800.00	
To credit the partners with their agreed salaries.		

Profit and loss.................................. 3,600.00		
J. L. Lane, capital...........................	1,800.00	
D. K. Burton, capital.......................	1,800.00	
To divide the remaining net income equally.		

(5) *Salaries, interest, and remainder in a fractional ratio.* Assume that Lane and Burton agree to make the following income • division:

Salaries:	
Lane...	$3,600.00
Burton..	4,800.00
Interest on capitals—6% on January 1 balances.	
Remainder equally.	

Following are the entries to close the Profit and Loss account:

Profit and loss.................................. 8,400.00		
J. L. Lane, capital...........................	3,600.00	
D. K. Burton, capital.	4,800.00	
To credit the partners with their agreed salaries.		

Profit and loss.................................. 1,800.00		
J. L. Lane, capital...........................	600.00	
D. K. Burton, capital.......................	1,200.00	
To credit the partners with 6% interest on their		
January 1 capitals:		
Lane —6% of $10,000.		
Burton—6% of $20,000.		

Profit and loss.................................. 1,800.00		
J. L. Lane, capital...........................	900.00	
D. K. Burton, capital.......................	900.00	
To divide the remaining net income equally.		

The methods of showing this division of profits in the working papers and in the statement of partners' capitals are illustrated on pages 230 and 231.

LANE AND BURTON
Working Papers
Year Ended December 31, 1954

	Trial Balance	Profit and Loss Statement	J. L. Lane, Capital	D. K. Burton, Capital	Balance Sheet
Cash.................................	17,000				17,000
Accounts receivable.................	15,000				15,000
Inventory, December 31, 1953........	4,000	4,000			
Accounts payable....................	3,000				3,000
J. L. Lane, capital.................	10,000		10,000		
J. L. Lane, drawings................	3,000		3,000		
D. K. Burton, capital...............	19,000			19,000	
D. K. Burton, drawings..............	4,000			4,000	
Sales...............................	90,000	90,000			
Discount on sales...................	200	200			
Purchases...........................	60,000	60,000			
Discount on purchases...............	700	700			
Selling expenses....................	13,000	13,000			
General expenses....................	6,500	6,500			
	122,700 122,700				
Inventory, December 31, 1954........		5,000			5,000
Net income..........................		12,000			
Divided as follows:					
Salaries............................			3,600	4,800	
Interest on capitals................			600	1,200	
Balance equally.....................			900	900	
		95,700 95,700			
Capitals at end of year:					
Lane................................			12,100		12,100
Burton..............................				21,900	21,900
			15,100 15,100	25,900 25,900	37,000 37,000

	J. L. Lane	D. K. Burton	Total
LANE AND BURTON			Exhibit B
Statement of Partners' Capitals			
For the Year Ended December 31, 1954			
Balances, January 1, 1954.......	$10,000.00	$20,000.00	$30,000.00
Add:			
Additional investments........	2,000.00	2,000.00	4,000.00
Net income for the year (Exhibit C):			
Salaries.................	3,600.00	4,800.00	8,400.00
Interest on capitals.........	600.00	1,200.00	1,800.00
Remainder equally.........	900.00	900.00	1,800.00
Total..................	$17,100.00	$28,900.00	$46,000.00
Deduct withdrawals...........	5,000.00	7,000.00	12,000.00
Balances, December 31, 1954....	$12,100.00	$21,900.00	$34,000.00

Interest on partners' capitals and salaries to partners are not expenses but are divisions of profits; therefore, they do not enter into the computation of the net income shown by the profit and loss statement, but are shown in the statement of partners' capitals.

Salaries and/or interest in excess of net income. The salaries and interest in the preceding illustration totaled $10,200. Suppose that the net income had been only $9,000; how should it have been divided?

The entries for the salaries and the interest must be made in accordance with the agreement, thus:

Profit and loss...................................	8,400.00	
J. L. Lane, capital..........................		3,600.00
D. K. Burton, capital.......................		4,800.00
To credit the partners with their agreed salaries.		

Profit and loss...................................	1,800.00	
J. L. Lane, capital..........................		600.00
D. K. Burton, capital.......................		1,200.00
To credit the partners with 6% interest on their capitals.		

After these entries are posted, the Profit and Loss account will have a debit balance of $1,200, because the salary and interest credits to the partners total $10,200, whereas the net income was only $9,000. Because the partners agreed to an equal division of the balance after salaries and interest, the $1,200 debit balance in the Profit and Loss account will be divided equally by the following entry:

J. L. Lane, capital...............................	600.00	
D. K. Burton, capital.............................	600.00	
Profit and loss..............................		1,200.00
To divide the debit balance in the Profit and Loss account equally, as agreed.		

The entries on the preceding page divide the $9,000 net income between the partners as follows:

	Lane	Burton	Total
Credits:			
Salaries.........................	$3,600.00	$4,800.00	$ 8,400.00
Interest on capitals..............	600.00	1,200.00	1,800.00
Total credits..................	$4,200.00	$6,000.00	$10,200.00
Less debit for remainder...........	600.00	600.00	1,200.00
Distribution of net income.........	$3,600.00	$5,400.00	$ 9,000.00

If partners' salaries and interest on their capitals are agreed upon, entries therefor must be made even though the operations of the business result in a loss. For instance, assume that the operations result in a loss of $5,000, and that salaries and interest are to be allowed as in the preceding illustration; the credits to the partners for salaries and interest, and the debits to them for the final balance of the Profit and Loss account, will be as indicated in the following tabulation:

	Lane	Burton	Total
Credits to partners:			
Salaries.........................	$3,600.00	$4,800.00	$ 8,400.00
Interest on capitals..............	600.00	1,200.00	1,800.00
Total credits to partners for salaries and interest..........	$4,200.00	$6,000.00	
Offsetting debit to Profit and Loss			$10,200.00
Net loss...........................			5,000.00
Debit balance in Profit and Loss.....			$15,200.00
Debits to partners to close Profit and Loss...........................	7,600.00	7,600.00	
Net debits to partners—equal to net loss............................	$3,400.00	$1,600.00	

The journal entries to close the Profit and Loss account are as follows:

```
Profit and loss................................ 8,400.00
    J. L. Lane, capital.........................          3,600.00
    D. K. Burton, capital.......................          4,800.00
    To credit the partners with their agreed salaries.

Profit and loss................................ 1,800.00
    J. L. Lane, capital.........................          600.00
    D. K. Burton, capital.......................          1,200.00
    To credit the partners with 6% interest on their
    capitals.

J. L. Lane, capital............................ 7,600.00
D. K. Burton, capital.......................... 7,600.00
    Profit and loss.............................          15,200.00
    To divide the debit balance in the Profit and Loss
    account equally, as agreed.
```

Changes in Personnel

Procedures generally applicable to changes in personnel.
Changes in the personnel of a partnership may be caused by the admission of a partner, or by the retirement or death of a partner.

It is important to realize that, in all such cases, the old partnership is dissolved. Therefore, the first of the following steps should usually be taken, and the second step may also be required.

(1) Close the books, to determine the capital of each partner.

(2) Make entries to adjust the asset valuations in accordance with any agreements with respect thereto. Asset valuations which are proper from the standpoint of a going concern may not be proper valuations to be used when changes occur in partners' interests. For instance, from the standpoint of a going concern, the proper valuation of a fixed asset is cost less depreciation; but if a partner dies or is withdrawing or a new partner is being admitted, there is, in effect, a transfer of assets from one group of people to another group, and equity requires that recognition be given to the market values of the fixed assets at the date of such transfer.

Any gains or losses reflected by such adjustments should be divided among all persons who were partners before the change in personnel, in their profit and loss ratio.

For example, assume that a change is to occur in the personnel of the partnership of A, B, and C, who share profits and losses equally, and that the following adjustments of asset valuations have been agreed upon:

```
Increase in Land account.................... $5,000.00
Increase in Building account................   8,000.00
Increase in Reserve for Bad Debts..........   1,000.00
```

The adjustments are made by the following journal entry:

```
Land..........................................  5,000.00
Building......................................  8,000.00
    Reserve for bad debts.......................            1,000.00
    A, capital..................................            4,000.00
    B, capital..................................            4,000.00
    C, capital..................................            4,000.00
```
To adjust the asset valuations in accordance with the agreement, crediting the partners in their profit and loss ratio.

If numerous adjusting entries are made, the gain or loss shown by each entry may be credited or debited to a Capital Adjustment account, and the final balance of this account will be closed to the partners' capital accounts.

In connection with asset valuations, it may be proper to give recognition to goodwill. The recognition of goodwill is illustrated later in the chapter.

It is also important to realize that, since a change in personnel dissolves the old partnership, the old articles of partnership no longer govern. New articles should be drawn up and signed. It is particularly important to realize that the old agreement regarding the division of profits is no longer in effect, and that, unless a new agreement is reached, the profits and losses of the new partnership will legally be divisible equally. For instance, if *A*, *B*, and *C* shared profits in the ratio of 60, 25, and 15, and *C* withdrew, it would be important for *A* and *B* (if they continued the business as a new partnership) to make a new agreement regarding the sharing of profits. In the absence of such an agreement, *A* might claim that the profits of the new partnership should be divided in the ratio of 60 and 25, whereas *B* could maintain that the profits were legally divisible equally.

Admission of a partner by purchase. A new partner may be admitted to the firm by purchase from an old partner or by purchases from two or more partners.

Purchase from one partner. Assume that *A* has a $10,000 capital interest in the partnership of *A*, *B*, and *C*. *D* desires to enter the partnership; *A*, with the consent of *B* and *C*, sells his interest to *D*. The price is a private matter between *A* and *D* and is not recorded on the firm's books. Regardless of the price paid, the entry on the partnership's books is:

A, capital	10,000.00	
D, capital		10,000.00
To record the transfer of *A*'s capital interest to *D*.		

Purchase from more than one partner. Assume that **three** partners had capital account balances as follows:

E	$10,000.00
F	15,000.00
G	20,000.00

H purchases one-quarter of the capital interest of each partner. *H*'s payment goes to *E*, *F*, and *G* personally, and not into the firm's cash; the prices paid are not recorded on the firm's books; and the entry for *H*'s admission is:

E, capital	2,500.00	
F, capital	3,750.00	
G, capital	5,000.00	
H, capital		11,250.00
Admission of *H* by purchase of one-fourth of capitals of *E*, *F*, and *G*.		

Admission of a partner by investment. A new partner may gain admission to a partnership by making a contribution to the firm's capital. The assets contributed are placed on the firm's books. A goodwill allowance may be made to the old partners in recognition of the profitability of their business. Or, if the new partner is turning over a profitable going business, an allowance may be made to him for his goodwill.

In the illustrations which follow, it is assumed that two partners, A and B, have capitals of $10,000 and $20,000, respectively, and that they share profits equally; C obtains a one-fourth interest in the firm's capital by making an investment. Although he obtains a one-fourth interest in the capital, he does not necessarily obtain a one-fourth interest in the profits; that is a matter for separate agreement.

No goodwill. Assume that C is to invest $10,000 in cash, and that no goodwill is to be allowed to the old partners or the new partner. The entry to record the admission of C is:

Cash	10,000.00	
C, capital		10,000.00
To record C's investment and his admission to the partnership with a one-fourth interest in the capital.		

Goodwill to old partners. A and B are allowed a goodwill of $3,000, making their total capitals $33,000; to obtain a one-fourth interest, C is required to invest $11,000. The required entries are:

Goodwill	3,000.00	
A, capital		1,500.00
B, capital		1,500.00
To record the agreed goodwill valuation, with credits to the old partners in their profit and loss ratio.		
Cash	11,000.00	
C, capital		11,000.00
To record C's investment and his admission to the partnership with a one-fourth interest in the capital.		

Goodwill to new partner. C has been conducting a profitable business, which is to be brought into the partnership. It is agreed that he is to be allowed a goodwill of $2,000, and that the goodwill plus $8,000 of miscellaneous assets is to entitle him to a one-fourth interest in the partnership capital.

Goodwill	2,000.00	
Miscellaneous assets	8,000.00	
C, capital		10,000.00
To record C's investment, including his goodwill, and his admission to the partnership with a one-fourth interest in the capital.		

Retirement of a partner. When a partner is to retire, it may be desirable, as previously indicated, to give recognition to the existence of unrecorded goodwill. There are two theories with respect to the proper procedure for recording partnership goodwill at the time of the retirement of a partner:

Place the entire goodwill on the books, with credits to all of the partners in their profit and loss ratio.

Record only the retiring partner's profit and loss percentage of the goodwill, with a credit to his capital account only.

To illustrate, assume that A and B are in partnership, sharing profits equally. It is agreed that the goodwill of the business is worth $5,000. B wishes to retire. If the entire goodwill is placed on the books, the entry is:

```
Goodwill....................................... 5,000.00
        A, capital..........................              2,500.00
        B, capital..........................              2,500.00
        To record the goodwill, prior to the retirement of B.
```

If only the retiring partner's share of the goodwill is recorded, the entry is:

```
Goodwill....................................... 2,500.00
        B, capital..........................              2,500.00
        To record B's share of the goodwill, prior to his
        retirement.
```

It is more conservative to record only the retiring partner's share of the goodwill.

A partner may retire from a partnership in the following ways:

By sale of his capital interest:
   To an outsider;
   To his partner or partners.

By payment from the partnership assets.

Sale to an outsider. Assume that H, I, and J are partners, sharing profits equally. Each capital account, after all adjustments prior to the retirement of J, has a balance of $10,000. With his partners' consent, J sells his capital interest to K. This is essentially the same situation as that in the first illustration on page 234 under the caption, "Admission of a partner by purchase." Regardless of the price paid by K to J, the entry is:

```
J, capital..................................... 10,000.00
        K, capital.........................              10,000.00
        To record J's sale of his capital interest to K.
```

Sale to other partners.　Assume that J sells his capital interest, in equal amounts, to H and I.　Regardless of the price, the entry is:

J, capital.....................................	10,000.00	
H, capital.................................		5,000.00
I, capital...................................		5,000.00
To record the purchase of J's capital interest by		
H and I.		

Payment from partnership assets.　When a partner retires and is paid from partnership assets, he may receive the amount of his capital balance, or more or less than his capital balance.

If he receives the amount of his capital account balance, the only entry required is a debit to his capital account and a credit to Cash, or credits to the accounts with whatever assets he accepts in settlement.　Referring to the preceding illustration, assume that J is paid $10,000 from partnership cash.　The entry is:

J, capital.....................................	10,000.00	
Cash......................................		10,000.00
To record the retirement of J.		

If a retiring partner receives more than the balance in his capital account, it may be because the accounts have not been adjusted for asset revaluations and/or goodwill, and the remaining partners prefer to treat the excess payment as a bonus.　Or the remaining partners may be willing to pay a bonus in order to get rid of an undesirable partner.　Continuing the illustration, assume that J is paid $12,000 from partnership cash.　As shown by the following entry, the bonus is debited to the remaining partners in their profit and loss ratio:

H, capital.....................................	1,000.00	
I, capital.....................................	1,000.00	
J, capital.....................................	10,000.00	
Cash......................................		12,000.00
J retires, receiving the amount of his capital		
and a $2,000 bonus.		

A retiring partner may receive less than the balance of his capital account because downward revaluations of assets have not been recorded, or because the retiring partner is willing to take a loss in order to get out of an unprofitable, or otherwise undesirable, partnership.　Assume, for instance, that J settles for $9,000.　The entry is:

J, capital.....................................	10,000.00	
Cash......................................		9,000.00
H, capital.................................		500.00
I, capital.................................		500.00
J retires, accepting $1,000 less than his capital		
credit.		

If a retiring partner is not paid in full immediately, the unpaid balance of his capital account should be transferred to an account payable or note payable account, which should be shown as a separate item in the balance sheet, with a clearly descriptive title, such as "Account payable to former partner." The unpaid balance of a retired partner's capital should not be allowed to remain in his capital account, because he is no longer a partner.

Death of a partner. The death of a partner dissolves the partnership; therefore, the surviving partners should take such action as is necessary for the determination of the net income from the date of the last preceding closing of the books to the date of the partner's death. If the articles of partnership provide for adjustments of asset values and a recognition of goodwill in the event of a partner's death, entries therefor should be made.

The immediate payment of the entire capital interest of a deceased partner might deplete the current assets of the business and seriously handicap it in its operations. Partners sometimes provide against such a contingency by carrying insurance on the lives of the partners, the firm being named as beneficiary; the collection of the insurance provides funds with which to make settlement with the deceased partner's estate. The articles of partnership may contain a provision that payments shall be made in installments; in the absence of such a provision, the surviving partners and the estate may reach such an agreement.

Liquidation of the Partnership

A partnership is *terminated* whenever there is any change in the members of the firm; the change in personnel creates a new partnership.

A partnership is *liquidated* when the business is discontinued or the assets are transferred to other parties.

Basis of illustration of liquidation. Assume the following balance sheet of a partnership:

A AND B
Balance Sheet
October 31, 19—

Assets			Liabilities and Net Worth	
Cash		$ 5,000	Accounts payable	$ 9,000
Accounts receivable	$25,000		A, loan	5,000
Less reserve for bad debts	1,000	24,000	A, capital	25,000
Inventory		30,000	B, capital	20,000
		$59,000		$59,000

In addition to investing $25,000, A has loaned the business $5,000.

Disposal of assets. Assume that X desires to acquire the business of A and B, and that the partners sell their inventory and accounts receivable to X for $52,000. A and B retain the $5,000 of cash shown in the foregoing balance sheet and are to pay the $9,000 of accounts payable. The sale of the inventory and receivables will be recorded as follows:

```
X.............................................  52,000.00
Loss on sale of business......................   2,000.00
Reserve for bad debts.........................   1,000.00
    Inventory..................................              30,000.00
    Accounts receivable........................              25,000.00
    To record the sale of the assets to X.

Cash..........................................  52,000.00
    X..........................................              52,000.00
    To record collection for assets sold.
```

Division of the profit or loss. Any profit or loss on the disposal of the assets should *always* be divided between the partners before any cash distribution is made to them, because the amounts of cash to which the partners are entitled cannot be determined until their shares of the profit or loss have been credited or charged to them. The profit or loss should be divided between the partners in their profit and loss ratio. Assuming that A and B share profits equally, the $2,000 loss on the sale of the assets to X will be divided by the following entry:

```
A, capital....................................  1,000.00
B, capital....................................  1,000.00
    Loss on sale of business...................              2,000.00
```

Distribution of cash. After the disposal of the inventory and the receivables, the collection of the cash, and the division of the loss between the partners, the balance sheet of the firm is as follows:

A AND *B*

Balance Sheet

November 3, 19—

Assets		Liabilities and Net Worth	
Cash....................	$57,000.00	Accounts payable..........	$ 9,000.00
		A, loan..................	5,000.00
		A, capital...............	24,000.00
		B, capital...............	19,000.00
	$57,000.00		$57,000.00

The distribution of cash should be made in the following order:

(1) In payment of liabilities to outside creditors:

```
Accounts payable.............................  9,000.00
    Cash.....................................              9,000.00
```

(2) In payment of partner's loan:

A, loan..	5,000.00	
Cash...		5,000.00

(3) In payment of partners' capitals:

A, capital..	24,000.00	
B, capital..	19,000.00	
Cash...		43,000.00

Partner with a debit balance. It sometimes happens that a partner has a debit balance in his capital account as a result of operating losses, drawings, and losses on the disposal of assets during liquidation. Three illustrative cases are now presented.

Case 1. Assume that, after the sale of all assets and the payment of liabilities, the trial balance of a partnership shows the following balances:

Cash...............................	20,000.00	
M, capital..........................	5,000.00	
N, capital..........................		25,000.00
	25,000.00	25,000.00

The entire cash balance should be paid to *N;* this payment would reduce his capital credit to $5,000. He has a right to collect $5,000 from *M.*

Case 2. Assume that, after the sale of all assets and the payment of liabilities to outside creditors, the trial balance of a partnership shows the following balances:

Cash.............................	25,000.00	
O, capital..........................	2,000.00	
O, loan.............................		3,000.00
P, capital.........................		24,000.00
	27,000.00	27,000.00

Enough of the credit in *O's* loan account should be transferred to his capital account to make good the debit balance in his capital account; this is accomplished by the following entry:

O, loan...	2,000.00	
O, capital..................................		2,000.00
To apply the right of offset, by transferring $2,000 of O's loan to his capital.		

The payments to partners will then be made as indicated by the following entries:

O, loan...	1,000.00	
Cash......................................		1,000.00
To record the payment of O's loan.		
P, capital....................................	24,000.00	
Cash......................................		24,000.00
To record the payment of P's capital.		

Case 3. In this case it is assumed that, after the sale of all assets and the payment of all liabilities, a partnership's trial balance appears as follows:

Cash..........................	20,000.00	
R, capital....................	5,000.00	
S, capital....................		15,000.00
T, capital....................		10,000.00
	25,000.00	25,000.00

Profits and losses were divided as follows: *R*, 20%; *S*, 40%; *T*, 40%.

R should pay $5,000 cash into the partnership to make good the debit balance in his capital account; if he does so, there will be $25,000 cash on hand, which will be sufficient to pay *S* and *T* in full.

But suppose that it is desired to distribute the $20,000 of cash on hand to *S* and *T* before it is known whether or not *R* will pay in the $5,000. In determining how to divide the cash between *S* and *T*, we should remember that, if *R* fails to pay in the $5,000, this loss will have to be borne by *S* and *T* in their profit and loss ratio. In the past, *S* and *T* each had 40% of the profits or losses; that is to say, their shares of profits or losses were equal. Therefore, if *R* should fail to pay in the $5,000, *S* and *T* would share the loss equally. Accordingly, they should be paid *down to* $2,500 each, thus leaving each of these partners with a capital balance sufficient to absorb his share of the loss if *R* fails to pay in the $5,000. The entry to record the payment is:

S, capital...................................	12,500.00	
T, capital...................................	7,500.00	
Cash..................................		20,000.00
To record the distribution of cash to *S* and *T*.		

The resulting trial balance will be:

R, capital....................	5,000.00	
S, capital....................		2,500.00
T, capital....................		2,500.00
	5,000.00	5,000.00

CHAPTER 17

Corporations

Nature of the corporation. Probably the most famous definition of the corporation is the one given in 1819 by Chief Justice Marshall in the Dartmouth College case decision, in which he described a corporation as "an artificial being, invisible, intangible, and existing only in contemplation of law."

This definition emphasizes the basic characteristic of the corporation—its separate legal entity. It is not a group of separate persons, as is the case with a partnership; it is itself a legal "person." It can make contracts in its own name; it can sue and be sued, even by its own stockholders; and it can own real estate. Within the limits of its charter, it can perform any business act which could be performed by a natural person.

Because a corporation is a legal entity, a stockholder usually is not liable for its debts unless his shares have a par value and were issued at a discount, and even under such circumstances he is liable only for the amount of the discount. Stockholders of certain classes of corporations, such as banks organized under the laws of some of the states, may have a personal liability in an amount not in excess of the par value of their shares. Although relief from personal liability is an advantage to the stockholders, it sometimes operates to the disadvantage of the corporation by limiting its borrowing power: banks frequently refuse to loan money to a corporation unless stockholders of means endorse the notes.

The separate legal entity of a corporation gives it a continuity of life. A partnership is dissolved by the death, insanity, insolvency, or withdrawal of a partner; therefore, the continued life of a partnership is constantly in jeopardy. A corporation can be dissolved only by agreement of the stockholders, by forfeiture of the charter by the state, by judicial decree, or by the expiration of the period stated in the charter. A charter may give a corporation an unlimited life; if the life is limited by the charter, a renewal usually can be obtained.

Continuity of corporate life notwithstanding changes in ownership is effected by the issuance of transferable shares. This transferability of interest gives a stockholder several advantages not enjoyed by a partner. (1) A partner cannot withdraw from a partnership or sell his interest without the consent of the other partners; if he undertakes to do so without their consent, he renders himself liable to a suit for damages. Unless there is an agreement among the stockholders to the contrary, a stockholder can sell his stock to any willing purchaser whenever he desires to do so; the consent of the other stockholders is not required. (2) If a partner dies, his heirs have a right to be paid the amount of his capital interest, but they have no right to enter the business as partners without the consent of the other partners. If a stockholder dies, his stock passes to his heirs, who thus acquire an interest in the business. (3) A stockholder can pledge his stock as collateral to a loan; a partner cannot easily pledge his partnership interest. Therefore, a stockholder is in a better position than is a partner to borrow needed funds.

These characteristics of the corporation make it an attractive form of business organization even for small enterprises. In large businesses, in which the capital requirements make it necessary to obtain funds from many investors, the adoption of the corporate form is virtually imperative. A partnership with hundreds of partners, subject to termination upon the death of any one of them, would be in an intolerable chaos of repeated dissolution and reorganization; the orderly conduct of business would be impossible, and capital could not be attracted.

On the other hand, the corporation has certain disadvantages, the chief of which are mentioned below.

Corporations are required to pay income taxes and the stockholders are required to pay income taxes on the dividends which they receive. This "double taxation" has induced a number of relatively small corporations to reorganize as partnerships.

The state requires the payment of a fee at the time the corporation is organized, and imposes an annual franchise tax for the privilege of continuing operations. Numerous reports, not required of partnerships, must be furnished to the state of incorporation and to other states where business is transacted.

A corporation has a right to conduct only the kind of business authorized in its charter; to engage in other lines of business, it must obtain an amendment of its charter.

Each state regards corporations organized in other states as *foreign* corporations. If a corporation desires to do business in states other than the one from which it obtained its charter, it may be required to obtain licenses from those states and pay a license fee to each of them. Failure to obtain such licenses may result in losses of far greater amount than the fees. For instance, a state may refuse unlicensed foreign corporations the privilege of bringing actions in its courts, and heavy losses may be incurred because of the inability to enforce claims by actions at law.

Restrictions of various kinds are placed upon corporations by the states. In some states, a corporation cannot own the stock of another corporation; in some states, it cannot own its own stock; in some states, its liabilities cannot exceed a certain percentage of its capital stock. Also, corporations frequently are prohibited from owning more real estate than they require for business uses.

Organization of a corporation. If a corporation is to be organized, an attorney should be consulted, because the laws of the various states differ regarding the rights and duties of corporations organized under their laws and the procedure for organizing corporations. Since the procedure differs in the various states, and since the organization of corporations is the work of an attorney rather than that of an accountant, the subject will not be discussed in detail here.

In general, and subject to the exceptions incident to the diversity of laws, the organization of a corporation involves steps somewhat as follows:

(1) An application, signed by a required number of incorporators, is filed with a designated state officer. This application states, among other things:
   (a) The name of the corporation.
   (b) The nature of the business which it is desired to conduct.
   (c) The amount of the authorized capital stock, and the number of shares into which it is to be divided.
   (d) The names and the addresses of the original subscribers to the stock.
   (e) The assets paid into the corporation by these subscribers.
(2) If the application is approved, a charter (which is often the approved application itself) is received from the state officer with whom the application was originally filed. This charter evidences the fact that the corporation has been organized and is authorized to conduct business.
(3) A meeting of the incorporators (or stockholders) is held for the purpose (among other things) of electing directors.
(4) A meeting of the directors is held, and officers are elected.
(5) Capital stock certificates are issued.

Organization costs. The organization of a corporation involves expenditures for attorneys' fees, the fee paid to the state at the time of incorporation, and other costs. Without organization expenditures, a corporation could not come into being and conduct operations; therefore, organization expenditures are the cost of an intangible asset which presumably will benefit the company during the entire period of its existence. This is the position taken by the Committee on Accounting Procedure of the American Institute of Accountants. In its bulletin on intangible assets, the committee mentions organization costs as one of the assets "as to which there is, at the time of acquisition, no indication of limited life," and which, therefore, need not be written off unless "it becomes reasonably evident that their term of existence has become limited." The committee further takes the position that, if such assets are written off, the write-off should be accomplished by periodical charges to income rather than by a charge to Earned Surplus. So long as organization expense remains on the books, it should be shown in the balance sheet as an asset, preferably as a separate item below the fixed assets.

Corporate management. If a business is organized as a corporation, the stockholders are its owners, but they have no authority to transact its business. The stockholders elect directors, to whom the general management of the business is committed. In most states, a person cannot serve as a director of a corporation unless he is one of its stockholders.

Although the directors are charged with responsibility for the general management of the business, their duties are to a considerable extent supervisory, since most of the work of management is performed by officers elected by them. The officers usually include a president, a vice-president, a secretary, and a treasurer. Sometimes one individual holds more than one office; for instance, one person may be secretary and treasurer. On the other hand, there may be several vice-presidents, an assistant secretary, and an assistant treasurer. The president usually is the ranking officer, but in some corporations there is an officer called the "chairman of the board," whose rank is superior to that of the president. The secretary is the official custodian of the corporate records and seal. The treasurer is the chief financial officer.

Although the officers have general control over the various functions of the business, other employees are charged with the responsibility of performing much of the detailed work. The kinds and number of employees differ in every business, and it is impossible, therefore, to draw up a standard personnel chart; the chart on page 246 is merely one illustration of the flow of authority.

Elements of net worth. Corporate accounts need not differ from the accounts of other types of business organization except in the manner of reflecting the elements of net worth. In accounting for the elements of net worth of a corporation, the emphasis is placed on *source*. How much of the net worth was produced by

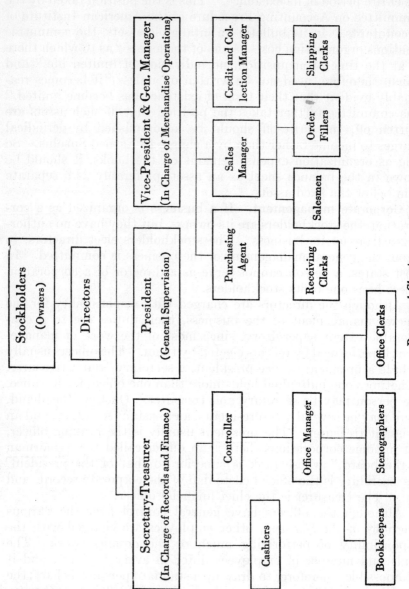

Personnel Chart

stockholders' capital contributions? How much consists of retained earnings? How much, if any, was produced in other ways?

Proper accounting for the elements of net worth according to their source requires a knowledge of the nature of capital stock and of the various classes of surplus. These matters are discussed in this and the following chapters.

Capital stock. The two principal classes of capital stock are common and preferred. Capital stock may have a par value or be without par value.

Recording the Issuance of Par Value Stock

Although $100 is a customary par value, any par may be authorized by the charter. Thus, a corporation with an authorized capital of $100,000 might have 100 authorized shares of $1,000 par value, or 100,000 authorized shares of $1 par value, or its shares might have any other desired par.

In the illustrations under this caption, it is assumed that a corporation's charter authorizes it to issue 1,000 shares of $100 par value common stock, and no preferred shares. The number of shares authorized may be shown by a memorandum in the Capital Stock account, thus:

Capital Stock

(Authorized issue, 1,000	shares of $100 par value.)

Group A illustrations—Immediate collection of subscriptions. In the four following illustrations it is assumed that the stock subscriptions are received and collected on the same day, and that the stock is immediately issued.

First illustration—All stock issued at par. In this illustration it is assumed that all of the authorized stock is subscribed for and issued at par. The entry for the issuance is:

```
Cash................................... 100,000.00
     Capital stock...........................        100,000.00
     Issuance of 1,000 authorized shares at their
     par value of $100.
```

When this entry is posted, the Capital Stock account appears as follows:

Capital Stock

(Authorized issue, 1,000	shares of $100 par value.)	
	Date	100,000.00

Second illustration—Part of stock issued at par.　In this illustration it is again assumed that subscriptions are taken at par, but that only half of the stock is subscribed, paid for, and issued. The entry is:

Cash..	50,000.00	
Capital stock.............................		50,000.00
Issuance of 500 of the authorized shares at their par value of $100.		

Third illustration—All stock issued at a premium.　In this illustration it is assumed that the stock is issued at $110 per share. The entry is:

Cash......................................	110,000.00	
Capital stock.............................		100,000.00
Premium on stock.........................		10,000.00
Issuance of 1,000 authorized shares at a premium of $10 per share.		

Stock may be issued at a premium at the time of the organization of the corporation, as illustrated above.　Stock premiums are probably more common, however, when additional shares are issued at a subsequent date.　For instance, assume that a company with 1,000 outstanding shares of capital stock with a total par value of $100,000 has been successful in its operations and has accumulated, over several years, an earned surplus of $50,000, thus giving the stock a book value of $150 per share.　It might not be fair to the old stockholders to allow new stockholders to acquire stock at par.　Moreover, because of the book value of the outstanding stock and the company's earnings record and prospects, its stock might be so attractive that investors would willingly pay a premium to obtain it.

Fourth illustration—All stock issued at a discount.　We shall now assume that all of the stock is issued at $90 per share.　The entry is:

Cash......................................	90,000.00	
Discount on stock.........................	10,000.00	
Capital stock.............................		100,000.00
Issuance of 1,000 authorized shares at a discount of $10 per share.		

Stock is rarely issued at a discount.　In many states the issuance of stock at a discount is illegal.　In states where it is legal, a discount may be allowed as an inducement to prospective investors. However, such an inducement is of doubtful value because, if stock is issued at a discount and the company becomes unable to pay its debts, the holders of such stock at the time of the corporation's insolvency (whether they be the original subscribers or subsequent transferees) may be held personally liable to the corporation's creditors for amounts equal to the original discount on the shares which they hold.

Group B illustrations—Stock issued before collection of subscriptions. We shall now assume that time elapses between the date when the stock subscriptions are received and the date when the subscriptions are collected. When the subscriptions are received, Subscriptions Receivable should be debited. What account should be credited? In general, it may be said that a person legally becomes a stockholder as soon as a valid stock subscription by him is accepted by the corporation. The law makes a distinction between a subscription to stock and a contract for the purchase of stock; we are here dealing only with stock subscriptions.

If a subscriber is immediately a stockholder, and if (as frequently happens) stock certificates are issued to subscribers before their subscriptions are fully collected, an immediate credit to the Capital Stock account appears to be justified.

In this chapter we shall show the entries to be made if stock certificates are issued when subscriptions are received although not yet collected. In the next chapter we shall show the entries to be made if the issuance of certificates is postponed until the subscriptions are collected.

First illustration—All stock subscribed for at par. If all of the authorized stock is subscribed for at par, and the subscriptions are subsequently collected, the entries are:

At date of subscription:

```
Subscriptions receivable.....................  100,000.00
     Capital stock...........................               100,000.00
     Subscriptions for 1,000 authorized shares at
     their par value of $100.
```

At date of collection of subscriptions:

```
Cash.......................................  100,000.00
     Subscriptions receivable.................               100,000.00
     Collection of subscriptions in full.
```

Second illustration—Subscriptions at a premium. This illustration is the same as the preceding one, except that it is now assumed that the subscriptions were at a premium.

At date of subscription:

```
Subscriptions receivable.....................  110,000.00
     Capital stock...........................               100,000.00
     Premium on stock........................                10,000.00
     Subscriptions for 1,000 authorized shares at
     $110 per share.
```

At date of collection of subscriptions:

```
Cash.......................................  110,000.00
    Subscriptions receivable..................            110,000.00
    Collection of subscriptions in full.
```

It should be observed that the premium is recorded at the date of the subscriptions, rather than at the date of collection. This is the correct procedure because the amount receivable is the par of the stock plus the premium.

Uncollected subscriptions in the balance sheet. If it is expected that the subscriptions will be collected in the near future, they may be shown in the balance sheet under the Current Asset caption, but they should be clearly shown as subscriptions to capital stock. The balance sheet will then appear as follows:

Balance Sheet

Current assets:		Net worth:	
Cash................	$ 60,000.00	Capital stock—$100 par value. Authorized, and issued, 1,000 shares..............	$100,000.00
Subscriptions receivable.	40,000.00		
	$100,000.00		$100,000.00

If there is no immediate intention to call on the subscribers for the uncollected balances of their subscriptions, the subscriptions receivable may still be shown on the asset side of the balance sheet, but under the caption of Other Assets.

Premium and discount in the balance sheet. The balances of Premium on Stock and Discount on Stock accounts should be shown in the Net Worth section of the balance sheet in the manner illustrated below:

```
Net worth:
    Capital stock—$100 par value; authorized and issued,
        1,000 shares.......................................  $100,000.00
    Premium on stock..................................      10,000.00
    Earned surplus....................................      25,000.00
```

or thus:

```
Net worth:
    Capital stock—$100 par value; authorized and issued,
        1,000 shares.......................................  $100,000.00
    Discount on stock.................................      10,000.00*
    Earned surplus....................................      25,000.00
        * Deduction.
```

If some shares are issued at a discount while other shares are issued at a premium, the amount of discount should be shown in a Discount on Stock account and the amount of premium should be shown in a Premium on Stock account.   They should not be offset, because the stockholder who acquired his stock at a discount is not relieved of his discount liability merely because some other stockholder acquired his stock at a premium.

Disposition of stock premium and discount accounts.   Stock premiums have customarily been carried indefinitely in the Premium on Stock account, and this procedure is correct.   The availability of such a credit for dividends depends on the laws of the state of incorporation.

In the past, many accountants advocated writing off stock discount as rapidly as possible, by charges to surplus.   This procedure was probably adopted because, although stock discount was customarily shown on the asset side of the balance sheet, it was realized that it had no valid asset status.   When stock discount was recognized for what it is—not an asset, but an item to be deducted in the net worth section of the balance sheet to show the net amount of the funds paid in by the investors—it became apparent that there was no particular reason for writing it off.   In fact, it appears definitely improper to write off stock discount. For one reason, the write-off beclouds the record of the capital investment and creates a confusion between the original investment and the accumulated earnings.   For another reason, writing off the discount against surplus does not relieve the stockholders of their discount liability, but merely conceals it.

Recording the Issuance of No-Par Stock

Prior to 1912, the capital stocks of all corporations in this country had a par value.   In that year, the first American law permitting the issuance of stock without par value was enacted in New York.   Other states have since passed similar laws, but, unfortunately, they are not uniform.

Advantages and disadvantages of no-par stock.   The par value of a share of stock is usually of little significance compared to the book value and the market value.   Printing a par value on a certificate has made it easy for promoters to extract money from the uninformed and the unsuspecting.   There is an inevitable attraction about a $100 share of stock offered for $50, and many people find it impossible to resist such an offer.   The omission of a par value may cause some prospective buyers to make inquiries regarding the issuing company's net assets and earnings.

No par value stock has another great advantage: it avoids the discount liability.   If a share of stock with a par value of $100 is issued for $90, the purchaser incurs a discount liability of $10, and may be required to furnish that amount of cash for the payment of the corporation's debts. But if a no par value share is sold for $90, there is no discount liability. Discount is the difference between a par value and a lower issuing price; if there is no par value, there can be no discount and, therefore, no discount liability.

No-par stock has some disadvantages. Transfer fees, organization fees, stock taxes, fees for operation in foreign states, and other taxes may be based on an arbitrary valuation of the stock very much in excess of its fair value. Laws not uncommonly provide that no-par shares shall, for tax purposes, be assumed to have a par of $100; such a provision might entail a very inequitable expense if the shares were issued at, say, $5.

Accounting procedures. The methods described above for recording issuances of par value stock can be used for recording issuances of no-par stock. But, in the absence of a par, this question arises: At what amount should the shares be recorded in the capital stock accounts? The answer depends on the law of the state of incorporation and on any resolution which the directors, with the permission of the law, may have passed.

The laws of some states require that the entire amount received for no-par stock shall (like the par of par value shares) be regarded as stated, or legal, capital, not to be impaired by distributions to stockholders; if a corporation is organized in a state with such a law, the entire amount received for its no-par stock should be credited to a capital stock account.

Some states allow corporations to credit a surplus account with a portion of the proceeds of the issuance of no-par stock, and some states even allow corporations to use such surplus for dividends. If a corporation is organized in a state which permits the crediting of a surplus account with a portion of the proceeds of the issuance of no-par shares, and if the directors pass a resolution stating the amount which is to be credited to the capital stock account, the accountant should be governed by the resolution; he should credit the capital stock account with the amount stated by the resolution, and should credit a paid-in surplus account with any excess of the proceeds over the stated capital amount. If the law permits such a division of the proceeds but the directors do not pass a resolution establishing a stated value for the stock, the entire proceeds of the stock issuance should be credited to the capital stock account.

Basis of illustrations. In all of the following illustrations of entries recording the issuance of no-par stock, it is assumed that the corporation is authorized to issue 1,000 shares of no par value. The number of shares authorized is recorded by a memorandum in the capital stock account, in the manner previously illustrated.

Group A illustrations—Immediate collection of subscriptions.
In the three following illustrations it is assumed that the subscriptions were collected on the day they were received and that the shares were immediately issued.

First illustration. In this illustration it is assumed that the corporation was organized in a state which requires that the entire proceeds of the issuance of shares be regarded as stated capital, and that all of the authorized shares were issued at $60 per share. The entry to record the issuance is:

```
Cash........................................ 60,000.00
    Capital stock...........................          60,000.00
    Issuance of 1,000 authorized shares at $60 per
    share.
```

After this entry is posted, the Capital Stock account appears as follows:

Capital Stock		
(Authorized issue, 1,000	shares of no par value.)	
	Date 1,000 shares issued	60,000.00

Second illustration. It is now assumed that the laws of the state of incorporation permitted the company to credit a portion of the proceeds of the issuance of no-par stock to a surplus account, but that the directors did not pass any resolution making an apportionment between capital stock and surplus. It is also assumed that all of the shares were issued for $60,000. The entry to record the issuance would be the same as the one shown in the immediately preceding illustration.

Third illustration. It is again assumed that all of the authorized stock was issued for $60,000, that the laws of the state of incorporation permitted the company to credit a surplus account with a portion of the proceeds, and that the directors established a $50 stated value for the shares. The entry to record the issuance is:

```
Cash........................................ 60,000.00
    Capital stock...........................          50,000.00
    Paid-in surplus.........................          10,000.00
    Issuance of 1,000 shares at $60 per share.
    Stated value of $50 per share established by the
    directors.
```

Paid-in surplus in the balance sheet. If only a portion of the proceeds of no-par stock is credited to a capital stock account, and the remainder is credited to a paid-in surplus account, the facts may be shown in the balance sheet in the manner illustrated on the following page.

Net worth:
Capital stock—No par value; authorized and
issued, 1,000 shares...................... $50,000.00
Paid-in surplus........................... 10,000.00 $60,000.00
Earned surplus.. 15,000.00

Or as follows:

Net worth:
Capital stock—no par value; authorized and
issued, 1,000 shares............................... $50,000.00
Surplus:
Paid-in............................... $10,000.00
Earned............................... 15,000.00 25,000.00

Group B illustrations—Stock issued before collection of subscriptions. As stated in connection with par value stock, certificates may be issued to subscribers before the subscriptions are collected in full, and an immediate credit to Capital Stock appears to be justified in such cases.

First illustration. If all of the authorized shares are subscribed for at $60 per share, the certificates are issued, the subscriptions are subsequently collected, and the law requires that the entire proceeds be regarded as stated capital, the entries are:

At the date of subscription:

Subscriptions receivable....................... 60,000.00
    Capital stock............................   60,000.00
Subscriptions for 1,000 authorized shares at $60
per share.

At the date of collection of subscriptions:

Cash... 60,000.00
    Subscriptions receivable...................   60,000.00
Collection of subscriptions in full.

Second illustration. This illustration is the same as the preceding one except that it is now assumed that the law permits the company to credit a surplus account with part of the proceeds of issuance, and that the directors establish a stated value of $50 per share. The entries are:

Subscriptions receivable....................... 60,000.00
    Capital stock............................   50,000.00
    Paid-in surplus..........................   10,000.00
Subscriptions, at $60 per share, for 1,000 authorized shares; stated value established by directors, $50 per share.

Cash... 60,000.00
    Subscriptions receivable...................   60,000.00
Collection of subscriptions in full.

Stock issued for property. When par value stock is issued for property other than cash, the question arises whether the property is really worth the par of the stock issued. If it is not worth the par of the stock, a Discount on Stock account should be debited with the excess of the par of the stock over the value of the property. Such a debit to Discount on Stock is not likely to be made, however, because directors are disposed to value the property at the par of the stock, and in so doing they are acting within their legal powers, for the law allows directors great latitude in exercising their discretion regarding the valuation of property acquired by issuance of shares of stock.

One of the advantages of no-par stock is that it reduces the incentive to overvalue assets, because it is not necessary to inflate the valuation of property received for stock in order to balance the par value of the stock. If stock without par value is issued, the property can be recorded at its fair value, and a capital stock account can be credited with the same amount. However, the use of no-par stock has not done away entirely with the overvaluation of assets issued for stock.

CHAPTER 18

Corporations (Continued)

Stock not issued until collection of subscriptions. Stock certificates may not be issued when the subscriptions are received. The subscriber may not acquire the status of stockholder until his subscription is paid in full; or, even though he acquires the legal status of stockholder when his subscription is received, the corporation may adopt the policy of deferring the issuance of certificates until subscriptions are collected.

If certificates are not issued until subscriptions are collected in full, it is advisable to keep two accounts, as follows:

Capital Stock Subscribed:
> When subscriptions are received, this account is credited with the par or stated value of the shares subscribed for.
> When stock certificates are issued, this account is debited and Capital Stock Issued is credited.
> The credit balance in this account shows the par or stated value of the shares subscribed for but not issued.

Capital Stock Issued:
> The number of shares authorized is shown by a memorandum entry in this account. When certificates are issued, this account is credited with the par or stated value of the shares represented by the certificates.

Illustrations—Par value stock. In the two following illustrations it is assumed that the corporation has an authorized issue of 1,000 shares of stock of $100 par, and that all of these shares are subscribed for at par. Shares of stock are not issued to a subscriber until he has paid his subscription in full.

First illustration—All subscriptions collected in full. The authorized issue is shown by a memorandum entry, as follows:

Capital Stock Issued
(Authorized issue, 1,000 shares of $100 par value.)

The subscriptions are recorded by the following entry:

Subscriptions receivable......................	100,000.00	
Capital stock subscribed.................		100,000.00
Subscriptions for 1,000 authorized shares at par		

When the subscriptions are collected, the following entries are made:

```
Cash................................... 100,000.00
    Subscriptions receivable.................        100,000.00
    Collection of subscriptions in full.

Capital stock subscribed.................... 100,000.00
    Capital stock issued....................        100,000.00
    Issuance of 1,000 shares after collection of
    subscriptions in full.
```

Second illustration—Some subscriptions fully, others partially, collected. The authorized issue should be recorded by a memorandum entry in the Capital Stock Issued account, as in the preceding illustration, and the same entry as in the preceding illustration should be made for the subscriptions:

```
Subscriptions receivable..................... 100,000.00
    Capital stock subscribed.................        100,000.00
    Subscriptions for 1,000 authorized shares at
    par.
```

It is now assumed that, at a subsequent date, half of the subscriptions are collected in full. The following entries are made:

```
Cash...................................... 50,000.00
    Subscriptions receivable...................        50,000.00
    Collection in full of subscriptions for 500 shares.

Capital stock subscribed..................... 50,000.00
    Capital stock issued......................        50,000.00
    Issuance of 500 shares for which subscriptions
    have been fully collected.
```

It is further assumed that $10,000 is collected on the other subscriptions. An entry is made to record the collection, but the certificates are not issued.

```
Cash...................................... 10,000.00
    Subscriptions receivable...................        10,000.00
    Collection on subscriptions for 500 shares.
```

Illustrations—No-par stock. If certificates for no-par stock are not issued until the subscriptions are collected in full, the Capital Stock Subscribed and Capital Stock Issued accounts may be used in the same manner as just described in connection with par value stock. It is assumed, in the two following illustrations, that the company has an authorized issue of 1,000 shares of no par value.

First illustration—All subscriptions collected in full. It is assumed that all of the authorized shares are subscribed for at $60 per share, and that they are given a stated value of $50. The authorized issue is shown by a memorandum in the Capital Stock

Issued account. The entries for the subscriptions, the collection of the subscriptions, and the issuance of the certificates are shown below:

Subscriptions receivable.........................	60,000.00	
Capital stock subscribed...................		50,000.00
Paid-in surplus............................		10,000.00
Subscriptions for 1,000 authorized shares at $60.		
Stated value, $50.		
Cash...	60,000.00	
Subscriptions receivable....................		60,000.00
Collection of subscriptions in full.		
Capital stock subscribed........................	50,000.00	
Capital stock issued.......................		50,000.00
Issuance of fully paid shares.		

Second illustration—Some subscriptions fully, others partially, collected. Assume that subscriptions were received as in the immediately preceding illustration. Also assume that, at a later date, subscriptions for half of the shares were collected in full and the certificates were issued.

Subscriptions receivable.........................	60,000.00	
Capital stock subscribed...................		50,000.00
Paid-in surplus............................		10,000.00
Subscriptions for 1,000 shares at $60. Stated		
value, $50.		
Cash...	30,000.00	
Subscriptions receivable....................		30,000.00
Full collection of half of the subscriptions.		
Capital stock subscribed........................	25,000.00	
Capital stock issued.......................		25,000.00
Issuance of 500 shares for which subscriptions		
have been fully collected.		

Assume further that $10,000 is collected on the remaining subscriptions. The following entry is made to record the collection, but the certificates were not issued.

Cash...	10,000.00	
Subscriptions receivable....................		10,000.00
Collection of portion of subscription price on		
500 shares.		

Records Peculiar to Corporations

Subscribers' ledger. If stock subscriptions are not immediately collected, the Subscriptions Receivable account in the general ledger should be supported by a subsidiary ledger containing an account with each subscriber. The subscriber's account is debited with the amount of his subscription, and is credited with the amounts collected from him.

Stock certificate and stub. Blank stock certificates are bound in books with stubs, like check books. The certificate illustrated on page 3 (Chapter 1) appears again on page 260, still attached to its stub. The certificate has been signed by the secretary and the president of the corporation, and is ready to be detached, stamped with the corporation's seal, and given to Dobson. The stub, which will remain in the certificate book, shows the essential facts about the certificate.

The important facts shown by the certificate and the stub are:

	Shown by Certificate	Shown by Stub
Certificate No.................	1	1
Number of shares...............	10	10
Authorized capital..............	$5,000.00	
Number of authorized shares.....	50	
Par value per share.............	$100.00	
Issued to..................	Henry Dobson	Henry Dobson
Transferred from......		Original
Date of issuance of certificate.....	July 20, 19—	July 20, 19—

The word "Original" appearing on the "Transferred from" line means that Dobson obtained the certificate by making an investment in the corporation, and not by purchase from another stockholder.

The use of the blank spaces in the stub is explained later.

Stockholders' ledger. A stockholders' ledger should be kept by corporations with numerous stockholders, and may be kept by any corporation. It contains an account with each stockholder, showing the number of shares issued in his name.

The issuance of the certificate to Henry Dobson is recorded in his account in the stockholders' ledger in the manner illustrated below:

Name   Henry Dobson

Address   173 Hickory Street, Chicago 40, Illinois

CERTIFICATES CANCELLED				CERTIFICATES ISSUED				Balance
Date	Ref.	Certificate Number	Number of Shares	Date	Ref.	Certificate Number	Number of Shares	
				19-┤ July 20		1	10	10

Transfer of shares. Assume that Henry Dobson wishes to sell two of his shares to Robert Dawson. Dobson will fill in the assignment form which is printed on the back of the certificate, as shown on page 261.

Certificate No. 1   10   Shares

CAPITAL STOCK $5,000.00
50 Shares of $100.00 Par Value

THIS CERTIFIES That   Henry Dobson   is the

owner of   Ten   Shares of the Capital Stock of

COMMUNITY TELEVISION

transferable only on the books of the Corporation by the holder hereof in person or by attorney upon the surrender of this Certificate properly endorsed.

IN WITNESS WHEREOF, the said Corporation has caused this Certificate to be signed by its duly authorized officers, and to be sealed with the seal of the Corporation at Chicago, Illinois this 20th day of July, 19 --

J. B. Hudson
Secretary

J. C. White
President

Certificate No. 1

For 10 Shares

Issued to

Henry Dobson

Transferred from

Original

Date July 20, 19 --

Original Certificate No.	Number of Original Shares	Number of Shares Transferred

Stock Certificate with Stub

For Value Received,_____I_____hereby sell,

transfer and assign to_____Robert Dawson_____

-----------------------------------Two-----------------------------------

_____

shares of stock within mentioned and hereby authorize

J. B. Hudson
_____

to make the necessary transfer on the books of the Corporation.

WITNESS__my__hand and seal this_____3rd_____day of

_____August_____, 19__--__

Witnessed by: (Seal)

Assignment Form on Back of Certificate

When the stock certificate is presented to the corporation for transfer of the stock, the certificate is canceled and attached to the stub from which it was originally taken. The open stubs (stubs to which no unissued or canceled certificates are attached) will indicate the certificates still outstanding.

In accordance with the terms of Dobson's assignment, two new certificates will be issued: one certificate to Robert Dawson for the two shares which Dobson sold to him, and another certificate to Dobson for the eight shares which he retained. At the right is the stub of the new certificate issued to Dawson; the stub of the certificate for eight shares issued to Dobson would be similarly filled in.

Certificate No._____5_____

For_____2_____Shares

Issued to

Robert Dawson

Transferred from

Henry Dobson

Date___August 3,___19__--__

Original Certificate No.	Number of Original Shares	Number of Shares Transferred
1	10	2

A record of the transfer is made in the transfer journal, in the manner illustrated on page 262.

Stock Transfer Journal

Page 1

Date	From				To		
	Name	Certificate Number	Number of Shares		Name	Certificate Number	Number of Shares
19-- Aug. 3	Henry Dobson	1	10		Robert Dawson	5	2
					Henry Dobson	6	8

After the entry in the transfer journal is posted, the stock-holders' ledger accounts affected appear as shown below.

Name				Robert Dawson				
Address				1369 Fortunata Street, Chicago 61, Illinois				

Certificates Cancelled				Certificates Issued				
Date	Ref.	Certificate Number	Number of Shares	Date	Ref.	Certificate Number	Number of Shares	Balance
				19-- Aug. 3	TJ 1	5	2	2

Name				Henry Dobson				
Address				173 Hickory Street, Chicago 40, Illinois				

Certificates Cancelled				Certificates Issued				
Date	Ref.	Certificate Number	Number of Shares	Date	Ref.	Certificate Number	Number of Shares	Balance
19-- Aug. 3	TJ 1	1	10	19-- July 20 Aug. 3	TJ 1	1 6	10 8	10 - 8

Transfer agent and registrar. Large corporations, particularly those whose stock is listed on a stock exchange, may (either by requirement of the stock exchange or voluntarily) engage a transfer agent and a registrar to perform the duties incident to the issuance and transfer of shares and the keeping of records showing the names and addresses of stockholders and the number of shares owned by each stockholder. A bank or trust company usually is engaged to perform the duties of transfer agent, and another bank or trust company is engaged to perform the duties of registrar.

The employment of a transfer agent and a registrar serves as a safeguard to the stockholders. When certificates are to be transferred, they are delivered to the transfer agent, who cancels the old certificates, signs the new certificates, and passes them to the registrar, who also signs them. Records of the stockholders are kept by the transfer agent. The registrar's chief function is to act as a control against any possible overissuance of stock, and for this purpose the registrar maintains a record showing the aggregate number of shares outstanding.

Minute book. A record of all the actions taken by the stockholders and directors at their meetings is kept by the secretary of the company in a minute book. This book does not contain debit and credit entries; it contains a record of events written in narrative form, or in the form of resolutions.

The minute book contains information which may be required by the company's accountant for purposes of making entries in the books, and by the public accountants when they audit the company's accounts. For instance, reference to the minutes may be necessary to validate the stated value of no-par stock, the amounts of officers' salaries, the valuations assigned to non-cash assets acquired for stock, and liabilities for dividends.

The minute book usually contains a copy of the company's by-laws. The rights and duties of the stockholders, directors, and officers are in general governed by the state corporation law; in many particulars, however, they are stipulated by the corporation's own by-laws. The by-laws contain other stipulations with respect to the management of the corporation, such as the dates on which the regular meetings of the stockholders and directors shall be held, the formalities to be complied with in calling special meetings, and any transactions (such as the issuance of new stock with special privileges) that require the approval of the stockholders. The by-laws are usually passed by the stockholders, but in some states they may be passed or amended by the board of directors.

Changing from Partnership to Corporation or Vice Versa

Basis of illustration. To illustrate the entries to be made to effect a change from partnership organization to corporate organization, let us assume that *A* and *B* are partners sharing profits and losses equally, and that their balance sheet appears as follows:

A AND *B*

Balance Sheet

December 31, 19—

Assets			Liabilities and Net Worth		
Cash		$ 5,000	Accounts payable		$ 9,000
Accounts receivable	$25,000		Net worth:		
Less reserve for bad			*A*, capital	$30,000	
debts	1,000	24,000	*B*, capital	20,000	50,000
Merchandise inventory		30,000			
		$59,000			$59,000

It is decided to incorporate. The corporation, to be known as The *A B* Company, is to obtain a charter authorizing the issuance of $100,000 of capital stock, consisting of 1,000 shares of $100 par value.

A and *B* expect to sell a portion of this stock later to other parties; in anticipation thereof, they make the following adjustments in the valuation of their assets:

The goodwill of the business is to be valued at $6,000.
The merchandise inventory is to be written down $2,000.
The reserve for bad debts is to be increased $500.

After making these adjustments, the two partners are to make additional cash investments sufficient to bring their capitals to $35,000 for *A* and $25,000 for *B*, and are to take capital stock in these amounts.

Adjustment of asset values; additional investments. The following entries will be made on the partnership books to adjust the asset values in accordance with the agreement, and to record the additional cash investments by the partners:

Goodwill...	6,000.00	
Merchandise inventory.............		2,000.00
Reserve for bad debts.......................		500.00
A, capital...................................		1,750.00
B, capital...................................		1,750.00
To make the adjustments indicated.		
Cash...	6,500.00	
A, capital...............................		3,250.00
B, capital...............................		3,250.00
To record additional cash investments prior to incorporation.		

After these entries are posted, the balance sheet of the partnership immediately prior to the incorporation will be:

A AND *B*
Balance Sheet
December 31, 19—

Assets			Liabilities and Net Worth		
Cash.......................		$11,500	Accounts payable.............		$ 9,000
Accounts receivable...	$25,000				
Less reserve for bad			Net worth:		
debts...........	1,500	23,500	*A*, capital.........	$35,000	
Merchandise inventory........		28,000	*B*, capital.........	25,000	60,000
Goodwill...................		6,000			
		$69,000			$69,000

Alternative procedures. The remaining entries to record the change from the partnership to the corporation will depend upon whether:

(1) The partnership books are to be retained for use by the corporation.

(2) The partnership books are to be closed and new books are to be opened by the corporation.

Partnership books retained. If the partnership books are to be retained as the books of the corporation, it is only necessary to:

Set up a Capital Stock account and make a memorandum notation of the number of authorized shares.

Make and post the following journal entry to close the partners' capital accounts and record the issuance of the stock:

A, capital...................................	35,000.00	
B, capital...................................	25,000.00	
Capital stock.............................		60,000.00
To close the parners' capital accounts and record the issuance of 600 shares of stock to A and B, in exchange for the net assets of the partnership.		

Partnership books closed; new books opened for corporation. If a new set of books is to be used by the corporation, the partnership books must be closed and the new books must be opened. This is accomplished as follows:

(1) Entries closing the partnership books by recording the transfer of the assets and the liabilities to the corporation, in exchange for stock of the corporation, as shown below:

The A B Company...........................	69,000.00	
Reserve for bad debts........................	1,500.00	
Cash....................................		11,500.00
Merchandise inventory....................		28,000.00
Accounts receivable......................		25,000.00
Goodwill................................		6,000.00
To record the transfer of the partnership's assets to The A B Company.		
Accounts payable............................	9,000.00	
The A B Company.......................		9,000.00
To record the assumption of our liabilities by the corporation.		
Stock of The A B Company...................	60,000.00	
The A B Company.......................		60,000.00
To record the receipt of 600 shares of the corporation stock in payment for the net assets transferred.		
A, capital...................................	35,000.00	
B, capital...................................	25,000.00	
Stock of The A B Company...............		60,000.00
To record the division of the stock between the partners, and to close their capital accounts.		

(2) A memorandum entry in the corporation's Capital Stock account showing the number of shares authorized and their par value, and the journal entry on the following page.

Cash..	11,500.00	
Merchandise inventory.......................	28,000.00	
Accounts receivable.........................	25,000.00	
Goodwill....................................	6,000.00	
Reserve for bad debts.....................		1,500.00
Accounts payable.........................		9,000.00
Capital stock............................		60,000.00

To record the assets, reserve, and liabilities taken
over from the partnership, and the stock issued.

Changing from a corporation to a partnership. Corporations with a few stockholders are sometimes changed to partnerships—usually for the purpose of obtaining a tax advantage, which is sometimes possible. To illustrate the accounting procedure involved, assume that a corporation's balance sheet immediately before the change appears as follows:

THE *X Y* COMPANY
Balance Sheet
June 30, 19—

Assets			Liabilities and Net Worth		
Cash........................		$ 6,000	Accounts payable.............		$15,000
Accounts receivable...	$30,000				
Less reserve for bad			Net worth:		
debts............	1,000	29,000	Capital stock......	$50,000	
Merchandise.................		40,000	Earned surplus....	10,000	60,000
		$75,000			$75,000

X owns $30,000 of stock, and *Y* owns $20,000. Hence, *X*'s interest in the surplus is $6,000, and *Y*'s interest is $4,000.

Entries if corporation books are retained. If the corporation's books are to be used by the partnership, the only entry is:

Capital stock...............................	50,000.00	
Earned surplus..............................	10,000.00	
X, capital..................................		36,000.00
Y, capital..................................		24,000.00

To record the change from corporate to partnership form of organization.

New books for the partnership. If a new set of books is to be used by the partnership, the corporation's books must be closed and new books must be opened. This is accomplished as follows:

(1) Entry on the corporation's books:

Capital stock...............................	50,000.00	
Earned surplus..............................	10,000.00	
Accounts payable............................	15,000.00	
Reserve for bad debts.......................	1,000.00	
Cash.....................................		6,000.00
Accounts receivable......................		30,000.00
Merchandise..............................		40,000.00

To record the dissolution of the corporation and distribution of the assets, subject to liabilities and reserve, to the stockholders.

(2) Entry to open the partnership books:

Cash...	6,000.00	
Accounts receivable............................	30,000.00	
Merchandise....................................	40,000.00	
Reserve for bad debts......................		1,000.00
Accounts payable..........................		15,000.00
X, capital................................		36,000.00
Y, capital................................		24,000.00

To open the books of the partnership.

Preferred Stock

Classes of stock. Shares of stock entitle their holders to four basic rights, namely:

(1) To share in the management; that is, to vote at the stockholders' meetings.

(2) To share in the profits; that is, to receive dividends when they are declared by the directors.

(3) To share in the distribution of the assets of the corporation if it is dissolved.

(4) To subscribe to any additional issues of stock of the class held. This is known as the *pre-emptive right.*

If there is only one class of stock, these four fundamental rights are enjoyed proportionately, share and share alike, by all stockholders.

If there are two or more classes of stock, one class may enjoy more than its proportionate share of some right, or may have some right curtailed. Thus, preferred stock may enjoy special privileges in the matter of dividends or in the distribution of assets in liquidation; on the other hand, the preferred stockholders may have no right to vote, or may have a right to vote only under certain conditions, such as the failure of the corporation to pay preferred dividends for a stated period of time.

Stock preferred as to dividends. Stock which is preferred as to dividends entitles its holders to a dividend at a stipulated rate on par, or to a stipulated amount per share in the case of no-par stock, before any dividend is paid on the common stock. Preferred stockholders have no right to dividends unless the directors declare them. Directors may decline to declare dividends on preferred as well as common stock on the ground that the funds are needed in the business; the stockholders then have no recourse except to elect a board which will pay dividends, or to bring action in the courts in the hope of proving that the retention of the funds is not justifiable.

Cumulative and non-cumulative stock. Stock which is preferred as to dividends may be:

(*a*) Cumulative, in which case all dividends in arrears on preferred stock must be paid before dividends can be paid on the common stock.

To illustrate, assume $100,000 par value of 6% cumulative preferred stock, $100,000 par value of common stock, and earned surplus of $30,000; no dividends have been paid on the preferred stock for four years—three prior years and the current year. Since the preferred stock is cumulative, the preferred stockholders are entitled to dividends of $24,000 before any dividends can be paid to the common stockholders.

(*b*) Non-cumulative, in which case a dividend lost in one year is lost forever.

Non-cumulative preferred stock is not a desirable investment because of the danger that dividends may be lost. This is particularly true if the preferred stock is non-voting, or if the voting power of the common stock exceeds that of the preferred stock and the directors are elected by the common stockholders.

Participating and non-participating stock. Stock which is preferred as to dividends may be:

(*a*) Fully participating, or entitled to dividends at as high a rate as the dividends paid on the common stock.

To illustrate, assume $100,000 par value of 6% fully participating preferred stock, $200,000 par value of common stock, no preferred dividends in arrears, and earned surplus of $27,000.

The preferred stock is entitled to a 6% dividend, or $6,000.

A 6% dividend (or $12,000) may then be paid to the common stockholders without any additional dividend payment being made to the preferred stockholders.

But if a 9% dividend ($18,000) instead of a 6% dividend is paid to the common stockholders, an extra 3% must be paid to the preferred stockholders.

(*b*) Partially participating, or entitled to participate with the common stock, but only to a limited degree. For instance, the preferred may carry a 6% preference rate, with a right to participate to 8%.

(c) Non-participating, or entitled to receive its stipulated preferred dividend but no more, regardless of the rate paid on the common stock.

Rights under various conditions of preference. If the preferred stock is non-cumulative and non-participating, its holders have a right to only the stipulated rate of return, regardless of the profits earned; and if a dividend is not paid in one year, the right to it is forever lost. On the other hand, if the stock is participating and cumulative, the preferred stockholders will receive as high a rate of dividend as the common stockholders receive, and the preferred dividend for every year must be paid before anything can be paid to the common stockholders.

If a corporation is successful, and its preferred stock is non-participating, the common stockholders may receive larger dividends than those paid to the preferred stockholders. As a consequence, the common stock may have a much higher market value than the preferred stock.

Stock preferred as to assets. In the event of dissolution and liquidation, stock that is preferred as to assets is entitled to payment in full (the par value of par stock or a stated liquidation value for no-par stock) before any distribution is made on the common stock.

To illustrate, assume $100,000 par value of preferred stock, $100,000 par value of common stock, and assets of only $150,000 after paying all liabilities. If the preferred stock is preferred as to assets, $100,000 should be paid to the preferred stockholders, and only $50,000 to the common stockholders. If the preferred stock is not preferred as to assets, the assets should be divided between the common and the preferred stockholders in the ratio of the par value of the two classes of stock—in this case, in equal amounts.

The preference as to assets may extend only to the par of the stock, or the preferred stockholders may have a right to receive par and all dividends in arrears. Just what the preferred stockholders' rights are must be determined in each case by reference to the stock certificate or the charter.

The fact that stock is preferred as to dividends does not make it preferred as to assets also, nor is stock which is preferred as to assets necessarily preferred as to dividends also.

Reasons for classes of stock. Different classes of stock with differing rights have been devised to meet the desires of management and to make the shares sufficiently attractive to investors. This fact can best be indicated by an illustration.

Assume that a group of men had an opportunity to buy a going business at a cost of $500,000, and that, on the basis of its past operations, the business could be expected to earn about $50,000 a year. They decided to organize a corporation to acquire the business. We shall assume that they wanted to keep their own investment down to about $250,000, perhaps because that was all they had available, or because they wanted to make other investments, or because they wanted to obtain a "leverage" on net income (this term is explained later).

If they obtained a charter which authorized the corporation to issue only common stock, they would not have control, because outsiders would have equal votes with them. They therefore decided to issue $250,000 par value of common stock and $250,000 par value of non-voting preferred stock.

The next matters which required their consideration were the rights and preferences to be given to the preferred stock. Would it be necessary to make the stock preferred as to assets as well as to dividends? Or was the business sufficiently safe to make preference as to assets unnecessary? What dividend rate would be necessary to make the stock attractive to investors? Could the stock be marketed without making it cumulative? Could it be marketed without making it participating?

We shall assume that the organizing group believed that the hazards of the business were so few and slight that preference as to assets would be unnecessary, and that a 7% cumulative preferred stock could be marketed without the participating feature. The organizing group wanted to avoid making the preferred stock participating, because non-participating preferred stock would give their common stock a leverage on the net income. To illustrate: If the preferred stock were participating and if the company earned $50,000 on the $500,000 investment, both the preferred and the common stocks would earn ten per cent; but if the preferred stock was non-participating, the allocation of earnings would be as follows:

Total net income	$50,000
Applicable to preferred stock—7% of $250,000	17,500
Remainder—applicable to common stock—equal to 13% of $250,000	$32,500

This illustration should serve to indicate the matters to which management gives consideration when planning the capital structure of a corporation.

Accounts with various classes of stock. The methods of recording the issuance of preferred stock are the same as those applicable to common stock, previously discussed.

If several classes of stock are issued, the account titles for each class should clearly indicate its nature. Thus, a ledger might contain accounts with titles similar to the following:

> Capital Stock—Common.
> Subscriptions Receivable—Common.
> Paid-in Surplus—Common Stock.
>
> Capital Stock Subscribed—7% Preferred.
> Capital Stock Issued—7% Preferred.
> Subscriptions Receivable—7% Preferred.
> Premium on Stock—7% Preferred.

If only one class of stock is authorized by the charter, it is common stock; the account titles need not include the word "Common."

Common and preferred stock in the balance sheet. If there are two classes of stock, the amounts thereof should be shown separately in the balance sheet, and the special rights of the preferred stock should be described briefly. No attempt need be made to divide the surplus in order to show the rights of the two classes of stock therein. The balance sheet presentation of the facts may, therefore, be as follows:

Net worth:
Capital stock:
Preferred, 6% participating, cumulative;
par value, $100; authorized and issued,
1,000 shares...................... $100,000.00
Common, no par value; stated value, $10;
authorized and issued, 10,000 shares... 100,000.00 $200,000.00
Surplus:
Premium on stock.................... $ 2,000.00
Paid-in surplus..................... 10,000.00 12,000.00
Earned surplus................................... 75,000.00
Total.. $287,000.00

Stock Values

The following terms are used in expressing different bases for the valuation of stock:

Par value. This is a nominal value, printed on the certificate. For instance, if a corporation is authorized to issue $100,000 of capital stock, represented by 1,000 shares, the par value of each share is $100.

Book value. The book value of a share of stock of a certain class is computed by dividing the total amount of capital stock and surplus applicable to the class by the number of shares of the class outstanding.

For instance, if a corporation has 1,000 shares of common stock (and no preferred stock) outstanding, and its balance sheet shows:

Capital stock	$100,000.00
Earned surplus	30,000.00
Total	$130,000.00

the book value of each share is $130,000 ÷ 1,000, or $130.

If there is preferred stock outstanding, the preferred stockholders' interest in the surplus will depend upon whether the stock is participating, and also upon whether the preferred stock is cumulative and there are preferred dividends in arrears.

Market value. This is the price at which a share of stock can be sold. It depends partly on the book value of the stock and partly on the corporation's earning record and the prospects of future earnings and dividends.

Liquidation value. This is the amount which a stockholder will be entitled to receive if the corporation goes out of business, disposes of its assets, pays its liabilities, and distributes the residue among its stockholders. If common stock only is outstanding, its liquidation value will depend only on the amount available for distribution to the stockholders after the realization of the assets and the payment of liabilities. If common and preferred stocks are outstanding, the liquidation values of both classes will also depend upon whether the preferred stock is preferred as to assets.

Redemption value. Corporations sometimes issue preferred stock with a right to redeem it. The redemption price may be stated in terms such as: *par, par and dividends in arrears,* or *par and a premium of $5.00 per share.*

Stated value. The concept of stated value is discussed at some length in Chapter 19.

CHAPTER 19
Corporations (Concluded)

The nature of surplus.   Surplus may be broadly defined as the portion of a corporation's net worth not represented by its capital stock.   Formerly, one surplus account was regarded as sufficient, and it was credited not only with the net income from operations, but with many other kinds of increments in net worth.   During recent years accountants have come to believe that two general classes of surplus should be recognized:

> Earned surplus—the portion of the owners' equity represented by retained earnings produced by operations and by extraneous transactions such as the sale of fixed assets and investments.
>
> Paid-in surplus*—including elements of the following nature:
>
> (A) Surplus resulting from transactions in the company's own stock, such as:
>> (1) Premiums on par value stock.
>> (2) Excess of amounts received for no-par stock over amounts credited to capital stock accounts.
>> (3) Reissuance of treasury stock at an amount greater than its acquisition cost.
>
> (B) Surplus resulting from stockholders' contributions:
>> (1) Donations by stockholders.
>> (2) Assessments on stockholders.
>
> (C) Surplus resulting from contributions by outsiders, including gifts of assets—such as the gift of a plant to a company to induce it to locate in the donor city.

Special points on paid-in surplus.   The term *paid-in surplus* is a generic term applicable to all surplus elements of the nature

---

* When the desirability of classifying the surplus was first recognized, the words *earned surplus* and *capital surplus* came into use.   There was, however, considerable coufusion as to the meaning of *capital surplus;* some accountants used the term to include items such as those here listed in the Paid-in Surplus category and *also* the credits resulting from writing up assets to an appraised valuation, credits which are now regarded as not properly to be considered as surplus.   There has been a growing tendency, in the interest of clarity of terminology, to discontinue the use of the term *capital surplus* and to use the term *paid-in surplus.*

mentioned above, but the student should not get the impression that all paid-in surplus elements should be recorded in a single Paid-in Surplus account. To do so would result in an inadequate classification of paid-in surplus according to source and a failure to maintain the detailed records necessary for proper accounting and statement-preparation purposes. Therefore, the ledger may contain several paid-in surplus accounts, in which the words "paid-in" may or may not appear, such as:

> Paid-in Surplus—No-par Common Stock.
> Premium on Preferred Stock.
> Paid-in Surplus—From Treasury Stock Transactions.

As one illustration of the importance of keeping separate accounts with the various elements of paid-in surplus, assume that preferred stock is issued at a premium of $50,000, and that common stock is issued at a discount of $20,000.   There is a net paid-in surplus of $30,000; but separate accounts should be used so that the books will show that the common stockholders are subject to a discount liability.

Another reason for setting up detailed paid-in surplus accounts is that some elements of paid-in surplus may be legally available for dividends whereas other portions are not.   Writers have sometimes expressed the opinion that dividends should never be charged to paid-in surplus. This is incorrect. Paid-in surplus may or may not be available for dividends, depending on how it was created and on the law of the state in which the company was incorporated. It probably would be better to say that stockholders should have a right to assume that dividends come from earned surplus unless they are informed to the contrary, and that, if dividends are charged to paid-in surplus, disclosure of that fact should be made to them.   There have been instances in which a corporation has been given a false appearance of prosperity by crediting a portion of the proceeds of stock issuances to a paid-in surplus account and by charging dividends to such surplus, thus merely giving back to the stockholders a portion of their investment but creating the impression that they are receiving dividends out of earnings.

Paid-in surplus should never be charged with asset write-downs and losses which normally would be charged to income or earned surplus. This rule was laid down in the first bulletin issued by the American Institute of Accountants' Committee on Accounting Procedure. Following are two illustrations of the application of the rule. If a reserve for bad debts is found to be inadequate, it should not be increased by an offsetting charge against paid-in surplus; to do so would relieve current income of a charge which normally should be made to it. Fixed assets should not be written down by charges to paid-in surplus; to do so would relieve future periods of depreciation charges which normally should be made against income.

Recommended discontinuance of use of the word "surplus." In 1949, the Institute's Committee on Accounting Procedure authorized the publication of a report of its subcommittee on terminology, in which the discontinuance of the use of the word "surplus" was recommended. Words indicating source, such as "retained income," "retained earnings," or "accumulated earnings" were suggested as suitable replacements for "earned surplus." No substitutes were suggested for "capital surplus" or "paid-in surplus." At the date of this writing, insufficient time has elapsed to determine the extent to which the recommendations of the Committee may modify traditional terminology.

Appropriated surplus. Corporations sometimes transfer, by journal entries, portions of their surplus to special-purpose reserves. Such appropriations of surplus may be classified as follows:

(A) Made in compliance with contracts:
    (1) With creditors.
        For instance, bond indentures may place a limitation on the amount of dividends which can be paid while the bonds are outstanding. To reflect this limitation in the accounts, the portion of the surplus not available for dividends may be transferred to a reserve. Such a reserve is still a part of the surplus, but is temporarily not available for dividends.
    (2) With preferred stockholders.
        If, under the terms of issuance, the preferred stock of a company is to be retired (periodically or otherwise) out of funds provided by the profits, the charter provisions for the retirement of the preferred stock may require the creation of an appropriated surplus reserve. Although not available for dividends until the preferred stock is retired, such a reserve is still a part of the surplus.

(B) Made by voluntary action of the directors:
    (1) To indicate that dividends will be limited in order to permit the accumulation of funds for general

purposes or for some specific purpose, such as the acquisition of additional plant assets. Such a segregation of surplus does not, of course, give any assurance that cash will be available for the expenditure to which the reserve is related.

(2) To provide a reserve for possible losses of so uncertain and contingent a nature that the creation of a reserve by charge to income would not be justified.

If such appropriations have been made from earned surplus, the earned surplus should be detailed in the balance sheet in some manner similar to the following:

Earned surplus:
Appropriated:
Bond sinking fund reserve....................	$ 60,000
Reserve for retirement of preferred stock.......	50,000
Reserve for plant extensions.................	75,000
Reserve for contingencies...................	10,000
Total appropriated surplus...............	$195,000
Free.......................................	115,000
Total earned surplus..............................	$310,000

The statement is sometimes made that appropriations of surplus should always be made from earned surplus and never from paid-in surplus. In most cases this probably is true; but, since an appropriation of surplus is usually intended to place a limitation on dividends, and since dividends are sometimes payable from paid-in surplus, occasions might arise in which an appropriation from paid-in surplus would not be improper.

Appraisal increments. Prior to 1940 it was not an uncommon practice for companies to write up their fixed assets to appraised values. The offsetting credit frequently was made to Capital Surplus, Appraisal Surplus, or Appreciation Surplus; but many accountants, believing that the word "surplus" should not be used in connection with unrealized increments in value, preferred an account title such as "Unrealized Increment in Valuation of Fixed Assets."

In 1940 the Institute's Committee on Accounting Procedure issued a bulletin containing the following statement: "Accounting for fixed assets should normally be based on cost, and any attempt to make property accounts in general reflect current values is both impracticable and inexpedient." As a consequence of the issuance of this bulletin, the practice of writing up fixed assets to appraised values has greatly diminished.

Stated capital. Among the advantages of the corporate form of business organization is that of limited liability: the stockholders cannot be held personally liable for the debts of the corporation. Since the law gives the stockholders this protection, it is only fair that the creditors should be given some assurance that the corporation will not make payments to its stockholders, either as dividends or for the acquisition or retirement of stock, which will reduce the net worth below a stipulated amount.

Originally the corporation laws placed restrictions only on dividends. Before the advent of no-par stock, the dividend restriction usually consisted of a prohibition against any dividend payment which would reduce the net worth below the par value of the shares outstanding. With the advent of no-par stock, such a basis of restricting dividends became inapplicable; obviously it could not be applied to distributions to the holders of no-par stock.

More recently it has been recognized that the protection of creditors was inadequate unless, in addition to a restriction on dividends, there was a restriction on the amount which could be paid to stockholders for the acquisition or retirement of their stock.

For the reasons indicated above, a definition of stated capital has been included in the laws of many states. Unfortunately, the concepts of stated capital are not uniform in all states. In some states, the stated capital includes the total amount received for par or no-par shares issued, including any amount credited to a premium or paid-in surplus account. In other states, the stated capital is measured by the par value of par shares or, with respect to no-par shares, the amount per share which the directors elect to establish as stated capital and credit to a capital stock account. In some states, the amount which the directors elect to establish as stated capital per share cannot be less than a minimum fixed by law.

Since it has come to be realized that a restriction as to dividends is only a partial protection to creditors, many state statutes prescribe that the stated or legal capital must not be impaired either by the payment of dividends or by disbursements for the acquisition or retirement of shares.

Since stated capital is a legal concept, and since there is a considerable variation in the state laws with respect thereto, it is impracticable to deal exhaustively with the subject here. It must suffice to call attention to the fact that dividends and transactions in the company's stock are usually restricted by the law of the state of incorporation.

Dividends. Dividends distributed by corporations to their stockholders may be classified as follows:

(A) Dividends out of surplus:*

(1) Decreasing net worth.

The customary dividend of this nature is a periodical distribution of cash. However, other assets may be distributed, or the company may issue scrip, which is an obligation to make payment at a later date.

(2) Not decreasing net worth.

This classification covers stock dividends. A stock dividend does not change the net worth of the corporation; it merely decreases the surplus element and increases the capital stock element.

(B) Dividends out of capital:

The principal dividends of this nature are liquidating dividends which are intended to return all of the capital to the stockholders because the company is discontinuing operations, or to return a portion of the capital because the scope of the business is being reduced and the total capital is no longer required.

In this chapter we shall be concerned only with dividends out of surplus.

Legality of dividends. Under what conditions does a company have a legal right to declare a dividend? It is difficult to state general rules which are not subject to exceptions because the laws of the various states differ in their regulations, especially with respect to dividends on no par value stock. In general, it may be said that a corporation has a right to pay a dividend if it has a surplus which has been produced by income from operations or from extraneous activities. Dividends must not reduce the net worth below the amount of the stated capital.

Financial policy with respect to dividends. In making their decisions with respect to the amounts of dividend payments, directors give consideration not only to the amount of surplus legally available for the payment of dividends, but also to matters of

---

* The expression "dividends out of surplus" is an abbreviation of "dividends paid out of surplus." These expressions are in common use and are therefore used in this text. However, they are subject to criticism. Since surplus is not an asset, nothing can literally be paid out of it. To avoid confusing the layman, it might be better to say "dividends which reduce surplus."

financial policy.   A dividend payment may be undesirable because the available cash is inadequate; but if there is only a temporary shortage of cash, the directors may consider it advisable to borrow money for dividend purposes in order to maintain a continuity of dividend payments.   Even when adequate cash is available, the directors may consider it advisable to pay no dividends, or dividends of only limited amounts, in order to conserve the funds for expansion of the business.

Significant dates applicable to dividends, and related entries. In the case of corporations with only a few stockholders and with infrequent transfers of shares, it may be practicable to declare and pay a dividend on the same day.   But for large corporations with many stockholders and frequent transfers of shares, such a procedure would be impracticable.   Under such conditions there are three significant dates applicable to dividends: the date of declaration, the date of record, and the date of payment.

Date of declaration.   On the date when the dividend is declared, the following entry is made:

```
Dividends................................. 100,000.00
    Dividends payable.....................           100,000.00
    To record the declaration of a dividend.
```

Date of record.   The directors' resolution authorizing the payment of a dividend states a date as of which the corporation, by an examination of its stock records, will determine the "stockholders of record."   For instance, a dividend may be declared on January 5, payable on January 30 to stockholders of record on January 20.   Between January 5 and January 20, the purchaser of stock obtains a right to the dividend; after January 20, the stock is sold "ex-dividend"—that is, the seller of the stock, rather than the purchaser, is entitled to receive the dividend payment.

No entry need be made by the company on the date of record.

Date of payment.   A period of time is usually required between the date of record and the date of payment because of the work involved in the determination of the stockholders of record and the preparation of the dividend checks.   When the checks are mailed, the following entry is made:

```
Dividends payable......................... 100,000.00
    Cash..................................           100,000.00
    Payment, to stockholders of record on January
    20, of dividend declared on January 5.
```

Unpaid declared dividends.   After a dividend has been legally declared and notice of the declaration has been given to the stockholders, by publication or otherwise, the unpaid dividend ranks as a liability and should be shown as such in the balance sheet, usually under the current liability caption.   The directors may

rescind the declaration of a dividend, but they can do so only in
case no one else has knowledge of the declaration.

Scrip dividends.   When it is desired to declare a dividend but
to defer the payment thereof, a corporation may issue scrip to its
stockholders.   "Scrip" is a certificate stating the rights of the
holder—usually to receive payment therefor with interest at a
stated future date.   Such scrip should be shown in the balance
sheet as a current liability, with some title such as "Dividend
Scrip Payable."   Issuance of scrip as a dividend is very rare.

Dividends in arrears on preferred stock.   Since even a preferred stockholder has no right to a dividend until it is declared,
preferred dividends do not accrue; no entry for them should be
made until the date of declaration.

But if dividends on cumulative preferred stock are in arrears,
there is an obligation to pay these arrearages before paying dividends to the common stockholders.   The amount of the cumulative dividends in arrears should, therefore, be shown in the balance
sheet.   This is usually done by adding a footnote below the balance sheet totals, thus:

> *Note:* Cumulative dividends on preferred stock were in arrears on (the balance sheet
> date) in the amount of $12,000.00.

Stock dividends.   Dividends are sometimes paid in capital
stock instead of in cash.   To illustrate, assume that a company
has 1,000 authorized shares of common stock of $100 par, of which
600 shares are outstanding; also assume that a 10% stock dividend
(60 shares) is declared and immediately issued.   The Committee
on Accounting Procedure of the American Institute of Accountants
has taken the position that, when such stock dividends are declared,
earned surplus in an amount equal to the fair value of the shares
issued as a dividend shall be capitalized by transfer to the Capital
Stock and Paid-in Surplus accounts.   Assuming that the shares
issued in this illustration have a fair value of $120 each, the entry
to record the distribution of the dividend is:

```
Stock dividends (to be closed to Earned Surplus)....  7,200.00
    Capital stock..............................             6,000.00
    Paid-in surplus—From stock dividend........             1,200.00
    Issuance of a 10% dividend: 60 shares of $100 par
    value stock having a fair value of $120 each.
```

Assume that the stock was without par value and that it had
been given a stated value of $75 per share; the entry would be:

```
Stock dividends (to be closed to Earned Surplus)....  7,200.00
    Capital stock..............................             4,500.00
    Paid-in surplus—From stock dividend........             2,700.00
    Issuance of a 10% dividend: 60 shares of no-par
    stock (stated value, $75 per share) having a fair
    value of $120 each.
```

If time intervenes between the declaration and payment of the stock dividend, the entries (for the dividend on par value stock, for instance) should be:

At date of declaration:

Stock dividends.................................	7,200.00	
Stock dividend payable......................		6,000.00
Paid-in surplus—From stock dividend.........		1,200.00
Declaration of 10% stock dividend to stockholders of record on December 31, 1953; shares to be issued February 1, 1954.		

At date of issuance:

Stock dividend payable.........................	6,000.00	
Capital stock................................		6,000.00
To record issuance of 60 shares as a stock dividend.		

If a balance sheet is prepared between the date of declaration and the date of distribution of a stock dividend, the net worth section should appear as illustrated below:

Net worth:		
Capital stock—$100 par value; authorized, 1,000 shares.		
Issued, 600 shares......................	$60,000.00	
To be issued February 1, 1954 as a stock dividend—60 shares................	6,000.00	$66,000.00
Surplus:		
Paid-in—Earned surplus capitalized in connection with a stock dividend...........	$ 1,200.00	
Earned...............................	11,000.00	12,200.00

Observe that an unpaid stock dividend is not shown as a liability.

Treasury stock. Treasury stock is a corporation's own stock which has been issued, reacquired, and not canceled in accordance with a formal procedure specified by law. It will be noted that there are three important elements of this definition:

(1) Treasury stock must be the company's own stock; holdings of the stocks of other companies are not treasury stock.
(2) The stock must have been issued.
(3) The stock, although reacquired, must not have been canceled. Cancellation of stock is effected by a procedure prescribed by law, and places the stock in the status of unissued, or even unauthorized, shares.

Unissued and treasury stock—Purchaser's liability for discount. A stockholder who acquires unissued stock at a discount assumes a contingent liability for the amount of the discount. This means that, if the corporation is unable to pay its debts, the creditors may demand that stockholders who acquired unissued stock at a discount pay the corporation the amount of the discount.

If a person acquires from a company, at a discount, par value treasury stock which was originally issued at par or more, he has no contingent liability for the discount.

Treasury stock is not an asset.   Treasury shares may have a ready marketability and may be reissued; but so may unissued stock be issued; and it seems obvious that treasury stock, like unissued stock, is not an asset but is merely a possible source of additional funds.

Although treasury stock has been shown in balance sheets as an asset (sometimes even combined with securities which *are* assets, under some title such as "Government Bonds and Other Securities"), accountants now generally recognize that the acquisition of treasury stock causes a reduction in the corporation's net worth.

Treasury stock in the balance sheet.   Since the acquisition of treasury stock causes a reduction of the corporation's net worth to the extent of the cost of the stock, the cost should be shown as a deduction in the net worth section of the balance sheet.   There are several ways of showing the deduction; the method illustrated below is generally regarded as acceptable.   The illustration is based on the following facts with respect to the capital stock:

The authorized issue is 1,000 shares of $100 par value.
All the authorized stock has been issued.
The corporation has reacquired 100 shares at a cost of $12,000.

You should note the distinction between "issued" and "outstanding."   All of the 1,000 shares have been issued, and are so shown.   The number of outstanding shares is not stated in the balance sheet, but can be easily determined; there are 900 outstanding shares: the difference between the 1,000 issued shares and the 100 treasury shares.

Net worth:
Capital stock—$100 par value; authorized
and issued, 1,000 shares, of which 100
shares are in the treasury.............. $100,000.00
Earned surplus........................ 25,000.00
Total............................. $125,000.00
Deduct cost of treasury stock.......... 12,000.00 $113,000.00

If a company has a paid-in surplus as well as an earned surplus, the facts may be shown in the balance sheet in the manner illustrated on the following page.

```
Net worth:
    Capital stock—$100 par value; authorized
        and issued, 1,000 shares, of which 100
        shares are in the treasury..............   $100,000.00
    Paid-in surplus.........................        10,000.00
    Earned surplus..........................        25,000.00
            Total...........................       $135,000.00
    Deduct cost of treasury stock...........        12,000.00   $123,000.00
```

If a company suffers a deficit after the acquisition of treasury stock, the facts may be shown as follows:

```
Net worth:
    Capital stock—$100 par value;
        authorized and issued, 1,000
        shares, of which 100 shares
        are in the treasury...................   $100,000.00
    Deduct:
        Deficit.................. $ 5,000.00
        Cost of treasury stock....  12,000.00     17,000.00
            Net worth...................................   $83,000.00
```

If treasury stock is acquired by donation, there is no cost to deduct; the facts may be shown as follows:

```
Net worth:
    Capital stock—$100 par value; authorized
        and issued, 1,000 shares, of which 100
        shares, acquired by donation, are in the
        treasury.............................   $100,000.00
    Earned surplus.........................        25,000.00
            Net worth....................................   $125,000.00
```

Recording treasury stock acquisitions—Cost basis. As indicated above, the cost of treasury stock may properly be shown in the balance sheet as a deduction in the net worth section. To provide the information for this balance sheet presentation, it is considered proper to debit the Treasury Stock account with the cost of the stock acquired. If this procedure is adopted, an acquisition of treasury stock is recorded as follows:

```
Treasury stock...............................  12,000.00
    Cash.....................................               12,000.00
    To record the acquisition of 100 shares of $100
    par value stock at a cost of $12,000.
```

An entry of this nature should be made regardless of whether the shares have a par value or are without par value, and regardless of the amount which was received for the shares when they were issued. The treasury stock account title should indicate the nature of the stock if there is more than one class of issued stock. If the company has only one class of stock, the account title may be merely Treasury Stock; otherwise, it might be Treasury Stock— Preferred, or Treasury Stock—Common, or Treasury Stock— Common—No Par Value.

Stockholders sometimes donate shares to the company; this may be done because the company is in a poor financial condition and the stockholders do not wish to invest additional funds; they, therefore, donate portions of their stock which possibly can be reissued to obtain additional funds. Since donated shares are acquired without cost, no debit and credit entries are made to record the acquisition. A memorandum notation is made in the Treasury Stock account, as shown below:

Treasury Stock

Date	50 shares donated							

Reissuance of treasury shares. When treasury stock is reissued, the Treasury Stock account should be credited with the acquisition price. Entries under various conditions are shown below.

Reissuance at cost. Assume that the treasury stock acquired for $12,000 is reissued for $12,000; the entry is:

```
Cash......................................  12,000.00
   Treasury stock...........................          12,000.00
```

Reissuance at a price in excess of cost. Assume that the shares were reissued for $13,500; the entry is:

```
Cash......................................  13,500.00
   Treasury stock...........................          12,000.00
   Paid-in surplus—From treasury stock trans-
     actions................................           1,500.00
```

Reissuance at a price less than cost. The method of recording reissuances of treasury stock at a price less than the original cost depends on the law of the state of incorporation and the kinds of surplus accounts on the company's books. Assume that shares acquired for $12,000 are reissued for $11,500. If a paid-in surplus exists as a result of treasury stock reissuances at more than cost, the entry may be:

```
Cash......................................  11,500.00
Paid-in surplus—From treasury stock transactions.     500.00
   Treasury stock...........................          12,000.00
```

If the company has a paid-in surplus resulting from the issuance of shares of the same class as those acquired as treasury stock, and if this paid-in surplus is not a part of the legal stated capital, the excess of the acquisition price over the reissuance price of the treasury shares may be charged to this paid-in surplus, thus:

```
Cash......................................  11,500.00
Premium on stock (or Paid-in surplus)..........     500.00
   Treasury stock...........................          12,000.00
```

In the absence of any applicable paid-in surplus accounts, the excess should be charged to Earned Surplus, thus:

```
Cash.......................................  11,500.00
Earned surplus.............................     500.00
    Treasury stock.........................              12,000.00
```

Reissuance of donated shares. If donated treasury stock is reissued, the entire proceeds of the reissuance should be credited to Paid-in Surplus—From Treasury Stock Transactions.

Recommended departure from the cost basis. In 1948 the executive committee of the American Accounting Association, in *Accounting Concepts and Standards Underlying Corporate Financial Statements,* expressed the following opinion:

> "An outlay by a corporation for shares of its own stock should be treated as a reduction of paid-in capital up to the pro-rata amount represented by the acquired shares, whether or not such shares are reissuable. If the outlay for the reacquired shares exceeds the pro-rata reduction in paid-in capital, the excess should be treated as a distribution of retained income. The reissue of acquired shares should be accounted for in the same manner as an original issue of corporate shares."

As an illustration of the recommended procedure, let us assume that a company's no-par stock was originally issued at $80 per share, of which $75 was credited to Capital Stock and $5 was credited to Paid-in Surplus. Also assume that a share of treasury stock is acquired at a cost of $85. If the recommended procedure is used, the entry is:

```
Treasury stock (Amount originally credited to Capital
    Stock)...........................................  75.00
Paid-in surplus (Amount originally credited to Paid-in
    Surplus).........................................   5.00
Earned surplus.......................................   5.00
    Cash.............................................          85.00
```

It is believed that this procedure is followed much less frequently than the cost-basis procedure.

Surplus restrictions resulting from treasury stock acquisitions. Assume that a company has issued capital stock of $100,000 par value and has an earned surplus of $25,000, but that it is holding treasury stock which it acquired at a cost of $12,000. Assume also that the law of the state of incorporation provides that dividend payments and treasury stock acquisitions, together, must not impair the stated capital*—which, in this illustration, is

---

* The state laws differ with respect to the effect of a treasury stock acquisition on earned surplus. In at least one state, the earned surplus is reduced; more commonly, it is merely restricted.

assumed to be the par value of the issued shares, including the treasury shares.   In effect, this means that $12,000 of the earned surplus is restricted so long as the treasury stock is retained, and that, so long as this restriction exists, future dividends and disbursements for treasury stock acquisitions must not, together, exceed the $13,000 unrestricted earned surplus.   The balance sheet should be prepared in such a way as to disclose this restriction.   The following net worth section of the balance sheet illustrates a method of making the disclosure:

Net worth:
    Capital stock—$100 par value; authorized and issued,
       1,000 shares, of which 100 shares are in the treasury.. $100,000.00
    Earned surplus:
       Not available for dividends—Equal to
         cost of treasury stock................. $12,000.00
       Free............................... 13,000.00   25,000.00
           Total.. $125,000.00
    Deduct cost of treasury stock........................ 12,000.00
         Net worth................................. $113,000.00

CHAPTER 20
Miscellaneous Matters

Purpose of the chapter. This chapter deals with a number of accounting devices and procedures with which the student should be familiar. They are presented in this chapter because they are used in a practice set of which the first transactions appear in the assignment material for this chapter.

Numerical Chart of Accounts

Account numbers. Most ledgers are kept on cards or in loose-leaf binders. Each account is given a number, and the cards or sheets are kept in numerical order.

It is advisable to number accounts in a systematic manner so that the account numbers indicate classifications and relationships. Numbering systems differ, but the following chart of accounts illustrates the general principle.

Observe that each account number contains four digits, and that the first digit at the left indicates a main classification, as shown below:

1---- Assets and related reserves.
2---- Liabilities and deferred credits.
3---- Net worth.
4---- Sales and related accounts.
5---- Accounts with manufacturing costs: materials, labor, and manufacturing expenses.
6---- Selling expenses.
7---- General expenses.
8---- Other income and expense.
9---- Closing accounts: Manufacturing and Profit and Loss.

The second digit indicates a main subclassification, thus:

11-- Current assets and related reserves.
12-- Other assets.
13-- Fixed assets and related reserves.
14-- Long-term deferred charges.

The third and fourth digits indicate further subclassifications and relationships, thus:

1130 Notes Receivable.
1135 Accrued Interest on Notes Receivable.

288

The third and fourth digits are not assigned haphazardly, but in many instances are selected for reasons of consistency, or to show relationships.

As illustrations of numbers chosen for purposes of consistency, observe the following account numbers. The first digit indicates whether the account represents an asset or a liability; the fact that the item is current is indicated by the second digit; the final 20 indicates an account receivable or payable; the final 30 indicates a note.

    1120   Accounts Receivable.
    2120   Vouchers Payable.

    1130   Notes Receivable.
    2130   Notes Payable.

Also observe that offset accounts, representing deductions from related accounts, are numbered with a final 8 or 9:

    1120   Accounts Receivable.
    1129   Reserve for Bad Debts.

    1331   Machinery and Equipment.
    1339   Reserve for Depreciation—Machinery and Equipment.

    4001   Sales.
    4008   Discount on Sales.
    4009   Returned Sales and Allowances.

As an illustration of account numbers assigned to show relationships, observe the following:

The account with bonds payable is:

    2350   6% First Mortgage Bonds.

Observe the numbers of the related accounts:

    1250   Sinking Fund Cash.
    1251   Sinking Fund Securities.
    2150   Accrued Bond Interest.
    2550   Bond Premium.
    3250   Sinking Fund Reserve.
    8250   Bond Interest.

Another illustration of account numbers assigned to show relationships is:

    1184   Unexpired Insurance.
    5384   Insurance (manufacturing expense).
    6084   Insurance (selling expense).
    7084   Insurance (general expense).

Illustrative chart of accounts. The following chart of accounts will be used in the practice set:

CURRENT ASSETS:

    1111   Cash.
    1112   Petty Cash.
    1120   Accounts Receivable.
    1129   Reserve for Bad Debts.
    1130   Notes Receivable.
    1135   Accrued Interest on Notes Receivable.
    1139   Notes Receivable Discounted.
    1151   Finished Goods.
    1161   Goods in Process.
    1171   Raw Materials.
    1181   Factory Supplies.
    1182   Postage.
    1183   Salesmen's Traveling Expense Advances.
    1184   Unexpired Insurance.

OTHER ASSETS:

    1250   Sinking Fund Cash.
    1251   Sinking Fund Securities.
    1271   Subscriptions to Capital Stock.

FIXED ASSETS:

    1311   Land.
    1321   Buildings.
    1329   Reserve for Depreciation—Buildings.
    1331   Machinery and Equipment.
    1339   Reserve for Depreciation—Machinery and Equipment.
    1341   Tools.
    1349   Reserve for Depreciation—Tools.
    1351   Delivery Equipment.
    1359   Reserve for Depreciation—Delivery Equipment.
    1361   Furniture and Fixtures.
    1369   Reserve for Depreciation—Furniture and Fixtures.
    1371   Patents.
    1379   Reserve for Patent Expiration.
    1381   Goodwill.

CURRENT LIABILITIES:

    2120   Vouchers Payable.
    2130   Notes Payable.
    2133   Dividends Payable.
    2135   Accrued Interest on Notes Payable.
    2137   Accrued Interest on Mortgages Payable.
    2150   Accrued Bond Interest.
    2161   Accrued Payroll.

2162   Federal Income Taxes Withheld.
2163   Federal O. A. B. Taxes Withheld.
2171   Federal O. A. B. Taxes Payable.
2172   State Unemployment Taxes Payable.
2173   Federal Unemployment Taxes Payable.
2180   Accrued Taxes Payable—General.
2181   Accrued Federal Income Taxes Payable.
2191   Rent Collected in Advance.

LONG-TERM LIABILITIES:

2310   Mortgage Payable—6%.
2320   Mortgage Payable—5%.
2350   5% First Mortgage Bonds.

LONG-TERM DEFERRED CREDITS:

2550   Bond Premium.

NET WORTH:

3171   Capital Stock.
3201   Earned Surplus.
3233   Dividends.
3250   Sinking Fund Reserve.

SALES AND RELATED ACCOUNTS:

4001   Sales.
4008   Discount on Sales.
4009   Returned Sales and Allowances.

PURCHASES AND RELATED ACCOUNTS:

5171   Purchases—Raw Materials.
5172   Freight In.
5174   Discounts Lost.
5179   Returned Purchases and Allowances.

DIRECT LABOR:

5201   Direct Labor.

MANUFACTURING EXPENSES:

5300   Manufacturing Expense—Control.
       5301   Indirect Labor.
       5302   Superintendence.
       5315   Heat, Light, and Power.
       5328   Repairs to Buildings.
       5329   Depreciation—Buildings.
       5338   Repairs to Machinery and Equipment.
       5339   Depreciation—Machinery and Equipment.
       5349   Depreciation—Tools.

5370   Payroll Taxes.
5379   Patent Expiration Expense.
5380   Taxes—General.
5381   Factory Supplies.
5384   Insurance.
5390   Miscellaneous.

SELLING EXPENSES:

6000   Selling Expense—Control.
   6001   Sales Salaries.
   6004   Delivery Salaries.
   6051   Delivery Expense.
   6059   Depreciation—Delivery Equipment.
   6061   Freight Out.
   6070   Payroll Taxes.
   6075   Advertising.
   6083   Salesmen's Traveling Expenses.
   6084   Insurance.
   6090   Miscellaneous.

GENERAL EXPENSES:

7000   General Expense—Control.
   7001   Officers' Salaries.
   7002   Office Salaries.
   7011   Office Supplies.
   7012   Printing and Stationery.
   7029   Bad Debts.
   7069   Depreciation—Furniture and Fixtures.
   7070   Payroll Taxes.
   7080   Taxes—General.
   7082   Postage.
   7084   Insurance.
   7090   Miscellaneous.

OTHER INCOME:

8135   Interest Income.
8151   Delivery Income.
8191   Rent Income.

OTHER EXPENSES:

8235   Sundry Interest Expense.
8250   Bond Interest.
8281   Federal Income Tax.

CLOSING ACCOUNTS:

9001   Manufacturing Account.
9002   Profit and Loss.

Organization of ledger. If the chart of accounts is well planned, the accounts will be arranged in the ledger in the sequence in which their balances will appear in the statements at the end of the period. For instance, all current asset accounts will be in one section of the ledger, and they will be arranged in the order in which they appear in the balance sheet. It is desirable to leave several unassigned numbers in each group, to provide for other accounts which may be added later in the sequence in which their balances will appear in the statements.

Use of account numbers instead of account names. Space can frequently be saved in the books of original entry by providing a narrow Account Number column instead of a wide Account Name column. The following paragraphs show the use of such Account Number columns in the voucher register, the cash disbursements book, and the cash receipts book.

Voucher register. Special columns are provided in the voucher register for accounts frequently debited. Previously it has been necessary to write (in the Sundry Accounts Debited section) the names of other accounts debited. The writing of these account names can be avoided by using an Account Number column instead of an Account Name column.

SUNDRY ACCOUNTS DEBITED		
Acct. No.	✓	Amount
1321		1,000 00
8235		25 00

Since the bookkeeper has used the account number to indicate the account to which the posting *is to be* made, it will be confusing to use the account number also to show that the posting *has been* made. Therefore, a check mark is used for that purpose. After the entries have been posted, the Sundry Accounts Debited section will appear as shown at the left.

SUNDRY ACCOUNTS DEBITED		
Acct. No.	✓	Amount
1321	✓	1,000 00
8235	✓	25 00

The only credit column in the voucher registers previously illustrated was Vouchers Payable. Occasionally it is necessary to credit some other account, and in such cases entries might be made in red ink in the Sundry Accounts Debited section. To avoid such red ink entries, a Sundry Credit section as well as a Sundry Debit section may be provided in the voucher register, as illustrated at the right.

SUNDRY ACCOUNTS					
Debits			Credits		
Acct. No.	✓	Amount	Acct. No.	✓	Amount

Cash disbursements book. A Sundry Accounts Debit section and a Sundry Accounts Credit section may be included in the cash disbursements book (sometimes called the "check register") for accounts other than Vouchers Payable and Cash. The form is illustrated below:

Cash Disbursements Book

				DEBITS			CREDITS		
Check No.	Date	Payee	Voucher Number	Vouchers Payable (2120)	Sundry Accounts		Sundry Accounts		Cash (1111)
					Acct. No. √	Amount	Acct. No. √	Amount	

Cash receipts book. The cash receipts books previously illustrated have contained a Sundry Accounts Credit section; it may also be desirable to have a Sundry Accounts Debit section. These two Sundry Accounts sections can be provided with columns to show account numbers instead of account names. The cash receipts book may then appear somewhat as shown on the next page.

The Explanation column does not contain the names of any accounts; the accounts to be debited and credited are indicated either by entering the amounts in special columns, or by entering account numbers in the Account Number columns of the Sundry Accounts Debit or Sundry Accounts Credit sections.

General Cash Receipts Book

Date	Explanation	CREDITS						DEBITS				
		Sundry Accounts			Sales (4001)	Interest Income (8135)	Accts. Receivable (1120)	Sundry Accounts			Discount on Sales (4008)	Freight Out (6061)	Cash (1111)
		Acct. No.	√	Amount				Acct. No.	√	Amount			

Use of account numbers, check marks, and X's. Account numbers, in column headings and in the Account Number columns of Sundry Accounts sections, indicate the accounts *to which* postings are to be made. To facilitate posting, general journal entries should show the account number as well as the account name, thus:

3233—Dividends
　　2133—Dividends payable

Check marks should be entered in the (√) columns and at the foot of special columns to indicate that postings *have been* made.

An X should be entered in the (√) column or at the bottom of a special column if the entry or the column total is not to be posted.

Expense Controls

Controlling accounts. In studying controlling accounts with customers and creditors, you learned that controlling accounts are introduced into the accounting system when the work becomes so heavy that it must be divided.

In a very large business, the controlling account procedure can also be applied to expense accounts, thus providing for further subdivision of the bookkeeping work. Controlling accounts with various classes of expense can be kept in the general ledger, and the details can be kept in a subsidiary expense ledger or other record.

Referring to the chart of accounts, it will be observed that expense controlling accounts are provided in the general ledger for Manufacturing Expense, Selling Expense, and General Expense, and detail accounts are in a subsidiary record.

When such a system of controlling accounts and subsidiary records is used, the voucher register may contain a debit section for each of the three controlling accounts (Numbers 5300, 6000, and 7000), and each of these controlling account sections will be provided with three subcolumns: Account Number, ($\sqrt{}$), and Amount, as shown at the bottom of page 297.

During the month, the bookkeeper in charge of the subsidiary expense record should post the individual entries from the expense control columns, and indicate by check marks in the ($\sqrt{}$) column (between the account number and the amount), that the postings were made. Thus, the check marks in the part of the register shown indicate that the bookkeeper has posted to accounts as shown at the top of page 297.

(Left page)   Voucher

Vo. No.	Date	Payee	Explanation	Terms	Paid Date	Ck. No.	Credit Vouchers Payable 2120	Purchases 5171	Freight In 5172
1	July 1	J. B. White...	Invoice, July 1	2/10, n/30	July 11	12	3,000 00	3,000 00	
2	2	C. N. W. Ry...			2	1	8 00		8 00
3	3	Payson & Co..	Invoice 1361	Cash	3	2	65 00		
4	3	C. R. Maynard	Circulars		3	3	200 00		
5	3	Basset & Co...	Note and interest		3	4	510 00		
6	3	Osborne & Co.	Invoice, July 2	1/10, n/30	12	14	850 00	850 00	
7	5	C. N. W. Ry...			5	5	25 00		
							18,222 00	14,590 00	375 00
							$\sqrt{}$	$\sqrt{}$	$\sqrt{}$

> 5381 Factory Supplies............... $ 65.00
> 6075 Advertising................... 200.00
> 6061 Freight Out................... 25.00

The general ledger bookkeeper posts from the voucher register as follows:

AT THE END OF THE MONTH—COLUMN TOTALS:

Credits:
    Vouchers payable............................ 2120 $18,222.00

Debits:
    Purchases—Raw materials..................... 5171 $14,590.00
    Freight in.................................. 5172   375.00
    Manufacturing expense (Control).............. 5300   995.00
    Selling expense (Control).................... 6000   882.00
    General expense (Control).................... 7000   870.00

DURING THE MONTH—ENTRIES IN SUNDRY ACCOUNTS SECTION:

Debits:
    Notes payable............................... 2130   500.00
    Interest expense............................ 8235   10.00
                                              $18,222.00

Since the subsidiary ledger bookkeeper posts all the items in the Manufacturing Expense column, the sum of the balances in the subsidiary manufacturing expense accounts should equal the balance in the Manufacturing Expense controlling account. The same agreement should exist between the Selling Expense controlling account and the subsidiary selling expense record, and between the General Expense controlling account and the subsidiary general expense record.

Register   (Right page)

	DEBITS						SUNDRY ACCOUNTS				
Manufacturing Expense 5300		Selling Expense 6000		General Expense 7000		Debit		Credit		Remarks		
Acct. No.	√ Amount	Acct. No.	√ Amount	Acct. No.	√ Amount	Acct. No.	√ Amount	Acct. No.	√ Amount			
5381	√ 65 00											
		6075	√ 200 00									
						2130	√ 500 00					
						8235	√ 10 00					
		6061	√ 25 00				—					
	995 00		882 00		870 00		510 00					
	√		√		√							

Subsidiary records.   The subsidiary expense records may be kept in columnar form, thus:

Selling Expense Analysis Record

Date	Vo. No.	Ref.	6001	6004	6051	6059	6061	6070	6075	6083	6084	6090
19—												
July 3	4						25 00					
5	7						45 00					
8	21								200 00			
9	28				50 00							
11	39				240 00							
23	82						32 00					
26	91									127 00		
28	99					25 00				138 00		
31	PR1		900 00	350 00				56 25				
31	J2										35 00	
31	J2											25 00
			900 00	350 00	290 00	25 00	102 00	56 25	200 00	265 00	35 00	25 00

"PR" stands for payroll record, a book explained and illustrated in connection with the practice set.

The last two entries, for depreciation of delivery equipment and expired insurance premiums, were made in the journal.

The "Ref." column shows the source of all entries not posted from the voucher register.

Credits in subsidiary expense record columns can be indicated by red ink or starred entries.

The controlling account with Selling Expense appears as follows:

Selling Expense (Control)   (6000)

Date		Ref.	Amount
19—			
July 31		VR1	882 00
31		PR1	1,306 25
31		J2	35 00
31		J2	25 00

The bookkeeper who posts to the subsidiary expense ledger or analysis record prepares a summary of the selling expense account balances at the end of the month in the following form:

Selling Expenses, July, 19—

6001	Sales salaries	$ 900.00
6004	Delivery salaries	350.00
6051	Delivery expense	290.00
6059	Depreciation—Delivery equipment	25.00
6061	Freight out	102.00
6070	Payroll taxes	56.25
6075	Advertising	200.00
6083	Salesmen's traveling expenses	265.00
6084	Insurance	35.00
6090	Miscellaneous	25.00
		$2,248.25

This summary is prepared for two reasons: first, to prove that the subsidiary record is in agreement with the controlling account; second, for use in connection with the periodic statements.

Posting from vouchers. If desired, the postings to the subsidiary expense records can be made directly from the vouchers instead of from the voucher register. If this is done, the Account Number and the ($\sqrt{}$) columns will not be needed in the expense controlling account sections of the voucher register.

Use of account numbers on vouchers. In the voucher illustrated on page 196, the names of the accounts most frequently debited were printed on the back of the voucher, and spaces were left in which to write the names of other accounts as required. It may be desirable to print account numbers instead of names on the back of the voucher. Since so much less space is required for numbers than for names, the back of the voucher can contain more printed account numbers than account names.

Note Registers as Books of Original Entry

Notes receivable register. If there are many transactions involving notes and drafts, the Notes Receivable and Notes Payable accounts may be controlling accounts and the note registers may be designed for use as books of original entry and subsidiary records rather than as merely supplementary memorandum records.

The illustration on page 301 shows how the notes receivable register may be used as a book of original entry in which to record the receipt of notes and acceptances receivable.

The total of the Accounts Receivable column is posted to the credit of the Accounts Receivable controlling account; postings to the credit of individual accounts in the subsidiary ledger are made as indicated by the check marks at the left of the names, and as more fully explained later.

The total of the Notes Receivable column is posted to the debit of the Notes Receivable controlling account. Since there are occasional interest and discount adjustments to be made in settling accounts by notes, Sundry Accounts sections are provided.

The entries in the notes receivable register are explained below. The debits and the credits in the register take the place of entries which would otherwise be made in the general journal.

First entry:

On July 2 we received a 30-day, 6% note dated July 1 from A. R. Lukins, the maker. We credited Lukins (the check mark in the L.F. column indicates the posting to his account) and Accounts Receivable control; Notes Receivable account was debited.

Second entry:

On July 6 we received a 60-day note from G. C. Walker with interest for 60 days at 6% included in the face. The note was received to apply on account. The entry in the register for the receipt of this note contained the following debits and credits:

Debit: Notes receivable...................... 1,010.00
Credit: Accounts receivable (and Walker)...   1,000.00
         Interest income (account 8135).....   10.00

Third entry:

James Hudson purchased merchandise from us on July 14. We allowed him to deduct 1% discount in consideration of his giving us a 30-day, interest-bearing note. The entry in the register for the receipt of the note was:

Debit: Notes receivable......................... 495.00
         Discount on sales (account 4008)............ 5.00
Credit: Accounts receivable (and Hudson)......   500.00

Fourth entry:

On July 21 we sold merchandise to C. F. Wilson under terms requiring him to accept a 30-day draft. The acceptance was received on July 25; it had been accepted on July 23 and was payable 30 days after sight. The acceptance was made payable at the Home National Bank of Atlanta. The entry was:

Debit: Notes receivable......................... 300.00
Credit: Accounts receivable (and Wilson).......   300.00

The postings to the general ledger from the register were:

	Debit	Credit
During the month—entries in Sundry Accounts columns:		
Discount on sales—account 4008......................	$ 5.00	
Interest income—account 8135......................		$ 10.00
At the end of the month:		
Notes receivable—account 1130........................	2,305.00	
Accounts receivable—account 1120....................		2,300.00
Total debits and credits to general ledger........	$2,310.00	$2,310.00

Notes Receivable Register

(Left Page)

Line	Date Received 19—	Date Made or Accepted 19—	N-A	Maker or Drawee (Name)	Drawer or Endorser (Name)	Time Mo.	Time Da.	Int. Rate	Where Payable	Credit Accounts Receivable 1120	Sundry Accounts Debit Acct. No.	Debit Amount	Sundry Accounts Credit Acct. No.	Credit Amount	Debit Notes Receivable 1130
1	July 2	July 1	N	A. R. Lukins		30		6%	Our office	500 00					500 00
2	6	6	N	G. C. Walker		60		6% in Face	Our office	1,000 00			8135	10 00	1,010 00
3	14	14	N	James Hudson		30		6%	Our office	500 00	4008	5 00			495 00
4	25	23	A	C. F. Wilson	Ourselves	30S			Home National—Atlanta	300 00					300 00
5															
6										2,300 00		5 00		10 00	2,305 00

Notes Receivable Register

(Right Page)

Line	When Payable Year	J	F	M	A	M	J	J	A	S	O	N	D	Discounted Date	With Whom	Date Collected	Remarks
1	19—							31								July 31 19—	
2	19—								4								
3	19—									13							
4	19—										22						
5																	
6																	

(The entries in the N-A column indicate whether the paper is a note or an acceptance. "30S" means 30 days after sight.)

Accounts in the accounts receivable subsidiary ledger were credited as indicated by the check marks at the left of the names.

Entries for the collection of notes receivable would be made in the cash receipts book in the usual way, with notations in the Date Collected column of the register. The cash receipts book should have a Notes Receivable credit column to facilitate posting to the controlling account.

Notes payable register. The entries in the notes payable register on page 303 are explained in the following comments:

First entry:
On November 1 we gave a 60-day, 6% note for $5,000 to Sidney Welch to apply on account.

Debit: Vouchers payable (No. 316)............ 5,000.00
Credit: Notes payable................... 5,000.00

Second entry:
On November 3 we accepted a 30-day sight draft for $1,000, without interest, drawn by George Mason, payable to himself.

Debit: Vouchers payable (No. 321)............ 1,000.00
Credit: Notes payable................... 1,000.00

Third entry:
On November 7 we gave a note to James Snowden, to whom we owed $2,000; the note was due in 30 days, and the face included interest at 6% for 30 days.

Debit: Vouchers payable (No. 330)............ 2,000.00
          Sundry interest expense (account 8235).. 10.00
Credit: Notes payable................... 2,010.00

Fourth entry:
On November 25 we borrowed from the bank, issuing a 60-day, non-interest note for $5,000, and receiving $4,950 as the proceeds. This transaction required a cash receipts book entry as well as a note register entry. These entries were as follows:

	Entries Not Posted	Entries Posted Debits	Credits
Notes payable register:			
Debit: Memo in Sundry Accounts column........	4,950.00		
Sundry interest expense (account 8235)....		50.00	
Credit: Notes payable....................			5,000.00
Cash receipts book:			
Debit: Cash.................................		4,950.00	
Credit: Memo in Sundry Accounts column....	4,950.00		

The entry in the cash receipts book appears on page 304 (all columns not required for the entry are omitted).

Notes Payable Register

(Left Page)

Line	Date of Entry	Date Made or Accepted	N A	Payee √	Payee Name	Int. Rate	Time Mo. Da.	Where Payable	Endorser or Drawer Name	Voucher No.	Voucher √	Voucher Amount	Sundry Debit Acct. No.	Sundry Debit √	Sundry Debit Amount	Sundry Credit Acct. No.	Sundry Credit √	Sundry Credit Amount	Credit Notes Payable 2130
1	19— Nov. 1	19— Nov. 1	N	√	Sidney Welch	6%	60	His office		316	√	5,000 00							5,000 00
2	3	3	A	√	George Mason		30S	His office		321	√	1,000 00							1,000 00
3	7	7	N	√	James Snowden	In Face	30	Farmers Bank	George Mason	330	√	2,000 00	8235 / CR	√ / X	10 00 / 4,950 00				2,010 00
4	25	25	N	√	First National Bank		60	First National Bank					8235	√	50 00				5,000 00
5																			
6											√	8,000 00			5,010 00				13,010 00

Notes Payable Register

(Right Page)

Line	Year	When Payable J F M A M J J A S O N D	Date Paid	Remarks
1	19—	31		See cash book entry
2	19—	3		
3	19—	7		
4	19—	24		
5				
6				

Cash Receipts Book

Date	Account	Explanation	SUNDRY ACCOUNTS (Credit)			Cash (Debit)
			Acct. No.	√	Amount	
						1111
Nov. 25	First National Bank	See notes payable register	X		4,950 00	4,950 00

The postings to the general ledger from the register were:

	Debit	Credit
During the month—entries in Sundry Accounts columns:		
Sundry interest expense—account 8235 (two entries)... $	60.00	
At the end of the month:		
Vouchers payable—account 2120.....................	8,000.00	
Notes payable—account 2130................... ...		$13,010.00
Total postings to general ledger................	$ 8,060.00	$13,010.00
Memo entry—not posted—balanced by unposted entry in		
cash receipts book.................................	4,950.00	
	$13,010.00	$13,010.00

When a voucher is paid by a note, notations should be made in the Date Paid and Check Number columns of the voucher register.

Date Paid	Check No.
Nov. 1	N.P.R.

These notations indicate that the voucher was paid by a note issued on November 1 and recorded in the notes payable register. After the notations are made in the voucher register, a check mark should be entered in the (√) column of the notes payable register, after the number of the voucher paid.

Entries for the payment of notes payable will be made in the voucher register and cash disbursements book in the usual way, with notations in the memorandum columns of the note register.

Alternative Treatments of Cash Discounts

Treatment as other income and expense. So far throughout this text, discounts on sales have been shown in the income and expense statements as a deduction from sales, and discounts on purchases have been shown as a deduction from purchases. They are sometimes shown under the captions, respectively, of "other expense" and "other income." Those who favor this procedure argue that, like interest expense and income, cash discounts are related to the use of money; they further maintain that discounts on sales are offered as an inducement to customers to pay their bills promptly, thus reducing the hazard of losses from bad debts.

The treatment of cash discounts as deductions from purchases and sales is coming to be recognized as theoretically preferable. The treatment of purchase discounts as other income is based on an absurdity: it assumes that, by purchasing merchandise and paying for it within the discount period, income is earned, regardless of whether or not the goods have been sold. With respect to both purchase and sales discounts, they are somewhat analogous to returns and allowances: both are deductions to determine the net cost of purchases and the net proceeds of sales.

Purchase discounts lost. Under the method of recording purchase discounts previously explained in this text, and commonly used in business, the credit balance in the Discount on Purchases account shows the amount of discount *taken*. The accounts do not show how much discount was *lost* by failure to pay bills within the discount period. An alternative method of recording purchases and purchase discounts, to disclose this important information, is illustrated below:

(1) Raw material is purchased with a billed price of $1,000, and with terms of 2/10; n/30. The purchase is recorded in the voucher register at the *net* price, by the following debit and credit:

```
5171—Purchases—Raw materials.................... 980.00
        2120—Vouchers payable................              980.00
```

(2) If the bill is paid within the discount period, the following entry is made in the cash disbursements book:

```
2120—Vouchers payable.......................... 980.00
        1111—Cash...........................              980.00
```

(3) If the bill is paid after the discount period has expired, the following entry is made in the cash disbursements book:

```
2120—Vouchers payable.......................... 980.00
5174—Discounts lost............................  20.00
        1111—Cash...........................            1,000.00
```

Adjusting entries for discounts lost. At the end of each period for which statements are prepared, an adjusting journal entry should be made for the discount on all unpaid vouchers for which the discount period has expired. A memorandum column should be provided in the voucher register to show the amount of the discount lost, so that the total liability on the voucher will be shown in the schedule of open vouchers payable. The procedure is illustrated on page 306.

General Journal

Date		General Ledger	Accounts Receivable 1120	Vouchers Payable 2120		General Ledger	Accounts Receivable 1120	Notes Receivable 1130
19— July 31	5174—Discounts lost	100 00						
	2120—Vouchers payable (No. 62).........					100 00		
	Discount period expired.							

Voucher Register

Voucher No.	Date	Payee	Terms	PAID		MEMO ENTRIES				
				Date	Check No.	Returns and Allowances Date	Discounts Lost	Vouchers Payable 2120	Purchases Raw Materials 5171	
62	19— July 8	Brown Company........	2/10;n/30			19— July 31	100 00	4,900 00	4,900 00	

(The purpose of the memo column for Returns and Allowances was explained in Chapter 14.)

Discussion of the method.   The method of recording purchases and purchase discounts lost, just described, is commonly referred to as the "net price" procedure.   Many accountants favor the net price procedure for three reasons: (1) it discloses very significant information—namely, the amount of discounts lost; (2) it records purchases at the price which will secure the goods; and (3) it results in presenting liabilities more nearly in terms of the amounts that will be expended for their settlement; if most invoices are paid before the discount period expires, the recording of purchases and liabilities in terms of gross invoice price tends to overstate the liabilities by the amount of the available purchase discounts on unpaid vouchers.   But since the procedure is unusual, if it is followed the balance sheet should indicate parenthetically that the liability on vouchers payable is stated net of available discounts.

There is some difference of opinion regarding the proper position of the Discounts Lost account in the periodic statements of operations.   Many accountants believe that, as a matter of theory, the net price is the correct measure of cost.   Following this theory, they would show the discounts lost in the profit and loss statement as an administrative expense, since, presumably, it is the responsibility of the administrative officers to see that obligations of the business are paid within the discount period.

Other accountants believe that cost is equal to the entire amount paid for an item.   Under this theory, the balance of the Discounts Lost account is added to the purchases.   The chart of accounts in this chapter is in accord with this theory.

CHAPTER 21
Bonds, Sinking Funds, and
Sinking Fund Reserves

Sources of corporate funds. When a corporation finds it necessary or desirable to raise additional funds, it may borrow them on a short-term note, on a long-term mortgage note, or on bonds, or it may issue additional stock. It usually is regarded as good business management to borrow on short-term notes only in case the funds are needed for current operations and the current operations presumably will produce the cash with which to repay the loan. If the funds are to be used for plant additions or permanent investments, they usually should be obtained by issuance of long-term securities.

Mortgage notes and bonds. If all the desired long-term funds can be borrowed from one lender, the borrower may issue a note and a mortgage; the note will recite the terms of the obligation (date, maturity, interest rate, and so forth) and the mortgage will effect a pledge of certain property as security. A mortgage originally was a conveyance of property from a debtor to a creditor or his representative, subject to the proviso that, if the debtor met his obligation, the conveyance would be nullified. In most states the form of the mortgage has been changed to give it the status of a lien instead of a conveyance or transfer of title.

If it is impossible to obtain the funds from one lender, an issue of bonds may be offered to the public. Since the bonds may be held by many people, who are not known at the time of arranging for the issue and who will change with each transfer of a bond from one holder to another, the lenders cannot be named in a mortgage. Therefore, the borrower selects a trustee, usually a bank or a trust company, to act as a representative of the bondholders; and a mortgage, or deed of trust, is executed conveying a conditional title to the pledged property to the trustee as agent for the bondholders. This trustee is called the *trustee under the mortgage.*

Since long-term borrowings by corporations are usually represented by bonds, the remainder of this chapter deals specifically with bonds. However, except as indicated above, long-term mortgage notes are essentially of the same nature as secured bonds. Therefore, what is said in the remainder of this chapter with respect to secured bonds may be regarded as also applying generally to long-term mortgage notes.

Stocks and bonds—advantages and disadvantages. Bond issues have certain advantages over stock issues:

(1) Bondholders have no vote; therefore, the stockholders do not have to share the management with them.

(2) The money cost may be lower. If common stock is issued, the contributors of new capital will share prorata with the old common stockholders in accumulated surplus and earnings. If preferred stock is issued, it may be participating, in which case the dividends may be greatly in excess of reasonable interest on bonds; or it may be nonparticipating, in which case it usually is necessary to give the preferred stock a dividend rate higher than the interest rate at which bonds could be sold, because bonds are a positive, and usually a secured, liability with a definite maturity, and also because bond interest is payable unconditionally, whereas the payment of preferred dividends is dependent upon earnings and the existence of surplus.

(3) The fact that bond interest is deductible as an expense in the computation of income taxes, whereas dividends are not, is frequently a deciding factor in the choice of securities to be issued, and has sometimes even influenced corporations to convert preferred stock into bonds.

On the other hand, if interest and principal payments on a bond issue are not made when due, the bondholders may institute foreclosure proceedings and the borrowing company may lose fixed assets which are essential to its operations and may even be forced into liquidation, with a consequent loss which will leave a very small equity for the stockholders.

Classes of bonds. It is impossible to discuss all the different kinds of bonds which have been devised for use in corporate financing. Some of the more common forms are:

(1) Secured bonds. These differ as to the nature of the property which is pledged as security. Three classes of secured bonds are in common use:

   (a) Real estate mortgage bonds. These are secured by mortgages on land, or on land and buildings.

   (b) Chattel mortgage bonds. These are secured by mortgages on tangible personal property, such as machinery, equipment of various kinds, and merchandise.

   (c) Collateral trust bonds. These are secured by a pledge of stocks, bonds, or other negotiable instruments.

(2) Unsecured bonds. Unsecured bonds are sometimes called *debentures*. Since they are not secured by a pledge of any specific property, their marketability depends upon the general credit of the borrower.

First and second mortgages. Bonds may be secured by first, second, or even third mortgages on the same property. If the obligations are not met, and foreclosure ensues, the proceeds of the mortgaged property must go first to the satisfaction of the first-mortgage bondholders, any residue to the satisfaction of the second-mortgage bondholders, and so on.

Second-mortgage bonds are thus obviously a less desirable investment than first-mortgage bonds, because they are secured by a secondary lien on the pledged assets. First-mortgage bonds are called *prior-lien* or *underlying* bonds; second-mortgage bonds are called *junior* bonds.

Registered and coupon bonds. Bonds may be classified in three groups on the basis of registry, as follows:

(1) Registered as to both principal and interest.

The name of the owner of the bond is recorded on the books of the issuing company or its fiscal agent, and the interest is paid by checks drawn to the order of the bondholders. This method has the advantage of safeguarding the owner against loss or theft, but it has two disadvantages: First, a sale and transfer can be made only by assignment and registry, instead of merely by delivery; second, the check method of paying interest is burdensome.

(2) Registered as to principal only.

By registering the bonds as to principal only, and attaching coupons for the interest, the owner is safeguarded against loss or theft of principal, and the debtor company is relieved of the burden of issuing numerous interest checks.

(3) Unregistered.

Such a bond is transferable by mere delivery; the owner's endorsement is not required. The danger from loss or theft is, of course, much greater than with a bond which is registered as to principal. The interest is collected by clipping the interest coupons and presenting them to a bank for deposit or collection.

Recording the bond issue. A separate liability account should be kept with each bond issue. If there is more than one issue, the account title for each issue should contain a comprehensive description of the issue, such as "First Mortgage, 6%, Bonds Payable, 1972," or "Collateral Trust, 7% Bonds Payable, 1975." The year is the year of maturity.

Assuming that a company has only one bond issue, all of which is sold for cash at par, the entry to record the issue is:

```
Cash...................................... 100,000.00
    Bonds payable.........................          100,000.00
```

The mortgage, or trust deed, states the amount of bonds which may be issued. Each bond is signed by the trustee under the mortgage to indicate that it is secured by the mortgage; this is called *authentication by the trustee*.

Very frequently, the amount of bonds immediately authenticated by the trustee and issued by the borrowing company is less than the total issue provided for under the trust deed. To illustrate, assume that a company's real estate is ample in value to secure an issue of $100,000 of first-mortgage bonds. Only $60,000 of funds are immediately required, but there may be future requirements for $40,000 more. If the trust deed were drawn to secure an issue of only $60,000, a subsequent loan of $40,000 could be secured only by a second mortgage; a second-mortgage issue, being less desirable, might require a higher interest rate and might be difficult to market. In anticipation of its future requirements, the company may authorize a total first-mortgage bond issue of $100,-000, drawing a trust deed as security for a loan of that amount. If $100,000 of bonds are authenticated, but only $60,000 are issued, the entries are:

```
Unissued bonds............................ 100,000.00
    First-mortgage bonds payable............          100,000.00
To record the authorized issue of first-mort-
gage, 6%, real estate bonds payable, due
March 1, 1970.

Cash...................................... 60,000.00
    Unissued bonds.........................          60,000.00
Issuance of $60,000 bonds at par.
```

The facts with respect to authorized, unissued, and issued bonds should be shown in the balance sheet as follows:

```
Long-term liabilities:
    First-mortgage, 6%, real estate bonds pay-
        able, due March 1, 1970:
        Authorized........................ $100,000.00
        Less unissued.....................   40,000.00 $60,000.00
```

Or thus:

```
Long-term liabilities:
    First-mortgage, 6%, real estate bonds payable, due
        March 1, 1970; authorized, $100,000.00; issued........ $60,000.00
```

The amount of unissued bonds should be shown in the balance sheet, because the bondholders have a right to know that $40,000 of additional bonds can be issued under the same trust deed which secures their bonds. Thus, if the real estate is carried in the balance sheet at $150,000, the holders of the $60,000 of issued bonds would be interested in knowing that an additional $40,000 of bonds could be issued. On the basis of the issued bonds only, the ratio of security to debt is 150 to 60; but on the basis of the total authorized issue, the ratio of security is only 150 to 100.

If the bonds are registered as to principal or interest, or both, subsidiary records should be kept, showing the names and addresses of the holders.

Issuances between interest dates. Bonds are often issued between interest dates, in which case the purchaser is usually required to pay the accrued interest. To illustrate, assume that $10,000 of 6% bonds are issued two months after the interest date, at par and accrued interest; the entry will be:

Cash..	10,100.00	
Bonds payable.............................		10,000.00
Bond interest expense......................		100.00

When the semiannual interest is paid four months later, the entry will be:

Bond interest expense........................	300.00	
Cash......................................		300.00

The $300 debit to Bond Interest Expense made at the time of paying the interest, minus the $100 credit to Bond Interest Expense made at the time of selling the bonds, leaves the account with a $200 debit balance, which is the interest expense for four months.

Payment of interest. Most bonds provide for the payment of interest semiannually. The methods of paying bond interest depend upon whether the bonds are registered as to interest. Two conditions are illustrated:

(1) The bonds are registered as to interest. If there are a large number of bondholders, it is advisable to draw a check for the entire amount of the bond interest and deposit it in a special bond interest bank account. The entry will be:

The X Bank—Bond interest account..............	6,000.00	
Cash....................................		6,000.00
To record deposit of funds in the account for payment of bond interest.		

Such a procedure has the advantage of simplifying the reconciliation of the principal bank account; also, the chief disbursing officer can be relieved of the task of signing a large number of interest checks by delegating the work of signing interest checks to a subordinate. Separate checks will then be drawn on the bond interest account, the total of these checks being debited to Bond Interest Expense and credited to The X Bank—Bond Interest Account.

(2) The bonds are not registered as to interest, but bear coupons which are clipped by the holders and presented for collection. The bondholder usually deposits the coupons in his own bank account, and the bank makes the collection. The coupons usually designate a bank at which collection can be made; when the semiannual interest is due, the company deposits the total amount of the interest in a special account at the bank where the coupons are payable; when coupons are presented for payment, the bank pays them and charges the amount to the company's account. The entries by the issuing company are as follows:

On or before the date when interest is payable:

```
The X Bank—Bond interest account.............  6,000.00
    Cash....................................                6,000.00
    Transfer of funds to special bank account for pay-
    ment of interest.
```

On the date when interest is payable:

```
Bond interest expense..........................  6,000.00
    Accrued bond interest payable...............            6,000.00
    To record the expense and liability for six months'
    interest.
```

At the end of the month or at any other date when the bank reports the amount of coupons paid:

```
Accrued bond interest payable..................  5,700.00
    The X Bank—Bond interest account..........            5,700.00
    To record the payment of interest coupons pre-
    sented to the bank.
```

Since some bondholders may be dilatory in presenting coupons for payment, balances may remain in the special bank account and in the Accrued Bond Interest Payable account. The balance sheet should show as an asset any balance in the special bank account, and should show as a liability any balance in the Accrued Bond Interest Payable account; the mere deposit of funds in a special bank account to be used for the payment of bond interest does not constitute payment of the liability.

Bond discount. If the bond interest rate is lower than the market rate for bonds of a similar nature (for instance, similar in the nature of the borrower's business and credit standing, and in the nature of the borrower's security), it may be impossible to obtain par for the bonds. Let us assume, by way of illustration, that a ten-year, 5% bond issue of $100,000 is disposed of for a net amount of $98,000. The issuance of these bonds will be recorded by the following entry:

```
Cash........................................ 98,000.00
Bond discount................................ 2,000.00
    Bonds payable...........................          100,000.00
    Issuance of bonds at 98.
```

Amortization of bond discount. In the preceding illustration, $98,000 was received, but $100,000 must be repaid. The $2,000 excess of the amount to be paid over the amount received is an expense to be spread over the life of the bonds. The total interest cost over the life of the bonds includes the discount as well as the semiannual interest payments.

The Bond Discount account should be written off to Bond Interest Expense in periodic installments; the write-off commonly is made in equal amounts each six months, at the semiannual interest-payment dates. Since there will be twenty semiannual interest payments during the ten-year life of the bonds, the discount will be written off in twenty equal installments of $100. The charges to Bond Interest Expense each six months will be as shown in the following entries:

```
Bond interest expense......................... 2,500.00
    Cash......................................          2,500.00
    Payment of semiannual interest.

Bond interest expense.........................  100.00
    Bond discount.............................          100.00
    To amortize 1/20 of the discount.
```

These semiannual amortizations will completely write off the Bond Discount account at the end of the tenth year, and will produce equal total semiannual charges to the Bond Interest Expense account.

If a semiannual interest-payment date does not coincide with the end of the issuing company's accounting period, an adjusting entry will be required for the accrued interest, and another entry will be required to amortize the portion of the discount applicable to the period between the last preceding interest date and the end of the accounting period. For example, referring to the preceding illustration, assume that interest was paid and an amortization entry made on September 30, and that the issuing company's accounting year ends on December 31.   The following entries will be required on December 31:

Bond interest expense............................	1,250.00	
Accrued bond interest payable................		1,250.00
Accrued interest for three months.		

Bond interest expense...........................	50.00	
Bond discount..............................		50.00
Amortization of discount for three months.		

Bond premium.   If bonds are issued at a premium, the premium reduces the interest charge.   For instance, if the bonds mentioned in the preceding illustration were sold for $102,000, the $2,000 premium received when the bonds were sold would not have to be repaid at their maturity, and should therefore be offset against the interest payments to determine the net cost of the use of the money.

The entry at the time of the issuance of the bonds would be as follows:

Cash.......................................	102,000.00	
Bonds payable..........................		100,000.00
Bond premium..........................		2,000.00
Issuance of bonds at 102.		

The payment of the bond interest and the amortization of the bond premium in equal semiannual installments would be recorded by the entries shown below:

Bond interest expense...........................	2,500.00	
Cash......................................		2,500.00
Payment of semiannual interest.		

Bond premium..................................	100.00	
Bond interest expense......................		100.00
Amortization of bond premium.		

If an interest-payment date does not coincide with the end of the issuing company's accounting period, end-of-period entries should be made for the accrued interest and for the amortization of premium for the fractional period.

Bond premium and discount in the balance sheet.   It has long been regarded as correct accounting procedure to show unamortized bond discount under a deferred charges caption at the bottom of the asset side of the balance sheet, and unamortized bond premium on the liability side under a caption of deferred credits, between the long-term liabilities and the net worth.   For instance, assume that a trial balance contained the following balances:

First-mortgage, 6%, real estate bonds, 1970......		100,000.00
First-mortgage equipment bonds, $5\frac{1}{2}$%, 1965.....		50,000.00
Premium on first-mortgage real estate bonds.....		3,000.00
Discount on first-mortgage equipment bonds.....	1,800.00	

The customary presentation of these facts in the balance sheet is:

Assets

Deferred charges:
Discount on first-mortgage equipment bonds...................... $ 1,800.00

Liabilities and Net Worth

Long-term liabilities:
First-mortgage, 6%, real estate bonds, 1970.......... $100,000.00
First-mortgage equipment bonds, 5½%, 1965..........   50,000.00
Total long-term liabilities.................................. 150,000.00

Deferred credits:
Premium on first-mortgage real estate bonds..................... 3,000.00

There has been some agitation in favor of showing unamortized premium as an addition to, and unamortized discount as a deduction from, the par of the bonds, thus:

Liabilities and Net Worth

Long-term liabilities:
First-mortgage, 6%, real estate bonds, 1970.......... $100,000.00
Add unamortized premium.......................   3,000.00 $103,000.00
First-mortgage equipment bonds, 5½%, 1965.......... $ 50,000.00
Deduct unamortized discount....................   1,800.00   48,200.00

This procedure has not been generally adopted by the accounting profession.

Retirement of bonds.   Bonds may be retired:

(1) In total at maturity, out of the borrowing company's general funds. The payment of the bonds under such conditions is recorded by debiting Bonds Payable and crediting Cash.

(2) In a series. Bonds retirable in this way are called *serial* bonds.

   To illustrate, assume that $100,000 is borrowed; nothing is to be paid off during the first five years; at the end of the sixth year, and each year thereafter, $20,000 is to be paid, so that the bonds will be retired serially by the end of the tenth year. Each retirement is recorded by a debit to Bonds Payable and a credit to Cash.

(3) In total at maturity out of a sinking fund created by periodic deposits with a sinking fund trustee. This method is discussed below.

Sinking funds.   If bonds are to be retired at maturity through the operation of a sinking fund, the borrowing company agrees, as one of the terms of the trust indenture, to make periodic deposits with a sinking fund trustee, who invests the deposited funds in securities. The sinking fund trustee may, or may not, be also the trustee under the mortgage. Sinking fund deposit agreements take various forms, particularly with respect to the amounts of the periodic contributions. As a simple illustration, we shall assume that a company borrows $100,000 which is repayable at the end of ten years. It agrees to deposit $10,000 with the sinking fund trustee at the end of the first year; the trustee is to invest the fund in securities and add the income earned on these securities to the fund. At the end of the second year, the company will deposit enough to bring the total fund up to $20,000. At the end of the third year, the company will deposit enough to bring the total fund up to $30,000; and so on to the end of the tenth year. The annual contributions by the company will decrease because the interest collected by the trustee on the accumulating fund will increase each year.

Assume that the trustee is able to earn 5% on the securities in the fund; the accumulation of the sinking fund may be tabulated in the manner illustrated below:

End of Year	Interest Earned	Deposit	Total Fund
1		$10,000.00	$ 10,000.00
2	$ 500.00	9,500.00	20,000.00
3	1,000.00	9,000.00	30,000.00
4	1,500.00	8,500.00	40,000.00
5	2,000.00	8,000.00	50,000.00
6	2,500.00	7,500.00	60,000.00
7	3,000.00	7,000.00	70,000.00
8	3,500.00	6,500.00	80,000.00
9	4,000.00	6,000.00	90,000.00
10	4,500.00	5,500.00	100,000.00
	$22,500.00	$77,500.00	

Annual entries for the deposit of funds with the trustee and the collection of interest by the trustee on sinking fund securities are indicated below:

End of first year:

Sinking fund cash............................. 10,000.00
   Cash......................................   10,000.00
   Deposit with sinking fund trustee.

End of second year:

Sinking fund cash............................. 500.00
   Sinking fund income.......................   500.00
   Income earned on sinking fund securities. (The Sinking Fund Income account will be closed to Profit and Loss.)

Sinking fund cash............................. 9,500.00
   Cash......................................   9,500.00
   Deposit with sinking fund trustee.

The trustee is expected to invest the sinking fund deposits in securities, but there usually will be some uninvested cash in the fund. The company's records should show what portion of the sinking fund is represented by cash and what portion is represented by securities. Therefore, when the trustee reports the purchase of securities, the company should make an entry debiting Sinking Fund Securities and crediting Sinking Fund Cash.

The sinking fund cash and securities may be shown in one total in the balance sheet, or they may be detailed as follows:

```
Sinking fund:
  Cash.....................................  $    300.00
  Securities...............................    19,700.00  $20,000.00
```

The sinking fund may be shown under the other assets caption or as a separate item.

When the bonds mature, the sinking fund securities will be disposed of by the trustee, who will pay the bonds from the cash in the sinking fund. Assuming that the entire $100,000 fund was invested in securities, that the securities were disposed of without loss, and that the bonds were paid, the trustee would report the facts to the debtor company, and the company would make entries as follows:

```
Sinking fund cash...........................  100,000.00
  Sinking fund securities...................               100,000.00
  Sale of sinking fund securities.

Bonds payable...............................  100,000.00
  Sinking fund cash.........................               100,000.00
  Retirement of the bonds.
```

If a loss is incurred in the disposal of the sinking fund securities, the company will be obliged to make another deposit with the trustee in an amount sufficient to bring the fund up to the required balance. Assume that the trustee loses $500 on the disposal of the securities; the company will be obliged to make up this loss by a deposit of $500, and its entries will be:

```
Sinking fund cash...........................   99,500.00
Loss on sale of sinking fund securities.........    500.00
  Sinking fund securities...................               100,000.00
  Sale of sinking fund securities at a loss.

Sinking fund cash...........................      500.00
  Cash.....................................                   500.00
  Additional deposit with trustee to cover the
  loss from the disposal of the securities in the
  fund.

Bonds payable...............................  100,000.00
  Sinking fund cash.........................               100,000.00
  Retirement of bonds by sinking fund trustee.
```

On the other hand, if the trustee makes a gain of $540 on the disposal of the sinking fund securities, the residue of the fund will be returned to the company.   The company's entries will be:

```
Sinking fund cash.........................  100,540.00
    Sinking fund securities..................              100,000.00
    Gain on sale of sinking fund securities.....                 540.00
    Sale of sinking fund securities at a gain.

Bonds payable............................  100,000.00
    Sinking fund cash......................              100,000.00
    Retirement of bonds by sinking fund trustee.

Cash.....................................      540.00
    Sinking fund cash......................                 540.00
    Excess in sinking fund received from trustee.
```

Sinking fund expense.   The service fee charged by the sinking fund trustee may be paid from the sinking fund cash.   If this is done, the issuing company should debit Sinking Fund Expense and credit Sinking Fund Cash.   Or the trustee's fee may be paid from the issuing company's general cash; if so, the entry will be: debit Sinking Fund Expense and credit Cash.

Sinking fund reserves.   In addition to requiring sinking fund deposits, the terms of the bond issue may restrict the amount of dividends which the borrowing company may pay during the life of the bonds.   One way of making this restriction is by requiring the establishment of a sinking fund reserve by transfers from earned surplus.

The sinking fund reserve requirement is intended to prevent the impairment of the company's working capital.   Suppose, for instance, that the company which issued the bonds mentioned in the foregoing illustration had a working capital (current assets minus current liabilities) of $100,000 after issuing its bonds, and that this amount was considered no more than adequate to carry on operations.   Assume that, during the first year of the life of the bonds, the company had a net income of $20,000, which increased the working capital an equal amount; if the company paid dividends to the full extent of the $20,000 net income and also paid $10,000 to the sinking fund trustee, the working capital would be reduced $10,000.   If this took place year after year, the company's working capital might be so impaired that it would not be able to carry on its operations profitably.   A year might soon come when, because of inadequate working capital, the company's operations would be so unprofitable that it would not be able to make its sinking fund deposit.

To restrict the payment of dividends, and thus to avoid a dangerous impairment of working capital, the terms of the bond issue may include a provision similar to the following: "In addition to increasing the sinking fund $10,000 each year, the company shall transfer $10,000 each year from its Earned Surplus account to a Sinking Fund Reserve account; the surplus set apart in this reserve shall not be available for dividends until the bonds have been paid."

Referring to the illustration in the section on sinking funds, and assuming that the company was obligated to set up a reserve in accordance with the provision just quoted, the following annual entries would be made:

End of first year:

Sinking Fund Entry:

Sinking fund cash...........................	10,000.00	
Cash..................................		10,000.00
Deposit with the sinking fund trustee.		

Sinking Fund Reserve Entry:

Earned surplus.............................	10,000.00	
Sinking fund reserve......................		10,000.00
To transfer a portion of the surplus to a reserve.		

End of second year:

Sinking Fund Entries:

Sinking fund cash..........................	500.00	
Sinking fund income......................		500.00
Income collected by sinking fund trustee on securities in the fund.		

Sinking fund cash..........................	9,500.00	
Cash..................................		9,500.00
Deposit with the trustee.		

Sinking Fund Reserve Entry:

Earned surplus.............................	10,000.00	
Sinking fund reserve......................		10,000.00
To transfer a portion of the surplus to a reserve.		

A sinking fund reserve is really a part of the earned surplus; for the time being, dividends cannot be charged to it, but it is earned surplus nevertheless. Therefore, it should be shown in the balance sheet under the net worth caption, as illustrated below:

Net worth:		
Capital stock...........................		$500,000.00
Earned surplus:		
Sinking fund reserve—Not available for dividends........................	$20,000.00	
Free—Available for dividends.......	15,000.00	
Total earned surplus.........		35,000.00
Total net worth..................		$535,000.00

It is sometimes difficult to understand that a sinking fund reserve is really a part of the earned surplus, because other reserves (such as the reserve for bad debts and the reserves for depreciation) represent decreases in the assets.   The nature of the sinking fund reserve would be more easily understood if it were called "Surplus Appropriated for Sinking Fund," or "Surplus Not Available for Dividends Until After the Bonds Have Been Paid."

After the bonds have matured and been paid, the bondholders have no further right to restrict the payment of dividends; therefore, an entry can be made debiting the Sinking Fund Reserve and crediting Earned Surplus.   Thus the balance in the Sinking Fund Reserve is returned to Earned Surplus, and is again free from any contractual limitations upon the payment of dividends.   However, it might be expedient for the directors to refrain voluntarily from the payment of dividends from this surplus in order to protect the company's working capital position.

A sinking fund requirement such as the one quoted on pages 319 and 320 may not be enough safeguard against an impairment of working capital.   If a company is required to deposit $10,000 in a sinking fund, it may not be sufficient to require that $10,000 also be transferred from Earned Surplus to a reserve; even though this requirement may be met, the borrowing company may still deplete its working capital by paying dividends and charging them against earned surplus accumulated before the long-term debt was incurred. For this reason, some bond indentures provide that, in addition to the creation of a sinking fund by periodic credits, the earned surplus at the date of the issuance of the obligations (or a stated portion thereof) shall be "frozen" and shall not be available for charges for dividends until the obligations are retired.

Some bond indentures restrict dividends in ways other than by a sinking fund reserve requirement.   For instance, the issuing company may agree to refrain from paying dividends which will reduce the net worth below a stipulated amount, or which will reduce the working capital below a stipulated amount, or which will reduce the working capital ratio (a company with $300,000 of current assets and $100,000 of current liabilities has a working capital ratio of 3 to 1) below the ratio existing when the bonds were issued.

Dividend restrictions not reflected by a sinking fund reserve should be stated parenthetically in the balance sheet in the manner illustrated below:

```
Net worth:
   Capital stock...........................   $100,000.00
   Earned surplus (of which $40,000 is not
      available for cash dividends because of
      restrictions in the bond indenture).......    65,000.00
                                                    _____
      Total.. ......................................   $165,000.00
```

CHAPTER 22
Cash

What is cash? In accounting usage, coin, paper money, bank balances, and other media of exchange, such as checks, bank drafts, cashier's checks, express money orders, and postal money orders, are referred to as "cash." I. O. U.'s and postage stamps, sometimes found with the contents of a cash fund, are not cash. An I. O. U. is a receivable. Postage stamps are a prepaid expense.

Although a business may have several cash accounts in its ledger, it is considered acceptable to combine the accounts for balance sheet purposes, describing the combined accounts as "Cash on hand and in banks." Or, the cash may be detailed as follows:

Cash on hand..............	$ xxx
Cash in bank..............	x,xxx

If some of the cash has been set aside for a special purpose or is otherwise not readily available for disbursement, such cash should be listed separately in the balance sheet.

As a general rule, cash is a current asset. There may be instances, however, where cash funds become so restricted or blocked that they should be excluded from the current assets section of the balance sheet. Cash in an insolvent closed bank is an example.

Internal check. The objectives of a good system of internal check, as it relates to assets, may be summarized as follows:

(1) To safeguard the assets.
(2) To achieve more accurate accounting.

The above objectives stand a greater chance of being achieved if, whenever it is feasible, the custody of assets and the recording of transactions affecting assets are assigned to two or more individuals in such a way that the work of one person is verified by another person. An irregularity, then, would require collusion.

In broad outline, a basic system of internal check with regard to cash would include the following:

(1) Establishing a definite routine for accounting for cash transactions.
(2) Separating the receiving and disbursing of cash from the recording function.

(3) Separating the activities associated with the disbursing of cash from those associated with the receiving of cash.

(4) Requiring that all cash received be deposited daily in the bank.

(5) Requiring that all disbursements be made by check.

The methods and procedures used to achieve internal check vary greatly in different organizations. The system described below is merely indicative of some of the methods and procedures in use.

Cash receipts. Some receipts may come *over the counter* as the proceeds of cash sales or as collections on account; other receipts may come through the mail. As to the cash received over the counter, prenumbered invoices should be made out for all cash sales, and it should be the duty of some person to see that the duplicates of these cash sales invoices or tickets agree with the recorded receipts, and that no invoices are missing and unaccounted for. Prenumbered receipts should be issued for all over-the-counter collections on account; if possible, these receipts should be issued by some person other than the one who receives the cash; and a third employee should compare the duplicates of the receipts with the cash record. All over-the-counter receipts should be recorded on a cash register, if possible. When this is done, all cash received over the counter should be counted and the total compared with the cash register tape by some person other than the one who collected the cash.

As noted above, the danger of misappropriations of cash is reduced if the system of internal check makes collusion necessary to conceal an abstraction of cash receipts. As to cash received *through the mail*, a system of internal control can be provided in which the perpetration and concealment of fraud would require the collusion of three people, whose records should be required to agree, as indicated below:

(1) All remittances received through the mail should go to an employee other than the cashier or bookkeeper for listing on an adding machine; this employee should also obtain the cash register readings so that his tape will include the total receipts for the day. After he has listed the mail receipts, he will turn the cash over to the cashier and will send the remittance letters to the bookkeeper.

(2) The cashier will prepare the deposit tickets and will deposit the funds. Since all funds received should be deposited daily, the total of the deposit tickets for the day should

equal the total of the adding machine tape prepared by the first employee. The cashier should prepare each deposit ticket in duplicate, request the receiving teller at the bank to receipt the duplicate, and present the receipted duplicate to the first employee for comparison with his tape.

(3) The bookkeeper will record the cash receipts from information shown by the remittance letters, cash register tapes, and other papers; the total recorded receipts for the day, as shown by the cash receipts book, should equal the first employee's tape and the cashier's deposit.

With such a system of internal check, fraud cannot be practiced with the cash receipts and remain undetected even for a day, without the collusion of three persons. The first employee has no access to the books and cannot falsify the records to conceal a misappropriation; he cannot expect to withhold funds received from debtors without detection, because the debtors will receive statements or letters from the credit department and will report their remittances.

If the cashier withholds any cash, his daily deposits will not agree with the first employee's list or with the bookkeeper's record of cash receipts made from the remittance letters and other sources of information. The bookkeeper, having no access to the cash, has no opportunity to misappropriate any of it, and therefore has no incentive to falsify his records unless he is participating in a three-party collusion.

Cash disbursements. Since all receipts are deposited daily in the bank, all disbursements must be made by check. The person authorized to sign checks should have no authority to make entries in the cash book; thus a fraudulent disbursement by check could not be concealed without the collusion of two persons. The collusion of a third person can be made necessary:

(1) Either by requiring that all checks shall be signed by one person and countersigned by another,

(2) Or by installing the voucher system, allowing the checks to be signed by one person, but only upon authorization evidenced by a voucher signed by some other person.

All checks should be prenumbered. All spoiled, mutilated, or voided checks should be preserved. Some companies even go so far as to require that such checks be recorded in their proper sequence in the cash disbursements record, without entry in the money column, but with a notation to the effect that the check is void.

Bank columns in the cash books. If all cash receipts are deposited daily and if all disbursements are made by check, the

Cash columns of the cash books will serve as a record of the deposits in, and the withdrawals from, the bank.   If several bank accounts are kept, the cash receipts book should be provided with as many columns as there are bank accounts.   This book may then appear somewhat as shown on page 326.

Instead of a single account with Cash, there should be a separate account with each bank, and the monthly totals of the Bank columns of the cash receipts record should be posted to the debit of the respective bank accounts.

The cash disbursements book (check register) may be similarly ruled, in which case the Bank credit columns should be provided with subcolumns to show check numbers, as shown on page 327.

Instead of a cash disbursements book with several bank columns, as in the illustration, a separate cash disbursements book may be used for each bank.

Petty, or imprest, cash.   In the discussion of the system of internal check on cash disbursements, the statement was made that all disbursements should be made by check.   How is this possible when certain disbursements of trifling amounts, for carfares and postage, for instance, must be made in cash?   Although such petty disbursements may not actually be made by check, their total can be covered by a check through operating a petty cash fund.   The petty cash fund, which is sometimes called the "imprest fund," is operated as follows:

(1) Establishment of fund:

> A check is drawn for a round amount ($10, $50, or such an amount as will provide for petty disbursements for a reasonable time) and cashed.   The cash is held in the office for use in making petty disbursements.   The establishment of a fund of $25 is recorded by entries indicated below.

> *Voucher register:*
> Debit Petty Cash, credit Vouchers Payable: $25.
> *Cash disbursements book:*
> Debit Vouchers Payable, credit Cash: $25.

These entries record a transfer from the general cash account to the petty cash account.

(2) Disbursements from fund:

> When expenditures are made out of the petty cash fund, receipts or other memoranda are put into the petty cash box to show what the money was spent for.

Cash Receipts Book

| Date | Account Credited | CREDITS | | | DEBITS | |
		Sundry Accounts L.F.	Sundry Accounts Amount	Accounts Receivable	Discount on Sales	First National Bank	First State Bank
19— July 1	1 James White			2,000 00	20 00	1,980 00	
	1 Notes receivable		2,000 00				2,000 00
	1 F. B. Lathrop			1,000 00	10 00	990 00	
	1 Sales		530 00			30 00	500 00
						3,000 00	2,500 00

Cash Disbursements Book

Date	Payee	Vo. No.	Debit Vouchers Payable	Discount on Purchases	CREDITS First National Bank Check No.	First National Bank Amount	First State Bank Check No.	First State Bank Amount
19—								
July 1	Rogers Brothers.........	327	1,000 00	20 00	39	980 00		
1	Victory Steel Company...	321	2,500 00	50 00			317	2,450 00
1	A. R. Bell...............	317	1,200 00	12 00			318	1,188 00
1	City Trust Company.....	334	1,500 00		40	1,500 00		
						2,480 00		3,638 00

In many businesses, the petty cashier is required to fill out a petty cash voucher for each expenditure. An example of a completed petty cash voucher is presented below. Petty cash vouchers usually provide space for the signature of the person receiving the cash from the petty cashier; thus, a receipt exists for each disbursement. Any documents received by the petty cashier supporting a petty cash disbursement can be attached to the petty cash voucher.

Petty Cash Voucher

No. *1*   Date *July 2, 19--*

Paid to *Ace Delivery Co.*

For *Freight in*

Account No. *5172*   Amount *$1.15*

Payment Approved   Payment Received

H. Smith   *John A. Doe*

In addition, memorandum entries may be made in a petty cash disbursements book, to show what accounts will be charged with the disbursements. Such a book might appear as follows:

Petty Cash Book

Date	Voucher Number	Amount	Freight In (5172)	Freight Out (6061)	Advertising (6075)	Office Supplies (7011)	Sundry	
							Acct. No.	Amount
July 2	1	1 15	1 15					
7	2	3 25	1 10	2 15				
13	3	7 00			5 00		6051	2 00
16	4	1 43	75			68		
20	5	5 70	1 20	4 00		50		
24	6	6 20	2 00	1 20	3 00			
		24 73	6 20	7 35	8 00	1 18		2 00

This is merely a memorandum book. No postings are made from it.

(3) Replenishment of fund:

> Whenever the petty cash expenditures have nearly exhausted the fund, it is necessary to replenish it. In the above illustration, the petty cash book is totaled and ruled because the expenditures (which total $24.73) have nearly exhausted the fund, and it is necessary to replenish it. It is replenished by a check for the exact amount of the expenditures: $24.73. The issuance of the check is recorded as follows:

>> *Voucher register:*
>> Debit the various expense (or other) accounts; credit Vouchers Payable: $24.73.
>> *Cash disbursements book:*
>> Debit Vouchers Payable; credit Cash: $24.73.

The expense accounts are debited when the fund is replenished, and not when the petty disbursements are made. Thus, numerous small disbursements can be recorded by one entry in the voucher register.

As a general rule, the petty cash vouchers covering disbursements must be presented by the petty cashier to a designated accounting officer for his review and approval. Such petty cash vouchers should equal the replenishment check, and, after being marked "cancelled," to prevent their re-use, they are filed as support for the replenishment check.

The foregoing procedure may be summarized as follows:

	Vouchers Payable	Cash	Petty Cash	Expense (or other) Accounts
Establishment of fund:				
Entry for voucher	25.00		25.00	
Entry for check	25.00	25.00		
Disbursements from fund:				
No entries, except perhaps memorandum entries.				
Replenishment of fund:				
Entry for voucher	24.73			24.73
Entry for check	24.73	24.73		

Ignoring the debits and credits to Vouchers Payable, which offset one another, we may state the procedure as follows:

Establishment of fund: Debit Petty Cash, credit Cash.
Replenishment for
expenditures made: Debit expense or other accounts. Credit Cash.

It will be noted that the only entry in the Petty Cash account is the one establishing the fund; other entries will be made in this account only if the established amount of the fund is increased or decreased.

The Petty Cash account is not debited for replenishments of the fund or credited for petty cash disbursements. The person in charge of the petty cash fund should always have cash or evidence of disbursements in his box equal to the balance of the Petty Cash account.

The petty cash fund should always be replenished at the end of a period before the statements are prepared and the books are closed, so that the effect of expenditures from the petty cash fund will be reflected in the accounts of the period in which the expenditures are made.

Cash over and short. In the process of handling cash receipts, making change, and making disbursements from the petty cash fund, it is possible that errors may be made, with the result that cash shortages or cash overages may develop.

Example of cash overage:

A cash register is used for cash sales. At the end of the day, the cash register shows that cash sales for the day equal $325.60. However, the cash in the drawer, when counted, amounts to $325.80. The cash overage of 20 cents is recorded in the following entry:

Cash..	325.80	
Sales...		325.60
Cash over and short...........................		.20

Example of cash shortage:

A $25 petty cash fund exists. The fund is down to $1.50 and is being replenished. However, the petty cashier has petty cash vouchers accounting for the disbursement of only $23.00. The cash shortage of 50 cents is recorded in the following entry:

Various expense (or other) accounts....................	23.00	
Cash over and short..................................	.50	
Vouchers payable.................................		23.50

If the cash shortages exceed the overages during an accounting period, the Cash Over and Short account will have a debit balance. A debit balance will show the net expense arising from cash shortages and overages. Such an expense may be treated as a general expense. If the Cash Over and Short account has a credit balance at the end of an accounting period, it may be treated as an item of miscellaneous income.

Dealings with the Bank

Opening a bank account. When an account is opened at the bank, the persons authorized to draw checks against the account will be requested to sign cards furnished by the bank, to show the signatures which they will use on checks. These signature cards will be filed by the bank, so that a teller who may be unfamiliar with a depositor's signature can test the authenticity of a check drawn on his account by comparing the depositor's signature on the card with the signature on the check.

```
                                                    CORPORATION

To CONTINENTAL ILLINOIS BANK AND TRUST COMPANY
You are hereby authorized to charge to our account all orders or obligations
for payment of money drawn on or payable at, or which shall be paid or hon-
ored by, your Bank, bearing any of the signatures below. You are also author-
ized to recognize any of said signatures in the transaction of all other business
for our account.

_____ WILL SIGN _____ PRESIDENT

_____ WILL SIGN _____ VICE-
                                                   PRESIDENT

_____ WILL SIGN _____ TREASURER

_____ WILL SIGN _____ SECRETARY

_____ WILL SIGN _____ ASS'T
                                                   TREASURER

_____ WILL SIGN _____ ASS'T
                                                   SECRETARY

                     PLEASE SIGN FOOTNOTE
It is hereby certified that the above signatures are the duly authorized signa-
tures of

_____
                 (TITLE OF CORPORATION)
_____President_____Secretary
                            (OR OTHER OFFICER)
Date_____19____
2-2-12                    ORIGINAL
```

Signature Card

If the depositor is a corporation, the bank will request that the directors pass a resolution authorizing certain officers or employees of the corporation to sign checks, and that a copy of this resolution be filed with the bank.

Deposits. Deposits should be accompanied by deposit tickets which describe the items deposited. Deposit tickets are of various forms; an illustration appears on page 332.

It was formerly a general custom for the depositor to be furnished with a pass book in which the bank teller recorded deposits; the entries in the pass book, initialed by the receiving teller, constituted receipts for the deposits.

It is now a more general custom for the depositor to prepare deposit tickets in duplicate, and for the teller to initial the carbon copy and return it to the depositor as a receipt.

Maintaining a record of the bank balance. Cash receipts and deposits are recorded in the cash receipts book, and disbursements are recorded in the cash disbursements book. At the end of the month, totals are posted from the two books to the bank account in the ledger, and the resulting balance in this account should show the balance in the bank.

But, during the month, how can one ascertain the balance in the bank? The record may be kept:

(1) On the stubs of the check book, or
(2) In a bank register.

A running record on the check book stub is shown below.

Balance brought forward _8,503.75_

Deposit____

Total

Check No. _93_

Date _July 17, 19--_

Payee _J.H.Guthrie_ _650.00_

Balance _7,853.75_

Deposit _7/17/--_ _2,300.00_

Total _10,153.75_

Check No. _94_

Date _July 17, 19--_

Payee _F.L.Kenyon_ _400.00_

Balance carried forward _9,753.75_

Deposit Ticket   Check Book Stub

If many checks are drawn, the computation of the bank balance after each deposit and each check is usually regarded as unnecessary. In some cases, unbound checks are used so that carbon copies can be prepared and handed to the bookkeeper for his information in recording disbursements. For either of these reasons, it may be expedient to eliminate the running record on the check book stubs, and keep a bank register which will not show the balance after *each* deposit and *each* check, but will show the balance at the end of each day.

The following is an illustration of a bank register:

Bank Register

Date	FIRST NATIONAL BANK			FIRST STATE BANK		
	Deposits	Withdrawals	Balance	Deposits	Withdrawals	Balance
19— June 30			5,000 00			4,850 00
July 1	3,000 00	2,480 00	5,520 00	2,500 00	3,638 00	3,712 00
2	4,500 00	3,500 00	6,520 00	4,000 00	3,200 00	4,512 00

This record is kept in the following way:

Each day enter pencil totals of the day's receipts (deposits) in the Bank debit columns in the cash receipts book (see page 326) and enter these totals in the Deposits columns of the bank register.

Similarly, enter, in pencil, daily totals of the disbursements in the Bank credit columns of the cash disbursements book, or check register (see page 327), and transfer these totals to the Withdrawals columns of the bank register.

Compute the resulting daily bank balances and enter them in the Balance columns of the bank register.

Miscellaneous transactions. In addition to providing the services of a checking account, with its benefits of a safe depository for funds and its conveniences in providing for remittances by check, the bank renders certain other services to its customers which will be merely mentioned here without discussion, since they are commented upon in other chapters. The bank will:

Through correspondent banks, collect sight drafts, notes, and acceptances, or present time drafts to the drawees thereof for acceptance; this service may involve a collection fee.

Sell cashier's checks or bank drafts to its customers for their use in making remittances to creditors who prefer not to accept personal checks; this service may involve an exchange fee.

Loan funds to its customers on their own notes payable or on notes and acceptances receivable owned by them; this service involves an interest or a discount charge.

The bank statement. Once a month the bank will render a statement to the depositor and return the checks which it has paid and charged to his account. The statement is usually a carbon copy of the bank's account with the depositor and shows the balance at the beginning of the month, the deposits, the checks paid, other debits and credits during the month, and the balance at the end of the month. A simple illustration of such a statement is shown on page 335.

The symbols on the statement require some explanation:

N.S.F.—On June 27 R. M. Walker Company received a check for $63.95 from Wm. Barnes; this check was included in the deposit of June 27. It was returned to The White National Bank because Barnes did not have a sufficient balance in his bank account to cover the check. The White National Bank therefore charged it back to R. M. Walker Company.

When a returned check marked "N.S.F." is received from the bank, an entry should be made crediting Cash and debiting the party from whom the check was received. Such a check should not be regarded as cash, even if it is redeposited, until it has been paid by the maker, unless the bank gives credit for it at the time it is redeposited.

Ex. —On June 5 the bank charged $.10 exchange on a check included in the deposit of that date.

Col. —On June 27 the bank credited the Walker Company with the proceeds of a note collected by the bank for the company's account, and charged a collection fee of $.25.

P.S. —(Payment stopped)—If the Walker Company received and deposited with The White National Bank a check from a customer who, for some reason, stopped payment on the check, the customer's bank would refuse to pay it and would return it to The White National Bank, which would charge it back to the account of the Walker Company.

S.C. —(Service charge)—Because of the expense involved in handling checking accounts, banks cannot profitably handle accounts with small balances; therefore, they frequently make a service charge on accounts with balances averaging less than a certain minimum amount. Instead of making a service charge if the balance falls below a minimum amount, many banks now base the service charge on a number of factors, such as the average balance of the account during the month, the number of deposits made, and the number of checks drawn.

<table>
<tr><td colspan="4" align="right">20 Vouchers Returned</td></tr>
</table>

_____20____ Vouchers Returned

_____June_____, 19_--

R. M. Walker Company,

135 West State Street,

Chicago, Illinois.

In Account with THE WHITE NATIONAL BANK

N.S.F. - Not sufficient funds	Int. - Interest on daily balance
Ex. - Exchange	P.S. - Payment stopped
Col. - Collection	S.C. - Service charge

Date	Checks			Deposits	Balance
		Balance brought forward			3,500.17
1	$100.00✓			310.00✓	3,710.17
4	96.00✓				3,614.17
5	Ex. .10			175.00✓	3,789.07
6	75.00✓	150.50✓			3,563.57
8				425.50✓	3,989.07
10	39.75✓				3,949.32
11	136.50✓				3,812.82
12				136.75✓	3,949.57
13	84.20✓				3,865.37
15	164.19✓			216.80✓	3,917.98
18	7.25✓				3,910.73
19				310.80✓	4,221.53
20	39.50✓				4,182.03
22	600.35✓				3,581.68
24				165.00✓	3,746.68
26	13.75✓	19.50✓	123.80✓		3,589.63
27			Col..25	138.20✓	3,727.58
29	76.35✓				3,651.23
30	12.60✓	N.S.F.63.95	109.11✓		3,465.57
		Balance end of month			3,465.57

Please examine at once; if no errors are reported within
ten days, the account will be considered correct.

Bank Statement

When the bank rendered this statement, it returned all paid checks to the depositor. Accompanying the statement and the canceled checks, there were debit memoranda for all charges to the depositor not represented by checks; these included charges for exchange, collection, and the check charged back (N.S.F.).

Reconciling the bank account. The balance shown by the bank statement rarely agrees with the balance shown by the depositor's books. Items may appear on the depositor's books which have not yet been taken up on the bank's books, such as:

Outstanding checks—not presented to and paid by the bank.
Deposits not yet received by the bank—perhaps in transit in the mails.
Paper left with the bank and charged to the bank as a deposit, but taken by the bank for collection only and not credited to the depositor until collected.

Similarly, items may appear on the bank's books which have not yet been taken up on the depositor's books, such as:

Service charges.
Charges for collection and exchange.
Charges for checks returned N.S.F. Although the bank notifies the depositor immediately of such returned checks, and also of checks returned because payment has been stopped, entries may not be made immediately on the depositor's books.
Charges for protest fees.

If a company keeps funds on deposit in several banks, contra errors are sometimes made in the bank accounts on the depositor's books. Checks drawn against one bank account may be recorded as disbursements from another bank, and deposits in one bank may be charged to another bank. The banks also occasionally make errors by charging or crediting one customer with another customer's checks or deposits, particularly if the customers' names are similar. For all these reasons, the bank statement should be reconciled as soon as possible after it has been received.

Illustration. The procedure of reconciling the bank account will depend to some extent upon the system of accounting and internal check. In some cases, the bank statement will be checked against the record of deposits and checks shown by the check book stubs. If all receipts are deposited daily, the deposits shown on the bank statement may be checked against the cash receipts book.

In this illustration, we shall reconcile the June bank statement of R. M. Walker Company (page 335) with the cash books shown on pages 337 and 338.

Cash Receipts Book

(Page 16)

Date	L.F.	Account	Explanation	CREDITS Sundry Accounts	CREDITS Accounts Receivable (1120)	DEBITS Discount on Sales (4008)	DEBITS Bank (1111)
19— June 5	4001	Sales	Cash sale	175 00			175 00 ✓
8	✓	John Smith	Invoice, June 1		300 00	3 00	297 00
8	✓	Wm. Barnes	Invoice, May 5		128 50		128 50 ✓
							425 50
12	4001	Sales	Cash sale	136 75			136 75 ✓
15	✓	D. E. McGuire	Invoice, June 8		150 00	1 50	148 50
15	4001	Sales	Cash sale	68 30			68 30 ✓
							216 80
19	1130	Notes receivable	E. F. Watson	250 00			250 00
19	4001	Sales	Cash sale	60 80			60 80 ✓
							310 80
24	4001	Sales	Cash sale	165 00			165 00 ✓
27	1130	Notes receivable	John Smith	74 25			74 25
27	✓	Wm. Barnes	Invoice, June 1		63 95		63 95
							138 20 ✓
30	4001	Sales	Cash sale	60 50			60 50
				990 60	642 45	4 50	1,628 55
				✓	✓	✓	✓

Cash Disbursements Book

(Page 23)

Check No.	Date	Payee	Vo. No.	Vouchers Payable (2120)	Discount on Purchases (8101)	Bank (1111)
	19— June					
131	1	C. R. Waterbury	123	75 00		75 00 √
132	2	O. F. Wharton	128	153 57	3 07	150 50 √
133	3	Bailey & Bayne	146	96 00		96 00 √
134	6	C. E. Whitely	147	136 50		136 50 √
135	9	R. E. Lathrop	130	39 75		39 75 √
136	13	Haines & Holmes	133	167 54	3 35	164 19 √
137	16	Geo. James	150	39 50		39 50 √
138	17	Horder & Co.	151	7 25		7 25 √
139	20	Davis & Co.	145	606 41	6 06	600 35 √
140	24	Petty cash	154	19 50		19 50 √
141	24	C. N. W. Ry.	149	13 75		13 75 √
142	26	O. F. Wharton	140	126 33	2 53	123 80 √
143	28	C. R. Waterbury	155	76 35		76 35 √
144	29	J. B. Magee	156	12 60		12 60 √
145	29	G. P. Oliver	158	109 11		109 11 √
146	30	C. E. Whitely	142	300 00		300 00
				1,979 16 √	15 01 √	1,964 15 √

The bank account in the ledger appears as follows:

The White National Bank

19—				19—			
May	31	Balance		3,625	97	June 30		CD23	1,964	15
June	30	3,290.37	CR16	1,628	55				
				5,254	52				

Steps in the reconciliation. The procedure of reconciling the bank account involves the following steps:

(1) Arrange in numerical order the paid checks returned from the bank.

(2) Refer to the reconciliation at the close of the preceding month; note the items which were outstanding at that date. The May 31st reconciliation appears below:

Bank Reconciliation
May 31, 19—

Balance, per books......................................		$3,625.97
Balance, per bank statement.............................		$3,500.17
Add deposit not credited by bank........................		310.00√
Total...		$3,810.17
Deduct outstanding checks:		
129..	$100.00√	
130..	84.20√	184.20
Adjusted balance......................................		$3,625.97

This reconciliation shows that $310 recorded by the company as a deposit in May had not been credited by the bank at the end of the month, and that checks for $100 and $84.20 were outstanding. Reference to the bank statement on page 335 shows that the deposit was credited by the bank on June 1, and that the checks were paid on June 1 and June 13. These items are now checked on the May 31st reconciliation and on the June 30th bank statement as follows: √. The use of the special check mark is not essential, but it has the advantage of identifying the items as applicable to May.

(3) See whether the daily totals of receipts (as shown by the cash receipts book) agree with the entries in the Deposits column of the bank statement. Place check marks in the cash receipts book and in the Deposits column of the bank statement beside the items which are in agreement.

Make a list of unchecked receipts in the cash book; these represent deposits not taken up by the bank. By reference to the cash receipts book, it will be noted that only one of the daily receipts is unchecked:

June 30 $60.50

This unchecked item is presumably a deposit in transit and must be taken into the bank reconciliation. Make a list of any unchecked items in the Deposits column of the bank statement, representing credits by the bank not taken up by the depositor. It will be noted that there are no unchecked items in the Deposits column of the bank statement.

(4) Compare the returned checks (which have been sorted in numerical order) with the entries in the cash disbursements book. Place a check mark in the cash disbursements book beside the entry for each check that has been returned by the bank.

Make a list of unchecked items in the cash disbursements book; these are outstanding checks. By reference to page 338, it will be noted that only one entry is unchecked: the $300 check drawn on June 30.

Make a list of any charges by the bank, as shown by the statement or by debit memos, that do not appear in the cash disbursements book. Such charges shown by the bank statement are:

Exchange......................................	$ .10
Collection.....................................	.25
N.S.F. check returned...........................	63.95

(5) Prepare the reconciliation statement, as follows:

Bank Reconciliation
June 30, 19—

Balance, per books..............................		$3,290.37
Deduct bank's charges not on the books:		
Exchange....................................	$ .10	
Collection....................................	.25	
N.S.F. check—Wm. Barnes....................	63.95	64.30
Adjusted balance...............................		$3,226.07
Balance, per bank statement.....................		$3,465.57
Add deposit not taken up by the bank.............		60.50
Total....................................		$3,526.07
Deduct outstanding checks:		
146..		300.00
Adjusted balance (as above)....................		$3,226.07

Certified checks. An ordinary check is deducted from the drawer's account when the check is presented to the drawer's bank for payment. In contrast, a certified check is deducted from the drawer's account when it is certified by the drawer's bank. Therefore, outstanding certified checks need not be included in the list of outstanding checks in the bank reconciliation.

Adjustments after reconciliation. The illustrative bank reconciliation discloses the fact that the bank has made certain deductions from the depositor's account which have not been taken up on the depositor's books. To take up these items, the company should debit Collection and Exchange $.35, debit William Barnes $63.95, and credit Cash $64.30.

The book of original entry to be used for such adjusting entries depends on whether the cash journals have been footed and posted prior to the preparation of the bank reconciliation.

Condition: Cash journals not ruled and posted prior to preparation of bank reconciliation.

Under such a condition, any required adjusting entry can be entered in the appropriate cash journal.

Condition: Cash journals ruled and posted prior to preparation of bank reconciliation.

Any required adjusting entry should be recorded in the general journal.

Payroll bank account. If a company pays a large number of employees by check, it is desirable for it to open a special payroll bank account. At each pay date, a voucher is prepared for the total payroll, and a check on the regular bank account is drawn and deposited in the payroll bank account. Individual checks for the employees are then drawn on this special account, which is thus immediately exhausted. If the payroll account and the general account are kept in the same bank, different-colored checks should be used.

This procedure has several advantages. In the first place, one voucher against the general bank account can be drawn for the entire payroll; the checks on the payroll account can be drawn without vouchers. In the second place, the officer authorized to sign checks on the general bank account can be relieved of the work of signing numerous payroll checks; these can be signed by some other employee. In the third place, the general bank account can be reconciled without cluttering the reconciliation statement with all the outstanding payroll checks. And, in the fourth place, the labor of recording the payroll disbursements is reduced; instead of recording all payroll checks in the cash disbursements book, check numbers may be entered in a payroll record.

The payment of the payroll is recorded as follows:

Make a voucher register entry, debiting Payroll Bank Account and crediting Vouchers Payable, for the amount needed for the payroll ($1,925).

Draw a check on the general bank account for the amount needed for the total payroll; deposit this check in the special payroll bank account.

Make a cash disbursements book entry, debiting Vouchers Payable and crediting Cash, $1,925.

Make general journal entries as follows (the amounts are assumed):

Salesmen's salaries	875.00	
Office salaries	533.44	
Officers' salaries	1,055.00	
Payroll bank account		1,925.00
Federal O. A. B. taxes withheld		36.95
Federal income taxes withheld		501.49
Payroll taxes	110.85	
Federal O. A. B. taxes payable		36.95
Federal unemployment taxes payable		7.39
State unemployment taxes payable		66.51

Instead of making and posting a general journal entry, the payroll record may be drawn up in such a form that postings to the various expense accounts and the Payroll Bank Account can be made directly from it.

When the statement of the payroll bank account is returned from the bank, the canceled checks are arranged in numerical order and checked off against the check numbers on the payroll record. The unchecked items will represent outstanding checks, and usually will be the only items to be taken into consideration in reconciling the payroll bank account.

Dividend bank account. If a company has a large number of stockholders, a special bank account may be used for the payment of dividends. A voucher for the total amount of the dividend will be prepared, and a check for that amount will be drawn and deposited in this special bank account. Checks payable to the individual stockholders will be drawn on this account.

Bank overdraft. If a bank account is overdrawn, the amount of the overdraft should be shown as a current liability.

CHAPTER 23

Accounts Receivable. Discounting Notes and Acceptances Receivable

Accounts Receivable

Accounts receivable in the balance sheet. The amount shown under the current assets caption as Accounts Receivable (without any further description) should include only amounts receivable on open account from trade debtors. Accounts receivable from stockholders, officers, or employees should be shown separately in the balance sheet unless the receivables arose from sales and are collectible in accordance with the company's regular terms; accounts with such individuals for loans or other advances may be listed under the current assets caption if the terms of such receivables and the company's experience with them indicate that they will be collected as soon as other current assets; otherwise, they should be shown under the caption of other assets, thus:

Other assets:
    Accounts receivable from officers and employees.............. $xx,xxx

Accounts receivable and payable with same party. If goods are purchased from and sold to the same party, it is advisable to keep two accounts: one in the accounts receivable ledger, thus:

James Smith

Date		Explanation	Folio	Debit		Credit		Balance	
19—									
Sept.	3	....	S1	500	00			500	00
	12	....	CR1			500	00		

and (unless a voucher system is in use) another in the accounts payable ledger, thus:

James Smith

Date		Explanation	Folio	Debit		Credit		Balance	
19—									
Sept.	7	....	P1			375	00	375	00
	15	....	CD1	200	00			175	00

343

If a voucher system is used, the receivable from Smith will be shown in the accounts receivable ledger, and the liability will be recorded in the voucher register.

It is recommended that such receivables and payables should not be offset when the balance sheet is prepared.

Ledger headings. The headings of the ledger sheets or cards used for accounts receivable usually are provided with spaces in which to enter certain general information relating to the debtor which may be useful for credit or sales purposes.   The data will vary in different businesses, but may include the following:

Sheet No. _____	Name _____
Rating _____	Address _____
Credit Limit _____	_____
Salesman _____	Business _____

The Sheet Number space is needed on active accounts extending over several pages kept in a loose-leaf binder; if the current sheet is number 7, it is known that six other sheets must be found, either in the current binder or the transfer binder, to include the entire account.

The Rating space is used to show the credit rating given the customer by rating agencies, such as Dun & Bradstreet, Inc.

The Credit Limit space shows the maximum amount fixed by the credit department.

The salesman's name may be desired on the account so that the sales manager can see whether the salesman appears to be neglecting his sales opportunity with the customer, and so that the credit and collection department can see which salesmen are making sales on accounts that become delinquent.

Account and statement at one impression. Many concerns which make a practice of sending monthly statements to their customers use bookkeeping machines to keep their accounts receivable.   Such machines can be used to type the entries and compute and enter the balance after each entry.   The three-column ledger ruling with debit, credit, and balance columns is generally used with these machines.

At the beginning of the month, a statement form is inserted in the binder with each customer's ledger sheet.   When an entry is to be recorded, the account and the statement are put into the machine, with a carbon between, so that the ledger account and the statement are duplicates.   At the end of the month, the statement is removed from the binder and mailed to the customer.

C.O.D. sales. Sales made on C.O.D. terms may be recorded in the sales book in the usual way, but a notation should be made

showing that the terms are C.O.D.   This can be done by merely
writing C.O.D. after the name of the customer.   From that point,
custom varies.   Three methods of procedure may be mentioned:

(1) The debtor's account is kept in its regular alphabetical posi-
     tion in the subsidiary accounts receivable ledger, with a
     notation in the heading of the account indicating that the
     customer is on a C.O.D. basis.
(2) The accounts of all customers who are on a C.O.D. basis are
     grouped together in one place in the ledger, where they
     can be more closely watched.
(3) Instead of keeping accounts with the debtors, the book-
     keeper posts the amounts of all C.O.D. sales to a C.O.D.
     accounts receivable register.   When the collection is
     received, it is recorded in the cash receipts book in the
     usual manner, and the date of the collection is entered
     in the Date Collected column of the register.   Such a
     register follows:

C.O.D. Accounts Receivable Register

Date	Invoice No.	Customer	Address	Amount	Date Collected
19—					
June 1	1387	J. B. White..........	Osborne, Iowa	50 00	June 5
6	1473	R. C. Luther..........	Dayton, Minn.	75 00	
7	1489	J. Y. Ritter..........	Oliphant, Tenn.	60 00	

The open items in the register (that is, the entries with no
notations in the Date Collected column) represent uncollected charges; in balancing the subsidiary records
against the accounts receivable controlling account, the
bookkeeper must include the open items in the register
with the balances in the subsidiary ledger.

Red balances in subsidiary ledgers.   The individual accounts
in the accounts receivable ledger normally have debit balances;
some accounts may run into credit balances because of overpay-
ments, credits for returns and allowances after payment of the
account in full, or for other reasons.   Such credit balances may be
entered in the accounts in red to distinguish them from the debit
balances; for this reason they are sometimes called *red* balances
even though written in black ink with a notation *Cr.* after them.

Assume that the debit balance in the Accounts Receivable controlling account is $6,325, which represents the subsidiary ledger
balances shown on the following page.

Debit balances	$6,500.00
Credit balances	175.00
Net debit	$6,325.00

The controlling account balance of $6,325 should not be used in the balance sheet; instead, the total debit balances and the total credit balances in the subsidiary ledger should be shown, thus:

Current assets:
  Accounts receivable....... $6,500.00

Current liabilities:
  Credit balances in customers' accounts................. $175.00

Similarly, if the subsidiary accounts payable ledger contains some debit balances, the balance sheet should not show the balance of the controlling account but should show the total credit balances and the total debit balances of the subsidiary ledger, thus:

Current assets:
  Debit balances in suppliers' accounts................ $135.00

Current liabilities:
  Accounts payable......... $7,800.00

Aging the receivables. As noted in Chapter 7, the amount to be added to the Reserve for Bad Debts is sometimes computed by giving consideration to the probable collectibility of each customer's account, thereby estimating the total probable reserve requirement. The age-distribution of the receivables is sometimes a reliable indication of collectibility, and may therefore be useful in estimating the reserve requirement. For example, experience may indicate that the following reserve balance would be desirable, considering the age-distribution of the receivables.

Accounts Receivable Balances	Estimated Per cent Uncollectible	Reserve Requirement
1–30 days old.................	$32,000	1	$ 320
31–60 days old.................	21,000	2	420
61–90 days old.................	14,000	8	1,120
91 days to 6 months old..........	8,000	20	1,600
Over 6 months old..............	2,000	50	1,000
	$77,000		$4,460

However, supplementary information must also be considered; some accounts which are not old may be of doubtful collectibility, whereas accounts long past due may be collectible.

The age-distribution may be obtained by preparing a schedule of the accounts receivable on columnar paper, with columns headed to indicate various ages, such as *1 to 30 days, 31 to 60 days, 61 to 90 days, 91 days to 6 months,* and *Over 6 months.* The balance of each debtor's account is analyzed to determine the age of the component elements, and the aging schedule is filled out by entries such as the following (which is based on the account with J. H. Boyce, presented below). After all the balances have been aged, the columns are totaled, thus completing the aging.

Accounts Receivable Aging, November 30, 19—

Name	Total	1–30 Days	31–60 Days	61–90 Days	91 Days to 6 Months	Over 6 Months
J. H. Boyce.....	775 00	525 00		250 00		

J. H. Boyce

Date	Explanation	Folio	Debit		Credit		Balance
19—							
Sept. 15	....	S1 a	250 00				250 00
Oct. 3	....	S2 b	500 00 ✓				750 00
9	....	CR1		b	500 00 ✓		250 00
15	....	S2 c	800 00 ✓				1,050 00
20	Note Receivable..............	J2		c	500 00 ✓		550 00
20	....	CR2		c	300 00 ✓		250 00
22	.... ✓	S3 d	750 00 ✓				1,000 00
25	.... ✓	S3 e	200 00 ✓				1,200 00
31	....	CR3		d, e	950 00 ✓		250 00
Nov. 5	....	S4 f	600 00 ✓				850 00
7	....	S4 g	250 00				1,100 00
9	....	CR4		f	200 00 ✓		900 00
10	Note Receivable..............	J3		f	400 00 ✓		500 00
11	....	S4 h	375 00				875 00
16	....	CR5		g	100 00		775 00

By reference to Boyce's account, it may be seen that the practice of lettering the entries in receivable accounts is very helpful in preparing the aging schedule. In this instance, the bookkeeper has also checked the offsetting items which do not enter into the balance of the account.

There are four unchecked items in the account, and these are, therefore, the only ones which enter into the balance; these items are:

Date		Debit	Credit
19—			
Sept. 15................................	(a)	$250.00	
Nov. 7................................	(g)	250.00	
11................................	(h)	375.00	
16................................			(g) $100.00

The $775 balance in the account consists of the $250 September item (which was between 61 and 90 days old on November 30), and two November debits and one November credit in a net amount of $525 (which was between 1 and 30 days old on November 30).

In addition to being useful in the computation of reserve requirements, data by age groups may be used by management to determine whether collections from customers are lagging. Such a trend would be revealed by a shift in the percentage relationships among the age groups, with the older balances making up a larger share of the total receivables than heretofore.

Bad debt recoveries. Suppose that an account receivable previously written off is collected. If subsequent developments indicate that the entry writing off the account against the reserve was an error, the write-off should be reversed. To illustrate, assume that P. K. Lane's account in the amount of $75 had been written off. The reversing entry, at the time of the collection from Lane, would be as follows:

```
P. K. Lane.........................................  75.00
    Reserve for bad debts...........................          75.00
    To reverse entry writing off Lane's account.
```

The cash collection will then be recorded in the cash book by an entry debiting Cash and crediting Lane.

The proper treatment of partial collections on written-off accounts is somewhat more difficult to determine because it depends upon the probability of further collections. To illustrate, assume that, after Lane's account was written off, he paid $30:

If this collection and other facts indicate that the account may be collected in full, the entries should be:

In the journal: Debit Lane, credit Reserve for Bad Debts: $75.00.

In the cash book: Debit Cash, credit Lane: $30.00.

If no more collections are expected, the entries should be:

In the journal: Debit Lane, credit Reserve for Bad Debts: $30.00.

In the cash book: Debit Cash, credit Lane: $30.00.

Reserves for returns and allowances, cash discounts, and freight. Let us assume that a company has total accounts receivable of $20,000 on December 31, and has provided a reserve of $1,000 for bad debts. This reserve may be an adequate provision for bad debt losses, but it does not necessarily follow that the company will collect $19,000 from the accounts. Customers may demand credits for returned merchandise and allowances on defective goods; many of the debtors will take the cash discounts to which they are entitled; and, if the goods are sold on terms which require the customers to pay the freight but allow them to deduct such payments in remitting for the merchandise, deductions will be taken for such freight.

Theoretically, all these prospective deductions should be provided for by reserves, so that the accounts receivable will be stated in the balance sheet at the estimated net amount which will be collected after allowing all such deductions. As a practical matter, however, such adjustments are rarely made, for the following reasons:

(1) Such prospective deductions are difficult to estimate.
(2) The omission of such adjustments normally will have no significant effect on net income.

> This might not be the case for the first year of a new business. Its accounts would show a full year's sales with something less than a full year's deductions from sales for discounts and returns and allowances. But in the second and succeeding years, since any deductions relating to prior years' sales are recorded when taken, the accounts for discounts and returns and allowances will show deductions covering a full period.
>
> Hence, unless large fluctuations occurred in sales deductions, the failure to adjust for prospective returns and allowances and discounts affects the financial statements only in that accounts receivable will be stated at an amount slightly above their cash realizable value. Most accountants feel that this is not serious, since the amounts involved are so small. If, in a given case, it should develop that the amounts involved were significant, then no doubt the accountant would make adjusting entries of the type indicated above.

Discounts on returned sales. Assume that a customer buys merchandise for $1,000 subject to a 2% discount, and that he pays the invoice within the discount period with a check for $980. Subsequently, he returns one-tenth of the goods, which had been billed to him at $100 and which were paid for at the net amount of $98. Should he receive credit for $100 or $98?

Although this is largely a matter of policy, it would seem that the credit should be $98 if he is to be reimbursed in cash, and $100 if the credit is to be traded out. The reasoning may be made clearer by assuming that the entire shipment is returned. Allowing a credit of $1,000 to be repaid in cash would open the way to abuses of the cash discount privilege, whereas allowing a credit of only $980 payable in merchandise would cause the customer to lose the benefit of having paid his bill within the discount period.

Freight paid and discount taken by customer. Assume that a customer buys merchandise amounting to $1,000. He is to pay the freight, which amounts to $40, and is allowed to deduct it in remitting for the merchandise; he is also allowed a 2% discount for cash within 10 days. Should the 2% discount be based on the $1,000 invoice, or on this amount less the $40 freight?

The discount should be based on the full amount of the invoice, because the customer is paying the freight for the seller, and is entitled to a cash discount for the funds so used. The settlement should, therefore, be made as follows:

Invoice...		$1,000.00
Deduct: Freight...............................	$40.00	
Discount—2% of $1,000.00...............	20.00	60.00
Net amount of remittance......................		$ 940.00

Sales discount on customers' partial payments. Assume that a customer buys merchandise for $1,000 subject to terms of 2/10; n/30. Suppose that he is not able to pay the entire invoice, but does send a check for $588 in partial settlement within the ten-day discount period. Since the partial payment was made within the discount period, the seller may, as a matter of policy, allow the discount on the partial payment.

If the discount is granted on partial payments, the amount paid is the net amount, and therefore it is necessary to determine the amount of the gross obligation settled by the partial payment. This can be computed as follows:

$$\$588 \div .98 = \$600$$

In general journal form, the collection would be recorded as follows:

Cash..	588.00	
Discount on sales................................	12.00	
Accounts receivable..........................		600.00
To record partial collection of an account receivable within the discount period.		

Uncollectible notes receivable. If a business has a large number of notes receivable, a separate reserve for bad debts account may be used. However, if there are only a few notes receivable, possible losses thereon are generally combined with the estimate of losses on accounts receivable. The debit to Bad Debts should cover estimated losses on both accounts and notes receivable. When a note is determined to be uncollectible, it should be written off against the reserve.

Discounting Notes and Acceptances Receivable

Purposes of discounting notes and acceptances receivable.
Instead of borrowing money from a bank by discounting our own
note payable, as discussed in Chapter 9, we may obtain funds from
a bank by endorsing, and transferring to the bank, any notes or
acceptances receivable held by us which are acceptable to the bank.

The payee of a note or an acceptance may endorse it and transfer it to a creditor to apply on account, if the creditor is willing to
take it.

Same methods apply to notes and acceptances.   The essential characteristics of a note and an acceptance are the same: they
are written obligations of a debtor, payable at a fixed or determinable date.   To simplify the presentation in this chapter, the
illustrations deal only with notes; it should be understood that the
procedures and entries applicable to the discounting of acceptances
are identical with those for notes.

Endorsements.   Paper which is payable to the order of a
named payee must be endorsed by the payee if it is to be transferred by him to some other party; thus, if F. K. Hamilton, the
payee of the illustrative note on page 114, wishes to transfer the
note to John Smith, Hamilton must endorse the note by writing
his name across its back.   The party who endorses a note is called
an *endorser;* the party to whom the note is transferred is called an
endorsee.

By the act of endorsement of a negotiable promissory note or
acceptance, the endorser assumes an obligation (subject to certain
defenses) to pay the paper to a subsequent holder if the maker fails
to pay it at maturity.   This obligation is called a *contingent liability.*   For a complete discussion of the nature of the contingent
liability of an endorser, and the nature of his defenses, you are
referred to any good text on the law of negotiable instruments.

Paper which is payable *to bearer* can legally be transferred by
delivery without endorsement; however, the party to whom the
paper is to be transferred may require that it be endorsed in order
to make the transferor contingently liable for its payment.

Endorsements are classified and illustrated as follows:

(1) *Unqualified endorsements* (the transferor assumes the full
    contingent liability imposed by law upon an endorser):

   (a) In full (shows the name of the party to whom the
       paper is transferred):

>   Pay to the order of
>   John Smith
>   F. K. Hamilton

The paper is still payable *to order;* that is, Smith must endorse it in order to transfer it.

(b) In blank (does not show the name of the party to whom the paper is transferred):

F. K. Hamilton

The paper is now payable to bearer and can legally be transferred by subsequent holders without endorsement.

(2) *Qualified endorsement* (the endorser limits his contingent liability by inserting the words *Without Recourse*):

(a) In full:

Pay to the order of
John Smith
Without Recourse
F. K. Hamilton

(b) In blank:

Without Recourse
F. K. Hamilton

One who endorses *without recourse* materially lessens his contingent liability as an endorser. He warrants that the paper is valid and that he has a good title to it, but he does not assume a legal obligation to pay the paper merely because the primary obligor does not do so.

(3) *Restrictive endorsement* (which must be in full):

(a) To prevent further transfers:

Pay to John Smith only
F. K. Hamilton

(b) To make the endorsee an agent for a special purpose:

Pay to the order of
First National Bank
For collection
F. K. Hamilton

Proceeds. The proceeds of a discounted note or acceptance receivable are computed as follows:

First, determine the value of the receivable at maturity (this is the amount which the holder will be entitled to collect at maturity).

The maturity value of non-interest paper is the face.

The maturity value of interest-bearing paper is the face plus the interest for the full period.

Second, determine the discount period, or time from the date of discount to maturity.

Third, compute the discount at the agreed rate, on the value at maturity, for the discount period.

Fourth, deduct the discount from the value at maturity.

Let us compute the proceeds of two notes receivable discounted.

	B. Bates	C. Cole
Maker....................................	B. Bates	C. Cole
Date of note..............................	August 1	August 1
Time from date of note to maturity............	60 days	60 days
Date of discount...........................	August 11	August 11
Discount period—or time from date of discount to maturity.............................	50 days	50 days
Rate of interest borne by the note..............	None	$5\frac{1}{2}\%$
Rate of discount charged.....................	6%	6%
Computation of proceeds:		
Face of note.............................	$6,000.00	$6,000.00
Add interest from date of note to maturity:		
The Bates note does not bear interest.		
Interest on the Cole note at $5\frac{1}{2}\%$ for 60 days is		55.00
Value at maturity.........................	$6,000.00	$6,055.00
Deduct discount at 6% for 50 days:		
50 days' interest on $6,000.00..............	50.00	
50 days' interest on $6,055.00..............		50.46
Proceeds.................................	$5,950.00	$6,004.54

Discounting notes receivable at the bank. Let us assume that we own the Bates and Cole notes, which are recorded in the Notes Receivable account as follows:

Notes Receivable

19—					
Aug.	1	B. Bates 60 da.	6,000	00	
	1	C. Cole 60 da. $5\frac{1}{2}\%$	6,000	00	

Let us now assume that we discount these notes at the bank on August 11. Since we part with the notes, it may seem that the Notes Receivable account should be credited. But we should remember that, in order to transfer the notes to the bank, we must endorse them, and thus render ourselves contingently liable for their payment. This contingent liability should be shown in the accounts. Therefore, we shall credit Notes Receivable Discounted, as illustrated in the entries* on the following page.

---

* The illustrative entries throughout this chapter are given in general journal form for simplicity of explanation; it will be understood that entries for cash receipts and disbursements would be made in the cash books.

Bates note—for which we receive less than the face:

```
Cash.......................................... 5,950.00
Interest expense..............................    50.00
    Notes receivable discounted.................          6,000.00
    Note of B. Bates discounted at bank at 6%.
```

Cole note—for which we receive more than the face:

```
Cash.......................................... 6,004.54
    Notes receivable discounted.................          6,000.00
    Interest income.............................              4.54
    C. Cole's 5½% note discounted at bank at 6%.
```

The Notes Receivable and Notes Receivable Discounted
accounts now appear as follows:

Notes Receivable

| 19—
Aug. | 1 | B. Bates 60 da. | | 6,000 | 00 | | | | | |
| | 1 | C. Cole 60 da. 5½% | | 6,000 | 00 | | | | | |

Notes Receivable Discounted

| | | | | | | 19—
Aug. | 11 | B. Bates | | 6,000 | 00 |
| | | | | | | | 11 | C. Cole | | 6,000 | 00 |

The *net* balance of the two accounts is zero, showing that we
own no notes receivable.

Discounting notes receivable with a creditor. Let us assume
that, instead of discounting the notes receivable at a bank, we
transferred them on August 11 to a creditor, J. B. Houston, to
apply on our account payable liability to him; let us also assume
that they were discounted at 6%; the proceeds, therefore, were the
same as computed above. Our entries to record the discounting
of the Bates and Cole notes with our creditor to apply on account
are shown below:

Bates note—for which we receive less than the face:

```
J. B. Houston................................. 5,950.00
Interest expense..............................    50.00
    Notes receivable discounted.................          6,000.00
    Note of B. Bates transferred on account, discounted
    at 6%.
```

Cole note—for which we receive more than the face:

```
J. B. Houston................................. 6,004.54
    Notes receivable discounted.................          6,000.00
    Interest income.............................              4.54
    C. Cole's 5½% note transferred on account, dis-
    counted at 6%.
```

Discounted note paid by maker at maturity. Assume that Bates and Cole paid their discounted notes at maturity. We no longer have any contingent liability, and can therefore make the following entries:

Notes receivable discounted......................	6,000.00	
Notes receivable............................		6,000.00
To eliminate the Bates note and contingent liability		
from the accounts.		
Notes receivable discounted......................	6,000.00	
Notes receivable............................		6,000.00
To eliminate the Cole note and contingent liability		
from the accounts.		

The two ledger accounts appear as follows:

Notes Receivable

19—				19—			
Aug.	1	B. Bates 60 da.	6,000 00	Sept.	30	B. Bates	6,000 00
	1	C. Cole 60 da. 5½%	6,000 00		30	C. Cole	6,000 00

Notes Receivable Discounted

19—				19—			
Sept.	30	B. Bates	6,000 00	Aug.	11	B. Bates	6,000 00
	30	C. Cole	6,000 00		11	C. Cole	6,000 00

Discounted note dishonored by maker. An endorser cannot be held on his contingent liability for the payment of a discounted note receivable unless the holder (endorsee) has presented it to the maker at maturity, demanded and not received payment, and given proper notice of dishonor to the endorser.

Let us assume that Bates and Cole dishonored their notes at maturity and that the holder took the proper steps to enforce collection from us. Our entries will be:

For payment of Bates note—which did not bear interest:

B. Bates.......................................	6,000.00	
Cash.......................................		6,000.00
Paid (bank or Houston) the Bates note discounted		
by us and dishonored by him.		

(The payment is charged to Bates because we have a right to enforce collection from him.)

Notes receivable discounted......................	6,000.00	
Notes receivable............................		6,000.00
To eliminate the Bates note and the contingent		
liability from the accounts.		

(This entry is made because there is no longer any contingent liability on the note. The contingent liability developed into a real liability, and was paid.)

For payment of Cole note—which bore interest:

```
C. Cole.......................................  6,055.00
    Cash......................................            6,055.00
    Paid (bank or Houston) the Cole note discounted
    by us and dishonored by him, and 5½% interest
    thereon for 60 days.

Notes receivable discounted.....................  6,000.00
    Notes receivable..........................            6,000.00
    To eliminate the Cole note and contingent liability
    from the accounts.
```

Disposition of Notes Receivable Discounted account. You should observe that the entry debiting Notes Receivable Discounted and crediting Notes Receivable is made by the endorser at the maturity of a discounted note, *regardless of whether the note is paid by the maker or by the endorser.* If the note is paid by the maker, the endorser has no further liability. If the note is dishonored, the contingent liability becomes a real liability.

Protest. In some cases, notice of dishonor can be given to the endorser informally, either orally or in writing. In other cases, protest and formal notice of dishonor are required.

Protest is a formal declaration in writing by a notary public to the effect that he has presented an instrument to the person primarily liable thereon and demanded payment, and that the instrument has been dishonored. Notice of protest is sent by the notary public to the maker and to all the endorsers.

The holder of the paper (the endorsee) engages the services of the notary public and pays his fee, which he charges to the endorser. The endorser is obligated to pay the face of the note, the protest fee, and any accrued interest.

Let us assume that the Cole note, discounted by us, was dishonored and protested, and that the protest fee was $2.04. Our entries at the time of payment will be:

```
C. Cole.......................................  6,057.04
    Cash......................................            6,057.04
    Payment of dishonored note, interest, and protest
    fee.

Notes receivable discounted.....................  6,000.00
    Notes receivable..........................            6,000.00
    To eliminate the C. Cole note and the contingent
    liability from the accounts.
```

Purpose of Notes Receivable Discounted account. It should be understood that the Notes Receivable Discounted account is used to show the contingent liability on paper which we have owned and have transferred to other parties, thus assuming a contingent liability as a result of our endorsement.

If we discount our own note payable, the transaction should be recorded by a credit to Notes Payable, to show the direct liability.

Notes receivable and notes receivable discounted in the balance sheet. Assume that a company's accounts with notes receivable and notes receivable discounted appear as follows:

Notes Receivable

19—						19—						
June	1	Smith—30 da.	J1	a	1,000	00	July	1	Smith	CR3	a	1,000	00
	10	Brown—30 da.	J2	b	2,000	00		10	Brown	J6	b	2,000	00
	20	White—60 da.	J3	c	2,500	00							
	25	Green—60 da.	J4	d	3,000	00							

Notes Receivable Discounted

19—							19—						
July	10	Brown	J6	b	2,000	00	June	15	Brown	J2	b	2,000	00
								25	White	J3	c	2,500	00

These accounts show the following facts:

The Smith note was received on June 1 and was collected on July 1.

The Brown note was received on June 10; it was discounted on June 15; it matured on July 10, and the contingent liability was eliminated.

The White note was received on June 20; it was discounted on June 25; it has not yet matured; therefore, there is a contingent liability of $2,500.

The Green note was received on June 25; it has not yet matured, and the company therefore has an asset of $3,000.

The balance sheet should show the note receivable asset of $3,000 and the contingent liability of $2,500. The asset and the contingent liability can be determined from the balances of the two accounts, as follows:

Debit balance of Notes Receivable account..................	$5,500.00
Credit balance of Notes Receivable Discounted account— amount to be shown as a contingent liability............	2,500.00
Net balance of the two accounts—amount to be shown as note receivable asset.......................................	$3,000.00

The note receivable asset is shown in the balance sheet on the asset side. The contingent liability on notes receivable discounted is usually stated in a footnote. The procedure is illustrated on the following page.

NAME OF COMPANY
Balance Sheet
July 31, 19—

Assets		Liabilities and Net Worth		
Cash	$ 750.00	Liabilities:		
Accounts receivable	2,850.00	Accounts		
Notes receivable	3,000.00	payable...	$ 2,000.00	
Inventory	6,780.00	Notes pay-able	1,000.00	$ 3,000.00
		Net worth:		
		Capital stock	$10,000.00	
		Earned sur-plus	380.00	10,380.00
	$13,380.00			$13,380.00

Note. On July 31, 19—, the company was contingently liable on a note receivable discounted in the amount of $2,500.

Discounted notes taken from debtor on account.
Assume that Fred Dutton is indebted to us on an account receivable, and that he wishes to transfer to us, to apply on account, two notes which he holds and which are described as follows:

Maker	Date	Time	Interest Rate	Face
James Magee	June 1	60 days	—	$3,000.00
Horace Heald	" 10	60 days	6%	6,000.00

We are willing to take these notes from Dutton on June 15 at a value determined by discounting them at 6%. The proceeds are computed as follows:

	Magee	Heald
Maker		
Date of note	June 1	June 10
Period of note	60 days	60 days
Maturity	July 31	Aug. 9
Date of discount	June 15	June 15
Discount period	46 days	55 days
Rate of interest on note	—	6%
Rate of discount charged by us	6%	6%
Computation of proceeds:		
Face of note	$3,000.00	$6,000.00
Add interest on note from date of issuance to maturity		60.00
Value at maturity	$3,000.00	$6,060.00
Discount at 6% deducted by us:		
On $3,000 for 46 days	23.00	
On $6,060 for 55 days		55.55
Proceeds	$2,977.00	$6,004.45

Entries at acquisition:

Notes receivable	3,000.00	
Interest income		23.00
Fred Dutton		2,977.00

James Magee 60-day, non-interest note due July 31, taken from Dutton on 6% discount basis, to apply on account.

The $23 credit to Interest Income is the amount we will earn by carrying the note from June 15, the date of discount, to July 31, the maturity.

```
Notes receivable...............................  6,000.00
Interest income................................     4.45
    Fred Dutton...............................            6,004.45
    Horace Heald 60-day, 6% note due August 9, taken
    from Dutton on 6% discount basis, to apply on ac-
    count
```

We charge the $4.45 to Interest Income because, when we collect the note and interest, the Interest Income account will be credited with $60.

The Interest Income account will then appear as follows:

Interest Income

June	15				4	45	Aug.	9				60	00

and the resulting credit balance of $55.55 will be the net amount we will earn by carrying the note from June 15, the date of discount, to August 9, the maturity.

Observe that, when we receive a note on a discounted basis, the debit is to Notes Receivable—not to Notes Receivable Discounted. The Notes Receivable Discounted account is used to show the contingent liability on notes which we endorse and transfer to others.

Entries at maturity if note is collected from the maker:

If, at the maturity of the notes, they are collected from the makers, the entries are as follows:

```
Cash..........................................  3,000.00
    Notes receivable...........................            3,000.00
    Collection of note from James Magee.
Cash..........................................  6,060.00
    Notes receivable...........................            6,000.00
    Interest income............................              60.00
    Collection of Horace Heald note and interest.
```

Entries at maturity if note is not collected from the maker:

If, at the maturity of the notes, they are not collected from the makers, but are *immediately* collected from Fred Dutton, the endorser, the entries will be the same as those shown just above, except that the explanatory comment will indicate that the collections were made from the endorser.

If the notes are dishonored by the makers, and are not immediately collected from the endorser, they should be charged back to the endorser from whom we received them, by entries as shown on the following page.

Fred Dutton.................................. 3,000.00
    Notes receivable...........................   3,000.00
    To charge Dutton with the Magee note taken from
    Dutton to apply on account, and dishonored by
    Magee.

Fred Dutton.................................. 6,060.00
    Notes receivable...........................   6,000.00
    Interest income............................   60.00
    To charge Dutton with principal of, and interest on,
    the Heald note taken from Dutton to apply on ac-
    count, and dishonored by Heald.

CHAPTER 24
Fixed Assets

Definitions. Fixed assets are assets of a relatively permanent nature used in the operation of the business and not intended for sale. A building used as a factory is a fixed asset; it is relatively permanent property; it is used in the operation of the business and it is not intended for sale. A factory building no longer in use is not a fixed asset because it is not used in operations. Land held as a prospective factory site is not a fixed asset; it is permanent property and it is not intended for sale, but it is not used in operations.

Fixed assets may be either tangible or intangible. An asset is tangible if it has bodily substance, like a building or a machine. An asset is intangible if, like a patent or a copyright, its value resides, not in any physical properties, but in the rights which its possession confers upon its owner.

Charging fixed asset costs to operations. Most fixed assets have a limited useful life. The cost of such an asset (less any scrap or residual value which may be realizable at the end of the asset's usefulness) should be charged off gradually against income during the period (known or estimated) of its useful life. The words most commonly used to describe such systematic assignment of fixed asset costs to expense are:

Depreciation, which is the systematic assignment of the cost of tangible assets other than natural resources to expense.

Depletion, which is the systematic assignment of the cost of natural resources to expense.

Amortization, which is the systematic assignment of the cost of intangible fixed assets to expense.

Classification of fixed assets. Fixed assets may be classified, with respect to their nature and the type of cost assignment to which they are subject, as follows:

(A) Tangible:
    (1) Plant property:
        (a) Subject to depreciation.
            Examples: Buildings, machinery, tools and equipment, delivery equipment, furniture and fixtures.

(b) Not subject to depreciation.
Example: Land.
(2) Natural resources, subject to depletion.
Examples: Timber tracts, mines, oil wells.

(B) Intangible:
(1) Normally subject to amortization.
Examples: Patents, copyrights, franchises, lease-hold improvements.
(2) Not normally subject to amortization.
Examples: Goodwill, trademarks.

These various classes of fixed assets will be discussed in the order in which they are mentioned in the foregoing classification.

Valuation of fixed assets. Fixed assets usually are carried in the accounts on one of the following bases of valuation:

Cost.
Cost less depreciation, depletion, or amortization.
Appraised value—usually replacement cost new less depreciation thereon.
(The use of appraisal data for accounting purposes is considered acceptable only under certain special conditions. Such conditions are encountered so infrequently that no general discussion of this valuation basis will be given in this volume; it is discussed in the authors' *Principles of Accounting, Intermediate.*

As a general statement, it can be said that the cost of a fixed asset includes all expenditures made in acquiring the asset and putting it into a place and condition in which it can be used as intended in the operating activities of the business. Thus, the cost of machinery includes such items as freight and installation costs in addition to its invoice price.

Separate accounts should be kept with land and buildings, because the buildings are subject to depreciation, whereas the land is not. If land and a building thereon are purchased for a lump-sum price, an appraisal may be necessary to provide a basis for dividing the cost between the land and the building. For instance, assume that land and a building are purchased at a lump-sum price of $50,000. An apportionment of the cost on an appraisal basis may be made as follows:

	Appraisal Valuation	Fraction	Cost Apportionment
Land	$15,000	¼	$12,500
Building	45,000	¾	37,500
Total	$60,000		$50,000

If, in order to obtain a desired building site, it is necessary to acquire land that has an unsuitable building thereon, the Land account should be charged with the entire purchase price. Under such circumstances, it will be necessary to demolish or remove the unsuitable building. Any costs incurred in this connection should also be charged to the Land account, since the costs were incurred to make the site suitable for building purposes. Any amounts received as salvage from the disposal of the building should be credited to the Land account.

The cost of land purchased without improvements includes the purchase price, broker's commission, fees for examining and recording title, surveying, draining, clearing (less salvage), and landscaping. Any interest accrued at the date of purchase on mortgages or other encumbrances, and paid by the purchaser and any accrued taxes paid by the purchaser are part of the cost of the land. If land and improvements are purchased, the broker's commission and any accrued interest or tax costs should be apportioned between the land and the buildings.

Expenditures for land improvements may be charged to the Land account if the expenditures result in the addition of costs which are not subject to depreciation. If depreciation must be considered in relation to such expenditures, an account with Land Improvements should be opened. Such an account would be charged with expenditures for fences, water systems, sidewalks, and paving. Special assessments for local improvements which benefit the property may be charged to the Land account.

Where a building is purchased, the Building account should be charged with any repair costs incurred to make good the depreciation prior to acquisition, and with the cost of any subsequent improvements.

The cost of a building constructed includes the payments to contractors, fees for permits and licenses, architects' fees, superintendents' salaries, and insurance and similar expenditures during the construction period. It is considered permissible to charge the Buildings account with interest costs incurred during the construction period on money borrowed for the payment of construction costs.

If a machine or other fixed asset is constructed by a company for its own use, it should be recorded at cost, and not at some higher price which it might have been necessary to pay if the asset had been purchased from outsiders.

Depreciation. Plant fixed assets do not last forever. They either wear out or become obsolete. The wearing out of a fixed asset is characterized by physical deterioration caused by use or the action of the elements. The nature of obsolescence is indicated by the following illustrations:

A company owns a hand machine capable of making 100 articles a day. The business has grown so that 1,000 articles must be made each day. Instead of buying nine more hand machines, it is better to dispose of the one machine owned and buy a power machine capable of making 1,000 units a day. The hand machine is obsolete.

The operation of the power machine requires the services of five men. A new automatic machine is invented. Because of the saving in labor, it may be economical business management to dispose of the recently acquired power machine and purchase the new automatic machine. If so, the power machine is obsolete.

The new automatic machine is capable of producing only one product. The market for this product suddenly ceases. The automatic machine is obsolete.

Whether the usefulness of a plant fixed asset is terminated by physical deterioration or by obsolescence, it is the objective of depreciation accounting to spread the cost of the asset over the years of its usefulness in a systematic and sensible manner. This notion of depreciation is supported by the following definition proposed by the Committee on Terminology of the American Institute of Accountants: "*Depreciation accounting is a system of accounting which aims to distribute the cost or other basic value of tangible capital assets, less salvage (if any), over the estimated useful life of the unit . . . in a systematic and rational manner. It is a process of allocation, not of valuation.*" It is important to stress the fact that depreciation, in the accounting sense, does not consist of measuring the effects of wear and tear. It is a systematic cost assignment procedure, determined primarily by the use-life expectancy of assets.

Fixed assets are, of course, subject to decreases in market value, but accountants do not consider it necessary to record such decreases, because fixed assets are not intended for sale. The market values may be up today and down tomorrow; such fluctuations in value may be ignored because the value of a fixed asset to a business normally lies in its usefulness rather than in its marketability. Hence, as noted in the above definition, measuring the decline in value attributable either to use or to obsolescence is not an objective of depreciation. To repeat, depreciation is not a valuation process.

Computing and recording depreciation. There are numerous methods of estimating depreciation. The *straight-line method*, which is the one most frequently used, will be discussed. Other methods are discussed in *Principles of Accounting, Intermediate*.

Theoretically, the periodic depreciation charge under this method should be computed as follows:

Cost of asset..	$2,500
Estimated residual or scrap value—amount which it is estimated can be realized from the asset when it is no longer usable....	300
Total depreciation to be charged to expense during the total useful life of the asset.....................................	$2,200
Estimated useful life.....................................	10 years
Estimated depreciation per year...........................	$ 220

As a practical matter, the residual value is frequently ignored, and the depreciation is based on the cost. Ignoring the residual value and writing off the total cost over a period of ten years would, in the foregoing illustration, result in an annual charge of $250.

Depreciation is recorded by:

Debiting a Depreciation account, which is an operating expense account.

Crediting either:

A Reserve for Depreciation, which will have a credit balance to be deducted in the balance sheet from the debit balance of the fixed asset account; or

The fixed asset account. This is called *writing down* the asset. This method usually is not desirable for two reasons:

First, if depreciation is credited to the asset account, the cost of the fixed asset will be lost sight of.

Second, the provision for depreciation is only an estimate; by crediting it to a reserve, the amount of depreciation provided can be shown in the balance sheet, where interested parties can get information on which to base their own opinions as to the adequacy of the provision.

Estimates of useful life may be based on the past experience of a business with assets of the same type, or experience data may be obtained from manufacturers or trade associations. Probably the most widely used reference source reporting on commonly accepted estimates of useful life for various assets is Bulletin F,

published by the Bureau of Internal Revenue. Presented below
are examples from Bulletin F.

Item	Useful life
Office equipment:	
Safes...	50 years
Furniture, fixtures, and filing cases............	20 years
Mechanical equipment.......................	8 years

Depreciation vs. provision for replacement. The nature of
depreciation accounting is often misunderstood. The misunderstanding arises from a tendency to assume that depreciation entries
somehow produce funds for the replacement of fixed assets; this
false assumption may have been caused by a misunderstanding of
the expression "provision for depreciation" frequently used by
accountants.

Depreciation entries merely charge operations, during a series
of periods, with the cost of an asset previously acquired. Depreciation entries in no way affect the Cash account. If it is desired
to provide a fund for the replacement of the assets, cash may be
set aside in a special bank account or invested in securities to be
held until money is required for replacement purposes. The creation of such a replacement fund is very unusual, because management usually believes that the cash can be more profitably used
in regular business operations.

Expenditures during ownership. An expenditure is the payment, or the incurring of an obligation to make a future payment,
for a benefit received. Expenditures incident to the ownership of
fixed assets are of two classes:

  Capital expenditures, which should be recorded by increasing
    the book value of the assets. In most cases, this is done by
    debiting the asset accounts; in some cases, it is done by debit-
    ing the depreciation reserves.
  Revenue expenditures, which should be charged to expense.

A careful distinction must be made between capital and revenue expenditures if a correct accounting for fixed assets and for
net income is to be maintained. If a capital expenditure is
charged to an expense account, the book value of the fixed asset
is understated, and the net income and net worth also are understated. On the other hand, if a revenue expenditure is charged
to an asset account instead of to an expense account, the book
value of the fixed asset is overstated and the net income and net
worth also are overstated.

The proper treatment of some of the more common types of
expenditures is indicated on the following page.

Particulars	Revenue Expenditures	Capital Expenditures Book Value of Assets Increased by Charges to	
	Charged to Expense Accounts	Asset Account	Reserve
Acquisition cost: A company purchased three second-hand machines; charge the fixed asset account. Expenditures to make good depreciation which took place prior to acquisition: Before the machines were put into use, they were thoroughly overhauled. This was a capital expenditure.............		$3,000 400	
Installation cost: This is a capital expenditure............		50	
Betterment: Additional accessories were purchased for use with the machines; this expenditure is chargeable to the asset account......		75	
Ordinary repair: At the end of the first month of operations, a repair bill was paid; this was a revenue expenditure or expense...............	$18		
Extraordinary repair: After three years of use, the machines were again thoroughly reconditioned at a cost of $400. This was a capital expenditure because it made good some of the depreciation subsequent to acquisition; it should not be recorded by a charge to the asset account because it is not an addition to cost; it should be recorded by a charge to the depreciation reserve because it is a reduction of accrued depreciation..............................			$400

Reinstallation expense:
  The first cost of installing machinery in a factory is a proper charge to the asset account. If machinery is rearranged in the factory for the purpose of improving the routing or otherwise reducing the time and cost of production, a question arises with respect to the proper treatment of the reinstallation expense. Presumably, the cost of one installation will already have been charged to the Machinery account. Theoretically, therefore, the cost, or the undepreciated remainder of the cost, of the first installation should be removed from the accounts (by crediting the fixed asset with the original cost and debiting the reserve with the accumulated depreciation thereon), and the reinstallation cost should be capitalized by charge to the Machinery account.

Disposal of fixed assets.

When a fixed asset subject to depreciation is disposed of, an entry should be made debiting Cash for the amount received, crediting the asset account with the cost of the asset, debiting the depreciation reserve with the depreciation provided against the asset, and debiting or crediting an account to show the loss or gain on the disposal. Three illustrations follow:

(1) *Price equal to book value:*
Assume that, at the date of disposal of a machine, the asset and reserve accounts had the following balances:

	Debit	Credit
Machinery...............................	$2,500.00	
Reserve for depreciation—Machinery......		$2,200.00

The asset had a net book value of $300 and was sold for $300. The entry to record the sale is:

	Debit	Credit
Cash.....................................	300.00	
Reserve for depreciation—Machinery......	2,200.00	
Machinery.........................		2,500.00

To record the sale of machinery, relieving the asset account of the cost and relieving the reserve of the depreciation provided thereon.

(2) *Price less than book value:*
Assume that the accounts had the following balances:

	Debit	Credit
Machinery...............................	$2,500.00	
Reserve for depreciation—Machinery....		$1,760.00

The asset had a net book value of $740 and was sold for $400; hence, there was a loss of $340. The entry to record the sale is:

	Debit	Credit
Cash.....................................	400.00	
Loss on disposal of machinery............	340.00	
Reserve for depreciation—Machinery......	1,760.00	
Machinery.........................		2,500.00

To record the sale of machinery.

(3) *Price more than book value:*
Assume that the accounts had the following balances:

	Debit	Credit
Machinery...............................	$2,500.00	
Reserve for depreciation—Machinery......		$2,200.00

The asset had a net book value of $300 and was sold for $500; hence, there was a gain of $200. The entry to record the sale of the machinery at a gain of $200 is shown below:

	Debit	Credit
Cash.....................................	500.00	
Reserve for depreciation—Machinery......	2,200.00	
Machinery.........................		2,500.00
Gain on disposal of machinery........		200.00

To record the sale of machinery.

Losses and gains on the disposal of fixed assets were formerly charged and credited to the Earned Surplus account. Some accountants supported this treatment by the following reasoning:

If depreciation were correctly estimated, no losses or gains would result from the disposal of fixed assets. Therefore, losses and gains arising from the disposal of fixed assets are in reality corrections of the earnings of prior years, which were incorrectly stated because the depreciation was incorrectly estimated. The earnings of prior years are now in the Earned Surplus account; a correction of prior years' earnings should therefore be debited or credited to Earned Surplus.

Other accountants justified the charge or credit to Earned Surplus as follows:

The profit and loss statement should show the results of regular operations; a loss or gain from the disposal of a fixed asset is an extraneous, non-operating item and therefore should be charged or credited direct to Earned Surplus.

Accountants are not in complete agreement on this matter at the present time. However, the following position, taken by the Committee on Accounting Procedure of the American Institute of Accountants, is widely supported:

There is a presumption that all items of profit and loss recognized during any given period should be used in determining the figure reported as net income. A possible exception may be justified in the case of extraordinary charges or credits resulting from the disposal of fixed assets, where the amount of such losses or gains is so large in relation to a company's net income that misleading inferences might be drawn unless such items were excluded from the profit and loss statement.

Deciding what is "extraordinary" and concluding that a certain gain or loss is so large that "misleading inferences" might be drawn from the profit and loss statement are matters of opinion. Therefore, it seems desirable for purposes of this text to regard all losses and gains from the disposal of fixed assets as being immaterial and hence not to be charged or credited to Earned Surplus.

If a fixed asset is disposed of during the year and it is the accounting policy to record depreciation for fractional periods, an entry for depreciation for the fractional period ending with the date of disposal is required. To illustrate, assume that the balances on page 370 appear in the accounts on June 30, 1954:

	Debit	Credit
Machinery....................................	$5,000.00	
Reserve for depreciation—Machinery—created by annual credits of $300.......................		$3,000.00

The asset is disposed of on June 30 for $1,500; no depreciation has been provided for since December 31, 1953. The following entries should be made:

Depreciation—Machinery......................	150.00	
Reserve for depreciation—Machinery......		150.00
To provide for depreciation as an operating expense of the six months ended June 30, 1954.		
Cash...	1,500.00	
Reserve for depreciation—Machinery............	3,150.00	
Loss on disposal of machinery..................	350.00	
Machinery..............................		5,000.00
To record the sale of machinery.		

Trade-ins. Frequently, a fixed asset is disposed of by trading it in on a new asset. Some trade-in allowance is generally granted by the dealer. The difference between the trade-in allowance and the book value of the asset being traded in, after recording depreciation to the date of disposal, is the gain or loss on disposal.

Trade-ins are illustrated by using the following data:

	Case A	Case B
Old asset:		
Cost...	$5,000	$5,000
Reserve for depreciation...........................	3,000	3,000
Book value.......................................	2,000	2,000
Trade-in allowance...............................	2,300	1,800
List price of new asset.............................	6,000	6,000
Cash payment......................................	3,700	4,200

Entries	Case A	Case B
Asset account (new asset)..................	6,000	6,000
Reserve for depreciation...................	3,000	3,000
Loss on disposal of old asset................		200
Gain on disposal of old asset............	300	
Asset account (old asset)................	5,000	5,000
Cash...................................	3,700	4,200
To record exchange of assets.		

In computing the federal income tax for a business, gains or losses resulting from trading in one asset on another are not allowed. Under the tax rule, the cost of the new asset, for purposes of computing depreciation and the gain or loss on subsequent disposal, is the sum of the book value of the old asset plus the additional expenditure made in acquiring the new asset. On this basis, the entry to record the exchange of assets in the foregoing cases would be as shown on the following page.

	Case A	Case B
Asset account (new asset).............	5,700	6,200
Reserve for depreciation.............	3,000	3,000
Asset account (old asset)...........		5,000 5,000
Cash................................		3,700 4,200

Many accountants, as a matter of convenience, prefer to follow the tax rule in the accounts.

Depreciation program revisions. After an asset has been in use for some time, it may be found that too much or too little depreciation has been provided. Such a condition may be due to an error in estimating the life of the asset or to an incorrect estimate of the residual value. In any event, it would be incorrect to continue with the existing depreciation program under such circumstances, unless, of course, the amount involved is so small that it can be ignored on practical grounds. If a change is warranted, either of the following alternatives is acceptable:

(1) Adjust the Reserve for Depreciation account to the amount which it would have contained if depreciation had originally been based on the estimates which now seem correct, and base subsequent depreciation charges on the revised useful life.

Data for example:

Asset cost......................................	$9,000
Estimated scrap value...........................	—0—
Estimated useful life...........................	10 years

Depreciation entries to date:

Year	
1..	$ 900
2..	900
3..	900
4..	900
5..	900
6..	900
Balance in Reserve for Depreciation at the end of the sixth year....................................	$5,400

During the seventh year, before recording any depreciation for the seventh year, it is established that the asset will probably last six more years (revised useful life = 12 years).

Computation of correction of Reserve for Depreciation:

Depreciation recorded during the first six years...........	$5,400
Revised annual charge for depreciation: $9,000 ÷ 12 = $750.	
Revised depreciation for the first six years: $750 × 6 = ...	4,500
Amount of adjustment................................	$ 900

Entry to adjust the Reserve for Depreciation account:

Reserve for depreciation...................... 900.00
  Earned surplus, or Correction of prior years' de-
    preciation.................................   900.00
  To adjust the Reserve for Depreciation to conform
  to the revised estimate of useful life.

Entry for depreciation for seventh and subsequent years:

Depreciation expense.......................... 750.00
  Reserve for depreciation....................   750.00
  Depreciation for the year.

Note: If the depreciation adjustment is immaterial in
amount, it may be shown in the profit and loss
statement. If the adjustment is material in
amount, some accountants would advocate carrying it direct to Earned Surplus, whereas other
accountants would still favor showing it in the
profit and loss statement.

(2) Spread the undepreciated cost of the asset over the remaining useful life of the asset by "revised" depreciation
provisions, without changing the current balance in the
Reserve for Depreciation account.

Data for example:
Same conditions as above.

*Computation of depreciation provision for the seventh and
subsequent years:*

Undepreciated cost:
  Cost.................................... $9,000
  Reserve for depreciation................ 5,400 $3,600
Revised remaining useful life...................... 6 years
Revised annual depreciation provision............... $ 600

Entry for depreciation for seventh and subsequent years:

Depreciation expense.......................... 600.00
  Reserve for depreciation...............   600.00
  Depreciation for the year.

The above illustration dealt with overdepreciation. If underdepreciation is discovered, the changes will be as follows:

For alternative (1):

The Reserve for Depreciation will be credited for the amount
of the underdepreciation, the debit being assigned either
to Earned Surplus or Correction of Prior Years' Depreciation, as discussed above.

The subsequent provisions for depreciation will be larger than the former annual provisions.

For alternative (2):

The subsequent provisions for depreciation will be larger than the former annual provisions.

The second alternative is found more commonly in practice, possibly for the following reasons:

(a) One reason has been well expressed by the Committee on Accounting Procedure in its Bulletin 27:

"Under most circumstances, costs once identified and absorbed through amortization or depreciation charges are not considered to be subject to further accounting, and corrections of estimates affecting the allocations are commonly reflected in revised charges during the remaining life of the property."

On another occasion, the committee expressed the same position in the following words:

"Corrections of (depreciation) estimates should normally be reflected in revised charges for later years."

(b) Alternative (1) is not acceptable for federal income tax purposes.

(c) Particularly if the difference between the former annual depreciation provision and the new annual depreciation provision is not large in relation to average net income, accountants are inclined to avoid an adjustment for the accumulated "error" resulting from past depreciation entries, since their effect on reported net income was immaterial. The "approximate" character of depreciation accounting does not seem to require such a precise treatment.

Subsidiary records. The general ledger should contain an account with each class of fixed assets, such as Land, Buildings, Machinery, Furniture and Fixtures, and Delivery Equipment. It is also desirable to maintain a subsidiary plant ledger containing considerable information with respect to the cost, depreciation, repairs, and so forth, of each unit. Thus, the subsidiary machinery record might contain a card or page for each machine, showing the following data:

Name of asset.
Identification number.
Location.

Manufacturer.
From whom purchased.
Date of installation.
Purchase cost.
Other incidental costs.
Depreciation data:
    Estimated life.
    Estimated residual value.
    Depreciation rate.
    Periodic and accumulated provision for depreciation.
Ordinary and extraordinary repairs, with information as to date, nature, and cost.
Actual life, residual value, and gain or loss on disposal.
Information as to abnormal operating conditions, such as overtime work, affecting rapidity of depreciation.

Such records furnish a good control over the fixed assets, as they are virtually a perpetual inventory showing all fixed assets which should be in the company's possession. The information regarding the cost and accumulated depreciation of each unit can be used in making entries to relieve the asset and depreciation reserve accounts of the correct amounts when a unit is fully depreciated. The subsidiary records are also useful in connection with insurance claims.

Natural Resources

Valuation. Natural resources, such as timber tracts, mines, and oil wells, should be carried in the asset accounts at cost. As the resources are converted, a portion of their cost is removed from the fixed asset account and assigned to other accounts, thereby reducing the book value of the fixed asset. Such cost transfers give recognition to depletion. Such assets are sometimes called *wasting assets*.

Development expenditures, such as those made for the removal of surface earth for strip mining operations, which do not result in the acquisition of tangible fixed assets, may be charged to the wasting asset account. Tangible fixed assets acquired for purposes of developing or extracting the wasting asset should be recorded in separate accounts; they should be depreciated in amounts proportionate to the depletion, if the developments will render service throughout the entire life of the wasting asset; they should be depreciated over a shorter period if their useful life will expire before the wasting asset is completely depleted.

Depletion. Depletion usually is computed by dividing the cost of the wasting asset by the estimated number of units (tons, barrels, thousand feet, and so forth) in the asset; thus a unit depletion charge is computed. The total depletion charge for each period is then computed by multiplying the unit charge by the number of units converted during the period.

To illustrate, assume that $90,000 was paid for a mine which was estimated to contain 300,000 tons of available deposit. The unit depletion charge is $90,000 ÷ 300,000, or $.30. If 60,000 tons are mined during a given year, the depletion charge for the year is $.30 × 60,000, or $18,000.

The depletion charge will be recorded as follows:

```
Depletion.................................. 18,000.00
    Reserve for depletion........................        18,000.00
```

If some of the units converted remain unsold at year-end, the depletion charge relating to such units is assignable to an inventory account. In other words, depletion is a charge against income when the units converted are sold, not when they are converted.

The credit balance in the Reserve for Depletion should be deducted in the balance sheet from the debit balance in the asset account.

Intangible Fixed Assets Normally Subject to Amortization

Reason for amortization. Some intangible fixed assets are subject to amortization because their lives are limited by law, regulation, contract, or their nature. Examples are patents, copyrights, franchises for limited periods, leaseholds, and leasehold improvements. It should be understood that the period fixed by law, regulation, or contract is the maximum period of life, and that the usefulness of such assets may cease prior to the expiration of that period; in such instances, the shorter useful life should be the period on which the amortization is based.

If the original estimate of useful life is subsequently regarded as incorrect, the accountant may either (1) adjust the book value of the asset to the amount which would be reflected by the accounts if amortization had originally been based on the estimates which now seem correct, and base the subsequent amortization on the revised useful life; or (2) spread the unamortized balance over the remaining useful life, as revised. These are the same alternatives that were discussed in connection with depreciation revisions, on pages 371 to 373.

Patents. If a patent is acquired by purchase, its cost is the purchase price. If it is obtained by the inventor, its cost is the total of the experimental expense and costs of constructing working models and obtaining the patent, including drawings, attorney's fees, and filing costs. Since a patent has no proven value until it has stood the test of an infringement suit, the cost of a successful suit may be charged to the Patents account. If the suit is unsuccessful, and the patent is thereby proved to be valueless, the cost of the suit and the cost of the patent should be written off.

A patent is issued for 17 years, and its cost should be amortized over that period, unless it was acquired after the expiration of a portion of the 17-year period, in which case it should be written off over its remaining life. If there is a probability that the patented device or the product of the device will become obsolete before the expiration of the patent, conservatism would suggest writing off the patent during a period shorter than its legal life.

A patent may give its owner a monopoly which enables him to develop his business to a point where, after the expiration of the patent, competitors will find it extremely difficult to enter the field and overcome the handicap. When this happens, a goodwill is created during the life of the patent. Nevertheless, the patent should be amortized, and no goodwill should be set up.

Copyrights. A copyright gives its owner the exclusive right to produce and sell reading matter and works of art. The fee for obtaining a copyright is only a nominal amount, too small to justify an accounting procedure of capitalization and amortization. Costs sufficient in amount to justify such an accounting procedure may be incurred, however, when copyrights are purchased.

Copyrights are issued for 28 years with a possibility of renewal for an additional 28 years. However, publications rarely have an active market for a period as long as 28 years, and it usually is regarded as advisable to write off copyright costs over a much shorter period.

Franchises. Franchises should not be set up in the books unless a payment was made in obtaining them. Franchises are sometimes perpetual, in which case their cost need not be amortized; usually they are granted for a definite period of time, in which case their cost should be amortized over that period.

Leaseholds and leasehold improvements. When property is rented for a period of years, an advance payment may be made which will apply against future rents; this payment may be charged to a Prepaid Rent account or a Leasehold account and amortized over the life of the lease by charges to Rent and credits to Prepaid Rent or Leasehold.

Sometimes a company will obtain a long-term lease on real estate, and property values will so increase that the rents payable under the lease are much smaller than they would be on the basis of current values. The lease may thus become very valuable because of the saving in rent or because the lease could be sold for a gain. It is not proper, however, to place this value in the accounts, because the offsetting credit to surplus would inflate the surplus by including an unrealized gain.

Leases for long periods frequently provide that the lessee (the party who acquired the right to occupy the property) shall pay the cost of any alterations or improvements which he may desire, such as new fronts, partitions, and built-in shelving. Such alterations and improvements become a part of the real estate and revert to the owner of the real estate at the expiration of the lease; all that the lessee obtains by the expenditure is the intangible right to benefit by the improvements during the life of the lease. The lessee should therefore charge such expenditures to a Leasehold Improvements account; the cost should be amortized over the life of the lease or the expected useful life of the improvements, whichever is shorter, by journal entries charging Rent and crediting Leasehold Improvements. The Rent account is, of course, also charged with the cash payments for rent made to the lessor.

Intangible Fixed Assets Not Normally Subject to Amortization

Some intangible fixed assets are not normally subject to amortization because they are assumed to have an unlimited useful life. Examples are trademarks, trade names, secret processes and formulas, and goodwill.

Such assets may be carried indefinitely at cost if there is no reason to believe that their useful lives will ever terminate. However, their amortization or complete write-off may be proper under several conditions. First, at the time of its acquisition there may be good reason to fear that the useful life of such an asset will terminate, even though there is no conclusive evidence to that effect; in such instances, periodic amortization charges may be made against income. Second, at some date subsequent to acquisition, the asset may be found to be valueless, in which case it should be written off; or conditions may have developed which indicate that the life of the asset will terminate, in which case its cost may be amortized over the estimated remaining life; or a portion of the cost may be charged off immediately (as representing amortization for prior periods) and the remainder may be amortized over the estimated remaining life.

Trademarks. The right to the use of a trademark may be protected by registry; the right does not terminate at the end of a definite period, and trademarks are, therefore, normally carried indefinitely in the accounts at cost, without amortization.

Goodwill.   The following statement, intended to indicate the nature of goodwill, is quoted from a court decision:

> "When an individual or a firm or a corporation has gone on for an unbroken series of years conducting a particular business, and has been so scrupulous in fulfilling every obligation, so careful in maintaining the standard of the goods dealt in, so absolutely fair and honest in all business dealings that customers of the concern have become convinced that their experience in the future will be as satisfactory as it has been in the past, while such customers' good report of their own experience tends continually to bring new customers to the concern, there has been produced an element of value quite as important as—in some cases, perhaps, far more important than—the plant or machinery with which the business is carried on. That it is property is abundantly settled by authority, and, indeed, is not disputed. That in some cases it may be very valuable property is manifest. The individual who has created it by years of hard work and fair business dealing usually experiences no difficulty in finding men willing to pay him for it if he be willing to sell it to them."

This quotation is interesting because it indicates some of the ways in which goodwill may be created. However, it does not adequately indicate the nature of goodwill for two reasons.

In the first place, it implies that goodwill is produced only by satisfactory customer relations; but since goodwill is dependent upon earnings, and since many things other than customer satisfaction contribute to earnings, there are many sources of goodwill. Some of these sources are: location; manufacturing efficiency; satisfactory relations between the employees and the management, which contribute to earnings through effective employee service and the reduction of losses from labor turnover; adequate sources of capital and a credit standing which is reflected in low money costs; advertising; monopolistic privileges; and, in general, good business management.

In the second place, in laying the emphasis on customer relations, the quotation fails to put the emphasis where it really belongs: on the relation between earnings and net assets. A company may be scrupulous, fair, and honest, and its good repute may tend continually to attract new customers, and yet the company may have no goodwill. The existence of goodwill depends upon the earning of excess profits.

"Goodwill" may be defined as the value of the earnings of a business which are in excess of a normal or basic return on the net assets exclusive of goodwill. To illustrate, let us assume the conditions shown on the following page.

	Company A	Company B
Net assets, exclusive of goodwill..............	$100,000	$100,000
Rate of net income which, for the particular industry, may be agreed upon by the purchaser and seller of a business as normal, or which a new company entering the field may reasonably be expected to earn—say.......	10%	10%
Net income earned........................	$ 10,000	$ 15,000
Income at "normal" rate on net assets exclusive of goodwill......................	10,000	10,000
Excess earnings...........................	—	$ 5,000

The excess earnings of Company B indicate that it has a goodwill; Company A apparently has none because it has no excess earnings.

Methods of computing goodwill. The price to be paid for goodwill in connection with the sale of a business may be an amount arbitrarily agreed upon by the purchaser and seller, without formal computation. On the other hand, it may be computed on the basis of past or anticipated earnings of the business. Three goodwill valuation bases are illustrated below:

(1) Some multiple of the average past annual earnings. For instance, assume that the average earnings for five years prior to the sale of the business have been $10,000, and that the goodwill is to be valued at twice the average earnings; the goodwill will be valued at $20,000. The price so computed is said to be "two years' purchase" of the average annual earnings.

This method is illogical because it fails to give recognition to the fact that the goodwill is not dependent upon total earnings, no matter how large, but upon the relation of the earnings to the net assets exclusive of goodwill, and that no goodwill exists unless the earnings are in excess of a normal income on the net assets other than goodwill. Recognition is given to this fact in the two following bases of goodwill valuation.

(2) Some multiple of the average past earnings in excess of a return at an agreed rate on the average investment. For instance, assume average annual earnings for five years of $10,000, an average investment of $100,000 and an agreement to pay for goodwill three years' purchase of the average earnings in excess of 8% on the average investment. The goodwill would be computed in the manner shown on the following page.

Average earnings..	$10,000
Less 8% on average investment...........................	8,000
Excess..	$ 2,000
Multiply by number of years' purchase....................	3
Goodwill...	$ 6,000

(3) The capitalized value of excess income. For instance, assuming the same facts as in (2) with respect to average income and investment, and assuming an agreement to compute goodwill by capitalizing, at 10%, the average annual earnings in excess of 8% on the average investment, we would compute the goodwill as follows:

Average earnings...	$10,000
Less 8% on average investment............................	8,000
Excess to be capitalized...................................	$ 2,000
Capitalized value:...................................$2,000 ÷ .10 =	$20,000

Proper book value of goodwill. A Goodwill account can properly appear on the books only if the goodwill was specifically paid for. The management of a company may believe that it has created goodwill by advertising expenditures or otherwise, and may desire to charge such items to a Goodwill account. Accountants do not approve of such charges to Goodwill because of the practical impossibility of identifying specific expenditures as representing the cost of goodwill.

It is usually considered good accounting to carry goodwill as an asset indefinitely at its cost. However, since the price paid for goodwill is generally based on a belief that better-than-average earnings will be produced by a given group of assets, what should the accountant do with the Goodwill account if better-than-average earnings fail to materialize or if the earnings decline?

As a general rule, accountants do not favor perpetuating an asset balance when there is no underlying value in support of the asset. And, where an accountant has convincing evidence that an asset is significantly overstated, such overstatement should be removed from the accounts, possibly by direct charge to Earned Surplus.

As a practical matter, there is no way of determining the "life" of goodwill. Many accountants believe that it is unlikely that goodwill will "last" over the entire life of an enterprise. For this reason, it is considered acceptable to amortize goodwill over a reasonable period of time. The Committee on Accounting Procedure has supported this practice in its Bulletin No. 24. The Committee's opinion is paraphrased below:

Where a corporation decides that goodwill may not continue to have value during the entire life of the enterprise, it may amortize the cost of such intangible despite the fact that there are no present indications that goodwill will have a limited life. In such cases the cost may be amortized over a reasonable period of time, by systematic charges in the income statement.

Fixed Assets in the Balance Sheet

It usually is considered desirable to show the total tangible fixed assets and the total intangible fixed assets separately in the balance sheet. One procedure is illustrated below:

Tangible fixed assets:			
Land...................................		$ 20,000.00	
Buildings...................	$150,000.00		
Less reserve for depreciation	30,000.00	120,000.00	
Machinery and equipment...	$ 90,000.00		
Less reserve for depreciation	12,000.00	78,000.00	
Tools......................	$ 15,000.00		
Less reserve for depreciation	4,000.00	11,000.00	
Delivery equipment.........	$ 5,000.00		
Less reserve for depreciation	2,000.00	3,000.00	
Furniture and fixtures.......	$ 5,500.00		
Less reserve for depreciation	2,200.00	3,300.00	
Total tangible fixed assets........................			$235,300.00
Intangible fixed assets:			
Patents...................	$ 8,000.00		
Less reserve for amortization...................	2,000.00	$ 6,000.00	
Goodwill............................		50,000.00	
Total intangible fixed assets.....................			56,000.00

If there are many fixed assets, space can be saved by a balance sheet presentation similar to the following:

	Cost	Depreciation or Amortization Reserve	Cost Less Depreciation or Amortization
Tangible fixed assets:			
Land....................	$ 20,000.00		$ 20,000.00
Buildings...............	150,000.00	$30,000.00	120,000.00
Machinery and equipment	90,000.00	12,000.00	78,000.00
Tools...................	15,000.00	4,000.00	11,000.00
Delivery equipment.......	5,000.00	2,000.00	3,000.00
Furniture and fixtures.....	5,500.00	2,200.00	3,300.00
Total tangible fixed assets................	$285,500.00	$50,200.00	$235,300.00
Intangible fixed assets:			
Patents.................	$ 8,000.00	$ 2,000.00	$ 6,000.00
Goodwill...............			50,000.00
Total intangible fixed assets................			56,000.00

CHAPTER 25

Inventories

Classes of inventories. The inventory of a concern that buys its goods in condition for sale is usually called a *merchandise inventory*. Merchandise inventories are found in wholesale and retail businesses. These businesses do not alter the form of the goods purchased for sale.

The following classes of inventories can be found in manufacturing businesses:

> Finished goods.
> Goods in process.
> Raw materials.

The above-mentioned inventories should be classified as current assets in the balance sheet, below the receivables and above the prepaid expenses.

Inventory all goods owned. What should be included in the inventory, and what should be excluded therefrom? The general rule is that the inventory should include all goods for which the company holds title, wherever they may be located.

If a business has received an order for goods but is holding them for future delivery, it is important to determine whether title has passed. The mere fact that the goods have been segregated from other merchandise may or may not mean that title has passed to the customer. If title has passed, the goods should be excluded from the inventory; if title has not passed, they should be included.

On the other hand, goods which have been ordered but not received at the inventory date may properly belong in the inventory. If the goods are in transit, the general rule as to passing of title is as follows: If the goods were shipped f. o. b. shipping point, they belong to the purchaser; if they were shipped f. o. b. destination and have not arrived at the destination, they belong to the seller.

A consignment is a shipment of merchandise from the owner (called the *consignor*) to another party (called the *consignee*) who is to attempt to sell the merchandise for the owner. Goods out on consignment should be included in the inventory of the consignor, who is the owner.

Importance of accuracy in taking and pricing the inventory. If the inventory is misstated, both the balance sheet and the profit and loss statement will be affected. For example, if the December

31, 1953 inventory is overstated $5,000, the current assets presented in the December 31, 1953 balance sheet will be overstated $5,000 and the net income appearing in the profit and loss statement for the year ended December 31, 1953 will be overstated the same amount. The effect on the profit and loss statement can be seen by the following illustration, in which two profit and loss statements have been presented; in the first profit and loss statement, the correct ending inventory, $30,000, has been used; in the second profit and loss statement, the ending inventory has been overstated $5,000.

DEUCE COMPANY
Profit and Loss Statement
For the Year Ended December 31, 1953

	Correct Ending Inventory		Incorrect (Overstated) Ending Inventory	
Sales...............................		$100,000		$100,000
Cost of goods sold:				
Beginning inventory, 12/31/52...........	$20,000		$20,000	
Purchases.........................	70,000		70,000	
Total........................	$90,000		$90,000	
Deduct ending inventory, 12/31/53........	30,000	60,000	35,000	55,000
Gross profit.........................		$ 40,000		$ 45,000
Operating expenses.....................		25,000		25,000
Net income...........................		$ 15,000		$ 20,000

Since the ending inventory of one year is the beginning inventory of the next year, a misstatement of an inventory will affect two profit and loss statements—the statement for the year in which the inventory error occurred, and the statement for the following year. This can be demonstrated by continuing the preceding illustration through 1954. It is assumed that the correct inventory for December 31, 1954 is $25,000.

DEUCE COMPANY
Profit and Loss Statement
For the Year Ended December 31, 1954

	Correct Beginning Inventory		Incorrect (Overstated) Beginning Inventory	
Sales...............................		$110,000		$110,000
Cost of goods sold:				
Beginning inventory, 12/31/53..........	$30,000		$ 35,000	
Purchases.........................	65,000		65,000	
Total........................	$95,000		$100,000	
Deduct ending inventory, 12/31/54......	25,000	70,000	25,000	75,000
Gross profit.........................		$ 40,000		$ 35,000
Operating expenses.....................		27,000		27,000
Net income...........................		$ 13,000		$ 8,000

If the amounts of net income reported above for the two years are added, it will be seen that the same total is reported for the two-year period.

	Net Income Computed With		
	Correct	An Inventory	Error in
Year	Inventories	Error	Net Income
1953.....................	$15,000	$20,000	$5,000 over
1954.....................	13,000	8,000	5,000 under
Total................	$28,000	$28,000	—0—

Although an inventory overstatement causes an overstatement of net income in the first year, it causes an offsetting understatement of net income in the second year. Thus, inventory errors are counterbalancing over a two-year period. The net income is misstated in each of the two years, but not in the aggregate.

If the December 31, 1953 inventory had been understated instead of overstated, just the opposite results would have occurred; the 1953 net income would have been understated and the 1954 net income would have been overstated.

The above observations may be summarized in the following manner:

If the ENDING inventory is: Net income for the period will be:
   Overstated   Overstated
   Understated   Understated

If the BEGINNING inventory is: Net income for the period will be:
   Overstated   Understated
   Understated   Overstated

Procedure of inventory taking. There is no universal procedure for taking an inventory. Probably the simplest procedure is as follows: Two people work as a team; one person counts, weighs, or otherwise measures the merchandise and calls the descriptions and quantities to the other person, who writes them on inventory sheets. Unit valuations are then entered on the sheets; extensions are made by multiplying quantities by these prices; and the sheets are footed.

Although this is a simple procedure, it does not provide safeguards against errors, because the work of one person is not checked by some other person. There are several ways of providing such safeguards. One such procedure is here described.

A team of two persons is assigned to a department, a section, or some other unit of space. Each team is provided with prenumbered, two-part, perforated inventory tags, which may be printed as illustrated at the top of the following page.

```
Tag No.  101
Location No._____
Article:
Identification
   number_____
Description_____
   _____

Quantity (    )_____
Taken by_____
-------------------------------------
Tag No.  101
Location No._____
Article:
Identification
   number_____
Description_____
   _____

Quantity (    )_____
Checked By_____
```

Each team is furnished with at least as many tags as there are different classes of articles that the team will inventory.

Each member of the team takes a complete inventory of the stock assigned to the team. One member of the team takes the tags and goes through the stock systematically, inventorying each class of merchandise, and entering the data for each class on the top section of the tag, which may then appear as shown below. The "Description" space is used if the article does not have an identifying number. The "Taken by" line may show the person's initials or his clock number. The per-

son who fills out the top section of the tag leaves the entire tag with the merchandise.

The second member of the team follows the first member, makes an independent identification and count of the articles, and fills out the bottom section of the tag. He compares the top and bottom sections of the

```
Tag No.  101
Location No._____B19_____
Article:
Identification
   number_____97_____
Description_____
Quantity (doz.)____4_____
Taken by_____924_____
----------------------------------------
```

tag and reports any differences to a supervisory employee. He also watches for any merchandise which the first member may have overlooked.

To deter the second member of the team from merely copying the data appearing on the top section of the tag without making a second count and without independently identifying the articles, the inventory plan frequently provides that supervisory personnel or members of the audit staff will make test checks of the tags and the items inventoried as a verification of the work of the inventory team. Such third parties should also check to see that nothing has been overlooked that should be included in the inventory.

After the inventory-taking has been completed, the bottom section of each tag is detached; the top section of the tag is left with the merchandise. The bottom sections are sent to the accounting office and are sorted in tag-number sequence. Any unused tags are sent with them, for purposes of control; if any tags are missing, they should be found, since they may contain data applicable to inventoried goods.

After the accounting department has determined that all pre-numbered tags have been accounted for, the tags are sorted by article number. This is necessary because the same kind of merchandise may be in several locations: for instance, the main department, the basement department, the display windows, the storeroom, and the receiving room. After the tags have been thus assembled, the data shown by them are entered on inventory sheets as follows:

INVENTORY

December 31, 19—

Department No. B 19   Sheet No. 1

Article No.	Tag No.	Unit of Measurement	Quantity		Price	Amount
			Detail	Total		
97	101	Doz.		4		
98	102	Pr.	8			
98	304	"	16			
98	419	"	31	55		

The inventory sheet shows that No. 98 articles are in three locations, as indicated by the tag numbers. The total is entered so that the total inventory valuation of all articles of this number can be computed by one multiplication and shown in one amount.

You will remember that the top half of the tag was left with the merchandise. This was done to provide a further check on the accuracy of the inventory. This is accomplished by giving all employees who handle the merchandise instructions to be on the alert, on the morning following the inventory-taking, for any merchandise not tagged or for merchandise improperly described or identified on the tag or incorrectly counted.

The unit valuations are then entered on the inventory sheets; these prices are multiplied by quantities, and the amounts are entered on the sheets; finally, totals are computed for each sheet, for each department, and for the inventory as a whole.

Inventory pricing. There are a number of acceptable bases for pricing inventories. Some are considered acceptable only under special circumstances, while others are widely applicable. The two bases most widely applicable are:

(1) Cost.
(2) Cost or market, whichever is lower.

Cost. Cost of merchandise or materials purchased includes not only the purchase price but also any additional costs necessary to put the goods into condition for sale or for use in manufacturing. These incidental costs include duties, freight, drayage, storage, insurance while the goods are being transported or stored, and costs incurred during any aging period.

Incidental costs frequently are omitted for inventory-pricing purposes. Such omission is sanctioned by accountants if the incidental costs are immaterial in amount and the effect of their exclusion on the financial statements would be negligible.

From a theoretical standpoint, purchase discounts are unquestionably cost reductions. However, as a general rule, it is impractical to attempt to relate discounts taken to the merchandise on hand. Furthermore, the amount involved is relatively small. Therefore, it does not seem reasonable for accountants to insist that purchase discounts be recognized in determining costs for inventory-pricing purposes.

Cost selection for inventory pricing. It is a readily observable fact that prices change. Therefore, identical goods may be acquired at different costs. Consequently, accountants are faced with the problem of determining which costs apply to the goods that have been sold, and which costs apply to the goods that remain in the inventory.

Several of the more widely used methods of selecting the costs which are to be regarded as applicable to the goods in the inventory are discussed in the following paragraphs.

For purposes of illustration, assume the following facts:

	Units	Unit Cost	Total
Beginning inventory	2	$10	$20
First purchase	1	11	11
Second purchase	1	10	10
Third purchase	1	12	12
Fourth purchase	1	13	13
Cost of goods available for sale			$66
Total quantity available for sale	6		
Sold during the period	4		
Ending inventory	2		

Specific identification. If the goods on hand can be identified as pertaining to specific purchases, they may be inventoried at the costs shown by the related invoices. Assume, for instance, that the two units in the ending inventory can be identified as having been acquired by the second and fourth purchases; the cost for inventory purposes would be:

Units	Unit Cost	Total
1	$10	$10
1	13	13
Ending inventory		$23

Weighted-average method. The cost of the goods available for sale is divided by the total units available for sale. The resulting average unit cost is used for pricing the ending inventory. Using the above facts, the weighted-average unit cost and the ending inventory would be computed as follows:

Cost of goods available for sale	$66
Total units available for sale	6
Average unit cost	$11
Ending inventory $11 × 2	$22

The costs determined by the weighted-average method are affected by purchases early in the period as well as toward the end of the period; therefore, on a rising market, the weighted-average unit cost will be less than current unit cost, and, on a falling market, the weighted-average unit cost will be in excess of the current unit cost.

First-in, first-out method. This method is based on the assumption that the first goods purchased are the first to be sold, and that the goods which remain are of the last purchases. This method, referred to as the *fifo* (initial letters of *first-in, first-out*) method, is probably the most commonly used method. Applying this method to the facts being used for illustrative purposes, the two units in the ending inventory would be regarded as having been acquired by the last two purchases. Thus, the ending inventory would be priced as follows:

Units	Unit Cost	Total
1	$12	$12
1	13	13
Ending inventory		$25

The assumption that the older stock is usually the first to be disposed of is generally in accordance with good merchandising policy. There are, of course, cases in practice where the assumption does not square with the facts; for instance, the first coal dumped on a dealer's pile will be the last sold.

This method has also been considered desirable because it produces an inventory valuation which is in conformity with price trends; since the inventory is assumed to consist of the most recent purchases and is priced at the most recent costs, the pricing follows the trend of the market.

Last-in, first-out method. Under this method, referred to as the *lifo* method, the oldest costs are assumed to be applicable to the goods on hand. In the case assumed here, the two units in the ending inventory would be priced at the unit cost used in pricing the two units in the beginning inventory. Thus, the ending inventory would be computed as follows:

Units	Unit Cost	Total
2	$10	$20

If the ending inventory had been composed of three units, the third unit would, under *lifo*, be priced by using the unit cost applicable to the first purchase. Thus, an ending inventory of three units would total $31 under *lifo*.

In the minds of the advocates of the *lifo* method, the expression "last-in, first-out" does not necessarily refer to an assumption regarding the flow of goods, but rather to an assumption regarding the flow of costs. The advocates of *lifo* maintain that, during periods of changing costs and selling prices, more meaningful profit and loss statements are produced if "current" costs are applied to current sales, thus achieving a better matching of costs and revenues.

Cost or market, whichever is lower. On the "cost or market, whichever is lower" basis for the valuation of inventories, cost is used except under certain conditions, described later, where market is lower than cost. The term "market," as used here, means current replacement cost—that is, the currently prevailing purchase price of merchandise purchased for resale and raw materials purchased for use in manufacture—and the reproduction cost, under prevailing conditions, of goods in process and finished goods.

In making the necessary comparisons to see whether market is lower than cost, the accountant may refer to some of the following sources for information regarding market prices.

(1) Current catalogues or other price lists.
(2) Recent invoices.
(3) Market price quotations as published in newspapers or trade journals.
(4) Specific quotations furnished by suppliers for this purpose.
(5) Current contracts for the purchase of like goods.
(6) Manufacturing cost data for a short period close to the inventory date.

Prices may vary depending on the quantity purchased. In the use of market prices for purposes of comparison with cost, if prices vary for different quantities, the accountant should use, for inventory purposes, the price for the quantity typically purchased by the business.

The lower-of-cost-or-market basis of inventory valuation was adopted as one of the earliest applications of an old rule of accounting conservatism often stated as follows: Anticipate no profit and provide for all possible losses. In the days when primary emphasis was placed on balance sheet conservatism, the cost-or-market rule required that inventories be priced at market whenever market was less than cost, regardless of whether the downward trend in replacement costs had been accompanied, or would probably be followed, by a decrease in selling prices. It was merely presumed that, when market purchase prices decreased, a loss of realizable value in the inventory was inevitable; this presumptive loss was "provided for" by reducing the inventory valuation to the market replacement price.

With the increasing emphasis on the income statement and the proper matching of income and related costs, accountants came to realize that decreases in replacement costs are not always and inevitably accompanied by decreases in selling prices, and that, when decreases in selling prices do occur, they may be proportionately less or greater than the decreases in replacement costs. Therefore, the old cost-or-market rule was somewhat modified. The general principles now governing the application of the cost-or-market rule may be stated as follows:

Inventories may be priced at cost, even though replacement cost is lower, if it appears probable that the inventory can be disposed of at a normal profit—that is, if there has been no decline, and there is no prospect of a decline, in selling prices.

If a decline in selling prices, actual or prospective, will probably reduce, but not entirely eliminate, the margin between the cost and the selling price of the inventory, the inventory may be priced at an amount, less than cost but greater than market, which will permit the realization of a normal gross profit on its disposal. For instance, assume that goods were purchased for $100 and were marked to sell for $150; that the market replacement price dropped to $80; and that it is expected that the goods in the inventory can be sold for $145. The inventory can properly be priced at $95 per unit, because its disposal for $145 per unit would yield the normal gross profit of $50.

The inventory valuation should not exceed the prospective selling price less reasonably predictable costs of completion and disposal. For instance, assume that goods were purchased for $100; that the replacement cost is $93; that selling prices have fallen to such an extent that it is doubtful whether the goods can be sold for more than $95; and that the costs of disposal are estimated at $5. The inventory valuation should be not more than $90.

Application of cost or market. There are three ways of applying the cost-or-market method:

(1) By comparing the cost and market for each item in the inventory, and using the lower figure in each instance, as shown below.

Determination of Lower of Cost or Market
Item-by-Item Method

	Quantity	Unit Price Cost	Unit Price Market	Extension at Lower of Cost or Market
Men's department:				
Suits....................................	200	$40	$37	$ 7,400
Coats....................................	100	31	35	3,100
Ladies' department:				
Dresses................................	300	10	12	3,000
Coats....................................	80	30	32	2,400
Inventory at lower of cost or market............................				$15,900

(2) By comparing the total cost and market for major inventory categories, and using the lower figure.

Determination of Lower of Cost or Market
Category Method

	Quantity	Unit Price Cost	Unit Price Market	Extended Cost	Extended Market	Lower of Cost or Market
Men's department:						
Suits......................	200	$40	$37	$ 8,000	$ 7,400	
Coats.....................	100	31	35	3,100	3,500	
Total..................				$11,100	$10,900	$10,900
Ladies' department:						
Dresses...................	300	10	12	$ 3,000	$ 3,600	
Coats.....................	80	30	32	2,400	2,560	
Total				$ 5,400	$ 6,160	5,400
Inventory at lower of cost or market............................						$16,300

(3) By comparing the total cost and market for the entire inventory, and using the lower figure, as shown on the following page.

Determination of Lower of Cost or Market
Total Inventory Method

	Quantity	Unit Price Cost	Unit Price Market	Extended Cost	Extended Market	Lower of Cost or Market
Men's department:						
Suits.....................	200	$40	$37	$ 8,000	$ 7,400	
Coats.....................	100	31	35	3,100	3,500	
Ladies' department:						
Dresses...................	300	10	12	3,000	3,600	
Coats.....................	80	30	32	2,400	2,560	
Total..................				$16,500	$17,060	
Inventory at lower of cost or market.................................						$16,500

For many years it was considered imperative to use the item-by-item method; the category and total inventory methods are now regarded as acceptable alternatives.

Effect of cost-or-market rule on gross profits. Although the cost-or-market rule is a conservative one and is generally accepted, the application of the rule distorts the gross profit of a period in which the market prices decline.

To illustrate, assume that a company buys goods at a cost of $10,000 and sells one-half of them for $7,500. The gross profit on the goods sold may be determined as follows:

```
Sales.......................................... $7,500.00
Less cost of goods sold (½ of $10,000)............  5,000.00
Gross profit on sales.........................  $2,500.00
```

But assume that the inventory valuation of the remaining half at the lower of cost or market is only $4,000. The profit and loss statement would usually be prepared thus:

```
Sales............................................... $7,500.00
Less cost of goods sold:
    Purchases............................. $10,000.00
    Less inventory at end of period...........  4,000.00  6,000.00
Gross profit on sales...................................  $1,500.00
```

A more comprehensive statement of facts would be:

```
Sales............................................... $7,500.00
Less cost of goods sold:
    Purchases............................. $10,000.00
    Less inventory—at cost..................  5,000.00  5,000.00
Gross profit on sales....................................  $2,500.00
Less decline in replacement cost of inventory..............  1,000.00
Gross profit less inventory adjustment.....................  $1,500.00
```

But, to prepare a statement in the latter form illustrated, it would be necessary to price the inventory at both cost ($5,000) and the lower of cost or market ($4,000) in order to determine the reduction. Computing the inventory on two bases would involve so much work that the procedure is usually regarded as impracticable.

Obsolete and damaged merchandise. Regardless of the inventory-pricing basis adopted, merchandise which has become obsolete or damaged should be excluded entirely from the inventory if it is unsalable. If it can be sold at a reduced price, a conservative estimate of realizable value may be assigned to it. Thus, the loss on goods remaining unsold which have been damaged or have become obsolete is taken in the period when the loss developed, not in the period in which the goods are sold.

Valuation basis should be disclosed. Either in the balance sheet itself or in comments or footnotes accompanying the balance sheet, the basis of the inventory valuation should be stated.

Gross profit method of estimating inventories. It is sometimes desired to estimate an inventory. Perhaps it is desired to prepare financial statements without taking a physical inventory, or to estimate the value of an inventory which has been destroyed by fire. The gross profit method is frequently used for this purpose.

To illustrate this method, assume that the goods on hand June 30, 1954 were destroyed by fire; no physical inventory had been taken since December 31, 1953. The books showed the following balances at the date of the fire:

Sales		$90,000.00
Returned sales and allowances	$ 700.00	
Inventory, December 31, 1953	20,000.00	
Purchases	65,000.00	
Returned purchases and allowances		1,000.00
Freight in	800.00	

Assume, further, that the company's records show that in prior years it made a gross profit of approximately 25% of net sales. Therefore, if it may be assumed that the same rate of gross profit was realized during the six months preceding the fire, the inventory at the date of the fire can be estimated as follows:

Inventory, December 31, 1953			$20,000.00
Add net purchases:			
Purchases	$65,000.00		
Freight in	800.00		
Total	$65,800.00		
Less returned purchases and allowances	1,000.00	64,800.00	
Total goods available for sale			$84,800.00
Less estimated cost of goods sold:			
Gross sales	$90,000.00		
Less returned sales and allowances	700.00		
Net sales	$89,300.00		
Less estimated gross profit—25% of $89,300.00	22,325.00	66,975.00	
Estimated inventory, June 30, 1954			$17,825.00

CHAPTER 26

Theory and Principles of Accounting

Purpose of chapter. Some of the principles which govern accounting have been stated and discussed in the preceding chapters in connection with the valuation of assets and the determination of income and expenses. Other principles, although not formally stated and discussed, have been implicitly recognized in the discussions of correct procedures. It is the purpose of this chapter to present a brief, but comprehensive, statement of generally accepted fundamental principles.

Accounting principles. What are these basic accounting principles? Although reference is frequently made to "generally accepted accounting principles," no authoritative compilation or code of principles exists.

A principle is a fundamental truth, a fundamental law, or a fundamental assumption which forms the basis of reasoning or conduct. But principles cannot be established in accounting, as they are in the realm of natural sciences, by experimentation. Nor have they been determined, as in the law, by authoritative pronouncement, although progress in that direction is being made. The American Institute of Accountants has issued bulletins dealing with matters which may be regarded as principles, but the opinions expressed in these bulletins are not law, nor have all of them been generally accepted by the profession. The American Accounting Association also has done commendable work in formulating statements of accounting standards, but the pronouncements of the Association, as well as those of the Institute, have not been unanimously accepted. The Securities and Exchange Commission has issued rules which touch the realm of accounting principles; these rules are binding only on those persons who are subject to the authority of the Commission, but they may be expected to exercise a pronounced influence on the practice of accounting generally.

Shift in emphasis. For many decades accountants regarded the balance sheet as of primary importance and the income statement as of secondary importance—a reflection of the attitude of bankers and other grantors of short-term credit. Grantors of credit were concerned with the margin of security for their loans; they were primarily interested in two questions: What assets does the applicant for credit own? What liabilities does he already owe?   The answers to these questions were found in the balance sheet.

With the increase in the number of investors in corporate securities, a shift in emphasis, from the balance sheet to the income statement, has taken place.   Investors and speculators are disposed to measure the desirability of securities in terms of the earnings of the issuing company.   As net income goes up, security values tend to increase; as net income goes down, security values tend to decrease.

When the balance sheet was regarded as of primary importance, *balance sheet conservatism* was the accounting principle which outranked all others.   As the governing principle, it was responsible, for instance, for the old (and now somewhat modified) cost-or-market rule which required writing down the inventory if replacement costs decreased, even though there was no prospect of a corresponding decrease in selling prices with a consequent loss of income.

With the increasing emphasis on the income statement, accountants are becoming increasingly interested in developing clear and precise concepts of net income, and in developing criteria for its determination.   Conservatism is one of these criteria, but accountants are now becoming increasingly concerned with the problems incident to a "sharp" determination of net income— with the proper "matching" of income and related costs applicable to a period.

Periodic statements.   The problems related to the matching of income and costs arise because of the custom of preparing periodic statements.   Most businesses are engaged in a continuing "stream" of activity.   Not until a business has ceased to function as a going concern and has disposed of its assets is it possible to compute with absolute accuracy the net income earned or the loss sustained.   But it obviously would be undesirable to make no computations of net income until the business completes its life span.   Unless interim computations of the results of operations are made, no adequate basis exists for reporting on the success of a business.

The matching of income and related costs means matching *for a period*.   Proper matching involves the following:

Determining what income has been earned during the period.
Determining what costs are properly chargeable against the income.

Matters affecting the determination of periodic income and related costs are considered in the remainder of this chapter.

Income

The nature of income. Income is an inflow of assets, but it must be recognized that there are inflows of assets which are not income. Obviously, an inflow of capital funds from stockholders is not income to a corporation, nor should a business regard as income an inflow of assets which is offset by an increase in liabilities. Income consists of an inflow of assets in the form of cash, receivables, or other property from customers and clients, and is related to the disposal of goods and the rendering of services. If income is earned by selling goods, it may also be called *profit;* the term *profit* is not properly applied to income derived from the rendering of services.

When is income earned? A basic criterion for the determination of the period in which income may be regarded as earned may be stated as follows: *Income should not be regarded as earned until an asset increment has been realized, or until its realization is reasonably assured.* There are also auxiliary criteria. The criteria which determine the period to which income from production and sales activities should be allocated differ somewhat from the criteria which govern the period-allocation of income from services. The two classes of income are therefore considered separately.

Income from production and sales activities. The earning of income from wholesale and retail operations involves a series of activities: the purchase of merchandise, the sale of merchandise, and sometimes the subsequent rendering of service or the fulfillment of guarantees. If a business is engaged in manufacturing, the series of activities includes the purchase of raw materials and the fabrication of the product. All of these activities are directed to the earning of income. At what point in the series should income be regarded as earned?

The point of sale. The sale is the step in the series of activities at which income is *generally* regarded as earned. The earning of income does not necessarily require a collection in cash, since a valid receivable from a solvent debtor is an asset in as good standing as cash.

The point of sale is generally regarded as the point when income is earned because (1) it is the point at which a conversion takes place—an exchange of one asset for another—and conversion is regarded as evidence of realization; and (2) it is the point at which the *amount* of the income is, in the normal case, objectively determinable from a sale price.

After the point of sale. The taking up of income at the point of sale, and before the collection of the resulting receivable, is justified only if there is a presumption that the receivable will be collected promptly and without material collection costs and losses. This presumption is subject to question in the case of installment sales in which there are high percentages of collection costs, repossessions, and collection losses. The *installment sales* accounting procedure defers the taking of income until collections are received. To illustrate the procedure, assume that goods which cost $100 are sold for $150, to be collected in 10 equal installments. If the installment sales procedure is adopted, the entire $50 difference between cost and selling price is credited to a deferred profit account; since one-third of the selling price is prospective profit, each $15 installment collection is regarded as including a $5 realization of profit; therefore, when each installment is collected, $5 is regarded as realized income to be transferred from the deferred profit account to an earned profit account.

Before the point of sale. Income is sometimes regarded as earned before a sale is completed. For instance, if goods are manufactured under a cost-plus contract and the amounts of income applicable to completed portions of the contract are determinable, realization of income may be reasonably assured even though delivery and transfer of title have not been made. But the taking up of profits on fixed-price contracts in process is of doubtful propriety, because completion costs usually cannot be estimated with accuracy; therefore, there is no certainty regarding an ultimate profit.

When the completion of a contract extends over two or more accounting periods, there may be a question as to whether the income statements fairly reflect the results of operations during these periods if the entire income is reported in the period of completion, particularly if the major portion of the work was done prior to the period of completion. Moreover, if the proprietorship personnel changes while the contract is in process, questions of equity to the changing partners or stockholders arise, and the accountant may feel that consideration should be given to these questions of equity as well as to accounting principles. But if a portion of the fixed price on contracts in process is taken into income, it should be evident that the reported income may be based to a greater degree on estimates and opinion than the accountant would prefer.

Income from services. When should income from services be regarded as earned? The theoretically correct answer seems to be: in the period in which the services are rendered. The accounting for service income on this basis frequently requires end-of-period adjustments for the unearned portion of charges billed in advance, or adjustments for accruals of unbilled charges.

Practical considerations may lead to the adoption of a policy of postponing the taking of any income from services until the services are completed. The rendering of services may extend over several periods and the amount to be charged for the entire service may not be determinable until completion; in such cases, the income applicable to services rendered during periods prior to completion cannot be known.

Unrealized appreciation. The accounting principle that income should not be regarded as earned until an asset increment has been realized, or until its realization is reasonably assured, is violated if unrealized appreciation is regarded as income.

Let us assume that a company purchases marketable securities for $50,000 and that, at the end of the accounting period, these securities have a market value of $60,000. Has $10,000 of income been realized? No. The securities have not been sold, and the market price may decline before they are sold; therefore, no asset increment has been realized and there is no reasonable assurance that an increment will be realized.

Income and savings. A saving, but not income, results from manufacturing a thing at a cost less than the price at which it could have been purchased. To regard such savings as income is a violation of the accounting principle relative to the realization of asset increments.

Companies which construct fixed assets for their own use at a cost less than the market purchase price sometimes desire to record the fixed assets at a theoretical purchase price and take up a "profit." The manufacture of fixed assets may increase the future profits by reducing future depreciation charges, but a present saving with a prospect of increased future profits should not be confused with realized income.

Ultimate profits on sales of merchandise may be increased by manufacturing the goods instead of purchasing them; but no profit should be regarded as realized until the goods are sold.

Costs

Terminology. The word *cost* is related to expenditure. An expenditure is a payment, in cash or otherwise, or the incurring of an obligation to make a future payment, for a benefit received. *Cost* is the measure of the expenditure. But when used without modifying words, *cost* does not always have a definite meaning. For precision of expression, we shall use several terms.

The expression *cost outlay* will be used with reference to expenditures and acquisitions, regardless of whether the benefit received is chargeable to an asset or an expense account.

The term *cost transformation* refers to such changes as the conversion of material, labor, and overhead costs into finished goods costs.

Expired costs are those which no longer have any asset status. Expired costs are of two classes: *utilized costs* and *lost costs*. *Utilized costs* include the cost of merchandise sold and the costs of services, utilities, and other benefits used for the purpose of producing income. *Lost costs* are costs which have expired without utilization or without contributing to the production of income.

A *cost residue* is the unexpired portion of a cost outlay; it may properly appear on the asset side of the balance sheet of a going concern.

The cost principle.   Cost is the generally accepted basis for accounting for assets and expenses.   Charges to asset and expense accounts should generally be made on the basis of cost—or, in other words, on the basis of actual expenditures.

It is a violation of the cost principle to value assets in the accounts at more than cost, because this would involve an anticipation of profits.   Actual costs should not be surcharged with theoretical additions by such practices as including interest on the investment in plant assets in the cost of goods manufactured, recording constructed fixed assets in the property accounts at a theoretical purchase price in excess of construction cost, valuing goods in process at various stages of completion at theoretical purchase prices, or charging operations with a theoretical rent on owned real estate in excess of the actual expenses incurred.

It is also a violation of the cost principle to value assets at less than cost *merely for purposes of conservatism*, because the profits and the net worth would thereby be understated.   It is, of course, necessary to give recognition to expired costs and lost costs in determining asset valuations.

The cost principle requires that assets, in general, shall be stated in the accounts at cost, or at cost minus the portions of cost which have been properly charged to operations by depreciation provisions or otherwise.   The cost principle also requires that the charges to operations for depreciation and other asset expirations shall be on the basis of cost.

The cost basis is sometimes criticized by people who believe that reports would be more informative if all assets were stated at market replacement prices at the date of the report.   Market values of plant and other assets may be information of significance, but it does not follow that the cost basis of accounting should be abandoned in favor of an accounting procedure which would require appraisals and revaluations of all assets at each balance sheet date. There are two reasons why such a procedure would not be desirable: First, it would introduce unrealized profits and losses into the accounts. Second, although there are many difficult problems involved in the determination of cost, there is more definite and objective evidence for the determination of costs than for the determination of market values; market or replacement values are often matters of pure opinion, estimate, and conjecture. It would seem that whatever benefits might be obtained by a periodic revision of the accounts to a current price basis could be obtained by stating such values parenthetically in the balance sheet.

Departures from the cost basis. Although cost is the generally accepted basis for accounting for assets and expenses, other bases are sometimes preferable or acceptable.

The gross amount of accounts receivable can scarcely be said to represent their cost, because of the profit element in the selling price of the merchandise for which the receivables were obtained. Moreover, the estimated realizable value of the receivables is the only significant basis for their valuation, and they are, therefore, properly valued at the gross amount less the reserve for losses.

Valuations of other current assets, such as inventories and temporary investments in marketable securities, at market values which are less than cost are generally recognized as acceptable departures from the cost basis. Or perhaps it might be more precise to say that the reduction from cost to market is a recognition of lost costs.

Classification of cost outlays. Expenditures chargeable to asset accounts and those chargeable to expense accounts should be clearly distinguished. An expenditure need not result in the acquisition of a tangible asset to justify charging it to an asset account. In general, it may be said that any expenditure for a service or other intangible which can reasonably be expected to benefit the business during at least one period beyond the period in which the expenditure is made can properly be charged to an asset account, and the asset, or diminishing portions thereof, may properly be regarded as continuing to exist so long as benefits are to be derived from the expenditure.

If it is known at the time of making a cost outlay that the benefit derived will not extend beyond the current accounting period (as when a month's rent is paid at the beginning of the month), it is customary and expedient to charge the cost immediately to an expense account. Although the cost may not have expired at the time of the outlay, the accounting entries are reduced by making an immediate charge to an expense account rather than charging an asset account and subsequently making a transfer from the asset account to an expense account.

If a cost outlay will presumably benefit more than one period, but only a few periods (as in the case of insurance costs), either of the following accounting procedures is acceptable. The outlay may be charged to an asset account (such as Unexpired Insurance); if this is done, the expired portions of cost are transferred periodically to an expense account (such as Insurance Expense). Or the cost outlay may be charged to an expense account; if this is done, cost residues are transferred periodically to an asset account.

If a cost outlay results in the acquisition of an asset which presumably will benefit a considerable number of periods (as in the case of the acquisition of a fixed asset), the cost should be charged to an asset account and the periodic cost expirations should be charged to expense.

Some of the most difficult problems of classification of cost outlays at the time when the outlays are made arise in connection with fixed assets. Some of these problems of differentiating between capital and revenue expenditures were discussed in the chapter dealing with fixed assets.

Determination of asset costs. The cost of an asset includes not only the basic, or purchase, price but also incidental costs such as the following: costs of title searches and legal fees incurred in the acquisition of real estate; transportation, installation, and breaking-in costs incident to the acquisition of machinery; storage, insurance, taxes, and other costs incurred in aging certain kinds of inventories, such as wine; and expenditures made in the rehabilitation of a plant purchased in a rundown condition.

Cash discount and interest. Although cash discounts on purchases are often shown in profit and loss statements as income, this procedure is coming to be recognized as a violation of the cost principle. Terms of 2/10; n/30 on an invoice dated, for instance, March 1, mean that 2% discount can be taken if payment is made on or before March 11, and that the gross amount of the invoice is payable on March 31. The purchaser gets the 2% discount for paying the invoice 20 days before it is due for payment. Two per cent for 20 days is equivalent to an interest rate of 36% a year. Such a rate is so high that purchase discounts cannot reasonably be regarded as income for the use of money; moreover, a profit cannot be made on a purchase. When cash discounts on merchandise purchases are treated in the operating statement as income rather than as a factor in the determination of the merchandise cost, the procedure is a violation of the cost principle; it is sanctioned partly because of custom and partly because of the difficulty of applying discounts as a reduction of purchase costs for purposes of inventory valuations. (The discount would have to be applied to each item in each invoice, to obtain the net price; and net prices, if accurately stated, would run into fractions of cents—for instance, the net price of an article purchased for $4.35, subject to a 1% cash discount, would be $4.3065.) But no such practical objection can be raised against applying cash discounts as a reduction in the cost of a fixed asset, and fixed assets should therefore be charged to the accounts at their net cost.

If time intervenes between the date of purchase and the date of payment and an interest charge is incurred, the interest should be recorded as an expense and not as an addition to the asset cost.

Assets acquired with securities. If assets are acquired by issuance of stocks or bonds, the price at which the securities could have been issued for cash is the true cost of the assets. For instance, if land was acquired by issuance of $50,000 par value of bonds which could have been sold for $55,000 cash, the entry to record the transaction should be:

```
Land...................................  55,000.00
    Bonds payable.......  ...................        50,000.00
    Premium on bonds........ ...............         5,000.00
```

If the cash value of the securities at the date of issuance cannot be determined, the price at which the asset could have been acquired for cash is an acceptable measure of cost.

Assets acquired for noncash assets. The determination of the cost of an asset acquired in a transaction in which some other non-cash asset is part or all of the consideration may present difficulties. For instance, assume that a machine is purchased at a price of $1,500; that $1,000 is paid in cash; and that the seller accepts, as the remainder of the price, an old machine which is carried at a depreciated cost of $400 and which could have been sold for $250. Did the new machine cost $1,500 (the nominal cost), or $1,400 (the sum of the cash and the undepreciated cost of the old machine), or $1,250 (the sum of the cash and the cash value of the old machine)? From a theoretical standpoint, $1,250 appears most truly to represent cost because it is the sum of cash and cash equivalent. A $1,500 cost, although commonly regarded as acceptable, is theoretically questionable because it involves the taking of a profit of $100; this "profit," although nominally arising from the disposal of the old asset, is so related to the purchase transaction that its realization is debatable. A $1,400 cost has some theoretical justification, since it is, in a sense, cost on a going-concern basis; that is, it is a valuation which includes an unexpired old plant cost plus an additional cost.

Cost apportionments.   If several kinds of assets are acquired by a cash payment at a lump price, the aggregate cost must be apportioned to the various assets.   This immediately introduces an element of opinion, and the effects upon current and subsequent income statements and balance sheets should be recognized. Thus, if land, buildings, and merchandise are acquired at a lump price, the apportionment of the cost affects the computation of merchandising profit during a relatively short period, the building depreciation charges during a relatively long period, and any gains or losses which may result from a disposal of the fixed assets.

Cost transformations and expirations.   Cost transformations and cost expirations must be differentiated.   During a period of operations, some costs will be transformed and others will expire; those which are transformed will remain as assets, although their nature will have changed; those which have expired should be charged against income or earned surplus.

Costs are transformed by the process of production.   Manufacturing costs are incurred initially for materials, labor, and overhead; by the transformations of the manufacturing process, these costs become merged into goods in process and finished goods.

Costs expire as a result of utilization; for instance, the cost of postage stamps expires when the stamps are used.   Although utilization is a cause of cost expiration, it should be clearly understood that utilization does not always result in an expiration of cost.   For instance, the cost of gasoline used in an engine which furnishes power for a factory becomes transformed into the cost of the finished goods; the cost of gasoline consumed in the motor of a truck used to deliver sold goods is an expired cost.   Similarly, the rent of a factory building for a month becomes a transformed cost; the rent of a salesroom becomes an expired cost.

Costs are regarded as lost if they disappear without utilization; for instance, the cost of stolen merchandise is a lost cost.

Cost favors and exemptions.   In the allocation of transformed costs, no special favors or cost exemptions should be granted.   One application of this principle was mentioned in Chapter 24 in the discussion of the propriety of including a charge for manufacturing expenses in the cost of fixed assets constructed.   Unless constructed fixed assets are charged with a proper portion of manufacturing expenses, a special favor or cost exemption is granted to the fixed assets.

Because of the labor and difficulties involved in the determination of their material, labor, and overhead costs, by-products are sometimes charged with only material costs, and sometimes with no costs at all.   This may be a case where departure from an accounting principle must be permitted because of the difficulty of obtaining the information which would be required to comply with the principle.

Because a certain company's operations were seasonal, its plant was comparatively idle for several months during the year. To keep its plant busy during this period, the company accepted an order for a special product at a price which included the costs of material and direct labor (but no overhead) and a "profit." The management requested its accountant to charge all the manufacturing expense for the year to the regular products and none to the special product, defending this procedure on the ground that no additional overhead was incurred because of the manufacture of the special product. Although the net income of the business as a whole presumably was increased by the manufacture and sale of the special product, a cost exemption was granted to the special product at the expense of the regular product. As a consequence, the profit on the regular product was understated and a profit on the special product was shown although a loss probably was incurred. That the total profits of a business can be increased by selling goods at a loss may at first seem anomalous; but it is obvious that over-all profits may be increased by the manufacture and sale (if without interference with the other activities of a business) of a product at a price sufficient to cover material and labor and a portion of overhead which otherwise would have to be charged to other products. Management may, therefore, regard such sales as good business policy, but they should not expect accountants to misstate the costs of, and profits on, the various products.

Cost expirations and residues. All costs expired during a period should be charged against the income for the period (or perhaps, in special instances, against earned surplus).

The balance sheet and income statement will not present fairly the financial position of a business and the results of operations unless a proper differentiation is made between costs which have expired and those which remain as assets.

In determining the amounts of cost expirations and cost residues, accountants attack the problem from two directions:

(a) By making decisions as to asset expirations and accepting the remainder as asset residues.
This is the procedure normally applied to fixed asset and expense prepayment costs. Provisions for depreciation, depletion, and amortization, and expense prepayment write-offs are intended to apportion costs over the periods benefited; the resulting asset net valuations are consid-

ered acceptable for balance sheet purposes because they represent unexpired cost, or value in use, there being no need for the asset residue shown by the balance sheet to represent a realizable value.

(b) By making decisions as to asset residues and accepting the remainders as asset expirations.

This is the theoretically correct procedure to be applied to most current assets, because, with respect to such assets, emphasis should be placed upon realization rather than use. For this reason, accountants apportion total merchandise costs between residues and expirations by placing a valuation on the inventory and regarding the excess of the total merchandise cost over the inventory valuation as the amount of the asset expiration.

The determination of the amounts of expired costs and cost residues should be made with the purpose of absorbing costs over the periods benefited (in the case of fixed assets and expense prepayments) or of valuing assets on a realization basis (in the case of some current assets). The amounts recorded as expirations should not be determined with the object of arbitrarily and unwarrantably affecting net income, or on the basis of the amount of "net income" available for reserve provisions. Depreciation should be recognized as a cost expiration for which provision must be made regardless of whether operations for the period are profitable or unprofitable. Costs of tangible assets, intangible assets, and expense prepayments which will be of no benefit to future periods should be written off, or written down to realizable values, and should not be carried along in the accounts for subsequent write-offs; the expired or lost costs should be immediately recognized.

General Considerations

Matching income and related costs. In the computation of net income *for a period*, it is important that:

If income is deferred because it is not regarded as earned, the related costs should also be deferred.

If future costs may be incurred which are applicable to the earnings taken into income, provisions for such future costs should be made by charges against income.

As a simple illustration of the first point, assume that commissions are paid to salesmen for sales for future delivery. If the commissions were charged against income in the period when paid, instead of being deferred until the period in which the sales are taken into income, there would not be a proper matching of income and related costs by periods.

With regard to the second point, companies sometimes sell their products with agreements to provide service for a period of time without cost to the purchaser; goods are sold with guarantees; a lessee may agree to return the leased property to the lessor at the end of the lease period in the condition in which it existed at the beginning of the lease; premium coupons redeemable in merchandise are issued. As a result of these and similar transactions and contracts, income may be received in one period and costs applicable thereto may be incurred in subsequent periods. Provisions for such future costs should be made by setting up reserves by charges to operations in the period in which the related income is taken up.

Basis of accounts. Accounts and statements should give expression, so far as possible, to facts evidenced by completed transactions and supportable by objective data.

For purposes of discussion, the statement of this principle may be divided into three elements:

(1) "by completed transactions"

For instance, as already pointed out, merchandising profits are not normally regarded as earned until the realization of income is evidenced by the completed transaction of a sale.

(2) "supportable by objective data"

For instance, the selling price in a bargained transaction is objective data supporting the computation of the profit.

(3) "so far as possible"

Many accounting entries, such as those providing for depreciation, bad debts, and contingencies, cannot be evidenced by completed transactions nor wholly supported by objective data, but must necessarily be based on estimates.

Fact, opinion, and policy. Audit reports rendered by certified public accountants formerly contained a "certificate," which was worded somewhat as follows:

"We hereby certify that, in our opinion, the accompanying balance sheet and related statements of profit and loss and surplus correctly reflect the financial condition of The *A B* Company on December 31, 19—, and the results of its operations for the year ended that date . . . ."

Audit reports now customarily contain an "opinion" expressed in language similar to that on the following page.

"In our opinion, the accompanying balance sheet and related statements of profit and loss and earned surplus present fairly the financial position of The *A B* Company on December 31, 19—, and the results of its operations for the year ended that date . . . "

The change in language from "correctly reflect" to "present fairly" is a recognition that periodic balance sheets and operating statements can rarely be statements of absolute fact, and therefore cannot be regarded as "correct" in any absolute sense.

Some of the amounts shown in the periodic statements (such as cash, sales, rent, and salaries) may be matters of fact. Other amounts, such as the provision for bad debts, are matters of opinion. Other amounts are affected by accounting policies; for instance, while the determination of the *quantity* of merchandise sold is a matter of ascertaining facts, the *cost* to be assigned to it, if identical goods were acquired at different costs, is affected by the choice between such methods as first-in, first-out and last-in, first-out, which is a matter of policy.

Conservatism. Attention was called, earlier in the chapter, to the fact that balance sheet conservatism was once the accounting principle that outranked all others. Accountants still believe that conservatism is a virtue and that, when matters of opinion or estimate are involved, it is commendable, in instances of doubt, to understate the net income and the net worth rather than to overstate them.

Conservatism may even be regarded as justifying a departure from procedures which could be defended from the standpoint of good accounting theory. For instance, in the preceding discussion of principles applicable to the recording of costs, it was pointed out that any expenditure for a service which can reasonably be expected to benefit the business during more than one period can properly be charged to an asset account, and the asset, or diminishing portions thereof, may properly be regarded as continuing to exist so long as benefits are to be derived from the expenditure. This is sound accounting theory. But suppose that large expenditures are made for an advertising campaign, the benefits of which may be expected to extend beyond the period in which the expenditures are made. It might be theoretically correct to carry forward part of the cost as a prepaid expense; but, because of the practical difficulty of determining the portion of the cost which could properly be deferred, most accountants probably would feel that they would be justified, on the ground of conservatism, in deferring no portion of the cost.

Although conservatism is still regarded as commendable, there is a growing tendency to question the time-honored beliefs that

408 THEORY AND PRINCIPLES OF ACCOUNTING [Ch. 26

balance sheet conservatism outweighs all other considerations, that a conservative balance sheet is a good balance sheet for all purposes, and that balance sheet conservatism automatically produces a proper statement of operations. Accountants are becoming increasingly aware that adherence to the doctrine of balance sheet conservatism may result in income statements which are:

(a) Incorrect.

It may be conservative from the balance sheet standpoint to charge operations with fixed asset expenditures which would more properly be capitalized, or to provide excessive reserves for depreciation and bad debts, but the net income is misstated.

(b) And sometimes unconservative.

For instance, some accountants have advocated writing off bond discount, by charge to Earned Surplus, during the period in which the bonds were issued, in order to clear the balance sheet of a deferred charge which has no realizable value. But the effect is to relieve the income statements of all periods throughout the life of the bonds of charges for an element of interest cost; as a result, the net income is overstated and the income statements are unconservative.

Conservatism can scarcely be regarded as a virtue if, as its consequence, the balance sheet and income statement do not "present fairly" the financial position and the results of operations.

Consistency. Increasing emphasis has been placed in recent years on the importance of consistency. There are many areas of accounting in which different procedures may be acceptable; for instance, inventory costs may be determined on a first-in, first-out basis or on a last-in, first-out basis. But a change from one basis to another will affect the net income for the period in which the change is made. In fact, changes in accounting bases may so materially affect the stated net income that a comparison of the operating statements of a company for two periods may be misleading unless the effect of the changes is known.

A proper regard for consistency need not preclude a desirable change in procedure; but if a change has a material effect on the statements, the nature of the change should be disclosed and the dollar effect thereof on the statements should be indicated, if determinable.

Disclosure. Statements should make full disclosure of significant information. It is the accountant's obligation to disclose all facts which, if not reported, might make the statements misleading.

The latitude of a profession.   As stated at the beginning of this chapter, there is no comprehensive code of accounting principles extending to the ramifications of procedural details. And it probably is not desirable that accounting procedures should be reduced to a rigid uniformity by any detailed statement of rules. Accounting must meet the varying requirements of different businesses operating under differing conditions, making proper choices between different procedures which are equally right for their various purposes, and must be unfettered and prepared to adjust itself to changes in the economic system. It seems desirable, therefore, that members of the accounting profession, like those of other professions, should exercise individual judgment and initiative within the framework of general principles.

The "Current Operating" and "Clean Surplus" Concepts of Net Income

For many years it was standard accounting procedure to show in the income statement only the results of *regular operations* for the *current period,* and to show in the surplus statement any corrections of the net income or loss of prior periods and any unusual, extraordinary, or nonrecurring gains and losses, such as those resulting from sales of investments and fixed assets. Statements prepared in this manner are said to be in accordance with the *current operating concept* of net income; they are illustrated below:

THE JONES CORPORATION
Statement of Income and Expense
For the Year Ended December 31, 1953

Net sales...	$1,204,960.00
Deduct cost of goods sold...........................	826,940.00
Gross profit on sales................................	$ 378,020.00
Deduct expenses.....................................	261,290.00
Net income..	$ 116,730.00

THE JONES CORPORATION
Statement of Earned Surplus
For the Year Ended December 31, 1953

Earned surplus, December 31, 1952..................		$ 326,215.00
Add:		
Net income for the year............................		116,730.00
Correction of net income for 1952—Undervaluation of inventory on December 31, 1952...............		19,600.00
Total..		$ 462,545.00
Deduct:		
Loss on sale of abandoned plant.........	$15,325.00	
Dividends.........................	90,000.00	105,325.00
Earned surplus, December 31, 1953..................		$ 357,220.00

At the present time many accountants advocate the *clean surplus concept;* that is, they believe that corrections of the net income or loss of prior periods and extraneous gains and losses should be shown in the income statement.   Statements prepared in accordance with the clean surplus concept of net income are shown below:

THE JONES CORPORATION
Statement of Income and Expense
For the Year Ended December 31, 1953

Net sales...		$1,204,960.00
Deduct cost of goods sold..........................		826,940.00
Gross profit on sales..............................		$ 378,020.00
Deduct expenses....................................		261,290.00
Net operating income..............................		$ 116,730.00
Add—deduct*:		
Correction of net income for 1952—		
Undervaluation of inventory on December 31, 1952...................	$19,600.00	
Loss on sale of abandoned plant.......	15,325.00*	4,275.00
Net income..		$ 121,005.00

THE JONES CORPORATION
Statement of Earned Surplus
For the Year Ended December 31, 1953

Earned surplus, December 31, 1952....................	$ 326,215.00
Add net income for the year.........................	121,005.00
Total..	$ 447,220.00
Deduct dividends...................................	90,000.00
Earned surplus, December 31, 1953...................	$ 357,220.00

Some of the arguments presented by the two schools of thought are briefly stated below.

Current operating concept.   The proponents of the current operating concept of net income support their position by the following arguments:

Investors are more interested in the net income of a business than in any other one figure shown by the annual statements. And the net income in which they are interested is that which resulted from normal operating transactions.   If extraneous gains and losses and corrections of the reported net income of prior periods are included, it is difficult to determine the trend of a company's operations.

If the stated net income of one year is affected by a material correction of the net income of a prior year, the error is compounded—the current year's net income is overstated or understated to the extent that the net income of the past was understated or overstated.   Indicated trends are therefore misleading.

Because of the danger that some readers of accounting reports are likely to assume that the income statement tells all that is to be told about profits and losses and are not aware of the significance of matters disclosed in the surplus statement, a combined statement of income and surplus is sometimes advocated. Such a statement, prepared in accordance with the current operating concept, is shown below:

THE JONES CORPORATION
Statement of Income and Earned Surplus
For the Year Ended December 31, 1953

Net sales...		$1,204,960.00
Deduct cost of goods sold...........................		826,940.00
Gross profit on sales................................		$ 378,020.00
Deduct expenses.....................................		261,290.00
Net income..		$ 116,730.00
Add:		
Earned surplus, December 31, 1952.................		326,215.00
Correction of net income for 1952—Under-		
valuation of inventory on December 31, 1952.......		19,600.00
Total...		$ 462,545.00
Deduct:		
Loss on sale of abandoned plant..........	$15,325.00	
Dividends.............................	90,000.00	105,325.00
Earned surplus, December 31, 1953..................		$ 357,220.00

Clean surplus concept. The proponents of the clean surplus concept present the following arguments:

The total of the amounts shown as net income in the statements for a series of years should be the aggregate net income for those years; this will not be the case if corrections of the reported net income of prior periods are shown in the surplus statement.

When an accountant charges earned surplus with a loss because he considers it extraordinary or extraneous, he implies that it is nonrecurring. But a study of business history indicates that such losses do recur.

The line of demarcation between operating items and extraordinary and extraneous items is not clear-cut, and is often a matter of opinion. Studies of annual reports have shown many inconsistencies in classifications between income and surplus made by different companies, and by the same company in different years. Wide variations in net income can be caused by such inconsistencies.

Many so-called extraordinary or extraneous charges and credits are closely related to operations—not to the operations of a single year, but to those of a series of years.

They may be regarded as corrections of the stated net income of a number of prior years; for instance, a gain or loss on the disposal of a fixed asset may be regarded as a correction of prior years' charges for depreciation.

Or extraordinary charges may relieve future periods of operating charges which otherwise would be required; this is the case when fixed assets are written down or written off, and future years are thereby relieved of depreciation and amortization charges.

Concluding note.   Accountants have not yet arrived at a unanimity of opinion with respect to these conflicting concepts of net income.   Differences exist in practice.   The American Accounting Association, in its official publications, has taken a strong position in favor of the clean surplus concept.   The Committee on Accounting Procedure of the American Institute of Accountants has taken a somewhat modified position; in its Bulletin No. 32, the committee stated:

"It is the opinion of the committee that there should be a general presumption that all items of profit and loss recognized during the period are to be used in determining the figure reported as net income. The only possible exception to this presumption in any case would be with respect to items which in the aggregate are materially significant in relation to the company's net income and are clearly not identifiable with or do not result from the usual or typical business operations of the period . . . "

In view of the fact that practice and authoritative opinion leave this matter still in a somewhat controversial state, it is perhaps undesirable for a textbook to take a firm, definite position on the question.   An accounting student should be familiar with both points of view, and should be adaptable enough to follow either approach, as directed.   Until the issue is more clearly resolved, an instructor is justified in suggesting the adoption of either point of view, if for no other reason than to achieve class uniformity.

CHAPTER 27

The Analysis of Financial Statements

Purpose of the chapter. Financial statements take on additional meaning when subjected to analytical procedures. It is the purpose of this chapter to discuss and illustrate some of the most widely adopted of these procedures and to point out their usefulness as well as the limitations inherent in some of them. Whole volumes have been written on this subject; it is obvious that, within the limitations of a single chapter of an introductory text, the treatment of the subject must be restricted to fundamentals.

Basis of the illustrations. The following statements serve as the basis of the illustrations in the chapter. Since comparison constitutes one of the major features of statement analysis, these statements cover two years.

SPECIALTY PRODUCTS COMPANY   Exhibit A

Balance Sheets

December 31, 1954 and 1953

Assets

	December 31, 1954	1953
Current assets:		
Cash......................................	$ 25,905	$ 25,330
Marketable securities.......................	10,000	8,000
Accounts receivable........................	98,600	80,250
Reserve for bad debts......................	2,500*	2,000*
Inventories:		
Finished goods............................	38,685	33,500
Goods in process..........................	15,800	14,000
Raw materials............................	25,940	22,865
Prepaid expenses..........................	3,600	3,400
Total current assets....................	$216,030	$185,345
Fixed assets:		
Land.....................................	$ 40,000	$ 40,000
Buildings.................................	245,350	198,675
Reserve for depreciation...................	61,000*	57,700*
Machinery and equipment...................	90,500	75,000
Reserve for depreciation...................	15,200*	10,050*
Furniture and fixtures......................	9,450	8,760
Reserve for depreciation...................	2,700*	1,800*
Total fixed assets......................	$306,400	$252,885
	$522,430	$438,230

413

Liabilities and Net Worth

Current liabilities:

Accounts payable...........................	$ 18,225	$ 12,500
Notes payable—Bank........................	40,000	25,000
Accrued taxes, wages, and other expenses......	35,250	24,300
Total current liabilities....................	$ 93,475	$ 61,800

Long-term liabilities:

Bonds payable—secured by real estate........	100,000	100,000
Total liabilities...........................	$193,475	$161,800

Net worth:

Capital stock—$100 par value:

Preferred—6%...........................	$ 50,000	$ 50,000
Common................................	250,000	200,000
Earned surplus—Exhibit B..................	28,955	26,430
Total net worth.........................	$328,955	$276,430
	$522,430	$438,230

SPECIALTY PRODUCTS COMPANY   Exhibit B

Statements of Income, Expense, and Earned Surplus
For the Years Ended December 31, 1954 and 1953

	Year Ended December 31,	
	1954	1953
Gross sales.....................................	$970,675	$786,500
Returned sales and allowances...................	21,045	29,650
Net sales......................................	$949,630	$756,850
Cost of goods sold—Schedule 1..................	685,320	582,700
Gross profit on sales...........................	$264,310	$174,150
Expenses—Schedule 2:		
Selling expenses..............................	$145,980	$ 89,050
Administrative expenses.......................	71,405	47,010
Total....................................	$217,385	$136,060
Net income from operations.....................	$ 46,925	$ 38,090
Income from securities.........................	500	400
Net income before interest and federal income tax....	$ 47,425	$ 38,490
Interest:		
On notes payable............................	$ 900	$ 750
On bonds payable...........................	6,000	6,000
Total....................................	$ 6,900	$ 6,750
Net income before federal income tax.............	$ 40,525	$ 31,740
Federal income tax............................	15,000	11,500
Net income....................................	$ 25,525	$ 20,240
Earned surplus—Beginning of year...............	26,430	25,190
Total...	$ 51,955	$ 45,430
Dividends:		
Preferred.....................................	$ 3,000	$ 3,000
Common......................................	20,000	16,000
Total...	$ 23,000	$ 19,000
Earned surplus—End of year....................	$ 28,955	$ 26,430

SPECIALTY PRODUCTS COMPANY   Exhibit B
Statements of Cost of Goods Sold   Schedule 1
For the Years Ended December 31, 1954 and 1953

	Year Ended December 31,	
	1954	1953
Cost of goods manufactured:		
Raw materials:		
Inventory—Beginning of year	$ 22,865	$ 20,850
Purchases	237,150	215,260
Total	$260,015	$236,110
Inventory—End of year	25,940	22,865
Materials used	$234,075	$213,245
Direct labor	316,500	253,200
Manufacturing expense	141,730	121,455
Cost of manufacturing	$692,305	$587,900
Goods in process—Beginning of year	14,000	12,700
Total	$706,305	$600,600
Goods in process—End of year	15,800	14,000
Cost of goods manufactured	$690,505	$586,600
Finished goods—Beginning of year	33,500	29,600
Total	$724,005	$616,200
Finished goods—End of year	38,685	33,500
Cost of goods sold	$685,320	$582,700

SPECIALTY PRODUCTS COMPANY   Exhibit B
Schedules of Selling and   Schedule 2
Administrative Expenses
For the Years Ended December 31, 1954 and 1953

	Year Ended December 31,	
	1954	1953
Selling expenses:		
Salesmen's salaries and payroll taxes	$ 28,000	$17,355
Salesmen's traveling expenses	27,610	17,690
Advertising	80,450	45,375
Freight out	7,865	6,350
Miscellaneous	2,055	2,280
Total	$145,980	$89,050
Administrative expenses:		
Officers' salaries and payroll taxes	$ 26,760	$13,765
Office salaries and payroll taxes	22,865	20,680
Stationery and supplies	1,250	1,140
Postage, telephone, and telegraph	2,535	1,950
Depreciation of furniture and fixtures	900	900
Bad debts	15,945	7,050
Miscellaneous	1,150	1,525
	$ 71,405	$47,010

Outline of chapter. The analytical procedures discussed and illustrated in the chapter are presented under the following main captions: The results of operations; Working capital: General financial position.

The Results of Operations

Ratio of net income to average net worth. Since capital is invested and business is conducted with the object of earning income, a basic measure of business success is the ratio of net income to the capital committed to the business. Because the amount of capital changes during the year, the ratio should be based on the average capital during the year. If the data were available, it would be desirable to compute the average capital by using the capital at the beginning of the year and the capital at each month-end during the year. Working with the available data, the computation of the ratios for Specialty Products Company is as follows:

Ratio of Net Income to Average Net Worth

		1954	1953
Net income—Exhibit B	(a)	$ 25,525	$ 20,240
Average net worth:			
Net worth—Beginning of year—Exhibit A		$276,430	$275,190
Net worth—End of year—Exhibit A		328,955	276,430
Average	(b)	$302,693	$275,810
Ratio (a ÷ b)		8.43%	7.34%

The ratio shows an improvement (from 7.34% to 8.43%); but, like most ratios, the ratio of net income to net worth would be more meaningful if there were some standard for comparison. How do the ratios for this company compare with the ratios of other companies in the same line of business? Information for the answer to this question is sometimes available in the form of statistics furnished by trade associations, or published in reference books such as *Moody's Manual of Investments* and *Standard & Poor's Corporation Records*.

Number of times preferred dividend earned. The ratio of net income to net worth gives no recognition to different classes of stock. Preferred stockholders, particularly if their shares are non-participating, are primarily interested, so far as earnings are concerned, in the relation of the net income to the preferred dividend requirement, which is computed as follows:

Number of Times Preferred Dividends Earned

		1954	1953
Net income	(a)	$25,525	$20,240
Preferred dividend requirement	(b)	3,000	3,000
Number of times preferred dividend earned (a ÷ b)		8.51	6.75

Earnings per share of common stock. Common stockholders are less interested in the total net income than in the net income applicable to the common stock—that is, in the net income minus the preferred dividend requirements. Assuming that the preferred stock of Specialty Products Company is non-participating, the earnings per share of common stock are computed as follows:

Per-Share Earnings on Common Stock Outstanding at End of Year

	1954	1953
Earnings applicable to common stock:		
Net income.....................................	$25,525	$20,240
Amount required for dividend on 6% non-participating preferred stock........................	3,000	3,000
Earnings applicable to common stock.....:.....(a)	$22,525	$17,240
Number of shares of common stock outstanding at end of year.................................(b)	2,500	2,000
Earnings per share (a ÷ b)........................	$9.01	$8.62

In appraising the significance of the increase in the earnings per share of common stock, it would be helpful to know how long the additional shares were outstanding during 1954.

It is, of course, understood that earnings per share are not always the same as dividends per share; but undistributed earnings increase the book value of the common stock, and thus tend to increase the value of the common stockholders' investments.

Earnings per share are often compared with market values of stock as an indication of the advisability of making or retaining an investment in the shares. Assume, for example, that the common stock of Specialty Products Company is quoted on the market at $150; a common stockholder who is considering the advisability of retaining his holdings, or a person who is considering investing in the common stock, will probably ask himself the question: Is $9.01 a satisfactory return on an investment of $150?

Number of times bond interest earned. Bondholders are interested in the debtor company's earnings as well as in the mortgaged security, because current income is the normal source of funds required for the payment of bond interest. Since the bond interest is a claim against revenue which takes precedence over income taxes, and since the earnings available for bond interest are, of course, the earnings before bond interest, the computation of the number of times the bond interest is earned is made as follows:

Number of Times Bond Interest Earned

	1954	1953
Net income before bond interest:		
Net income before income tax...................	$40,525	$31,740
Bond interest...................................	6,000	6,000
Income available for bond interest...........(a)	$46,525	$37,740
Bond interest................................(b)	$ 6,000	$ 6,000
Number of times bond interest earned (a ÷ b)........	7.75	6.29

Analysis of the profit and loss statement. Percentage computations are often helpful in the analysis of statements of operations. There are two classes of percentage analyses:

Vertical analysis.
Horizontal analysis.

Both classes are illustrated in this chapter.

Vertical analysis. Vertical percentage analysis is so called because the per cents apply to related amounts usually shown in a column. The illustrative statements below and on page 419, with vertical analysis, show the per cents of various items to the net sales. They answer the question: What became of the sales dollar?

SPECIALTY PRODUCTS COMPANY
Comparative Statements of Profit and Loss
With Per Cents of Net Sales
For the Years Ended December 31, 1954 and 1953

	1954 Amount	1954 Per Cent of Net Sales	1953 Amount	1953 Per Cent of Net Sales
Gross sales..........................	$970,675	102.22%	$786,500	103.92%
Returned sales and allowances............	21,045	2.22	29,650	3.92
Net sales..............................	$949,630	100.00%	$756,850	100.00%
Cost of goods sold......................	685,320	72.17	582,700	76.99
Gross profit on sales...................	$264,310	27.83%	$174,150	23.01%
Expenses:				
Selling expenses.................	$145,980	15.37%	$ 89,050	11.77%
Administrative expenses...............	71,405	7.52	47,010	6.21
Total..............................	$217,385	22.89%	$136,060	17.98%
Net income from operations..............	$ 46,925	4.94%	$ 38,090	5.03%
Income from securities..................	500	.05	400	.05
Net income before interest and federal income tax...........................	$ 47,425	4.99%	$ 38,490	5.08%
Interest...............................	6,900	.72	6,750	.89
Net income before federal income tax......	$ 40,525	4.27%	$ 31,740	4.19%
Federal income tax.....................	15,000	1.58	11,500	1.52
Net income...........................	$ 25,525	2.69%	$ 20,240	2.67%

Vertical analysis of a profit and loss statement for a single period is not very informative—there is no basis for judging the acceptability of the various per cents. For instance, referring to the profit and loss statement for 1954, is a 27.83% rate of gross profit good or bad in the industry? Are 15.37 cents of selling expenses per dollar of sales too high? Is a net income of 2.69 cents per sales dollar in line with the net income of other concerns in the same kind of business?

SPECIALTY PRODUCTS COMPANY
Comparative Schedules of Selling and Administrative Expenses
With Per Cents of Net Sales
For the Years Ended December 31, 1954 and 1953

| | 1954 | | 1953 | |
	Amount	Per Cent of Net Sales	Amount	Per Cent of Net Sales
Selling expenses:				
Salesmen's salaries and payroll taxes......	$ 28,000	2.95%	$17,355	2.29%
Salesmen's traveling expenses.............	27,610	2.91	17,690	2.34
Advertising.........................	80,450	8.47	45,375	6.00
Freight out.........................	7,865	.83	6,350	.84
Miscellaneous.......................	2,055	.21	2,280	.30
Total.............................	$145,980	15.37%	$89,050	11.77%
Administrative expenses:				
Officers' salaries and payroll taxes........	$ 26,760	2.82%	$13,765	1.82%
Office salaries and payroll taxes...........	22,865	2.41	20,680	2.73
Stationery and supplies.................	1,250	.13	1,140	.15
Postage, telephone, and telegraph.........	2,535	.27	1,950	.26
Depreciation of furniture and fixtures.....	900	.09	900	.12
Bad debts............................	15,945	1.68	7,050	.93
Miscellaneous.......................	1,150	.12	1,525	.20
Total.............................	$ 71,405	7.52%	$47,010	6.21%

Vertical analysis takes on more meaning when applied to a comparative statement. For instance:

It is interesting to observe that the per cent of returns and allowances has decreased; returns and allowances mean wasted sales effort and dissatisfied customers.

It is encouraging to note that the rate of gross profit has increased from 23.01% to 27.83%; the cause of the increase cannot be known without information about comparative volume, sales prices, and costs of goods sold.

It is disturbing to see that the selling and administrative expenses have increased from 17.98% of net sales to 22.89% of net sales. An inspection of the expense schedules shows material increases in the per cents of salesmen's salaries, salesmen's traveling expenses, advertising (indicating that the increased sales effort has been relatively unproductive), officers' salaries, and bad debt losses.

A word of caution is in order in connection with the vertical analysis of a comparative statement. Per cents are computed by dividing one number, called the *percentage* (for instance, the gross profit), by another number, called the *base* (the net sales in the foregoing statements). A change in a per cent can be caused by a change in the percentage, a change in the base, or changes in both. Therefore, changes in vertical analysis per cents have to be carefully interpreted. For instance, the foregoing statement shows that the per cent of administrative expenses increased from 6.21% to 7.52%; this might be thoughtlessly interpreted as indicating an inconsequential increase; actually, the administrative expenses increased about $25,000. This increase was nearly offset, per-centage-wise, by the increase in net sales. The vertical analysis per cents in the foregoing statement do not bring forcefully to the attention of the management this really significant question: Was the dollar increase in administrative expenses justified by the dollar increase in sales? Unless administrative expenses should normally increase in proportion to an increase in sales (an unusual situation), the per cent of administrative expenses to sales should have decreased in 1954.

Horizontal analysis. The determination of per cents of increase and decrease, as shown in the following statement, is sometimes called *horizontal* analysis, because the amounts used in the computation are usually shown on the same line of a statement.

SPECIALTY PRODUCTS COMPANY
Comparative Statements of Profit and Loss
With Per Cents of Increase and Decrease
For the Years Ended December 31, 1954 and 1953

	1954	1953	Increase-Decrease* Amount	Per Cent
Gross sales	$970,675	$786,500	$184,175	23.42%
Returned sales and allowances	21,045	29,650	8,605*	29.02*
Net sales	$949,630	$756,850	$192,780	25.47
Cost of goods sold	685,320	582,700	102,620	17.61
Gross profit on sales	$264,310	$174,150	$ 90,160	51.77
Expenses:				
Selling expenses	$145,980	$ 89,050	$ 56,930	63.93
Administrative expenses	71,405	47,010	24,395	51.89
Total	$217,385	$136,060	$ 81,325	59.77
Net income from operations	$ 46,925	$ 38,090	$ 8,835	23.20
Income from securities	500	400	100	25.00
Net income before interest and federal income tax	$ 47,425	$ 38,490	$ 8,935	23.21
Interest	6,900	6,750	150	2.22
Net income before federal income tax	$ 40,525	$ 31,740	$ 8,785	27.68
Federal income tax	15,000	11,500	3,500	30.43
Net income	$ 25,525	$ 20,240	$ 5,285	26.11

The per cents shown in this statement seem to be more infor-mative than the per cents of net sales shown in the statement on page 418. They show a number of interesting changes:

Although the gross sales increased 23.42%, the returned sales and allowances decreased 29.02%; as a result of both of these changes, the net sales increased 25.47%.

Although the net sales increased 25.47%, the cost of goods sold increased only 17.61%; as a result, the gross profit increased 51.77%. We cannot tell from the statement why the per cent of increase in cost of goods sold was less than the per cent of increase in sales; it was, of course, due to a change in the relationship between unit selling prices and unit costs, or a shift in sales from low-profit merchandise to high-profit merchandise, or perhaps both.

Although the net sales increased 25.47%, the selling and administrative expenses increased 63.93% and 51.89%, respectively; as a consequence, the 25.47% increase in net sales was accompanied by an increase of only 23.20% in net income from operations.

Computation of per cents of increase and decrease. Following are illustrations of some problems which arise in the determination of per cents of increase and decrease; the asterisks indicate entries in red ink.

	This Year	Last Year	Increase—Decrease* Amount	Increase—Decrease* Per Cent
Cases in which there were positive amounts last year: Statement item				
A..........................	$1,500.00	$1,000.00	$ 500.00	50%
B..........................	500.00	1,000.00	500.00*	50*
C..........................	—	1,000.00	1,000.00*	100*
D..........................	500.00*	1,000.00	1,500.00*	150*
Cases in which there were no amounts last year: Statement item				
E..........................	1,500.00	—	1,500.00	—
F..........................	500.00*	—	500.00*	—
Cases in which there were negative amounts last year: Statement item				
G..........................	1,500.00*	1,000.00*	500.00*	—
H..........................	500.00	1,000.00*	1,500.00	—
I..........................	—	1,000.00*	1,000.00	—

The computations of the per cents for items A, B, C, and D are obvious. No per cents can be computed for items E and F because, in each instance, there is no last-year amount to serve as a base; and none can be computed for items G, H, and I because the last-year amounts are negative.

Positive and negative (black and red) amounts sometimes appear on the same line (as in item H) in comparative statements which, for reasons of condensation, show only differences between certain debit and credit balances. For instance, assume that a complete profit and loss statement shows the following items:

	This Year	Last Year
Net income from operations	$31,500.00	$29,860.00
Add interest income	3,700.00	3,000.00
Net income from operations and other income	$35,200.00	$32,860.00
Deduct interest expense	2,950.00	3,900.00
Net income	$32,250.00	$28,960.00

A condensed statement might show the net amounts of interest income and expense, thus:

	This Year	Last Year
Net income from operations	$31,500.00	$29,860.00
Interest income (expense*)—net	750.00	900.00*
Net income	$32,250.00	$28,960.00

Comparison of more than two statements. If comparative statements include data for more than two periods or as of more than two dates, there are two available bases for computing amounts of increases and decreases.

(1) Comparisons may be made with data for the immediately preceding period or date, thus:

	Year Ended December 31,			Increase—Decrease*	
	1954	1953	1952	1954 1953	1953 1952
Sales	$205,000	$180,000	$210,000	$25,000	$30,000*

(2) Or comparisons may be made with data for the earliest date or period, thus:

	Year Ended December 31,			Increase—Decrease*	
	1954	1953	1952	1954 1952	1953 1952
Sales	$205,000	$180,000	$210,000	$5,000*	$30,000*

It might seem that the same two bases of comparison could also be used to show per cents of increase and decrease. That is:

(1) The per cents might be based on data for the immediately preceding date or period, thus:

	Year Ended December 31,			Per Cent of Increase—Decrease*	
	1954	1953	1952	1954 1953	1953 1952
Sales..........	$205,000	$180,000	$210,000	14%	14%*

(2) Or the per cents might be based on data for the earliest date or period, thus:

	Year Ended December 31,			Per Cent of Increase—Decrease*	
	1954	1953	1952	1954 1952	1953 1952
Sales..........	$205,000	$180,000	$210,000	2%*	14%*

Per cents of increase and decrease based on the data for the immediately preceding date or period are likely to be misleading. For instance, the statement prepared by method 1 above shows that the sales decreased 14% in 1953 and increased 14% in 1954; if one considered only the per cents, he might jump to the incorrect conclusion that the increase in 1954 offset the decrease in 1953. The method 2 statement shows that, although some of the 1953 decrease was recovered in 1954, the sales for 1954 were still 2% below those for 1952.

The confusion which may result from the use of method 1 arises, of course, from the fact that the per cents were computed on two bases: the per cent of decrease in 1953 was computed on a base of $210,000, whereas the per cent of increase in 1954 was computed on a base of $180,000.

Ratios expressed decimally. The relation of an amount for a later date or period to an amount for an earlier date or period may be expressed decimally, as shown in the comparative statements on the next page. The ratios are computed by dividing the amounts for the later period by the amounts for the earlier period.

Although such ratios are less commonly used than per cents of increase and decrease, they have some advantages. In the first place, per cents of decrease must be shown in red ink or in some other manner to distinguish them from per cents of increase;

this fact somewhat increases the work of preparing the statement and may cause some confusion in interpreting it. In the second place, it is probably difficult for many persons to grasp the significance of large per cents, such as a 1,400% increase; it is much easier to understand that one item is 15 times as large as another item.

SPECIALTY PRODUCTS COMPANY
Comparative Profit and Loss Statement
For the Years Ended December 31, 1954 and 1953

	1954	1953	Increase Decrease*	Ratio, 1954 to 1953
Gross sales	$970,675	$786,500	$184,175	1.23
Returned sales and allowances	21,045	29,650	8,605*	.71
Net sales	$949,630	$756,850	$192,780	1.25
Cost of goods sold	685,320	582,700	102,620	1.18
Gross profit on sales	$264,310	$174,150	$ 90,160	1.52
Expenses:				
Selling expenses	$145,980	$ 89,050	$ 56,930	1.64
Administrative expenses	71,405	47,010	24,395	1.52
Total	$217,385	$136,060	$ 81,325	1.60
Net income from operations	$ 46,925	$ 38,090	$ 8,835	1.23
Income from securities	500	400	100	1.25
Net income before interest and federal income tax	$ 47,425	$ 38,490	$ 8,935	1.23
Interest	6,900	6,750	150	1.02
Net income before federal income tax	$ 40,525	$ 31,740	$ 8,785	1.28
Federal income tax	15,000	11,500	3,500	1.30
Net income	$ 25,525	$ 20,240	$ 5,285	1.26

SPECIALTY PRODUCTS COMPANY
Comparative Schedules of Selling and Administrative Expenses
For the Years Ended December 31, 1954 and 1953

	Amounts			Ratio, 1954 to 1953
	1954	1953	Increase Decrease*	
Selling expenses:				
Salesmen's salaries and payroll taxes	$ 28,000	$17,355	$10,645	1.61
Salesmen's traveling expenses	27,610	17,690	9,920	1.56
Advertising	80,450	45,375	35,075	1.77
Freight out	7,865	6,350	1,515	1.24
Miscellaneous	2,055	2,280	225*	.90
Total	$145,980	$ 89,050	$56,930	1.64
Administrative expenses:				
Officers' salaries and payroll taxes	$ 26,760	$13,765	$12,995	1.94
Office salaries and payroll taxes	22,865	20,680	2,185	1.11
Stationery and supplies	1,250	1,140	110	1.10
Postage, telephone, and telegraph	2,535	1,950	585	1.30
Depreciation of furniture and fixtures	900	900	—	1.00
Bad debts	15,945	7,050	8,895	2.26
Miscellaneous	1,150	1,525	375*	.75
	$ 71,405	$ 47,010	$24,395	1.52
Net sales	$949,630	$756,850		1.25

Working Capital

In the analysis of the statements of a business, great stress is laid on the analysis of working capital. Some of the applicable analytical procedures are discussed below.

Amount of working capital. The working capital of a business is the excess of its current assets over its current liabilities. The following schedule shows the working capital of Specialty Products Company at two dates and the changes in the elements thereof in the interval.

Schedule of Working Capital

	December 31,		Increase
	1954	1953	Decrease*
Current assets:			
Cash.......................................	$ 25,905	$ 25,330	$ 575
Marketable securities........................	10,000	8,000	2,000
Accounts receivable..........................	98,600	80,250	18,350
Reserve for bad debts.................... ..	2,500*	2,000*	500*
Inventories:			
Finished goods.........................	38,685	33,500	5,185
Goods in process........................	15,800	14,000	1,800
Raw materials............................	25,940	22,865	3,075
Prepaid expenses...........................	3,600	3,400	200
Total current assets ....(a)	$216,030	$185,345	$30,685
Current liabilities:			
Accounts payable...........................	$ 18,225	$ 12,500	$ 5,725
Notes payable—Bank.......................	40,000	25,000	15,000
Accrued taxes, wages, and other expenses.......	35,250	24,300	10,950
Total current liabilities...............(b)	$ 93,475	$ 61,800	$31,675
Working capital (a − b)......................	$122,555	$123,545	$ 990*

The working capital is an indication of the ability of a business to pay its current liabilities as they mature. It is sometimes called a measure of short-term solvency. The schedule shows that the working capital decreased slightly, but not significantly, during the year.

Working capital ratio. The working capital should be sufficient to provide for the payment of current liabilities as they mature and for the financing of current operations. But the *amount* of working capital is not an adequate measure of sufficiency; this fact can be demonstrated by comparing the working capital positions of two companies, as follows:

	Company A	Company B
Current assets............................	$10,000	$100,000
Current liabilities.........................	5,000	95,000
Working capital...........................	$ 5,000	$ 5,000

Both companies have the same amount of working capital, but their current positions differ radically. Any test of the adequacy of working capital must give consideration to the possibility of shrinkages in the realizable values of the current assets; in the event of forced liquidation, the inventory may have to be disposed of at a loss, and in the event of a general business recession, it may be difficult to dispose of the inventory and to collect the receivables. The current assets of Company A, even with a 50% shrinkage, are sufficient to pay the current liabilities; Company B can suffer only a 5% shrinkage.

For the reasons indicated above, it is important to know, not only the amount of the working capital, but also the ratio of current assets to current liabilities. These ratios, for Specialty Products Company, are computed below:

Working Capital Ratio

	December 31,	
	1954	1953
Total current assets..........................(a)	$216,030	$185,345
Total current liabilities........................(b)	93,475	61,800
Working capital ratio—Dollars of current assets per dollar of current liabilites (a ÷ b)..............	2.31	3.00

Although the decrease in the amount of working capital did not appear significant, the decrease in the ratio may be significant.

Window dressing. Since businessmen know that banks are interested in the working capital ratio, they sometimes conduct their affairs just prior to the statement date in such a manner as to increase the working capital ratio. To illustrate, assume that Specialty Products Company, late in December of each year, had done three things:

(1) Sold the marketable securities at their carrying value and applied the proceeds to the payment of the accounts payable.
(2) Used $10,000 of cash to reduce the bank loans.
(3) Postponed $10,000 of raw material purchases on account until the following January.

By these procedures, the current assets and current liabilities were reduced by equal amounts, as follows:

	December 31,	
	1954	1953
Reduction in current assets:		
Sale of marketable securities for payment of accounts payable.......................................	$10,000	$ 8,000
Use of cash to reduce bank loans..................	10,000	10,000
Postponement of raw material purchases..........	10,000	10,000
Offsetting reduction in liabilities...................	$30,000	$28,000

The effect of the window dressing is shown below; observe that the amounts of working capital are not affected, but that the working capital ratios are increased:

| | December 31, | |
	1954	1953
Current assets	$186,030	$157,345
Current liabilities	63,475	33,800
Working capital	$122,555	$123,545
Working capital ratio	2.93	4.66
Instead of	2.31	3.00

Effect of seasonal business.   If business activities vary radically during different seasons of the year, the working capital ratio is likely to vary also.   During a relatively active season, the inventories, accounts receivable, and accounts payable are apt to be large, and bank loans may be needed to finance the operations; during a relatively slack season, the inventory may be reduced, the accounts receivable should be relatively small, and there should be a corresponding reduction in the accounts payable and any bank loans.   The *amounts* of working capital may be approximately the same during both periods; but since, as we have seen, an equal increase in current assets and current liabilities reduces the working capital ratio, the *ratio* is likely to be smaller during the rush season than during the slack season.   For this reason (and because it is easier to take a small inventory during the slack season than a large inventory during a busy season), many concerns close their books and prepare statements at the close of the slack season, which is known as *the close of the natural business year*.

Effect of good and bad times.   Periods of boom and periods of depression affect the working capital ratio in the same manner that it is affected by seasonal activity.   A boom period is a busy period, and the working capital ratio tends to be relatively low; a depression period, with slack business, tends to increase the ratio. Therefore, an increase in the working capital ratio of a given business is not necessarily a good sign; the increase may have been caused by a slump in business.

Distribution and movement of current assets.   For many years the appraisal of the working capital position was pretty much limited to a rule of thumb: a working capital ratio of 2 to 1 was generally considered satisfactory.   Reliance on this ratio as an adequate measure of short-term credit standing is rapidly disappearing.   Analysts now recognize that the working capital ratio alone is not sufficiently informative; information is also needed with respect to the two matters mentioned on the following page.

The distribution of current assets—What kinds of current assets does the business own?

The movement of current assets—How rapidly are the current assets converted from raw materials to finished goods to accounts receivable to cash?

Distribution. Two computations which give consideration to the distribution of current assets are discussed below, under the captions:

Acid-test ratio.

Percentage distribution.

Acid-test ratio. In the computation of the acid-test ratio, a distinction is made between quick current assets (cash, temporary investments in marketable securities, and accounts and notes receivable) and other current assets. The acid-test ratios for Specialty Products Company are computed below. A ratio of at least 1 to 1 is considered desirable.

Acid-Test Ratio

| | | December 31, | | Increase |
		1954	1953	Decrease*
Quick current assets:				
Cash......................................		$ 25,905	$ 25,330	$ 575
Marketable securities........................		10,000	8,000	2,000
Accounts receivable—Less reserve for bad debts...		96,100	78,250	17,850
Total quick current assets.................	(a)	$132,005	$111,580	$20,425
Current liabilities............................	(b)	93,475	61,800	31,675
Excess of quick current assets over current liabilities.		$ 38,530	$ 49,780	$11,250*
Acid-test ratio—Dollars of quick current assets per dollar of current liabilities (a ÷ b)...............		1.41	1.81	.40*

Distribution of current assets. The acid-test ratio is sometimes supplemented by a list of the current assets showing what per cent each current asset is of the total. Such a statement for Specialty Products Company appears below:

Distribution of Current Assets

	December 31,			
	1954		1953	
	Amount	Per Cent of Total	Amount	Per Cent of Total
Cash......................................	$ 25,905	11.99%	$ 25,330	13.67%
Marketable securities....................	10,000	4.63	8,000	4.32
Accounts receivable—Less reserve.........	96,100	44.48	78,250	42.22
Finished goods..........................	38,685	17.91	33,500	18.07
Goods in process........................	15,800	7.31	14,000	7.55
Raw materials...........................	25,940	12.01	22,865	12.34
Prepaid expenses........................	3,600	1.67	3,400	1.83
	$216,030	100.00%	$185,345	100.00%

This schedule shows that there have been no shifts of material consequence in the *percentage* distribution of current assets.   But the per cents, like all vertical analysis per cents, must be carefully interpreted to avoid unwarranted conclusions.   The per cents applicable to the inventories have all decreased, and the per cent applicable to accounts receivable has increased.   At first glance, this may be interpreted as an improvement in distribution.   But we should remember that the change in a vertical-analysis per cent applicable to an item is the result of the change in that item and the change in the total of all items; and we should observe that the amounts of the inventory items have increased although the per cents have decreased, and that the total of the current assets was affected by the increase in the accounts receivable—an increase which may have been caused in part by a slowing up of collections.

An increase in inventories may be good or bad.   It is good if the increased inventories are necessitated by an increase in sales volume or if larger-than-normal purchases have been made in advance of price rises; it is bad if the increase is not justified by increased volume or if it is due to an accumulation of unsalable or obsolete items.

Movement.   In the following sections we shall consider tests of the movement of accounts receivable, finished goods, and raw materials.

Accounts receivable.   The question with which we are concerned here is: How rapidly are the accounts receivable collected, or how old are the accounts?

The ideal source of information for the answer to this question is found in an aging schedule of the accounts.   Following is such a schedule for Specialty Products Company:

Age of Accounts Receivable

	December 31, 1954		December 31, 1953	
	Amount	Per Cent of Total	Amount	Per Cent of Total
30 days or less	$38,059.60	38.6%	$32,340.75	40.3%
31 to 60 days	26,917.80	27.3	26,402.25	32.9
61 to 90 days	16,367.60	16.6	13,803.00	17.2
91 to 120 days	14,494.20	14.7	6,500.25	8.1
Over 120 days	2,760.80	2.8	1,203.75	1.5
	$98,600.00	100.0%	$80,250.00	100.0%

This schedule shows that the accounts on December 31, 1954 were relatively older than those on December 31, 1953.

The preparation of an aging schedule requires access to the accounts.   Outsiders, who do not have access to the accounts, sometimes compute the ratio of accounts receivable at the end of the year to the net sales during the year. The following ratios for Specialty Products Company show that a smaller per cent of the year's sales remained uncollected at the end of 1954 than at the end of 1953, *but they give no indication of the relative ages of the uncollected balances.*

Per Cent of Year's Sales Uncollected

		1954	1953
Accounts receivable at end of year.............. (a)		$ 98,600	$ 80,250
Net sales for the year......................... (b)		949,630	756,850
Per cent of year's sales uncollected (a ÷ b).........		10.38%	10.60%

Theoretically, the ratio should be computed by dividing the accounts receivable by the charge sales, rather than by the aggregate sales, for the period. Usually this information is not available in published statements. The use of aggregate sales will still disclose trends, unless there is a shift in the relative amounts of charge sales and cash sales.

Finished goods. The movement of finished goods is measured by their turnover. The following computation for Specialty Products Company is illustrative of the procedure.

Finished Goods Turnovers
(Data Obtained from Exhibit B—Schedule 1)

		1954	1953
Cost of goods sold........................... (a)		$685,320	$582,700
Average finished goods inventory:			
Inventory at beginning of year..................		$ 33,500	$ 29,600
Inventory at end of year......................		38,685	33,500
Average inventory.......................... (b)		$ 36,093	$ 31,550
Turnovers (a ÷ b)........................... (c)		18.99	18.47
Average number of days per turnover (365 ÷ c)....		19	20

If there is a seasonal variation in inventories, a more accurate turnover computation can be made by the use of the average of the inventory at the beginning of the year and all month-end inventories during the year.

A high turnover of finished goods is desirable because it increases the liquidity of the inventory; moreover, given a certain per cent of gross profit, the total amount of gross profit earned during a year increases as the turnovers increase. However, increasing the turnover by reducing the inventory may ultimately have the disastrous effect of alienating customers who become dissatisfied with the assortment.

Raw materials. The movement of raw materials is measured by their turnover, as is illustrated by the computation for Specialty Products Company shown on the following page.

Raw Materials Turnovers
(Data Obtained from Exhibit B—Schedule 1)

		1954	1953
Raw materials used	(a)	$234,075	$213,245
Average raw materials inventory:			
Inventory at beginning of year		$ 22,865	$ 20,850
Inventory at end of year		25,940	22,865
Average inventory	(b)	$ 24,403	$ 21,858
Turnovers (a ÷ b)	(c)	9.59	9.76
Average number of days per turnover (365 ÷ c)		38	37

What was said about the ˙use of an average of monthly inventories of finished goods if there are seasonal variations in the inventories applies equally to the use of an average of monthly inventories of raw materials in the raw material turnover computations.

General Financial Condition

Some balance sheet analysis procedures in addition to those concerned with working capital are discussed in following sections of this chapter.

Ratio of worth to debt.   The ratios of the net worth of Specialty Products Company to its total liabilities at the two year-ends are computed below:

Ratio of Worth to Debt

		December 31,	
		1954	1953
Net worth	(a)	$328,955	$276,430
Total liabilities	(b)	193,475	161,800
Ratio of worth to debt (a ÷ b)		1.70	1.71

From the creditors' standpoint, a high ratio of worth to debt is desirable; since, in the event of trouble, the stockholders stand to lose their investment before the creditors suffer any loss, a high ratio means a large capital cushion of protection to the creditors of the business.

From the stockholders' standpoint, a high ratio may not be desirable. To the extent that a company can obtain creditors' funds at an interest cost lower in rate than the per cent of net income on total assets, the stockholders benefit by an increased rate of return on their investment.

While a low ratio of worth to debt may be advantageous to stockholders from the standpoint of the rate of income on the investment, too low a ratio is hazardous; in a period of business recession, a shrinkage of assets and the pressure of creditors may be disastrous.

Analysis of equities. More detailed information about the equities of various classes of creditors and stockholders is furnished by a statement similar to the following:

Analysis of Equities

	December 31, 1954		December 31, 1953	
	Amount	Per Cent of Total	Amount	Per Cent of Total
Current liabilities	$ 93,475	17.89%	$ 61,800	14.10%
Long-term liabilities	100,000	19.14	100,000	22.82
Preferred stock	50,000	9.57	50,000	11.41
Common stock equity	278,955	53.40	226,430	51.67
	$522,430	100.00%	$438,230	100.00%

The most significant trend disclosed by this statement is shown by the ratios of current liabilities and common stock equity. The common stock equity increased from 51.67% to 53.40%—an increase of 1.73 percentage points. However, the current liabilities increased from 14.10% to 17.89%—an increase of 3.79 percentage points. Thus, notwithstanding the issuance of common stock of $50,000 par value during the year, the claims of current creditors increased percentagewise as well as in amount.

Security for long-term debt. A ratio which once had more significance than it has now is computed in the manner illustrated below, using data of Specialty Products Company:

Ratio of Pledged Fixed Assets to Long-Term Debt

	December 31,	
	1954	1953
Pledged fixed assets—Book value:		
Land	$ 40,000	$ 40,000
Buildings	245,350	198,675
Reserve for depreciation	61,000*	57,700*
Total (a)	$224,350	$180,975
Long-term debt (b)	$100,000	$100,000
Ratio of pledged fixed assets to long-term debt (a ÷ b)	2.24%	1.81%

The change in the ratio shows an increased degree of protection, but the ratio has no positive significance because the security is governed by market values rather than by book values.

Possible overinvestment in fixed assets. Investments in fixed assets impose upon a business fixed charges such as depreciation, insurance, and taxes. Although many expenses can be reduced in a period of business depression, fixed charges often cannot be reduced. Hence, the greater the amount of fixed expenses, the greater the danger that a business may not be able to ride out a business recession. This can be shown by an illustrative "break-even point" computation. Assume the facts stated on the following page.

	Company A	Company B
Sales...	$500,000	$500,000

Costs and expenses:
Fixed expenses:

	Company A	Company B
Incident to ownership of fixed assets....	$ 60,000	$ 10,000
Other fixed expenses.................	20,000	20,000
Total.............................	$ 80,000	$ 30,000

Variable costs and expenses (Assumed to vary in direct proportion to sales):

	Company A	Company B
Merchandise costs....................	$350,000	$350,000
Other variable expenses...............	20,000	70,000
Total.............................	$370,000	$420,000
Per cent of variable expenses to sales.........	74%	84%

The sales points at which the companies will break even (have neither a net income nor a net loss) are computed below; S represents the sales at the break-even point.

For Company A:

$$S = \$80,000 + .74S$$
$$.26S = \$80,000$$
$$S = \$307,692$$

For Company B:

$$S = \$30,000 + .84S$$
$$.16S = \$30,000$$
$$S = \$187,500$$

Company A, in order to avoid a net loss, must keep its sales up to a level of $307,692. Company B's sales can drop to $187,500 before it will incur a loss.

An overinvestment in fixed assets is also dangerous because, in a period of depression, fixed assets are likely to become frozen assets.

Obviously there can be no standard per cent or ratio to mark the danger point in investments in fixed assets; the fixed asset requirements of different businesses vary. Two ratios which indicate trends are illustrated.

Ratio of worth to fixed assets. The computation of this ratio is illustrated below:

Ratio of Worth to Fixed Assets

	December 31,	
	1954	1953
Net worth...................................(a)	$328,955	$276,430
Fixed assets.................................(b)	306,400	252,885
Ratio of worth to fixed assets (a ÷ b).............	1.07	1.09

Ratio of sales to fixed assets. Changes in the ratio of sales to fixed assets are an indication (but not a conclusive one) of whether sales are moving toward or away from the break-even point.

Only a major decrease in the ratio would be a cause for immediate concern.

Ratio of Sales to Fixed Assets

		December 31,	
		1954	1953
Net sales	(a)	$949,630	$756,850
Fixed assets	(b)	306,400	252,885
Ratio of sales to fixed assets (a ÷ b)		3.10	2.99

Horizontal and vertical analysis of the balance sheet. The comparative balance sheets on pages 435 and 436 illustrate the application of both horizontal and vertical analysis.

The horizontal analysis shows increases and decreases in dollar amounts, and the ratios of 1954 amounts to 1953 amounts. Sales data are included so that the analyst can compare the sales ratio with the ratios of changes in assets and liabilities. For instance, with a sales ratio of 1.25, are a cash ratio of only 1.02 and a total current liability ratio of 1.51 matters for concern?

The vertical analysis discloses much the same information. Probably the most significant change disclosed is the increase in current liabilities from 14.10% to 17.89% of the balance sheet totals.

Conclusion

Several words of caution need to be expressed before closing the discussion of statement analysis:

(1) Avoid meaningless ratios. With the increasing interest in statement analysis during recent years, there has been a tendency to develop a multiplicity of ratios, some of which have little or no significance. If two dollar amounts have little or no significance in relation to each other, a ratio expression of their relation is no more significant. For instance, it is claimed by some that the ratio of current assets to long-term debt is meaningful, but it is difficult to see any reason for regarding it as significant.

(2) Avoid ratios which may be misinterpreted. The turnover of working capital, often regarded as a very significant ratio, is a good example. It is computed by dividing the net sales by the working capital; an increase in the ratio is usually interpreted as desirable. But an increase in turnover may be caused by either an increase in the sales or a decrease in the working capital. An increase in working capital turnover caused by a decrease in working capital may be an undesirable trend.

(3) Appraise related ratios. For instance, the comparative balance sheet on page 435 shows that, with a 25% increase in sales, the accounts receivable increased 23%. Instead of jumping to the conclusion that the receivables have the same collectibility at the

SPECIALTY PRODUCTS COMPANY
Comparative Balance Sheets
December 31, 1954 and 1953

Assets	Amounts December 31, 1954	Amounts December 31, 1953	Increase Decrease*	Ratio 1954 to 1953	Per Cents of Total December 31, 1954	Per Cents of Total December 31, 1953
Current assets:						
Cash	$ 25,905	$ 25,330	$ 575	1.02	4.96%	5.78%
Marketable securities	$ 10,000	$ 8,000	$ 2,000	1.25	1.91%	1.82%
Accounts receivable	$ 98,600	$ 80,250	$18,350	1.23		
Reserve for bad debts	2,500	2,000	500	1.25		
Net	$ 96,100	$ 78,250	$17,850	1.23	18.39%	17.86%
Inventories:						
Finished goods	$ 38,685	$ 33,500	$ 5,185	1.15	7.41%	7.65%
Goods in process	15,800	14,000	1,800	1.13	3.02	3.19
Raw materials	25,940	22,865	3,075	1.13	4.97	5.22
Total	$ 80,425	$ 70,365	$10,060	1.14	15.40%	16.06%
Prepaid expenses	$ 3,600	$ 3,400	$ 200	1.06	.69%	.77%
Total current assets	$216,030	$185,345	$30,685	1.17	41.35%	42.29%
Fixed assets:						
Land	$ 40,000	$ 40,000	—	1.00	7.66%	9.13%
Buildings	$245,350	$198,675	$46,675	1.23		
Reserve for depreciation	61,000	57,700	3,300	1.06		
Net	$184,350	$140,975	$43,375	1.31	35.29	32.17
Machinery and equipment	$ 90,500	$ 75,000	$15,500	1.21		
Reserve for depreciation	15,200	10,050	5,150	1.51		
Net	$ 75,300	$ 64,950	$10,350	1.16	14.41	14.82
Furniture and fixtures	$ 9,450	$ 8,760	690	1.08		
Reserve for depreciation	2,700	1,800	900	1.50		
Net	$ 6,750	$ 6,960	$ 210*	.97	1.29	1.59
Total fixed assets	$306,400	$252,885	$53,515	1.21	58.65%	57.71%
	$522,430	$438,230	$84,200	1.19	100.00%	100.00%
Net sales	$949,630	$756,850		1.25		

SPECIALTY PRODUCTS COMPANY
Comparative Balance Sheets—Concluded
December 31, 1954 and 1953

	Amounts		Increase Decrease*	Ratio 1954 to 1953	Per Cents of Total, December 31,	
	December 31,					
	1954	1953			1954	1953
Liabilities and Net Worth						
Current liabilities:						
Accounts payable	$ 18,225	$ 12,500	$ 5,725	1.46	3.49%	2.85%
Notes payable—Bank	40,000	25,000	15,000	1.60	7.65	5.70
Accrued taxes, wages, and other expenses	35,250	24,300	10,950	1.45	6.75	5.55
Total current liabilities	$ 93,475	$ 61,800	$31,675	1.51	17.89%	14.10%
Long-term liabilities:						
Bonds payable	100,000	100,000	—	1.00	19.14	22.82
Total liabilities	$193,475	$161,800	$31,675	1.20	37.03%	36.92%
Net worth:						
Capital stock:						
Preferred	$ 50,000	$ 50,000	—	—	9.57%	11.41%
Common	250,000	200,000	$50,000	1.25	47.86	45.64
Earned surplus	28,955	26,430	2,525	1.10	5.54	6.03
Total net worth	$328,955	$276,430	$52,525	1.19	62.97	63.08
	$522,430	$438,230	$84,200	1.19	100.00%	100.00%
Net sales	$949,630	$756,850		1.25		

end of 1954 as they had at the end of 1953, observe that the schedule of administrative expenses (page 419) shows that bad debt charges in 1954 were 1.68% of net sales in 1954 as compared with .93% in 1953. This suggests a greater degree of possible loss in the receivables at the end of 1954 than in the receivables at the end of 1953. Then observe that, although the bad debt losses doubled in 1954 ($15,945 compared with $7,050), the reserve for bad debts has not been increased proportionately. Then consider the possibility that an additional loss provision should have been made in 1954, and note the effect of such an additional provision on the net income for 1954.

(4) Be aware that undesirable business operations or conditions may account for apparently favorable ratios, and vice versa. For instance, it was pointed out earlier in the chapter that a higher working capital ratio is more likely to exist in a period of poor business than in a period of good business.

(5) Be aware that facts not disclosed by the statements might affect the interpretation placed on the statements. For instance, assume that the management informed you that the large bad debt charge in 1954 was principally the result of the bankruptcy of one customer; the line of reasoning in (3) above would be affected.

(6) Bear constantly in mind the fact that changes in vertical-analysis per cents are affected by changes in the items being measured and changes in the base—for instance, changes in expense items and a change in net sales. Changes in vertical-analysis per cents cannot safely be interpreted without a constant awareness of this fact.

(7) Remember, also, that horizontal-analysis per cents and ratios must often be interpreted in the light of supplementary information. For instance, if net sales increased 25%, it does not necessarily follow that any expense increases of 25% or less are satisfactory. The propriety of that conclusion depends on whether the expense is relatively fixed or relatively variable.

(8) Weigh the results of the analysis of a given business against the trends in the industry and in business in general. It may be that, although conditions in the specific business have worsened, they are better than the average.

(9) Give consideration to changes in price levels and in the purchasing power of the dollar. For instance, if sales have been uniform for two years and there has been no change in the dollar amount of the inventory, but there has been a 25% increase in unit purchase costs, a 20% decrease in inventory quantities is indicated. But before accepting such a conclusion, find out whether the business uses *fifo* or *lifo*.

CHAPTER 28

Manufacturing Cost Controls

Perpetual Inventories

Under the method of accounting for manufacturing concerns described in Chapter 13, it is necessary to take physical inventories before the statements can be prepared. Because of the labor involved in taking these physical inventories, it may be impracticable, under this method, to prepare statements more frequently than once a year. The following pages contain a description of methods of keeping perpetual inventories of raw materials, goods in process, and finished goods, and the related controlling accounts.

RAW MATERIALS

Materials purchased. Let us assume that a company, at the beginning of its operations, purchased the following materials: 500 units of Material A at $4 per unit, and 1,500 units of Material B at $2 per unit.

Material A							

Date	Quantity			Price	Cost		
	In	Out	Balance		In	Out	Balance
19-- Feb. 3	500		500	4 00	2,000 00		2,000 00

Material B							

Date	Quantity			Price	Cost		
	In	Out	Balance		In	Out	Balance
19-- Feb. 3	1,500		1,500	2 00	3,000 00		3,000 00

438

The perpetual inventory of raw materials will contain a page or a card for each kind of material.   After the invoice has been recorded in the voucher register, it may be used by the perpetual inventory clerk to make entries on the cards as shown on page 438.

Materials used.   Materials should not be taken from the storeroom for use in the factory without a written order, called a *requisition*, approved by some person in authority.   Let us assume that the two following material requisitions were issued in February:

Material Requisition			No. 1
For Production Order No. 1		Date	2/5/19--
Material	Number of Units	Cost per Unit	Amount
A	200	4 00	800 00
B	700	2 00	1,400 00
			2,200 00

Approved _Q. H. Z._

Material Requisition			No. 2
For Production Order No. 2		Date	2/16/19--
Material	Number of Units	Cost per Unit	Amount
A	150	.4 00	600 00
B	100	2 00	200 00
			800 00

Approved _Q. H. Z._

The unit costs and the extended amounts were entered on the requisitions by the perpetual inventory clerk.

The material items shown by these requisitions were entered by the inventory clerk in the Out columns of the raw materials perpetual inventory records, and the balances were computed and entered on the cards by the perpetual inventory clerk, as shown on page 440.

Material __A__									
Date	Quantity			Price		Cost			
	In	Out	Balance			In		Out	Balance
19--									
Feb. 3	500		500	4	00	2,000	00		2,000	00
5		200	300					800	00	1,200	00
16		150	150					600	00	600	00

Material __B__									
Date	Quantity			Price		Cost			
	In	Out	Balance			In		Out	Balance
19--									
Feb. 3	1,500		1,500	2	00	3,000	00		3,000	00
5		700	800					1,400	00	1,600	00
16		100	700					200	00	1,400	00

GOODS IN PROCESS

Production orders. The perpetual inventory of goods in process is kept on sheets called *production orders*. A production order is kept for each job or kind of product going through the factory.

Let us assume that the company worked on two products during February: Product X and Product Y. Product X was started first, and is represented by production order 1; Product Y is represented by production order 2. The method of recording the material, labor, and overhead costs on these production orders is explained in the following paragraphs.

Raw materials. The cost of materials used is shown by the material requisitions. Copies of the requisitions are given to cost clerks for entry on the production orders.

> Requisition Number 1 (page 439) shows that materials costing $2,200 were taken from stock on February 5, for use on production order 1. This amount was entered in the Raw Materials column of production order 1 (page 441).
>
> Requisition Number 2 shows that materials costing $800 were taken from stock on February 16, for use on production order 2. See entry on production order 2.

		Production Order	1
For 800 Product X		Date Completed	

Date	Raw Materials	Direct Labor	Overhead
19-- Feb. 5	2,200 00		

		Production Order	2
For 200 Product Y		Date Completed	

Date	Raw Materials	Direct Labor	Overhead
19-- Feb. 16	800 00		

Direct labor. Each factory workman keeps a record of the time spent on each production order, by punching time cards. He uses a separate card each day for each production order on which he is engaged. When the card is turned in at the office, it shows the workman's number, the production order number, and the time worked. Clerks compute the elapsed time, enter the hourly wage rate, and compute the total labor cost. Following are two cards turned in by one workman.

Date	FEB 20	Date	FEB 20
Employee's Number	21	Employee's Number	21
Hour In	8 00	Hour In	1 00
Hour Out	12 00	Hour Out	4 00
Elapsed Time	4:00	Elapsed Time	3:00
Hourly Rate	$2.25	Hourly Rate	$2.25
Amount	$9.00	Amount	$6.75
Production Order	1	Production Order	2

These cards are used in making up the payroll. The cards are then sorted according to the production order numbers, and a summary is prepared showing the total direct labor cost applicable to each production order. The summary shows the direct labor cost incurred during February on each production order.

Production Order Direct Labor Cost Summary				
		Payroll Periods		
Production Order		Feb. 1 to 15		Feb. 16 to 28
1		1,000 00		200 00
2				800 00
		1,000 00		1,000 00

The direct labor costs shown by the labor cost summary were entered on the two production orders as shown below:

Production Order___1___

For ___800 Product X___   Date Completed _____

Date	Raw Materials	Direct Labor	Overhead
19-- Feb. 5	2,200 00		
15		1,000 00	
28		200 00	

Production Order___2___

For ___200 Product Y___   Date Completed _____

Date	Raw Materials	Direct Labor	Overhead
19-- Feb. 16	800 00		
28		800 00	

Production order 1 was charged with $1,000 and $200 of direct
labor.

Production order 2 was charged with $800 of direct labor.

Manufacturing expense, or overhead. The material and labor
costs applicable to each production order can be definitely determined by the methods just explained. Overhead expenses must
be estimated. This may be done as follows: If, in the past, the
annual manufacturing expense has been about 50% of the annual
direct labor cost, it may be assumed (unless conditions indicate
otherwise) that this ratio will continue. Therefore, when the
labor cost is entered on the production orders, the manufacturing
expense may be estimated as 50% of the labor cost.

It is assumed that 50% is a fair overhead rate for the concern
under illustration. Therefore, the cost clerk, after entering the
direct labor cost on the production orders, enters overhead charges
equal to 50% of the direct labor costs, as shown below:

Production Order____1____

For ____800 Product X____   Date Completed _____

Date		Raw Materials		Direct Labor		Overhead	
19-- Feb.	5	2,200	00				
	15			1,000	00	500	00
	28			200	00	100	00

Production Order____2____

For ____200 Product Y____   Date Completed _____

Date		Raw Materials		Direct Labor		Overhead	
19-- Feb.	16	800	00				
	28			800	00	400	00

Product X has been completed, and the production order is
removed from the work in process binder. Product Y is still in

process at the end of February; production order 2 shows the total cost of work in process—$2,000.

FINISHED GOODS

Completed production orders. After Product X (see production order 1) was completed, the production order was summarized to determine the total cost and the unit cost, as shown below:

			Production Order ___1___			
For ____800 Product X____				Date Completed__2/20__		
Date		Raw Materials		Direct Labor		Overhead
19-- Feb.	5	2,200	00			
	15			1,000	00	500	00
	28			200	00	100	00
Total		2,200	00	1,200	00	600	00

Summary:		
Material	2,200	00
Direct Labor	1,200	00
Overhead	600	00
Total	4,000	00
Unit cost (Quantity produced ___800___)	5	00

This production order furnishes the information for the following entry on the perpetual inventory card for Product X:

	Product___X___						
Date	Quantity			Unit Cost	Cost		
	In	Out	Balance		In	Out	Balance
19-- Feb. 20	800		800	5 00	4,000 00		4,000 00

Finished goods sold. On February 27, a sale of 500 units of Product X was made. The carbon copy of the invoice is provided with a Cost column at the right of the Amount (selling price) column. The carbon copy is sent to the inventory clerk, who performs the following operations:

(1) Looks up the unit price on the finished goods inventory card.
(2) Computes the total cost of the goods sold and enters this cost in the Cost column of the carbon copy of the invoice, thus:

Number	Description	Unit Price	Amount	Cost
(Heading of the Invoice)				
500	Article X	7 00	3,500 00	2,500 00

(3) Makes entries in the Out columns of the inventory card, showing the number and the cost of the articles sold, and computes the new quantity and cost balances. (See below.)
(4) Sends the carbon copy of the invoice back to the office for entry in the sales book.

The inventory card for Product X now appears as follows:

Product __X__

Date	Quantity			Unit Cost	Cost		
	In	Out	Balance		In	Out	Balance
19-- Feb. 20	800		800	5 00	4,000 00		4,000 00
27		500	300			2,500 00	1,500 00

Since Product X is the only article of finished goods on hand, this one card shows the total cost of the finished goods inventory at the end of February—$1,500.

Inventory Controlling Accounts

The raw material inventory cards show the units and costs of raw materials on hand; the production orders show the units and accumulated costs of goods in process; the finished goods inventory cards show the units and costs of finished goods on hand.

In a large business there may be thousands of these inventory cards and production orders, and the preparation of monthly statements will be greatly facilitated if the following controlling accounts are kept in the general ledger:

Raw Materials —with a balance equal to the sum of all the balances on the raw material inventory cards.

Goods in Process—with a balance equal to the sum of all the balances on the production orders for goods still in process.

Finished Goods —with a balance equal to the sum of all the balances on the finished goods inventory cards.

Such controlling accounts not only facilitate the preparation of the monthly profit and loss statements and balance sheets but also serve as checks upon the accuracy of the subsidiary perpetual inventory records of raw materials, goods in process, and finished goods.

We shall now see how such accounts can be produced. For purposes of illustration, we shall begin with expenditures for material, labor, and overhead, and trace the flow of these costs through goods in process into finished goods. The illustration will be based on the same assumed facts as those used on the preceding pages in illustrating the perpetual inventory records.

Material, labor, and overhead accounts. Assume that the expenditures during February for material, labor, and manufacturing expenses were:

```
(a) Raw materials..............................    $5,000.00
(b) Direct labor................................     2,000.00
(c) Manufacturing expenses:
      Indirect labor...........................  $500.00
      Factory supplies.........................   300.00
      Power....................................   220.00   1,020.00
```

These expenditures are recorded exactly as they were under the method of accounting described in Chapter 13, with one exception: one Raw Materials account is used instead of a Raw Materials Purchases account and a Raw Materials Inventory account. The accounts showing charges for these costs appear below:

Raw Materials	Direct Labor	Manufacturing Expense (Control)
(a)Cost 5,000	(b)Paid 2,000	(c) 1,020

Raw materials used. The raw materials taken from stock for use in the factory are shown by the material requisitions. (See illustrative requisitions on page 439.) These requisitions should be listed in a requisition register, as follows:

Requisition Register

Date		Requisition No.	Amount	
19--				
Feb.	5	1	2,200	00
	16	2	800	00
			3,000	00

The requisition register is footed at the end of the month, and the following journal entry is made:

(d) Goods in process............................ 3,000.00
        Raw materials.......................... 3,000.00
        To transfer the cost of raw materials used
        during the month out of the Raw Materials
        account and into Goods in Process.

Direct labor spent on goods in process. The production order direct labor cost summary (see page 442) shows the amount of direct labor charged to each production order. The totals of the summary show that $2,000 of direct labor was charged to the production orders during the month. Therefore, at the end of the month, the following journal entry is made transferring the labor cost shown by the summary into the Goods in Process account:

(e) Goods in process............................ 2,000.00
        Direct labor........................... 2,000.00
        To charge Goods in Process with the total
        direct labor cost entered on the production
        orders.

Manufacturing expenses charged to goods in process. This company is using an overhead rate of 50%; that is, the estimated overhead charged to each production order is 50% of the direct labor. Since $2,000 of direct labor was charged to the production orders, the total overhead charge was $1,000. This amount is charged into Goods in Process by the following journal entry:

(f) Goods in process............................ 1,000.00
        Manufacturing expense applied.......... 1,000.00
        To charge Goods in Process with the total over-
        head applied to the production orders.

Ledger accounts after transfer of costs into goods in process.
After the material, labor, and applied overhead costs for the month
are charged to the Goods in Process account, the accounts affected
contain the following amounts:

Raw Materials		Direct Labor		Manufacturing Expense (Control)	
(a)Cost 5,000	(d)Used 3,000	(b)Paid 2,000	(e)Used 2,000	(c)	1,020

	Manufacturing Expense Applied
	(f) 1,000

Goods in Process	
(d) Raw materials............	3,000.00
(e) Direct labor..............	2,000.00
(f) Manufacturing expense....	1,000.00

The Raw Materials account has a debit balance of $2,000,
representing the cost of all raw materials on hand at the end of
February. The costs of the individual items of raw material are
shown by the perpetual inventory cards (see page 440): Material A,
$600; Material B, $1,400.

The Direct Labor account has no balance. All of the direct
labor has been applied to the cost of goods in process.

The Manufacturing Expense account has a debit balance of
$1,020; the Manufacturing Expense Applied account has a credit
balance of $1,000. Twenty dollars of expense has not been applied
because of a slight error in the estimated burden rate of 50%.
Methods of disposing of this $20 are discussed on page 455.

The Goods in Process account (produced by posting the three
journal entries illustrated) shows the total material, labor, and
overhead charged to production during the month.

Cost of goods finished. When goods are finished, the production order is summarized (see production order No. 1, page 444)
and taken from the goods in process binder. The total cost is
entered in a register of completed production orders, thus:

Register of Completed Production Orders

Date		Production Order Number	Total Cost	
19-- Feb.	20	1	4,000	00

At the end of the month, the register is totaled, and the cost of goods finished during the month is transferred out of Goods in Process into Finished Goods by the following journal entry:

```
(g) Finished goods............................. 4,000.00
      Goods in process........................           4,000.00
      Total cost of goods completed during the
    month.
```

After this entry is posted, the two accounts affected contain the following amounts:

Goods in Process

(d) Raw materials............ 3,000.00	(g) Finished goods............ 4,000.00
(e) Direct labor.............. 2,000.00	
(f) Manufacturing expense.... 1,000.00	

Finished Goods

(g) Manufactured............ 4,000.00

The Goods in Process account has a debit balance of $2,000, representing the cost of goods in process at the end of February. Details are shown on production order 2, which is the only order in process at the end of the month.

Cost of goods sold. As shown on page 445, the carbon copies of the invoices are provided with a column in which a clerk enters the cost of the goods sold. Invoices are recorded in the manner shown in the following sales book:

Sales Book

Date		Name	Invoice Number	Selling Price		Cost	
19-- Feb.	27	Henderson & Riley	1	3,500	00	2,500	00

At the end of the month the two columns are totaled, and the totals are posted as follows:

```
Total of Selling Price column:
    (h) Debit Accounts Receivable controlling account
        Credit Sales
Total of Cost column:
    (i) Debit Cost of Sales
        Credit Finished Goods
```

The accounts affected (except Accounts Receivable) will contain the following amounts:

Finished Goods		
(g) Manufactured............ 4,000.00	(i) Sold....................	2,500.00

The debit balance of this account shows the cost of finished goods still on hand. Details are shown on the finished goods perpetual inventory cards.

Sales	
	(h)........................ 3,500.00

Cost of Sales	
(i) 2,500.00	

The difference between the debit balance in the Cost of Sales account and the credit balance in the Sales account is the gross profit for the month. Thus, the gross profit on sales can be determined from the books, without taking physical inventories.

Freight In, Discount on Purchases, and Returned Purchases and Allowances

For purposes of simplicity, no consideration has been given in the preceding pages to the problems of accounting for freight in, purchase discounts, and returned purchases and allowances in the raw materials perpetual inventory and controlling account. These matters will now be considered.

Freight in. Since freight in is part of the cost of raw materials purchased, the freight cost should be charged to the Raw Materials controlling account and included in the cost entered on the inventory card. Also, the unit costs entered in the Price column of the raw material perpetual inventory cards should include the freight element. Assume, for instance, that the freight on Material A (see page 438) was $50; the unit cost would be computed as follows:

$2,000 (purchase cost) + $50 (freight) = $2,050 (total cost)
$2,050 ÷ 500 (units purchased) = $4.10 (unit cost)

Purchase discounts. Cash discounts on purchases may or may not be reflected in the raw materials perpetual inventory and controlling account, depending on the general accounting policy adopted. Three policies are considered on the opposite page.

(1) Discounts *taken* may be shown in the profit and loss statement as income. If this procedure is followed, cash discounts do not affect the raw material perpetual inventory records or the Raw Materials controlling account.

(2) Discounts *taken* may be regarded as a deduction from the gross costs of raw materials. If this procedure is followed, cash discounts taken are credited to the Raw Materials controlling account. But an awkward situation arises in connection with the perpetual inventory records. Since, at the time of the purchase, it presumably is not known whether the discount will be taken, the purchase will be entered at the gross amount and the unit cost will be computed at the gross amount. Later, if the discount is taken, the unit cost and the amount in the Cost Balance column will have to be adjusted. The necessity for these adjustments may make this accounting procedure impracticable if perpetual inventories are maintained.

(3) Discounts *available* are regarded as a cost deduction; the net price is debited to the Raw Materials controlling account and entered on the perpetual inventory card, and the unit cost is computed on the basis of the net price. (This is the procedure discussed in Chapter 20.) To illustrate the computation of the net unit cost, assume that Commodity B was purchased subject to a 2% cash discount; then,

98% of $3,000 (gross price) = $2,940 (net price)
$2,940 ÷ 1,500 (units purchased) = $1.96 (unit cost)

To avoid the necessity of making adjustments for discounts lost, such discounts should not be debited to the Raw Materials controlling account (as a cost correction) but should be debited to Discounts Lost, which should be shown in the profit and loss statement as an expense.

Returned purchases and allowances. Returns and allowances should be credited to the Raw Materials controlling account. The entry in the perpetual inventory record is a simple matter if the transaction is a return of materials; it is recorded in the Out columns, and new quantity and cost balances are computed; the unit cost is not affected. If the credit is for an allowance, it is recorded in the Out column of the Cost section of the inventory card, and an adjusted unit cost and cost balance are entered on the card.

Summary

The entries in the general ledger cost control accounts and the subsidiary records under the system of accounting described in this chapter are summarized below, and the methods of accounting described in Chapter 13 and in this chapter are compared on page 454.

Summary of Entries in the General Ledger Accounts and in the Subsidiary Records, Using the Method of Accounting Described in This Chapter

	GENERAL LEDGER	SUBSIDIARY RECORDS
Purchase of materials..........	Debit Raw Materials—total of Raw Materials column of voucher register.	Enter details in the In columns of the perpetual inventory cards, using facts shown by suppliers' invoices.
Direct labor payments..........	Debit Direct Labor—total of Direct Labor column of voucher register.	
Payment of manufacturing expenses..........	Debit Manufacturing Expense—voucher register entries, etc.	
Materials put into process..........	Credit Raw Materials and Debit Goods in Process—journal entry using total of material requisition register.	Enter details in Out columns of raw material inventory cards, from material requisitions. Enter in Material column of production orders, from material requisitions.
Direct labor on goods in process..........	Debit Goods in Process and credit Direct Labor—journal entry using amount shown by direct labor cost summary.	Enter in Labor column of production orders, from direct labor cost summary.
Manufacturing expense applied..........	Debit Goods in Process and credit Manufacturing Expense Applied—journal entry, amount being based on labor cost summary.	Enter in Overhead column of production orders, amounts being obtained by multiplying the labor cost on the production order by an overhead rate.

Finished goods completed.............	Credit Goods in Process and Debit Finished Goods—journal entry using total of register of completed production orders.	Foot the production orders for the completed goods and remove them from the goods in process binder. Enter in In columns of finished goods perpetual inventory cards, using amounts shown by production orders.
Finished goods sold............	Debit Cost of Sales and credit Finished Goods—total of Cost column of sales book. Debit Accounts Receivable and credit Sales —total of Selling Price column of sales book.	Enter in Out column of finished goods perpetual inventory record, using information shown by the invoice.

Comparison of Method Described in This Chapter with Method Described in Chapter 13

	METHOD DESCRIBED IN CHAPTER 13	METHOD DESCRIBED IN THIS CHAPTER
Profits and losses on various commodities....	Although the statement of cost of goods manufactured illustrated in Chapter 13 shows the cost of *all* finished goods manufactured during the period, the accounting system does not show the cost of *each kind* of product manufactured. Therefore, the profit or loss on the sale of each kind of commodity cannot be ascertained with accuracy, and the management is left with inadequate information as to the profit derived from each product.	The cost of each product is shown by the production orders. Each invoice shows the selling price of the articles sold, and also the cost thereof. The gross profit on each commodity and the gross profit on each sale can thus be easily ascertained.
Physical *vs.* perpetual inventories.............	Under the Chapter 13 method, it is necessary to take physical inventories of raw materials, goods in process, and finished goods before a statement of cost of goods manufactured, a profit and loss statement, and a balance sheet can be prepared. Because of the labor involved in taking these inventories, it may be impracticable to prepare statements more frequently than once a year.	Under the method of accounting described in this chapter, the costs of raw materials, goods in process, and finished goods can be determined from the books, without taking physical inventories. This facilitates the preparation of monthly statements, which are of great importance if the management is to keep a close watch over the operations of the business. (Periodical physical inventories should be taken to check the perpetual inventories.)
Inventory valuations..........	Since the accounting system described in Chapter 13 does not show the cost of each kind of product manufactured, and the accumulated cost of goods in process, the valuations applicable to physical inventories of finished goods and goods in process are often mere estimates of the cost.	Since the accounting system described in this chapter shows the cost of each product and the costs incurred on goods still in process, costs for inventory purposes can be much more accurately determined.

Underabsorbed and Overabsorbed Burden

To illustrate the various methods of dealing with underabsorbed and overabsorbed manufacturing expense, let us assume that the manufacturing expense accounts at the end of the year have the following balances:

```
Manufacturing expense (control).............. $11,000.00
Manufacturing expense applied...............            $10,500.00
```

The actual expenses were $11,000; the amount applied to the production orders was only $10,500.

The $500 balance of unabsorbed burden may be treated in two ways, as follows:

(1) Theoretically, it should be apportioned to finished goods manufactured and sold during the period, finished goods on hand, and goods in process, by a journal entry similar to the following:

```
Cost of sales........................................ 425.00
Finished goods....................................... 60.00
Goods in process..................................... 15.00
    Manufacturing expense applied.................        500.00
```

(2) If the greater portion of the finished goods manufactured has been sold, it is reasonably correct to charge the entire unabsorbed burden to Cost of Sales, as follows:

```
Cost of sales........................................ 500.00
    Manufacturing expense applied.................        500.00
```

Adjustments for overabsorbed burden may be made similarly; that is, (1) by credits to Cost of Sales, Finished Goods, and Goods in Process; (2) by credit to Cost of Sales.

After one of the foregoing entries has been made at the end of the year to bring the credit balance of the Manufacturing Expense Applied account into agreement with the balance in the Manufacturing Expense control account, these accounts are closed by an entry similar to the following:

```
Manufacturing expense applied................ 11,000.00
    Manufacturing expense....................        11,000.00
    To close the manufacturing expense accounts.
```

The two entries may be combined, thus:

```
Cost of sales.................................    500.00
Manufacturing expense applied................ 10,500.00
    Manufacturing expense....................        11,000.00
    To close the manufacturing expense accounts
    and assign the unapplied expense to cost of
    sales.
```

Working Papers

Adjustments for accrued and deferred items are made in the working papers on page 457 in the manner with which you are already familiar. (See entry *a*.) The Adjustments columns also contain the debits and credits of the entries:

(b) Applying the unabsorbed manufacturing expense against the cost of sales.

(c) Closing the Manufacturing Expense account against the Manufacturing Expense Applied account.

Closing the Books

The procedure of closing the books at the end of the period is illustrated below:

The adjusting and closing entries follow:

(1) Make adjustments for any deferred and accrued items. Salesmen's salaries in the amount of $200 are accrued and unpaid at the end of the year.

```
Selling expense.....................................  200.00
    Accrued salaries payable........................           200.00
        To set up accrual.
```

(2) Write off the unabsorbed manufacturing expense. For purposes of illustration we shall write off the entire unabsorbed manufacturing expense to Cost of Sales.

```
Cost of sales.....................................  1,000.00
    Manufacturing expense applied.................           1,000.00
        To apply the unabsorbed manufacturing expense to
        cost of goods sold.
```

Close the Manufacturing Expense account and Manufacturing Expense Applied account.

```
Manufacturing expense applied.................. 14,000.00
    Manufacturing expense.....................          14,000.00
        To close.
```

(3) Make the general closing entries:

```
Sales.....................................  100,000.00
    Profit and loss.......................           100,000.00
        To close the Sales account.

Profit and loss...........................   93,200.00
    Cost of sales..........................           76,000.00
    Selling expense........................           12,200.00
    General expense........................            5,000.00
        To close debit-balance accounts.

Profit and loss...........................    6,800.00
    Earned surplus.........................            6,800.00
        To transfer the net income to Earned Surplus.
```

THE X Y Z COMPANY
Working Papers
Year Ended December 31, 19—

Account	Trial Balance Dr	Trial Balance Cr	Adjustments Dr	Adjustments Cr	Profit and Loss Dr	Profit and Loss Cr	Earned Surplus Dr	Earned Surplus Cr	Balance Sheet Dr	Balance Sheet Cr
Cash	75,000								75,000	
Accounts receivable	10,000								10,000	
Finished goods	15,000								15,000	
Goods in process	1,500								1,500	
Raw materials	5,000								5,000	
Vouchers payable		6,000								6,000
Capital stock		50,000								50,000
Earned surplus		43,500						43,500		
Sales		100,000				100,000				
Cost of sales	75,000		(b) 1,000		76,000					
Manufacturing expense	14,000			(c) 14,000						
Manufacturing expense applied		13,000	(c) 14,000	(b) 1,000						
Selling expense	12,000		(a) 200		12,200					
General expense	5,000				5,000					
	212,500	212,500								
Accrued salaries payable				(a) 200						200
			15,200	15,200						
Net income—to Earned Surplus					6,800			6,800		
					100,000	100,000				
Earned surplus, December 31, 19—							50,300			50,300
							50,300	50,300	106,500	106,500

Statements

The following statement of profit and loss, statement of earned surplus, and balance sheet were prepared from the working papers.

THE X Y Z COMPANY   Exhibit C
Statement of Profit and Loss
For the Year Ended December 31, 19—

Sales		$100,000.00
Cost of goods sold		76,000.00
Gross profit on sales		$ 24,000.00
Deduct expenses:		
Selling	$12,200.00	
General	5,000.00	17,200.00
Net income		$ 6,800.00

THE X Y Z COMPANY   Exhibit B
Statement of Earned Surplus
For the Year Ended December 31, 19—

Balance, December 31, 19—	$43,500.00
Net income, per Exhibit C	6,800.00
Balance, December 31, 19—	$50,300.00

THE X Y Z COMPANY   Exhibit A
Balance Sheet
December 31, 19—

Assets		Liabilities and Net Worth	
Cash	$ 75,000.00	Vouchers payable	$ 6,000.00
Accounts receivable	10,000.00	Accrued salaries payable	200.00
Finished goods	15,000.00	Capital stock	50,000.00
Goods in process	1,500.00	Earned surplus, per Exhibit	
Raw materials	5,000.00	B	50,300.00
	$106,500.00		$106,500.00

APPENDIX 1
Matters Related to Payrolls

Federal old age benefits taxes. The Social Security Act of 1935, as amended, provides for federal government disbursements called, variously "old age benefits," "old age and survivors' benefits," "old age insurance," and "old age annuities." These payments include monthly benefits to workers who retire at age sixty-five, supplementary benefits to their wives and dependent children, benefits for survivors of wage earners who die, and lump-sum payments in some cases.

The funds required for these disbursements are obtained from taxes (generally called "O. A. B. taxes") levied under the Federal Insurance Contributions Act on employers and employees, in amounts based on wage payments for services performed in the United States, Alaska, and Hawaii, and on American vessels. Certain services are excepted. Payments made to an independent contractor for services performed are not wages.

The taxes levied on employees are withheld by the employers from wage payments; these tax withholdings, as well as the taxes levied on the employers, are remitted by the employers to the Director of Internal Revenue for the district in which the principal place of business of the employer is located. At the time of this writing, the rate is $1\frac{1}{2}\%$, to increase to 2% in 1954, to $2\frac{1}{2}\%$ in 1960, to 3% in 1965, and to $3\frac{1}{4}\%$ in 1970. Because of possible revisions in the law, you should ascertain the rate currently in effect.

The tax is not levied on wages in excess of $3,600.00 paid to a worker by one employer during a calendar year. However, if an individual works for two or more employers during a calendar year, each employer is required to pay the tax on his wage payments to the employee up to $3,600, and to make similar deductions from the employee's wages. The employee can obtain a refund from the government for deducted taxes on his aggregate wages for the year in excess of $3,600; the employers cannot obtain a refund.

Each employer must apply to the Social Security Administration for an "identification number," to be shown on his tax return. Each worker must apply to the Administration for an "account number"—often referred to as his *social security number;* the employer must be informed of the account number of each of his employees, for use in his records and reports.

The law specifies that every employer withholding taxes must furnish the employee with an annual statement on or before January 31 of the succeeding year which shows the total social security tax withheld.

If employment is terminated, the employer must give a final statement to the employee on the date of the final wage payment. Many employers find it convenient to report the tax deduction at the time of making each wage payment; methods of making such reports to employees are illustrated on pages 468 and 470.

The employer is required to maintain records which show, as to each employee, his name, address, and social security number; the total compensation due him at each pay date; any portion thereof not subject to tax; the period covered by the payment; and the amount of old age benefit insurance tax deducted. The employer must also keep copies of all returns and reports filed by him with government authorities.

Self-employed persons. Self-employed persons other than farmers and certain professional groups became covered by the old age and survivors' insurance program on and after January 1, 1951. The tax on self-employment income is handled in all particulars as an integral part of the federal income tax.

Federal unemployment insurance taxes. Taxes are levied against employers (but not against employees) under the Federal Unemployment Tax Act to obtain funds required to meet the provisions of the Social Security Act relative to unemployment insurance, sometimes called *unemployment compensation.* Unemployment compensation payments are not made by the federal government directly to unemployed persons; the funds obtained by the collection of federal unemployment insurance taxes are used to make grants to the various states to assist them in carrying out their own unemployment compensation programs. Laws providing for unemployment compensation payments have been enacted by all the states and territories.

Unlike the federal old age benefit tax, which is assessed against an employer with one or more employees in covered employment, the federal unemployment insurance taxes are assessed against only certain employers, as defined in the law, as follows:

> "The term 'employer' does not include any person unless on each day of some twenty days during the taxable year, each day being in a different calendar week, the total number of individuals who were employed by him in employment for some portion of the day (whether or not at the same moment of time) was eight or more."

The expression "employed by him in employment" has the significance of *employed by him in covered employment,* or, in other words, not employed in the performance of exempt services. A person is not subject to the federal unemployment insurance tax unless he has employed at least eight individuals for the performance of nonexempt services on at least one day during at least twenty different weeks of the taxable year; and an employer who is subject to the tax is assessed on the basis of wages paid to only those employees who are engaged in the performance of nonexempt services.

The federal unemployment insurance tax rate is 3%; wages in excess of $3,000 paid to any one individual during the taxable year are not subject to the tax. Although the tax rate is 3%, the employer is entitled to a credit for taxes paid to the states and territories under their unemployment compensation laws. This credit cannot be more than 90% of the tax assessed by the federal government at the 3% rate. Because of this provision in the federal law, the states have generally established a 2.7% unemployment compensation tax rate. Since taxable wages are generally (though subject to some minor exceptions) computed in the same manner for both federal and state taxes, the tax rates are usually considered to be as follows:

Federal tax	.3%
State tax	2.7
Total	3.0%

Although the basic rate for state taxes is 2.7%, the tax actually payable to a state may be computed at a lower rate. Since one of the purposes of state unemployment legislation is to stabilize employment, the state laws contain provisions for merit-rating plans; under these provisions, an employer who establishes a good record for stable employment (thus reducing the claims upon state funds for unemployment compensation) may obtain the benefit of a state tax rate much lower than 2.7%. In order to assure the employer of the enjoyment of the tax saving resulting from the reduced state rate, the federal law provides that an employer paying a state tax at a rate less than 2.7%, as a result of the state's merit-rating plan, may deduct as a credit an amount computed at the 2.7% rate or at the highest rate applicable to any taxpayer in the state, whichever is lower; the amount of the credit cannot, of course, be more than 90% of the federal tax.

The employer must file his federal unemployment tax return with the Director of Internal Revenue on or before January 31 following the taxable calendar year. To assure himself of obtaining the credit for state taxes, he should pay these taxes not later than January 31.

The federal tax may be paid at the time the return is filed, or in four equal installments on January 31, April 30, July 31, and October 31 of the year following that for which the tax is assessed.

The employer's records should contain all information required to support his tax return.

State unemployment compensation taxes. Stimulated by the enactment of the federal unemployment insurance legislation, which provided for federal grants to the states as an aid in financing their unemployment compensation programs, all the states and territories have passed laws which have, in general, the following principal objectives:

(1) The payment of compensation, of limited amounts and for limited periods, to unemployed workers.

(2) The operation of facilities to assist employers in obtaining employees, and to help workers obtain employment.

(3) The encouragement of employers to stabilize employment; the inducement offered is a reduction in the tax rate, through the operation of merit-rating systems.

Since the laws of the several states differ in many particulars, it is possible here to give only a general discussion. All the states levy a tax on employers; a very few also levy a tax on employees. The list of exempt services in the federal law is rather closely followed in most of the state laws. Whereas the federal unemployment insurance tax is assessed against only those employers who have eight or more employees, many of the states assess taxes on employers of a smaller number of individuals—even as few as one. In most states the tax is not assessed on salaries in excess of $3,000. In general, the state tax rate is basically 2.7%, but provision is made in some of the laws for increased rates if they are essential to meet disbursement requirements. All state laws include a merit-rating plan of some kind; these plans are intended to effect lower taxes by a reduction of the tax rate or by a credit against taxes for employers who have established (during an experience period, usually of three years) a favorable record of stable employment. The reserve ratio plan is typical; in principle it operates as follows:

Assume that an employer's average annual payroll for three years has been $100,000.

Assume, also, that the balance in the state's reserve account with this employer is $5,000; this is the excess of the taxes paid by this employer over the amounts of benefits paid by the state to his former employees.

The reserve ratio ($5,000 ÷ $100,000) is 5%.

The higher the reserve ratio, the lower the tax rate.

Most states require employers to file returns quarterly and to pay the tax by the end of the month following the close of the quarter. Since the amount of taxable wages paid to an individual is usually one of the factors determining the amounts of benefits payable to him when he is unemployed, employers are required to file information returns showing the amount of compensation paid to each employee during the period.

The states require employers to maintain a compensation record for each employee, showing, among other things, the period of employment, the reason for termination of employment, the cause of lost time, and the amounts of periodical payments of compensation to him during the period of employment. The specific requirements of each state are shown in its published regulations.

Federal income tax withholding. Employers of one or more employees are required to withhold federal income taxes from the wages of employees, except certain exempt wage payments.

The amount withheld from an employee's wages is affected by the amount of his income and the number of exemptions ($600 each).

An individual is entitled to:

(1) An exemption for himself.
(2) An additional exemption if he is over 65 or will become 65 on or before January 1 of the following year.
(3) An additional exemption if he is blind.

If the employee is married, he can claim any of the above exemptions which his spouse could claim if she were employed—unless, of course, she is employed and claims them herself.

(4) An exemption for each dependent. No *additional* exemptions are allowed for aged or blind *dependents*.

A dependent is a person who is closely related to the taxpayer, who has a gross income of less than $600 for the year, and who received more than half of his support for the year from the taxpayer.

In order to determine the amount of tax which he should withhold from an employee's compensation, the employer must know the number of exemptions claimed by the employee. Therefore, the employee is required to furnish an Employee's Withholding Exemption Certificate to his employer.

If the employee's status as to exemptions changes during the year, he should give his employer an amended certificate; he is required to do so if the number of exemptions decreases, and he is permitted to do so if the number of exemptions increases.

The employer's report and payment procedures are summarized below:

Each employer must file a quarterly combined return for O. A. B. taxes and withheld income taxes. Except as noted in the following paragraph, the return and taxes are due and payable on or before the last day of the month following the calendar quarter covered by the return.

If the combined O. A. B. taxes and withheld income taxes of any employer exceed $100 in any month other than the last month of a quarter (March, June, September, or December), the employer is required to deposit them in an authorized depositary bank by the 15th of the following month. For March, June, September, or December, the employer may deposit the taxes in an authorized bank on or before the end of the following month. If all these monthly deposits have been made on time, the due date for the quarterly return is extended to the 10th day of the second month following the calendar quarter covered.

On or before January 31, the employer should give each of his employees a withholding receipt showing the employee's total wages for the preceding year and the amount of income tax and social security tax withheld therefrom. If an employee's employment is terminated, the employer should give him, at the time of the last wage payment, a withholding receipt covering the portion of the year during which he was employed.

With the return for the last calendar quarter, each employer should file with the Director of Internal Revenue a Reconciliation of Quarterly Returns, which summarizes the amounts of taxes shown by the quarterly returns. It should be accompanied by carbon copies of all withholding receipts given to employees, and by a listing (which may be in the form of an adding machine tape) of the amounts of withheld taxes as shown by the copies of the withholding receipts.

Other payroll deductions. Employers may make other deductions from payrolls, such as the following: deductions for premiums for group hospital insurance, deductions for purchases of government bonds for the employees, and deductions for payment of union dues.

Requirements of Federal Fair Labor Standards Act. This act establishes a minimum hourly wage rate and maximum hours of work per week for certain classes of employees engaged directly or indirectly in interstate commerce, and provides that payment for overtime hours in excess of 40 hours during any work week shall be at the rate of $1\frac{1}{2}$ times the regular hourly wage. The act also requires that employers subject to it shall maintain a record for each subject employee showing his name, address, date of birth (if under 19), occupation, work week, regular rate of pay per hour, basis of wage payment (hour, week, month, piecework, and so on), hours worked per day and per work week, daily or weekly wages at his regular rate, weekly excess compensation for overtime worked, miscellaneous additions to or deductions from wages, total periodical wage payments, and date of payment.

Following are some illustrations of the application of the requirement for the payment of wages at $1\frac{1}{2}$ times the regular hourly rate for hours of work in excess of 40 hours during any work week:

(1) A's regular hourly rate is $2.00. He works 45 hours during one week. His wages are computed as follows:

```
45 hours at $2.00............................. $90.00
 5 hours at  1.00.............................   5.00
    Total....................................  $95.00
```

(2) B's wages are $58.50 a week for a regular work week of 39 hours (7 hours a day for 5 days, and 4 hours on Saturday). He works 45 hours during one week.

```
$58.50 ÷ 39 = $1.50 regular hourly rate.
45 hours at $1.50 = $67.50
 5 hours at  .75  =   3.75 (Excess payment for hours over 40)
   Total            $71.25
```

(3) C accepts a position with the understanding that he is to work 7 hours per day during each of the 6 days of his work week, and is to receive a weekly wage of $86. He works 50 hours during one week. To determine his regular hourly rate, we must remember that his regular work week consists of 42 hours, and that for 2 of these hours he is being paid $1\frac{1}{2}$ times the regular hourly rate; in other words, for the 2 hours regularly worked in addition to 40 hours, he is given the equivalent of 3 hours' pay. Therefore,

$86.00 ÷ 43 = $2.00, the regular hourly rate.

If he works the regular 42 hours, his wage is (theoretically) computed as follows:

```
42 hours at $2.00 = $84.00
 2 hours at  1.00 =   2.00 (Excess for hours over 40)
   Total            $86.00
```

For the week that he works 50 hours, his wage is:

```
50 hours at $2.00  =  $100.00
10 hours at  1.00  =    10.00  (Excess for hours over 40)
       Total          $110.00
```

If wages are paid monthly or semimonthly, recognition must be given to the fact that the time-and-one-half requirement applies to each work week separately. To illustrate, assume that an employee, whose regular hourly rate is $2.00, was paid for the half-month ended Wednesday, July 15, and that he was entitled to no overtime payment for that period. We are now to compute his wage payment for the last half of July; we require the following information as to hours worked:

In prior payroll period:

```
Monday,     July 13................................. 8
Tuesday,      "  14................................. 8
Wednesday,    "  15................................. 8
```

In current payroll period:

```
Thursday,  July 16................................. 8
Friday,      "  17................................. 7
Saturday,    "  18................................. 5
Monday,      "  20................................. 6
Tuesday,     "  21................................. 7
Wednesday,   "  22................................. 7
Thursday,    "  23................................. 8
Friday,      "  24................................. 6
Saturday,    "  25................................. 7
Monday,      "  27................................. 8
Tuesday,     "  28................................. 8
Wednesday,   "  29................................. 8
Thursday,    "  30................................. 8
Friday,      "  31................................. 8
```

His total wage payment for the semimonthly period is computed as follows:

(a) For the portion of the work week ended July 18:
Considering that work week as a whole, he worked 44 hours. Since, at the time of making the payment for the period ended July 15, it was not known whether he would work over 40 hours during the entire week, he was paid for the first 3 days at the regular rate. We now find that he worked 44 hours during that week, 20 of them during the current payroll period. Therefore, the payment to him now should be:

```
20 hours at $2.00  =  $40.00
 4 hours at  1.00  =    4.00
       Total          $44.00
```

(b) For the work week ended July 25:
During this week he worked 41 hours.   For it he should be
paid:

41 hours at $2.00 = $82.00
1 hour at 1.00 =   1.00
Total $83.00

(c) For the portion of the work week ended July 31:
Although he had already worked 40 hours during the week,
there was no certainty on Friday night that he would
work on Saturday.   Therefore, he should be paid an
amount computed as follows:

40 hours at $2.00 = $80.00

His total wage payment for the semimonthly period is the
total of the items shown below:

For partial work week ended July 18..........	$ 44.00
For work week ended July 25.................	83.00
For partial work week ended July 31..........	80.00
Total................................	$207.00

Payroll procedures.   The payroll summary on page 469
furnishes information required for the entries in the ledger accounts
applicable to wages and payroll deductions.   Postings of column
totals may be made directly from the payroll summary to the
ledger; the debits and credits are shown below.

Wages (if it is desired to debit various accounts for amounts of wages payable for different services, an analysis must be made to obtain the information for this purpose)................................	3,265.20	
Federal O. A. B. taxes withheld from employees.		45.86
Federal income taxes withheld from employees..		381.80
Wages payable.............................		2,837.54

Some companies consider it satisfactory to use one account,
"Federal Taxes Withheld from Employees," for both the O.A.B.
and the income tax withholdings.   If this is done, the entries in the
account should be identified, so that the liability on each class of
tax can be determined.

It will be observed that the amount shown in the payroll summary for O.A.B. withholdings is not exactly $1\frac{1}{2}\%$ of the payroll;
this is presumably because some of the wage payments represented
excesses over $3,600, which therefore were not subject to the social
security taxes.

The employer should compute his own liability for social security taxes in the manner shown on page 469.

```
Total wages.................................. $3,265.20 $3,265.20
Wages not subject to social security taxes........    208.10
Wages (in excess of $3,000) not subject to unem-
  ployment taxes............................              608.10
Wages subject to taxes....................... $3,057.10 $2,657.10
Taxes:
  Federal O.A.B.—1½% of $3,057.10..................... $    45.86
  Federal unemployment—0.3% of $2,657.10..............      7.97
  State unemployment—2.7% of $2,657.10................     71.74
                                                      $   125.57
```

The entry to record the expense and the liabilities for these taxes may be as follows:

```
Payroll taxes (separate expense accounts may be used if
  desired)........................................... 125.57
    Federal O.A.B. taxes payable.....................         45.86
    Federal unemployment taxes payable...............          7.97
    State unemployment taxes payable.................         71.74
```

THE BROWN COMPANY

Employee's name_____

Employee's number_____

Date paid_____ 19____

	Hours	Wages
Regular		
Overtime		
Total		

Deductions:

O.A.B. tax _____

U. S. Inc. tax _____

Savings bonds _____

Insurance _____

Total deductions _____

Cash enclosed _____

To meet the requirements of the social security legislation, it is also desirable to keep, for each employee, an individual employment and compensation record, similar to that illustrated on page 469.

To comply with legal requirements, payroll records, with supporting data, should be retained for four years.

Wage payment reports to employees. As previously stated, many employers make reports to employees of payroll deductions at the time of each wage payment.

If wages are paid by check, a stub may be attached to the check and the data may be shown on the stub, as illustrated on page 470.

If wages are paid in cash, the pay envelope may be printed as in the illustration above.

PAYROLL SUMMARY

For the Week Ended August 7, 1953 — Date of Payment August 9, 1953

Employee No.	Income Tax Exemptions	Name	1	2	3	4	5	6	7	Total Hours	Hours Over 40	Hourly Wage Rates Regular	Excess	Wages Regular	Excess	Total	O.A.B.	Income Tax	Hospital Insurance	Net	Check No.
					Hours Worked																
85	1	John Jones	7	8	6	8	7	7		43	3	1 95	9 75	83 85	2 93	86 78	1 30	11 10		74 38	5216
86	3	Frank Brown	7	7	7	7	7	7		42	2	2 15	10 75	90 30	2 15	92 45	1 39	8 10		82 96	5217
														3,128 40	136 80	3,265 20	45 86	881 80		2,837 54	

INDIVIDUAL EMPLOYMENT AND COMPENSATION RECORD

Name ____ *John Jones* ____ Employee No. ____ *85* ____

Address ____ *2913 So. Burns Ave.,* ____ Social Security Acct. No. ____ *325-10-0876* ____

____ *Chicago* ____ Date of Birth ____ *8-17-28* ____

Phone ____ *BA 9-4631* ____

Date Employed ____ *8-1-53* ____

Date of Severance ____

Cause ____

For Week In 1953 Ended	Income Tax Exemptions	Lost Time Hours	Cause	Hours Worked Total	Over-time	Regular Hourly Rate	Total Wages	O.A.B.	Income Tax	Hospital Insurance	Net	Check No.
Aug. 7	1	1	V	43	3	1 95	86 78	1 30	11 10		74 38	5216
14				42	2		83 85	1 26	10 50		72 09	5273

V—Voluntary time off.

PAYROLL CHECK

DETACH BEFORE CASHING CHECK

STATEMENT OF EARNINGS AND DEDUCTIONS FOR EMPLOYEE'S RECORD COVERING PAY PERIOD TO AND INCLUDING DATE SHOWN BELOW

HUDSON & DUTTON
210 S. LA SALLE ST.
CHICAGO, ILL.

DATE _____ 195__

TO

TOTAL WAGES	
OLD AGE BENEFIT	
WITHHOLDING U. S. INCOME TAX	
SAVINGS BONDS	
INSURANCE	
TOTAL DEDUCTIONS	
AMOUNT THIS CHECK	

NO. A 210

HUDSON & DUTTON
210 SOUTH LA SALLE STREET

CHICAGO 4, _____ 195__

PAY TO THE ORDER OF _____

$_____

PAY ROLL

FIDELITY NATIONAL BANK
OF CHICAGO

DOLLARS

HUDSON & DUTTON

BY

APPENDIX 2
Locating Errors

It is impracticable to attempt to state a procedure which can invariably be followed, step by step, in locating errors in the general ledger or in the subsidiary records. Experience is the best guide, but the following suggestions may be helpful.

Checking the general ledger. It is usually advisable to locate any errors in the general ledger before looking for errors in the subsidiary records. Until the general ledger is in balance, there can be no assurance that the controlling accounts are correct. Suppose, for instance, that the general ledger is out of balance and that the accounts receivable ledger is not in agreement with its control; it may be that the Accounts Receivable controlling account is incorrect and that, after the error in that account has been located, the subsidiary ledger and the controlling account will be in agreement.

If the general ledger is out of balance, the following procedure may be followed by the bookkeeper:

(1) Refoot the general ledger trial balance.
(2) See that the ledger balances have been correctly transcribed to the trial balance, watching for errors in amounts, for debit balances entered on the credit side of the trial balance or vice versa, and for ledger balances omitted from the trial balance.
(3) Recompute the ledger balances and refoot the debit and credit sides of the accounts.
(4) Check the postings from the books of original entry to the ledger, watching for errors in amounts and for postings to the wrong side of an account. As mentioned in Chapter 11, entries affecting controlling accounts are sometimes made in books of original entry which do not contain special columns for the controlling accounts affected; the amounts are entered in the General Ledger column and are posted twice: to the controlling account and to the subsidiary ledger. In checking the postings, give special attention to such items to be sure that they have been properly posted.

As each item in a book of original entry is traced to the ledger, place a check mark beside the amount in the book of original entry and also beside the amount in the ledger. After this work has been completed, look for unchecked items in the books of original entry (indicating items which have not been posted), and for unchecked items in the ledger (indicating entries which have been posted twice, or which, for some other reason, do not belong in the ledger).

(5) Refoot the books of original entry. If a book contains debit and credit columns (as in the voucher register, which contains a Vouchers Payable and a General Ledger credit column and numerous debit columns), cross-foot the column totals to see that the sum of the debit column totals is equal to the sum of the credit column totals.

Posting to work sheets. If the procedure described above does not result in locating the error, it may be necessary to post all the entries to work sheets. Using sheets as large as can easily be handled, head up skeleton accounts, thus:

Cash	Accounts Receivable	Notes Receivable

Provide skeleton accounts for all the accounts in the ledger, putting as many accounts as possible on one page, and allowing only as much space as is necessary in each account. Copy into the skeleton accounts all the ledger balances at the beginning of the period; take a trial balance of the skeleton accounts, thus proving that the accounts were in balance at the beginning of the month or the year. Post all the entries from the books of original entry, entering only the reference to the book of original entry and the amount, thus:

Accounts Receivable	
Bal....... 10,000	RS........ 1,090
S......... 30,000	CR....... 27,000
	J......... 1,500

After completing the posting to the work sheets, compute the balance of each work sheet account and compare it with the balance of the corresponding ledger account. If the balance of a work sheet account does not agree with the balance of the corresponding ledger account, compare the entries in the ledger account with the entries in the work sheet account.

This procedure is called *abstracting the books of original entry*, and will often locate an error after all other methods have failed.

Checking the subsidiary ledgers. After the general ledger has been balanced, if a subsidiary ledger does not agree with its control:

(1) It may be tentatively assumed that the general ledger is correct and that the error lies in the subsidiary ledger.

(a) Refoot the schedule of the subsidiary ledger.

(b) See that the balances of the subsidiary ledger accounts have been correctly transcribed from the ledger to the schedule, watching for errors in amounts and for balances omitted from the schedule. In some cases, subsidiary ledgers which normally contain only debit balances (as the accounts receivable ledger) have a few credit balances, and ledgers which normally contain only credit balances (as the accounts payable ledger) have a few debit balances; such exceptional balances should be watched for.

(c) Recompute the ledger balances and refoot the two sides of the accounts.

(d) Trace all postings from the books of original entry to the subsidiary ledgers, place check marks beside the entries in the books of original entry and the accounts, and look for unchecked items.

(2) The assumption that the error is in the subsidiary ledger may be incorrect. Suppose, for instance, that a sales book appears as follows:

Sales Book

Date		Name	√	Amount	
19—					
July	3	John Smith.....................	√	500	00
	15	William Brown.................	√	600	00
	29	Fred White....................	√	300	00
				1,500	00
				(10) (501)	

This sales book has been incorrectly footed; the total should be $1,400 instead of $1,500. The error in footing resulted in an excess debit to Accounts Receivable control and a similar excess credit to Sales, and left the general ledger in balance—but incorrect. The subsidiary accounts receivable ledger will not agree with its control; but the error is in the general ledger, notwithstanding the fact that the general ledger is in balance.

Because of such possibilities, all column totals posted to controlling accounts should be refooted.

Checking other subsidiary records. The voucher register is a subsidiary record, but postings are not made to it as they are to a subsidiary accounts receivable or accounts payable ledger. The open or unpaid items consist of those entries which have no notations in the Date Paid column. If the schedule of open items in the voucher register does not agree with the balance of the Vouchers Payable account:

(1) Refoot the Vouchers Payable column to see that the total posted to the controlling account is correct.
(2) See whether there are any debits to Vouchers Payable in the Sundry Accounts column, recording cancellations of vouchers on account of partial payments or other adjustments; if any such debits to Vouchers Payable are found, see that they have been correctly posted.
(3) The cash disbursements book shows the numbers of all paid vouchers; working from the cash disbursements book, see that notations have been made in the Date Paid column for all paid vouchers.
(4) Vouchers are sometimes canceled by the issuance of notes, with entries in the journal or the notes payable register debiting Vouchers Payable and crediting Notes Payable; in such cases, notations should be made in the Date Paid column of the voucher register. See that all such notations have been made.
(5) Other journal entries, such as for purchase returns and allowances, may affect the balance of the Vouchers Payable account; be sure that they were given proper recognition when the schedule of open vouchers was prepared.

The note registers may be subsidiary records; if so, the open items should agree with the balances in the Notes Receivable and Notes Payable accounts. If the notes receivable register is out of agreement with the controlling account:

(1) See that there is an entry in the register for each note received and recorded in the journal (notes received on account) or in the cash disbursements book or voucher register (notes received for money loaned).
(2) See that a notation in the Date Paid column of the register has been made for each note collected (recorded in the cash receipts book) or otherwise canceled (recorded in the journal or elsewhere).

If the notes payable register is out of agreement with its control, similar procedures may be followed.

Expense ledgers or analysis records are also subsidiary records. If they do not agree with their controls:

(1) Refoot the summaries prepared at the end of the month, or recompute the balances of the accounts (if accounts are kept).

(2) Check all postings from the voucher register (or from the vouchers, if postings are made from the vouchers) and watch particularly for charges or credits to expense controls from other books, seeing that entries have also been made in the subsidiary records. For instance, depreciation charges will be recorded in the journal, expense adjustments may also be made in the journal, and refunds credited to expense accounts may be recorded in the cash receipts book.

Special tests. Certain special tests may be applied in locating errors in the general ledger or in finding differences between the subsidiary ledgers and the controls. These tests, which are illustrated below, may be applied before beginning the routine already described.

(1) Determine the exact difference to be located; for instance, assume that the debit total of the general ledger trial balance is $50,200 and that the credit total is $50,000; the difference is $200—too little credit or too much debit.

    (a) Look for a credit balance of $200 in the ledger; it may have been omitted from the trial balance.

    (b) Look for a $200 error in transcribing the balances from the ledger accounts; for instance, a debit balance of $2,000 entered in the trial balance as $2,200, or a credit balance of $2,200 entered in the trial balance as $2,000.

    (c) Look for an entry of $200 in the books of original entry; if it is a credit, it may not have been posted; if it is a debit, it may have been posted twice.

(2) Treating a debit as a credit (or vice versa) either in posting or in transferring balances to the trial balance will produce a trial balance difference of twice the amount of the item incorrectly treated. Therefore, divide the trial balance difference by two; in the foregoing illustration,

the quotient will be $100. Since we have too much debit (or too little credit):

(a) Look for a credit balance of $100 in the ledger and see whether it may have been entered on the debit side of the trial balance.

(b) Look for a credit entry of $100 in the books of original entry and see if it may have been posted to the debit side of the ledger.

(3) Transpositions of figures (for instance, $78.50 posted as $75.80) are errors frequently and easily made; they should be constantly guarded against and may be sought for if the books are out of balance. A transposition of two figures will produce an error of an amount exactly divisible by nine; if the transposed figures are in adjacent decimal positions, the significant figure of the quotient after dividing by nine will be the difference between the figures transposed; and the decimal position of this significant figure will be that of the right of the two numbers transposed.

As an illustration:

An entry of...	$78.50
Posted as...	75.80
Will cause a difference of..	$ 2.70
Dividing this difference by 9 will produce a quotient of........	.30

Since the difference ($2.70) is exactly divisible by 9, a transposition is indicated; the difference between the figures transposed appears to be 3; and these figures appear to be in the dimes column and the column at its left. Hence we may look for items (ledger balances or entries) where the difference between the two figures in the dimes and dollars places is 3, as in the number $78.50.

As another illustration:

An entry of...	$613.50
Posted as...	163.50
Will produce a difference of..	$450.00
The quotient after dividing by 9 is................................	50.00

Suggesting a transposition (in the tens and hundreds columns) of two figures with a difference of 5.

These special tests for transpositions are sometimes helpful in locating errors, but the other methods described are more likely to be effective.

Correcting errors. Erasures in accounting books should be avoided, since they tend to discredit the records. Corrections should be made by drawing a line through the incorrect entry and making the correct entry above it, or by a journal entry, thus:

```
Machinery and equipment........................  500.00
     Buildings...................................         500.00
To correct improper posting of voucher register entry
of June 15.   Debit was posted to Buildings account;
should have been posted to Machinery and Equip-
ment.
```

APPENDIX 3

Preparation of Monthly Statements When Books Are Closed Annually

On pages 480 and 481 are working papers prepared at the end of January, 1954. The books of the company were closed on the preceding December 31. They were not closed on January 31. Therefore, in the February 28, 1954 working papers (pages 482 and 483),

The Inventory account balance shows the amount of the inventory on December 31.

The Earned Surplus account balance shows the balance on December 31.

The balances of the income and expense accounts show results of operations for the two months ended February 28.

The asset and liability account balances show assets (other than inventory) and liabilities at the end of February.

If it is desired to prepare statements for the two months ended February 28, the working papers can be prepared in the manner with which you are already familiar.

However, if it is desired to prepare operating statements for February, the account balances will not show operating results for that month, and it will be necessary to deduct January 31 balances of operating accounts from February 28 balances to determine the changes in the account balances during February. Refer to the working papers on pages 482 and 483 and observe the following:

The trial balances after adjustment, on January 31 and February 28, are entered in the first two pairs of columns.

The balances in the income and expense accounts (beginning with Sales and ending with Federal Income Tax) on January 31 are deducted from the balances on February 28, and the differences (resulting from February transactions) are extended to the February Profit and Loss columns.

The inventory on December 31 is not extended to any column.

The inventory at the end of January (which was shown in the January working papers) is entered in the Profit and Loss debit column; and the inventory at the end of February is entered in the Profit and Loss credit and the Balance Sheet debit columns.

The balance in the Profit and Loss columns then shows the net income for February. This is entered as a balancing figure in the Profit and Loss debit column and is extended to the Earned Surplus credit column.

The balance of the Earned Surplus account as of December 31 is entered in the Earned Surplus credit column. The net income for January, shown by the working papers for that month, is also entered in the Earned Surplus credit column. The balance of the Earned Surplus columns then shows the surplus at the end of February; the amount is entered in the Earned Surplus debit column as a balancing figure, and is extended to the Balance Sheet credit column.

The February 28 balances in the asset, liability, and capital stock accounts are extended to the Balance Sheet columns, and these columns are footed.

The statements for January and February are not shown; they would be prepared from the working papers in the usual manner.

THE BAILEY COMPANY
Working Papers
For the Month of January, 1954

	Trial Balance January 31, 1954 After Adjustments	Profit and Loss	Earned Surplus	Balance Sheet
Cash	3,417.00			3,417.00
Accounts receivable	8,956.00			8,956.00
Reserve for bad debts	460.00			460.00
Notes receivable	3,000.00			3,000.00
Accrued interest receivable	21.00			21.00
Inventory (December 31, 1953)	23,650.00	23,650.00		
Unexpired insurance	180.00			180.00
Land	10,000.00			10,000.00
Buildings	25,000.00			25,000.00
Reserve for depreciation—Buildings	3,083.00			3,083.00
Furniture and fixtures	6,000.00			6,000.00
Reserve for depreciation—Fur. & Fix.	1,050.00			1,050.00
Accounts payable	5,860.00			5,860.00
Notes payable	6,000.00			6,000.00
Accrued interest payable	18.00			18.00
Reserve for federal income tax	800.00			800.00
Capital stock	50,000.00			50,000.00
Earned surplus (December 31, 1953)	10,308.00		10,308.00	

Sales		11,975.00		11,975.00		11,918.00
Returned sales and allowances	212.00		212.00			
Discount on sales	207.00		207.00			
Purchases	6,730.00		6,730.00			
Returned purchases and allowances		115.00		115.00		
Discount on purchases		58.00		58.00		
Freight in	196.00		196.00			
Selling expense (Control)	862.00		862.00			
General expense (Control)	493.00		493.00			
Interest income		15.00		15.00		
Interest expense	18.00		18.00			
Federal income tax	800.00		800.00			
Inventory, January 31, 1954				22,615.00		22,615.00
	89,742.00	89,742.00	34,778.00	34,778.00	11,918.00	11,918.00
Net income for January			1,610.00		1,610.00	
			34,778.00	34,778.00	11,918.00	79,189.00
Earned surplus, January 31, 1954					11,918.00	79,189.00

THE BAILEY COMPANY
Working Papers
For the Month of February, 1954

	Adjusted Trial Balances		Profit and Loss, February	Earned Surplus	Balance Sheet
	January 31, 1954	February 28, 1954			
Cash	3,417.00	5,095.00			5,095.00
Accounts receivable	8,956.00	9,329.00			9,329.00
Reserve for bad debts	460.00	525.00			525.00
Notes receivable	3,000.00	3,000.00			3,000.00
Accrued interest receivable	21.00	36.00			36.00
Inventory (December 31, 1953)	23,650.00	23,650.00			
Unexpired insurance	180.00	165.00			165.00
Land	10,000.00	10,000.00			10,000.00
Buildings	25,000.00	25,000.00			25,000.00
Reserve for depreciation—Buildings	3,083.00	3,166.00			3,166.00
Furniture and fixtures	6,000.00	6,000.00			6,000.00
Reserve for depreciation—Fur. & Fix.	1,050.00	1,100.00			1,100.00
Accounts payable	5,860.00	5,320.00			5,320.00
Notes payable	6,000.00	6,000.00			6,000.00
Accrued interest payable	18.00	46.00			46.00
Reserve for federal income tax	800.00	1,520.00			1,520.00

Account	January Dr	January Cr	February Dr	February Cr	Two Months Dr	Two Months Cr
Capital stock		50,000.00				50,000.00
Earned surplus (December 31, 1953)		10,308.00				10,308.00
Sales		11,975.00		9,865.00		21,840.00
Returned sales and allowances	212.00		175.00		387.00	
Discount on sales	207.00		187.00		394.00	
Purchases	6,730.00		5,840.00		12,570.00	
Returned purchases and allowances		115.00		92.00		207.00
Discount on purchases		58.00		51.00		109.00
Freight in	196.00		111.00		307.00	
Selling expense (Control)	862.00		847.00		1,709.00	
General expense (Control)	493.00		470.00		963.00	
Interest income		15.00		15.00		30.00
Interest expense	18.00		28.00		46.00	
Federal income tax	800.00		720.00		1,520.00	
	89,742.00	89,742.00	100,171.00	100,171.00	32,423.00	32,423.00

Inventories:
January 31 ... 22,615.00
February 28 ... 22,400.00
Net income for February ... 1,430.00
Net income for January ... 1,610.00
Earned surplus, February 28, 1954 ... 13,348.00

	13,348.00	81,025.00
	13,348.00	81,025.00

ASSIGNMENT MATERIAL

ASSIGNMENT MATERIAL

Ruled forms especially adapted to the solutions of all Group A problems are provided in the envelopes of laboratory material accompanying the text.

Journal, ledger, and analysis paper is suitable for solutions to most of the Group B problems. A pad of such paper, as well as some ruled forms more specifically adapted to the solutions of some problems, is available.

If no year is stated in the questions, problems, and practice sets, use the current year.

ASSIGNMENT MATERIAL FOR CHAPTER 1

Questions

1. Define assets, liabilities, and owners' equity.

2. What are the sources of owners' equity?

3. What facts are shown by the heading of a balance sheet?

4. Should the amount receivable from each debtor and the amount payable to each creditor be shown in the balance sheet? Why?

5. Give rules for debiting and crediting: (a) asset accounts; (b) liability accounts; (c) owners' equity accounts.

6. In what way or ways is a trial balance useful?

7. Describe posting.

8. Mention transactions that would cause the changes set forth below:

    (a) Assets increased; owners' equity increased.
    (b) Assets increased; liabilities increased.
    (c) Assets decreased; liabilities decreased.
    (d) Asset total unchanged; liabilities and owners' equity total unchanged.

Problems—Group A

Problem A-1. Prepare a balance sheet for Acme Corporation after each of the following transactions.

1954
May 1—The corporation was organized and $10,000 par value capital stock was issued for cash.

    3—Repair supplies were purchased for $1,000 cash.

    5—The corporation issued $2,000 additional par value stock for cash.

    6—The corporation acquired a tract of land for $5,000, paying $2,000 in cash and promising to pay the remaining $3,000 within thirty days.

Problem A-2. The following transactions relate to the affairs of The Mosher Company, a newly organized corporation.

April 1—$15,000 par value capital stock was issued for cash.

    2—Service parts costing $1,200 were purchased on account from *A B C* Company.

    8—Paid $600 to *A B C* Company to apply on account.

    10—Purchased additional service parts for $500 cash.

    18—Paid the balance owed to *A B C* Company.

    24—Purchased a U. S. Government bond for $1,000.

    30—Acquired land for a building site, paying $3,000 in cash and giving a note payable for $10,000.

Required:

Enter the above transactions in skeleton (T) accounts.

Problem A-3. Enter the following transactions of the *E Z* Company in skeleton (T) accounts.

May   1—$8,000 par value capital stock was issued for cash.
    13—Paid $800 to American Supply Company for service supplies.
    19—Purchased land for $5,000 cash.
    24—Service supplies costing $600 were purchased on account from McVee Corporation.
    27—The land was sold for $5,000 cash.
    29—Additional par value capital stock in the amount of $7,000 was issued for cash.
    31—A larger tract of land was acquired for $9,000 cash.
    31—Paid $300 on account to McVee Corporation.

Problem A-4. The transactions listed below are those of the Smith Do-all Company, which was organized on August 1, 1954. Journalize these transactions and post to ledger accounts. Take a trial balance.

1954
August   1—Capital stock of a par value of $10,000 was issued for cash.
    3—Land was acquired for $3,000 cash.
    5—Repair parts costing $900 were purchased on account from James Brown.
    8—A more suitable piece of land was purchased for $4,000 cash.
    14—The land acquired on August 3 was sold for $3,000. No cash was received on this date. The buyer, R. S. Jones, agreed to pay for the land within ten days.
    18—$900 was paid to James Brown for the repair parts purchased on August 5.
    21—The company received $3,000 from R. S. Jones, the buyer of the land.
    27—Additional repair parts were purchased for $600 cash.
    31—$2,000 was invested in U. S. Government bonds.

Problem A-5. The following chart of accounts is planned for the Arbana Company.

	Account Number
Assets:	
Cash	1
Parts and supplies	10
Land	15
Patent	20
Liabilities:	
General Supply Co	31
Notes payable	35
Owners' equity:	
Capital stock	50

Perform the following: (*a*) Journalize the transactions, (*b*) post to ledger accounts, (*c*) take a trial balance, and (*d*) prepare a balance sheet as of December 31, 1954.

1954
December   3—The company was organized and $20,000 of cash was received for the issuance of the same amount of par value capital stock.

1954

December   5—The company paid $3,000 to an inventor for a patent.

8—Purchased on account from General Supply Co. parts and supplies costing $3,000.

12—Purchased land for $4,500, cash.

16—Paid $1,500 to General Supply Co. to apply on account.

18—Purchased for cash parts and supplies costing $850.

24—Paid the balance owed to General Supply Co.

26—Purchased additional parts and supplies on account from General
Supply Co.; cost, $1,800.

29—Purchased additional land for $6,000, paying $1,000 in cash and
giving a $5,000 note payable for the balance.

Problems— Group B

Problem B-1.   Using the following data, prepare the balance sheet of Pierpont
Service Enterprises as of December 31, 1954.

Cash	$3,000
Accounts payable	2,000
Accounts receivable	1,000
Repair parts	500
Capital stock	4,000
Land	1,500

Problem B-2.   Balance sheets have been prepared for Iowa Company after
each transaction.   From an analysis of the balance sheets, prepare a list of the
transactions that occurred.

IOWA COMPANY
Balance Sheet
November 1, 1953

Assets		Owners' Equity	
Cash	$4,000.00	Capital stock	$4,000.00
	$4,000.00		$4,000.00

IOWA COMPANY
Balance Sheet
November 2, 1953

Assets		Liabilities and Owners' Equity	
Cash	$4,000.00	Liabilities:	
Repair parts	1,000.00	Accounts payable	$1,000.00
		Owners' equity:	
		Capital stock	4,000.00
	$5,000.00		$5,000.00

IOWA COMPANY
Balance Sheet
November 3, 1953

Assets		Liabilities and Owners' Equity	
Cash	$2,000.00	Liabilities:	
Repair parts	1,000.00	Accounts payable	$1,000.00
Land	5,000.00	Notes payable	3,000.00
		Owners' equity:	
		Capital stock	4,000.00
	$8,000.00		$8,000.00

IOWA COMPANY
Balance Sheet
November 4, 1953

Assets		Liabilities and Owners' Equity	
Cash	$1,500.00	Liabilities:	
Repair parts	1,000.00	Accounts payable	$ 500.00
Land	5,000.00	Notes payable	3,000.00
		Owners' equity:	
		Capital stock	4,000.00
	$7,500.00		$7,500.00

IOWA COMPANY
Balance Sheet
November 5, 1953

Assets		Liabilities and Owners' Equity	
Cash	$3,500.00	Liabilities:	
Repair parts	1,000.00	Accounts payable	$ 500.00
Land	5,000.00	Notes payable	3,000.00
		Owners' equity:	
		Capital stock	6,000.00
	$9,500.00		$9,500.00

IOWA COMPANY
Balance Sheet
November 6, 1953

Assets		Liabilities and Owners' Equity	
Cash	$3,000.00	Liabilities:	
Repair parts	1,500.00	Accounts payable	$ 500.00
Land	5,000.00	Notes payable	3,000.00
		Owners' equity:	
		Capital stock	6,000.00
	$9,500.00		$9,500.00

Problem B-3. Record the following transactions in skeleton (T) accounts. Allow five lines for each ledger account.

May 1—O. N. Sterling and R. N. Dunne organized a corporation known as the Midwest Motor Company. Sterling paid in $30,000, Dunne paid in $40,000, and shares of capital stock were issued.

2—Land was bought for use as a used-car lot for $15,000, paid in cash.

3—A small frame building was purchased and moved to the lot to serve as an office building. Cost, $3,500, paid in cash.

4—Automobiles were purchased at auction for $40,000 cash.

5—A building was purchased to serve as a repair shop. The cost was $10,000. $3,000 cash was paid down and the Midwest Motor Company owed the balance of $7,000 to John R. Hicks on account. The land on which the building was located was purchased for an additional $2,000 cash. (Use separate accounts for the building and the land.)

8—Two automobiles costing $2,000 each were traded for service equipment worth $4,000.

May 9—Title to an automobile was transferred to James West, a competitor, at cost, $2,100.   Mr. West did not pay any cash, but agreed to pay the full amount in thirty days.

11—John R. Hicks agreed to accept capital stock in the amount of $7,000 in payment of the amount due him.   The stock was issued.

Problem B-4.   John A. Burke and William R. Hutchins completed the organization of the Good Housekeeping Service Store on June 17, 1954.

Record the following transactions, which occurred during the remainder of June, in a journal, post the entries to a ledger, and take a trial balance.   Allow seven lines for the Cash account and four lines each for all other ledger accounts.

1954
June 17—Capital stock of $35,000 in total was issued to Burke and Hutchins for cash.

18—A building was acquired for $27,000 cash.   The land on which the building was located was purchased for an additional $3,000 cash. (Make two entries and use separate accounts for the building and the land.)

19—Service equipment was purchased from the Whirlaway Company on account for $8,500.

20—Store equipment was purchased for cash in the amount of $3,000.

23—Borrowed $15,000 from the First National Bank, giving a note payable.   (Credit Notes Payable.)

25—Paid $5,000 cash to the Whirlaway Company as part payment on the purchase of June 19.

27—Additional capital stock was issued to John A. Burke for $10,000 cash.

30—Repair parts with a wholesale list price of $18,500 were purchased from the Better View Company for $17,000 cash.   The Better View Company, currently short on storage space, was giving liberal terms in order to move existing inventories.

Problem B-5.   Enter the following transactions occurring during the latter part of March, 1954, in a journal; post to ledger accounts; take a trial balance; and prepare a balance sheet.

March 20—J. B. Webster and A. O. Snyder completed the organization of the Economy Service Company, and each invested $12,500 cash; $25,000 of capital stock was issued.

23—Purchased land for $4,000 cash.

24—Issued additional capital stock to J. R. Derby for $5,000 cash.

25—Service supplies costing $2,000 were purchased from the Dunham Company on account.

30—$5,000 cash was invested in U. S. Treasury notes.

31—Building and land were acquired for $20,000.   A cash payment of $16,000 was made and a mortgage payable was given for the remainder.   The land was valued at $5,000.

31—Land acquired on March 23 was exchanged for service equipment costing $4,000.

31—Paid the Dunham Company $1,200 on account.

31—Additional service supplies were acquired for $800 cash.

ASSIGNMENT MATERIAL FOR CHAPTER 2

Questions

1. How does the trial balance differ from the balance sheet?
2. What is meant by "closing the books"?
3. What is the purpose of closing the books?
4. What accounts are closed to Earned Surplus?
5. What is the function of the Profit and Loss account?
6. What are dividends?
7. Give a rule for debiting and crediting income and expense accounts.
8. What facts appear in the heading of a statement of income and expense? Does the heading of a balance sheet differ in any particular from the heading of a statement of income and expense?
9. What are the rules for the use of dollar signs?
10. What is the purpose of taking a trial balance after closing the books?
11. After the books are closed:

   What classes of accounts have no balances?
   What classes of accounts have balances?

Problems—Group A

Problem A-1. The transactions listed below are those of Landscapers, Incorporated, which was organized on May 1, 1954. Journalize these transactions.

1954
May 1—Capital stock of a par value of $8,000 was issued for cash.
　　2—$100 was paid for the use of office facilities for May.
　　5—A landscaping job was finished today and $250 was collected.
　　6—Paid $60 for materials used on the landscaping job.
　　10—A bill was delivered to O. A. Smith in the amount of $500 for landscaping work completed today. Smith agreed to pay in ten days.
　　11—Paid $90 for materials used on the Smith job.
　　15—Paid wages in the amount of $225.
　　17—Purchased land as a future building site, paying $3,000.
　　19—Received $500 from O. A. Smith for the work completed on May 10.
　　22—A landscaping job was finished today; the bill was $600. The customer, R. J. Blank, promised to pay half of the bill before the end of the month and the balance within thirty days.
　　23—Paid $95 for materials used on the Blank job.
　　27—Received $300 from R. J. Blank.
　　31—Paid wages in the amount of $350.
　　31—Stockholders were paid a dividend of $80.
　　31—Purchased a tractor for $1,000 cash.

Problem A-2. The Ad Corporation was organized on April 1, 1954. The corporation is a service enterprise, prepared to help clients with their advertising programs. The corporation's primary source of income will be from fees. The following transactions occurred during the month of April.

1954
April 1—Par value stock in the amount of $6,000 was issued to the organizers for cash.

3—Office facilities were rented. Rent, for the balance of April, was paid, $195.

6—A bill in the amount of $75 was mailed to The Corner Store for work performed on its advertising program.

8—The Mid-town Drug Company, another client, was billed $225 for work performed on its advertising program.

12—$75 was collected from The Corner Store.

15—Salaries of the corporation's employees for the first half of April were paid, $325.

18—The plans for an extensive advertising campaign for Tri-State Stores were completed. According to the terms of the agreement, the bill, amounting to $600, was to be paid within thirty days from the date of the completion of the plans.

24—Received $100 from Mid-town Drug Company, in part payment of their account.

25—Paid miscellaneous expenses in the amount of $24.75.

29—Submitted a bill to The Corner Store for work performed on its advertising program, $225.

30—Paid salaries for the last half of April, $325.

30—Paid miscellaneous expenses, $75.82.

Required:

(a) Journalize the above transactions.
(b) Post to ledger accounts.
(c) Take a trial balance.

Problem A-3. The following trial balance was taken from the ledger of Moon Corporation, a corporation which was organized on June 1, 1954. Journalize the closing entries.

MOON CORPORATION
Trial Balance
June 30, 1954

Cash	3,302.20	
U. S. Government bonds	1,000.00	
J. R. Richards	532.50	
Installation and repair parts	647.25	
Land	3,000.00	
Brown Supply Company		327.25
Capital stock		8,000.00
Dividends	60.00	
Selling commissions earned		925.00
Miscellaneous expense	185.30	
Office facilities expense	125.00	
Wages expense	400.00	
	9,252.25	9,252.25

Problem A-4. Brown Corporation was organized on January 1, 1954. The trial balance presented below was taken after one month of operations. The accounts are presented in alphabetical order.

BROWN CORPORATION
Trial Balance
January 31, 1954

Black Coal Co.	115.25	
Capital stock		7,000.00
Cash	3,005.00	
Commissions earned		2,100.00
Dividends	140.00	
Land	3,550.00	
Miscellaneous expense	312.25	
O & C Company		228.80
Ohio Corporation		319.20
Rent expense	280.00	
Repair parts on hand	925.50	
Wages expense	1,100.00	
White Company	220.00	
	9,648.00	9,648.00

Required:

(a) Present the January 31, 1954 trial balance in more useful order.
(b) Prepare the statement of income and expense, the statement of earned surplus, and the balance sheet.
(c) Journalize the closing entries.

Problem A-5. The following transactions are those of King Company, a newly organized business, during its first month of operations.

1954
November 1—$4,000 of par value stock was issued for cash.
2—Paid office rent for November, $150.
10—Received $750 in commissions.
12—Paid miscellaneous expenses of $35.65.
20—Received $600 in commissions.
28—Paid miscellaneous expenses of $43.22.
30—Paid salaries for the month, $800.
30—Billed Acme Brokers per agreement for commissions earned during last ten days of November, $650.
30—Paid a dividend, $80.
30—Received a bill for $17.50 from the State Telephone Co. for telephone service for November.

Required:

(a) Journalize the transactions.
(b) Post.
(c) Take a trial balance.
(d) Prepare the statement of income and expense, the statement of earned surplus, and the balance sheet.
(e) Make and post the journal entries necessary to close the books. Rule the income and expense accounts.
(f) Take an after-closing trial balance.

Problems—Group B

Problem B-1. Journalize the following transactions of Borders Company.

1954

August   1—Repair parts costing $1,400 were purchased on account from A. K. Wilson.

10—Paid J. R. Swanson, a creditor, $800 on account.

15—Miscellaneous expenses paid, $300.

17—Paid A. K. Wilson $700 on account.

25—A non-interest-bearing note receivable was accepted from D. R. Meeks, a customer, in lieu of payment on his account. The note was for $600. (Debit Notes Receivable.)

31—Salaries and wages paid in cash for August amounted to $2,500.

31—Paid a cash dividend of $150 to stockholders.

31—Miscellaneous expenses paid, $250.

31—Commissions collected for services performed, $4,000.

Problem B-2. Cascade Laundry, Inc., was organized on November 1, 1954, by E. M. Sowell and R. H. Gregory. Transactions occurring during November are given below. Journalize, post, and take a trial balance.

November   1—Sowell and Gregory each invested $5,000 for capital stock.

1—An agreement was made whereby laundry equipment and facilities were rented on a monthly basis. Rent of $1,100 was paid for November. Cascade assumed responsibility for repairs.

5—Capital stock of $4,000 par value was issued to G. S. Davis for land of equal value.

10—Paid $80 for a newspaper advertisement.

15—Billed City Restaurant $300 and Exclusive Hotel $2,500 for laundry work performed during first half of month.

18—Received bill for $12 from the Electrical Fixit Shop for repairs to equipment.

20—Received $2,000 from the Exclusive Hotel on account.

25—Paid miscellaneous expenses of $60.

30—Billed City Restaurant $400 and Exclusive Hotel $2,600 for laundry work performed during last half of month.

30—Salaries and wages of $3,800 were paid in cash.

30—Invested $6,000 in U. S. Treasury notes.

Problem B-3. Statements of income and expense and earned surplus are given below. Journalize the closing entries as they would appear in the books of the company on July 31.

KOLDAIR FROZEN FOOD LOCKERS, INC.
Statement of Income and Expense
For the Month of July, 1954

Income:		
Locker rentals earned...		$1,650.00
Expenses:		
Salaries expense.....................................	$800.00	
Other expense..	300.00	1,100.00
Net income..		$ 550.00

KOLDAIR FROZEN FOOD LOCKERS, INC.
Statement of Earned Surplus
For the Month of July, 1954

Earned surplus, June 30, 1954	$1,800.00
Add net income for the month—per statement of income and expense	550.00
Total	$2,350.00
Deduct dividends	400.00
Earned surplus, July 31, 1954	$1,950.00

Problem B-4. The balance sheets of the Gem Servicing Company as of October 31, 1954, and November 30, 1954, are given below.

The company earns its income entirely from services performed. Its expenses for the month of November consisted of salaries and wages of $4,000, office expenses of $300, and miscellaneous expenses of $1,700. A cash dividend of $800 was paid in November.

GEM SERVICING COMPANY
Balance Sheet
October 31, 1954

Assets		Liabilities and Owners' Equity	
Cash	$ 5,000.00	Liabilities:	
Accounts receivable	10,400.00	Accounts payable	$ 400.00
		Owners' equity:	
		Capital stock	10,000.00
		Earned surplus	5,000.00
	$15,400.00		$15,400.00

GEM SERVICING COMPANY
Balance Sheet
November 30, 1954

Assets		Liabilities and Owners' Equity	
Cash	$ 4,800.00	Liabilities:	
Accounts receivable	12,000.00	Accounts payable	$ 600.00
		Owners' equity:	
		Capital stock	10,000.00
		Earned surplus	6,200.00
	$16,800.00		$16,800.00

Prepare the statement of income and expense and the statement of earned surplus of the company for the month of November.

Problem B-5. The transactions occurring during June, 1954, in the business of Roofing Repair Company, organized June 1, are given below:

1954
June 1—Issued capital stock for cash, $8,000.

     5—Paid $100 for two days' rental of a derrick and pulley assembly used on a repair job.

  10—Paid $200 for repair materials used on a job.

  17—Collected $1,100 upon completion of roofing repair work.

  22—Purchased repair materials costing $180 on account from O. P. Adams. These materials were used immediately on a job.

  24—Paid cash dividend of $125 to stockholders.

  25—Collected $2,000 for roofing repair work completed on this date.

1954

June 30—Paid salaries and wages of $2,700.

　　　30—Completed roofing repair work for G. B. Armstrong in the amount of $500. Mr. Armstrong promised to pay for the work on July 10.

　　　30—Purchased government bonds for $5,000 cash.

Required: (a) Journalize the transactions; (b) post to ledger accounts; (c) prepare a trial balance; (d) prepare a statement of income and expense, a statement of earned surplus, and a balance sheet; (e) journalize and post closing entries; (f) rule the accounts having no balances; and (g) take an after-closing trial balance.

Suggested account titles are:

Cash	Dividends
G. B. Armstrong	Profit and Loss
Government Bonds	Repair Service Income
O. P. Adams	Salaries and Wages
Capital Stock	Repair Materials Expense
Earned Surplus	Rental Expense

ASSIGNMENT MATERIAL FOR CHAPTER 3

Questions

1. Is the following statement correct? Adjusting entries, since they do not record transactions, are entered directly in the ledger accounts without being journalized.

2. When are adjusting entries made?

3. Does the depreciation expense account balance always equal the balance in the reserve for depreciation account?

4. Discuss the validity of the following statement: The net income of a business equals the increase in its Cash account balance.

5. Depreciation reserves have credit balances. Then why are they not shown on the right side of the balance sheet where other balance sheet accounts with credit balances are shown?

6. Assume that, when an income transaction is being recorded, the accountant is justified in believing that the amount will be earned before the end of the current accounting period, and that he accordingly credits it to an income earned account. Suppose, however, that a delay is experienced, and that, at the end of the current accounting period, a portion of the amount has not been earned. What should the accountant do under such circumstances?

7. Will the column totals of the after-closing trial balance always equal the totals appearing in the balance sheet for the same date?

8. Do accounts with the word *accrued* in their titles appear in the profit and loss statement or the balance sheet?

Problems—Group A

Problem A-1. From the trial balance and other data provided below, prepare adjusting entries for the Blanding Company at the end of operations for the month of March, 1954. The books were closed on February 28, 1954.

BLANDING COMPANY
Trial Balance
March 31, 1954

Cash	2,400.17	
Parts	1,600.50	
Prepaid rent	1,800.00	
Equipment	18,000.00	
Reserve for depreciation—Equipment		6,000.00
Accounts payable		2,300.00
Unearned fee income		3,000.00
Capital stock		10,000.00
Earned surplus		1,621.50
Commissions earned		4,000.00
Salaries and wages expense	3,015.50	
Miscellaneous expense	105.33	
	26,921.50	26,921.50

Data for adjustments:

(1) The equipment had an expected useful life of six years when purchased new.

(2) Parts on hand at the end of March totaled $1,100.50.

(3) Rent expense for March was $200.

(4) Salaries and wages earned by employees but not paid amounted to $105.

(5) Of the balance in the Unearned Fee Income account, $1,500 has not been earned.

(6) No entry had been made to record the rental of equipment by the Blanding Company to J. M. White on March 1. One month's rent of $200 was due. (Credit Rent Income.)

Problem A-2. The trial balance of the ledger of Waring Renovators, Inc., on September 30, 1954, was as follows:

WARING RENOVATORS, INC.
Trial Balance
September 30, 1954

Cash..	1,500.00	
Government bonds.............................	5,000.00	
Prepaid insurance.............................	600.00	
Land..	3,000.00	
Building......................................	12,000.00	
Reserve for depreciation—Building..............		1,500.00
Mortgage payable.............................		6,000.00
Capital stock.................................		12,000.00
Earned surplus................................		1,334.00
Service income................................		4,350.00
Wages expense................................	2,884.00	
Equipment rent expense.......................	200.00	
	25,184.00	25,184.00

Adjustments were required for the following:

(1) The government bonds were acquired on September 1 as an investment, and interest in the amount of $7 has accrued.

(2) On September 1 insurance was prepaid for twelve months.

(3) Depreciation of building for September was $50.

(4) The mortgage was signed on September 15 and accrued interest payable as of September 30 was $15.

(5) Accrued wages payable totaled $95.

(6) On September 29, $150 cash was collected for work to be performed in October. This amount was erroneously credited to the Service Income account; Unearned Service Income should have been credited.

Prepare adjusting entries.

Problem A-3. J. W. Dewing and A. R. Gray completed the organization of the Resort Motels Company on June 1, 1954, and engaged in the following transactions during June.

1954

June 1—Dewing and Gray each paid in $30,000. Capital stock of $60,000 par value was issued.

1—A motel was purchased for $51,000 cash, including land and supplies. The land was valued at $10,000 and the supplies at $1,000. When acquired, the motel was fully occupied by guests who had reserved space for the entire summer season.

June 17—Purchased supplies on account from the Davis Company for $500.

20—Received $2,000 cash for a portion of the land, sold at cost.

30—Laundry expense for the month was $110, paid in cash.

30—Rent earned during June totaled $2,400, all collected in cash on this date.

30—Salaries and wages amounted to $1,400, all paid in cash.

30—A dividend of $200 was paid in cash.

Adjustments were required on June 30 for the following:

(1) Depreciation of motel, $180.
(2) Supplies expense, $300.
(3) Salaries and wages earned by employees but unpaid, $90.
(4) A floor-sanding machine was rented on June 28 at a rate of $10 per day. Three days' rent was unpaid on June 30.

Required:

(a) Journalize the transactions and post.
(b) Take a trial balance.
(c) Journalize and post adjusting entries.
(d) Prepare a statement of income and expense, a statement of earned surplus, and a balance sheet.
(e) Journalize and post closing entries.
(f) Rule ledger accounts having no balances.
(g) Take an after-closing trial balance.

Problem A-4. The after-closing trial balance of the Merriam Company at the end of October, 1954, was as follows:

MERRIAM COMPANY
After-Closing Trial Balance
October 31, 1954

Cash	4,000.00	
Supplies	800.00	
Prepaid rent	1,200.00	
Equipment	15,000.00	
Reserve for depreciation—Equipment		4,500.00
Capital stock		15,000.00
Earned surplus		1,500.00
	21,000.00	21,000.00

Transactions during November were as follows:

1954

November 1—Paid advertising expense of $60 in cash.

8—Issued capital stock for land, $2,000.

15—Purchased supplies costing $400 on account from R. N. Devoe.

18—Billed R. M. Bain $250 for commissions earned.

20—Paid dividend of $150 in cash.

28—Paid R. N. Devoe $200 on account.

30—Collected $4,800 in commissions from a transaction completed today.

30—Salaries expense paid in cash amounted to $950.

The following data were available for adjustments at the end of November:

(1) Rent expense for November was $1,000.
(2) Depreciation of equipment amounted to $1,500.
(3) Supplies used during November totaled $500.
(4) Salaries earned by employees but not paid amounted to $88.

Required: (See note below.)

    (a) Journalize the November transactions and post.
    (b) Take a trial balance.
    (c) Journalize and post adjusting entries.
    (d) Prepare a statement of income and expense, a statement of earned surplus, and a balance sheet.
    (e) Journalize and post closing entries.
    (f) Rule ledger accounts having no balances.
    (g) Take an after-closing trial balance.

Note. Students using the forms prepared for the solution of the "A" problems will find the after-closing balances as of October 31, 1954, entered in the appropriate ledger accounts.

For those students not using the prepared forms, it will be necessary to enter the after-closing balances as of October 31, 1954, in appropriate ledger accounts. An example showing how this should be accomplished is given below:

Cash   No. 1

1954				
Oct.	31	Balance	4,000 00	

Problems—Group B

Problem B-1. The trial balance of the Libby Printing Company at the end of October, 1954, was as follows:

LIBBY PRINTING COMPANY
Trial Balance
October 31, 1954

Cash	500.00	
Supplies	700.00	
Mortgage receivable	2,000.00	
Land	2,500.00	
Building	10,000.00	
Reserve for depreciation—Building		500.00
Accounts payable		300.00
Capital stock		10,000.00
Earned surplus		3,900.00
Printing service income		4,000.00
General expenses	2,500.00	
Selling expenses	500.00	
	18,700.00	18,700.00

Supplementary data:

(1) Depreciation of building, $10.
(2) Supplies used during month, $350.
(3) Wages accrued at end of month, $75.

(4) The mortgage was received on October 15.   Interest accrued for the half-month, $6.67.

(5) A section of the building was rented on October 10 to L. R. Smith. Smith owed $90 rent on October 31.

Prepare adjusting entries.

Problem B-2.   Prepare adjusting entries from the following information pertaining to the accounts of the Larry Motor Freight Lines at the end of June, 1954:

(1) Accrued wages payable, $350.

(2) Depreciation of trucks and vans during June, $1,600.

(3) Accrued interest on U. S. Government bonds owned, $110.

(4) Two-year insurance coverage was purchased on June 1 for $480 and entered as an asset.

(5) A tow truck was rented during June from the Wescott Company at the rate of fifteen cents a mile.   This truck was driven 1500 miles during the month and no rental had been paid as of June 30.

(6) Supplies used during June totaled $970.

(7) On June 1 a trailer was rented to the Gilbert Company for a two-month period at a rate of $200 per month.   No cash had been received as of June 30 and no entry had been made.

(8) Accrued interest payable, $20.

Problem B-3.   The Hammond Plumbing Company, engaged in inspection and repair work only, has been in business several years.   It closes its books on December 31.   The company's trial balance at the end of the year 1954 was:

HAMMOND PLUMBING COMPANY
Trial Balance
December 31, 1954

Cash...	1,200.00	
Note receivable.............................	1,000.00	
Prepaid insurance...........................	800.00	
Land..	7,300.00	
Building....................................	14,400.00	
Reserve for depreciation—Building..............		2,160.00
Automotive equipment.........................	5,000.00	
Reserve for depreciation—Automotive equipment.		1,000.00
Accounts payable.............................		300.00
Unearned inspection income...................		6,000.00
Capital stock................................		15,000.00
Earned surplus...............................		3,290.00
Dividends....................................	2,000.00	
Repair service income........................		13,250.00
Salaries and wages expense...................	8,000.00	
Miscellaneous expense........................	1,300.00	
	41,000.00	41,000.00

The building had an expected useful life of twenty years when new, and the automotive equipment an expected life of five years when new.   The accrued interest on the note receivable amounted to $5 as of December 31, 1954.   The insurance coverage was acquired on January 1, 1954, and the policy was effective for two years.   Half of the balance in the Unearned Inspection Income account had been earned on December 31.

Prepare adjusting and closing entries.

Problem B-4. The trial balance given below was taken from the ledger of the Willet Company before adjusting entries were posted at the end of operations for the year 1954.

WILLET COMPANY
Trial Balance
December 31, 1954

Cash	800.00	
Notes receivable	2,500.00	
Supplies	750.00	
Land	3,000.00	
Building	18,000.00	
Reserve for depreciation—Building		2,160.00
Unearned service income		3,500.00
Mortgage payable		5,000.00
Capital stock		10,000.00
Earned surplus		2,590.00
Commissions income		9,000.00
Salaries and wages expense	6,500.00	
Miscellaneous expense	700.00	
	32,250.00	32,250.00

The following adjusted trial balance was taken from the ledger after adjusting entries had been posted but before closing entries were recorded.

WILLET COMPANY
Adjusted Trial Balance
December 31, 1954

Cash	800.00	
Notes receivable	2,500.00	
Accrued interest receivable	12.50	
Supplies	275.00	
Land	3,000.00	
Building	18,000.00	
Reserve for depreciation—Building		2,880.00
Accrued interest payable		100.00
Salaries and wages payable		100.00
Unearned service income		700.00
Mortgage payable		5,000.00
Capital stock		10,000.00
Earned surplus		2,590.00
Commissions income		9,000.00
Salaries and wages expense	6,600.00	
Miscellaneous expense	700.00	
Interest income		12.50
Supplies expense	475.00	
Depreciation of building	720.00	
Service income		2,800.00
Interest expense	100.00	
	33,182.50	33,182.50

Make the adjusting entries which were entered in the journal of the Willet Company at the end of 1954.

Problem B-5. Statements of the Whittaker Company are presented below:

WHITTAKER COMPANY
Statement of Income and Expense
For the Month of January, 1954

Income:

Commissions income	$6,200.00	
Service income	1,800.00	$8,000.00

Expenses:

Salaries and wages expense	$5,900.00	
Supplies expense	800.00	
Depreciation of service equipment	167.00	
Rent expense	150.00	7,017.00
Net income		$ 983.00

WHITTAKER COMPANY
Statement of Earned Surplus
For the Month of January, 1954

Earned surplus, December 31, 1953	$ 650.00
Add net income for January, 1954—per statement of income and expense	983.00
Total	$1,633.00
Deduct dividends	250.00
Earned surplus, January 31, 1954	$1,383.00

WHITTAKER COMPANY
Balance Sheet
January 31, 1954

Assets			Liabilities and Owners' Equity	
Cash		$ 1,200.00	Liabilities:	
Supplies		100.00	Accrued salaries and wages	$ 200.00
Servicing equipment	$16,000.00		Accrued rent payable	150.00
Less reserve for depreciation	4,167.00	11,833.00	Unearned service income	1,400.00
			Owners' equity:	
			Capital stock	10,000.00
			Earned surplus	1,383.00
		$13,133.00		$13,133.00

The data from which adjusting entries were made before the above statements were prepared are summarized below:

(1) Supplies used during January, $800.
(2) Depreciation of servicing equipment, $167.
(3) Of the unearned service income, $1,800 was earned during January.
(4) Salaries and wages earned by employees but unpaid on January 31, $200.
(5) Rent payable for use of building during January, $150.

Required: Reconstruct the January 31, 1954 trial balance of the ledger of the Whittaker Company before adjusting entries were made.

ASSIGNMENT MATERIAL FOR CHAPTER 4

Questions

1. What are working papers?

2. Is it always desirable to prepare working papers before preparing the financial statements?

3. After entering the account balances in the Adjusted Trial Balance columns of the working papers, to what column would you extend the balance of each of the following accounts?

> Capital stock.
> Income from services.
> Prepaid insurance.
> Dividends.
> William Hill (an account receivable).
> Salaries expense.
> Accrued interest receivable.
> Unearned rent income.

4. In what columns is the net income entered in the working papers?

5. In what columns is the earned surplus entered in the working papers?

6. Give the sequence of procedures for the accounting cycle.

7. Describe the type or types of debit entries that normally will appear in an accrued expense payable account.

8. Are accrued receivable and payable accounts ever closed?

Problems—Group A

Problem A-1. A trial balance after the journal entries for the August transactions had been posted was as follows:

FIELDING BALER COMPANY
Trial Balance
August 31, 1954

Cash	4,800.00	
Prepaid insurance	1,000.00	
Prepaid rent	4,000.00	
Equipment	24,000.00	
Reserve for depreciation—Equipment		4,800.00
J. K. Morten		875.00
Capital stock		21,000.00
Earned surplus		4,825.00
Dividends	500.00	
Service income		9,800.00
Salaries expense	6,000.00	
Miscellaneous expense	1,000.00	
	41,300.00	41,300.00

Adjustments were required as follows:

(1) Insurance expense for August, $188.50.
(2) The equipment had an expected useful life of five years when new.
(3) Prepaid rent on August 31 was $3,150.35.
(4) Accrued salaries payable, $115.08.

Prepare working papers.

Problem A-2.   The trial balance of the Oil Well Servicing Company at the end of the calendar year 1954 was as follows:

OIL WELL SERVICING COMPANY

Trial Balance

December 31, 1954

Cash................................	5,700.00	
U. S. Treasury notes....................	30,000.00	
Chemicals.............................	200,000.00	
Prepaid insurance......................	3,200.00	
Land.................................	9,000.00	
Building..............................	50,000.00	
Reserve for depreciation—Building........		10,000.00
Equipment............................	560,000.00	
Reserve for depreciation—Equipment......		105,200.00
Note payable..........................		18,000.00
Capital stock..........................		400,000.00
Earned surplus.........................		27,700.00
Dividends.............................	30,000.00	
Oil-well servicing income.................		775,000.00
Salaries expense.......................	440,000.00	
Gasoline and oil.......................	8,000.00	
	1,335,900.00	1,335,900.00

Adjusting data at the end of the year comprised the following:

(1) The treasury notes were purchased in November. Interest of $85 has accrued.
(2) Chemicals used during the year, $180,000.
(3) Insurance expense for the year, $2,600.
(4) The building had an expected useful life when new of twenty-five years; the equipment, an expected life of ten years.
(5) The note payable was given on December 1. Interest accrued for one month amounts to $90.

Prepare working papers.

Problem A-3.   The organization of Excavators, Inc., was completed on April 1, 1954. The following transactions occurred during the first month of operations:

1954
April 1—Issued $90,000 par value capital stock to W. J. Jenness and T. J.
        Wagner for cash.
       1—Equipment with an expected useful life of five years and costing
        $80,000 was purchased for cash.
      15—Rent was paid for the use of land and building from April 15, 1954 to
        April 15, 1955, $1,800.
      19—Paid repair expense on equipment, $170.85.
      23—Received bill from W. K. Alexander for supplies which had been used
        on jobs, $217.15.

1954
April 28—Paid dividend of $800.
      30—Paid salaries and wages of $6,112.18 for the month.
      30—Completed an excavation contract for Downing Corporation, earning
$10,014.22 from the job.   Of this amount, $6,000 was collected in
cash and the Downing Corporation has agreed to pay the balance
within thirty days.

Adjustments were required, in addition to those indicated above, as follows:

(1) Accrued salaries and wages, $104.80.
(2) Unreimbursed traveling expenses, paid from personal funds by an officer
of Excavators, Inc. while negotiating for one of the jobs completed in April,
amounted to $125.30.   (Credit Traveling Expenses Payable.)

Required:

(a) Journalize transactions and post to ledger accounts.
(b) Take a trial balance.
(c) Prepare working papers.
(d) Prepare statements.
(e) Make and post journal entries for adjustments.
(f) Make and post journal entries to close the books.
(g) Rule ledger accounts having no balances.
(h) Take an after-closing trial balance.

Problem A-4.   Bowlanes Corporation was organized on June 1, 1954, to
acquire and operate a bowling center.   June transactions follow:

1954
June 1—$80,000 par value of capital stock was issued to R. H. Marshall and
          B. W. Chamberlin for cash.
      1—Bowling equipment, building, and land were acquired for $75,000 cash.
          The cost was apportioned as follows:

Bowling equipment	$50,000
Building	20,000
Land	5,000

      5—A bill was received from C. M. Whiting for supplies costing $510.25.
          It is estimated that these supplies will last two months.
     12—Paid advertising expense, $75.
     24—Paid C. M. Whiting $300 on account.
     30—Wages for the month were paid in cash, $2,102.50.
     30—Dividends in the amount of $100 were paid.
     30—During June the bowling facilities were used exclusively by the State
          Bowling Club for a regional tournament.   Bowlanes Corporation
          received $3,720 today from the club for the use of the facilities
          during June.

Adjustments were required as follows:

(1) Bowlanes is required to pay the city an operator's tax of one per cent of
its gross bowling income earned each month.   (Credit Accrued Taxes Payable.)
(2) The bowling equipment has an expected useful life of five years.
(3) The building has an expected useful life of twenty years.
(4) Supplies on hand, $208.70.

Required:

(a) Journalize the transactions and post to ledger accounts.
(b) Take a trial balance.
(c) Prepare working papers.
(d) Prepare a statement of income and expense, a statement of earned surplus, and a balance sheet.
(e) Make and post journal entries for adjustments.
(f) Make and post journal entries to close the books.
(g) Rule ledger accounts having no balances.
(h) Take an after-closing trial balance.

Problems—Group B

Problem B-1. Drive-in Movies, Inc., had the following trial balance at the end of August, 1954:

DRIVE-IN MOVIES, INC.
Trial Balance
August 31, 1954

Cash	1,875.00	
Prepaid rent	4,400.00	
Equipment	15,000.00	
Reserve for depreciation—Equipment		2,500.00
Capital stock		10,000.00
Earned surplus		705.45
Dividends	300.00	
Admissions income		11,000.00
Salaries expense	2,630.45	
	24,205.45	24,205.45

Adjustments were required as follows:

(1) Film rental expense amounted to 60% of admissions income. No payments had been made on August rental.
(2) Depreciation of equipment, $250.
(3) Rent expense, $400.
(4) Accrued commissions income on refreshment stand amounted to $75.08 for the month.

Required:

(a) Working papers.
(b) Adjusting entries.
(c) Closing entries.

Problem B-2. The Johnson Company's trial balance as of April 30, 1954, is given on the following page.

Data for adjustments:

(1) Service income in the amount of $1,200 has been earned.
(2) Supplies used during April, $600.
(3) Depreciation of building was $75.
(4) Equipment was rented on April 1. One month's rental was $300 and no payment had been made as of April 30.

Prepare working papers.

JOHNSON COMPANY
Trial Balance
April 30, 1954

Cash..	500.00	
A. B. Hunt.....................................	1,200.00	
Supplies.......................................	750.75	
Land...	4,000.00	
Building.......................................	18,000.00	
Reserve for depreciation—Building.............		5,400.00
R. C. Holt.....................................		1,200.00
Unearned service income.......................		1,600.00
Capital stock..................................		15,000.00
Earned surplus.................................		1,286.58
Dividends......................................	225.00	
Fee income.....................................		6,300.00
Wages expense..................................	6,000.00	
Other expense..................................	110.83	
	30,786.58	30,786.58

Problem B-3. Using the trial balance and the data for adjustments given below, prepare working papers for Bauer Laundry, Inc., for the month of August:

BAUER LAUNDRY, INC.
Trial Balance
August 31, 1954

Cash...	1,520.00	
Note receivable...............................	2,000.00	
Supplies......................................	2,660.00	
Land..	11,000.00	
Building......................................	20,000.00	
Reserve for depreciation—Building.............		12,000.00
Laundry equipment.............................	56,000.00	
Reserve for depreciation—Laundry equipment....		14,000.00
Ebb Soap Company..............................		5,500.00
Capital stock.................................		50,000.00
Earned surplus................................		7,550.00
Dividends.....................................	500.00	
Laundry income................................		9,000.00
Salaries expense..............................	4,220.00	
Advertising expense...........................	150.00	
	98,050.00	98,050.00

Data for adjustments:

(1) Accrued interest on the note receivable, $10.

(2) Supplies costing $625 were on hand.

(3) Depreciation of building was $90, and depreciation of laundry equipment was $583.

(4) Salaries accrued, $60.

(5) On August 1 Barton Delivery Service was engaged at the rate of $30 per day used. The service was employed eight days in August and no payments were made.

Problem B-4. The Rotary Drilling Company was organized on September 1, 1954, to drill for oil on a contract basis. Transactions occurring during September are stated on the following page.

1954

September 1—A. R. Southworth and J. K. Silk each paid in $50,000.   Capital
stock of $100,000 par value was issued to them.

1—Drilling equipment costing $160,000 and having an expected use-
ful life of five years was purchased from the Oil Well Equipment Company. $90,000 cash was paid.

1—Insurance coverage for two years was purchased for $1,440 cash.

5—Received $60,000 as an advance payment on footage to be drilled
for the Mid-State Oil Company.   (Credit Unearned Drilling
Income.)

8—Paid cash for drilling supplies costing $11,000.

17—Paid Oil Well Equipment Company $50,000 on account.

25—Completed a shallow well for the Devonian Production Company at a contract price of $9,000.   Devonian paid $7,500
cash.

30—Paid dividend of $600.

30—Paid salaries and wages for the month, $6,200.

Information for adjustments, in addition to that provided above, was as
follows:

(1) One-sixth of the payment advanced by Mid-State Oil Company had been
earned.

(2) Drilling supplies costing $3,000 were on hand.

Required:

(a) Journalize the transactions and post the journal entries to ledger
accounts.

(b) Take a trial balance.

(c) Prepare working papers.

(d) Prepare a statement of income and expense, a statement of earned
surplus, and a balance sheet.

(e) Make and post journal entries for adjustments.

(f) Make and post journal entries to close the books.

(g) Rule ledger accounts having no balances.

(h) Take an after-closing trial balance.

Problem B-5.   Following is the after-closing trial balance of The Lee Company.

THE LEE COMPANY
After-Closing Trial Balance
December 31, 1953

Cash	3,600.00	
Note receivable	1,200.00	
Accrued interest receivable	30.00	
Prepaid insurance	60.00	
Equipment	18,000.00	
Reserve for depreciation—Equipment		4,500.00
J. A. Mohr		720.00
Accrued rent payable		120.00
Capital stock		16,000.00
Earned surplus		1,550.00
	22,890.00	22,890.00

Journalize the following transactions that occurred during January, 1954.

1954

January   2—Paid $720 to J. A. Mohr.

4—Paid the December, 1953 rent, $120.

7—Collected $1,000 in fees for work completed today.

15—Paid January rent, $120.

20—Collected the note receivable, which matured today, principal and interest amounting to $1,233.

22—Paid wages, $700.

Problem B-6. The after-closing trial balance of Hilldale Corporation appears below.

HILLDALE CORPORATION
After-Closing Trial Balance
December 31, 1953

Cash..	8,900.00	
Accrued rent receivable......................	200.00	
Land..	2,000.00	
Building....................................	7,000.00	
Reserve for depreciation—Building.............		3,500.00
Accrued salaries payable.....................		400.00
Accrued taxes...............................		105.00
Capital stock...............................		12,000.00
Earned surplus..............................		2,095.00
	18,100.00	18,100.00

Journalize the following transactions and adjustments for January, 1954.

1954

January   3—Paid the accrued taxes of $105.

7—Collected $800 in cash for repair services completed today.

11—Paid salaries for the month ending January 10, 1954, $600.

18—Received $900 cash for repair services completed today.

27—Paid miscellaneous expenses, $120.

31—Data for adjustments:

Accrued taxes, $9.

Depreciation, $12.

Accrued salaries, $410.

Repair services performed, not billed, $310.

Accrued rent receivable, $300.

(Storage space in the building is rented for $100 a month. As of January 31, 1954, three months' rent is uncollected.)

ASSIGNMENT MATERIAL FOR CHAPTER 5

Questions

1. How is the gross profit computed?
2. State an alternative heading for the statement of income and expense.
3. Describe the entries normally appearing in the Inventory account.
4. When are entries made in the Cost of Goods Sold account?
5. Are the adjusting and closing entries for a merchandising company using the perpetual inventory method made in the same manner as those for a service enterprise?
6. How does a deficit arise?
7. How is a deficit shown in the balance sheet?
8. If there is a net loss for the period, where will it appear in the working papers?
9. In what ways are the following accounts similar?

> Inventory
> Prepaid insurance

Problems—Group A

Problem A-1. Journalize the following transactions of Central Television Sales Corporation, a newly organized corporation.

1954
July 1—Issued $10,000 par value stock for cash.
     2—Paid rent for July, $110.
     3—Purchased from Wholesale Supply Company, on account, five television sets for $200 each.
     7—Sold one television set for $300 cash.
     8—Paid $40 as commission to the salesman.
    10—Sold a television set for $300 to R. S. Brown on account.
    15—Paid $1,000 to Wholesale Supply Company.
    18—Purchased for cash four television sets for $200 each.
    20—Paid $30 for newspaper advert sing.
    24—Collected $300 from R. S. Brown.
    24—Paid $40 commission to the salesman.
    28—Cash sale of three television sets to Local Hospital for $860.

Problem A-2. The after-closing trial balance of Air Distributors, Inc., is presented on the following page.

The inventory on December 31, 1953, consisted of two airplanes costing $3,500 each.

(a) Journalize the January, 1954 transactions listed after the trial balance on the following page.

AIR DISTRIBUTORS, INC.
After-Closing Trial Balance
December 31, 1953

Cash...	7,105.20	
Inventory.......................................	7,000.00	
Prepaid rent...................................	300.00	
Accrued commissions payable..................		400.00
Accrued taxes.................................		135.80
Capital stock..................................		15,000.00
Earned surplus (Deficit).......................	1,130.60	
	15,535.80	15,535.80

1954

January   2—Sold an airplane and collected cash for the sales price, $4,800.

         5—Purchased from Willow Aircraft Company on account two airplanes costing $3,600 each.

         7—Paid the taxes accrued on December 31, 1953.

     10—One of the salesmen sold the remaining airplane that was on hand December 31, 1953. He collected $4,800 from the customer. He deducted his commission on this sale and the commission owed to him as of December 31, 1953, and turned in $4,000 to the company.

     15—Delivered one of the airplanes acquired from Willow Aircraft Company to a customer and collected the sales price, $4,950.

     18—Paid the amount owed to Willow Aircraft Company.

     31—Purchased from Willow Aircraft Company on account three airplanes costing $3,650 each.

(b) Compute the balance in the Inventory account as of January 31, 1954.

Problem A-3. Following is the trial balance of the Johnson Tractor Sales Company at the end of operations for the month of October, 1953:

JOHNSON TRACTOR SALES COMPANY
Trial Balance
October 31, 1953

Cash......................................	6,000.00	
Inventory.................................	22,000.00	
Prepaid insurance.........................	300.00	
Land......................................	19,000.00	
Building..................................	60,000.00	
Reserve for depreciation—Building...........		18,000.00
Earth-Mover Tractor Company..............		10,000.00
Capital stock.............................		60,000.00
Earned surplus............................		14,600.00
Dividends.................................	3,000.00	
Sales.....................................		61,000.00
Cost of tractors sold......................	43,000.00	
Advertising expense.......................	2,100.00	
Miscellaneous expense.....................	2,200.00	
Salaries and wages expense.................	6,000.00	
	163,600.00	163,600.00

Accrued salaries and wages amount to $400. The building when new had an expected useful life of forty years. Insurance premium unexpired at the end of October is $250.

Prepare adjusting and closing entries as of October 31, 1953, and a profit and loss statement for the month of October, 1953.

Problem A-4. Using the following information, prepare working papers for the year ended June 30, 1954.

ARBORVIEW CORPORATION
Trial Balance
June 30, 1954

Cash..	3,200.00	
U. S. Government bonds......................	5,000.00	
Inventory...................................	9,500.00	
Land..	2,750.00	
Building....................................	9,000.00	
Reserve for depreciation—Building.............		3,000.00
Equipment..................................	2,800.00	
Reserve for depreciation—Equipment............		1,200.00
Accrued taxes...............................		500.00
Capital stock...............................		25,000.00
Earned surplus (Deficit).....................	3,750.00	
Sales.......................................		35,000.00
Cost of goods sold..........................	25,000.00	
Advertising expense.........................	350.00	
Salaries expense............................	2,400.00	
Miscellaneous expense.......................	950.00	
	64,700.00	64,700.00

Depreciation:
  (a) Depreciation of building, $225.
  (b) Depreciation of equipment, $140.
Accrued amounts as of June 30, 1954:
  (c) Accrued interest receivable, $25.
  (d) Accrued salaries, $300.
  (e) Total accrued taxes, $750.

Problem A-5. The following adjusted trial balance was prepared at the end of the company's fiscal year.

PARKSIDE COMPANY
Adjusted Trial Balance
August 31, 1954

Cash..	7,000.00	
A. B. Jones.................................	2,100.00	
R. W. Bird..................................	800.00	
Inventory...................................	4,450.00	
Land..	2,800.00	
Building....................................	10,500.00	
Reserve for depreciation—Building.............		4,800.00
Equipment..................................	4,000.00	
Reserve for depreciation—Equipment............		1,150.00
Accrued salaries payable.....................		75.00
Accrued taxes...............................		150.00
Capital stock...............................		30,000.00
Earned surplus (Deficit).....................	2,765.00	
Sales.......................................		34,000.00
Cost of goods sold..........................	26,000.00	
Salaries expense............................	8,000.00	
Taxes.......................................	900.00	
Advertising.................................	250.00	
Depreciation of building....................	210.00	
Depreciation of equipment...................	400.00	
	70,175.00	70,175.00

Required:

   (a) Profit and loss statement, earned surplus statement, and balance sheet.
   (b) Journal entries to close the books.

Problems—Group B

Problem B-1. Determine the cost of goods purchased by Central Stores, Inc., from the following data:

Inventory at the beginning of the period	$12,113.98
Sales	19,769.40
Sales returns	425.60
Cost of goods sold	12,430.24
Selling commissions	1,976.94
Inventory at end of period	12,498.33

Problem B-2.

TONE COMPANY
Trial Balance
December 31, 1953

Cash	18,000.00	
Accounts receivable	42,400.00	
Notes receivable	22,500.00	
Inventory	55,000.00	
Advertising	6,300.00	
Insurance	2,400.00	
Building	60,000.00	
Reserve for depreciation—Building		5,000.00
Delivery equipment	15,000.00	
Reserve for depreciation—Delivery equipment		5,500.00
Notes payable		15,000.00
Accounts payable		25,000.00
Mortgage payable		25,000.00
Capital stock		100,000.00
Earned surplus		32,000.00
Sales		143,000.00
Cost of goods sold	88,500.00	
Selling expense	20,800.00	
Administrative expense	19,600.00	
	350,500.00	350,500.00

Adjustment information for the year ended December 31, 1953:

Depreciation of building, 4% of cost.
Depreciation of delivery equipment, 20% of cost.
Unexpired insurance, $800.
Advertising paid in advance, $1,350.
Interest accrued on the mortgage, $1,000.
Interest accrued on the notes receivable, $1,350.
Wages payable to office workers amounted to $483 on December 31, 1953.

Required:

Working papers.

Problem B-3. The trial balance on the following page was taken from the books of The Newton Company at the close of business for the year 1954.

THE NEWTON COMPANY
Trial Balance
December 31, 1954

Cash...................................	5,438.00	
Accounts receivable........................	12,720.00	
Inventory.................................	6,500.00	
Materials and supplies.....................	2,250.00	
Prepaid insurance.........................	270.00	
Land......................................	5,000.00	
Buildings.................................	50,000.00	
Allowance for depreciation—Buildings.........		10,000.00
Equipment................................	60,000.00	
Allowance for depreciation—Equipment.......		32,000.00
Accounts payable..........................		4,450.00
Notes payable—5%, due 12/31/57............		16,000.00
Taxes payable.............................		2,520.00
Capital stock.............................		60,000.00
Earned surplus............................		12,500.00
Dividends.................................	3,600.00	
Sales.....................................		138,430.00
Cost of goods sold.........................	82,400.00	
Selling commissions........................	6,900.00	
Delivery expense..........................	2,380.00	
Wages and salaries........................	33,500.00	
Property taxes............................	4,542.00	
Interest expense..........................	400.00	
	275,900.00	275,900.00

The following information was also obtained from the records maintained by The Newton Company.

(1) The building was put into operation on January 1, 1949, and is expected to have a useful life of 25 years from that date.

(2) The equipment is to be depreciated at 20% per year.

(3) A count of the materials and supplies shows $460 as the cost of those on hand.

(4) The insurance policy was purchased on June 30, 1953, and expires on June 30, 1956.

(5) The notes payable bear interest of 5% per year. Interest was last paid on July 1, 1954.

(6) Accrued wages payable amount to $110.

(7) Sales commissions payable are $332.

Required:

Working papers.

Problem B-4. On July 31, 1954, Mr. Sam Teed and Mr. John Tokay received a charter from the State of Wisconsin authorizing the Totee Corporation to issue five hundred shares of $50 par value stock and to engage in the purchase, sale, and servicing of refrigerators and allied products.

1954

August 1—The Totee Corporation issued 300 shares of stock to Mr. Teed upon the investment of $15,000, and 200 shares of stock to Mr. Tokay upon the investment of $10,000.

1—A showroom and warehouse-servicing building was rented from the May Real Estate Agency for $300 per month, payable in advance. The August rent was paid.

1954

August 3—Received, per order, 15 O. K. Specials at an invoice price of $175 each, from the O. K. Cooling Equipment Co.

4—Purchased for cash from Johnstone Hardware Co. tools and light repair equipment for $600. It is expected that these items will last approximately two years.

5—Paid O. K. Cooling Equipment Co. $2,000 on account and ordered $850 worth of service supplies and parts.

6—Sales for the day totaled two O. K. Specials. One was sold for $255 cash installed and the other was sold for $273 on credit to J. B. Stonehue.

8—Supplies and parts ordered on August 5 from O. K. Cooling Equipment Co. were received.

9—Collected $15 for repairs of refrigerators.

10—Billed D. R. Tompkins $28 for general overhaul of his air conditioner.

11—Paid balance owing O. K. Cooling Equipment Co. and ordered 12 O. K. Specials.

12—Paid $48 for newspaper advertising for the week ended August 6.

13—Paid employees' wages for the week, $350.
      Sales for the day: Cash—three units at $255 each.
                         Credit—one unit at $273 to Frank Rae.

15—Collected $15 from J. B. Stonehue.

16—Paid $83 for window posters advertising next week's sale.

17—Received the 12 O. K. Specials ordered on August 11, at an invoice price of $175 each.

18—Collected D. R. Tompkins' account.

19—Billed the Stuart Hotel $818 for general overhaul of its refrigerator system.

20—Paid employees' wages for the week, $350.
      Sales for the day: Cash —four units at $255 each.
                         Credit—one unit at $273, to Henry Peel.
                             —one unit at $273 to H. E. Roberts.

22—Collected $15 from J. B. Stonehue and $15 from Frank Rae.

23—Paid newspaper advertising for the week ended August 13, $63.

24—Cash received for servicing of equipment, $38.

25—Paid O. K. Cooling Equipment Co. $1,000 on account.

26—Paid Local Drayage Co. $180 for deliveries of refrigerators to customers during the first three weeks.

27—Paid employees' wages for the week, $350.
      Sales for the day: Cash—four units at $255 each.

29—Purchased repair parts and supplies for $2,500 cash.

30—Received ten O. K. Specials from O. K. Cooling Equipment Co. at an invoice price of $175 each.
      Paid advertising for the week ended August 20, $105.

31—Paid salaries of $400 each to Mr. Teed and Mr. Tokay.
      Collected $15 each from J. B. Stonehue, Frank Rae, Henry Peel, and H. E. Roberts.

Adjustment data:

(1) The corporation owes $130 for advertising.

(2) The corporation owes one-half week's wages to employees.

(3) The tools and equipment are to be depreciated for one full month. See transaction of August 4.

(4) The cost of supplies and parts used on repair jobs amounted to $438.
(5) Delivery expense incurred but not yet paid amounts to $60.

Required:

(a) Journalize, post, and prepare a trial balance.
(b) Prepare working papers.
(c) Journalize and post the adjusting and closing entries.
(d) Prepare a balance sheet and a profit and loss statement.

ASSIGNMENT MATERIAL FOR CHAPTER 6

Questions

1. State the differences in the bookkeeping procedures between the perpetual inventory method and the periodical inventory method.

2. How is the cost of goods sold determined under the periodical inventory method?

3. Why might an accountant find it convenient to list in the trial balance accounts having no balances?

4. Are adjusting entries affected by the inventory method? Explain.

5. Are the closing entries affected by the inventory method? Explain.

6. Which inventory method is better? Give reasons.

7. The terms of an invoice are: 1/10; n/30. What does this mean?

8. What is meant by internal control?

9. What purpose is served by purchase requisitions?

10. Describe the procedure of checking an invoice for goods purchased.

Problems—Group A

Problem A-1. Journalize the March, 1954 transactions of Motor Sales Company. The management decides to separate engine sales and repair income in the accounts but not to keep a perpetual inventory.

1954
March   1—Issued $10,000 par value stock for $5,000 cash, land valued at $500, and equipment valued at $4,500.
2—Paid March rent, $200.
3—Purchased six factory-rebuilt automobile engines for $68.50 each from Morris Company, on account.
6—Purchased shop supplies for $1,800 cash.
8—Billed A. B. Sneed $100 for one rebuilt engine and $38.75 for repairs on his car.
9—Paid shop wages of $85.
13—Collected $600 for repairs and rebuilding of wrecked car.
15—Billed J. C. Aster $100 for one rebuilt engine and $39.20 for repairs on his car.
    Collected $95 for one rebuilt engine and $30 for repairs on another job.
16—Paid shop wages of $85.
17—Purchased four rebuilt engines for $72.80 each on account from Morris Company and paid for those received on March 3.
20—Truck overhauled for $400 cash.
22—Collected $195 for two rebuilt engines.
23—Paid shop wages of $85.
27—Billed R. P. Cutter $104 for one rebuilt engine and $24.75 for repairs.
30—Paid shop wages of $87.

Problem A-2. The balance sheet of Southhold Company as of December 31, 1953, is presented below:

SOUTHHOLD COMPANY
Balance Sheet
December 31, 1953

Assets		Liabilities and Owners' Equity		
Cash....................	$ 3,471.40	Liabilities:		
Accounts receivable.......	3,562.18	Accounts pay-		
Inventory...............	4,919.20	able........	$4,468.58	
Prepaid insurance........	108.00	Accrued taxes		
		payable.....	1,132.92	$ 5,601.50
		Owners' equity:		
		Capital stock..	$5,000.00	
		Earned surplus	1,459.28	6,459.28
	$12,060.78			$12,060.78

The accounts receivable and accounts payable totals were made up of the following individual accounts:

R. T. Wright...	$	562.18
W. R. Smith...		428.00
X. B. James...		2,572.00
Total accounts receivable............................	$3,562.18	
Double Supply Company...............................	$	468.50
Jones and Jones......................................		950.08
Over Supply Company.................................		3,050.00
Total accounts payable...............................	$4,468.58	

The transactions for the month are presented below.

1954

January 1—Paid month's rent, $250.

4—Sale on account to X. B. James, $310.

6—Paid Double Supply Company $468.50 on account.

9—Cash sales, $215.45.

14—Purchased merchandise from Over Supply Company on account, $612.90.

16—Made payment of $300 on accrued taxes.

18—Cash collected from R. T. Wright on account, $562.18.

20—Sold merchandise on account to R. T. Wright, $448.19.

24—Paid $950.08 owed to Jones and Jones.

27—Cash sales, $448.92.

29—Purchase from Over Supply Company on account, $842.18.

30—Sale on account to W. R. Smith, $562.20.

31—Received $428 from W. R. Smith on account.

A physical count reveals $5,102.95 of merchandise on hand at the close of business this date.

Required:

(a) Journalize the above transactions for January.

(b) Present the Cost of Goods Sold section of the statement of income and expense for January.

Problem A-3.   Using the data below, prepare working papers.

HOLDAND CORPORATION
Trial Balance—December 31, 1954

Cash...	1,562.50	
Notes receivable.............................	2,000.00	
Accounts receivable..........................	5,450.00	
Inventory, December 31, 1953.................	6,000.00	
Supplies......................................	1,570.00	
Furniture and fixtures........................	3,500.00	
Reserve for depreciation—Furniture and fixtures..		800.00
Notes payable................................		3,000.00
Accounts payable.............................		2,250.00
Capital stock................................		8,000.00
Earned surplus...............................		246.00
Sales..		53,000.00
Purchases....................................	34,702.00	
Wages..	8,627.50	
Rent...	2,600.00	
Taxes..	1,214.00	
Interest on notes payable.....................	90.00	
Interest on notes receivable..................		20.00
	67,316.00	67,316.00

Additional information:

(1) Accrued interest receivable, $20.
(2) Supplies on hand, $430.
(3) Depreciation of furniture and fixtures, $262.
(4) Accrued interest payable, $90.
(5) Accrued wages payable, $225.
(6) Accrued taxes, $1,262.
(7) End-of-period inventory, $6,245.

Problem A-4.   From the trial balance and other information given below, prepare working papers and closing entries.

THE BARTON CORPORATION
Trial Balance—June 30, 1954

Cash......................................	4,592.40	
Accounts receivable........................	5,351.20	
Inventory, June 30, 1953....................	7,849.00	
Supplies...................................	2,600.00	
Land......................................	3,500.00	
Building...................................	40,000.00	
Reserve for depreciation—Building...........		4,000.00
Equipment.................................	15,200.00	
Reserve for depreciation—Equipment..........		4,560.00
Mortgage payable—6%......................		10,000.00
Capital stock.............................		30,000.00
Earned surplus.............................		2,566.18
Sales......................................		68,863.22
Purchases..................................	27,219.42	
Advertising expense.........................	3,120.00	
Wages and salaries..........................	9,693.18	
Interest expense............................	600.00	
Taxes......................................	264.20	
	119,989.40	119,989.40

Other information:

  (a) Supplies on hand, $355.
  (b) Equipment depreciation, 10%.
  (c) Building depreciation, 4%.
  (d) Accrued wages payable, $192.63.
  (e) Inventory, June 30, 1954, $7,231.50.

Problems—Group B

Problem B-1. The entries given below were recorded in the journal of Mathews Company for September, 1954. The company uses the perpetual inventory method.

Journal

1954				
Sept.	5	Repairs expense..............................	64 00	
		Cash.......................................		64 00
		Paid cash for repairs to building.		
	10	Inventory....................................	4,800 00	
		Bishop Company........................		4,800 00
		Purchased 8 pumping units on account.		
	14	D. E. Sells.................................	4,000 00	
		Sales......................................		4,000 00
		Sold 5 pumping units on account.		
	14	Cost of goods sold..........................	3,000 00	
		Inventory.................................		3,000 00
		Cost of 5 pumping units transferred from Inventory to Cost of Goods Sold.		
	15	Bishop Company............................	4,000 00	
		Cash.......................................		4,000 00
		Paid on account.		
	17	Supplies....................................	310 40	
		Cash.......................................		310 40
		Purchased supplies for cash.		
	21	Inventory....................................	4,200 00	
		A. N. Mentor............................		4,200 00
		Purchased 7 pumping units on account.		
	26	Cash..	5,600 00	
		Sales......................................		5,600 00
		Sold 7 pumping units for cash.		
	26	Cost of goods sold..........................	4,200 00	
		Inventory.................................		4,200 00
		Cost of 7 pumping units transferred from Inventory to Cost of Goods Sold.		
	30	Dividends...................................	200 00	
		Cash.......................................		200 00
		Paid cash dividend.		

Show how the journal of Mathews Company for September would appear if the company had used the periodical inventory method of accounting instead of the perpetual inventory method.

Problem B-2.

BAKER COMPANY
After-Closing Trial Balance—July 31, 1954

Cash	760.75	
J. E. Dunham	425.60	
Inventory	5,000.00	
Equipment	12,500.00	
Reserve for depreciation—Equipment		4,850.00
C. D. Bain		500.00
Accrued rent payable		150.00
Capital stock		10,000.00
Earned surplus		3,186.35
	18,686.35	18,686.35

The Baker Company sells engine units and uses the perpetual inventory method to account therefor.

Journal entries to record the company's transactions and to adjust and close the books for August, 1954, are given below:

Journal

1954				
August	3	C. D. Bain	100 00	
		Cash		100 00
		Paid on account.		
	10	Inventory	6,000 00	
		J. A. Duncan		6,000 00
		Purchased 15 engine units on account.		
	12	Cash	5,000 00	
		Sales		5,000 00
		Sold 10 engine units for cash.		
	12	Cost of goods sold	4,000 00	
		Inventory		4,000 00
		Cost of 10 engine units sold transferred from Inventory to Cost of Goods Sold.		
	15	Accrued rent payable	150 00	
		Rent expense	150 00	
		Cash		300 00
		Paid rent for one month ending August 15.		
	24	Inventory	5,200 00	
		C. D. Bain		5,200 00
		Purchased 13 engine units on account.		
	27	Johnson Company	6,000 00	
		Sales		6,000 00
		Sold 12 engine units on account.		
	27	Cost of goods sold	4,800 00	
		Inventory		4,800 00
		Cost of 12 engine units sold transferred from Inventory to Cost of Goods Sold.		
	31	Salaries expense	1,194 79	
		Cash		1,194 79
		Paid salaries for month of August.		
	31	Dividends	40 00	
		Cash		40 00
		Paid cash dividend.		

Journal

1954					
August	31	Depreciation expense—Equipment............	230	00	
		Reserve for depreciation—Equipment....			230	00
		Depreciation of equipment for August.			
	31	Rent expense......	150	00	
		Accrued rent payable..................			150	00
		Accrual of rent for last half of August.			
	31	Sales...................................	11,000	00	
		Profit and loss.....................			11,000	00
		To close the income account.			
	31	Profit and loss...........................	10,524	79	
		Cost of goods sold....................			8,800	00
		Salaries expense.....................			1,194	79
		Rent expense.......................			300	00
		Depreciation expense—Equipment........			230	00
		To close the expense accounts.			
	31	Profit and loss...........................	475	21	
		Earned surplus.....................			475	21
		To close the Profit and Loss account.			
	31	Earned surplus...........................	40	00	
		Dividends.........................			40	00
		To close the Dividends account.			

Show how the journal of Baker Company for August would appear if the company had used the periodical inventory method of accounting.

Problem B-3. From the closing entries given below, prepare a statement of income and expense for Perrin Company for October, 1954.

1954					
October	31	Sales...................................	18,750	30	
		Inventory...............................	6,063	10	
		Profit and loss.......................			24,813	40
		To close the Sales account and set up the ending inventory.			
	31	Profit and loss...........................	24,013	60	
		Inventory...........................			7,135	00
		Purchases..........................			16,005	00
		Supplies expense.....................			30	10
		Depreciation expense—Building..........			170	00
		Insurance expense....................			53	60
		Repairs expense......................			140	30
		Salaries expense.....................			479	60
		To close the expense accounts and to remove the beginning inventory from the Inventory account.			
	31	Profit and loss...........................	799	80	
		Earned surplus.....................			799	80
		To close the Profit and Loss account.			
	31	Earned surplus...........................	75	00	
		Dividends.........................			75	00
		To close the Dividends account.			

Problem B-4. Partially completed working papers for The Gilbert Company appear below:

Prepare completed working papers. Essential data, in addition to the information given above, are as follows:

(1) Accrued interest expense, $30.
(2) Accrued interest income, $10.
(3) Accrued rent payable, $1,000.
(4) Inventory, June 30, 1954, $7,000.

THE GILBERT COMPANY
Working Papers
For the Month of June, 1954

	Trial Balance	Adjustments	Income and Expense Statement	Earned Surplus Statement	Balance Sheet
Cash	2,000.00				2,000.00
Note receivable	5,000.00				
Inventory, June 1, 1954					
Prepaid insurance	600.00				550.00
Equipment	30,000.00				30,000.00
Reserve for depreciation— Equipment					5,200.00
Note payable	5,000.00				6,000.00
Capital stock	6,000.00				20,000.00
Earned surplus	20,000.00				
Dividends	6,120.00				
Sales	300.00				
Purchases	30,000.00				
Salaries	4,120.00				
	67,120.00				
Earned surplus, June 30, 1954.				7,430.00	

ASSIGNMENT MATERIAL FOR CHAPTER 7

Questions

1. Define current assets.

2. What is an operating cycle?

3. Define current liabilities.

4. Give the meaning of the following: F.o.b. destination.

5. Distinguish between trade discounts and cash discounts.

6. How should depreciation and bad debt charges be classified in the profit and loss statement?

7. Describe two basic methods of estimating bad debt provisions.

8. Why are accounts receivable not charged to an expense account when they are found to be bad, instead of being charged to a Reserve for Bad Debts?

9. The account receivable of Paul Smith, amounting to $85, is considered worthless. Give the journal entry to write it off.

10. The ledger of *X* Company on July 31, before the books were closed for the month, contained the following data:

Accounts receivable (total)		35,000.00
Reserve for bad debts		800.00
Sales		50,500.00
Returned sales and allowances	500.00	

The $800 in the bad debt reserve is the balance remaining from credits in previous months.

The company provides for bad debt losses by monthly charges of 1% of sales less returns and allowances. Make the July 31 adjustment for bad debts.

What amount will appear in the statement of profit and loss as the bad debt expense for July, and where will it be shown? How will the accounts receivable be shown in the balance sheet for July 31?

11. The ledger of *Y* Company on December 31, before the books were closed for the year, contained the following data:

Accounts receivable (total)	75,000.00
Reserve for bad debts	1,100.00

It was estimated that the total loss to be incurred in collecting the accounts would not exceed $1,750. Make the December 31 adjustment for bad debts.

What amount will appear in the statement of profit and loss as the bad debt expense for the year, and where will it be shown? How will the accounts receivable be shown in the December 31 balance sheet?

12. After year-end adjustments for bad debt losses were made, the ledger of a certain company contained the following data:

Accounts receivable (total)		75,000.00
Reserve for bad debts		2,500.00
Bad debts	1,500.00	

Why is the credit balance of the reserve greater than the debit balance in the Bad Debts account?

In which statement (balance sheet or statement of profit and loss) will the balance of the Reserve for Bad Debts be shown?   In which statement will the balance of the Bad Debts account be shown?

Which account will be closed to Profit and Loss when the books are closed?

13. Describe a system of accounting for sales taxes.

14. Describe a system of accounting for employees' income taxes withheld by the employer.

Problems—Group A

Problem A-1.   Prepare working papers and journal entries to close the books of The Amican Company as of December 31, 1953.

THE AMICAN COMPANY
Trial Balance
December 31, 1953

Cash	9,100.50	
Accounts receivable	11,719.50	
Reserve for bad debts		28.00
Inventory, December 31, 1952	7,320.00	
Equipment	23,000.00	
Reserve for depreciation—Equipment		11,200.00
Accounts payable		14,000.00
Capital stock		15,000.00
Earned surplus		1,052.00
Sales		55,250.00
Returned sales and allowances	250.00	
Discount on sales	50.00	
Purchases	22,190.00	
Returned purchases and allowances		190.00
Discount on purchases		110.00
Freight in	420.00	
Salesmen's salaries	14,500.00	
Advertising expense	480.00	
Rent expense	2,400.00	
Office salaries	4,800.00	
Property taxes	210.00	
Miscellaneous office expense	390.00	
	96,830.00	96,830.00

Other data:

(a) Provision for bad debt losses, $\frac{1}{2}$ of 1% of sales less returns and allowances and cash discount.

(b) The equipment is depreciated at the rate of 8% per annum. $3,000 of the machinery was acquired on June 30, 1953.

(c) Accrued salesmen's salaries, $125.

(d) Unrecorded bill for advertising, $28.

(e) Federal income tax, $3,240.

(f) Inventory, December 31, 1953, $7,545.

Problem A-2. Prepare completed working papers of The Lanrue Company.

Additional information:

(1) Expired insurance, $80.
(2) Bad debt expense, $\frac{1}{2}$ of 1% of gross sales.
(3) Depreciation of equipment and furnishings, 7%.
(4) Accrued rent payable, $300.
(5) Accrued freight out payable, $38.
(6) Inventory, December 31, 1954, $6,395.

THE LANRUE COMPANY
Working Papers
For the Year Ended December 31, 1954

	Trial Balance	Adjustments	Profit and Loss	Earned Surplus	Balance Sheet
Cash	3,211.00				
Accounts receivable	7,940.00				
Reserve for bad debts					
Inventory, December 31, 1953	6,210.00				
Prepaid insurance	160.00				
Equipment and furnishings	11,500.00				
Reserve for depreciation	2,500.00				
Accounts payable	7,450.00				
Capital stock	12,000.00				
Earned surplus	3,000.00				
Dividends	1,200.00				
Sales					
Returned sales and allowances	460.00				
Purchases	48,050.00				
Purchase discounts	480.00				
Returned purchases and allowances	270.00				
Freight in	2,100.00				
Advertising	4,200.00				
Salesmen's salaries	10,500.00				
Freight out	780.00				
Office salaries	6,200.00			4,450.00	
Rent	3,300.00			6,275.00	
	105,811.00	1,948.24	1,948.24		
Net income				3,444.76	

Problem A-3. Following is the summary of the payroll of Acme Corporation for the payroll period ending February 15:

	Gross Pay	O.A.B. Tax Withheld	Income Tax Withheld	Net Pay
Wages................	$4,319.62	$ 64.79	$475.16	$3,779.67
Salaries...............	3,000.00	45.00	360.00	2,595.00
Totals..............	$7,319.62	$109.79	$835.16	$6,374.67

Submit the following journal entries:

(a) To record the liability for wages and salaries and the withholding taxes thereon.

(b) To record the payment of the wages and salaries.

(c) To record the liability for payroll taxes on the employer. The state unemployment insurance tax rate is 2.7%. The federal unemployment insurance tax rate is 0.3%. Assume that all wages and salaries are subject to unemployment insurance taxes.

Problems—Group B

Problem B-1. The ledger of *X Y* Company contains the following data on December 31:

Accounts receivable (total)...................	35,867.80	
Reserve for bad debts........................		918.30
Sales..		421,873.80
Returned sales and allowances................	2,707.00	

(a) Assume that the estimated amount of bad debt losses is $3,000. Give the adjusting entry, and show how the accounts receivable should appear in the balance sheet.

(b) Assume that bad debts, according to past experience, are adequately provided for by making provisions of ½ of 1% of sales less returns and allowances. Give the adjusting entry, and show how the accounts receivable should appear in the balance sheet.

Problem B-2. (a) How would the following items appear in the balance sheet of Zee Company:

Reserve for bad debts.....................................	3,805.50
Accounts receivable......................................	84,689.35

(b) A $315.60 account receivable from D. C. Woods is determined to be uncollectible and is to be written off. Make the journal entry to write off the account and show how the accounts receivable should appear in the balance sheet after such write-off.

Problem B-3. From the following data, determine the purchases made by Block Company: Sales, $18,748.40; selling expenses, $2,173.38; freight in, $983.59; purchase returns, $339.60; sales returns, $340.20; cost of goods sold, $11,960.24; beginning-of-period inventory, $5,984.38; end-of-period inventory, $6,348.87.

Problem B-4. From the following data, determine the discount on purchases taken by Circle Company: Sales, $48,000; purchase returns, $750; selling expenses, $1,800; freight in, $840; reserve for bad debts, $2,000; beginning inventory, $10,400; ending inventory, $9,730; purchases, $35,700; cost of goods sold, $35,780; discount on sales, $900.

Problem B-5. Journalize the following transactions of The Neway Corporation, using the periodical inventory method.

1954
July 1—Purchased merchandise from Andrews Company on account, $1,820; terms, 2/10; n/30.
   3—Sold merchandise to A. E. Smith on account, $100; terms, 1/10; n/30.
   5—Returned to Andrews Company merchandise billed at invoice price of $140.
   7—Sold merchandise to R. A. Roth on account, $230; terms, 1/10; n/30.
   9—Paid Andrews Company the balance owing on the purchase of July 1.
  13—Received a check for $99 from A. E. Smith.
  15—Cash sales, $828.
  17—Paid freight bill on purchases, $23.
  19—Purchased merchandise from White Stores on account; $2,300 list price; trade discounts, 15% and 10%; terms, 3/10; n/30.
  20—R. A. Roth returned merchandise billed to him at $30. The merchandise was defective.
  23—Sold merchandise to B. A. Baker on account, $219; terms, 1/10; n/30.
  28—Paid White Stores in full for purchase of July 19.
  30—R. A. Roth paid his account in full.
  30—B. A. Baker returned defective merchandise billed to him at $45.

Problem B-6. Journalize the following transactions of The Established Corporation, using the periodical inventory method.

1954
April 1—Purchased merchandise from Black Company, $1,600; terms, 2/10; n/30.
   4—Sold merchandise to Robert White on account, $300; terms, 2/10; n/30.
   5—Returned to Black Company merchandise billed at $500.
   6—Wrote off R. R. Lund's account as uncollectible, $75.
   8—Paid Black Company the balance owing on the purchase of April 1.
  13—Received a check from Robert White, $294.
  17—Purchased merchandise from Corner Supply Company on account, $2,000 list price; trade discounts of 10%, 5%, and 5%; terms, 2/10; n/30.
  20—Sold merchandise to John Ames on account, $220; terms, 2/10; n/30.
  24—John Ames returned $50 of the merchandise and received credit therefor.
  25—Paid the amount owing to the Corner Supply Company.
  28—John Ames settled his account by check.

Problem B-7. Using the following data, prepare the adjusting entry for depreciation for the year ending December 31, 1954.

Equipment	
1951	
Jan. 1	10,000.00
1952	
July 1	5,000.00
1954	
April 1	4,000.00
Aug. 15	8,000.00

Reserve for Depreciation—Equipment

1951		
Dec. 31		1,000.00
1952		
Dec. 31		1,250.00
1953		
Dec. 31		1,500.00

Problem B-8. The William Matteson Company operates a retail department store. It employs a total of 50 salesmen and saleswomen at a rate of $1.50 per hour; they work a total of 40 hours per week and are paid weekly.

In addition to the hourly paid sales employees, the company employs four department heads, called buyers, one general sales manager, ten office clerks, and one office manager. All employees other than salespersons are paid a monthly salary as follows:

Buyers..	$300 per month
General manager.................................	500 per month
Office clerks......................................	220 per month
Office manager...................................	400 per month

The store is subject to a state unemployment tax rate of 2.7%.
Compute the employer's federal and state unemployment taxes:

(a) For the first week's hourly payroll.
(b) For the January salary payroll.
(c) For the October salary payroll.
(d) For the December salary payroll.

Assume no turnover in salaried personnel during the year.

Problem B-9. (a) Using the data shown in Problem B-8, compute the old age benefits tax to be withheld from the employees' pay:

(1) For the first week's hourly payroll.
(2) For the January salary payroll.
(3) For the August salary payroll.
(4) For the December salary payroll.

Assume no turnover in salaried personnel during the year.

(b) For each of the four payrolls of part (a) state the amount of old age benefits tax levied on the employer.

Problem B-10. From the following accounts, select those that would appear in the December 31, 1954 balance sheet of Max Corporation and prepare a classified balance sheet.

Cash..	$ 9,702.20
Sales...	94,588.00
Earned surplus, December 31, 1954......	22,318.00
Accounts receivable (total)......................... ...	31,700.50
Discount on purchases............................	555.50
Capital stock.............................	80,000.00
Reserve for bad debts......................	2,004.40
Reserve for depreciation—Equipment....................	3,333.00
Property tax expense...................................	840.00
Mortgage payable—due December 31, 1960..	30,000.00
Accrued taxes.............	785.60
Accrued rent receivable	100.00

Advertising expense	443.70
Accounts payable (total)	7,201.80
Inventory, December 31, 1954	35,740.40
Prepaid insurance	30.30
Accrued salaries	374.60
Land	6,000.00
Equipment	18,744.00
Reserve for depreciation—Building	10,000.00
Depreciation of building	2,000.00
Building	50,000.00
Land (held for future use)	4,000.00

Problem B-11. The following amounts, with the exception of one inventory amount, were taken from the adjusted trial balance of The Americo Corporation. The accounts are listed in alphabetical order. Prepare the adjusted trial balance, with the accounts listed in statement order, and classified statements.

Accounts payable (total)	$ 7,000.00
Accounts receivable (total)	7,080.00
Accrued federal income taxes	6,702.00
Accrued interest receivable	40.00
Accrued wages payable	65.00
Advertising expense	680.00
Advertising materials inventory	30.00
Bad debts	210.00
Building	34,000.00
Capital stock	50,000.00
Cash	5,646.00
Depreciation of building	1,700.00
Depreciation of equipment	1,400.00
Discount on purchases	580.00
Discount on sales	300.00
Dividends	5,000.00
Earned surplus, December 31, 1953	27,611.00
Equipment	26,000.00
Federal income taxes	6,702.00
Freight in	2,000.00
Freight out	960.00
Government bonds (temporary investment)	2,000.00
Insurance expense	70.00
Interest income	210.00
Inventory, December 31, 1953	14,800.00
Inventory, December 31, 1954	13,500.00
Investments (long-term)	4,500.00
Land	3,500.00
Land held for future use	5,000.00
Notes receivable	2,000.00
Office expenses	570.00
Office salaries	3,800.00
Prepaid insurance	160.00
Property taxes	380.00
Purchases	31,000.00
Reserve for bad debts	270.00
Reserve for depreciation—Building	6,000.00
Reserve for depreciation—Equipment	2,700.00
Returned sales and allowances	200.00
Sales	62,000.00
Sales salaries and commissions	2,700.00
Salesmen's traveling expenses	710.00

ASSIGNMENT MATERIAL FOR CHAPTER 8

Questions

1. Name the accounts used to record the following matters:

    (a) Capital investments of:
        (i) An individual proprietor.
        (ii) Partners.
        (iii) Stockholders.
    (b) Withdrawals of profits by:
        (i) An individual proprietor.
        (ii) Partners.
        (iii) Stockholders.

2. State the differences in procedure of closing the books of:

    (a) An individual proprietorship.
    (b) A partnership.
    (c) A corporation.

3. James Dudley is in business as an individual proprietor. He takes merchandise from the store for his personal use. The merchandise cost $100 and he has marked it to sell for $150. What entry should be made?

4. What is one of the chief disadvantages of a partnership as compared with a corporation?

5. Name the alternative account titles for the drawing account.

6. How is income tax treated in the financial statements of an individual proprietor?

7. May a partner's drawing account be debited for anything other than a cash withdrawal? For what purpose is his drawing account credited?

8. Are all accounts with partners presented in the net worth section of the balance sheet?

Problems—Group A

Problem A-1. The trial balance (see page 534) for Peter Urban as of June 30, 1955, has been set up on working papers provided in the materials for type A problems. Assume that all year-end adjustments have been made and that the inventory on June 30, 1955, is $35,000.

The capital account of Peter Urban is reproduced below:

Peter Urban, Capital

					1954 July 1	Balance			47,100	00
					1955 May 20	Additional investment	18		10,000	00

PETER URBAN
Trial Balance—June 30, 1955

Cash	10,000.00	
Accounts receivable	20,000.00	
Inventory, June 30, 1954	25,000.00	
Fixtures	15,000.00	
Reserve for depreciation		5,000.00
Accounts payable		8,000.00
Notes payable		2,000.00
Peter Urban, capital		57,100.00
Peter Urban, drawings	12,000.00	
Sales		80,000.00
Purchases	65,000.00	
Returned purchases and allowances		3,000.00
Operating expenses	8,000.00	
Interest expense	100.00	
	155,100.00	155,100.00

Complete the working papers and prepare a statement of profit and loss, a statement of proprietor's capital, a balance sheet, and closing journal entries.

Problem A-2. The following trial balance as of December 31, 1955, has been set up on eight-column working papers in the laboratory material. Complete the working papers; prepare a statement of profit and loss, a statement of proprietor's capital, and a balance sheet. Prepare the journal entries which would be necessary to close the books. Assume that all adjustments have been made.

JAMES MATSON
Trial Balance—December 31, 1955

Cash	13,000.00	
Accounts receivable	25,000.00	
Reserve for bad debts		1,000.00
Inventory, December 31, 1954	15,000.00	
Unexpired insurance	500.00	
Equipment	10,000.00	
Reserve for depreciation		2,000.00
Accounts payable		11,000.00
Accrued interest payable		100.00
Notes payable		5,000.00
James Matson, capital		45,400.00
James Matson, drawings	6,000.00	
Sales		150,000.00
Discount on sales	3,000.00	
Purchases	120,000.00	
Freight in	5,000.00	
Discount on purchases		1,200.00
Selling expenses	12,000.00	
General expenses	6,000.00	
Interest expense	200.00	
	215,700.00	215,700.00

James Matson, Capital

		1955				
		Jan.	1	Balance	25,400	00
		Apr.	3	Additional invest-ment	23 20,000	00

The inventory on December 31, 1955, was $20,000.

Problem A-3. The following trial balance was taken from the books after they were partially closed on December 31, 1955.

ALLMAN AND FERNDON
Trial Balance—December 31, 1955

Cash...	125,000.00	
Notes payable......................................		25,000.00
James Allman, capital (including additional investment of $10,000)..		40,000.00
Henry Ferndon, capital (including additional investment of $8,000)...		30,000.00
James Allman, current..............................	10,000.00	
Henry Ferndon, current.............................	15,000.00	
Profit and loss.....................................		55,000.00
	150,000.00	150,000.00

Prepare journal entries necessary to complete the closing of the books, post, and prepare a statement of partners' capitals.

Problem A-4. C. H. Royce and R. P. Smith prepared the following trial balance after the books were partially closed on June 30, 1955, the end of the accounting year.

ROYCE AND SMITH
Trial Balance—June 30, 1955

Cash...	110,000.00	
R. P. Smith, loan..................................		10,000.00
C. H. Royce, capital (including additional investment of $13,000)..		38,000.00
R. P. Smith, capital...............................		60,000.00
C. H. Royce, personal..............................	3,000.00	
R. P. Smith, personal..............................	5,000.00	
Profit and loss.....................................		10,000.00
	118,000.00	118,000.00

Prepare journal entries needed to complete the closing process, post, and prepare a statement of partners' capitals. The partners have agreed that profits and losses shall be shared as follows: Royce, 50%; Smith, 50%.

Problem A-5. Stanley Judson and Walter Pike, partners, have prepared the following trial balance as of December 31, 1955.

JUDSON AND PIKE
Trial Balance—December 31, 1955

Cash...	10,000.00	
Accounts receivable................................	25,000.00	
Inventory, December 31, 1954......................	50,000.00	
Equipment...	10,000.00	
Reserve for depreciation...........................		2,000.00
Accounts payable..................................		18,000.00
Stanley Judson, capital............................		40,000.00
Walter Pike, capital...............................		45,000.00
Stanley Judson, drawings...........................	6,000.00	
Walter Pike, drawings..............................	5,000.00	
Sales..		90,000.00
Purchases...	75,000.00	
Expenses..	14,000.00	
	195,000.00	195,000.00

The inventory on December 31, 1955, is $69,000. The partners share profits and losses equally. Neither partner made additional investments during 1955. Prepare working papers, statement of profit and loss, statement of partners' capitals, and a balance sheet, and draft the journal entries needed to close the books. The capital accounts are not kept with a fixed balance.

Problem A-6. Following is the trial balance of Abrams and Hicks as of March 31, 1955, the end of their accounting year. Assume that all necessary adjustments have been made. The closing inventory was $15,000.

ABRAMS AND HICKS
Trial Balance
March 31, 1955

Cash.......................................	10,000.00	
Accounts receivable.........................	15,000.00	
Loan receivable—J. H. Hicks.................	5,000.00	
Inventory, March 31, 1954...................	30,000.00	
Accounts payable............................		6,000.00
Loan payable—H. P. Abrams.................		4,000.00
H. P. Abrams, capital.......................		20,000.00
J. H. Hicks, capital........................		25,500.00
H. P. Abrams, personal.....................	3,000.00	
J. H. Hicks, personal......................	2,500.00	
Sales......................................		50,000.00
Returned sales and allowances...............	2,000.00	
Purchases..................................	20,000.00	
Expenses...................................	18,000.00	
	105,500.00	105,500.00

The partners agree to share profits and losses as follows: Abrams, 50%; Hicks, 50%.

The partners' capital accounts are reproduced below:

H. P. Abrams, Capital

				1954 March	31	Balance		20,000	00

J. H. Hicks, Capital

				1954 March	31	Balance		20,500	00
				1955 Jan.	25	Additional investment	6	5,000	00

Complete the working papers and prepare a statement of profit and loss, a statement of partners' capitals, a balance sheet, and the journal entries necessary to close the books.

Problems—Group B

Problem B-1. On page 537 is the trial balance of Adams and Parker on September 30, 1955, the close of their fiscal year, and a reproduction of their capital accounts showing the changes during the year. Prepare journal entries to close the books, a balance sheet, a statement of profit and loss, and a statement of partners' capitals. Assume that no adjustments are necessary. The closing inventory was $25,000.

ADAMS AND PARKER
Trial Balance—September 30, 1955

Cash....................................	13,000.00	
Accounts receivable.......................	12,000.00	
Loan—P. E. Adams.......................	5,000.00	
Inventory, September 30, 1954...............	30,000.00	
Fixtures.................................	15,000.00	
Reserve for depreciation....................		3,000.00
Accounts payable..........................		12,000.00
Notes payable............................		10,000.00
P. E. Adams, capital......................		23,000.00
R. A. Parker, capital......................		33,500.00
P. E. Adams, current......................	7,000.00	
R. A. Parker, current......................	6,000.00	
Sales....................................		80,000.00
Purchases................................	50,000.00	
Returned purchases and allowances...........		2,000.00
Operating expenses........................	25,000.00	
Interest expense..........................	500.00	
	163,500.00	163,500.00

P. E. Adams, Capital

1954				
Oct.	1	Balance		20,000 00
Dec.	15	Additional invest-ment	32	3,000 00

R. A. Parker, Capital

1954				
Oct.	1	Balance		30,000 00
1955				
Feb.	23	Additional invest-ment	41	3,500 00

Problem B-2. James Rogers has the following after-closing trial balance.

JAMES ROGERS
After-Closing Trial Balance
December 31, 1955

Cash.......................................	20,000.00	
Accounts receivable.........................	30,000.00	
Inventory..................................	10,000.00	
Patent.....................................	25,000.00	
Accounts payable...........................		15,000.00
James Rogers, capital.......................		70,000.00
	85,000.00	85,000.00

At this time a new partnership is formed with Thomas Alf. It is intended that the books used by Rogers shall be continued in use. but that, before Alf is admitted, the following changes will be made:

(1) Inventory is to be restated at $11,000.
(2) Patent is to be restated at $15,000.
(3) Goodwill of $5,000 is to be recorded.

After these changes, Alf invests $66,000 cash.

Make the entries that are necessary to record the partnership formation. Prepare a balance sheet immediately after the partnership is organized on December 31, 1955.

Problem B-3.   J. P. Maynard and R. T. Norton decide to form a partnership on May 3, 1955.   Maynard invests the following assets:

Description	Value
Cash	$ 2,000
Accounts receivable	8,000
Notes receivable	1,000
Building	15,000
Total	$26,000

The partnership also assumes certain of Maynard's liabilities, as follows:

Accounts payable	$ 3,000
Notes payable	8,000
Total	$11,000

Norton invests furniture and fixtures valued at $10,000.

It is also decided that Norton's goodwill is worth $5,000, and that this amount should be entered on the books.

Prepare journal entries to record the formation of the partnership and a balance sheet as of May 3, 1955, after the partnership is formed.

Problem B-4.   The Western Corporation has the following trial balance on June 30, 1955, after the books are closed.

WESTERN CORPORATION
After-Closing Trial Balance
June 30, 1955

Cash	75,000.00	
Accounts receivable	25,000.00	
Inventory	40,000.00	
Fixtures	15,000.00	
Accounts payable		20,000.00
Capital stock		100,000.00
Earned surplus		35,000.00
	155,000.00	155,000.00

The entire capital stock is owned by three individuals, as follows:

Peter Roe	40%
Henry Starr	40%
William Tucker	20%

On June 30, 1955, an agreement is reached among the stockholders to terminate the corporation's existence and distribute assets as follows:

(1) Tucker will receive $30,000 cash.
(2) Roe and Starr will continue to operate as a partnership, using the same books as the corporation.
(3) Fixtures will be revalued to $20,000.
(4) Goodwill will be entered on the books at $10,000.

Prepare a balance sheet for Roe and Starr as of June 30, 1955.

ASSIGNMENT MATERIAL FOR CHAPTER 9

Questions

1. What is the maturity of a note dated December 22, 1954, due

    (a) Four months after date?
    (b) 120 days after date?

2. If the maker of a note dishonors it at maturity, the payee should charge it to the maker's account. Why?

3. Why is it unnecessary for the maker of a note to make a similar entry, if he dishonors it, transferring the liability from the Notes Payable account to a personal account with the payee?

4. We sold goods to James Keegan and received a note; the bookkeeper recorded the transaction as follows:

```
Notes receivable.................................  300.00
     Sales......................................             300.00
```

State how you think the transaction should have been recorded, and give your reason.

5. Interpret the following journal entries. (The transactions are unrelated.)

```
(a) Notes receivable........................  1,000.00
        Cash..................................             1,000.00
(b) Cash....................................  5,050.00
        Notes receivable.....................             5,000.00
        Interest income.......................               50.00
(c) Horace Magee............................  2,020.00
        Notes receivable.....................             2,000.00
        Interest income.......................               20.00
(d) Interest expense.........................     30.00
        Accrued interest payable.............                30.00
(e) Notes payable............................  1,500.00
        Notes payable.........................             1,500.00
(f) Cash....................................    990.00
    Prepaid interest expense..................     10.00
        Notes payable.........................             1,000.00
```

6. What is a trade acceptance?

7. Give the sequence of entries on the books of the seller and the purchaser when the terms of sale require the purchaser to accept a time draft for the amount of the invoice.

8. When and for what purpose are the following accounts debited and credited: Accrued Interest Payable and Accrued Interest Receivable?

9. Interpret the following entry:

Interest expense... 5.00
    Prepaid interest expense............................   5.00

Under what circumstances might the following entry be made at the end of an accounting period?

Prepaid interest expense.............................. 12.00
    Interest expense...................................   12.00

Problems—Group A

Problem A-1. Journalize the following transactions in the order in which they are presented. In all interest computations, use 360 days as a year. The company closes its books annually on December 31.

(1a) July 1—Borrowed $5,000 from March and Company on a 30-day, non-interest-bearing note.
(1b) July 31—Paid the above note.
(2a) July 3—Borrowed $5,000 from J. R. Barton on a 30-day, 6% note.
(2b) Aug. 2—Paid the above note and interest.
(3a) July 5—Borrowed $5,000 from the First National Bank by giving them our 30-day, non-interest-bearing note. The bank discounted the note at 6%.
(3b) Aug. 4—Paid the above note.
(4a) July 6—Loaned $1,000 to Ralph Smith on a 60-day, non-interest-bearing note.
(4b) Sept. 4—Smith paid his note due today.
(5a) July 10—Loaned $1,000 to Frank Jones on a 60-day, 6% note.
(5b) Sept. 8—Jones paid his note due today.
(6a) July 7—Loaned John Black $1,000 on a 60-day note. We deducted discount at 6%.
(6b) Sept. 5—Black paid his note due today.
(7a) July 9—Sold merchandise to Frank White on account, $800.
(7b) July 11—White gave us a 30-day, 6% note for the amount of the sale to him on July 9.
(7c) Aug. 10—White paid his note due today.
(8a) July 17—Purchased merchandise on account from Bowen and Company, $1,200.
(8b) July 17—Gave Bowen and Company a 30-day, 6% note for the amount of today's purchase.
(8c) Aug. 16—Paid the above note.
(9a) July 17—Received a 30-day, non-interest-bearing note for $900 from George Whitely to apply on account.
(9b) Aug. 16—Whitely dishonored the note due today.
(10a) Nov. 10—Received a 30-day, 6% note for $500 to apply on the account of Henry Cronk.
(10b) Dec. 10—Cronk dishonored the note due today.
(11a) Jan. 9—Gave Gibbons & Company a 30-day, non-interest-bearing note for $600 to apply on account.
(11b) Feb. 8—Dishonored the note due today to Gibbons & Company.
(12a) Mar. 10—Gave Kelly Brothers a 30-day, 6% note for $500 to apply on account.

(12b) Apr.   9—Dishonored the note due today to Kelly Brothers.

(13a) May   6—Received a 30-day, non-interest-bearing note for $1,500 from Joseph French to apply on account.

(13b) June   5—Received a 30-day, non-interest-bearing note from French in renewal of the note due today.

(14a) June 20—Gave Victor Burton a 30-day, non-interest-bearing note for $2,000 to apply on account.

(14b) July 20—Gave Burton a 30-day, non-interest-bearing note in renewal of the note due him today.

(15a) Aug. 13—Received a 30-day, 5% note for $800 from Louis Clark to apply on account.

(15b) Sept. 12—Clark dishonored his note due today.

(16a) Oct. 18—Gave Charles Norton a 30-day, 4% note for $450 to apply on account.

(16b) Nov. 17—Dishonored the Norton note due today.

(17a) Dec. 11—Received a 45-day, 5% note for $1,500 from Thomas Dutton to apply on account.

(17b) Jan. 25—Collected the interest on the Dutton note, collected $500 on the principal of the note, and received a 45-day, 5% note for the balance.

(18a) Feb.   2—Gave a 20-day, 4% note for $440 to Alvin Webster to apply on account.

(18b) Feb. 22—Paid the interest on the Webster note and $240 of the principal, and gave him a new 20-day, 4% note for the balance.

(19a) July   2—Purchased $900 worth of merchandise from Fall Company; terms, trade acceptance due 30 days after sight. The merchandise was received and the draft was accepted.

(19b) Aug.   1—Dishonored the draft due today.

(19c) Aug. 10—Gave a 4%, 30-day note dated August 1 to cover the dishonored trade acceptance.

(19d) Aug. 31—Paid the note to Fall Company.

(20a) June   5—Sold merchandise to K. F. Willow in the amount of $300; terms, 10-day sight draft.

(20b) June   7—Received accepted draft from K. F. Willow, dated June 6.

(20c) June 16—Received $300 from K. F. Willow.

Problem A-2.   Make journal entries to record the following transactions, and make supplementary entries in note registers. Assume that the books are closed as of December 31.

19—

June 10—Received a 30-day, 6% note dated June 8 for $2,500 from Homer Jones to apply on account.

June 25—Discounted our $4,000, 60-day note payable at the Second State Bank. Discount rate, 6%.

June 28—Our bank notified us that it held a $400, 30-day sight draft drawn on us by Moss Company, with bill of lading attached. We accepted the draft and received the bill of lading from the bank. We presented the bill of lading to the railroad and received the merchandise.

July   2—We drew a $500, 30-day sight draft on S. L. Ost and mailed it today. Ost's account is past due.

July   7—Received $500 from S. L. Ost.

July   8—Homer Jones paid his note in full today.

July 15—Sold merchandise to D. K. Fuller in the amount of $880; terms, 10-day sight draft.

July 17—Received the draft accepted by D. K. Fuller on July 16.

July 23—Received a 60-day, 4% note dated July 22 for $1,000 from Jackson Johnson to apply on account.

July 26—D. K. Fuller dishonored his acceptance.

July 28—Sent Moss Company $400 in payment of our acceptance.

July 30—Received a 30-day, 3% note dated July 26 for $880 from D. K. Fuller to cover the dishonored acceptance.

Aug. 24—Paid Second State Bank for the note due today.

Aug. 29—D. K. Fuller dishonored his note due today.

Problem A-3. Using the following information,

  (a) Journalize the January, 1954 transactions.
  (b) Post to ledger accounts.
  (c) Prepare working papers for the month of January, 1954.
  (d) Prepare financial statements.
  (e) Journalize and post the adjusting and closing entries.
  (f) Prepare an after-closing trial balance.

MIDDLE CORPORATION
After-Closing Trial Balance
December 31, 1953

Cash	3,450.00	
Notes receivable (Balance consists of one 4%, 60-day note from City Supply Co., dated December 1, 1953.)	1,200.00	
Smith Supply Co.	200.00	
Accrued interest receivable	4.00	
Merchandise inventory	5,700.00	
Prepaid rent expense (prepaid for six months)	900.00	
Equipment (Depreciation rate: 10% per annum)	9,000.00	
Reserve for depreciation—Equipment		5,400.00
Notes payable (Balance consists of one 6%, 90-day note to Jarvis Company, dated December 21, 1953.)		6,000.00
Accrued interest payable		10.00
Liability for sales taxes		600.00
Federal income taxes withheld		165.00
Capital stock		9,000.00
Earned surplus (Deficit)	721.00	
	21,175.00	21,175.00

(*Note:* If the student is not using the laboratory material for the A problems, the above balances must be entered in ledger accounts.)

Transactions

1954

Jan. 2—Paid $240 for a two-year fire insurance policy.

  4—Cash sale, $300 plus 3% sales tax.

  5—Purchase from Jones Brothers, Inc., $800; 2/10; n/30.

  8—Paid for advertising, $60.

  10—Sale to Smith Supply Co., $1,100 plus 3% sales tax.
    Remitted the federal income taxes withheld from employees' pay.

  14—Paid amount owing to Jones Brothers, Inc., less discount.

  15—Paid $2,400 for an additional item of equipment.

1954
Jan. 17—Cash sale, $400 plus 3% sales tax.
    20—Collected $200 from Smith Supply Co.
    22—Accepted a 4%, 60-day note for $1,000 from Smith Supply Co. to apply on account.
    25—Discounted at 6% a 60-day, $2,000 non-interest-bearing note with the State Bank.
    28—Paid the December 31, 1953 liability for sales taxes.
    29—Cash purchase, $400.
    30—Collected the amount due from City Supply Co. on its note receivable.
    31—Paid January salaries and recorded payroll taxes thereon. (*Note:* The corporation is not subject to unemployment taxes.)

Data: Gross salaries		$600
O.A.B. taxes withheld	$ 9	
Federal income taxes withheld	105	114
Amount paid		$486

Additional Information

The January 31, 1954 inventory amounts to $5,900.
The Smith Supply Co. account is believed to be fully collectible. All other data necessary for the adjustments are given in the problem.

Problems—Group B

Problem B-1. Journalize the following transactions in the order in which they are presented. In all interest computations, use 360 days as a year. The company closes its books annually on December 31.

(1a) Jan. 2—Loaned $1,600 to Wayne Kasserman on a 30-day, non-interest-bearing note.
(1b) Feb. 1—Kasserman paid the note due today.
(2a) Mar. 10—Borrowed $300 from Andrew Byrnes on a 60-day, non-interest-bearing note.
(2b) May 9—Paid the above note due today.
(3a) Apr. 11—Loaned $700 to Ed Moore on a 30-day, 6% note.
(3b) May 11—Moore paid the note due today.
(4a) Apr. 13—Borrowed $800 from Henry Gilman on a 60-day, 6% note.
(4b) June 12—Paid the note due to Gilman.
(5a) May 17—Borrowed $1,000 from the City National Bank on a 30-day, non-interest-bearing note. The bank deducted discount at 6%.
(5b) June 16—Paid the above note.
(6a) June 14—Loaned $3,600 to Ralph Matus on a 60-day, non-interest-bearing note, deducting discount at 6% and giving him cash for the proceeds.
(6b) Aug. 13—Matus paid the note due today.
(7a) July 7—Purchased a delivery truck from Central Motors Company for $4,000, on account.
(7b) July 7—Gave the Central Motors Company a 60-day, non-interest-bearing note for the cost of the truck.
(7c) Sept. 5—Paid the above note due today.

(8a) Aug. 15—Sold merchandise to Robert Johnston on account, $250.

(8b) Aug. 15—Johnston gave us a 30-day, non-interest-bearing note for amount of today's sale.

(8c) Sept. 14—Johnston paid the above note due today.

(9a) Sept. 8—Received a 45-day note, bearing 6% interest, for $900 from William Martin to apply on his account.

(9b) Oct. 23—Martin paid the above note due today.

(10a) Oct. 18—Gave a 45-day, 5% note for $700 to Alan Ackerman to apply on account.

(10b) Dec. 2—Paid the above note due today.

(11a) Nov. 13—Received a 30-day, non-interest-bearing note for $750 from William Shaw to apply on account.

(11b) Dec. 13—Shaw dishonored the note due today.

(12a) Nov. 3—Gave a 45-day, non-interest-bearing note for $550 to Mel Foerster to apply on account.

(12b) Dec. 18—Dishonored the note due to Foerster today.

(13a) Dec. 11—Received a 60-day, 6% note for $1,800 from Henry Fox to apply on account.

(13b) Feb. 9—Fox dishonored the note due today.

(14a) Dec. 21—Gave a 45-day, 6% note for $1,300 to William O'Donnell to apply on account.

(14b) Feb. 4—Dishonored the note due to O'Donnell today.

(15a) Jan. 4—Received a 30-day, non-interest-bearing note for $400 from Donald Scotton to apply on account.

(15b) Feb. 3—Received a 30-day, non-interest-bearing note from Scotton in renewal of the note due today.

(16a) Mar. 2—Gave a 60-day, non-interest-bearing note for $880 to Henry Hoffman to apply on account.

(16b) May 1—Gave a 60-day, non-interest-bearing note to Hoffman in renewal of the note due to him today.

(17a) Dec. 6—Received a 90-day, 5% note for $4,400 from Joseph Thompson to apply on account.

(17b) Mar. 6—Received the interest and $1,400 on the principal of the note due from Thompson today, and a 60-day, 6% note for the balance.

(18a) Dec. 11—Gave a 45-day, 4% note for $6,300 to Albert Cranston to apply on account.

(18b) Jan. 25—Paid the interest and $3,300 of the principal on the note due to Cranston, and gave him a 30-day, 5% note for the balance.

(18c) Feb. 24—Paid the note due today.

(19a) June 1—Purchased $700 worth of merchandise from Cramer Company; terms, trade acceptance due 45 days after sight. The merchandise was received and the draft was accepted.

(19b) July 15—Issued our check for $700 in payment of acceptance held by Cramer Company.

(20a) Jan. 14—X. P. Henry has owed us $350 for several months. We drew a draft on Henry today, payable to ourselves 15 days after sight, for $350, and mailed it to Henry with a request that he accept it.

(20b) Jan. 16—The accepted draft was received from Henry today. It was accepted under date of January 15.

(20c) Jan. 30—Henry dishonored the acceptance due today.

Problem B-2. Make journal entries to record the following on the books of State Supply Company and Carl Smith.

19__

Aug. 13—State Supply Company sold merchandise to Carl Smith for $240. The terms of sale were bill of lading attached to 15-day sight draft. The goods were shipped today.

     15—Carl Smith accepted the draft and obtained the goods today.

     16—State Supply Company received the accepted draft.

     30—Carl Smith mailed a check for $240 to State Supply Company.

     31—Check from Carl Smith was received today by State Supply Company.

Problem B-3. Make journal entries to record the following on the books of Aviation Supplies Company and those of Smith and White, a partnership operating a flying service.

19__

July   7—Aviation Supplies Company sold supplies to Smith and White for $304.56; terms, trade acceptance due 30 days after date. The goods were shipped today.

     9—Smith and White received the merchandise. The trade acceptance was received, accepted, and returned to Aviation Supplies Company.

     11—Aviation Supplies Company received the acceptance.

Aug.   6—The acceptance was dishonored.

     12—Smith and White sent a 4%, 30-day note dated August 6 to cover the dishonored acceptance.

     13—The note from Smith and White was received by Aviation Supplies Company.

     31—Aviation Supplies Company's fiscal year ended today.

Sept.   4—Smith and White mailed a check to Aviation Supplies Company for the amount due at maturity on the note.

     5—Aviation Supplies Company received the check from Smith and White.

ASSIGNMENT MATERIAL FOR CHAPTER 10

Questions

1. What is the principal advantage of having special columns in the journal?

2. What are some of the advantages of controlling accounts?

3. If controlling accounts are kept, why is it desirable to have special columns for them in the books of original entry?

4. Before posting the column totals of a book of original entry, what should be done to check the correctness of these totals?

5. Why is a check mark used in place of an account number to designate that a posting has been made to a subsidiary ledger?

6. If you were designing a system of accounts, what facts would influence you in deciding what controlling accounts should be used?

7. What is the procedure for proving subsidiary ledgers?

8. If a business used only a two-column journal, would there be any advantage in using controlling accounts?

Problems—Group A

Problem A-1. The account balances of the Tours Grocery on February 1, 1954, follow:

Cash	850.00	
Accounts receivable	1,698.00	
Inventory	4,561.00	
Fixtures	2,800.00	
Reserve for depreciation		450.00
Accounts payable		1,238.00
Capital stock		7,500.00
Earned surplus		721.00
	9,909.00	9,909.00

Accounts Receivable

A. C. Arturo	$ 68.92	R. E. Lowler	$296.44
D. P. Barker	532.20	J. P. Munfort	182.20
W. T. Colman	319.70	W. R. Ormano	218.25
C. F. Jones	72.14	T. F. Tulls	8.15

Accounts Payable

G. G. Wholesale Company	$429.60	Tompkins Products	$138.50
Peters & Sons Company	342.15	Waltham Wholesale Company	327.75

February transactions were as follows:

Feb. 2—Cash sales, $128.00.

4—Collected $532.20 from D. P. Barker.

7—Sale on account to T. F. Tulls, $148.60.

Feb. 9—Paid G. G. Wholesale Company balance of account.
10—Purchase on account from Tompkins Products, $393.20.
12—Cash sales, $362.00.
14—Purchase on account from G. G. Wholesale Company, $368.75.
16—Sale on account to C. F. Jones, $54.80.
18—Sale on account to J. P. Munfort, $73.20.
23—Returned damaged goods to G. G. Wholesale Company, $15.00.
24—Made payments to:
      Peters & Sons Company, $342.15;
      Waltham Wholesale Company, $327.75.
26—Collections from:
      C. F. Jones, $72.14;
      J. P. Munfort, $182.20.
27—Sales on account to:
      W. R. Ormano, $129.40;
      D. P. Barker, $210.50.

Journalize the transactions for February using a 10-column journal; post, using subsidiary ledgers for the accounts receivable and accounts payable.

Problem A-2. Trend Corporation was organized during the latter part of December, 1953, but did not commence operations until January, 1954. The first month's transactions are listed below.

1954
January 2—Issued $10,000 par value stock for $10,000.
               Rented a building, paying $200 for January occupancy.
4—Paid $3,600 for furniture and fixtures.
5—Purchased merchandise from Retail Suppliers for $2,200, paying
      $1,000 in cash.
7—Sale on account to P. T. Smith, $28.
9—Cash sale, $33.
11—Sale on account to R. M. Burforth, $47.
14—Purchased merchandise on account from Loft Corporation, $350.
16—Sale on account to C. F. Toms, $73.
17—Returned merchandise to Retail Suppliers, $65.
19—Purchased a delivery truck from Hanson Company for $2,193, cash.
20—Sale on account to T. P. Ekton, $120.
21—Cash sale, $29.
23—Purchased merchandise on account from R and S Company, $664.
24—Sale on account to A. A. Parker, $79.
25—Paid service station bill for gasoline, $18.
26—Paid Retail Suppliers the balance of account.
27—Sale on account to R. X. Pero, $134.
28—Purchased merchandise on account from RePeto Company, $465.
30—Sale on account to J. P. Younger, $129.
31—Paid salaries, $420.
      Cash sales, $183.

Journalize the above in a 10-column journal and post. The corporation uses an accounts receivable ledger and an accounts payable ledger.

Problem A-3. Post from the journal of Topper Company on pages 548 and 549, and submit a schedule proving the subsidiary ledger as of August 31, 1954.

Journal   Page 28

Date	L.F.	Account	DEBITS Cash	DEBITS Purchases	DEBITS Accounts Receivable	DEBITS Sundry	CREDITS Cash	CREDITS Sales	CREDITS Accounts Receivable	CREDITS Sundry
1954										
Aug. 1		Purchases		270 15						
		Cash					270 15			
		Cash purchase.								
4		J. B. Brown			87 30					
		Sales						87 30		
		Sale on account, 2/10; n/30.								
9		Cash	17 62							
		Sales						17 62		
		Cash sale.								
12		Purchases		187 40						
		National Company								187 40
		Purchase on account.								
14		Cash	85 55							
		Discount on sales				1 75				
		J. B. Brown							87 30	
		Collection of account, less discount.								
19		B. T. Johnson			43 21					
		Sales						43 21		
		Sale on account.								
21		Cash	990 00							
		Prepaid interest expense				10 00				
		Notes payable								1,000 00
		Discounted note at bank.								

Date	Account			
22	Reserve for bad debts	50 00		
	S. V. Werner		50 00	
	Account written off.			
24	S. P. Jones	39 94		39 94
	Sales		39 94	
	Sale on account.			
27	Purchases	187 40		187 40
	National Company		187 40	
	Purchase on account.			
29	National Company	550 00		
	Cash		550 00	
	Payment on account.			
31	Salaries	150 00		
	Cash		150 00	
	Salaries for August.			
31	Rent expense			
	Cash			
	Rent for the month.			

137 17   137 30   188 07   1,157 55   1,324 57

949 15   170 45   594 72   1,093 17

Problems—Group B

Problem B-1. Zulauf Corporation uses controlling accounts and a columnar journal similar to the one illustrated on pages 137 and 138. On July 25, the bookkeeper of Zulauf Corporation made an error in posting a $1,219.72 purchase of merchandise from the Porter Company as $1,217.92. All other postings during the month and those at the end of the month were made correctly. The Zulauf Corporation closes its books monthly.

Required:
   (a) At what stage, if any, of the bookkeeping cycle would the above error be discovered?
   (b) Would this error cause the trial balance as of July 31 to be out of balance? Why?
   (c) How would this error be corrected when discovered?

Problem B-2. From the following information, secured from the company's special-column journal, prepare the Accounts Receivable and the Accounts Payable controlling accounts of the Certified Company in T-account form.

Sales on account	$10,000
Bad debts charged off	100
Purchases on account	16,000
Discount on sales	180
Discount on purchases	120
Purchase returns	200
Cash paid to creditors	4,000
Cash received from customers	5,000
Notes issued to creditors	8,000
Notes received from customers	1,000
Annual adjusting entry to provide for uncollectible accounts	300

Problem B-3. The Short Company uses a 10-column journal and subsidiary ledgers for accounts receivable and accounts payable. The following data are taken from page 11 of its journal and relate to the month of January, 1954.

Column totals:

Debit columns:		
Cash	$5,621.15	
Purchases	3,405.20	
Accounts Receivable	5,707.80	
Accounts Payable	2,000.00	
Sundry	825.00	$17,559.15
Credit columns:		
Cash	$2,825.00	
Sales	6,707.80	
Accounts Receivable	4,321.15	
Accounts Payable	3,405.20	
Sundry	300.00	17,559.15

Column details:

	Date	
Debit columns:		
Accounts Receivable:		
A. J. Brown	Jan. 3	$1,307.80
R. S. Woods	7	2,100.00
T. W. Zan	18	2,300.00
Accounts Payable:		
Winter Wholesale Co.	21	2,000.00

Sundry:

Rent expense...........................	2	200.00
Salaries................................	31	600.00
Advertising expense......................	31	25.00

Credit columns:

Accounts Receivable:

R. S. Woods............................	18	2,100.00
T. W. Zan.............................	30	2,221.15

Accounts Payable:

Winter Wholesale Co......................	8	2,000.00
Hepworth Company......................	28	1,405.20

Sundry:

Notes payable..........................	25	300.00

Show all ledger accounts as they would appear at the end of January after the posting had been completed. Use three-column paper for the subsidiary ledger.

Problem B-4. Smith Enterprises uses an eight-column journal and a subsidiary ledger for accounts payable. The following data are taken from the journal and relate to the operations of the first month, July, 1954.

Column totals:

Debit columns:

Cash..................................	$14,703.00	
Purchases.............................	8,472.00	
Accounts Payable.......................	5,372.00	
Sundry...............................	4,030.00	$32,577.00

Credit columns:

Cash..................................	$ 9,402.00	
Sales.................................	8,703.00	
Accounts Payable.......................	8,472.00	
Sundry...............................	6,000.00	$32,577.00

Column details:

Purchases:

Date	Description	Amount
July 5	Merchandise purchased from Brown Company.............	$1,720.00
8	Merchandise purchased from Red Company...............	980.00
13	Merchandise purchased from White Company.............	2,000.00
17	Merchandise purchased from Brown Company.............	1,372.00
21	Merchandise purchased from Red Company...............	1,300.00
28	Merchandise purchased from Brown Company.............	1,100.00

Accounts Payable:

Date	Description	Amount Debit	Amount Credit
July 5	Brown Company............................		$1,720.00
8	Red Company.............................		980.00
10	Brown Company............................	$1,720.00	
12	Red Company.............................	980.00	
13	White Company............................		2,000.00
17	Brown Company............................		1,372.00
21	Red Company.............................		1,300.00
23	Brown Company............................	1,372.00	
28	Brown Company............................		1,100.00
31	Red Company.............................	1,300.00	

Sundry:

Date	Description	Amount Debit	Credit
July 1	Capital investment by the owner, R. D. Smith...		$5,000.00
2	Paid rent..	$ 150.00	
6	Purchased store equipment.....................	3,000.00	
17	Paid for advertising...........................	80.00	
22	Sales return...................................	100.00	
31	Salaries.......................................	700.00	
31	Borrowed money on a note.....................		1,000.00

Show the ledger accounts as they would appear at the end of July, 1954, after the posting had been completed. Use three-column paper for the subsidiary ledgers.

Prepare a trial balance and a schedule of the subsidiary ledger.

ASSIGNMENT MATERIAL FOR CHAPTER 11

Questions

1. In what two ways do the special books of original entry reduce bookkeeping work?

2. When special books of original entry are used, what entries are made in the general journal?

3. If a business received many notes, do you think it would be desirable to have a special Notes Receivable credit column in the cash receipts book, so that the face of each note collected could be entered in the Notes Receivable column instead of in the Sundry credit column? If you think it would be advantageous, give your reason. If you do not think such a special column would be desirable, state your reason.

4. Assume that a cash receipts book contains a special Accounts Receivable controlling account column; state the procedure for making postings from it.

5. If the journal were not provided with special controlling account columns for Accounts Receivable, and you wished to credit J. S. Smith, a customer, for a note received from him, how would the credit entry be posted?

6. Under what circumstances would you suggest having an Accounts Receivable debit column in the cash disbursements book?

7. Describe the posting procedure where a given transaction must be journalized in two journals.

Problems—Group A

Problem A-1. The Excello Dry Goods Company has been in business for a number of years. On December 31, 1953, the books were closed for the calendar year 1953 and complete financial statements were prepared.

The general and subsidiary ledger accounts and the balances on January 1, 1954, are set up in the ledgers in the accompanying forms. Record the transactions for January, 1954, in the books of original entry listed below.

    (a) General journal.
    (b) Purchase book.
    (c) Sales book.
    (d) Cash receipts journal.
    (e) Cash disbursements journal.

1954

Jan. 2—Paid dividends payable—$1,500.
          Purchased merchandise from Edwin Nugent for $3,000 on account. Invoice dated January 2.
     3—Sold merchandise to Homer Ferris for $3,200. Invoice No. 1063.
          Paid $125 express on merchandise purchased from Nugent.
     4—Received a check from James Altman for $7,350 in full payment of his account. ($7,500 less 2% cash discount.)

553

Jan. 4—Paid Arthur Mooney $1,980 in full of account. ($2,000 less 1% cash discount.)

Bought office supplies for cash, $120.

7—Sold securities for $1,300. These common stocks had cost $1,000 and had been held as a temporary investment.

Recorded and paid weekly sales salaries—$300. Withheld federal income tax of $70 and federal O.A.B. taxes of $4.50. Employers' O.A.B. tax is also $4.50.

8—Sold merchandise to Michael Eldridge for $3,600. Invoice No. 1064.

Returned merchandise costing $300 to Edwin Nugent and received credit on account.

9—Received checks from Peter Davis, Homer Ferris, and Charles Gant in full payment of their January 1 balances less 2% discount.

10—Paid Harry Oren, Robert Quinlan, Alvin Rogers, and Roy Stanton in full, less 1% cash discount.

11—Purchased merchandise from Lawrence Pope, $1,300. Invoice dated January 10.

Purchased for cash a 3-year fire insurance policy costing $270.

14—Sold merchandise to John Clark for $3,200. Invoice No. 1065.

Recorded and paid weekly sales salaries—$300. Taxes were the same as on the January 7 payroll.

15—Recorded and paid bi-monthly office salaries—$200. Withheld $53 federal income taxes and $3 federal O.A.B. taxes. Employers' O.A.B. tax is $3.

16—Received a check from James Hawkins, trustee for the creditors of William Bowman, who had gone bankrupt. The check is for $1,150. In an accompanying letter, Mr. Hawkins explains that creditors will receive only 50 cents on the dollar. The remaining balance in Bowman's account is written off as uncollectible.

18—Purchased a bookkeeping machine for $1,200 cash.

21—Sold merchandise to Charles Gant for $2,200. Invoice No. 1066.

Sold merchandise to Peter Davis for $1,300. Invoice No. 1067.

Paid weekly sales payroll. Amounts identical with other sales payrolls.

22—Paid $1,275 in settlement of fourth quarter 1953 taxes withheld and payable.

23—Received merchandise billed at $500 from Michael Eldridge, who claims the items are unsatisfactory. It is decided to accept the return. Eldridge is issued credit memo No. 336 for $500.

24—Sold merchandise to James Altman for $2,100. Invoice No. 1068.

Purchased merchandise from Alvin Rogers for $7,200. Invoice dated January 23.

25—Purchased merchandise from Harry Oren for $1,300. Invoice dated January 23.

Made a sale for cash—$350.

28—Recorded and paid weekly sales payroll—same data as for other weeks.

29—Purchased merchandise from Arthur Mooney for $850. Invoice dated January 28.

Sold merchandise to Homer Ferris for $1,000. Invoice No. 1069.

30—Paid note payable of $2,000 plus interest of $20. Interest of $10 had accrued prior to January 1 and $10 interest accrued during January.

Paid monthly gas bill—$120.

Paid monthly telephone bill—$60.

Jan. 31—Paid $100 on mortgage. Of this amount, $41.67 represents interest and
          $58.33 represents principal.
          Recorded and paid bi-monthly office payroll. Amounts are same as
          on January 15.
          Declared a $750 dividend to be paid February 5, 1954.

   Post the above entries and prepare a general ledger trial balance as of January
31. Prove the balances in the control accounts by preparing subsidiary ledger
schedules.

   Problem A-2. The Arthur Company began operations on July 5, 1954.
Record the transactions for the remainder of the month, post, and take a trial
balance. Prove the balances in the control accounts by preparing schedules of
accounts receivable and accounts payable.

   The following books of original entry are used:

   General journal
   Cash receipts book
   Cash disbursements book
   Sales book
   Purchase book

   The accounts to be used are indicated in the ledger in the accompanying
forms.

1954
July 5—Capital stock of $20,000 was issued for cash.
          A store building and site were purchased for $40,000, of which $10,000
          is considered land cost. A $5,000 cash payment was made and a
          mortgage of $35,000 was given for the balance.
          Fixtures were purchased for $6,000 cash.
      6—Merchandise was received from James Bently on account, $5,500.
          Invoice date, July 5. Terms, 2/10; n/60.
          Merchandise was received from William Burton on account, $7,300.
          Invoice date, July 5. Terms, 1/10; n/30.
      7—Office supplies were purchased for cash, $375.
          Fire insurance for five years was purchased for cash, $1,000.
      8—Merchandise was purchased for cash, $3,000.
          Office equipment was purchased from Otis Company for $6,500. Cash
          in the amount of $3,000 was paid and a 30-day non-interest note was
          given for the balance.
      9—Merchandise was sold for cash, $1,000.
          Unsatisfactory merchandise was returned to James Bently and full
          credit was received on account, $1,200.
     12—Merchandise was received from Peter Carlson on account, $5,300.
          Invoice date, July 12. Terms, 3/10; n/30.
          Merchandise was sold to Wilbur Matson on account, $6,200. Invoice
          No. 2. Terms, 1/10; n/30.
     13—Merchandise was sold to Roger Simmons on account, $7,900. Invoice
          No. 3. Terms, 1/10; n/30.
     14—A $15,000, 15-day, non-interest-bearing note was discounted at the
          bank. The discount rate was 6%. (Record in general journal and
          cash receipts book.)
          James Bently and William Burton were paid the amounts due them
          after deduction of the applicable discounts.

July 15—Merchandise was sold for cash, $1,200.

Merchandise was sold to Henry Tucker on account, $6,500. Invoice No. 5. Terms, 1/10; n/30.

16—Recorded and paid salaries for period July 5–15, $1,700. Withholdings for federal income taxes were $300 and for federal old-age benefits were $25.50. (Use both the general journal and the cash disbursements book with an X posting procedure.)

Employers' old-age benefits tax was $25.50.

19—Sold merchandise to John Urban on account, $5,700. Invoice No. 6. Terms, 1/10; n/30.

20—Received merchandise on account from Jack Dill, $3,600. Invoice date, July 20. Terms, 1/10; n/30.

Sold merchandise to Samuel Victor on account, $6,500. Invoice No. 7. Terms, 1/10; n/30.

21—Purchased a used delivery truck for cash, $1,500.

Purchased new tires for delivery truck for cash, $225.

22—Paid Peter Carlson for July 12 invoice, less discount.

Received merchandise returned by John Urban. Issued credit memo No. 1 for $1,000.

Received cash from Wilbur Matson for invoice No. 2, less discount.

23—Received cash from Roger Simmons for invoice No. 3, less discount.

Paid note to bank, $15,000.

• 26—Received merchandise from Phillip Edgar on account, $7,600. Invoice date, July 23. Terms, 3/10; n/30.

Paid freight charges on above order, $375.

27—Received cash from Henry Tucker, $6,500.

Sold merchandise on account to Wilbur Matson, $2,300. Invoice No. 8. Terms, 1/10; n/30.

28—Paid electricity bill in cash, $120.

Sold merchandise on account to Henry Tucker, $2,100. Invoice No. 9. Terms, 1/10; n/30.

29—Paid Jack Dill for his invoice of July 20, less discount.

Received cash from John Urban for the balance of invoice No. 6, less discount.

Purchased office supplies for cash, $75.

30—Received cash from Samuel Victor for invoice No. 7, less discount.

Received merchandise from William Burton on account, $3,100. Invoice date, July 29. Terms, 1/10; n/30.

Recorded and paid salaries for period July 16–30, $2,000. Withheld income taxes of $325 and federal O.A.B. taxes of $30.

Employers' federal O.A.B. taxes were $30.

Paid gas and oil bills for delivery truck, $85.

Problem A-3. Howard Walker is the sole proprietor of an electrical appliance distributorship. His accounting system includes the following books of original entry:

Sales book—in the form illustrated on page 142.

Purchase book—in the form illustrated on page 144.

Cash receipts book—in the form illustrated on page 145.

Cash disbursements book—in the form illustrated on page 147.

General journal—in the form illustrated on page 149.

In the interest of brevity, the following transactions are assumed to be all of the transactions for the year 1955. Record these transactions in the books of original entry. Set up whatever accounts are necessary and post these entries, including column totals, to general ledger and subsidiary ledger accounts. For purposes of this problem, assume that columns are totaled and posted at the end of the year and not at the end of each month. Allow five lines for each account.

1955
Jan. 10—Sold merchandise on account to Patrick Bell, $5,000. Invoice No. 1384. Terms, 1/10; n/30.
Feb. 15—Purchased for cash 200 shares of the common stock of Millroad Corporation for $10 per share as a short-term investment.
27—Accepted a return of merchandise from Patrick Bell and issued credit memo No. 186 for $1,000.
Mar. 29—Purchased merchandise for cash, $6,300.
May 30—Purchased office equipment for $10,000. Paid $1,000 in cash and gave a 1-year, 6% note for the balance.
June 25—Borrowed from City Bank by discounting a $20,000, 1-year note at 6%.
Aug. 10—Received a 5%, 60-day note for $4,000 from Patrick Bell on account.
Sept. 25—Sold 100 shares of Millroad stock for $12 per share, cash.
Oct. 3—Howard Walker withdrew merchandise costing $250 for his personal use.
9—Collected the Patrick Bell note plus interest.
Nov. 28—Purchased merchandise on account from William Seely, $3,000. Terms, 3/10; n/30. Invoice date, Nov. 27.
Dec. 7—Paid William Seely in full less discount.
10—Sold 100 shares of Millroad stock for $9 per share. Received half of selling price in cash and half in notes due in 30 days without interest.
31—Accounting period ends.

Problem A-4. Harrison Mercantile Corporation has the following trial balance on November 30, 1954, after all posting has been completed for November.

HARRISON MERCANTILE CORPORATION
Trial Balance
November 30, 1954

Cash	10,000.00	
Securities	5,000.00	
Accounts receivable	8,000.00	
Notes receivable	2,000.00	
Inventory	20,000.00	
Prepaid interest		
Unexpired insurance		
Office equipment	5,000.00	
Sales equipment	15,000.00	
Accounts payable		6,000.00
Notes payable		3,000.00
Capital stock		25,000.00
Earned surplus		32,600.00
Dividends	500.00	
Sales		60,000.00
Returned sales and allowances	1,000.00	
Discount on sales	500.00	
Purchases	35,000.00	
Freight in	1,000.00	

Returned purchases and allowances............		600.00
Discount on purchases.......................		300.00
Delivery expense............................	4,000.00	
Rent..	5,500.00	
Salaries....................................	15,000.00	
Taxes.......................................		
Interest expense............................		
Interest income.............................		
Gain on sale of securities...................		
	127,500.00	127,500.00

The accounts receivable balance of $8,000 represents November 30, 1954 invoices as follows:

James Hawk.............. $3,000.00
Peter Jenks.............. 5,000.00

Jack Kiel's account in the subsidiary ledger has no balance as of November 30.

The accounts payable balance of $6,000 represents an invoice dated November 25, 1954, payable to William Logan. Creditors' accounts are needed also for Robert Mass and Henry Opal.

No posting has been done for the month of December, 1954. The entries for December are summarized below. If the A forms are not used, set up the necessary accounts, allowing five lines each; post to the ledgers; and prepare a trial balance as of December 31, 1954. Reconcile the control accounts and subsidiary ledgers.

General Journal (page 9)—*column totals:*

Accounts receivable (debit)...........................	$ -0-
Accounts payable (debit).............................	500.00
General ledger (debit)...............................	19,500.00
General ledger (credit)..............................	18,500.00
Accounts payable (credit)............................	-0-
Accounts receivable (credit).........................	1,500.00

General Journal (page 9)—*column details:*

Accounts payable (debit):
Henry Opal (Dec. 15)..............................	$ 500.00

General ledger (debit):
Returned sales and allowances (Dec. 7)................	$ 1,500.00
Cash (Dec. 10)......................................	2,000.00
Notes receivable (Dec. 10)..........................	6,000.00
Cash (Dec. 20)......................................	9,900.00
Prepaid interest (Dec. 20)..........................	100.00
	$19,500.00

General ledger (credit):
Securities (Dec. 10)................................	$ 5,000.00
Gain on sale of securities (Dec. 10)..................	3,000.00
Returned purchases and allowances (Dec. 15)..........	500.00
Notes payable (Dec. 20).............................	10,000.00
	$18,500.00

Accounts receivable (credit):
Jack Kiel (Dec. 7).................................	$ 1,500.00

Sales Book (page 15)—*column total*.....................	$11,800.00

140 000
.4
———
56.000.00

125 000
4
———
50 0000

5 0
1 2 5
5 6
———
6 9

1 3 6
6 9
———
6 7

Quiz

Inventory Jan 1	40,000
Sales	140,000
Purch.	100,000
Ret. Sales & Allow	5,000
Ret. Purch & Allow	4,000
Gross Profit 40% of net sales	

Sales Book (page 15)—*column details:*

Jack Kiel (Dec. 4)	$ 3,500.00
James Hawk (Dec. 15)	2,500.00
Peter Jenks (Dec. 18)	3,200.00
Jack Kiel (Dec. 23)	2,600.00
	$11,800.00

Purchase Book (page 12)—*column total* ... $17,500.00

Purchase Book (page 12)—*column details:*

Robert Mass (Dec. 6)	$ 3,100.00
Henry Opal (Dec. 10)	3,000.00
William Logan (Dec. 18)	7,200.00
Robert Mass (Dec. 24)	4,200.00
	$17,500.00

Cash Disbursements Book (page 16)—*column totals:*

General ledger	$11,540.00
Accounts payable	18,800.00
Discount on purchases	376.00
Cash	29,964.00

Cash Disbursements Book (page 16)—*column details:*

General ledger:

Rent (Dec. 1)	$ 500.00
Unexpired insurance (Dec. 3)	250.00
Notes payable (Dec. 5)	3,000.00
Interest expense (Dec. 5)	90.00
Taxes (Dec. 18)	700.00
Purchases (Dec. 23)	2,000.00
Dividends (Dec. 31)	5,000.00
	$11,540.00

Accounts payable:

William Logan (Dec. 4)	$ 6,000.00
Robert Mass (Dec. 16)	3,100.00
Henry Opal (Dec. 20)	2,500.00
William Logan (Dec. 28)	7,200.00
	$18,800.00

Cash Receipts Book (page 8)—*column totals:*

General ledger	$16,050.00
Accounts receivable	15,700.00
Discount on sales	157.00
Cash	31,593.00

Cash Receipts Book (page 8)—*column details:*

General ledger:

Sales (Dec. 5)	$ 2,100.00
No title (Dec. 10)	2,000.00
No title (Dec. 20)	9,900.00
Notes receivable (Dec. 21)	2,000.00
Interest income (Dec. 21)	50.00
	$16,050.00

Accounts receivable:

James Hawk (Dec. 8)	$ 3,000.00
Peter Jenks (Dec. 9)	5,000.00
Jack Kiel (Dec. 14)	2,000.00
James Hawk (Dec. 24)	2,500.00
Peter Jenks (Dec. 28)	3,200.00
	$15,700.00

Problems—Group B

Problem B-1. Portions of the general journal and cash disbursements book of the Iowa Company are reproduced below and on page 561. Set up ledger accounts and make whatever postings are necessary.

General Journal

(Page 9)

	DEBITS					CREDITS	
Accounts Receivable	Accounts Payable	General Ledger	Date	L.F.	General Ledger	Accounts Payable	Accounts Receivable
		10,000 00	1955 May 5		Land		
					Cash............... 2,000 00		
					Notes payable...... 8,000 00		
					Purchased land.		
		1,000 00	15		Salaries		
					Cash............... 835 00		
					Federal income taxes withheld.... 150 00		
					Federal O.A.B. taxes withheld.... 15 00		
					Paid bi-monthly payroll.		
2,100 00	3,900 00	50,000 00	(Month's total)		43,000 00	8,000 00	5,000 00

Cash Disbursements Book   (Page 6)

Date	Account Debited	Explanation	L.F.	DEBITS — General Ledger Amount	DEBITS — Accounts Payable ✓	DEBITS — Accounts Payable Amount	CREDITS — Discount on Purchases	CREDITS — Cash
1955 May 5		Land purchase—see journal.		2,000|00				2,000|00
10	Notes payable	Paid note and interest.		3,000|00				3,090|00
	Interest expense			90|00				
15		Payroll—see journal.		835|00				835|00
23	Purchases	Cash purchase.		500|00				500|00
	(Month's totals)			18,000|00		6,000|00	120|00	23,880|00

Problem B-2. Below and on page 563 are reproduced portions of the general journal and cash receipts book of the Allman Corporation for the month of September, 1955. Set up the necessary ledger accounts (general and subsidiary) and post the items that should be posted. Assume that no postings have been made during the month.

General Journal

(Page 82)

	DEBITS					CREDITS		
	Accounts Receivable	Accounts Payable	General Ledger	Date	L.F.	General Ledger	Accounts Payable	Accounts Receivable
				1955				
Cash			1,980 00	Sept. 10				
Prepaid interest			20 00					
Notes payable........................						2,000 00		
Discounted 60-day note at 6%.								
Cash			2,000 00	15				
Loss on sale of land			1,000 00					
Land........................						3,000 00		
Sold land for cash.								
Notes receivable			1,200 00	20				
Jack Roberts........................								1,200 00
Accepted customer's note; 60-day, 6%.								
(Month's totals)	2,600 00	3,900 00	8,000 00			10,000 00	3,300 00	1,200 00

Cash Receipts Book

(Page 90)

Date	Account Credited	Explanation	L.F.	General Ledger Amount	Accounts Receivable Amount	Discount on Sales	Cash
1955							
Sept. 10		Discounted note—see journal		1,980 00			1,980 00
15		Sold land—see journal		2,000 00			2,000 00
18	Notes receivable	Collected note		2,000 00			2,120 00
	Interest income	and interest		120 00			
25	Sales	Cash sale		500 00			500 00
(Month's totals)				16,800 00	3,200 00	320 00	19,680 00

Problem B-3. The Robbins-Hickham Textile Company was organized on August 3, 1955. A summary of the books of original entry at the end of August is presented below. No postings have been made to ledger accounts.

Post the entries for the month, allowing five lines for each account, take a trial balance, and reconcile the controlling account balances with the subsidiary ledgers.

General Journal—column totals:

Accounts receivable (debit)............................	$ 1,002.50
Accounts payable (debit).............................	500.00
General ledger (debit)...............................	6,750.00
General ledger (credit)..............................	6,802.50
Accounts payable (credit)............................	250.00
Accounts receivable (credit).........................	1,200.00

General Journal—column details:

Accounts receivable (debit):
James Benson (Aug. 30)............................	$ 1,002.50

Accounts payable (debit):
Roger Mills (Aug. 20).............................	$ 500.00

General ledger (debit):
Purchases (Aug. 5)................................	$ 5,000.00
Returned sales and allowances (Aug. 12)..............	200.00
Notes receivable (Aug. 15).........................	1,000.00
Harold Hickham, drawing (Aug. 25).................	300.00
Office supplies (Aug. 28)..........................	250.00
	$ 6,750.00

General ledger (credit):
John Robbins, Capital (Aug. 5)......................	$ 5,000.00
Returned purchases and allowances (Aug. 20).........	500.00
Purchases (Aug. 25)...............................	300.00
Notes receivable (Aug. 30).........................	1,000.00
Interest income (Aug. 30)..........................	2.50
	$ 6,802.50

Accounts payable (credit):
Pace Stationery Store (Aug. 28).....................	$ 250.00

Accounts receivable (credit):
Arthur Call (Aug. 12).............................	$ 200.00
James Benson (Aug. 15)............................	1,000.00
	$ 1,200.00

Sales Book:

Column total......................................	$16,700.00

Column details:
Arthur Call (Aug. 8)...............................	$ 2,200.00
Jack Devon (Aug. 10)..............................	6,000.00
William Fair (Aug. 11).............................	2,500.00
James Benson (Aug. 15)............................	1,000.00
Arthur Call (Aug. 23).............................	2,000.00
Jack Devon (Aug. 25)..............................	3,000.00
	$16,700.00

Purchase Book:

Column total....................................... $25,000.00
Column details:
   Andrew Norton (Aug. 6)........................... $10,000.00
   Ralph Sill (Aug. 11)............................... 4,000.00
   Roger Mills (Aug. 16)............................. 3,000.00
   Ralph Sill (Aug. 19)............................... 3,000.00
   Andrew Norton (Aug. 22)......................... 5,000.00
                                  $25,000.00

Cash Disbursements Book—column totals:

General ledger..................................... $14,575.00
Accounts payable.................................. 19,500.00
Discount on purchases............................. 195.00
Cash.. 33,880.00

Cash Disbursements Book—column details:

General ledger:
   Rent expense (Aug. 5)............................ $ 500.00
   Store fixtures (Aug. 6)........................... 10,000.00
   Purchases (Aug. 8)............................... 3,000.00
   John Robbins, drawing (Aug. 15) 250.00
   Freight in (Aug. 20).............................. 175.00
   Harold Hickham, drawing (Aug. 23) 300.00
   Returned sales and allowances (Aug. 25).......... 350.00
                                   $14,575.00

Accounts Payable:
   Andrew Norton (Aug. 15).......................... $10,000.00
   Ralph Sill (Aug. 21).............................. 4,000.00
   Roger Mills (Aug. 26)............................. 2,500.00
   Ralph Sill (Aug. 28).............................. 3,000.00
                                   $19,500.00

Cash Receipts Book—column totals:

General ledger..................................... $48,000.00
Accounts receivable............................... 10,500.00
Discount on sales................................. 210.00
Cash.. 58,290.00

Cash Receipts Book—column details:

General ledger:
   John Robbins, capital (Aug. 5) $20,000.00
   Harold Hickham, capital (Aug. 5) 25,000.00
   Sales (Aug. 20).................................. 3,000.00
                                   $48,000.00

Accounts receivable:
   Arthur Call (Aug. 18)............................. $2,000.00
   Jack Devon (Aug. 20)............................. 6,000.00
   William Fair (Aug. 21)............................ 2,500.00
                                   $10,500.00

Problem B-4. Hendricks Corporation is formed on May 1, 1954. The transactions described below occurred during the first month of operations. Books of original entry such as are described in this chapter are to be used to record the month's transactions. Set up general ledger accounts and subsidiary ledger accounts, allowing five lines to each account, and post these entries. Number your general ledger accounts. After posting the month's entries, prepare a trial balance and reconciliations of the accounts receivable and accounts payable controlling accounts.

1954

May 1—Issued capital stock for cash, $25,000.
  3—Purchased store fixtures for cash, $3,000.
  Purchased office fixtures for cash, $1,000.
  4—Purchased merchandise from Able Brothers, Inc., on account, $2,500. Invoice date, May 2. Terms, 2/10; n/30.
  Paid rent for May, $750.
  5—Paid freight on Able Brothers' order, $100.
  8—Purchased merchandise from Jackson Company on account, $3,000. Invoice date, May 8. Terms, 2/10; n/30.
  9—Sold merchandise for cash, $300.
  Purchased office supplies for cash, $125.
  11—Sold merchandise to Peter Mumford on account, $2,000. Invoice No. 2. Terms, 1/10; n/30.
  12—Purchased for $26,000 the entire inventory of Harrison Company, which is going out of business. Paid $16,000 in cash and gave a 5%, 2-year note for the balance.
  Sold merchandise to Ralph Peters for $3,000 on account. Invoice No. 3. Terms, 1/10; n/30.
  13—Returned merchandise costing $350 to Able Brothers and received full credit on account.
  16—Sent a customer a check for $75 as an allowance to apply on the cash sale of May 9.
  17—Purchased merchandise from Lanway Co. for $2,700 on account. Invoice date, May 16. Terms, 2/10; n/30.
  18—Paid Jackson Company $3,000 less 2% cash discount.
  19—Accepted returned merchandise from Peter Mumford and issued him credit memo No. 1 for $150.
  21—Received a check from Peter Mumford for $1,831.50 representing a payment of $1,850 less 1%.
  22—Sold merchandise to John Roberts for $7,200 on account. Invoice No. 4. Terms, 1/10; n/30.
  Sold merchandise to James Sanley for $3,200 on account. Invoice No. 5. Terms, 1/10; n/30.
  Received a check for $990 from Ralph Peters. This amount represents a partial payment of $1,000 on his May 12 purchase less 1%; the discount was allowed.
  23—Discounted a 60-day note for $5,000 at the bank; discount rate, 6%.
  26—Received a 30-day, 5% note from Ralph Peters for $2,000, the balance of his account.
  27—Paid Lanway Co. $2,700 less 2% cash discount.
  29—Purchased merchandise from Arthur Leland for $2,300 on account. Invoice date, May 27. Terms, 2/10; n/30.
  30—Purchased a 3-year fire insurance policy for $630 cash.
  31—Recorded and paid salaries of employees, $1,000. Withholdings for federal income taxes were $225 and for federal old-age benefits tax were $15. (Note: Record salaries payable in general journal and payment in cash disbursements book.)
  Employers' federal old-age benefits tax is $15.

Problem B-5.   The trial balance and schedules shown below were drawn off by the bookkeeper before recording adjusting entries after one month of operations.   The general ledger trial balance does not balance and the subsidiary ledger schedules do not agree with their respective controls.

JOSEPH CORPORATION
Trial Balance—July 31, 19—

Cash	15,749.00	
Accounts receivable	1,720.00	
Accounts payable		3,510.00
Capital stock		25,000.00
Sales		3,430.00
Returned sales and allowances	40.00	
Discount on sales	13.00	
Purchases	15,900.00	
Returned purchases and allowances		150.00
Discount on purchases		52.00
Salesmen's salaries	220.00	
Advertising	100.00	
	33,742.00	32,152.00

Schedule of Accounts Receivable—July 31, 19—

S. E. Batts	600.00
G. O. Dana	280.00
R. E. Waterman	350.00
Total	1,230.00

Schedule of Accounts Payable—July 31, 19—

Harvey's, Inc.	1,300.00
Otto Company	2,100.00
Rice and Smith	650.00
	4,160.00

Following are the ledgers from which these balances were taken:

GENERAL LEDGER

Cash   (1)

19—					19—				
July	31		CR1	28,097 00	July	31		CD1	12,448 00

Accounts Receivable   (10)

19—					19—				
July	31		S1	3,280 00	July	31		CR1	1,560 00

Notes Receivable   (15)

19—					19—				
July	5	R. E. Waterman	J1	500 00	July	20	R. E. Waterman	CR1	500 00

Accounts Payable   (20)

19—					19—				
July	31		CD1	4,850 00	July	31		P1	10,050 00
	31		J1	1,150 00					
	31		J1	540 00					

Notes Payable (21)

19—						19—					
July	25	Rice and Smith	CD1	1,000	00	July	7	Rice and Smith	J1	1,000	00

Capital Stock (30)

						19—					
						July	1		CR1	25,000	00

Sales (40)

						19—					
						July	3		CR1	150	00
							12		CR1	500	00
							31		CR1	400	00
							31		S1	3,280	00

Returned Sales and Allowances (41)

19—											
July	3		J1	40	00						

Discount on Sales (42)

19—											
July	31		CR1	13	00						

Purchases (50)

19—											
July	1		CD1	5,000	00						
	10		CD1	500	00						
	26		CD1	350	00						
	31		P1	10,050	00						

Returned Purchases and Allowances (51)

						19—					
						July	5		J1	150	00

Discount on Purchases (52)

						19—					
						July	31		CD1	52	00

Store Rent (61)

19—											
July	1		CD1	300	00						

Salesmen's Salaries (62)

19—											
July	16		CD1	20	00						
	31		CD1	200	00						

Advertising   (63)

19—					
July	31	CD1	100 00		

ACCOUNTS RECEIVABLE LEDGER

S. E. Batts

19—					
July	12	S1	600 00		600 00

G. O. Dana

19—					
July	7	S1	450 00		450 00
	15	CR1		450 00	
	23	S1	280 00		280 00

R. E. Waterman

19—					
July	2	S1	800 00		800 00
	3	J1		40 00	760 00
	5	CR1		260 00	500 00
	5	J1		500 00	
	18	S1	850 00		850 00
	24	CR1		850 00	50 00
	30	S1	300 00		350 00

ACCOUNTS PAYABLE LEDGER

Harvey's, Inc.

19—					
July	9	P1		3,500 00	3,500 00
	16	CD1	3,500 00		
	24	P1		1,300 00	1,300 00

Otto Company

19—					
July	13	P1		2,600 00	2,600 00
	19	CD1	500 00		2,100 00

Rice and Smith

19—					
July	1	P1		2,000 00	2,000 00
	5	J1	150 00		1,850 00
	7	CD1	850 00		1,000 00
	7	J1	1,000 00		
	18	P1		650 00	650 00

On the following pages are the books of original entry from which postings were made to the foregoing accounts.

Cash Receipts Book (Page 1)

Date	Account Credited	Explanation	L.F.	General Ledger Amount	Accounts Receivable Amount	Discount on Sales	Cash
19—							
July 1	Capital stock........	Investment	30	25,000 00			25,000 00
3	Sales.............	Cash sale	40	150 00			150 00
5	R. E. Waterman....	Invoice, July 2			260 00		260 00
12	Sales.............	Cash sale	40	500 00			500 00
15	G. O. Dana........	Invoice, July 7, less 1%			450 00	4 50	445 50
20	Notes receivable...	R. E. Waterman note	15	500 00			500 00
24	R. E. Waterman....	Invoice, July 18, less 1%			850 00	8 50	841 50
31	Sales.............	Cash sale	40	400 00			400 00
				26,550 00	1,560 00	13 00	28,097 00
					(10)	(42)	(1)

Cash Disbursements Book

(Page 1)

Date	Account Debited	Explanation	DEBITS General Ledger L.F.	General Ledger Amount	Accounts Payable √	Accounts Payable Amount	CREDITS Discount on Purchases	Cash
19— July 1	Purchases	Cash purchase	50	5,000 00				5,000 00
1	Store rent	For July	61	300 00				300 00
7	Rice and Smith	Invoice, July 1, less 2%			√	850 00	17 00	833 00
10	Purchases	Cash purchase	50	500 00				500 00
16	Harvey's, Inc.	Invoice, July 9, less 1%			√	3,500 00	35 00	3,465 00
16	Salesmen's salaries		62	200 00				200 00
19	Otto Company	On account			√	500 00		500 00
25	Notes payable	Rice and Smith	21	1,000 00				1,000 00
26	Purchases		50	350 00				350 00
31	Salesmen's salaries		62	200 00				200 00
31	Advertising	For July	63	100 00				100 00
				7,650 00		4,850 00	52 00	12,448 00
						(20)	(52)	(1)

Journal   (Page 1)

DEBITS			Date	L.F.		CREDITS		
Accounts Receivable	Accounts Payable	General Ledger				General Ledger	Accounts Payable	Accounts Receivable
		40 00	19— July 3	41 √	Returned sales and allowances R. E. Waterman............ Credit Memo No. 1.			40 00
		500 00	5	15 √	Notes receivable R. E. Waterman............ Received 15-day, non-interest bearing note to apply on account.			500 00
	150 00		5	√ 51	Rice and Smith Returned purchases and allowances........... Return of portion of goods purchased July 1.	150 00		
	1,000 00		7	√ 21	Rice and Smith Notes payable........... Gave 18-day, non-interest note to apply on account.	1,000 00		
	1,150 00 (20)	540 00				1,150 00		540 00 (10)

Sales Book (Page 1)

Date	√	Name	Invoice No.	Amount	
19—					
July 2	√	R. E. Waterman............................	1	800	00
7	√	G. O. Dana...............................	2	450	00
12	√	S. E. Batts..............................	3	600	00
18	√	R. E. Waterman............................	4	850	00
23	√	G. O. Dana...............................	5	280	00
30	√	R. E. Waterman............................	6	300	00
				3,280	00
				(10)	(40)

Purchase Book (Page 1)

Date	√	Name	Invoice Date		Amount	
19—						
July 1	√	Rice and Smith...........................	July	1	2,000	00
9	√	Harvey's, Inc............................		8	3,500	00
13	√	Otto Company............................		10	2,600	00
18	√	Rice and Smith...........................		16	650	00
24	√	Harvey's, Inc............................		23	1,300	00
					10,050	00
					(50)	(20)

Make a list of the errors and prepare a trial balance of the general ledger and schedules of the subsidiary ledgers showing what the balances in the accounts in the three ledgers should have been. You are not required to correct the books. The procedures on page 163 are to be followed.

A suggested form for the solution is on page 574.

JOSEPH CORPORATION
Schedule of Errors
July 31, 19—

	GENERAL LEDGER	ACCOUNTS RECEIVABLE		ACCOUNTS PAYABLE	
	Trial Balance	Control	Subsidiary	Control	Subsidiary
	33,742|00 32,152|00	1,720|00	1,230|00	3,510|00	4,160|00
	−10|00				
	33,742|00 32,142|00				

The general ledger trial balance totals are..................

The controlling account balances are..................

The totals of the subsidiary ledgers are..................

Refoot the general ledger trial balance:

(a) The credit column is overfooted..................

Compare the balances shown by the trial balance with those shown by the accounts in the general ledger:

Practice Set

Barker and Carroll, a partnership, sells the office equipment products of National Brand Co.   The partnership has been in operation for about four years. The firm uses the books of original entry shown on page 576.

The firm uses a general ledger, an accounts receivable ledger, and a notes receivable register.   All purchases on account are made from National Brand Co., and therefore no subsidiary ledger is needed for accounts payable.   A schedule of notes receivable as of March 31, 1954 is presented below:

Date	Maker	Time	Int. Rate	Due Date	Amount
1954					
Feb. 19	Thomas Roland	60 days	6%	Apr. 20	$2,700
Mar. 16	August Benson	60 days	6%	May 15	1,500
Mar. 27	Philip Hawley	30 days	6%	Apr. 26	520
Mar. 31	Martin Warner	60 days	6%	May 30	340

No register is maintained for notes payable, since the firm issues few notes.
The accounts used by the firm, with their March 31, 1954 balances, are presented below:

Acct. No.	Account Title	March 31, 1954 Balance
101	Cash	$ 2,275.00
201	Accounts receivable	5,160.00
202	Reserve for bad debts	432.08
203	Notes receivable	5,060.00
204	Accrued interest receivable	22.10
300	Inventory of office equipment	1,706.00
400	Unexpired insurance	317.50
401	Prepaid advertising	
402	Sales supplies	27.00
403	Office supplies	63.00
404	Prepaid interest expense	
501	Sales fixtures	9,600.00
502	Reserve for depreciation—Sales fixtures	2,220.00
503	Office fixtures	2,592.00
504	Reserve for depreciation—Office fixtures	1,151.00
601	National Brand Co	540.00
602	Notes payable	
603	Salaries payable	239.35
604	Federal OAB taxes withheld	28.35
605	Federal OAB taxes payable	28.35
606	Federal income taxes withheld	186.20
701	K. L. Barker, capital	9,756.97
702	K. L. Barker, drawings	
703	T. J. Carroll, capital	12,240.30
704	T. J. Carroll, drawings	
705	Profit and loss	
801	Sales	
802	Returned sales and allowances	
901	Purchases	
902	Returned purchases and allowances	
903	Discount on purchases	
904	Freight in	
1001	Store rent	

Cash Receipts Book

			CREDITS					DEBIT
					General Ledger	Accounts Receivable		
Date	Account Credited	Explanation	Notes Receivable	Sales	Interest Income	L.F.	Amount	L.F.	Amount	Cash

Cash Disbursements Book

				DEBITS		CREDITS			
				General Ledger	National Brand Co.	Freight In	Fed. Inc. Tax Withheld	FOAB Withheld	Discount on Purchases	Cash
Date	Account Debited	Explanation	L.F.	Amount						

Sales Book

| Date | Name | L.F. | Invoice No. | Amount |

Purchase Book

| Date | Name | Invoice Date | Amount |

General Journal

| | | | DEBITS | | CREDITS | |
| Date | Account and Explanation | L.F. | National Brand Co. | General Ledger | General Ledger | Accounts Receivable |

1002 Delivery truck rent.....................................
1003 Advertising..
1004 Depreciation expense—Sales fixtures.....................
1005 Sales salaries...
1006 Miscellaneous selling expense..........................
1101 Bad debts...
1102 Payroll taxes...
1103 Insurance expense.....................................
1104 Office salaries.......................................
1105 Depreciation expense—Office fixtures...................
1106 Office expense..
1107 General expense.......................................
1201 Interest income.......................................
1202 Interest expense......................................

The accounts receivable to be used will be:

Name	March 31 Balance
Anderson Coke Co.............	$ 372.00
Richard Chamberlain.........	832.00
Courtland and Sparks..............	—0—
Richard C. Lawson..................	—0—
Vincent Mercer Grocery.............	—0—
Thomas Outland....	1,475.00
Wilson R. Trenach.................	326.00
Wayne Shops......................	730.00
Welliston Electric Co...............	1,425.00
Wiseheart Rug Service..............	—0—

The firm hires two clerks, who are paid on the 4th of each month for the last half of the preceding month and on the 18th of each month for the first half of the current month. The payroll data are scheduled below:

| | | | | Withholding | | |
Name	Position	Pay Period	Semimonthly Gross Wage	O.A.B.	Income Tax	Net Wage
Theo. Lewis.............	Office clerk	Semi-monthly	$120.00	$1.80	$13.30	$104.90
Robert Schmidt.........	Sales clerk	Semi-monthly	150.00	2.25	13.30	134.45

The books of Barker and Carroll are closed monthly, and this practice set will cover the operations of the firm for the month of April, 1954.

Instructions

(1) Journalize the transactions for the month of April, 1954.
(2) Post the journal entries to the ledger accounts; also enter the necessary information in the notes receivable register.
(3) Prepare the April 30, 1954 trial balance. (Use the Trial Balance columns of the working papers.)
(4) Complete the working papers.
(5) Prepare the following monthly statements:

Statement of profit and loss.
Statement of partners' capitals.
Balance sheet.

(6) Journalize the adjusting and closing entries.
(7) Post

1954

April 3—An invoice is received from National Brand Co. for the purchase of office equipment, $2,400; terms, 2/10; n/30.

Freight on the above shipment is paid to the carrier, $68.

Store rent for April is paid, $230.

Sale of office equipment is made on account to Vincent Mercer, $127. (Start with invoice number 783.)

Cash sales for the day, $327.50.

    4—Semimonthly salaries for the last half of March are paid to the clerks. (See the payroll schedule for the amounts.)

Collection is received from Thomas Outland, $1,475.

A sales agreement is made with Wayne Shops whereby, during the next several weeks, Wayne Shops will purchase equipment for all its retail outlets on account. When all of the purchases have been made, a note will be given covering the total purchases under this agreement. Wayne Shops also agrees that the amount owing Barker and Carroll on March 31, 1954, shall be paid before April 10. The first sale under this agreement is completed today, $1,300.

    5—Telephone bill is paid, $11.25.

Sales supplies are purchased for cash, $64.

An invoice from National Brand Co. dated March 28, in the amount of $540, is paid. The terms were 2/10; n/30.

Office equipment is sold to Vincent Mercer, $520.

Cash sales for the day, $125.

    6—Vincent Mercer returns the office equipment purchased on April 3 in order to get a larger-model machine, which is placed on order. A credit memorandum is issued.

Cash sales for the day, $296.70.

    7—Federal O.A.B. taxes withheld and payable for the first quarter are remitted to the federal depositary. The amounts, based on salaries paid, are $24.30 each.

Federal income taxes withheld for the first quarter are remitted to the federal depositary. The amount withheld on salaries paid is $159.60, and this is the amount remitted.

Sale of office equipment to Wayne Shops, $1,235.

Collection of the March 31 balance in the account of Wayne Shops is received, $730.

  10—Collections are received from:

> Welliston Electric Co.............. $1,425
> Wilson R. Trenach............... 326

Gas and oil for the delivery truck are purchased for cash, $8.25.

Cash sales for the day, $89.

  11—An invoice is received from National Brand Co. for the purchase of office equipment, $2,000; terms, 2/10; n/30.

Freight on the above shipment is paid to the carrier, $38.20.

The new machine ordered for Vincent Mercer is delivered to him, $175.

  12—Newspaper advertising for two days is purchased for cash, $25.

Sale of office equipment to Wayne Shops, $936.

Cash sales for the day, $136.

April 12—Premium on a three-year insurance policy is paid, $180. The policy date is April 15.

13—The National Brand Co. invoice of April 3 is paid.

Office equipment is removed from the inventory to be used in the office of Barker and Carroll; cost, $72.

Cash sales for the day, $286.

14—Barker withdraws cash for his personal use, $300.

Janitor services are paid, $12.

Sales of office equipment on account:

> Richard C. Lawson............ $832
> Wayne Shops................. 439

17—Semimonthly rental for the delivery truck is paid to Argo Rental Co., $35.

Carroll withdraws cash for his personal use, $450.

Richard Chamberlain pays $332 on his March balance of $832 and signs a 60-day, 6% note for the balance.

Office supplies are purchased for cash, $117.

18—Semimonthly salaries for the first part of April are paid to the clerks. The semimonthly accrual for the Federal O.A.B. tax liability is recorded at this time.

An invoice is received from National Brand Co. for the purchase of office equipment, $3,000; terms, 2/10; n/30.

Freight on the above shipment is paid to the carrier, $63.

Sale of office equipment is made on account to Richard C. Lawson, $465.

Cash sales for the day, $217.30.

19—Sale of office equipment is made on account to Courtland and Sparks, $176.

A defective machine included in the latest shipment is returned to National Brand Co. Full credit is taken in line with an agreement with the supplier. The amount is $79.

20—The National Brand Co. invoice of April 11 is paid.

Thomas Roland's note dated February 19 is collected.

Sales of office equipment on account:

> Courtland and Sparks............ $1,250
> Wilson R. Trenach.............. 158

21—Advertising supplies to be used for the next several months are purchased for cash, $230.

Gas and oil for the delivery truck is purchased for cash, $7.30.

Sale of equipment is made on account to Courtland and Sparks, $375.

24—Newspaper advertising for three days is purchased for cash, $38.

The firm signs a 60-day, $1,200 note at the bank. The note is discounted by the bank at 5%.

Sale of office equipment on account is made to Wayne Shops, $570.

25—An invoice is received from National Brand Co. for the purchase of office equipment, $1,300; terms, 2/10; n/30.

Freight on the above shipment is paid to the carrier, $24.

Sale of office equipment is made on account to Wiseheart Rug Service, $465.

Cash sales for the day, $169.

April 26—As per the agreement of April 4, August Wayne signs a 60-day, 6%
    note for the sum of the purchases by Wayne Shops.
    Cash sales for the day, $147.
    27—Philip Hawley's note dated March 27 is collected.
    A defective typewriter is returned by a cash customer and a cash
    refund is given for the sales price, $65.
    The defective typewriter is returned to National Brand Co. and credit
    is taken for its cost, $36.   This item was in the April 25 purchase.
    28—The National Brand Co. invoice of April 18 is paid, less the credit for
    the equipment returned.
    The semimonthly delivery truck rental is paid, $35.
    Janitor services are paid, $12.
    30—Utilities for April are paid, $15.60.
    Cash sales for the day, $182.

Required Adjustments

(a) Accrued salaries for the last half of the month.
(b) Accrued federal O.A.B. tax payable for the last half of the month.
(c) The insurance policies are:

Date Purchased	Protection	Term	Total Premium
April 15, 1951	Fire on merchandise	3 years	$180
January 1, 1953	Public liability	3 years	144
January 1, 1954	Fire and theft on fixtures	2 years	264
April 15, 1954	Fire on merchandise	3 years	180

(d) Accrued interest on the notes receivable outstanding at the end of the month.
(e) Interest expense on the note payable.
(f) The annual depreciation rates are:

Asset	Rate
Sales fixtures	10%
Office fixtures	$12\frac{1}{2}$%
Office fixture transferred from inventory to fixed assets during the month	$12\frac{1}{2}$%

(g) It is estimated that the monthly provision for uncollectible accounts should
    be 1% of the net credit sales (total credit sales less credit returns).
(h) The account of Anderson Coke Co. is found to be uncollectible and is written
    off.
(i) Inventories of prepaid expenses are:

Sales supplies	$ 41
Office supplies	76
Advertising supplies	196

Other Data

The ending merchandise inventory is $2,871.
The partners share profits as follows:

K. L. Barker	40%
T. J. Carroll	60%

ASSIGNMENT MATERIAL FOR CHAPTER 12

Questions

1. Explain what is meant by the phrase "departmental contribution to overhead."

2. If the method described in this chapter for recording cash sales in a business with various departments is used, why are the totals of the Sales column in the cash receipts book and the Cash column in the sales book not posted?

3. What departmental accounts should be kept if it is desired to determine merely the gross profit on sales by departments?

4. What additional information must be obtained to determine net income by departments?

5. What is the danger in apportioning selling expenses to departments on the basis of sales?

6. Describe the journalizing procedure for recording cash purchases if the business has several departments and maintains a separate Purchases account for each department. Explain how such entries would be posted.

7. Suggest a basis for apportioning each of the following expenses to departments, and state your reason for selecting the basis used:

> Delivery expense
> Rent expense
> Advertising expense
> Freight in

8. If the operations of a department result, year after year, in a net loss, after charging the department with reasonable amounts of selling and general expenses, could there be any possible reason for continuing its operations?

Problems—Group A

Problem A-1. Using the information in the following adjusted trial balance, prepare working papers showing the gross profit on sales by departments. Apportion the freight in on the basis of purchases.

MAX CORPORATION
Adjusted Trial Balance
December 31, 1954

Cash....................................	17,830.00	
Accounts receivable..........................	14,600.00	
Allowance for bad debts......................		690.00
Inventories—December 31, 1953:		
Dept. A..................................	15,000.00	
Dept. B..................................	27,000.00	
Unexpired insurance........................	640.00	
Store equipment............................	4,000.00	
Allowance for depreciation—Store equipment...		1,200.00

Accounts payable.............................		11,800.00
Federal income tax payable...................		5,000.00
Capital stock................................		40,000.00
Earned surplus..............................		8,325.00
Dividends..................................	2,000.00	
Sales:		
Dept. A..................................		72,000.00
Dept. B..................................		118,000.00
Returned sales and allowances:		
Dept. A..................................	400.00	
Dept. B..................................	800.00	
Purchases:		
Dept. A..................................	56,000.00	
Dept. B..................................	84,000.00	
Discount on purchases:		
Dept. A..................................		560.00
Dept. B..................................		840.00
Freight in.................................	2,000.00	
Store rent.................................	4,800.00	
Delivery expense...........................	1,125.00	
Advertising................................	500.00	
Depreciation of store equipment..............	400.00	
Selling commissions.........................	14,000.00	
Office salaries..............................	6,500.00	
Bad debts..................................	410.00	
Insurance..................................	285.00	
Miscellaneous office expense.................	1,125.00	
Federal income tax.........................	5,000.00	
	258,415.00	258,415.00

Inventories—December 31, 1954:

Dept. A.......................	$17,000.00
Dept. B.......................	22,500.00

Problem A-2. Following is the trial balance of the Brighton Company as of December 31, 1954

BRIGHTON COMPANY
Trial Balance
December 31, 1954

Cash.......................................	32,176.44	
Accounts receivable.........................	24,914.62	
Reserve for bad debts........................		228.15
Notes receivable............................	5,000.00	
Accrued interest receivable...................	—0—	
Inventory—Department A....................	14,207.50	
Inventory—Department B....................	17,108.62	
Unexpired insurance.........................	1,200.00	
Delivery equipment.........................	9,560.00	
Reserve for depreciation—Delivery equipment..		1,728.00
Accounts payable............................		14,738.09
Notes payable..............................		15,000.00
Federal income tax payable...................	—0—	
Accrued salaries payable.....................	—0—	
Accrued interest payable.....................	—0—	
Capital stock..............................		60,000.00
Earned surplus.............................		7,447.94
Dividends..................................	3,000.00	

Sales—Department A......................		75,000.00
Sales—Department B......................		125,000.00
Returned sales and allowances—Department A.	1,310.12	
Returned sales and allowances—Department B.	1,129.88	
Discount on sales—Department A............	1,280.00	
Discount on sales—Department B............	1,892.50	
Purchases—Department A..................	59,712.00	
Purchases—Department B..................	95,788.00	
Returned purchases and allowances—Department A...............................		750.0ι
Returned purchases and allowances—Department B...............................		1,050.00
Discount on purchases—Department A........		620.00
Discount on purchases—Department B........		1,775.00
Freight in...............................	1,555.00	
Store rent...............................	4,000.00	
Advertising..............................	5,050.00	
Salesmen's salaries—Department A...........	5,000.00	
Salesmen's salaries—Department B...........	7,000.00	
Delivery expense..........................	2,957.50	
Depreciation—Delivery equipment...........	—0—	
Officers' salaries.........................	5,000.00	
Office salaries............................	3,075.00	
Insurance................................	—0—	
Bad debts................................	—0—	
Miscellaneous general expenses..............	1,380.00	
Interest income...........................		98.00
Interest expense..........................	138.00	
Federal income tax........................	—0—	
	303,435.18	303,435.18

Investigation discloses that the following facts have to be taken into consideration before the formal statements can be prepared:

(a) The $1,200 in the Unexpired Insurance account is the premium on a fire insurance policy which was acquired on January 1, 1954, covering a period of three years.

(b) The following salaries had been earned but were unpaid as of December 31, 1954:

Salesmen of Department A...............................	$ 600.00
Salesmen of Department B...............................	800.00
Deliveryman..	50.00
Office clerks..	125.00
Total...	$1,575.00

(c) The $5,000 in the Notes Receivable account represents a 60-day, 6% note received from A. Bobbs, a customer, on December 16, 1954.

(d) The $15,000 in the Notes Payable account represents two notes as follows:

(1) A 5%, 60-day note for $7,200, dated December 1, 1954, given to Champion Corporation.

(2) A 6%, 30-day note for $7,800, dated December 21, 1954, given to H. R. Davies and Sons.

(e) Bad debts are estimated to be $\frac{1}{2}$ of 1% of sales less returned sales and allowances.

(f) The delivery equipment is depreciated at the rate of 10% a year.

(g) Federal income taxes are to be recorded at $1,000 for the year 1954.

(h) The inventories on hand on December 31, 1954, as determined by actual count, were as follows:

Department A..: $11,667.02
Department B... 18,622.86

(i) The company has decided that the freight in should be allocated on the basis of purchases.

Required:

(1) Working papers for the year ended December 31, 1954, showing gross profit on sales by departments.
(2) The statement of profit and loss for the year ended December 31, 1954, showing gross profit by departments.

Problem A-3. Supplementing all of the data included in Problem A-2 with the following data relative to the apportionment of the selling and general expenses and interest income and expense, prepare (1) a schedule of apportionments, (2) a work sheet showing net income by departments, and (3) a statement of profit and loss showing net income by departments.

(a) The following expenses are to be apportioned on the basis of sales:

1. Delivery expense.
2. Depreciation of delivery equipment.
3. Officers' salaries.
4. Office salaries.
5. Miscellaneous general expenses.
6. Interest income.

(b) Interest expense is to be apportioned on the basis of purchases.
(c) Insurance expense is to be apportioned on the basis of average inventories.
(d) Store rent should be apportioned on the basis of floor space occupied; Department A covers 5,200 square feet and Department B covers 7,800 square feet of floor space.
(e) Advertising expense should be allocated on the basis of advertising space occupied in the display windows, newspapers, magazines, and so forth. The statistical department has apportioned the $5,050 of advertising as follows: $3,000 to Department A, and $2,050 to Department B.
(f) Bad debts expense should be apportioned on the basis of net sales (exclusive of discount on sales).
(g) The income tax department has stated that $1,500 of income tax would have been levied on the profits of Department B. (On the work sheet, extend the $1,000 debit for federal income taxes as a $500 credit in Department A's columns and a $1,500 debit in Department B's columns.)

All apportionments should be carried to the nearest cent.

Problem A-4. The officers of Brighton Company have asked you to determine whether it would be advisable for them to discontinue the operations of Department A, since the apportionment of selling and general expenses as per Problem A-3 has resulted in showing Department A as operating at a loss.

An investigation made by you has disclosed the following facts:

(a) The store has been leased for a period of 25 years; therefore, the entire space would have to be retained under the lease.

(b) The advertising and salesmen's salaries charged to Department A would be eliminated if the operations of that department were discontinued.

(c) There would be no reduction of either delivery expense or depreciation of delivery equipment, since the company has only one delivery truck and employs only one driver.

(d) Officers' salaries would not be reduced.

(e) Office salaries would be reduced by $1,000, the salary of one part-time employee.

(f) Insurance costs applicable to inventories presently carried in Department A would be eliminated.

(g) All bad debt losses charged to Department A would be eliminated.

(h) Approximately 20% of the total miscellaneous general expenses would be eliminated.

(i) Both the interest received on receivables arising from Department A's sales and the interest expense incurred to finance the purchases of Department A would disappear.

Required:

(1) Determine the total amount of expenses that would be eliminated if operations of Department A were discontinued.

(2) Determine by what amount the expenses eliminated would exceed or be less than the gross profit on sales made by Department A.

(3) Determine what the net income before federal income tax would be if Department A were discontinued.

Problems—Group B

Problem B-1.   Refer to Problem A-1 and prepare journal entries to close the books as of December 31, 1954.

Problem B-2.   Set up the necessary general ledger accounts and make all postings from the journals on pages 586 and 587 to the general ledger of Arbor Company.

Sales Book (Page 1)

Date	Name	Invoice No.	Accounts Receivable ✓	Amount	Cash	Sales Dept. A	Sales Dept. B	Sales Dept. C
19— Jan. 3	J. B. McVaugh	1		100 00				100 00
5	Cash sale				40 00		40 00	
8	L. A. Lee	2		80 00				80 00
11	C. D. Woods	3		75 00		75 00		
12	Cash sale				30 00	30 00		
27	P. M. Garrison	24		20 00			20 00	
28	Cash sale				25 00		25 00	
31	C. J. Dodge	25		60 00				60 00
				1,125 00	450 00	630 00	460 00	485 00

Cash Receipts Book

(Page 1)

Date	Account Credited	Explanation	Sundry L.F.	Sundry Amount	Sales	Interest Income	Accounts Receivable √	Accounts Receivable Amount	Collection and Exchange	Discount on Sales	Cash
19— Jan. 5	Sale............				40 00						40 00
7	Notes receivable.......	6% note collected		500 00		5 00					505 00
9	J. B. McVaugh.......	Invoice No. 1						100 00		2 00	98 00
12	Sale............	Invoice No. 2			30 00						30 00
14	L. A. Lee.......							80 00	15	1 60	78 25
28	Sale............	Invoice No. 18			25 00						25 00
31	C. D. Woods......							60 00		1 20	58 80
31	Investments..........	Sale of bond at a gain		1,000 00		20 00					1,045 00
	Gain on sale of investments......			25 00							
				1,525 00	450 00	25 00		985 00	30	18 00	2,966 70

Problem B-3. The profit and loss statement of The Hedges Corporation is shown on page 589.

The following expenses and income are fully variable, meaning that the portion thereof allocated to each department would be eliminated if the department were discontinued: advertising, salesmen's salaries, insurance, bad debts, miscellaneous general expenses, interest expense, and interest income.

The following expenses are fixed charges, meaning that they would not be reduced if a department were discontinued: store rent, depreciation of delivery equipment, officers' salaries, and office salaries.

Determine the effect on net income before income taxes which would result from a discontinuance of Department I.

Problem B-4. Using the information presented in Problem B-3, prepare a profit and loss statement for The Hedges Corporation showing each department's contribution to non-departmental overhead.

Problem B-5. The officers of Brighton Company are considering the discontinuance of the operations of Department A, since the report submitted in the solution to Problem A-3 showed that Department A was operating at a loss. An analysis of the expenses charged to Department A was made and the following results were obtained:

(a) If Department A were discontinued, all of Department B would be located on the first floor. The second floor could then be rented out at a yearly rent of $1,000.

(b) Most of the advertising expense of the company is for advertisements in newspapers, whose charges include both a fixed and a variable fee. Advertising only the merchandise sold in Department B would reduce the total advertising expense from $5,050 to $2,550.

(c) The salaries of the salesmen of Department A would be eliminated.

(d) The cost of the gas and oil used by the delivery truck in making deliveries of sales of Department A is estimated to be $200. The other expenses included in the Delivery Expense account would not be eliminated.

(e) The depreciation expense on the delivery truck would not be reduced.

(f) Officers' salaries would not be affected.

(g) The discontinuance of the operations of Department A would eliminate the necessity of paying the office clerks overtime pay, which would reduce the office salaries payroll by $300.

(h) Insurance costs applicable to inventories presently carried in Department A would be eliminated.

(i) All bad debt losses charged to Department A would be eliminated.

(j) Approximately one-third of the total miscellaneous general expenses would be eliminated.

(k) Both the interest received on receivables arising from Department A's sales and the interest expense incurred to finance the purchases of Department A would disappear.

Required:

(1) Determine the total amount of expenses that would be eliminated if operations of Department A were discontinued.

(2) Determine by what amount the expenses eliminated would exceed or be less than the gross profit on sales made by Department A.

(3) Determine what the net income before federal income tax would be if Department A were discontinued.

THE HEDGES CORPORATION
Profit and Loss Statement
(Showing Net Income by Departments)
For the Year Ended December 31, 1954

	Department I			Department II			Total		
Gross sales			$25,000			$50,000			$75,000
Deduct: Returned sales and allowances	$ 100			$ 200			$ 300		
Discount on sales	200	$ 300		300	$ 500		500		$ 800
Net sales			$24,700			$49,500			$74,200
Deduct cost of goods sold:									
Purchases		$15,000			$30,000			$45,000	
Deduct: Returned purchases and allowances	$ 350			$ 400			$ 750		
Discount on purchases	250	600		550	950		800	1,550	
Net cost of purchases		$14,400			$29,050			$43,450	
Add freight in		900			1,200			2,100	
Total		$15,300			$30,250			$45,550	
Add inventory—December 31, 1953		10,500			16,300			26,800	
Total cost of goods available for sale		$25,800			$46,550			$72,350	
Deduct inventory—December 31, 1954		8,200			9,800			18,000	
Cost of goods sold			17,600			36,750			54,350
Gross profit on sales			$ 7,100			$12,750			$19,850
Deduct operating expenses:									
Selling expenses:									
Store rent	$ 750			$ 750			$1,500		
Advertising	900			600			1,500		
Salesmen's salaries	600			400			1,000		
Depreciation of delivery equipment	250	$ 2,500		125	$ 1,875		375	$ 4,375	
General expenses:									
Officers' salaries	$2,000			$1,500			$3,500		
Office salaries	600			600			1,200		
Insurance	1,000			900			1,900		
Bad debts	900			1,500			2,400		
Miscellaneous general expenses	650	5,150		450	4,950		1,100	10,100	
			7,650			6,825			14,475
Net operating income (loss*)			$ 550*			$ 5,925			$ 5,375
Deduct net interest expense:									
Interest expense	$ 80			$ 70			$ 150		
Interest income	50	30		65	5		115	35	
Net income (loss*) before federal income tax			$ 580*			$ 5,920			$ 5,340
Federal income tax (credit#)		50#			300			250	
Net income (loss*)			$ 530*			$ 5,620			$ 5,090

ASSIGNMENT MATERIAL FOR CHAPTER 13

Questions

1. What are the three elements of manufacturing cost?

2. Distinguish between direct labor and indirect labor.

3. Tell in which element of manufacturing cost the following would be classified:

    (a) Floor-sweeping material.
    (b) Wages paid the factory timekeeper.
    (c) A machine operator's wages.
    (d) Lumber to be used in making desks to be sold.
    (e) Lumber to be used in making desks for the office.
    (f) First-aid kit for the factory.
    (g) Towels for the factory office.
    (h) Parts to be used in a machine to be sold.

4. How do the working papers of a manufacturing business and those of a trading business differ?

5. If you were given the amount for the cost of goods sold, what would you do to compute the cost of goods manufactured?

6. If an expense account balance is to be apportioned, how is such apportionment handled in the working papers?

7. The *X* Machinery Co. manufactured a machine for use in its own furnace room. At what figure should the machine be set up in the fixed asset account:

    Materials cost?
    Prime cost (materials plus direct labor)?
    Total manufacturing cost (materials, labor, and overhead)?
    Selling price?
    The price at which the *X* Machinery Co. would be able to purchase the machine elsewhere?

Problems—Group A

Problem A-1. Following is the December 31, 1955 trial balance of the Mulligan Corporation, whose accounting period is the calendar year.

MULLIGAN CORPORATION
Trial Balance
December 31, 1955

Cash	20,000.00	
Raw materials inventory—December 31, 1954	30,000.00	
Goods in process inventory—December 31, 1954	15,000.00	
Finished goods inventory—December 31, 1954	12,000.00	
Unexpired insurance	1,000.00	
Factory equipment	25,000.00	
Reserve for depreciation—Factory equipment		5,000.00
Furniture and fixtures	8,000.00	
Reserve for depreciation—Furniture and fixtures		3,200.00
Accounts payable		15,000.00

Accrued salaries and wages payable......................		
Capital stock...		75,000.00
Earned surplus..		35,300.00
Dividends..	2,000.00	
Sales..		200,000.00
Purchases—Raw materials.............................	70,000.00	
Direct labor..	50,000.00	
Indirect labor..	10,000.00	
Factory rent...	5,000.00	
Heat, light, and power................................	4,000.00	
Insurance expense....................................		
Depreciation—Factory equipment......................		
Advertising..	3,000.00	
Salesmen's salaries...................................	42,000.00	
Office supplies.......................................	1,500.00	
Officers' salaries.....................................	30,000.00	
Office salaries.......................................	5,000.00	
Depreciation—Furniture and fixtures..................		
	333,500.00	333,500.00

Information for adjustments and allocations is as follows:

Adjustments:

1. Insurance amounting to $800 has expired.
2. Accrued salaries and wages as of December 31, 1955 are as follows:

Direct labor..................	$2,000
Indirect labor...............	700
Salesmen's salaries...........	500
Officers' salaries.............	400
Office salaries...............	100
	$3,700

3. Annual depreciation rates are as follows:

Factory equipment.................	10%
Furniture and fixtures.............	20%

4. Inventories—December 31, 1955:

Raw materials..............	$25,000
Goods in process...........	23,000
Finished goods.............	20,000

Allocations:

1. Insurance expense should be allocated 50% to manufacturing, 10% to selling, and 40% to general.
2. Depreciation of furniture and fixtures should be allocated 40% to selling and 60% to general.

Required:

(a) Working papers for the year ended December 31, 1955.
(b) Statement of cost of goods sold for the year ended December 31, 1955.
(c) Closing entries.

Problem A-2. On pages 592 and 593 is a trial balance of The Pardee Company on December 31, 1954.

THE PARDEE COMPANY
Trial Balance
December 31, 1954

Cash	32,987.50	
Notes receivable	2,400.00	
Accounts receivable	250,900.00	
Reserve for bad debts		13,000.00
Accrued interest receivable		
Raw materials inventory, 12/31/53	27,000.00	
Goods in process inventory, 12/31/53	25,000.00	
Finished goods inventory, 12/31/53	30,000.00	
Unexpired insurance	3,600.00	
Land	25,000.00	
Buildings	50,000.00	
Reserve for depreciation—Buildings		5,250.00
Machinery	40,000.00	
Reserve for depreciation—Machinery		12,500.00
Furniture and fixtures	5,700.00	
Reserve for depreciation—Furniture and fixtures		2,500.00
Notes payable		87,000.00
Accounts payable		42,800.00
Federal income tax payable		
Accrued salaries and wages payable		
Accrued interest payable		
Capital stock		200,000.00
Earned surplus		95,327.50
Dividends	15,000.00	
Sales		990,000.00
Returned sales and allowances	42,000.00	
Discount on sales	15,900.00	
Purchases—Raw materials	320,000.00	
Discount on purchases		9,700.00
Freight in	23,000.00	
Direct labor	299,500.00	
Indirect labor	52,000.00	
Depreciation—Buildings		
Depreciation—Machinery		
Insurance—Buildings		
Insurance—Machinery		
Taxes—Real estate	4,100.00	
Heat, light, and power	23,700.00	
Repairs—Buildings	950.00	
Repairs—Machinery	1,310.00	
Factory supplies	12,875.00	
Miscellaneous factory expenses	3,010.00	
Salesmen's commissions and salaries	43,000.00	
Salesmen's traveling expenses	17,500.00	
Advertising	19,600.00	
Freight out	11,000.00	
Insurance—Merchandise	900.00	
Miscellaneous selling expenses	10,250.00	
Officers' salaries	15,000.00	
Office salaries	18,000.00	
Postage	2,000.00	
Telephone and telegraph	1,800.00	
Stationery and printing	3,950.00	
Depreciation—Furniture and fixtures		
Bad debts	9,400.00	

Miscellaneous general expenses......................	695.00	
Interest expense...................................	6,600.00	
Interest income....................................		7,550.00
Federal income tax.................................		
	1,465,627.50	1,465,627.50

The following data must also be taken into consideration:

(a) Depreciation rate on buildings is set at 4% per annum.

(b) Depreciation rate on machinery is set at 10% per annum.

(c) Depreciation rate on furniture and fixtures is set at 10% per annum.

(d) The amount shown in the Notes Payable account represents the following two notes:

    (1) $37,000—60-day, non-interest-bearing note, dated November 23, 1954, given to Steel Industries, Inc.

    (2) $50,000—6%, 60-day note, dated December 16, 1954, given to the General Factory Products Co.

(e) The following insurance costs have expired during 1954:

    (1) $400—on policy covering buildings.

    (2) $300—on policy covering machinery.

(f) Accrued wages and salaries on December 31, 1954, were as follows:

Direct labor........................	$10,300
Indirect labor.......................	3,000
Salesmen's commissions..............	2,500
Total...........................	$15,800

(g) The amount in the Notes Receivable account represents a $2,400 note dated December 1, 1954, received from one of our customers. The note bears interest at 5% and is due on February 1, 1955.

(h) The bad debts expense is to be adjusted to bring the total expense for bad debts for the year to equal $12,480.

(i) The liability for the 1954 income tax is to be set up in the amount of $6,500.

(j) The following apportionments of expenses are to be made:

	Manufacturing	Selling	General
Insurance—Buildings..................	95%	.	5%
Depreciation—Buildings...............	95%		5%
Repairs—Buildings...................	95%		5%
Taxes—Real estate...................	95%		5%
Heat, light, and power...............	90%	5%	5%
Insurance—Merchandise..............	50%	50%	
Telephone and telegraph..............		50%	50%
Depreciation—Furniture and fixtures...		25%	75%

(k) The inventories on hand December 31, 1954, were as follows:

Raw materials..............	$25,500
Goods in process............	20,000
Finished goods..............	35,000

Prepare working papers, statement of cost of goods manufactured, statement of profit and loss, statement of earned surplus, and balance sheet.

Problem A-3. Following is a trial balance of the Pareed Corporation as of December 31, 1954:

PAREED CORPORATION
Trial Balance
December 31, 1954

Cash	121,287.43	
Accounts receivable	973,912.00	
Reserve for bad debts		4,139.00
Notes receivable	30,400.00	
Accrued interest receivable		
Raw materials inventory	22,000.00	
Goods in process inventory	27,500.00	
Finished goods inventory	31,600.00	
Unexpired insurance	23,500.00	
Prepaid garage rent	3,600.00	
Land	50,000.00	
Buildings	100,000.00	
Reserve for depreciation—Buildings		13,750.00
Machinery	73,000.00	
Reserve for depreciation—Machinery		17,255.00
Delivery equipment	27,000.00	
Reserve for depreciation—Delivery equipment		9,870.00
Furniture	38,000.00	
Reserve for depreciation—Furniture		7,315.00
Notes payable		55,000.00
Accounts payable		73,917.72
Federal income tax payable		
Accrued wages and salaries payable		
Accrued interest payable		
Capital stock		1,000,000.00
Earned surplus		79,169.26
Dividends	60,000.00	
Sales		2,417,318.72
Returned sales and allowances	9,239.28	
Discount on sales	15,312.80	
Purchases—Raw materials	1,218,738.27	
Returned purchases and allowances		4,294.44
Discount on purchases		11,216.38
Freight in	17,319.82	
Direct labor	482,917.00	
Indirect labor	58,917.00	
Depreciation—Buildings		
Depreciation—Machinery		
Insurance—Buildings		
Insurance—Machinery		
Taxes—Real estate	4,860.00	
Heat, light, and power	28,500.00	
Repairs—Buildings	12,500.00	
Repairs—Machinery	39,178.41	
Factory supplies	17,111.11	
Miscellaneous factory expenses	9,319.00	
Salesmen's salaries	48,917.28	
Salesmen's traveling expenses	11,975.00	
Advertising	39,100.75	
Freight out	8,173.92	
Insurance—Merchandise		
Insurance—Delivery equipment		

Repairs—Delivery equipment.............	1,007.50	
Depreciation—Delivery equipment........		
Other delivery expenses..................	7,117.00	
Miscellaneous selling expenses...........	9,182.00	
Officers' salaries.......................	25,000.00	
Office salaries.........................	28,190.00	
Postage...............................	3,171.00	
Telephone and telegraph.................	1,650.00	
Stationery and printing.................	2,800.00	
Depreciation—Furniture.................		
Bad debts.............................		
Miscellaneous general expenses...........	9,173.70	
Interest expense.......................	4,148.75	
Interest income........................		2,073.50
Federal income tax.....................		
	3,695,319.02	3,695,319.02

Additional data:

(a) The depreciation rate on buildings is $2\frac{1}{2}\%$ per annum.

(b) The depreciation rate on machinery is 10% per annum.

(c) The depreciation rate on delivery equipment is 20% per annum.

(d) The depreciation rate on furniture is 5% per annum.

(e) Insurance policies, purchased on January 1, 1954, were as follows:

Property insured	Term of policy	Premium paid
Buildings..........................	5 years	$ 5,000
Machinery..........................	5 years	15,000
Merchandise........................	2 years	1,500
Delivery equipment..................	4 years	2,000
Unexpired insurance as of 1/1/54.................		$23,500

(f) On July 1, 1954, the company entered into a lease for additional garage space. The lease covered three years and cost $3,600.

(g) The data on the notes receivable are as follows:

From whom received	Date of note	Time of note	Rate	Face value
B. R. Reigel............	12/16/54	60 days	6%	$ 1,000
Wilson and Sons........	9/ 1/54	6 months	6%	15,000
C. R. Creamer.........	12/ 1/54	90 days	5%	14,400
Notes receivable on hand 12/31/54......,............				$30,400

(h) The data on the notes payable are as follows:

To whom given	Date of note	Time of note	Rate	Face value
Lester Steel Corp.......	11/18/54	3 months	—	$30,000
Truex Products.........	11/ 1/54	4 months	6%	25,000
Notes payable outstanding 12/31/54..................				$55,000

(i) Wages and salaries earned but unpaid on 12/31/54:

Assembly-line workers...............	$ 8,500
Indirect laborers...................	770
Salesmen........................	1,420
Deliverymen.....................	345
Office clerks.....................	912
Total........................	$11,947

(j) The company estimates that, of the $973,912 of accounts receivable on 12/31/54, only $947,802 will be collected.

(k) Federal income tax for 1954 is estimated at $110,000.

(l) The company has decided on the following apportionments of expenses:

	Manufacturing	Selling	General
All expense on buildings...............	90%		10%
Taxes on real estate....................	90%		10%
Heat, light, and power................	80%	10%	10%
Telephone and telegraph..............		50%	50%
Depreciation—Furniture..............		20%	80%
Insurance—Merchandise..............	Average inventories		

(m) The inventories on hand on 12/31/54 were as follows:

Raw materials..............	$18,000
Goods in process............	22,500
Finished goods..............	28,400

Prepare:

(1) Working papers.
(2) Statement of cost of goods manufactured.
(3) Statement of profit and loss.
(4) Statement of earned surplus.
(5) Balance sheet.

Problems—Group B

Problem B-1. From the following information, prepare a statement of cost of goods manufactured for Cramer Creamery Company.

December 31, 1953 inventories:	
Raw materials..	$ 10,000
Goods in process......................................	15,000
Finished goods..	5,000
December 31, 1954 inventories:	
Raw materials..	12,000
Goods in process......................................	9,000
Finished goods..	7,000
Raw material purchases...............................	100,000
Direct labor...	200,000
Freight in...	3,000
Selling expenses.....................................	25,000
Freight out..	2,000
Indirect labor.......................................	15,000
Insurance on factory.................................	12,500
Heat, light, and power—Factory......................	22,000
Depreciation—Machinery..............................	3,000
Factory supplies expense.............................	4,000
Returned purchases and allowances...................	5,000
Sales..	350,000
Discount on purchases................................	800
Discount on sales....................................	2,000

Problem B-2. Using the information given in Problem A-2, prepare (1) adjusting entries, and (2) closing entries.

Problem B-3.   Using the information given in Problem A-3, prepare (1) adjusting entries, and (2) closing entries.

Problem B-4.   The following information pertains to the operations of the C. L. Moore Company for the fiscal year ended June 30, 1954:

Inventories, June 30, 1953:
Raw materials	$ 22,000
Goods in process	16,225
Finished goods	77,500

Inventories, June 30, 1954:
Raw materials	24,500
Goods in process	17,100
Finished goods	58,425
Net purchases	300,000
Freight in	4,000
Direct labor	400,500
Total manufacturing expenses	235,700

From the information given above, compute the following:

(a) The cost of manufacturing.
(b) The cost of goods manufactured.
(c) The cost of goods sold.

Problem B-5.   The account balances of Sun Corporation after year-end adjustments are presented below.

SUN CORPORATION
Adjusted Trial Balance
December 31, 1954

Cash	11,000.00	
Accounts receivable	56,500.00	
Reserve for bad debts		4,500.00
Finished goods inventory	31,000.00	
Goods in process inventory	12,000.00	
Raw materials inventory	20,000.00	
Unexpired insurance	2,800.00	
Prepaid advertising	1,200.00	
Machinery and equipment	50,000.00	
Reserve for depreciation—Machinery and equipment		12,500.00
Furniture and fixtures	20,000.00	
Reserve for depreciation—Furniture and fixtures		7,500.00
Accounts payable		34,300.00
Accrued interest payable		900.00
Accrued salaries and wages payable		12,600.00
Accrued income tax		8,000.00
Mortgage payable		30,000.00
Capital stock		75,000.00
Earned surplus		13,700.00
Dividends	7,500.00	
Sales		206,500.00
Returned sales and allowances	3,500.00	
Discount on sales	2,300.00	
Purchases	54,000.00	
Returned purchases and allowances		3,000.00
Discount on purchases		1,100.00
Freight in	2,000.00	

Direct labor................................	40,000.00
Indirect labor..............................	14,000.00
Heat, light, and power......................	2,000.00
Factory rent...............................	6,000.00
Factory insurance..........................	1,200.00
Depreciation—Machinery and equipment......	5,000.00
Miscellaneous manufacturing expense.........	1,800.00
Advertising................................	4,000.00
Freight out................................	2,500.00
Salesmen's salaries.........................	12,500.00
Delivery expense...........................	4,000.00
Miscellaneous selling expense................	1,000.00
Officers' salaries...........................	18,000.00
Office salaries.............................	6,000.00
Stationery and supplies expense..............	1,400.00
Bad debts..................................	3,600.00
Depreciation—Furniture and fixtures..........	2,000.00
Miscellaneous general expense...............	1,000.00
Interest expense...........................	1,800.00
Income tax................................	8,000.00

409,600.00   409,600.00

Inventories, December 31, 1954:

Finished goods...............	$25,500.00
Goods in process.............	17,500.00
Raw materials...............	18,000.00

The heat, light, and power is allocated as follows:

Factory...................	70%
Selling...................	20%
Administration.............	10%

Prepare entries to close the books.

ASSIGNMENT MATERIAL FOR CHAPTER 14
Questions

1. Name a major advantage of the voucher system.

2. How does a voucher system permit the elimination of the accounts payable subsidiary ledger?

3. If you were designing a voucher system, how would you determine what debit columns to have in the voucher register?

4. Why is it necessary to have a Sundry Accounts Debited section in the voucher register? When are the entries in this section posted? When are all other entries posted?

5. When a voucher system is used, what is the procedure:

    (a) When a purchase is made on account?
    (b) When a purchase is made for cash?

6. What is the procedure when a voucher is paid by note?

7. If at the time when a liability is incurred it is known that it will be paid in installments, what is the accounting procedure with a voucher system?

8. Would you recommend the use of a voucher system if a company is in such a poor financial condition that its liabilities are usually paid in installments?

9. How are the following situations handled when a voucher system is in use?

    (a) A voucher is partially paid.
    (b) Part of a purchase for which a voucher has been made is returned and credit is received.

10. What is the purpose of the Deduction columns in the voucher register?

Problems—Group A

Problem A-1. The following are selected transactions of the Pillar Corporation during January, 1955. The corporation uses the voucher system. Record these transactions in the books of original entry. Assume appropriate voucher and check numbers.

1955
Jan. 6—Merchandise is received from A. Hawk, $3,000. A 6%, 20-day note is given in payment.

    12—Merchandise is received on account from H. Stell, $5,000. Terms, 2/10; n/30.

    15—Merchandise costing $1,000 is returned to H. Stell and a credit memo is received.

    19—A machine costing $6,000 is purchased from Beekman Co. Cash in the amount of $2,000 is paid down, and the balance is payable in monthly installments of $1,000 each.

    20—H. Stell is paid the amount due, $4,000 less 2% discount.

    21—Merchandise is received on account from P. R. Prince, $1,000. Terms, n/10.

Jan. 26—The note payable to A. Hawk is paid with interest.

28—A cash customer, R. Williams, returned merchandise for which he had paid $700. A bank draft for that amount is purchased from the White Bank and forwarded to him. The bank charged $700.75 for the draft, the $.75 representing an exchange charge. The voucher was made for $700.75.

31—A check for $400 is mailed to P. R. Prince in partial payment of his invoice of January 21.

Problem A-2. The transactions below represent a selection from the July, 1955 transactions of Smith and Smart, partners. The firm uses a voucher system. Record these transactions in the books of original entry. Assume appropriate voucher and check numbers.

1955

July 6—A machine costing $8,000 is purchased from Alexander Co. Cash in the amount of $4,000 is paid and the balance will be paid in four monthly installments of $1,000 each.

10—Merchandise is received from J. Peters on account, $3,000. Terms, n/10.

15—Merchandise is received on account from L. A. Moore, $2,500. Terms, 2/10; n/30.

18—Merchandise costing $500 is returned to L. A. Moore and a credit memo for that amount is received.

20—J. Peters is paid $1,800 cash and a 6%, 10-day note for $1,200 is given him for the balance owed.

22—Merchandise is purchased for cash from Rowland Co., $700.

24—L. A. Moore is paid the amount due, $2,000 less 2% discount. In order to make the remittance, a bank draft for $1,960 was purchased. The State Bank charged $1,961 for the draft.

30—The note payable to J. Peters is paid with interest.

31—Jack Smart withdraws $600.

Problem A-3. J. P. Mast and P. R. Sanders form a partnership on February 15, 1955, to operate a cash-and-carry wholesale hardware business. The transactions for the first two weeks of operations are given below. Record these transactions in the books of original entry listed below, post, and prepare a trial balance and a list of unpaid vouchers at the end of the month. The company uses the following books of original entry:

Journal
Voucher register
Check register
Cash receipts book

1955

Feb. 15—J. P. Mast invests $60,000 cash.

P. R. Sanders invests non-cash assets with values as follows:

Equipment............. $20,000
Merchandise............ 40,000

Rent for a building is paid to Peters Realty Co. for three months in advance, $600. The partners plan to adopt a calendar year for accounting purposes.

16—Cash sale—$2,000.

Feb. 16—A five-year fire insurance policy is purchased from Hitchcock Mutual for cash, $2,000.

Merchandise is received from A. Punt on account, $4,500. Terms, 2/10; n/30. Invoice date, February 15.

Merchandise is purchased for cash from Abel Bros., $3,000.

17—Supplies are purchased from Hunt Supply Co. for cash, $300.

Merchandise is received from P. Jenkins on account, $5,000. Terms, 3/10; n/30. Invoice date, February 17.

18—Additional equipment (storage bins) is purchased from Carter Co., $10,000. Cash in the amount of $2,000 is paid and the balance is payable in four monthly installments of $2,000 each.

19—Cash sale, $5,000.

Merchandise is purchased for cash from Besser Co., $6,000.

Merchandise is received on account from John Regan, $8,300. Terms, 1/10; n/30. Invoice date, February 18.

22—Transportation charges on an incoming order are paid to the Vulcan Express Company, $900.

Merchandise is received from Arthur Jackson on account, $7,900. Terms, 2/10; n/30. Invoice date, February 21.

Merchandise is purchased for cash from Simpson Steel Co., $3,500.

23—Cash sale, $2,000.

Cash in the amount of $800 is refunded to a customer, Jack Bret, who returned merchandise.

24—Merchandise is received from Wilson Corp. on account, $2,500. Terms, 1/10; n/30. Invoice date, February 23.

Merchandise is returned to John Regan and a credit memo for $300 is received (see February 19).

25—A. Punt is paid $4,500 less 2% for invoice of February 15.

J. P. Mast withdraws cash, $500.

P. R. Sanders withdraws cash, $750.

26—P. Jenkins is paid $5,000 less 3% for invoice of February 17.

A loan is secured at bank by discounting a one-year, $1,000 note. The discount rate is 5%.

27—Cash sale, $2,000.

John Regan is paid $8,000 less 1% for invoice of February 18.

Problems—Group B

Problem B-1. The Farriday and Johnson Company uses the following books:

Journal
Voucher register (with "Deductions" section)
Check register
Cash receipts book
Sales book

For the following selected transactions, indicate the books in which entries would be made. If a notation is required to be made in one of the books of original entry in addition to other entries, state this fact and name the book in which the notation is made.

Example: Merchandise is returned to a creditor and a credit memo is received.
Answer: Entered in Journal.
        Notation in Voucher Register.

1. Made a sale to a customer, accepting part payment in cash and a note for the balance.
2. Purchased merchandise for cash.
3. Gave a note to a creditor for a past-due balance.
4. Borrowed money by discounting a note at the bank.
5. Purchased equipment on the installment plan. Made a cash down payment and agreed to pay the balance in equal monthly installments.
6. Collected a customer's note, plus interest.
7. Made a partial payment to a creditor on an invoice which had been received and recorded previously.
8. Paid a note at bank. (Note bore no interest and had been discounted at the bank.)
9. Paid a note to a creditor plus interest.
10. Returned merchandise to a vendor and received a credit memo.

Problem B-2. Pilot Corporation began operations on October 1, 1955. At the end of October, no general ledger postings had been made from the books of original entry, which are presented in summary below. Set up the necessary general ledger accounts, post, and prepare a general ledger trial balance as of October 31, 1955.

Journal:

Column totals:
Debit.. $22,725
Credit... $22,725

Column details:
Debits:

Notes receivable	(Oct. 7)........................	$ 3,000
Vouchers payable	(Oct. 12)...........................	4,000
Cash	(Oct. 16)............................	9,900
Prepaid interest	(Oct. 16)............................	100
Vouchers payable	(Oct. 23)...........................	500
Salaries	(Oct. 31)............................	5,000
Payroll taxes	(Oct. 31)............................	225
		$22,725

Credits:

Accounts receivable	(Oct. 7)..........	$ 3,000
Notes payable	(Oct. 12)...........	4,000
Notes payable.	(Oct. 16)...........	10,000
Returned purchases and allowances	(Oct. 23)...........	500
Accrued payroll	(Oct. 31)...........	4,000
Federal O. A. B. taxes withheld	(Oct. 31)...........	75
Federal income taxes withheld	(Oct. 31)...........	925
Federal O. A. B. taxes payable	(Oct. 31)...........	75
Federal unemployment taxes payable	(Oct. 31)...........	15
State unemployment taxes payable	(Oct. 31)...........	135
		$22,725

Voucher register:

Column totals:
Vouchers payable.. $64,000
Purchases... 42,000
Sundry accounts... 22,000

Column details:
Sundry accounts:

Freight in	(Oct. 7)	$ 1,000
Rent	(Oct. 8)	400
Supplies	(Oct. 12)	500
Equipment	(Oct. 12)	10,000
Delivery expense	(Oct. 20)	2,000
Unexpired insurance	(Oct. 25)	600
Returned sales and allowances	(Oct. 30)	1,000
Advertising	(Oct. 30)	2,500
Accrued payroll	(Oct. 31)	4,000
		$22,000

Check register:

Column totals:

Vouchers payable	$53,000
Discount on purchases	750
Cash	52,250

Cash receipts book:

Column totals:

General ledger	$69,900
Accounts receivable	40,000
Discount on sales	400
Cash	109,500

Column details:
General ledger:

Capital stock	(Oct. 5)	$60,000
Untitled	(Oct. 16)	9,900
		$69,900

Sales book:

Column total	$63,000

Problem B-3. Libby-Westcott and Company, a partnership, uses the voucher system. Its voucher register has, in addition to other columns, a provision for noting deductions against the amounts of outstanding vouchers. Two debit columns, one for Purchases and one for Sundry accounts, are provided.

Below are selected transactions for the month of August, 1955. Construct the voucher register for Libby-Westcott and Company and record therein all the entries and notations which would be necessary for these selected transactions. Assume appropriate voucher, check, and page numbers. You are not required to prepare any of the other books of original entry, although the company does use a journal, check register, cash receipts book, and sales book in addition to the voucher register.

1955

Aug. 4—Merchandise is received from J. Armin on account, $6,000. Terms, 2/10; n/30.

6—Office supplies are purchased on account from United Stationers, $700. Terms, n/30.

7—Merchandise costing $1,000 is returned to J. Armin (see August 4) and a credit memo is received.

Aug. 9—A check for $500 is paid to a customer, Julian Ross, who returned goods he had bought for cash on August 2.

12—J. Armin is paid the balance due on the August 4 purchase, less discount.

15—Merchandise is received from James Eddy on account, $2,000. Terms, 1/10; n/30.

17—A bookkeeping machine is purchased from Bliss Co. for $3,000. Cash in the amount of $1,000 is paid down and the balance is payable in four monthly installments of $500 each, beginning on September 17.

19—A note payable to Arthur Jinks for $3,000 plus interest of $60 is paid. (This note was given Jinks in June, 1955.)

20—Merchandise is purchased for cash from Randolph Corp., $2,000.

21—Merchandise is received from Silver Bros. on account, $4,000. Terms, n/10.

25—Ronald Westcott, a partner, withdraws $600 cash.

27—A check for $500 is sent to James Eddy in partial payment of the amount owing on the August 15 purchase. The discount period ended on August 24.

31—A 4%, 30-day note for $4,000 is given Silver Bros. in settlement of the August 21 purchase.

Problem B-4. Dixie Corporation is organized on September 4, 1955. The transactions for September are given below.

The corporation uses the following books of original entry:

Journal
Voucher register
Check register
Cash receipts book

Set up the books of original entry, record the transactions, post to general ledger accounts, and prepare a trial balance and a schedule of vouchers payable as of September 30, 1955.

All sales are for cash, and hence the cash receipts book has a credit column for sales rather than for accounts receivable. The voucher register has columns in which deductions may be noted and has debit columns for Purchases, and Sundry accounts.

1955

Sept. 5—Capital stock of $50,000 is issued to John Jones. Cash of $30,000 is collected and a 15-day, 6% note is accepted for the balance.

7—Rent for the balance of the month of September is paid to J. Regan, $275.

Equipment costing $5,000 is purchased from the Millward Co. A $2,000 down payment is made, with the balance payable in monthly installments of $1,000 each.

8—Office supplies are purchased from the Efficiency Co. on account, $300. Terms, n/10.

10—Merchandise is received from Burt Co. on account, $6,000. Terms, 1/10; n/30.

Merchandise is purchased for cash from Hingle Bros., $2,000.

11—A three-year fire insurance policy is purchased from Security Insurance Co. for cash, $630.

12—Cash sale, $2,300.

Sept. 13—Merchandise is received from Roll, Inc., on account, $4,200. Terms, 2/10; n/30.

    15—Freight is paid to the R. E. Truck Company on Burt and Hingle orders, $225.

    16—Merchandise costing $1,000 is returned to Burt Co. and a credit memorandum is received.

       Merchandise is purchased from Joten, Ltd., for cash, $3,700.

    17—Efficiency Co. is paid $300 for invoice of September 8.

       Freight on Joten order is paid to Chapel Van Company, $340.

    18—A check for $2,970 is sent to Burt Co. in partial payment of the amount owed. It is Burt's policy to allow discounts on partial payments.

    19—Cash of $700 is refunded to R. Ralt, a customer who had purchased for cash.

    20—The note given by the stockholder is collected, with interest.

    22—Roll, Inc., is paid $4,200 less 2% discount.

       Merchandise is received on account from Mendel Mills, $4,900. Terms, 1/10; n/30.

    24—Cash sale, $1,700.

    26—A note for $2,000, bearing interest at 6% and dated September 20, 1955, is sent to Burt Co. in settlement of the balance owed to them.

    28—Delivery charges for the month are paid to the Safe Haul Co., $325.

ASSIGNMENT MATERIAL FOR CHAPTER 15

Questions

1. A business follows the practice of reversing all adjustments for the accrual of income. Describe an alternative procedure to avoid the use of reversing entries.

2. When should an expenditure be charged to an asset account, and when should it be charged to an expense account?

3. Would it be a mistake to charge an expense account for an expenditure that benefits a three-year period?

4. Describe two procedures by which income collected in advance and applicable in part to future periods may be recorded in the accounts.

5. How does an accountant determine when adjustments are required?

6. Is it possible to adopt accounting procedures that will result in making reversing entries unnecessary?

7. If reversing entries are used, must they be recorded on the first business day of the new accounting period?

8. Assume that you wish to record all expenses by one or the other of the following methods:

   (a) Charge all expense expenditures to expense accounts and set up prepaid expense accounts at the end of the period, if necessary.
   (b) Charge all expense expenditures to prepaid expense accounts and write off the expired portion of each expense at the end of the period by a charge to an expense account.

Which method would you adopt?

Problems—Group A

Problem A-1. The trial balance of Ward Company, before adjustments, at the end of the year 1954, is given below:

WARD COMPANY
Trial Balance
December 31, 1954

Cash	800.00	
Accounts receivable	15,700.00	
Reserve for bad debts		173.00
Notes receivable	7,000.00	
Inventory	32,000.00	
Unexpired insurance	600.00	
Land	17,000.00	
Building	30,000.00	
Reserve for depreciation—Building		12,000.00
Equipment	26,950.00	
Reserve for depreciation—Equipment		9,625.00
Accounts payable		4,000.00
Notes payable		8,000.00
Capital stock		80,000.00

Earned surplus......................................		2,857.00
Sales..		103,000.00
Purchases..	71,150.00	
Salaries..	17,500.00	
Advertising expense.............................	1,125.00	
Miscellaneous selling expense.................	3,330.00	
Lease income......................................		3,500.00
	223,155.00	223,155.00

Data required for adjusting the accounts are as follows:

(1) The Reserve for Bad Debts should be increased to $300.

(2) The balance of the Notes Receivable account is the face of a 6%, 60-day note carrying the date December 1, 1954.

(3) The insurance was purchased on July 1, 1954, to run for 18 months.

(4) The expected useful life of the building when new was 20 years; the equipment, 7 years.

(5) The balance of the Notes Payable account is the face of a 5%, 90-day note dated December 16, 1954.

(6) Salaries accrued amounted to $375.

(7) The advertising expense is the cost of printed matter, one-third of which has been used.

(8) A portion of the building was leased on July 1, 1954, for a two-year period, at a total rental of $3,500.

Prepare entries required to adjust the accounts on December 31, 1954, and prepare reversing entries as of January 2, 1955.

Problem A-2. The trial balance before adjustments of the Superior Company, at the end of operations for the year 1954, is presented below:

SUPERIOR COMPANY
Trial Balance
December 31, 1954

Cash.......................................	2,020.00	
Accounts receivable........................	21,230.00	
Reserve for bad debts......................		180.00
Notes receivable...........................	11,000.00	
Inventory..................................	24,700.00	
Prepaid insurance..........................	450.00	
Land.......................................	19,000.00	
Building...................................	40,000.00	
Reserve for depreciation...................		9,600.00
Long-term equipment rental prepaid.....	10,000.00	
Accounts payable...........................		6,730.00
Notes payable..............................		5,000.00
Capital stock..............................		90,000.00
Earned surplus.............................		18,340.00
Sales......................................		87,690.00
Purchases..................................	63,400.00	
Salaries...................................	16,720.00	
General expense............................	3,200.00	
Delivery expense...........................	4,320.00	
Supplies expense...........................	1,700.00	
Interest income............................		200.00
	217,740.00	217,740.00

Data required for adjustments follow:

(1) Five per cent of the accounts receivable are estimated to be bad.

(2) The notes receivable bear a 5% rate. Interest on an $8,000 six-month note was collected in advance and was one-half earned on December 31, 1954. The remaining notes were dated December 1, 1954, and mature sixty days from that date.

(3) One-half of the insurance has expired.

(4) The building had an expected useful life when new of 25 years.

(5) The equipment rental was paid on January 1, 1954, for five years in advance.

(6) The notes payable are 6%, 90-day notes and were given December 1, 1954.

(7) Salaries accrued amount to $410.

(8) A delivery service was engaged during the year on a per-mile contract basis. On December 31, 1954, the company had paid in advance for 400 miles of service at a rate of 12 cents a mile.

(9) Supplies on hand total $350.

Using a six-column work sheet, enter the trial balance, make the adjustments, and complete the adjusted trial balance. Also, using journal paper, prepare reversing entries as of January 2, 1955.

Problem A-3. The unadjusted trial balance of Clark Publishing Company on December 31, 1954, follows:

CLARK PUBLISHING COMPANY
Trial Balance
December 31, 1954

Cash	21,850.00	
Subscriptions receivable	23,780.00	
Reserve for uncollectible subscriptions		380.00
U. S. Government bonds	7,500.00	
Lease of building and land prepaid	28,290.00	
Equipment	69,760.00	
Reserve for depreciation—Equipment		27,440.00
Accounts payable		15,700.00
Unearned subscriptions income		110,000.00
Mortgage payable		20,000.00
Capital stock		60,000.00
Earned surplus		10,578.00
Materials and supplies expense	74,600.00	
Salaries	14,750.00	
Rent expense—Office equipment	936.00	
Insurance expense	2,632.00	
	244,098.00	244,098.00

Adjustments were required as follows:

(1) Three per cent of the uncollected subscriptions are estimated to be uncollectible.

(2) The bonds were acquired at par on October 1, 1954, and bear 3% interest.

(3) On January 1, 1954, the lease covering the building and the land had two years to run.

(4) A rate of 12½% is used in recording depreciation of the equipment.

(5) Subscriptions income earned for the year amounts to $107,500.

(6) The mortgage was given November 1, 1954, and carries a 6% rate.

(7) Salaries accrued amount to $427.

(8) The rent expense was paid April 1, 1954, for an 18-month rental of an addressing machine.

(9) The insurance was acquired on January 1, 1954, for a two-year period.

(10) The company accepted for the first time an advertising contract effective December 1, 1954, for a two-year period. The contract calls for the payment to Clark Publishing Company of a monthly fee of $8,750.

Prepare the adjusting entries and indicate, by writing the letter "R" in the ledger folio column, which of the entries are reversed on January 1, 1955.

Problems—Group B

Problem B-1. Unique Company uses a fiscal year ending June 30 in accounting for its operations.

Transactions involving the company's Insurance Expense account were:

July 1, 1953—Paid a one-year premium, $444, on an equipment policy, and a three-year premium, $1,548, on a policy covering the buildings. Both payments were charged to Insurance Expense.

July 1, 1954—Paid a one-year renewal premium, $444, on the equipment policy. Payment was charged to Insurance Expense.

Prepare all entries affecting the Insurance Expense account from July 1, 1953, through July 1, 1955, assuming that no new premiums were paid on July 1, 1955.

Problem B-2. The unadjusted trial balance and the adjusted trial balance of the Phoenix Company, as of December 31, 1954, are given below.

Prepare the reversing entries as of January 1, 1955, assuming that the financial statements for the year 1954 have been completed.

PHOENIX COMPANY
Unadjusted and Adjusted Trial Balances
December 31, 1954

	Unadjusted		Adjusted	
Cash	1,550		1,550	
Accounts receivable	20,000		20,000	
Reserve for bad debts		450		850
Accrued interest receivable			100	
U.S. Government bonds	10,000		10,000	
Inventory	18,000		18,000	
Prepaid rent	1,200		800	
Unexpired insurance			2,700	
Land	8,000		8,000	
Building	35,000		35,000	
Reserve for depreciation—Building		5,500		7,250
Delivery equipment	28,000		28,000	
Reserve for depreciation—Delivery equipment		6,080		9,580
Notes payable		5,000		5,000
Accounts payable		12,560		12,560
Accrued salaries payable				650
Accrued interest payable				25
Unearned rent income				4,500
Capital stock		70,000		70,000
Earned surplus		11,760		11,760

	Unadjusted		Adjusted	
Sales..	125,000		125,000	
Purchases.......................................	95,000		95,000	
Salesmen's salaries.........................	10,000		10,300	
Rent expense..................................			400	
Depreciation expense—Delivery equipment.....			3,500	
Administrative salaries......................	12,000		12,350	
Insurance expense............................	3,600		900	
Bad debts.......................................			400	
Depreciation expense—Building..............			1,750	
Rent income....................................		6,000		1,500
Interest income...............................				100
Interest expense..............................			25	
	242,350	242,350	248,775	248,775

Problem B-3. Commercial Standard Company purchased a new office building on January 1, 1954. Rents were collected in advance during a two-year period as follows:

1954		Term	Term Rental Collected
January 1........................		Two years	$ 4,800.00
March 1.............................		Three years	9,000.00
June 1..............................		Two years	6,000.00
October 1...........................		One year	1,200.00
1955			
February 1.........................		Three years	10,800.00
April 1.............................		Two years	7,200.00
August 1...........................		One year	1,500.00
September 1.........................		Six months	600.00

Required:

(a) Assuming that the collections were credited to Rental Income Earned, make all the entries necessary to account for the rent through January 1, 1956, except that entries need not be made to record the collections.

(b) Assuming that the collections were credited to Unearned Rental Income, make the entries for the same period as in (a) above. Entries need not be made to record the collections.

The company uses the calendar year in accounting for its operations.

Problem B-4. Adjusting and closing entries are given below for the Dawson Company. The company is on a calendar-year basis.

Adjusting Entries

1954

Dec. 31	Bad debts.....................................	150.00	
	Reserve for bad debts......................		150.00
	To provide for estimated uncollectible accounts.		

31	Accrued interest receivable.....................	15.00	
	Interest income.............................		15.00
	To record interest income accrued.		

31	Store supplies on hand...........................	160.00	
	Store supplies expense......................		160.00
	To adjust for store supplies on hand.		

Dec. 31 Depreciation expense—Equipment................ 2,500.00
               Reserve for depreciation—Equipment.........   2,500.00
         To record depreciation of equipment for the year.

     31 Interest expense................................   20.00
               Accrued interest payable...................   20.00
         To adjust for unrecorded interest expense.

     31 Salaries.......................................   276.00
               Accrued salaries payable...................   276.00
         To record accrued salaries.

     31 Prepaid rent...................................   1,200.00
               Rent expense..............................   1,200.00
         To adjust the Rent Expense account.

     31 Insurance expense..............................   1,000.00
               Unexpired insurance.......................   1,000.00
         To record insurance expired.

Closing Entries

     31 Sales.. 60,000.00
         Inventory......................................   9,300.00
         Interest income................................   215.00
               Profit and loss...........................   69,515.00
         To close the Sales and Interest Income accounts
         and set up the ending inventory.

     31 Profit and loss................................ 63,546.00
               Inventory.................................   8,000.00
               Purchases.................................   35,000.00
               Salaries..................................   13,076.00
               Rent expense..............................   3,600.00
               Insurance expense.........................   1,000.00
               Bad debts.................................   150.00
               Store supplies expense....................   200.00
               Depreciation expense—Equipment............   2,500.00
               Interest expense..........................   20.00
         To close the expense accounts and remove the
         beginning inventory from the Inventory account.

     31 Profit and loss................................   5,969.00
               Earned surplus............................   5,969.00
         To close the Profit and Loss account.

From the information provided by these entries:

(a) Make reversing entries as of January 1, 1955.

(b) Compute the balances of the accounts given below as they appeared in the December 31, 1954 trial balance before adjustments:

> Bad debts
> Interest income
> Store supplies expense
> Depreciation expense—Equipment
> Interest expense
> Salaries
> Rent expense
> Insurance expense

If the trial balance amount cannot be determined, so state.

Problem B-5. Hayes Company rented a store building for five years on January 1, 1954, for $30,000 paid in advance. On March 1, 1954, the company started another store, paying in advance rent of $14,400 for a two-year period. A third store was opened on November 1, 1954, and a rental of $12,600 was paid in advance for one and one-half years. On July 1, 1955, the company rented a building for its fourth store, paying a rental of $9,450 for one year.

The company uses the calendar year in accounting for its operations.

Required:

(a) Make all entries in connection with the company's rent beginning January 1, 1954, and carrying through January 1, 1956, assuming that Rent Expense is charged at the time the rent is paid.

(b) Make all entries in connection with the rent for the same period as in (a) above, assuming that Prepaid Rent is charged at the time the rent is paid.

Problem B-6. The books of Bonnie Company contained the following accounts before adjustments, at the end of the year 1954:

Prepaid interest expense	200.00
Interest expense	50.00
Rent received in advance	1,350.00
Rent income	2,400.00

The ledger accounts appeared as follows:

Prepaid Interest Expense (9)

1953				
Dec.	31	Adjusting entry	28	200 00

Rent Received in Advance (29)

			1953				
			Dec.	31	Adjusting entry	28	1,350 00

Interest Expense (38)

1953					1953				
Oct.	15	Interest on 60-day note	25	150 00	Dec.	31	Adjusting entry	28	200 00
Dec.	1	Interest paid in advance on 3-month note	26	300 00		31	To Profit and Loss	29	250 00
				450 00					450 00
1954									
June	30	Interest on 30-day note	51	50 00					

Rent Income (43)

1953					1953				
Dec.	31	Adjusting entry	28	1,350 00	Oct.	1	12 mos. rent rec'd in advance	23	1,800 00
	31	To Profit and Loss	29	450 00					
				1,800 00					1,800 00
					1954				
					Oct.	1	12 mos. rent rec'd in advance	72	2,400 00

Required:

(a) What was wrong with the accounts?

(b) What entries should the bookkeeper make on December 31, 1954, in connection with these accounts?

(c) What additional entry or entries should be made to put the accounts in condition to receive entries for transactions for the year 1955?

ASSIGNMENT MATERIAL FOR CHAPTER 16

Questions

1. Mention some of the things which should be given consideration in the determination of an equitable division of partnership profits.

2. If partners' salaries and interest on their capitals are agreed upon, must allowances therefor be made even though the operations of the business result in a loss? Devise an example to illustrate the procedure which conforms with your answer.

3. How may a change in the personnel of a partnership be caused?

4. If a partner is to withdraw:

(a) Why should the books be closed?
(b) Why may it be proper to revise the valuations of the fixed assets? (In answering this question, assume that the fixed assets are carried at cost in the fixed asset accounts, and that the depreciation reserves have been computed properly.)

5. If the valuations of partnership assets are revised at the time of a change in the firm's personnel, how should the increase or decrease in valuation be divided among the partners?

6. If a partner retires and is not paid in full immediately, should the unpaid balance be left in his capital account?

7. A new partner may be admitted either by purchase or by investment. Explain the basic difference in accounting for these alternatives.

8. Why is it imperative to divide all profits or losses between the partners before distributing any assets to them when the partnership is dissolved?

9. A partnership's books show the following liabilities and partners' capitals:

Accounts payable	$15,000.00
J. P. Olive, loan	6,000.00
F. R. Tutt, capital	20,000.00
J. P. Olive. capital	25,000.00
Total	$66,000.00

All the assets have been sold for $50,000, and this amount is on hand in cash. Losses on the disposal of the assets have not been charged to the partners. How should the cash be paid out?

Problems—Group A

Problem A-1. Following is a trial balance of the ledger of Clark and Foster, a partnership, on December 31, 1954:

Cash	4,520.00
Accounts receivable	9,404.00
Inventory (December 31, 1953)	12,400.00

Furniture and fixtures.........................	2,200.00	
Reserve for depreciation—Furniture and fixtures..		330.00
Goodwill......................................	10,000.00	
Accounts payable......		4,100.00
Notes payable...............................		5,000.00
K. L. Clark, capital...........................		10,000.00
James Foster, capital..........................		5,000.00
K. L. Clark, drawings..........................	2,800.00	
James Foster, drawings........................	3,600.00	
Sales...		55,106.00
Sales returns and allowances...................	280.00	
Purchases....................................	30,527.00	
Salesmen's salaries............................	2,600.00	
Insurance expense.............................	360.00	
Taxes..	120.00	
Office expense................................	650.00	
Interest expense..............................	75.00	
	79,536.00	79,536.00

The inventory on the trial balance date was $5,025.

K. L. Clark invested $5,000 on February 1. The other capital account remained unchanged throughout the year.

The partnership agreement provided that the profits be shared as follows:

(1) Interest to be allowed partners at 6% per annum on their capital account balances at the beginning of the year.
(2) Foster to be allowed a salary of $3,200 for his active management of the business.
(3) The remainder of the profits to be shared in the following ratio: Clark 60%; and Foster, 40%.

Prepare:

Working papers.
Statement of partners' capitals.

Problem A-2.   Following is a trial balance of the books of Kelly, Stone, and Court, a partnership, on June 30, 19—:

Cash...	7,500.00	
Accounts receivable...........................	17,500.00	
E. Kelly, capital.............................		5,000.00
J. R. Stone, capital...........................		10,000.00
Frank Court, capital..........................		10,000.00
	25,000.00	25,000.00

Stone decides to withdraw from the partnership, and it is agreed that his interest shall be disposed of as follows:

One-fourth of his interest to Frank Court for $4,000.
One-half of his interest to E. Kelly for $8,000.
One-fourth of his interest to D. L. Sweeney for $4,500.

Prepare the journal entries to be placed on the partnership books to record the withdrawal.

Problem A-3. The after-closing trial balance of the firm of W, X, Y, and Z is presented below:

W, X, Y, and Z

After-Closing Trial Balance

December 31, 1954

Cash..	3,000.00	
Real estate..................................	31,000.00	
Accrued taxes payable........................		4,200.00
X, loan...................................		3,000.00
Z, loan...................................		500.00
W, capital................................		4,800.00
X, capital................................		3,000.00
Y, capital................................		12,600.00
Z, capital................................		5,900.00
	34,000.00	34,000.00

The partnership is liquidated. Prepare a statement showing the distribution of cash in each of the following cases.

Case 1.   The real estate is sold for $35,000.
Case 2.   The real estate is sold for $18,600.
Case 3.   The real estate is sold for $8,200.

Problem A-4. Dole, Gorman, and Paine are partners. Their capital accounts for 1954 appear below:

Ralph Dole, Capital

1954				1953			
Aug.	10	2,115	00	Dec.	31	16,000	00
				1954			
				June	13	3,430	00

James Gorman, Capital

1954				1953			
May	3	590	00	Dec.	31	22,000	00
Aug.	9	215	00				

J. L. Paine, Capital

1954				1953			
May	13	385	00	Dec.	31	12,000	00
Dec.	12	265	00	1954			
				Feb.	8	5,135	00

Make journal entries as of December 31, 1954, to divide the $14,280 of net income under the following agreements:

(a) The first $6,000 of net income is to be divided in the ratio of 5, 4, and 3, and the remainder is to be divided equally.
(b) Net income is to be divided in the ratio of the partners' capitals at the beginning of the year.
(c) Net income is to be divided in the ratio of the partners' capitals at the end of the year.

(d) Interest at 6% is to be allowed on partners' capitals at the beginning of the year, and the remainder is to be divided equally.

(e) Remainder is to be divided in the ratio of 5, 4, and 3, after crediting the partners with salaries of $4,000 each.

(f) Remainder is to be divided equally after allowing salaries as follows:

Dole	$5,500
Gorman	6,500
Paine	7,500

Problem A-5. Make journal entries for the distribution of cash in liquidation in the following cases.

Case 1:

Cash	19,000.00	
A, loan		3,000.00
A, capital	1,000.00	
B, capital		17,000.00
	20,000.00	20,000.00

Case 2:

Cash	13,000.00	
Accounts payable		2,000.00
C, capital		12,000.00
D, capital	1,000.00	
	14,000.00	14,000.00

Case 3:

Cash	16,000.00	
Notes payable		10,000.00
Accrued interest payable		1,000.00
E, loan		5,000.00
E, capital	3,000.00	
F, capital	3,000.00	
G, capital		6,000.00
	22,000.00	22,000.00

Case 4:

Cash	21,000.00	
Taxes payable		3,000.00
H, loan		3,000.00
H, capital		8,000.00
I, capital		7,000.00
	21,000.00	21,000.00

Problems—Group B

Problem B-1. Using the capital accounts given in Problem A-4, make journal entries as of December 31, 1954, to divide net income of $11,280 under the following agreements:

(a) The first $9,000 of net income is to be divided in the ratio of 3, 4, and 5, with any remainder divided equally.

(b) Net income is to be divided in the ratio of the partners' capitals at the beginning of the year.

(c) Interest at 4% is to be allowed on partners' capitals at the beginning of the year, with any remainder divided equally.

(d) Salaries of $3,000 each are to be allowed, with any remainder divided in the ratio of 4, 3, and 3.

(e) Interest at 3% on partners' capitals at the beginning of the year and salaries of $3,000 each are to be allowed, with any remainder divided in the ratio of 3, 3, and 4.

(f) Interest at 5% on partners' capitals at the beginning of the year and salaries of $5,000 each are to be allowed, with any remainder divided in the ratio of 1, 2, and 1.

Problem B-2. The firm of Ace, Jack, and King earned $2,412 during the year. The capital account balances as of the beginning of the year are given below.

> Ace................ $25,000
> Jack.............. 20,000
> King............. 15,000

The profit-sharing agreement provides that the partners shall share profits in the ratio of 30–30–40 after allowing for salaries and interest on beginning capital balances at 5%. The salary allowances are as follows:

> Ace................ $4,500
> Jack.............. 5,400
> King............. 3,900

Prepare journal entries to close the Profit and Loss account.

Problem B-3. The Profit and Loss account of the firm of Smith, Nelson, and Paige shows a net loss of $3,400 for the year. The capital account balances at the beginning of the year are shown below.

> O. E. Smith........... $30,000
> P. R. Nelson.......... 20,000
> G. F. Paige............ 15,000

The articles of partnership provide that the partners shall share annual profits equally after allowing interest at 4% on opening capital account balances and after crediting the partners with salaries as follows:

> Smith.............. $8,000
> Nelson............. 6,000
> Paige.............. 4,000

Prepare journal entries to close the Profit and Loss account, and a statement showing each partner's net participation.

Problem B-4. Three partners. who divide profits in their capital ratio, have the following balances in their capital accounts:

> Raymond Cole.............. $10,000
> Arnold Howes.............. 10,000
> Harold Smith.............. 20,000

Make journal entries to record Charles Johnson's admission to the partnership under the following conditions:

(a) Johnson buys Cole's interest for $10,000.

(b) Johnson invests $10,000 for a one-fifth interest in the capital of the firm.

(c) Johnson allows $4,000 as goodwill to the old partnership and invests $11,000 for a one-fifth interest in the capital of the firm.

(d) Johnson is granted goodwill; he invests $8,000 for a one-fifth interest in the capital of the new partnership.

Problem B-5. The net worth on June 30, 19— of Jones and Sons, a partnership, is represented by the following balances in the capital accounts:

James Jones................ $22,000
Henry Jones................ 20,000
William Jones.............. 18,000

The only asset of the firm is an investment in real estate. There are non-interest-bearing notes payable of $4,000.

Land Corporation agrees to buy the real estate from Jones and Sons for $100,000 in cash, after which the partnership is to be dissolved. Give the entries necessary to record the sale of the real estate and the dissolution of the partnership.

Problem B-6. Following is a trial balance of the books of Green and Hill, a partnership, on June 30, 19—:

Cash...................................	500.00	
Accounts receivable.....................	3,250.00	
Reserve for bad debts...................		125.00
Inventory..............................	5,610.00	
Land...................................	4,900.00	
Building...............................	3,840.00	
Reserve for depreciation—Building.......		765.00
Accounts payable.......................		450.00
Frank Green, capital...................		9,000.00
John Hill, capital.....................		7,760.00
	18,100.00	18,100.00

Henry Farmer was admitted as a partner, and a new partnership, known as Green, Hill, and Farmer, was formed on the following terms:

(1) Certain assets of the old partnership were restated as follows:

Inventory... $4,500.00
Land... 5,500.00
Buildings (adjust by an entry in the reserve).............. 3,000.00

(2) The old partnership was granted goodwill in the amount of $2,000.
(3) Farmer contributed $10,000 as follows:

Cash... $5,000.00
30-day, non-interest note............................... 2,500.00
Accounts receivable, of a face value of $3,000, valued at..... 2,500.00

(4) John Hill and Frank Green contributed sufficient cash to bring their capital account balances to $10,000 each.

Prepare the journal entries to record these transactions, and prepare the opening balance sheet of the new partnership.

Problem B-7. The partnership of *A*, *B*, and *C*, who share profits equally, closed its books on December 31; their accounts on that date had credit balances as follows:

A, capital............ $9,000.00
B, capital............ 5,000.00
C, capital............ 2,000.00
C, loan.............. 500.00

The partnership went into liquidation. All of its assets were turned into cash, and losses were charged to a Loss on Liquidation account. Prepare a statement with columns as follows:

A, Capital B, Capital C, Capital C, Loan   Total

For each of the following cases, enter the December 31st balances; show deductions for the loss on liquidation; show any transfers from C's loan account to his capital account; and show the amounts paid to each partner as a distribution of cash on hand.

Case 1.   Loss on liquidation, $3,300; cash to divide, $13,200.
Case 2.   Loss on liquidation, $6,690; cash to divide, $9,810.
Case 3.   Loss on liquidation, $8,400; cash to divide, $8,100.

ASSIGNMENT MATERIAL FOR CHAPTER 17

Questions

1. List several characteristics of a corporation that make it an attractive form of business organization.

2. What are organization costs? How should such costs be recorded in the accounts?

3. The *M* Corporation was organized with authorized capital stock of $100,000 divided into 10,000 shares of $10 par value each. Half of the stock was sold at $9, and the following entry was made: Debit Cash and credit Capital Stock, $45,000.

Have you any criticism of the above entry?

4. What kind of account is Subscriptions Receivable?

5. Illustrate how premium and discount on capital stock are presented in the financial statements.

6. Assume that you are appointed chief accountant of a small corporation. You discover the following account in the ledger: Discount on Capital Stock. What action, if any, would you take in connection with this account?

7. Does the par value of stock represent its real value?

8. If you purchased a share of no-par capital stock for $25, and two years later purchased another share of the same stock for $16, would you necessarily believe that the second acquisition was more advantageous?

Problems—Group A

Problem A-1. Journalize the following transactions of Barton Chemical Company, a newly organized corporation, in general journal form, and show how the Capital Stock account would appear in the general ledger after the entries were posted: (a) assuming that authorization was obtained for the issuance of 10,000 shares of $10 par value stock, and (b) assuming that authorization was obtained for the issuance of 10,000 shares of no-par stock, with the directors voting to assign a stated value of $10 a share to the no-par stock.

1954
Nov. 12—Cash subscriptions were received for 3,000 shares at $10 per share. The cash was collected and stock certificates were issued.

15—Subscriptions were received for 2,000 shares at $11 per share. Stock certificates were issued.

30—The subscriptions of November 15 were collected in full.

Problem A-2. (a) Give entries in general journal form for the following transactions of Hicks Corporation, a newly organized corporation. Authorization was obtained for 5,000 shares of $25 par value stock. Show how the Capital Stock account would appear in the general ledger after the above entries were posted.

1954

May   1—1,000 shares of stock were issued for $24,000 cash.

7—Subscriptions were received for 1,500 shares at $26.50 per share. Stock certificates were issued.

9—Paid organization costs, $3,000.

15—The subscriptions of May 7 were collected in full.

20—Subscriptions were received for 100 shares at $26 per share. Stock certificates were issued.

(b) Complete the above requirements under the assumption that the authorized shares had no par value.

(c) Assuming that the corporation had $1,800 of earned surplus after the books were closed on May 31, prepare the net worth section of the balance sheet as of May 31, 1954, for (a) and (b).

Problem A-3.   Booth Corporation was organized on June 1, 1954, and was authorized to issue 5,000 shares of $100 par value stock.

Subscriptions were taken on June 1 from M. A. Frederick for 2,000 shares and from R. B. Booth for 2,200 shares at $110 per share. The stock certificates were issued.

On June 8 Frederick transferred the following assets and liabilities to the corporation:

Notes receivable................	$ 8,000
Accounts receivable............	35,250
Inventory.....................	60,370
Accounts payable..............	7,340

The net assets were accepted in partial payment of Frederick's subscription.

Booth transferred assets to the corporation on June 10 in partial payment of his subscription as follows:

Land..................	$18,000
Building..............	90,000

A subscription was taken on June 12 from R. B. Wood for 100 shares at $112 per share. The certificate was issued.

Frederick and Booth paid the remainder of their subscriptions on June 13 in cash and Wood paid his subscription in cash on June 14. On June 15, the corporation paid $7,000 for legal fees and other organization costs.

Prepare entries in journal form to record the subscriptions and issuance of the shares and prepare a balance sheet of the corporation on June 15.

Problems—Group B

Problem D-1.   Acers Corporation was organized on May 1, 1954, and was authorized to issue 1,000 shares of $100 par value stock. On May 1, A. K. Powell and C. D. Lockwood paid cash for 150 shares each at $90 per share. By May 15, the officers had entered into several contracts which were advantageous to the company, and 400 shares were issued to J. K. Morris for cash at par. By May 25, the corporation needed additional funds and, because of the favorable earnings outlook, it secured $110 a share cash for the issuance of 200 shares to J. A. Taylor.

Journalize the transactions involving the issuance of shares of stock as indicated above.

Problem B-2. Hughes Paint Company was organized on July 1, 1954, and was authorized to issue 1,000 shares of no-par stock. The entire issue was sold for cash on the date of organization for $90 a share.

Make journal entries to record the sale of the stock under the following conditions:

(a) The company was organized in a state in which the laws require that the entire amount received for no-par shares shall be regarded as legal capital.

(b) The company was organized in a state in which the laws permit the crediting of a surplus account with a portion of the proceeds from the sale of no-par shares, and the directors of the company passed a resolution stipulating that $75 per share should be credited to the Capital Stock account.

Problem B-3. Great Western Lumber Company was organized on September 1, 1954, and was authorized to issue 3,000 shares of $100 par value stock. Prepare journal entries to record the issuance of the stock on the organization date, assuming that (a) all of the authorized stock was issued for cash at par, (b) all of the authorized stock was issued for cash at 105, and (c) all of the authorized stock was issued for cash at 95.

Problem B-4. Federal Sign Company was organized on January 2, 1954. The company was authorized to issue 10,000 shares of no-par stock. The laws of the state in which the company was organized require a stated value for such stock of at least $3 per share. The company issued 8,000 shares at $12 per share on the date of organization and on January 31 issued 1,000 shares at $15 per share. The directors did not pass any resolution concerning stated value.

The company paid $5,000 in organization fees.

Assuming earnings of $2,200 for January and the payment of no dividends, prepare the net worth section of the balance sheet of Federal Sign Company as of January 31, 1954.

Problem B-5. Garner Corporation was organized on March 1, 1954, and was authorized to issue 6,000 shares of $100 par value stock.

On March 1, subscriptions to 3,000 shares at par were received and the certificates were issued. On March 5, one-half of the subscriptions of March 1 was collected in cash. On March 10 subscriptions were received for 500 shares at $108 per share and certificates were issued. On March 15 the remainder of the March 1 subscriptions was collected. Eleven shares were issued to an attorney on March 17 in payment of $1,210 of costs incurred in the organization of the corporation. A tract of land costing $8,000 was purchased for cash, and inventory in the amount of $12,000 was acquired on account on March 22 from Jones Company. The subscriptions of March 10 were collected in full on March 29.

Give entries in journal form to record the above transactions, and prepare a balance sheet as of March 31, 1954.

Problem B-6. J. R. Hadley and A. M. Nelson organized the Arctic Refrigeration Company on February 1, 1954, with an authorized capitalization of 4,000 shares of no-par value stock. The state in which the company was incorporated allowed a portion of the proceeds of the sale of stock to be credited to a surplus account. A resolution stipulating that $20 per share would be regarded as stated capital was passed.

On the date of organization, Hadley subscribed for 1,000 shares and Nelson subscribed for 1,200 shares at $25 per share. The stock certificates were issued.

On February 10, Hadley transferred land worth $15,000 to the company in part payment of his subscription and paid cash for the balance. On the same date Nelson paid cash for his entire subscription.

Fifty shares were issued on February 16 to pay attorneys' costs of $1,250 incurred in connection with the organization of the company.

On February 27, J. N. Wilson paid in $30 per share cash for 100 shares.

Required:

(a) Prepare journal entries to record the subscriptions and the issuance of the shares.

(b) Assuming that the net income for February was $1,620 and that no dividends were declared, prepare the net worth section of the Arctic Refrigeration Company's balance sheet as of February 28, 1954.

ASSIGNMENT MATERIAL FOR CHAPTER 18
Questions

1. Does a Capital Stock Subscribed account normally have a debit or a credit balance? Where does such an account appear in the financial statements? What does its balance show?

2. Contrast the accounting under the following circumstances:

(1) Stock certificates are issued when subscriptions are received.
(2) Stock certificates are not issued until subscriptions are collected in full.

3. Suppose that a stockholder sells a portion of his shareholdings to another person. Describe how the transfer is recorded by the corporation. What accounts are debited and credited?

4. A partnership decides to incorporate. Describe the accounting procedure:

(a) If the partnership books are retained by the corporation.
(b) If the corporation opens new books.

5. What basic rights does the ownership of shares of stock confer upon a stockholder? Are these rights always enjoyed proportionately by all classes of stockholders?

6. (a) In what two general ways may stock be preferred?
(b) What is meant by the words "cumulative" and "participating" as applied to preferred stock?

7. Express an opinion on the following statement: "No stock is worth more than its par value."

8. Give some reasons why a partnership might wish to incorporate. Is there any reason why the stockholders of a corporation might wish to change to a partnership?

Problems—Group A

Problem A-1. On November 1, 1954, Crown Corporation was authorized to issue 3,000 shares of no-par stock. A resolution was passed establishing $12 per share as the stated value. On November 2, subscriptions were received for 1,400 shares at $15 per share. On November 10, subscriptions were received for 800 shares at $16 per share. The subscriptions of November 2 were collected in full on November 15 and the certificates were issued. On November 24, collection was made in full for 600 of the shares subscribed for on November 10. The certificates were issued. There was no immediate intention to call on the subscribers for the uncollected balances of their subscriptions.

Give entries in journal form to record the above transactions, and prepare a balance sheet as of November 30, 1954, for Crown Corporation.

Problem A-2. A description of the capital stock of the Cobb Corporation appears on the following page.

5% preferred stock: $100 par value; participating to the extent of 2% above the 5% preference rate, and cumulative; 1,000 shares outstanding.
Common stock: $100 par value; 1,000 shares outstanding.

Information concerning the earnings and earned surplus during the first five years of the company's existence follows:

Year	Net Income	Portion of Year's Net Income Retained	Total Earned Surplus at End of Year
1950	$25,000.00	$7,000.00	$ 7,000.00
1951	3,000.00	—	7,000.00
1952	26,000.00	5,000.00	12,000.00
1953	11,000.00	1,000.00	13,000.00
1954	18,000.00	6,000.00	19,000.00

Prepare a statement showing the dividend payments of the company for each of the years shown above.

Problem A-3. On August 31, 1954, the ledger of the partnership of Wingate and Wilson had the following balances:

Assets

Cash...	$ 6,500.00
Accounts receivable................................	31,000.00
Inventory...	37,000.00
Land..	8,000.00
Building..	25,000.00
Equipment..	22,000.00
	$129,500.00

Liabilities and Owners' Equity

Accounts payable..................................		$ 15,000.00
Notes payable.........		7,500.00
Owners' equity:		
Wingate, capital........................	$65,800.00	
Wilson, capital...........................	41,200.00	107,000.00
		$129,500.00

The partners had taken action to form a corporation on August 31, to be known as the *W* Company. The profit and loss ratio of the partners was: Wingate, 60 per cent, and Wilson, 40 per cent.

The goodwill of the partnership was valued at $12,000. The valuations of certain of the partnership assets were to be adjusted, as indicated below:

Accounts receivable (by establishing a reserve).............	$30,000.00
Building...	19,000.00
Equipment...	14,000.00
Cash (Wingate withdrew $4,000)........................	2,500.00

The new corporation was authorized to issue 1,000 shares of $100 stock.

Required:

(a) Prepare journal entries to adjust the partnership's accounts.
(b) Prepare the journal entry to record the change from the partnership to the corporate form, assuming that the books of the partnership were to be used by the corporation.
(c) Prepare journal entries to close the books of the partnership and to open new books for the corporation.

Problem A-4. Dover Corporation was incorporated on June 1, 1954, with an authorized capital consisting of 5,000 shares of 5% cumulative preferred stock of $100 par value and 2,000 shares of common stock of $50 par value.

Prepare (a) journal entries to record the transactions and (b) the owners' equity section of the balance sheet as of June 8, 1954. In making entries for the subscriptions, show subscribers' names, number of shares subscribed, the price, and the amount of the subscriptions in the explanation.

On June 1, shares were subscribed for as follows:

Preferred

Subscriber	Shares	Price	Amount
W. H. Prince	300	$100.00	$ 30,000.00
A. A. Rainbolt	700	98.00	68,600.00
J. A. Campbell	1,000	99.00	99,000.00
J. B. Blair	200	102.00	20,400.00
	2,200		$218,000.00

Common

Subscriber	Shares	Price	Amount
C. R. Raley	500	$48.00	$24,000.00
W. H. Prince	600	49.00	29,400.00
J. A. Campbell	300	48.00	14,400.00
E. L. Odom	50	47.00	2,350.00
	1,450		$70,150.00

On June 8, the subscriptions were collected as follows:

Rainbolt transferred equipment valued at $50,000 to the corporation and paid the balance in cash.

Campbell transferred land valued at $50,000 and a building valued at $40,000, and paid cash for the remainder.

The remaining subscriptions were collected in cash.

All certificates were issued at the same time.

Make individual entries for the collection on subscriptions from Rainbolt and Campbell. Make only one entry for the cash receipts from the other subscribers and show names of subscribers paying their subscriptions and other details in the explanation of the journal entries.

Problems—Group B

Problem B-1. It was decided that the Bell Corporation should be liquidated. The capitalization of the corporation was as follows:

Preferred stock—$100 par value; authorized and issued, 1,000 shares. (Dividends in arrears on preferred stock, $5 per share.)
Premium on preferred stock, $10 per share.
Common stock—$100 par value.

The preferred stock is preferred as to assets. The charter of the corporation provides that, in the event of dissolution and liquidation, the preferred stockholders have the right to receive all dividends in arrears before the common stockholders receive anything.

After the payment of all liabilities, assets of $112,500 remained. Show how these assets should be distributed to the stockholders.

Problem B-2. Nabors Corporation was organized on May 1, 1954, and was authorized to issue 4,000 shares of $100 par value stock. On May 3, subscriptions for 1,500 shares at par were received. On May 10, subscriptions for 1,800 shares at $110 per share were received. On May 15, two-thirds of the May 3 subscriptions were collected in full and certificates were issued. On May 25, one-half of the May 10 subscriptions was collected in full and certificates were issued.

Journalize the above transactions and prepare a balance sheet as of May 31 for Nabors Corporation, assuming that the uncollected subscriptions will be collected in the near future.

Problem B-3. Azle Company has 1,000 shares of $100 par value 5% preferred and 2,000 shares of $50 par value common stock outstanding.

With the understanding that the directors declare all dividends possible each year, show how profits of $4,000 in 1953, $10,000 in 1954, and $14,000 in 1955 will be distributed to each class of stockholders if the preferred stock is:

(a) Non-cumulative and non-participating.
(b) Cumulative and non-participating.
(c) Cumulative and fully participating.

Problem B-4. Osburn Corporation was organized on October 1, 1954, with authorization to issue 1,000 shares of 6% participating, cumulative, preferred stock of $100 par value, and 1,000 shares of no par value common stock.

Subscriptions were received for 300 shares of preferred at par on October 1. On the same date, 840 shares of common were issued for assets as follows:

Notes receivable.............	$ 2,500.00
Inventory....................	14,800.00
Land........................	10,000.00
Building....................	30,000.00
Equipment..................	18,300.00

One-half of the subscriptions was collected in cash on October 15. No subscriptions were collected in full.

Attorneys' fees for organizing the corporation amounted to $1,038. The corporation paid the fees on October 16 by issuing 10 shares of preferred stock at par and giving cash for the balance.

On October 31, the directors passed a resolution establishing $75 a share as the stated value for the common stock. On this date, the preferred subscriptions were collected in full. Certificates were issued.

Required:

(a) Prepare journal entries to record the stock transactions.
(b) Prepare the corporation's balance sheet as of October 31, 1954.

Problem B-5. The Triangle Company's balance sheet is presented below.

TRIANGLE COMPANY
Balance Sheet—November 30, 1954
Assets

Cash...		$ 5,400.00
Accounts receivable.........................	$8,750.00	
Less reserve for bad debts.................	1,100.00	7,650.00
Inventory..		25,000.00
Land..		10,000.00
Building...		30,000.00
Equipment...		15,800.00
		$93,850.00

Liabilities and Owners' Equity

Current liabilities:
Accounts payable.................................... $ 8,740.00
Owners' equity:
Capital stock............................ $60,000.00
Paid-in surplus.......................... 10,000.00
Earned surplus.......................... 15,110.00   85,110.00
                                                      $93,850.00

The stockholders decided to change to the partnership form of organization on November 30.

The stockholders own shares as follows:

Fain................ $30,000.00
Farmer............. 15,000.00
Farley............. 15,000.00

It was decided that a new set of books would be opened for the partnership.

Give necessary journal entries on the books of the corporation and of the partnership to record the change.

Problem B-6. Prince and Price, a partnership, received authorization to establish a corporation on June 30, 1954. Prince has been receiving 60 per cent of the profits and Price 40 per cent. The balance sheet of the partnership on June 30 was as follows:

PRINCE AND PRICE
Balance Sheet
June 30, 1954
Assets

Cash... $ 7,500.00
Accounts receivable......................... $12,500.00
Less reserve for bad debts................. 1,800.00   10,700.00
Inventory... 30,000.00
Land... 8,000.00
Building.. 27,000.00
                                                $83,200.00

Liabilities and Owners' Equity

Accounts payable.................................... $ 9,350.00
Owners' equity:
Prince, capital........................... $33,690.00
Price, capital........................... 40,160.00   73,850.00
                                                      $83,200.00

Before the change was made, it was decided to reduce the valuation of the land to $6,000 and increase the valuation of the building to $30,300.

The charter authorized 2,000 shares of $50 par value stock, and the new company was named the Gandy Corporation. 1,002 shares were issued for the net assets of the partnership.

Required:

(a) Journal entries on the partnership's books to adjust the assets and close the books.

(b) Journal entries to open the new books for the corporation.

ASSIGNMENT MATERIAL FOR CHAPTER 19

Questions

1. What items are properly credited to Paid-in Surplus?

2. Explain "stated capital."

3. What is a stock dividend? Will the issuance of a stock dividend affect the book value per share of the class of stock distributed by the dividend?

4. Are all declared dividends liabilities?

5. When are dividends "in arrears"?

6. Under what conditions might a corporation prefer to declare a stock dividend rather than a cash dividend?

7. Which would you prefer to acquire from a corporation for $90:

    (a) A share of unissued stock of a par value of $100?
    (b) A share of treasury stock of the same class?

8. Is there any relationship between dividends and treasury stock? Explain.

9. Tell how the Earned Surplus account is affected by the following:

    (a) Declaration of a scrip dividend.
    (b) Payment of a previously declared cash dividend.
    (c) Declaration of a stock dividend.
    (d) Acquisition of treasury shares.

10. What is appropriated surplus? Give some examples.

Problems—Group A

Problem A-1. General Corporation has 10,000 shares of $10 par value stock outstanding. Give necessary journal entries for the following, omitting explanations.

    (1) Declared a stock dividend amounting to 1,000 shares. In this instance, the fair value of the stock is equal to par value.
    (2) Received a donation of 1,000 shares of treasury stock.
    (3) Established a reserve for contingencies in the amount of $5,000.
    (4) Sold the donated treasury stock for $12 per share.
    (5) Issued the stock dividend previously declared.
    (6) A building site worth $15,000 was donated to the corporation.
    (7) Declared a cash dividend in the amount of $1 per share.
    (8) Established a reserve for plant extension in the amount of $40,000.
    (9) Paid the dividend previously declared.
    (10) Acquired 1,000 shares of treasury stock for $15,000.
    (11) Eliminated the reserve for contingencies.
    (12) Sold 200 shares of the treasury stock for $16 per share.
    (13) Increased the reserve for plant extension by $10,000.
    (14) Sold 300 shares of the treasury stock for $18 per share.
    (15) Sold the remaining treasury shares for $7,000.

Problem A-2. The following balances were taken from the ledger of the Sabine Company on August 31, 1954:

Cash	$14,720.00
Accounts receivable	55,000.00
Subscriptions receivable—Common	15,000.00
Subscriptions receivable—Preferred	40,000.00
Land	30,000.00
Building	180,000.00
Organization cost	3,120.00
Discount on stock—Common	7,430.00
Treasury stock—Common	9,480.00
Treasury stock—Preferred	6,000.00
Common stock issued	100,000.00
Preferred stock issued	80,000.00
Reserve for bad debts	2,300.00
Earned surplus	21,230.00
Paid-in surplus—Treasury stock transactions	14,990.00
Reserve for depreciation—Building	10,000.00
Subscribed stock—Common	30,000.00
Subscribed stock—Preferred	60,000.00
Accounts payable	19,730.00
Reserve for plant expansion	30,000.00
Inventory	20,000.00
Dividends payable—Common	12,500.00

The treasury stock of both classes is carried at cost. There are 50 shares of preferred and 70 shares of common in the treasury. Under the laws of the state of incorporation, earned surplus is restricted to the extent of the cost of the treasury stock.

The stock subscriptions are due in the near future.

Both classes of stock have a par value of $100 per share. Of the 1,600 authorized shares of preferred, 800 shares are issued. There are 2,000 shares of common authorized and 1,000 shares are issued. The preferred carries a dividend rate of 5%, it is cumulative and participating, and there are no dividends in arrears.

Prepare a classified balance sheet for the Sabine Company as of August 31, 1954.

Problem A-3. Gliders Corporation operated profitably in the early years of its history. In recent years, sales have declined and operating deficits have been incurred.

A portion of the corporation's balance sheet is reproduced below:

GLIDERS CORPORATION
Partial Balance Sheet
December 31, 1954

Net worth:		
Capital stock:		
5% cumulative preferred—$100 par value; 4,000 shares authorized; 3,000 shares issued		$270,000.00
Common—$10 par value; 50,000 shares authorized; 42,600 shares issued, of which 1,000 shares are in the treasury		420,000.00
Earned surplus:		
Operating deficit	$111,500.00	
Deduct premium on common stock	14,000.00	97,500.00*
		$592,500.00

* Deduction.

The corporation is seeking a bank loan. The corporation's accountant has come to you for advice concerning the desirability of giving the bank the balance sheet in the present form.

During the early years of operation, the corporation issued common stock at premiums totaling $50,000. Later, additional common stock was issued at discounts totaling $36,000. Last month the corporation paid $6,000 for 1,000 shares of its own common stock.

The preferred stock was issued on January 1, 1952. No dividends have been declared to date on this stock.

Prepare the net worth section of the corporation's balance sheet in more acceptable form.

Problems—Group B

Problem B-1. The following were taken from the records of the Hendrix Corporation, after closing, on December 31, 1954:

Capital stock—$100 par value; authorized, 2,000 shares; issued, 1,600 shares	$160,000.00
Reserve for plant extensions	40,000.00
Reserve for contingencies	16,000.00
Capital stock to be issued, January 8, 1955, as a stock dividend, 320 shares	32,000.00
Paid-in surplus	8,000.00
Bond sinking fund reserve	70,000.00
Unappropriated earned surplus	185,000.00

Prepare the net worth section of the balance sheet as of December 31, 1954.

Problem B-2. Following are certain transactions of the Mason Company:

1954

June 1—The company purchased 88 shares of its stock at $105 per share. These shares had been issued at their par of $100.

15—Reissued at $108 per share 55 of the shares purchased on June 1.

24—Reissued at $103 per share the remaining 33 shares purchased on June 1.

Required:

(a) Journalize the above transactions.

(b) Journalize the transaction of June 24, assuming that the company had no paid-in surplus on that date.

Problem B-3. From the following account balances taken from the ledger of Mixture Corporation, compute the total earned surplus.

Premium on preferred stock	$11,000.00
Earned surplus	81,000.00
Dividends payable	10,000.00
Reserve for plant extension	30,000.00
Reserve for bad debts	7,000.00
Surplus from donations	15,000.00
Cash	33,000.00
Discount on common stock	9,500.00
Reserve for the retirement of preferred stock	22,000.00
Organization costs	5,000.00
Reserve for contingencies	20,000.00
Surplus arising from treasury stock transactions	3,700.00

Problem B-4. The owners' equity section of the balance sheet of the Household Equipment Company on May 31, 1954, appears below:

Owners' equity:
Capital stock—no-par value: Authorized, 4,000 shares;
    issued, 3,000 shares at a stated value of $75 per share.. $225,000.00
Paid-in surplus...................................... 75,000.00
Earned surplus....................................... 125,000.00

Assume that the books are closed monthly. In each case, prepare the journal entry to record the transaction and any related closing entry on June 30. Deal with each case independently of all other cases.

(a) The directors declared a dividend of $5 per share on June 15, 1954, to be paid in cash on July 25 to stockholders of record on July 10.

(b) The directors declared a dividend of $5 per share on June 15, 1954, to be paid in cash on July 25 to stockholders of record on July 10; one-third of the dividend was to be charged to paid-in surplus.

(c) On June 15, 1954, the directors declared a stock dividend of $\frac{1}{10}$ of a share for each share held on July 10, to be issued on July 25. The shares are regarded as having a fair value of $100 each.

(d) The directors declared a dividend on June 15, 1954, to distribute to stockholders of record on July 10 inventory items costing $12,000. The date set for distribution was July 25.

Problem B-5. The net worth sections of the Big Gap Corporation as of December 31, 1953 and December 31, 1954 are presented below. It is the corporation's policy to accept no subscriptions for its shares unless they are collectible immediately in cash.

By comparing the net worth sections, determine the transactions that occurred to account for the changes in the corporation's net worth. Give journal entries for these transactions.

BIG GAP CORPORATION
Net Worth Section of Balance Sheet
December 31, 1953

Common stock—$10 par value; 10,000 shares authorized;
    5,000 shares issued.................................. $50,000.00
Premium on stock..................................... 5,000.00
Earned surplus....................................... 18,000.00
                                                $73,000.00

BIG GAP CORPORATION
Net Worth Section of Balance Sheet
December 31, 1954

Common stock—$10 par value; 10,000 shares authorized;
    6,000 shares issued, of which 100 shares are in the treasury $ 60,000.00
Common stock—To be issued, January 10, 1955, as a stock
    dividend, 590 shares............................... 5,900.00
Premium on stock..................................... 6,000.00
Earned surplus:
    Appropriated: Reserve for contingencies.... $ 5,000.00
    Free................................... 28,000 00   33,000.00
        Total... $104,900.00
Deduct cost of treasury stock.......................... 1,200.00
                                                  $103,700.00

Problem B-6.   Linn Corporation presented the net worth section of its June 30, 1954 balance sheet in the following form:

Net worth:
   Capital stock, $10 par value; 25,000 shares
   authorized; 15,000 shares issued and out-
    standing............................. $150,000.00
   Surplus...............................   184,413.00 $334,413.00

An analysis of the records of the corporation showed that the surplus resulted from the transactions summarized below:

Net income..	$381,997.00
Dividends declared and paid............................	130,000.00
Net losses...	107,384.00
Premium on issuance of capital stock...................	21,000.00
Proceeds from the sale of donated treasury shares........	30,000.00
Excess of cost of purchased treasury stock over proceeds from sale thereof....................................	3,200.00
Discount on the issuance of capital stock...............	8,000.00

During their June meeting, the board of directors approved the establishment of a reserve for plant expansion in the amount of $40,000.

Restate the net worth section of the balance sheet in more acceptable form.

ASSIGNMENT MATERIAL FOR CHAPTER 20
Questions

1. Explain the use of check marks and X's as posting references.

2. What advantages result from the use of expense controlling accounts?

3. If expense controlling accounts are kept and special columns are provided therefor in the voucher register, how should expenses be recorded and how should postings be made?

4. If expense controls are used, what is the purpose of the summary of expenses prepared from the subsidiary expense records at the end of the month?

5. What kinds of entries affecting the expense analysis records are likely to be made in books of original entry other than the voucher register? How will such entries be posted?

6. When the note registers are used as books of original entry:

    (a) Are special columns for the note controlling accounts required in the journal? Why?

    (b) Are special columns required in the cash books? Why?

7. Give a reason in support of the classification of cash discounts as other expense and other income.

8. Describe a method of accounting by which discounts lost by failure to pay bills within the discount period may be shown in the accounts.

Problems—Group B

Problem B-1. Street Corporation maintains an account to show purchase discounts lost; the corporation does not use a voucher system. The corporation's fiscal year ends on June 30. Prepare entries required during June in general journal form for the following transactions.

1954

June 2—Merchandise is purchased from General Supply Company with a billed price of $800 and with terms of 2/10; n/30.

     8—Merchandise is purchased from James Black with a billed price of $300 and terms of 1/10; n/30.

     9—Paid the June 2 purchase within the discount period.

   12—Office supplies are purchased for $80; the seller, Ace Supply Company, offers terms of 2/10; n/30.

   14—Merchandise is purchased from Hill Corporation with a billed price of $710 and terms of 2/10; n/30.

   19—The office supplies are paid for.

   20—Merchandise is purchased from A. B. Company for cash. The merchandise has a list price of $400, but a discount of 2 per cent is granted for all cash transactions.

   28—Paid $300 to James Black for purchase of June 8.

Problem B-2. Young Corporation was organized on June 1, 1954. Its adjusted trial balance as of June 30, 1954, is as follows:

YOUNG CORPORATION
Adjusted Trial Balance
June 30, 1954

Cash..	7,000.00	
Accounts receivable..........................	13,500.00	
Store fixtures................................	12,000.00	
Reserve for depreciation......................		120.00
Vouchers payable.............................		6,880.00
Capital stock.................................		15,000.00
Sales..		60,000.00
Purchases....................................	47,040.00	
Returned purchases and allowances..............		2,940.00
Discounts lost................................	80.00	
Selling expenses..............................	2,200.00	
General expenses.............................	3,000.00	
Depreciation expense.........................	120.00	
	84,940.00	84,940.00

Additional facts:

(1) All merchandise is purchased under terms of 2/10; n/30.

(2) All merchandise returned by Young Corporation is returned within five days.

(3) On June 30, two adjusting entries were made. One was for depreciation, in the amount of $120. The other is given below.

Discounts lost..	20.00	
Vouchers payable..................................		20.00

To record discount lost on an unpaid invoice for merchandise purchased from Admiral Supply Company. The invoice was recorded at the net price of $980.

Required:

The June 30, 1954 adjusted trial balance as it would have appeared if the corporation had not used the net price procedure.

Practice Set

This practice set is based on the transactions of Dale Corporation for the month of August. The current year should be used in all dates.

CHART OF ACCOUNTS. SUBSIDIARY RECORDS.

Charts of the general ledger accounts and the subsidiary expense accounts appear on the inside covers of the general ledger and the books of original entry. The general ledger contains the following controlling accounts:

1120—ACCOUNTS RECEIVABLE.

    This account controls an accounts receivable subsidiary ledger.

2120—VOUCHERS PAYABLE.

    Vouchers should be recorded net of the available cash discounts, in the manner described in Chapter 20.

1130—Notes Receivable.
2130—Notes Payable.

These accounts control note registers, which are also used as books of original entry.

5300—Manufacturing Expense—Control.
6000—Selling Expense—Control.
7000—General Expense—Control.

These accounts control expense analysis records, or distribution sheets, containing columns for the subsidiary accounts. You will make postings to the selling expense analysis record. It is assumed that your assistant makes the postings to the other analysis records.

Books of Original Entry

You will record transactions in the following books of original entry:

Sales book.
Voucher register.
Cash receipts from customers book.
General cash receipts book.
Cash disbursements book (Check register).
Notes receivable register.
Notes payable register.
General journal.

Payroll summaries will be prepared by an assistant; postings from the summaries will be made by you. At some time before payroll entries are posted, you should read the material in Chapter 7 and in the appendix dealing with payroll deductions and taxes.

Postings, except column totals, should be made daily from all books of original entry.

Expenses and income wholly applicable to August should be recorded directly in expense and income accounts. Expense and income items not wholly applicable to August should be recorded in prepaid expense and deferred income accounts. Transfers from these accounts to expense and income accounts will be made by adjusting entries at the end of the month.

Transactions

(The numbers in parentheses are transaction numbers.)

August 1:

(1) Dale Brothers have been in business for some time, operating as a partnership. They decide to incorporate, and Dale Corporation is organized with an authorized capital of 4,000 shares of $100 par value. Subscriptions are received for these shares as follows:

John Dale................ 2,250
Robert Dale............. 1,750
                         4,000

Make an entry to record the subscriptions.

(2) In settlement of the stock subscriptions, the corporation takes over the assets and assumes the liabilities of the partnership of Dale Brothers, as stated on the following page.

Assets:

Cash		$ 1,151.68
Accounts receivable	$ 16,763.42	
Less reserve for bad debts	597.90	16,165.52
Finished goods		74,854.35
Goods in process		34,347.83
Raw materials		58,930.62
Land		52,000.00
Buildings		142,000.00
Machinery and equipment		155,000.00
Tools		2,400.00
Delivery equipment		6,000.00
Furniture and fixtures		4,800.00
Patents		9,000.00
Goodwill		20,000.00
Total assets		$576,650.00

Liabilities:

Notes payable	$ 65,000.00	
Accrued interest on notes payable	400.00	
Mortgage payable—Land and buildings—6%	50,000.00	
Mortgage payable—Machinery and equipment—5%	60,000.00	
Accrued interest on mortgages payable	1,250.00	
Total liabilities		176,650.00

Partners' interests:

John Dale	$225,000.00	
Robert Dale	175,000.00	
Total partners' interests		$400,000.00

(a) Make a journal entry recording all of the assets except cash, and all of the liabilities except notes payable, crediting account 2201—Dale Brothers.

(b) Make an entry for the cash in the general cash receipts book, crediting account 2201.

(c) The $65,000 liability on notes payable is detailed as follows:

Date	Payee	Time	Interest Rate	Face
July 8	Citizens State Bank	90 days	6%	$25,000
June 17	First State Bank	60 "	6%	40,000
				$65,000

Record these notes in the notes payable register, debiting account 2201.

(d) Open an account in the subsidiary accounts receivable ledger with each of the debtors listed below:

C. E. Bruce	$ 8,424.30
J. C. Burns	3,215.60
C. W. Finley	219.80
C. L. Murphy	113.85
Rowley and Company	1,789.87
Stinson Motor Sales	3,000.00
	$16,763.42

(e) Make a journal entry debiting Dale Brothers and crediting Subscriptions to Capital Stock for the subscriptions paid by the transfer of the net assets of the partnership.

ASSIGNMENT MATERIAL FOR CHAPTER 21
Questions

1. Give two advantages of the use of a separate bank account for the payment of bond interest.

2. Discuss the relative advantages of unregistered and registered bonds, from the point of view of (a) the issuing corporation, and (b) the bondholder.

3. A $500,000 bond issue has been authorized, but only $300,000 of the bonds have been sold. How should these facts appear in the balance sheet?

4. Unissued bonds of a face value of $5,000, bearing 6% interest, are sold for $5,050 one month after the interest payment date. Give the entry or entries required to record this transaction.

5. From the bondholders' standpoint, what is the object of:

    (a) The sinking fund provision?
    (b) The sinking fund reserve provision?

6. What is the difference in the nature of a sinking fund reserve and a depreciation reserve?

7. Why are bond discount and bond premium written off to the Interest Expense account over the life of the bonds?

8. Where do the following appear on the balance sheet?

    Unissued Bonds.
    Sinking Fund Cash.
    Sinking Fund Securities.
    Bond Discount.
    Bond Premium.
    Accrued Bond Interest.
    Sinking Fund Reserve.
    Bonds Payable.

9. Give an appraisal of the effectiveness of a sinking fund reserve in achieving the objective for which it is established.

10. What disposition should be made of the following accounts at the maturity of a bond issue?

    Sinking Fund Reserve.
    Sinking Fund Securities.

Problems—Group A

Problem A-1. Culver Corporation uses the calendar year as its accounting year. On May 15, 1955, the corporation was authorized to issue $1,000,000 of 5% first-mortgage bonds. The bonds mature in twenty years from June 30, 1955, and interest is to be paid semiannually on June 30 and December 31. All of the bonds were issued on July 1, 1955.

Prepare journal entries to record the authorization of the bond issue, the issuance, and the payment of interest and the amortization on December 31, 1955, assuming that the bonds were issued at:

(a) 97.
(b) 103.

Problem A-2. On December 31, 1954, Wiley Company issued $500,000 of 4%, 10-year debenture bonds. The indenture provides for the establishment of a sinking fund with the Foundation Trust Company as trustee. Beginning in 1955, Wiley Company is to deposit with the trustee, on each December 31 during the life of the bonds, an amount of cash which, when added to the fund earnings after trustee fees, will increase the fund by $50,000. The trustee is able to invest in securities which provide a return of 4% on the fund principal at the beginning of each year. The trustee fee charged by Foundation Trust Company is 1% per year on the fund balance at the beginning of each year.

Required:

(a) Prepare a table showing, by years, the following:
1. Fund balance, beginning of year.
2. Fund earnings.
3. Trustee fees.
4. Annual contribution.
5. Fund balance, end of year.
(b) Prepare journal entries regarding the sinking fund for Wiley Company through December 31, 1956, assuming that the trustee immediately invests all cash in securities.

Problems—Group B

Problem B-1. On January 23, 1955, Kilroy Corporation's stockholders and directors authorized the issuance of $200,000 of 6%, 20-year bonds secured by a first mortgage. Interest was to be paid semiannually on January 31 and July 31. The bonds were dated February 1, 1955.

Interest was to be paid by means of interest coupons, the first of which came due July 31, 1955. A deposit, against which interest coupons will be charged, is to be made with Liberty Bank each interest date.

All of the bonds were issued on March 1, 1955, at par plus accrued interest to that date.

Prepare journal entries to record the authorization of the bonds, their issuance, the July 31, 1955 interest payment to Liberty Bank, the payment by Liberty Bank of $3,000 in honoring interest coupons, and the entries necessary to adjust the books on December 31, 1955, the close of Kilroy Corporation's accounting period.

Problem B-2. Tibbs Manufacturing Company is authorized to issue $100,000 of 4%, 10-year debentures on March 1, 1956. Interest is to be paid semiannually on February 28 and August 31. On March 1, 1956, all of the debentures are issued at 97.

Prepare all entires through December 31, 1956, the close of the company's accounting period.

Problem B-3. From the after-closing trial balance on page 641, prepare the balance sheet of Hamilton Corporation.

HAMILTON CORPORATION
After-Closing Trial Balance
December 31, 1955

Cash....................................	20,000.00	
Notes receivable.........................	10,000.00	
Inventory...............................	40,000.00	
Investments (non-current)................	30,000.00	
Land (for future expansion)..............	20,000.00	
Machinery and equipment.................	240,000.00	
Discount on 4% first-mortgage bonds.........	1,000.00	
Unissued 6% sinking fund debentures..........	5,000.00	
Unissued 5% collateral trust bonds............	2,000.00	
Sinking fund securities......................	5,000.00	
Reserve for depreciation.....................		60,000.00
Premium on collateral trust bonds.............		500.00
Vouchers payable..........................		38,000.00
Accrued taxes.............................		2,000.00
4% first-mortgage bonds payable, 1970........		70,000.00
6% sinking fund debentures payable, 1965.....		30,000.00
5% collateral trust bonds payable, 1961........		20,000.00
Sinking fund reserve.........................		5,000.00
Preferred stock, $10 par, 8%.................		40,000.00
Common stock, no-par, 100,000 shares authorized, 97,500 shares issued and outstanding....		60,000.00
Earned surplus.............................		47,500.00
	373,000.00	373,000.00

Problem B-4. Prepare entries in journal form covering the following, through December 31, 1955. Omit all closing entries. The company is on a calendar-year basis.

On July 1, 1954, Orson Company was authorized to issue $100,000 of 4%, 10-year bonds, interest payable on June 30 and December 31. The bond indenture required the company to establish a sinking fund and a sinking fund reserve. On each interest date, a deposit of $5,000 less sinking fund earnings since the last interest date was required. The indenture provided that the sinking fund reserve should equal the sinking fund.

On July 1, 1954, $50,000 of the bonds were issued at 101. On September 1, 1954, $48,000 of the bonds were issued at par plus accrued interest. On July 1, 1955, $2,000 of the bonds were issued for $2,036.

The company established a special bank account for the payment of bond interest. Cash equal to the interest obligation was deposited in the special account on each June 28 and December 29. Interest checks were issued on the interest-payment dates.

During the first six months of 1955, the sinking fund trustee, who immediately invests all cash receipts in securities, reported earnings of $200. During the second six months of 1955, the trustee reported earnings of $410; the trustee also submitted a bill for services, in the amount of $150, which the company paid on December 31, 1955.

Practice Set (Continued)

August 1—*Continued:*

(3) The stockholders and directors have authorized an issue of $240,000 of first-mortgage bonds, to be dated August 1, to mature in ten years, and to bear interest at 6%, payable semiannually. The indenture requires the

creation of a sinking fund by monthly additions of $2,000, and the transfer to a sinking fund reserve of an amount equal to the monthly addition to the sinking fund. The bonds are to be secured by a mortgage on all of the company's real estate and machinery and equipment. Details regarding the bonds issued today are shown below:

(a) To retire the 6% mortgage on land and buildings:

Principal of mortgage...............................	$50,000
Accrued interest on mortgage........................	500
Face of bonds issued................................	$50,500

(b) To retire 5% mortgage on machinery and equipment:

Principal of mortgage...............................	$60,000
Accrued interest on mortgage........................	750
Total..	$60,750
Face of bonds issued................................	60,500
Premium (allowed because the bonds bear 6% interest, whereas the mortgage bore 5%).....................	$ 250

(c) To Citizens State Bank, to pay note:

Principal of note...................................	$25,000
Accrued interest on note............................	100
Face of bonds issued................................	$25,100

(d) To First State Bank, to pay note:

Principal of note...................................	$40,000
Accrued interest on note............................	300
Face of bonds issued................................	$40,300

(e) To Lakewood Investment Association, for cash:

Proceeds...	$63,950
Face of bonds issued................................	63,600
Premium..	$ 350

August 2:

(4) Receive a 10-day, non-interest note from C. E. Bruce for $8,424.30, the amount of the account receivable from him taken over from Dale Brothers. (In order to compress within the limits of one month the transactions which it is desired to include in this practice set, the time periods of notes are unusually short.)

(5) Issue a check for $1,000 to sales manager T. R. Price as an advance for salesmen's traveling expenses.

August 3:

(6) Collect the $1,789.87 receivable from Rowley and Company, less 2% cash discount.

(7) Purchase from Morley Company (terms, 2/10; n/30):

	Gross	Net
Materials..................................	$41,380.25	$40,552.64
Factory supplies...........................	2,900.50	2,842.49
	$44,280.75	$43,395.13

August 4:

(8) Sale to James Greathead, $35,000; terms, 2/10; n/30.

August 5:

(9) Receive from Stinson Motor Sales a 15-day note for $3,007.50, the amount of the $3,000 account receivable taken over from Dale Brothers plus interest at 6%.

(10) Insurance policies expiring one year from August 1 are received today from Scott and Scott, together with their bill for $4,920. The bill is paid.

August 6:

(11) Sale to Henry Wright, $20,000; terms, 2/10; n/30.

(12) Issue a check for $22,878.80 to Lippert Reduction Company for materials purchased today. Terms, cash.

August 8:

(13) Purchase materials from Hubbard and Laurel, $6,354.70. Terms, 2/10; n/30. Net, $6,227.61.

ASSIGNMENT MATERIAL FOR CHAPTER 22

Questions

1. What are the objectives of a system of internal check in relation to assets?

2. What is the purpose of a petty cash fund? Describe the procedure of setting up and operating a petty cash fund.

3. List several basic requirements for a good system of internal check with regard to cash.

4. If a company operates a payroll bank account by drawing a check on the regular bank account for the exact amount of the payroll and depositing this check in the payroll bank account, what might be indicated by:

    (a) A balance in the payroll bank account in the general ledger?
    (b) A balance in the payroll account per the bank statement?

5. Under what circumstances may adjusting entries resulting from a bank reconciliation be made in the cash journals?

Problems—Group A

Problem A-1. Portions of the September cash receipts book and cash disbursements book of McAuliffe-Moore Corporation are shown below:

Cash Receipts Book		Cash Disbursements Book			
Date	Debit Cash	Check No.	Date		Credit Cash
1954			1954		
Sept. 1	372 18	426	Sept. 3		678 00
2	176 34	427	5		31 58
3	192 82	428	10		111 72
3	44 50	429	12		73 82
3	310 00	430	15		414 14
5	422 18	431	15		100 73
8	322 47	432	15		7 92
8	50 00	433	18		15 48
12	428 39	434	22		179 97
15	730 00	435	25		33 03
15	217 32	436	29		212 72
17	109 23	437	29		314 76
18	15 28				
18	317 60				2,173 87
22	57 77				
24	182 91				
29	50 00				
29	177 38				
30	62 57				
30	378 01				
	4,616 95				

440.58

The company maintains one bank account with the Manufacturers' National Bank. The company deposits all cash receipts. The statement submitted by the bank covering the transactions for the month of September follows:

Manufacturers' National Bank

Date 1954	Checks				Deposits		Balance	
Aug. 31	Balance brought forward						3,913	39
Sept. 2					372	18	4,285	57
3	678.00				176	34	3,783	91
4	Col.	.25	Ex.	.35	547	32	4,330	63
8	31.58				422	18	4,721	23
9					372	47	5,093	70
11	111.72						4,981	98
15	414.14				428	39	4,996	23
16	100.73				947	32	5,842	82
18	73.82				109	23	5,878	23
19	15.48				332	88	6,195	63
23	Ex.	.50			57	77	6,252	90
25	179.97		33.03		182	91	6,222	81
30	314.76				227	38	6,135	43

The bank balance as of August 31, 1954, as shown by the bank statement, agreed with the balance as shown by the company's ledger account.

Required:

  (a) The company's bank reconciliation as of September 30, 1954.

  (b) Necessary journal entries as of September 30, assuming that the cash journals have been ruled and posted.

Problem A-2. McAuliffe-Moore Corporation opened an account with the First State Bank during the following month (see Problem A-1). The transactions recorded during the month of October, 1954, on the books of the company were as shown on pages 646 and 647.

The statements from the two banks for the month of October, 1954, together with lists of returned checks and debit memos, are as shown below and on page 648.

Manufacturers' National Bank

Date 1954	Checks				Deposits		Balance	
Oct. 1	Balance brought forward						6,135	43
1					440	58	6,576	01
2					706	13	7,282	14
4	38.30		132.00		902	03	8,013	87
6	765.07						7,248	80
11	202.00	Col.	.35		2,114	04	9,160	49
14	212.72	Ex.	.25		433	81	9,381	33
18	390.07		129.54		1,617	17	10,478	89
21	Col.	1.25	384.04		4,000	00	14,093	60
24	38.20		728.00		171	98	13,499	38
25					1,007	93	14,507	31
31	500.00		550.00				13,457	31
	Balance at end of month						13,457	31

Cash Receipts Book

Date	Account Credited	CREDITS			DEBITS		
		Sundry Accounts L.F.	Sundry Accounts Amount	Accounts Receivable	Discount on Sales	Manufacturers' National Bank	First State Bank
1954 Oct. 1	Triangle Vacuum Co.			713 26	7 13	706 13	
3	Sales	✓	902 03			902 03	
8	National Products Co.			319 28	3 19		316 09
8	William Cramer			2,098 73	20 99		2,077 74
10	Sales	✓	1,716 27			1,716 27	
10	James Cronin			397 77		397 77	
13	National Products Co.			438 19	4 38	433 81	
13	Notes receivable	✓	1,000 00				1,010 00
13	Interest income	✓	10 00				
17	Sales	✓	1,117 17			1,117 17	
17	Henry Stimson			505 05	5 05	500 00	
20	Land	✓	4,000 00			4,000 00	
20	Kinsteel Co.			58 50			58 50
20	National Products Co.			573 39	5 73		567 66
23	Louis Wayne			173 72	1 74	171 98	
24	Sales	✓	1,007 93				1,007 93
31	Notes receivable	✓	650 00				
31	Interest income	✓	6 50				656 50
31	Alberta Porter Co.			212 50		212 50	
31	Sales	✓	919 47			919 47	
			11,329 37	5,490 39	48 21	11,077 13	5,694 42

Cash Disbursements Book

Date	Payee	Voucher No.	Debit Vouchers Payable	CREDITS Discount on Purchases	Manufacturers' National Bank Check No.	Manufacturers' National Bank Amount	First State Bank Check No.	First State Bank Amount
1954 Oct. 3	Peoples' Gas & Light	417	38 30		438	38 30		
4	Office Supply Co.	414	123 00		439	123 00		
5	Prengel Supplies	407	132 18	2 64	440	129 54		
5	Simpson Retailers	418	202 00		441	202 00		
5	Carl Bergner Co.	420	772 80	7 73	442	765 07		
10	Banicki & Letko	421	307 09		443	307 09		
10	Briggs-Lerchen Co.	422	95 00				1	95 00
11	Office Equipment Co.	426	772 00	14 44			2	757 56
11	Johnson & Johnson	435	390 07		444	390 07		
15	Western Telephone	437	28 82				3	28 82
15	See-It Television	428	387 92	3 88	445	384 04		
15	City Water Works	434	13 82		4	13 82		
17	Central Mfg. Co.	429	728 00		446	728 00		
20	Square Supply Co.	433	38 59	39	447	38 20		
20	Bill Williams Corp.	432	132 04				5	132 04
23	Bell & Co.	436	903 82	9 04			6	894 78
31	Carl L. McAuliffe	438	500 00		448	500 00		
31	John W. Moore	439	550 00		449	550 00		
31	National Supply	431	73 82				7	73 82
31	Cranfall Products	415	119 50		450	119 50		
			6,308 77	38 12		4,288 63		1,982 02

Checks and debit memos returned by Manufacturers' National Bank (rearranged in numerical order) were:

Checks:		Debit memos:	
No. 436	$212.72	Exchange charge......... $ .25	
438	38.30	Collection charge........ .35	
439	132.00	Collection charge........ 1.25	
440	129.54		
441	202.00		
442	765.07		
444	390.07		
445	384.04		
446	728.00		
447	38.20		
448	500.00		
449	550.00		

First State Bank

Date 1954		Checks	Deposits	Balance
Oct.	1	Balance brought forward		00
	10		2,393 83	2,393 83
	11	95.00		2,298 83
	15	Col. .45 13.82 757.56	1,010 00	2,537 00
	22	28.82	626 16	3,134 34
	25	894.78		2,239 56
	31	Balance at end of month		2,239 56

Returned checks and debit memos (rearranged in numerical order):

Checks:		Debit memos:	
No. 1	$ 95.00	Collection charge......... $.45	
2	757.56		
3	28.82		
4	13.82		
6	894.78		

From the information presented above and in Problem A-1, prepare reconciliations of the two bank accounts and any necessary journal entries, assuming that the company's fiscal year ends on October 31.

Problem A-3. The H & M Company, which uses a voucher system, decides to pay for miscellaneous small expenses out of a special fund, which is to be maintained on an imprest basis. The following transactions relative to the fund have taken place during the month of September. The numbers in parentheses indicate the number of the petty cash voucher used.

1954

Sept. 10—A petty cash fund of $25 is established.

(1) Sept. 11—Paid Acme Truckers for freight on merchandise purchased, $7.20, and for freight on merchandise sold, $2.22.

(2) Sept. 14—Paid Office Supplies Company for stationery for office, $5.15.

(3) Sept. 15—Paid Truex Print Shop for miscellaneous posters advertising special sale, $3.17.

(4) Sept. 21—Paid freight bill to CW & SR Railroad as follows: on merchandise purchased, $3.19; on merchandise sold, $2.21.

Sept. 22—The cash on hand in the petty cash fund is $1.86. The fund is replenished; because of the rapidity with which the fund has been exhausted, the amount of the fund is increased to $40.

(5) Sept. 23—Paid the Acme Truckers for freight on merchandise purchased, $2.38, and for freight on merchandise sold, $2.72.

(6)   Paid the Western Union telegraph boy for a collect telegram, $.85.

(7) Sept. 25—Gave Jerry Daugherty, office boy, $5 for 100 3¢ stamps and 100 2¢ stamps. (Charge to an expense account.)

(8) Sept. 27—Paid $6 to Tom Donohue for overtime meal allowances.

(9) Sept. 28—Gave Jerry Daugherty $.52 for the purchase of five desk blotters.

(10) Sept. 30—Paid Acme Truckers for freight on merchandise purchased, $1.73, and for freight on merchandise sold, $4.14.

(11)   Paid 4 boys $2 each for delivering sales circulars house-to-house.

(12)   Gave delivery truck driver, Sam Baker, $2.50, to have advertising sign on truck repainted.

Sept. 30—Because the company closes its books and prepares statements monthly, the petty cash fund is replenished today. The cash on hand amounts to $6.06.

On the basis of the above information, prepare (1) a petty cash book (similar to the one illustrated in the chapter), and (2) entries in general journal form which would be made relative to the above entries, indicating in which book of original entry the transactions would be recorded.

Problems—Group B

Problem B-1. Using the following information, prepare a bank reconciliation for J. B. Field and Son, as of March 31, 1954. J. B. Field and Son maintains a bank account with the Chitaqua Bank.

(1) The balance of the Cash account in the ledger as of March 1, 1954, was $4,130.56.

(2) The cash receipts book for March shows a total debit to cash of $13,-512.23; the cash disbursements book for the month shows a total credit to cash of $14,382.12.

(3) The statement received from the bank shows a balance of $3,277.98 as of March 31.

(4) The cash on hand, representing receipts for the day, amounts to $289.29.

(5) An examination of the cancelled checks shows that the following checks have not yet been paid by the bank: #1874 for $59.70; #1907 for $209.40; and #1908 (a certified check) for $200.

(6) The cancelled checks returned by the bank include a check of J. C. Folder and Sons for $50.

(7) The bank returned a check for $12.50, which was received from George Pire; the check is marked "N.S.F." and a bank debit slip for this amount is enclosed with the bank statement.

(8) On March 30, the bank credited the account of J. B. Field and Son with $100, which represents the proceeds of a $101.50 non-interest-bearing note of George Roberts. The bank deducted $1.50 for collection charges. No entry had been made by J. B. Field and Son for this collection.

Problem B-2. Prepare a bank reconciliation for Kaye and Company on March 31, 1954, based on the following information.

(1) The balance per books of Kaye and Company is $3,895.82.

(2) The bank statement shows a balance of $5,738.73 as of March 31.

(3) Accompanying the bank statement was a check of W. W. Ward for $77.32, which was marked N. S. F. by the bank.

(4) Checks outstanding as of March 31 were as follows: #C57 for $902.68 and #C62 for $1,005.

(5) Also accompanying the bank statement was a cancelled check for $57.62 of King Company; the bank had deducted this check from the account of Kaye and Company erroneously.

(6) On March 29, 1954, the bank collected a non-interest-bearing note for Kaye and Company. The note was for $152.50; the bank charged a collection fee of $2.50.

(7) A deposit of $157.63 was in transit; it had been mailed to the bank on March 31.

(8) The bookkeeper of Kaye and Company had recorded a check received on account from Baker Company erroneously; he recorded a $90 check as $9.

(9) The service charges on the account for March amount to $3.20; a debit memo in this amount was returned with the bank statement.

Prepare necessary journal entries under the assumption that the company's fiscal year ends on March 31.

Problem B-3. The Walt Kell Paint Distributors Company has the following payroll for the week ending January 7:

Salesmen's salaries............	$ 738.00
Office salaries................	419.75
Officers' salaries..............	1,925.00

The income tax withheld amounted to $612.32. The F.O.A.B. tax rates are $1\frac{1}{2}\%$; the state unemployment insurance tax rate is 2.7%; the federal unemployment insurance tax rate is .3%. All salaries paid were subject to taxes.

The company maintains a special payroll account with the National Bank and Trust Company.

Prepare the general journal entries to record: (1) the payroll for the week ending January 7, and (2) the employer's taxes on the payroll.

Problem B-4. Prepare entries in general journal form to record the following, including any necessary adjusting entries, in the books of Hex Corporation, which uses the voucher system and closes its books annually on December 31.

1954

November 20—The corporation established an imprest cash fund of $50.

November 30—An examination of the imprest cash fund disclosed the following composition:

Currency and coin..............................	$ 3.50
Vouchers showing disbursements for:	
Telephone and telegraph......................	9.75
Postage......................................	27.00
General office expense........................	9.55

Owing to the rapid exhaustion of the fund, a check was drawn to replenish the fund and to increase its amount to $100.

December 31—The composition of the imprest fund was as follows:

Currency and coin..............................	$19.14
Vouchers showing disbursements for:	
Telephone and telegraph......................	13.25
Postage......................................	40.00
General office expense........................	17.61
Traveling expense............................	10.00

The fund was not replenished as of December 31.

Practice Set (Continued)

August 9:

(14) Sale to Henry Barton, $25,000; terms, 2/10; n/30.

(15) Purchase raw materials from Weber and Fields, $9,400; terms, 10-day acceptance for amount of invoice less 2% discount. We accept the draft today.

(16) Purchase raw materials from F. J. Donovan, Inc., for $20,691.40. Terms, 30 days net.

August 10:

(17) Write off C. W. Finley's $219.80 account as uncollectible.

(18) Sale to Burroughs and West, $16,400; terms, 2/10; n/30. Also bill them $175.75 for delivery charges.

(19) Draw a $200 check to the order of the petty cashier to establish a petty cash fund.

August 11:

(20) Give a $29,750 note to C. D. Fulton & Co. for a purchase of machinery. The note bears 6% interest and is due in 30 days.

August 12:

(21) Collect from C. E. Bruce the $8,424.30 non-interest note received from him on August 2.

(22) Sale to Kenneth Dutton, $7,500; terms, 10-day sight draft less 2% discount. Receive the acceptance, in the face amount of $7,350.

(23) Pay Morley Company voucher No. 2 for $44,280.75, less 2% cash discount.

(24) Discount our 10-day note for $10,000 at the First State Bank. Proceeds, $9,983.33.

August 13:

(25) Collect from James Greathead the $35,000 invoice of August 4, less 2% discount.

(26) Receive a credit memo for $500 from F. J. Donovan, Inc., for goods returned to that company.

August 15:

(27) On August 5, C. L. Murphy's account, $113.85, was placed in the hands of an attorney for collection. The attorney collected the account. The proceeds are received today, less $20 attorney's fee.

(28) Pay East and West Railroad freight bill, which is detailed below:

$125.76   On sale to Henry Barton on August 9. Since the terms of this sale required that Barton bear the expense of the freight, the $125.76 should be charged to him. The charge should be entered in the Sundry Debits column of the voucher register; the customer's name should be written in the Remarks column to indicate the account in the subsidiary ledger to which the item should be posted.

315.67   On sales.

219.60   On materials purchased.

$661.03

August 16:

(29) Sale to Fred Madison, $12,000; terms, 10-day sight draft less 2% cash discount. The acceptance is received.

(30) The payroll clerk has prepared the payroll summary for the first half of August. Your work in connection with the payroll consists of the following:

(a) Post to the general ledger accounts and to the selling expense analysis record. (It is assumed that your assistant posts to the manufacturing and general expense analysis records.) The accounts to be debited and credited are indicated on the payroll summary.

(b) Record a voucher and a check payable to Payroll for the net payroll amount shown by the payroll summary in the pamphlet of books of original entry.

If you have not read Appendix 1, do so at this time.

(31) Sale to Henry Fowler, $20,000; terms, 30-day, 6% note. The note is received.

August 17:

(32) Sale to Rowley and Company, $14,700; terms, 2/10; n/30.

(33) Pay Daily News $23.45 for want ads for factory labor. (Charge account 5390.)

August 18:

(34) Sale to Charles Lathrop, $30,250; terms, 2/10; n/30.

(35) The discount period on the Hubbard and Laurel voucher expires today, and we want to take advantage of the 2% discount. However, we have reported some unsatisfactory materials and have not yet arrived at an agreement regarding the amount of credit we should receive. By agreement with Hubbard and Laurel, we now make a partial settlement of $5,000, being allowed a discount of $100, and sending them a check for $4,900. We expect to claim the discount on the balance, on the grounds of their delay in issuing a credit memorandum for the unsatisfactory goods.

August 19:

(36) A credit memorandum is issued to Rowley and Company to correct a $400 error in overfooting their invoice of August 17. Since this credit memorandum was not issued for either a return or an allowance, but to correct an error in the billed amount, the record of the credit memorandum should not involve a debit to Returned Sales and Allowances.

(37) Receive a bill from Davison Job Printers, terms 15 days, detailed as follows:

Sales forms (account 6090)............................... $ 69.80
Bookkeeping supplies and office forms (account 7012)........ 95.30
Total... $165.10

(38) Pay Weber and Fields acceptance.

ASSIGNMENT MATERIAL FOR CHAPTER 23

Questions

1. What is a red balance in a subsidiary ledger? How are such balances presented in financial statements?

2. Explain the nature and operation of a reserve for sales discounts.

3. How would you interpret each of the entries in the following account?

Reserve for Bad Debts

1952					1951			
Aug.	1		J12	225 36	Dec.	31	J8	2,000 00
					1952			
					Dec.	31	J15	2,200 00
					1953			
					Feb.	24	J20	225 36

4. The following entry was made for an account considered uncollectible:

Reserve for bad debts............................... 200.00
    R. F. Burns.................................... 200.00

Assume that $100 is collected. What entries should be made if: (a) It is thought the account may now be collected in full? (b) No more collections are expected?

5. Describe the circumstances that would justify the following entry:

Notes receivable discounted............................. xxxx
    Notes receivable.................................... xxxx

6. Describe the circumstances that would justify the following entry, made at the end of the accounting period:

Interest income... xxxx
    Deferred interest income........................... xxxx

7. What is the purpose of the Notes Receivable Discounted account?

8. What transactions are recorded in the following accounts? How should the facts shown by these accounts appear in the balance sheet?

Notes Receivable

19—					19—				
July	1	A. Jones	1,500 00		Aug.	12	A. Tillman	200 00
	9	J. Griffin	750 00			21	J. Griffin	750 00
	28	A. Tillman	200 00					
Aug.	4	J. P. Clark	100 00					

Notes Receivable Discounted

19—					19—				
Aug.	21	J. Griffin	750 00		Aug.	12	J. Griffin	750 00
						14	J. P. Clark	100 00

654

9. Compute the proceeds of the following $6,000 notes:

Date of Note	Time of Note	Rate of Interest on Note	Date Discounted	Rate of Discount Charged by Bank
(a) June 9, 1954	60 days		June 15	6%
(b) June 9, 1954	60 days	5%	June 15	6%
(c) June 9, 1954	2 months		June 15	6%
(d) June 9, 1954	2 months	5%	June 15	6%

Problems—Group A

Problem A-1. Make entries in journal form to record the following transactions on the books of G. H. Haines Company. Assume that the company closes its books annually on December 31. Prepare the entries in the order presented.

(1a)　March 1—Discounted our $5,000, 30-day note payable at the bank. Discount rate, 6%.

(1b)　March 31—Paid the above note.

(2a)　March 1—Discounted our $5,000, 60-day note payable at the bank. Discount rate, 6%.

(2b)　April 30—Paid the above note.

(3a)　March 1—Received a 30-day, non-interest note from T. Usher, $3,000, to apply on account.

(3b)　March 11—Discounted the Usher note at the bank. Discount rate, 6%.

(3c)　March 31—Usher paid his note at the bank.

(4a)　March 25—Discounted at bank a 60-day, non-interest note, signed by Paul LeBreton, dated March 5. Face of note, $5,400. Discount rate, 5%.

(4b)　May 4—LeBreton dishonored his note and we paid the bank.

(4c)　May 31—Received a check from LeBreton for payment of his note of March 5.

(5a)　May 25—Discounted at the bank a 60-day, 6% note for $7,200, received from Webb Johnson, dated May 19. Discount rate, 5%.

(5b)　July 18—Johnson paid his note at the bank.

(6a)　July 25—Discounted at bank a 90-day, 5% note for $8,000, received from O. C. Schnicker. Note dated July 7. Discount rate, 6%.

(6b)　Oct. 5—Schnicker dishonored his note and we paid the bank the amount due, together with a protest fee of $2.75.

(7a)　Aug. 16—Received a 30-day, non-interest note for $4,800 from T. Hoffmann to apply on account.

(7b)　Aug. 22—Transferred the Hoffmann note to F. R. Farrell to apply on account. Discount rate, 6%.

(7c)　Sept. 15—Hoffmann paid Farrell for the note due today.

(8a)　Sept. 20—Received a 60-day, 6% note for $8,000 from D. Demors to apply on account.

(8b)　Sept. 30—Transferred the Demors note to R. Biggs to apply on account. Discount rate, 5%.

(8c)　Nov. 19—Demors dishonored the note and we made payment to Biggs, including a protest fee of $3.15.

(9a)　Oct. 16—D. Barath sent us, to apply on account, a 30-day, non-interest note, signed by B. Birch, dated October 11, for $3,600. The note was taken at discounted value; rate, 6%.

(9b)　Nov. 10—Collected the above note from Birch.

(10a)　Sept. 27—Sold merchandise to W. Savage, $5,000; terms, n/30.

(10b) Oct. 27—Savage transferred to us a 60-day, 6% note for $3,000, dated October 21, signed by R. Sherman, which we took on a 5% discount basis. Savage paid us the remainder due (on the September sale) in cash.

(10c) Dec. 20—Sherman dishonored his note. Savage paid it in full.

Problem A-2. Make entries in journal form to record the following transactions on the books of Snow and Harris.

Oct. 13—Jacob Snow sold merchandise to Frank Harris, $2,400, and received a 30-day, non-interest note from Harris for the amount of the sale.

Oct. 19—Snow discounted the note at the bank; discount rate, 6%.

Nov. 12—Harris paid the note at the bank.

Problem A-3. Make entries in journal form to record the following transactions on the books of Dempsey, Rogers, and Walton.

May 16—James Dempsey sold merchandise to B. E. Rogers, $2,400, and received a 30-day, 6% note for the amount of the sale.

28—David Walton sold merchandise to James Dempsey, $5,400, and received the following:

(1) The note from Rogers, which he took on a 6% discount basis;
(2) A 60-day, 6% note for $2,000, signed by Dempsey;
(3) Cash for the balance.

June 15—Rogers dishonored the note and Walton collected it from Dempsey. Dempsey collected $1,000 from Rogers.

July 27—Walton collected the $2,000 note from Dempsey.

Problem A-4. (a) Prepare an aging schedule for the following accounts of Mid-States Corporation.

Winter Furnace Company

1954										
July	7	S8	a	660	00				660	00
Aug.	10	S9	b	1,020	00				1,680	00
	17	CR7				a	660	00	1,020	00
Sept.	20	S10	c	840	00				1,860	00
Oct.	15	S11	d	900	00				2,760	00
Nov.	7	CR9				d	900	00	1,860	00
Dec.	8	S12	e	420	00				2,280	00
	20	J5				e	40	00	2,240	00

Coal and Ice Company

1954										
June	10	S7		310	00				310	00
July	7	J3					30	00	280	00

H. C. Motor Company

1954										
Aug.	15	S9	m	370	00				370	00
	20	J4				m	50	00	320	00
Nov.	12	S11	n	272	50				592	50
Dec.	7	S12	o	301	00				893	50
	15	Note Receivable	J5			n	272	50	621	00

Green Corporation

1954												
Oct.	13		S11	x	372	10					372	10
Nov.	7		S11	y	181	00					553	10
	21		J4				x	40	00		513	10
	25		CR9				x	232	10		281	00
Dec.	7		S12	z	222	00					503	00

(b) Mid-States Corporation provides a reserve for bad debts at the end of each year equal to 50 per cent of all amounts over six months old and 20 per cent of all amounts 91 days to six months old. There is a credit balance in the reserve account on December 31 in the amount of $38. Prepare the journal entry to record the provision for bad debts.

Problems—Group B

Problem B-1. Record the following transactions of T. N. Bands Company in general journal form. Assume that the company closes its books annually on December 31. Prepare journal entries in the order presented.

(1a) Aug. 1—Received a 30-day, non-interest note for $3,900 from W. Jennings to apply on account.

(1b) Aug. 16—Discounted the Jennings note at the bank. Discount rate, 6%.

(1c) Aug. 31—W. Jennings paid his note at the bank.

(2a) Aug. 15—Discounted at the bank a 90-day, 5% note for $9,000, signed by P. Whelan, dated August 5. Discount rate, 4%.

(2b) Nov. 3—Whelan dishonored his note due today and we paid the bank.

(3a) Sept. 4—Discounted at the bank a 72-day, non-interest note for $8,500, signed by W. Tate, dated August 29. Discount rate, 6%.

(3b) Nov. 9—Tate paid his note at the bank.

(4a) Mar. 11—Discounted at the bank a 60-day, 4% note from W. Coyer for $2,400, dated March 5. Discount rate, 6%.

(4b) May 4—Coyer dishonored his note and we paid the bank the amount due, including a protest fee of $2.60.

(5a) Mar. 7—Discounted with W. Woodman, a creditor, a 60-day, 6% note from L. Townsend for $6,600, dated March 1. Discount rate, 7%.

(5b) Apr. 30—Townsend paid Woodman for the note due today.

(6a) Apr. 17—Discounted with R. Plumley, a creditor, a 30-day, 6% note from G. Bailey for $5,000, dated March 28. Discount rate, 5%.

(6b) Apr. 27—Bailey dishonored his note due today and we made a payment to Plumley for the amount due, including a protest fee of $5.15.

(7a) May 12—R. Hall sent us, to apply on his account, a 60-day, 6% note for $4,200, signed by S. Rodman, dated May 6. The note was accepted at discounted value; rate, 7%.

(7b) July 5—Collected the above note from Rodman.

(8a) June 7—H. Shields sent to us, to apply on his account, a 60-day, 6% note for $7,000, signed by W. Jensen, dated May 1. The note was taken at discounted value; rate, 5%.

(8b) June 30—Jensen dishonored the note and we collected it from the endorser, H. Shields.

Problem B-2. Make entries in journal form to record the following transactions on the books of Brennan and Ward. Brennan is on a calendar-year basis; Ward closes his books each June 30.

Dec. 19—Patrick Brennan sold merchandise to Samuel Ward, $6,000, and received a 60-day, 6% note from Ward for the amount of the sale.
Dec. 31—Brennan discounted the note at the bank; discount rate, 4%.
Feb. 17—Ward dishonored the note. Brennan paid the bank the face of the note, the interest, and a protest fee of $2.87.
Feb. 23—Ward gave Brennan a new 30-day, 6% note for $3,500 and paid Brennan the remainder of his indebtedness in cash.

Problem B-3. Make entries in journal form to record the following transactions on the books of Walsh, Voss, and Hartman.

March 13—Emil Hartman sold merchandise to Homer Voss, $4,500, and received a 60-day, non-interest note for the amount of the sale.
24—Peter Walsh sold merchandise to Emil Hartman, $6,200. Hartman transferred the Voss note to Walsh; Walsh took it on a 6% discount basis. Hartman paid the balance of the invoice in cash.
May 12—Walsh collected the note from Voss.

Problem B-4. Make entries in journal form to record the following transactions on the books of Vance, Howard, and Spencer.

Aug. 15—Oliver Vance sold merchandise to Richard Howard, $3,000, and received Howard's 60-day, 6% note for the amount of the invoice.
Aug. 21—L. H. Spencer sold merchandise to Oliver Vance, $4,800, and received:
    (1) The Howard note, which he took on a 5% discount basis;
    (2) A 60-day, 5% note for $1,500, signed by Vance;
    (3) Cash for the balance.
Aug. 24—Spencer discounted both of the notes at the bank; discount rate, 4%.
Oct. 14—Howard dishonored his note and Spencer paid the bank the face, the interest, and a protest fee of $1.92.
Oct. 15—Spencer collected from Vance the amount he paid the bank for the dishonored Howard note.
Oct. 17—Vance received from Howard a new 30-day, 6% note for $2,000 and cash for the remainder of the amount owed.
Oct. 20—Vance paid his discounted note at the bank.

Problem B-5. The June 30, 1954 balance sheet of Semi Corporation shows the following item under current assets: Accounts receivable, $40,647.49. An examination of the accounts reveals that the amount is composed of the following:

Regular customers—controlling account balance	$33,702.33	
Less amount owing to customers—recorded in accounts payable ledger	1,501.11	$32,201.22
Subscriptions receivable (collected in July, 1954)		3,500.00
Advances to employees		1,875.00
Accrued interest receivable		87.61
C. O. D. customers		301.56
Discount on preferred stock		2,500.00
Red balances in accounts payable	$903.54	
Less red balances in accounts receivable	721.44	182.10

What amount should be reported in the balance sheet as accounts receivable?

Practice Set (Continued)

August 20:

(39) Collect the note receivable from Stinson Motor Sales.

(40) Effective today, part of one of the buildings has been rented to Millen Hardware Company for one year, at $300 per month. The first month's rent is collected today. Credit account 2191—Rent Collected in Advance. Monthly transfers will be made to account 8191—Rent Income.

(41) Discount at First State Bank the 10-day acceptance for $11,760 received from Fred Madison on August 16. Proceeds, $11,748.24.

(42) Machinery is purchased for $39,500 from Johnson Machine Company. A cash payment of $19,500 is made today; the balance is payable September 20.

August 22:

(43) Merchandise in the amount of $7,500 was sold to Kenneth Dutton on August 12, and a 10-day acceptance was received from Dutton for the amount of the invoice less 2% discount. Dutton dishonors the acceptance today, and thereby forfeits the discount.

(44) Pay the First State Bank the $10,000 note given on August 12.

August 23:

(45) Sale of merchandise to Ostrander & Company, $43,325; terms, 2/10; n/30.

August 24:

(46) Issue credit memorandum for $725 to Charles Lathrop because of defective goods sold him on August 18.

August 25:

(47) Collect from Henry Wright the amount of the invoice of August 6, $20,000. The discount period has expired.

(48) Purchase materials from Watson Refineries, $7,941.23. Terms, 1/5; n/30.

August 26:

(49) On August 17 a sale was made to Rowley and Company in the billed amount of $14,700; on August 19 a credit memorandum for $400 was issued to correct an overfooting of the invoice. A check for $14,406 is received from Rowley and Company today. They apparently overlooked the credit memorandum, overpaid their account, and incidentally took too much discount. Rowley and Company is notified.

(50) Collect from Charles Lathrop the amount of the invoice of August 18, less the credit memorandum issued on August 24, and less 2% cash discount.

(51) The bank informs us that Fred Madison paid his $11,760 acceptance which we discounted at the bank on August 20.

August 27:

(52) Purchase materials from Wagner and Hobson, $28,985.40; terms, 2/10; n/30.

(53) On August 8 we purchased raw materials from Hubbard and Laurel at a gross amount of $6,354.70 and a net amount of $6,227.61. On August 18 we sent Hubbard and Laurel a check for $4,900, and recorded a new voucher for the remaining $1,327.61 of the net amount of the purchase. Today we receive a credit memorandum for $1,000 and issue a check for $347.61.

August 29:

(54) Receive a check for $24,625.76 from Henry Barton for the sale on August 9 and $125.76 freight charge on August 15. He is informed that the discount period has expired.

ASSIGNMENT MATERIAL FOR CHAPTER 24
Questions

1. Should the following assets owned by a manufacturing company be classified in its balance sheet as fixed assets?
   - (a) Land on which its factory is situated.
   - (b) Land used as an experimental farm for the improvement of grain used as one of its raw materials.
   - (c) Land and buildings formerly used as the company's factory, but now leased to another company.
   - (d) Land which the company purchased two years ago and which it hopes to sell at a profit; the land is not in use.
   - (e) Land which is not at present in use but is being held for possible plant expansion.

2. Describe a situation in which appraisal data are considered acceptable for purposes of establishing the amount to be charged to a fixed asset account.

3. Is it ever acceptable to charge the cost of a building to the Land account?

4. Should the following be charged to the asset account, to the related depreciation reserve, or to expense?
   - (a) Broker's commission in connection with the purchase of real estate.
   - (b) Taxes accrued at the date of purchase.
   - (c) Taxes after purchase.
   - (d) Cost of remodeling a section of the building to convert it into an office.
   - (e) Annual painting and decorating costs.

5. What is your opinion regarding the practice of charging losses and crediting gains resulting from the disposal of fixed assets direct to the Earned Surplus account?

6. Why is it unnecessary to amortize the cost of a trademark?

7. Contrast depreciation and depletion.

8. Why is depreciation not ordinarily credited to the fixed asset account?

9. Describe two methods of accounting for depreciation program revisions.

10. Describe the types of charges that may be assigned to the following accounts: (1) Leaseholds; (2) Leasehold Improvements. Explain the accounting procedures applicable to these accounts.

Problems—Group A

Problem A-1. L. Wayne Company was organized on January 1, 1954. At the end of the year, its ledger contained a Land and Buildings account, with debit and credit entries as shown on page 662. The bookkeeper stated that the entries in this account had been made in accordance with the accounting principle that all costs during the construction period should be capitalized.

Debits:

Incorporation fees and expenses.......................... $	500.00
Other organization expenses............................	300.00
Cost of land and old buildings. (There were three buildings: the values assigned to the buildings were: Building A—$20,000; Building B—$20,000; Building C—$30,000. The land was valued at $50,000. Buildings A and B were to be demolished; only Building C was to be retained.).....................................	100,000.00
Broker's commission on above purchase	1,000.00
Attorney's fees for the year:	
Incorporating company.....:......................	300.00
Examination of real estate title....................	100.00
Patent investigation..............................	500.00
Real estate taxes accrued at date of acquisition.........	1,800.00
Paving assessments:	
1953..	250.00
1954..	250.00
Cost of rehabilitation of Building C, completed on June 30, 1954...	6,300.00
Contract cost of new building completed June 30, 1954..	350,000.00
Real estate taxes for 1954...........................	3,000.00
Cost of demolishing Buildings A and B...............	7,500.00
Interest on $350,000 for six months at 6% (The new building was paid for with the funds obtained from the sale of preferred stock.)............................	10,500.00
Semiannual dividend on preferred stock...............	12,500.00
Material, labor, and overhead costs of partitions, shelving, etc., installed by company employees...............	12,400.00
Excess of price quoted by a contractor in bid for partitions, shelving, etc., over the $12,400 stated above.........	2,600.00
Salary of John Smith for first six months of the year. Smith supervised the building construction; after June 30 he served as factory superintendent..............	1,500.00
Discount on $475,000 of preferred stock issued for cash to obtain funds for purchase of land and old buildings and construction of new building......................	9,500.00
Par value of preferred stock given to a contractor (on the same date on which the preferred stock mentioned immediately above was sold) for filling in swamp land, grading, landscaping, paving roads, laying sidewalks, etc..	25,000.00
Replacement of windows broken in August.............	35.00
Repairs necessitated by cyclone in September..........	5,000.00
Cost of building fence around property................	2,000.00
Total debits................................... $	552,835.00

Credits:

Recovery from insurance company for cyclone damages.. $	4,000.00
Proceeds of sale of salvage from buildings demolished....	6,000.00
Proceeds of sale of portion of land....................	10,000.00
Total credits.................................. $	20,000.00
Balance.. $	532,835.00

Required:

An analysis and reclassification of items charged to the Land and Buildings account, indicating the account which should be charged for each separate item included in the above account.

Problem A-2. L. W. Thomas Company started in business on January 1, 1952; on that date it purchased the following machines:

Machine *A*, $4,200, estimated life, 5 years, with a scrap value of $200.
Machine *B*, $5,400, estimated life, 6 years, with no scrap value.
Machine *C*, $4,800, estimated life, 10 years, with no scrap value.

On September 1, 1952, Machine *D* (estimated life, 8 years; scrap value, $200) was purchased from the K. Wayne Company for $10,000; terms, 2/10; n/30. The machine was paid for on September 5, 1952.

On July 1, 1953, Machine *E* (estimated life, 10 years; no scrap value) was purchased for $7,200, cash.

On December 30, 1955, it was decided that Machine *C* would become obsolete by the end of 1958, and that the undepreciated cost would be written off over the newly estimated remaining life.

On April 1, 1956, Machine *A* was traded in for Machine *F*, which had a list price of $6,000. An allowance of $1,000 was received on Machine *A*, the balance of the list price being paid in cash. The life of Machine *F* was estimated at 10 years, with a scrap value of $200. (Follow the income tax procedure.)

On September 1, 1956, Machine *E* was sold for $4,000.

You are asked (1) to prepare journal entries in chronological sequence for all of the transactions above and also the depreciation entry made at the end of each year; (2) to post the entries above and to submit the Machinery and Reserve for Depreciation—Machinery accounts, showing their balances as of December 31, 1956; (3) to prepare a schedule showing (a) the cost of the machines on hand on December 31, 1956 and (b) the depreciation charged to date on those machines.

Problems—Group B

Problem B-1. On January 2, 1956, you are hired by Kass Company as their accountant. In your preliminary investigation of the accounts as of December 31, 1955, you notice that the Machinery account has a balance of $4,723.92, and that there is no related Reserve for Depreciation—Machinery account.

Inquiry uncovers the facts that the former accountant kept a very inadequate set of records and that he had been computing depreciation by taking 10% of the balance in the account as of January 1 of each year and crediting the asset account with the depreciation thus computed instead of using a reserve.

The balance in the Machinery account represents the undepreciated portion of the cost of a single machine purchased on January 1, 1951. The life of the machine had been estimated at 10 years, with no salvage value. No entries had been made in the account except the entry recording the acquisition and the entries recording the depreciation for each year.

After bringing the error to the attention of the president of the company, you are asked to submit to him a schedule showing the amount of underdepreciation for each year. He also asks you to submit the entry necessary to correct the accounts and to place them on the basis of the accepted method of computing and recording depreciation.

Problem B-2. The articles of partnership of the firm of *A*, *B*, and *C*, who share profits and losses in the ratio of 40%, 35%, and 25%, respectively, contained the following provision: "In the event of the death of a partner, the goodwill of the firm shall be computed by capitalizing at 12½% the excess of the average earnings for the three full years prior to his death over 10% of the net worth of the firm per the books at the end of the year prior to his death."

B died on May 3, 1955. The profits for the three preceding years were: 1952, $11,356.20; 1953, $12,287.95; 1954, $12,355.85. The balances in the capital accounts on December 31, 1954, were: *A*, $30,000; *B*, $25,000; *C*, $20,000.

Make the proper entry for the goodwill.

Problem B-3. The K & L Wayne Company purchased a used machine on July 1, 1952, at a cost of $4,000. The machine was immediately overhauled at a cost of $550. The company also paid an electrician a fee of $150 to check the electric wiring in the machine and to help install the machine.

The balance sheet prepared by the company on December 31, 1955, contained the following balances:

Machinery.................................... $4,000.00
Less reserve for depreciation................ 1,400.00 $2,600.00

The annual profits, as shown by the profit and loss statements, were:

1952.............. $2,470.00
1953.............. 3,508.00
1954.............. 3,392.00
1955.............. 3,238.00

Compute the effect of the above errors on the profits as reported and show what the profits would have been if the above expenditures had been given the proper accounting treatment.

Problem B-4. Universal Mining Corporation purchased a coal mine at a cost of $70,000. When the mine was purchased in 1953, it was estimated to contain 350,000 tons of coal. The quantities of coal mined during 1953 and the two following years were:

1953.......... 40,000 tons
1954.......... 57,000 tons
1955.......... 78,000 tons

In 1956, a new vein of coal was discovered, containing an estimated 75,000 tons of coal.

Make the journal entry recording the depletion charge for the year 1956, if 80,000 tons of coal were mined in that year.

Problem B-5. K-X Tile Company leased a store building from Blake Realty Company for a period of 20 years. The cost of the lease was $100,000, payable in 20 equal installments on the first day of each year. The lease agreement stipulated that K-X Tile Company would pay the cost of any alterations or improvements made.

K-X Tile Company built partitions in the store at a cost of $4,000. The partitions were estimated to last the remaining life of the building, 30 years. K-X Tile Company also built shelving at a cost of $1,200; the shelving would have to be replaced at the end of 5 years. All of these improvements were made just prior to occupancy by K-X Tile Company under the lease.

Prepare journal entries for the following:

(1) To record the cost of the partitions.
(2) To record the cost of the shelving.
(3) To record the first annual payment of rent under the lease.
(4) To record the first annual amortization of the cost of the partitions.
(5) To record the first annual amortization of the cost of the shelving.

Practice Set (Continued)

August 30:

(55) Pay East and West Railroad freight bill, which is detailed below:

$319.50	On machinery purchased from Johnson Machine Company.
427.95	On materials purchased.
139.43	On sales.
$886.88	
15.00	Railroad's overcharge, on bill paid August 15, for freight charged to Henry Barton on goods sold to him.
$871.88	

August 31:

(56) Pay Benson Corporation for the following:

Trailer for truck...........................	$875
Tires—to replace tires worn out.............	70
	$945

(57) Pay City Abstract Company $200 for title search relative to real estate acquired from the predecessor partnership.

(58) Pay Hanson Construction Co. $415 for installing machinery purchased August 20.

(59) City Garage bills us for the following items, payable September 10:

Gas and oil.................	$108.56
Repairs....................	93.40
	$201.96

(60) Because the discount period on the Watson Refineries invoice was five days instead of the customary ten days, we inadvertently failed to take advantage of the $79.41 discount. Make an entry to record the loss of the discount. Payment will be deferred.

(61) Issue a check for $451.90 to the petty cashier to increase the fund to $500 after replenishing it for the following expenditures:

Account		Amount
6057	Sales circulars.....................	$ 73.15
7011	Typewriter supplies................	28.75
1182	Postage...........................	50.00
		$151.90

(62) The August bill received from Central Power Co., payable September 10, is analyzed as follows:

Factory light and power.............	$825.00
Office light........................	31.65
	$856.65

(63) A check for $2,000, the regular monthly sinking fund deposit, is given to Midland Trust Company, the sinking fund trustee.

(64) Midland Trust Company informs us that it has purchased securities for the sinking fund at a cost of $1,500.

(65) Credit the sinking fund reserve $2,000.

(66) The directors declare a 1% cash dividend, payable September 10 to stockholders of record August 31.

(67) Post from the August 16–31 payroll summary to the general ledger and the selling expense analysis record.

ASSIGNMENT MATERIAL FOR CHAPTER 25

Questions

1. What is a consignment? Should goods on consignment be included in the inventory of the one in possession of the goods?

2. Devise an illustration to show how inventory misstatements affect net income.

3. List some of the incidental costs that are proper additions in determining cost for inventory-pricing purposes.

4. Explain the following:

Fifo.
Lifo.

5. If prices are rising, will the last-in, first-out inventory method have any effect on net income different from the first-in, first-out method? Explain.

6. If the cost-or-market method is used for inventory pricing, name some of the sources that an accountant might use in securing market-price data.

7. Describe the acceptable ways of applying the cost-or-market method.

8. If the inventory of finished goods is valued at market purchase prices, because they are lower than cost, does the profit and loss statement correctly state the gross profit on goods sold?

9. Describe the gross profit method of estimating inventories. Cite some circumstances under which the method might prove useful.

Problems—Group A

Problem A-1. On January 1, 1955, the Ellis Corporation had on hand three units of Part No. 1316 which cost $20 per unit. During 1955 purchases of Part No. 1316 were made as follows:

Date	Quantity	Unit Cost
January 31	4	$19
April 20	6	22
July 30	4	23

At the end of 1955, a periodical inventory was taken, and it was determined that there were five units on hand.

Compute the closing inventory by the following methods:

(1) First-in, first-out.
(2) Last-in, first-out.
(3) Weighted average.

Problem A-2. Warner Appliance Mart maintains two departments—main salesroom and bargain basement.

On December 31, 1955, the inventory was composed of the items shown on the following page.

		Unit Price	
	Quantity	Cost	Market
Main salesroom:			
Refrigerators...............................	75	$170	$173
Stoves.....................................	120	85	85
Washers...................................	50	60	65
Television sets............................	30	160	150
Bargain basement:			
Refrigerators.............................	15	140	142
Stoves....................................	25	50	50
Washers..................................	40	40	42
Television sets...........................	60	100	90

Compute the closing inventory at the lower of cost or market, applying the method to: (a) each item in the inventory; (b) the inventory in each department; (c) the entire inventory.

Problems—Group B

Problem B-1. During the calendar year 1956, Mally Fuel Corporation sold 6,000 tons of coal for $120,000. In its inventory on December 31, 1955, the company had 750 tons of coal which had cost $13 per ton. Purchases during 1956 were as follows:

Date	Quantity (Tons)	Unit Price	Total
January 25...........................	1,000	$12	$12,000
March 30............................	500	13	6,500
June 25..............................	1,500	13	19,500
July 13..............................	2,000	15	30,000
August 20............................	500	16	8,000
September 5..........................	500	17	8,500
November 3..........................	300	18	5,400
Total purchases....................	6,300		$89,900

Compute the gross profit on sales, assuming the use of the following methods of determining cost: (a) first-in, first-out; (b) last-in, first-out; (c) weighted average.

Problem B-2. Following is the after-closing trial balance of Stacy Manufacturing Company as of December 31, 1955, the close of its first year of operations:

Cash..	10,000.00	
Accounts receivable..........................	20,000.00	
Raw materials................................	15,000.00	
Goods in process.............................	30,000.00	
Finished goods...............................	12,000.00	
Machinery and equipment....................	20,000.00	
Reserve for depreciation—Machinery and equipment.....................................		1,000.00
Accounts payable.............................		4,000.00
Bonds payable...............................		15,000.00
Preferred stock..............................		20,000.00
Common stock...............................		40,000.00
Reserve for plant expansion..................		10,000.00
Earned surplus—free.........................		17,000.00
	107,000.00	107,000.00

An audit of the inventory accounts and procedures of the company reveals the following data:

(1) $3,000 of raw materials in transit on December 31, 1955, were not included in the closing inventory amount, although, through an oversight, the invoice from the vendor had been entered in the purchase journal. The goods were shipped f. o. b. shipping point.

(2) The inventory of goods in process was properly taken and computed.

(3) Finished goods costing $4,000 were shipped on consignment to Cabot Wholesale Company. None of these goods had been sold by the consignee as of December 31, 1955, but, since the goods were not on hand when the inventory count was made, they were not included in the closing inventory.

(4) Finished goods costing $2,000 had been sold to Jeeper Brothers, and the sale recorded. Jeeper Brothers had requested that delivery be postponed until January 12, 1956. The cost of these goods was included in the finished goods inventory on December 31, 1955, although title had passed to Jeeper Brothers.

Required:

(a) Prepare the December 31, 1955 balance sheet in the light of these additional data. Ignore any income tax adjustments which might be necessary.

(b) Prepare a schedule showing your computation of earned surplus on December 31, 1955.

Problem B-3. Mayfair Company sells ladies' dresses. During its first year of operations, it purchased one lot of 1,000 Type A dresses at a cost of $10 per dress, another lot of 1,500 Type B dresses at $20 per dress, and a third lot of 500 Type C dresses at $30 per dress. During that year its sales amounted to $70,000.

At the close of its first year, an inventory count revealed the following quantities on hand:

Type A............ 300
B............ 200
C............ 50

The company computes its inventory at the lower of cost or market, applied to each class of merchandise.

Type A dresses are standard styles and patterns, but the market has become so saturated that these dresses could be replaced for $7 per dress, and, while these dresses normally would be sold by Mayfair for $17, those on hand are marked down to $15. They are selling well at this price.

Type B dresses are higher-priced standard styles, and the market has been quite steady. Replacement cost per dress would be $21.

Type C dresses are strictly style merchandise, and it is customary in the trade to dispose of season-end stock at a significant reduction in price. It is expected that these 50 dresses can be sold for approximately $17.50 per dress, but that a special full-page newspaper advertisement will be needed. The cost of such an advertisement is $350.

Required:

Prepare a statement of gross profit on sales for Mayfair Company for its first year, supporting your statement with a schedule showing the computation of the closing inventory.

Problem B-4. When Carlton Corporation, dealer in automotive parts, took an inventory on April 30, 1955, the management was surprised to discover that it amounted to only $12,000, at cost. An investigation revealed that Donald Crow, the night watchman, had co-operated with thieves systematically to loot the warehouse. Since Crow was bonded, no loss would be borne by the corporation, but the amount of the thefts had to be determined. Since Crow had been hired in February, there was reasonable certainty that the thefts all occurred during 1955.

The corporation's books showed the following account balances on April 30, 1955:

Sales.....................................	$60,000
Returned sales and allowances................	2,000
Inventory, December 31, 1954...............	25,000
Purchases.................................	45,000
Returned purchases and allowances...........	1,000
Freight in..................................	2,000

For the past several years, Carlton Corporation has averaged a gross profit of 35% of net sales.

Required:

Compute the amount of the theft claim to be submitted to the bonding company.

Practice Set (Continued)

(68) Foot and complete the posting of all of the books of original entry.
(69) Take a trial balance of the general ledger. Enter the account balances in the Trial Balance columns of the working papers provided in the laboratory material.

ASSIGNMENT MATERIAL FOR CHAPTER 26
Questions

1. What is income? When is income earned?

2. A company has received orders for future delivery amounting to $5,000; it has goods on hand, which cost $3,500, which are sufficient to fill these orders. The management of the company wishes to include $1,500 as profits in its operating statement. Would you approve this procedure?

3. A printer received an order for 10,000 textbooks, which he completed and had ready for delivery before the end of the year. As an accommodation to the publisher, the printer agreed to hold these books in his warehouse and make shipments to schools as directed to do so by the publisher. The printer desired to include the profit on this work in his operating statement for the year. Would you approve?

4. How is cost computed when a noncash asset is acquired for noncash assets?

5. A company has its fixed assets appraised at each year-end and adjusts its accounts to show the values disclosed by the appraisal; the adjustments of the asset valuations are shown in the operating statement as income or expense. What comment do you have to make on this procedure?

6. A manufacturing company has expended a total of $3,000 worth of its own material, labor, and expense in constructing a machine for its own use. This machine, if bought in the open market, would have cost $4,000. Is it sound accounting to capitalize this machine at the market price?

7. In determining the amount of cost expirations and cost residues, accountants attack the problem from two directions. Explain the two directions referred to in this connection.

8. Is it regarded as good accounting to take up profits on uncompleted work under the following conditions:

    (a) The product is being made for stock?
    (b) The work is being done under a contract at a fixed price?
    (c) The work is being done on a cost-plus basis?

9. A company purchases for $75,000 a plant which has been in use for fifteen years. It is in a run-down condition, and the company spends $15,000 to put it into condition for use. The expenditures are principally for repairs, painting, and similar work that would have been considered operating charges had the plant been maintained properly by the previous owner. Should the $15,000 be recorded as a capital or a revenue expenditure?

10. At certain times of the year, a company has large amounts of cash which it invests in bonds; these are sold when the cash is needed. How should these bonds be valued in the balance sheet if their market value at the balance sheet date is considerably above cost? How should they be valued if their market value is considerably below cost?

11. A company issued $1,000,000 of 4% bonds at 95, and immediately wrote off the discount to Earned Surplus. Do you consider this procedure correct?

12. Why is the accountant interested in consistency in relation to the application of accounting procedures?

13. Explain the clean surplus concept and give some of the arguments that have been developed in support of the concept.

Problems—Group A

Problem A-1. In an examination of the books of the Connell Company, it is found that ordinary repairs to equipment have been charged to the Equipment account during each of the years 1953 and 1954. Repairs in the amount of $5,220 in 1953 and in the amount of $4,830 in 1954 were so charged. Net income as reported was $138,432 for 1953 and $143,672 for 1954. The company applies a rate of 10% to the balance in the Equipment account at the end of each year in its determination of depreciation charges.

Prepare a schedule showing the correct net income for these two years.

Problem A-2. The bookkeeper of Burnett Company prepared the following balance sheet:

BURNETT COMPANY
Balance Sheet
December 31, 1954
Assets

Current assets:		
Cash	$ 2,850.00	
Accounts receivable	28,920.00	
Inventory	17,200.00	$48,970.00
Other assets		2,000.00
Fixed assets:		
Land and buildings		30,000.00
		$80,970.00

Liabilities and Net Worth

Current liabilities:		
Accounts payable	$ 7,800.00	
Notes payable	4,000.00	$11,800.00
Reserves:		
Reserve for bad debts	$ 320.00	
Reserve for plant expansion	14,040.00	
Reserve for depreciation	4,900.00	19,260.00
Net worth:		
Capital stock, $10 par	$40,000.00	
Earned surplus	9,910.00	49,910.00
		$80,970.00

The account Other Assets consists entirely of 160 shares of the company's own stock which was purchased for $2,000. The amount shown for the inventory represents the sales value of the merchandise on hand. Gross profit for the company has averaged 25% of selling price. The land cost $9,000 in 1948. The notes payable are not due for three years.

In addition, it was discovered, after the above balance sheet had been prepared, that an invoice in the amount of $3,720, for a portion of the original cost of the building, had been charged to expense on January 1, 1948. The building had an expected useful life when new on January 1, 1948, of thirty years.

Reconstruct the balance sheet in a more acceptable form, making any corrections which you believe to be required.

Problem A-3. In an examination of the Westcott Company's books, the auditors discovered that net income had been incorrectly reported by the bookkeeper for the calendar years 1953 and 1954, as a result of the following:

(1) The Store Supplies Expense account had not been adjusted on December 31, 1953, to reflect supplies on hand amounting to $325. The records properly showed that no store supplies were on hand at the end of 1954.

(2) Major repairs, amounting to $12,000, completed on July 1, 1953, on second-hand equipment installed on the same date, were charged to expense. At the date of installation, the equipment had an expected useful life of four years.

(3) The physical inventory of merchandise taken on December 31, 1953, understated the actual inventory by $1,500.

(4) Unrecorded accrued wages on December 31, 1953, amounted to $380.

(5) The company does not have a Reserve for Bad Debts account in its ledger. A Reserve for Bad Debts should have been set up for $640 of receivables believed to be worthless on December 31, 1953. These accounts were written off in 1954. Also, no entry was made at the end of 1954 concerning $480 of accounts about which the management was doubtful of collection.

The reported net income was:

$$\text{For 1953} \ldots \ldots \ldots \ \$17,381$$
$$\text{For 1954} \ldots \ldots \ldots \ \ 26,483$$

Prepare a statement showing the computation of corrected net income for 1953 and 1954.

Problem A-4. Wallace Company, publishers of a monthly magazine, began operations on July 1, 1954, and established the calendar year as the time period to be used in accounting for its operations.

The publication, issued at the end of each month, was available by the copy for thirty-five cents, by a one-year subscription for $4, or by a two-year subscription for $7. Magazines were sent to subscribers in the month in which subscriptions were received.

All receipts from single-copy sales and from subscriptions were credited to income. The statement of profit and loss for the six months ended December 31, 1954, showed Magazine Income Earned to be $64,985. Details for single-copy sales and subscriptions are given below:

Month	Single Copy Sales	One-Year Subscriptions	Two-Year Subscriptions
July	$ 1,750.00	$ 4,000.00	$ 1,400.00
August	2,625.00	6,000.00	1,750.00
September	3,500.00	4,800.00	2,100.00
October	3,150.00	6,400.00	1,960.00
November	3,850.00	6,800.00	2,100.00
December	3,570.00	7,200.00	2,030.00
	$18,445.00	$35,200.00	$11,340.00

Compute the correct amount of magazine income earned for the six months ended December 31, 1954.

Problems—Group B

Problem B-1. Statements of earned surplus for Dalworth Company are given below:

DALWORTH COMPANY
Statement of Earned Surplus
For the Year Ended December 31, 1953

Balance, December 31, 1952		$ 64,500.00
Additions:		
Net income for the year	$48,700.00	
Gain on sale of marketable securities	1,250.00	49,950.00
Total		$114,450.00
Deductions:		
Dividends paid	$ 9,000.00	
Storm loss in October, 1953	5,100.00	14,100.00
Balance, December 31, 1953		$100,350.00

DALWORTH COMPANY
Statement of Earned Surplus
For the Year Ended December 31, 1954

Balance, December 31, 1953		$100,350.00
Additions:		
Net income for the year	$51,300.00	
Correction for overdepreciation of equipment during		
1951, 1952, and 1953	3,600.00	54,900.00
Total		$155,250.00
Deductions:		
Dividends paid	$10,000.00	
Payment of assessment for additional income taxes for		
year 1952	6,000.00	16,000.00
Balance, December 31, 1954		$139,250.00

Dividends paid in 1953 included $3,000 of dividends declared in 1952. Dividends paid in 1954 included $4,000 of dividends declared in 1953. An additional $4,000 of dividends were declared in 1954 to be paid in 1955. No entries were made on the dates of declaration.

Prepare corrected statements of earned surplus for the years 1953 and 1954, as they would have appeared if the company had followed the clean surplus theory.

Problem B-2. The comparative statement of earned surplus on page 675 was prepared by the bookkeeper of Grand Company.

Additional data:

(1) Payment of $1,080 was made in 1954 for merchandise which was on hand and included in the inventory on December 31, 1953. The liability and charge for this merchandise were unrecorded at the end of 1953. When the invoice was paid in 1954, the Purchases account was debited.

(2) Interest income earned but unrecorded on December 31, 1954, amounted to $830.

(3) Rent expense accrued but unrecorded on December 31, 1954, amounted to $1,150.

GRAND COMPANY
Comparative Statement of Earned Surplus
For the Years Ended December 31, 1953 and 1954

	Year Ended December 31,	
	1953	1954
Balances, end of previous year......................	$ 87,500.00	$147,570.00
Additions:		
Net income.......................................	$ 54,700.00	$ 63,400.00
Interest income earned in 1953 but not recorded—		
collected in 1954.................................		1,100.00
Gain on sale of treasury stock....................	700.00	
Gift of land from the city of Arlington..............	20,000.00	
Total additions.............................	$ 75,400.00	$ 64,500.00
Total.................................	$162,900.00	$212,070.00
Deductions:		
Dividends declared...............................	$ 12,000.00	$ 14,000.00
Payment of rent expense accrued but unrecorded at end		
of previous year.....	830.00	950.00
Provision for reserve for contingencies..............	2,500.00	
Total deductions............................	$ 15,330.00	$ 14,950.00
Balances, end of year.............................	$147,570.00	$197,120.00

Prepare statements of earned surplus for the years 1953 and 1954 as they would have appeared if the company had adopted the clean surplus theory and had made all year-end adjustments under the accrual method of accounting.

Problem B-3. Parker Company engaged a new bookkeeper on September 1, 1954, the start of its fiscal year. At the end of September, the Sales account appeared as follows:

Sales

1954					1954				
Sept.	15	Return of merchandise by a cash customer	CD8	80 00	Sept.	7	Merchandise shipped on consignment	J3	19,500 00
						22	Order received from U.S. Government	J4	32,000 00
						23	Collection from a customer whose account was written off as uncollectible in 1953	CR7	350 00
						25	Sale of treasury stock	CR7	1,800 00
						30	Cash sales for September	CR7	38,010 00
						30	Cash collections from credit customers for September sales	CR7	61,360 00
						30	Appreciation of inventory	J4	9,400 00

The company maintains a perpetual inventory. Sales on account for the month were $65,700. The bookkeeper made no entry for any of the charge sales.

The bookkeeper, in observing that wholesale prices had increased, recognized the increase in the replacement cost of the goods on hand September 30 by adjusting the inventory upward.

The treasury stock disposed of on September 25 cost the company $1,500.

Upon receipt of the order from the U. S. Government calling for the shipment on November 1 of merchandise having a selling price of $32,000, the bookkeeper debited the account "Due from U. S. Government."

When the merchandise on consignment, which cost $16,000, was shipped, the bookkeeper made the following entries:

Consignments out—Azle Company	19,500.00	
Sales		19,500.00
Cost of sales	16,000.00	
Inventory		16,000.00

As of September 30, Azle Company had not disposed of any of the merchandise received on consignment.

Prepare entries to correct the Sales account.

Problem B-4. James Rockwall, an individual proprietor, keeps only a few records. Assume that he has asked you to prepare a statement of profit and loss for him for the calendar year 1954.

You discover the following:

(1) A balance sheet was prepared at the end of the previous year, as follows:

Assets

Cash		$ 3,200.00
Accounts receivable	$25,400.00	
Less reserve for bad debts	1,350.00	24,050.00
Inventory		18,700.00
Fixtures	$12,000.00	
Less reserve for depreciation	4,000.00	8,000.00
		$53,950.00

Liabilities and Net Worth

Accounts payable	$18,400.00
James Rockwall, capital	35,550.00
	$53,950.00

(2) All cash receipts are deposited and all payments are made by check.

(3) Accounts receivable at the end of the year arising from 1954 sales amounted to $21,500. It was believed that only $600 of these accounts were likely to be uncollectible. Of the accounts at the beginning of the year, $24,100 were collected. The remainder should be written off as uncollectible.

(4) Accounts payable at the end of the year amounted to $19,370. Creditors at the beginning of the year were paid in full during 1954.

(5) Cancelled checks and check stubs showed payments, in addition to disbursements to creditors, as follows:

Rent	$7,800
Insurance	800
Store supplies	250
Store salaries	4,800
Payment on principal of note given during year	6,000
Interest expense	70

(6) Cash receipts from all sources for the year amounted to $78,300.

(7) Rockwall borrowed $6,000 on a note during the year.

(8) From a reconciliation of the bank account, the cash balance as of December 31, 1954, was determined to be $2,805.

(9) Other essential data were as follows:

Merchandise inventory at cost on December 31, 1954..........	$23,800
Depreciation of fixtures for 1954............................	1,000
Rent prepaid..	2,800
Store supplies on hand....................................	75

(10) There was no income other than that derived from sales of merchandise.

Show the computations you made in determining the sales and purchases for the year as reflected in the profit and loss statement.

Practice Set (Continued)

(70) Apply the following adjustments in the working papers:

   (a) Expired insurance, chargeable as follows:

Account	Amount
5384..............	$300
6084..............	100
7084.............	10
	$410

   (b) Postage used, $32.65.

   (c) Salesmen's traveling expenses for the month amounted to $863.50.

   (d) Factory supplies used, $623.14.

   (e) Provision for bad debts—1% of gross sales.

   (f) Accrued interest on notes receivable, $50.

   (g) Accrued interest on notes payable, $99.17.

   (h) Depreciation, computed for a full month on August 1 balances and for one-half month on increases during the month, at the following annual rates:

Asset	Rate	Amount
Buildings...	3%	$ 355.00
Machinery and equipment..........................	12	1,899.92
Tools..	24	48.00
Delivery equipment...............................	18	96.56
Furniture and fixtures............................	12	48.00

   (i) The patents had a life of 15 years from August 1.

   (j) Accrued property taxes: Factory, $325; general, $40.

   (k) Of the rent collected in advance, $100 has been earned.

   (l) Accrued bond interest, $1,200.

   (m) Amortization of bond premium.

(71) Complete the working papers.

The following schedules of subsidiary records, assumed to have been prepared by your assistant, will be found in the laboratory material:

Accounts receivable.	Notes payable.
Notes receivable.	Vouchers payable.

See that they are in agreement with the related controlling accounts. Observe that the accounts receivable schedule shows that one account has a credit balance. Instead of entering the balance of the controlling account in the Balance Sheet debit column of the working papers, enter the total debit balances of the subsidiary ledger in the debit column and the credit balance in the credit column.

The inventories on August 31 were:

Finished goods...............	$57,705.96
Goods in process.............	39,872.50
Raw materials...............	40,026.95

The working papers should show a net income of $11,904.69 before income tax. Assume that the income tax provision should be $4,000; enter this provision in the working papers as follows:

	Profit and Loss Debit Column	Balance Sheet Credit Column
Provision for federal income tax........	4,000.00	4,000.00

(72) Make and post (to the general ledger and the selling expense analysis record) adjusting journal entries for the matters mentioned in (70). Also make and post an adjusting entry for the estimated provision for income tax. Use the journal form provided for adjusting entries.

ASSIGNMENT MATERIAL FOR CHAPTER 27

Questions

1. What is meant by horizontal analysis? Vertical analysis?

2. How is it customary to compute the ratio showing the number of times bond interest has been earned?

3. Why may comparisons of analytical per cents be misleading?

4. Assume that two companies have the same amount of working capital and the same working capital ratio. Why may one company be in a better working capital position than the other?

5. Would you consider the following as reflecting improvements, or not?

   (a) Increase in the ratio of receivables to net sales.
   (b) Increase in the finished goods turnover.
   (c) Increase in the ratio of net worth to debt.
   (d) Increase in the ratio of net worth to net fixed assets.
   (e) Increase in the ratio of net sales to net fixed assets.

6. Compute the working capital ratio for the following case.

Cash:

On hand	$ 500	
State Bank	7,500	
National Bank (overdraft)	3,000*	$ 5,000
Accounts receivable—net		10,000
Inventory		15,000
Vouchers payable		12,000
Accrued expenses		3,000

7. Distinguish between the working capital ratio and the acid-test ratio.

8. What is meant by the term "window-dressing?"

9. What is meant by the term "break-even point?" Develop an example to illustrate the determination of the break-even point.

Problems—Group A

Problem A-1. A comparative statement of profit and loss and a comparative balance sheet for Barnes Company are given below:

BARNES COMPANY
Comparative Profit and Loss Statement
For the Years Ended December 31, 1954 and 1953

	1954	1953
Sales	$318,500.00	$310,400.00
Deduct cost of goods sold	231,400.00	228,600.00
Gross profit on sales	$ 87,100.00	$ 81,800.00
Deduct:		
Selling expenses	$ 35,214.00	$ 32,513.00
General expenses	31,184.00	27,404.00
Total expenses	$ 66,398.00	$ 59,917.00
Net income	$ 20,702.00	$ 21,883.00

BARNES COMPANY
Comparative Balance Sheets
December 31, 1954 and 1953

	December 31,	
	1954	1953
Assets		
Current assets:		
Cash...............................	$ 12,600.00	$ 10,840.00
Accounts receivable—net................	64,270.00	58,750.00
Inventory...........................	82,570.00	84,885.00
Prepaid expenses......................	7,685.00	7,120.00
Total current assets..................	$167,125.00	$161,595.00
Fixed assets:		
Land................................	$ 14,000.00	$ 14,000.00
Buildings—net........................	89,790.00	92,415.00
Equipment—net.......................	31,350.00	24,625.00
Total fixed assets....................	$135,140.00	$131,040.00
	$302,265.00	$292,635.00
Liabilities and Net Worth		
Current liabilities:		
Accounts payable......................	$ 46,835.00	$ 50,038.00
Notes payable........................	20,000.00	14,000.00
Total current liabilities..............	$ 66,835.00	$ 64,038.00
Net worth:		
Capital stock........................	$200,000.00	$200,000.00
Earned surplus.......................	35,430.00	28,597.00
Total net worth......................	$235,430.00	$228,597.00
	$302,265.00	$292,635.00

Apply the horizontal-analysis technique, using the above statements. For the income statement, express the changes in ratios; use per cents in analyzing the balance sheet.

Problem A-2. A statement of profit and loss and a balance sheet for Idiom Company follow:

IDIOM COMPANY
Statement of Profit and Loss
For the Year Ended December 31, 1954

Net sales...	$188,000.00
Deduct cost of goods sold...........................	132,600.00
Gross profit on sales...............................	$ 55,400.00
Deduct:	
Selling expenses....................................	$ 23,200.00
General expenses....................................	17,400.00
Total expenses......................................	$ 40,600.00
Net income...	$ 14,800.00

IDIOM COMPANY
Balance Sheet
December 31, 1954
Assets

Current assets:

Cash	$ 25,470.00
Accounts receivable—net	65,000.00
Inventory	42,800.00
Total current assets	$133,270.00

Fixed assets:

Land	$ 15,000.00
Building—net	48,700.00
Store equipment—net	30,800.00
Total fixed assets	$ 94,500.00
	$227,770.00

Liabilities and Net Worth

Current liabilities:

Accounts payable	$ 31,970.00
Notes payable	10,000.00
Total current liabilities	$ 41,970.00

Net worth:

Capital stock	$150,000.00
Earned surplus	35,800.00
Total net worth	$185,800.00
	$227,770.00

Apply the vertical-analysis technique, using the above statements.

Problem A-3. The following are statements of United Company as prepared at the end of 1954:

UNITED COMPANY
Profit and Loss Statement
For the Year Ended December 31, 1954

Gross sales		$600,000.00
Returned sales and allowances		13,000.00
Net sales		$587,000.00
Cost of goods sold		397,000.00
Gross profit on sales		$190,000.00
Expenses:		
Selling expenses	$80,000.00	
General expenses	65,000.00	145,000.00
Net income from operations		$ 45,000.00
Income from sinking fund securities		240.00
Net income before interest expense and federal income tax		$ 45,240.00
Interest on mortgage payable		3,600.00
Net income before federal income tax		$ 41,640.00
Federal income tax		16,560.00
Net income		$ 25,080.00

UNITED COMPANY
Balance Sheet
December 31, 1954
Assets

Current assets:

Cash...		$ 25,000.00	
Accounts receivable.........	$210,000.00		
Less reserve for bad debts..	8,000.00	202,000.00	
Inventory.................................		140,000.00	
Prepaid expenses.........................		15,000.00	
Total current assets....			$382,000.00

Other assets:

Investment in sinking fund securities..................		8,000.00

Fixed assets:

Land..................................		$ 18,000.00	
Buildings....................	$100,000.00		
Less reserve for depreciation	20,000.00	80,000.00	
Equipment..................	$ 15,000.00		
Less reserve for depreciation	4,000.00	11,000.00	
Total fixed assets.............................			109,000.00
			$499,000.00

Liabilities and Net Worth

Current liabilities:

Accounts payable......................	$108,700.00	
Accrued salaries payable.............	12,000.00	
Total current liabilities.........................		$120,700.00

Long-term liabilities:

Mortgage payable (secured by land and buildings)......		60,000.00
Total liabilities...............................		$180,700.00

Net worth:

Preferred stock—5%, par value, $100......	$ 50,000.00	
Common stock—Par value, $100..........	200,000.00	
Earned surplus.........................	68,300.00	
Total net worth................................		318,300.00
		$499,000.00

At the end of 1953, the inventory was $120,000 and the total net worth was $305,960.

Compute the following: (Carry computation to two decimal places; for example, 6.78%.)

Working capital ratio.
Acid-test ratio.
Inventory turnover.
Per cent of year's net sales uncollected.
Ratio of net worth to debt.
Ratio of net worth to net fixed assets.
Ratio of net sales to net fixed assets.
Ratio of pledged fixed assets to long-term debt.
Earnings per share of common stock.
Ratio of net income to average net worth.
Number of times preferred dividends earned.
Number of times mortgage interest earned.

Problem A-4. The amounts shown below were taken from the comparative statement of profit and loss of Differential Corporation for the years ended December 31, 1954 and 1955.

	1955	1954
Sales	$21,840	$20,090
Rent expense	920	1,200
Advertising	1,360	1,240
Bonuses—officers	1,200	—0—
Research and development expense	—0—	840
Returned sales and allowances	310	460
Gain (loss*) on disposal of equipment	440	120*

Compute the amount and (when possible) the per cent of change for each of the items above.

Compute per cents to two decimal places; for example, 4.87%.

Problem A-5. Tempo Corporation has issued preferred stock under an agreement to maintain net assets (assets minus liabilities) at an amount not less than 300% of the preferred stock outstanding, to maintain current assets at not less than 200% of the current liabilities, and to maintain working capital at not less than 125% of the preferred stock outstanding.

On December 31, 1954, the corporation's adjusted trial balance was as follows:

TEMPO CORPORATION
Adjusted Trial Balance
December 31, 1954

Cash	12,000.00	
Accounts receivable	41,000.00	
Reserve for bad debts		1,000.00
Inventory	46,000.00	
Prepaid expenses	2,000.00	
Land	6,000.00	
Building	52,000.00	
Reserve for depreciation—Building		7,000.00
Equipment	63,000.00	
Reserve for depreciation—Equipment		14,000.00
Accounts payable		23,000.00
Notes payable—due 1960		25,000.00
Accrued expenses		2,000.00
Preferred stock		50,000.00
Common stock		50,000.00
Earned surplus		50,000.00
	222,000.00	222,000.00

As an accountant engaged by the preferred stockholders, you discover that the notes payable were issued on December 29, 1954, and that the proceeds were used to settle current accounts payable, and that, on December 31, 1954, $25,000 cash was disbursed to settle a tax liability.

Contrast, by means of ratios, the existing conditions with those that would have existed if the transactions discovered had not occurred, so far as they relate to the agreement with the preferred stockholders.

Comment briefly on your findings.

Problems—Group B

Problem B-1. The following data are from the accounts of Selector Corporation.

	December 31, 1954	December 31, 1953	Year 1954
Cash......................................	$20,000		
Accounts receivable......................	12,000		
Reserve for bad debts....................	1,000		
Inventory................................	8,000	$7,000	
Accounts payable........................	12,000		
Notes payable—due in six months...........	3,000		
Sales....................................			$53,000
Discount on sales........................			1,000
Returned sales and allowances..............			800
Purchases................................			34,000
Returned purchases and allowances..........			750

On the basis of the information presented above, compute the following:

Working capital ratio.
Acid-test ratio.
Inventory turnover.

Problem B-2. Modern Company's working capital ratio was 3 to 1 on December 31, 1953. Assume that the following additional transactions had occurred on that date, and indicate whether each transaction would have increased, decreased, or not affected the working capital ratio.

1. Borrowed cash on a note.
2. Purchased inventory for cash.
3. Paid a note.
4. Sold merchandise for cash.
5. Paid cash for a delivery truck.
6. Declared a cash dividend.
7. Purchased inventory on account.
8. Returned merchandise, for which no payment had been made to creditor.
9. Sold fully depreciated fixed asset for a gain.
10. Discounted a non-interest-bearing note receivable at the bank.

Problem B-3. Statements for Marathon Company follow:

MARATHON COMPANY
Profit and Loss Statement
For the Year Ended December 31, 1954

Gross sales..	$235,800.00
Returned sales and allowances......................	4,500.00
Net sales..	$231,300.00
Cost of goods sold.................................	160,000.00
Gross profit on sales................................	$ 71,300.00
Expenses...	57,300.00
Net income from operations.........................	$ 14,000.00
Interest on mortgage payable.......................	2,800.00
Net income before federal income tax.................	$ 11,200.00
Federal income tax.................................	3,800.00
Net income...	$ 7,400.00

MARATHON COMPANY
Balance Sheet
December 31, 1954
Assets

Current assets:

Cash		$10,000.00
Accounts receivable	$85,000.00	
Less reserve for bad debts	6,000.00	79,000.00
Inventory		60,000.00
Total current assets		$149,000.00

Fixed assets:

Land		$12,000.00
Buildings	$60,000.00	
Less reserve for depreciation	12,000.00	48,000.00
Store equipment	$15,000.00	
Less reserve for depreciation	7,000.00	8,000.00
Total fixed assets		68,000.00
		$217,000.00

Liabilities and Net Worth

Current liabilities:

Accounts payable	$74,600.00	
Accrued expenses payable	29,000.00	
Total current liabilities		$103,600.00

Long-term liabilities:

Mortgage payable (secured by land and buildings)		40,000.00
Total liabilities		$143,600.00

Net worth:

Preferred stock, 6%—par value, $100	$20,000.00	
Common stock—Par value, $100	40,000.00	
Earned surplus	13,400.00	
Total net worth		73,400.00
		$217,000.00

On December 31, 1953, the inventory was $40,000 and the total net worth was $69,800.

Compute the following (Carry computations to two decimal places; for example, 14.71%):

Working capital ratio.
Acid-test ratio.
Inventory turnover.
Per cent of year's net sales uncollected.
Ratio of net worth to debt.
Ratio of net worth to net fixed assets.
Ratio of net sales to net fixed assets.
Ratio of pledged fixed assets to long-term debt.
Earnings per share of common stock.
Ratio of net income to average net worth.
Number of times preferred dividends earned.
Number of times mortgage interest earned.

Problem B-4. Determine the break-even point for the following cases:

	(1)	(2)	(3)
Fixed expenses	$80,000	$74,000	$35,000
Per cent of variable expenses to sales	75%	68%	55%

Problem B-5. The following ratios and other data are based on the financial statements of Booster Corporation.

Working capital ratio: $18,800 ÷ $7,800 = 2.41
Acid-test ratio: $8,800 ÷ $7,800 = 1.13
Inventory turnover: $36,000 ÷ $9,000 = 4.0
Number of times bond interest earned: $1,800 ÷ $200 = 9.0
Gross profit rate: $11,000 ÷ $51,000 = 21.57%

A review of the records of the corporation discloses that the following entries were made as of December 31, 1954, the last day of the accounting period. Recompute any of the above ratios that were affected by the entries.

```
1954
Dec. 31  Cash...................................  1,000.00
             Sales...............................            1,000.00
         Cash sales for January 2, 1955.

     31  Cash...................................  1,400.00
             Accounts receivable.................            1,400.00
         Collections  on  account  received  on
         January 2, 1955.

     31  Accounts payable......................  2,200.00
             Cash...............................            2,200.00
         Checks issued January 2, 1955, dated
         December 31, 1954.

     31  Purchases..............................    900.00
             Accounts payable...................              900.00
         To record invoices received January 2,
         1955.  The  merchandise  covered  by
         the invoices was received on December
         30, 1954, and was included in the Decem-
         ber 31, 1954 inventory.
```

Problem B-6. You are engaged by the bank holding the $30,000 of notes payable of Jackson Corporation to determine the following:

(a) The distribution of current assets.
(b) Working capital ratio.
(c) Acid-test ratio.
(d) Inventory turnover.
(e) Per cent of sales uncollected.
(f) Earnings per share.

Carry computations to two decimal places; for example, 7.18%.
Jackson Corporation submitted the following financial statements.

JACKSON CORPORATION
Balance Sheet
December 31, 1954
Assets

Cash...	$ 16,000.00
Marketable securities..................................	10,000.00
Accounts receivable....................................	15,000.00
Inventory...	18,000.00
Prepaid expenses......................................	1,200.00
Machinery and equipment.............................	50,000.00
Treasury stock, 100 shares at cost......................	1,400.00
	$111,600.00

Liabilities and Net Worth

6% notes payable...................................	$ 30,000.00
Accounts payable..................................	15,000.00
Accrued income taxes..............................	4,300.00
Accrued expenses.................................	1,800.00
Allowance for doubtful accounts.....................	900.00
Allowance for depreciation..........................	8,000.00
Reserve for contingencies...........................	2,000.00
Capital stock, $10 par value........................	40,000.00
Earned surplus....................................	9,600.00
	$111,600.00

JACKSON CORPORATION
Profit and Loss Statement
For the Year Ended December 31, 1954

Net sales..		$130,000.00
Cost of sales:		
Inventory, December 31, 1953.............	$15,000.00	
Purchases..............................	82,000.00	
Freight in..............................	800.00	
Total..................................	$97,800.00	
Inventory, December 31, 1954.............	18,000.00	79,800.00
Gross profit on sales................................		$ 50,200.00
Selling expense............................	$19,000.00	
Administrative expense.....................	18,500.00	37,500.00
Net operating income................................		$ 12,700.00
Interest expense.....................................		1,950.00
Net income before income taxes.......................		$ 10,750.00
Federal income taxes—40%...........................		4,300.00
Net income..		$ 6,450.00

In connection with the above statements, you discover the following. The corporation kept open the cash receipts book, the check register, and the voucher register until the middle of January, 1955. As a result, checks for $20,000 received in January in payment of merchandise purchased by customers during November and December were included in the cash receipts book; checks for $15,000 issued in January in payment of vendors' December invoices were entered in the check register; and $8,000 of vendors' invoices received in January for goods delivered and services rendered in December were recorded in the voucher register. Of the latter amount, $5,000 represented goods included in the ending inventory and $3,000 was for selling expense items.

The corporation uses the periodical inventory method. On December 30, 1954, a customer returned merchandise which had been sold to him for $600. The following entry was made on December 30:

Returned sales and allowances........................	600.00	
Accounts receivable.............................		600.00

The returned merchandise was included in the ending inventory at $600; its cost was $400. The notes payable become due at the rate of $10,000 each July 1st.

Practice Set (Concluded)

(73) The following schedules of subsidiary records, assumed to have been prepared by your assistant, will be found in the laboratory material: Manufacturing expenses; General expenses. See that they are in agreement with the related controlling accounts.

Prepare a schedule of the selling expenses, and see that it is in agreement with the controlling account.

(74) Prepare the following statements:

Statement of cost of goods manufactured.
Profit and loss statement.
Statement of earned surplus.
Balance sheet.

(75) Close the books. Use the journal pages allotted to closing entries.
(76) Take an after-closing trial balance.

ASSIGNMENT MATERIAL FOR CHAPTER 28

Questions

1. Name the records subsidiary to the following controlling accounts:

Raw Materials.
Goods in Process.
Finished Goods.

2. Discuss the alternative policies for accounting for cash discounts on purchases when a perpetual inventory system is being used.

3. State what entries, under the accounting procedure described in this chapter, affecting general ledger accounts should be made when:

(a) Raw materials are purchased for cash.
(b) Raw materials are used on a production order.
(c) Direct labor is charged to a production order.
(d) Overhead is charged to a production order.
(e) A production order is completed.
(f) A sale is made.

4. Discuss two methods of disposing of underabsorbed and overabsorbed burden.

5. Describe the functions of:

(a) Raw material perpetual inventory cards.
(b) Material requisitions.
(c) Production orders.
(d) Finished goods perpetual inventory cards.

6. Are manufacturing expenses assigned to production orders in the same manner as material and direct labor?

Problems—Group A

Problem A-1. Patman Products keeps perpetual inventory records in terms of quantities and costs. On December 31, 1955, there were on hand 100 units of material 3623 which had cost $5 per unit. During January, 1956, the following purchases and requisitions of material 3623 were made.

Date	Purchases Quantity	Cost per Unit	Requisitions (Quantity)
January 5			50
12	80	$6	
17			70
23			10
25	60	4	
30			20

Required: Prepare perpetual inventory cards as they would appear for material 3623, assuming that the company uses: (a) First-in, first-out; (b) Last-in, first-out.

Problem A-2. Harmon Foundry manufactures castings on special order from customers. When a contract is received, a production order is filled out on which cost data are accumulated. Since Harmon Foundry produces only on order and delivers immediately upon the completion of production, no inventory of finished goods is maintained.

On April 15, 1956, an order is received for 100 pulley housings from the Western Winch Company. The specified sales price to apply to the order is $7.50 per unit.

On April 18, production is begun. Pig iron costing $100 is sent to the furnace for melting. Other materials costing $25 for making molds (not reused) are requisitioned on April 19. Direct labor in melting, pouring, and cleaning for this order amounts to $400. It is assumed that overhead amounts to 25% of direct labor.

On April 28, the order is completed and delivered, and an invoice is prepared for $750 and sent to Western Winch Company.

Required:

(a) Prepare production order 1864 as it would appear after reflecting all of the information above.

(b) Give journal entries which would be made to reflect the production and delivery of these castings, assuming that perpetual inventory accounts are maintained by the company for raw materials and goods in process.

Problem A-3. The following is the trial balance of Lyons Manufacturing Company on December 31, 1956, the close of its fiscal year.

LYONS MANUFACTURING COMPANY
Trial Balance
December 31, 1956

Cash....................................	12,000.00	
Accounts receivable.........................	40,000.00	
Finished goods........................... ...	15,000.00	
Goods in process..	20,000.00	
Raw materials.............................	13,000.00	
Unexpired insurance........................	1,000.00	
Machinery and equipment....................	50,000.00	
Reserve for depreciation—Machinery and equipment..		10,000.00
Vouchers payable...........................		25,000.00
Capital stock..............................		80,000 00
Earned surplus.............................		27,000.00
Dividends.................................	5,000.00	
Sales.....................................		150,000.00
Cost of sales..............................	110,000.00	
Manufacturing expense......................	20,000.00	
Manufacturing expense applied..............		24,000.00
Selling expense............................	20,000.00	
General expense...........................	10,000.00	
	316,000.00	316,000.00

Additional information:

(1) Depreciation of $3,200 on machinery and equipment has not yet been recorded. All depreciation is considered a manufacturing expense.

(2) Insurance costing $500 has expired. Insurance is allocated 60% to manufacturing expense, 30% to general expense, and 10% to selling expense.

(3) Underabsorbed or overabsorbed manufacturing expense is treated as an adjustment of cost of sales.

Required:

Prepare working papers, journal entries to adjust and close the books, and financial statements.

Problem A-4. Following is the trial balance of Westcott Machine Company on January 1, 1956. Prepare journal entries for the January transactions, post to general ledger accounts, prepare adjusting and closing entries for January 31, post, and prepare financial statements for the month of January.

WESTCOTT MACHINE COMPANY
Trial Balance
January 1, 1956

Cash..	10,000.00	
Accounts receivable.........................	25,000.00	
Finished goods..............................	20,000.00	
Goods in process............................	12,000.00	
Raw materials...............................	15,000.00	
Equipment..................................	30,000.00	
Reserve for depreciation—Equipment..........		9,000.00
Accounts payable............................		21,000.00
Capital stock...............................		60,000.00
Earned surplus..............................		22,000.00
	112,000.00	112,000.00

Summarized transactions during January were as follows:

(1) Raw materials were purchased on account, $35,000.
(2) Sales were made on account, $60,000. The goods sold cost $40,000 to manufacture.
(3) Payments were made for: direct labor, $15,000; indirect labor, $2,000; other manufacturing overhead costs, $4,000; selling expense, $3,000; general expense, $1,000.
(4) Collections on account were $63,000.
(5) Payments for material purchases, $32,000.
(6) Raw materials requisitioned for production, $30,000.
(7) Direct labor applied to production, $15,000.
(8) Estimated overhead assigned to production, $6,500.
(9) Production orders completed, $60,000.

Additional data as of January 31, 1956:

(a) Depreciation of equipment for January, $250. Depreciation is considered to be chargeable 80% to manufacturing expense and 10% each to general expense and selling expense.

(b) Underabsorbed or overabsorbed manufacturing expense is treated as an adjustment of cost of sales.

Problem A-5. Hartford Company's trial balance on January 1, 1956 appears on the following page.

HARTFORD COMPANY
Trial Balance
January 1, 1956

Cash.....................................	10,000.00	
Accounts receivable.........................	20,000.00	
Finished goods.............................	22,000.00	
Goods in process...........................	12,000.00	
Raw materials..............................	15,000.00	
Machinery and equipment...................	21,000.00	
Reserve for depreciation.....................		10,000.00
Vouchers payable...........................		15,000.00
Capital stock..............................		50,000.00
Earned surplus.............................		25,000.00
Sales.....................................		
Cost of sales..............................		
Direct labor...............................		
Manufacturing expense......................		
Manufacturing expense applied..............		
Selling expense............................		
General expense............................		
	100,000.00	100,000.00

The company keeps the following records and books of original entry, from which the information below has been summarized.

1. *Journal:*
   No January entries as yet made.
2. *Check register:*
   Cash column total.................................... $80,000.00
   Vouchers Payable column total........................ 80,000.00
3. *Voucher register:*
   Raw Materials column total........................... $30,000.00
   Manufacturing Expense column total................... 8,000.00
   Direct Labor column total............................ 25,000.00
   Selling Expense column total......................... 3,000.00
   General Expense column total......................... 5,000.00
   Vouchers Payable column total........................ 71,000.00
4. *Sales book:*
   Selling Price column total........................... $80,000.00
   Cost column total.................................... 60,000.00
5. *Cash receipts book:*
   Cash column total.................................... $75,000.00
   Accounts Receivable column total..................... 75,000.00
6. *Production order direct labor cost summary:*
   Column total... $25,000.00
7. *Requisition register:*
   Column total... $33,000.00
8. *Register of completed production orders:*
   Column total... $70,000.00

No postings to general ledger accounts have been made since taking the January 1, 1956 trial balance. The company estimates that manufacturing expenses are equal to 40% of direct labor costs, and estimated manufacturing expense is entered on individual production orders at the same time as direct labor costs are entered.

Required:

(a) Prepare journal entries necessary to record the information reflected on the production order direct labor cost summary, the requisition register, and the register of completed production orders, and to record the manufacturing expense applied.

(b) Set up a working paper with the following eight columns:

Trial balance, January 1, 1956 (2 columns)
Debits
Debit references
Credits
Credit references
Trial balance, January 31, 1956 (2 columns)

Enter the January 1, 1956 trial balance in the appropriate columns (allowing 4 lines for goods in process), make all January postings in the debit and credit columns, indicating the source in the reference columns, and extend the balances representing the trial balance on January 31, 1956.

Problems—Group B

Problem B-1. On June 30, 1956, the close of its fiscal year, Robinson Corporation prepares the following trial balance. Prepare journal entries to adjust and close the books; also prepare financial statements for the year ended June 30, 1956.

ROBINSON CORPORATION
Trial Balance
June 30, 1956

Cash.....................................	10,000.00	
Accounts receivable.........................	20,000.00	
Finished goods.............................	18,000.00	
Goods in process...........................	20,000.00	
Raw materials..............................	15,000.00	
Prepaid rent...............................	300.00	
Machinery and equipment...................	40,000.00	
Reserve for depreciation.....................		18,000.00
Accounts payable...........................		15,000.00
Capital stock..............................		50,000.00
Earned surplus, June 30, 1955...............		21,500.00
Sales.....................................		120,000.00
Cost of sales...............................	92,000.00	
Direct labor...............................		2,500.00
Manufacturing expense......................	30,000.00	
Manufacturing expense applied..............		32,300.00
Selling expense............................	10,000.00	
General expense...........................	4,000.00	
	259,300.00	259,300.00

Supplementary data:

(1) Accrued wages and salaries are $3,000. Of this amount, $2,500 represents direct labor, $100 represents manufacturing expense, $200 represents selling expense, and $200 represents general expense.

(2) There is no prepaid rent on June 30, 1956. Rent cost is allocable 50% to production, 25% to selling expense, and 25% to general expense.

(3) Depreciation of fixed assets is $4,000 and is allocable on the same basis as rent.

Problem B-2. Using the data given in Problem B-1, prepare working papers for Robinson Corporation. (Allow 3 lines each for manufacturing expense, selling expense, and general expense.)

Problem B-3. Zelden Manufacturing Company uses the following books of original entry:

1. Journal
2. Voucher register
3. Sales book
4. Cash receipts book
5. Check register

In addition, the company keeps the following records upon which journal entries are based:

1. Materials requisition register
2. Production order direct labor cost summary
3. Register of completed production orders

Below are selected transactions of Zelden Manufacturing Company during April, 1956. For each transaction, indicate the book of original entry or other record in which the transaction would be recorded and indicate the final debit-credit effect that each transaction would have on the general ledger accounts.

Example:

Accounts receivable of $500 are collected.
Enter in cash receipts book.

Debit—Cash........................... $500
Credit—Accounts Receivable............   500

(1) Raw materials are purchased on account, $1,000.
(2) Invoices representing manufacturing expense items are received from creditors, $2,000.
(3) Direct labor payroll is paid, $5,000.
(4) Sales are made on account, $3,000. These goods cost $2,000 to manufacture.
(5) Manufacturing operations are completed on goods costing $750.
(6) Creditors are paid for outstanding invoices, $300.
(7) Raw materials are requisitioned for production, $900.
(8) Direct labor cost is assigned to production orders, $3,200.
(9) Manufacturing expense is estimated to be 50% of direct labor costs and is assigned to production orders at the same time as is direct labor cost. A summary entry reflecting the application of manufacturing expense to production orders is made at the end of each month. Total direct labor assigned to production orders during April, 1956, is $16,000.

Index

Index

A

697

Profit and loss (*Cont.*)
statement (*Cont.*)
gross profit:
by departments, 166
less selling expenses, departments, 177
income tax in, 178, 180
manufacturing company, 186–187
partial, 85
partnership, 111, 113
periodical inventory, 75
vertical analysis of, 418–420
Profits:
departmental, 165
division of, partnership, 107
gross (*see* Gross profits)
Promissory notes, 114 (*see also* Notes)
Property, stock issued for, 255
Proprietorships, individual:
capital account, 102
closing the books, 103
accounts after, 103–104
drawing account, 102–103
statements, 104, 106
working papers, 104, 105
Protest, defined, 356
Punctuating numbers, 30
Purchase:
admission of partner by, 234–235
book, 142, 143–144
cash credit column, 171
discounts, 450–451
journal, 142
order, 78–79
requisitions, 77–78
routine, 77–83
checks, advices, 82
invoice, 79–83 (*see also* Invoice)
orders, 78–79
receipts, 82
requisitions, 77–78
Purchaser, verification of invoice, 80
Purchases:
cash, departmental, 169–171
in cash disbursements book, 158, 159
cash discounts on, 89–90
debited to Inventory account, 57
returned (*see* Returns and allowances)

R

Ratio:
acid-test, current assets, 428
capital, 228
expressed decimally, 423–424
meaningless, 434
misinterpretation of, 434
net income to average net worth, 416

Ratio (*Cont.*)
partnership division of profits and losses, 227–231
pledged fixed assets to long-term debt, 432
profit and loss, partnership, 110
related ratios, appraisal of, 434
sales to fixed assets, 433–434
working capital, 425–427
worth to debt, 431
worth to fixed assets, 433
Raw materials:
inventories, 382
movement of, 430–431
purchased, 438–439
requisition, 439, 440–441
register, 447
used, 439–440, 447
Real estate:
acquisition of, costs, 401
mortgage bonds, 309
Receivables, age distribution of, 346–348
Receiving record, 80
Reconciliation of bank account, 336–340
adjustments after, 341
statement, 340
steps in, 339–340
Records:
bank balance, 332–333
compensation, for employees, 463
corporation, 258–264 (*see also* Corporation: records)
individual employment and compensation, form, 470
inventory, 59
payroll, 298
receiving, 80
subsidiary (*see* Subsidiary records)
wage payment, to employees, 469–470
Redemption value of stock, 273
Registered bonds, 310
Registers, 128–131
bank, 332, 333
check (*see* Check register)
completed production orders, 448–449
note (*see* Note register)
notes payable, 130, 131
notes receivable, 128–130, 131
requisition, 447
voucher (*see* Voucher: register)
Registrar, 263
Reinstallation expense, 367
Repairs:
cost of, 363
apportionments, 37
extraordinary, 367, 369
income, 32
ordinary, 367